# What Is PSYCHOLOGY? ESSENTIALS

## 2nd EDITION

**Ellen Pastorino**

Valencia College

**Susann Doyle-Portillo**

Gainesville State College

WADSWORTH
CENGAGE Learning™

Australia • Brazil • Japan • Korea • Mexico • Singapore • Spain • United Kingdom • United States

***What Is Psychology? Essentials,*** **Second Edition**

Ellen Pastorino and Susann Doyle-Portillo

Publisher: Linda Schreiber-Ganster

Executive Editor: Jon-David Hague

Senior Acquisitions Editor: Jaime Perkins

Senior Developmental Editor: Kristin Makarewycz

Freelance Development Editor: Shannon LeMay-Finn

Assistant Editor: Paige Leeds

Editorial Assistant: Jessica Alderman

Media Editor: Mary Noel

Senior Marketing Manager: Elisabeth Rhoden

Marketing Assistant: Janay Pryor

Marketing Communications Manager: Laura Localio

Senior Content Project Manager: Christy Frame

Creative Director: Rob Hugel

Senior Art Director: Vernon Boes

Senior Print Buyer: Karen Hunt

Rights Acquisitions Account Manager, Text and Image: Don Schlotman

Production Service: Lachina Publishing Services

Text Designer: Marsha Cohen

Photo Researcher: Roman Barnes

Copy Editor: Margaret Tropp

Illustrator: Lachina Publishing Services

Cover Designer: Marsha Cohen

Cover Image: age fotostock/Superstock

Compositor: Lachina Publishing Services

> For product information and technology assistance, contact us at
> **Cengage Learning Customer & Sales Support, 1-800-354-9706.**
>
> For permission to use material from this text or product,
> submit all requests online at **www.cengage.com/permissions**.
> Further permissions questions can be emailed to
> **permissionrequest@cengage.com**.

Library of Congress Control Number: 2011939003

Student Edition:

ISBN-13: 978-1-111-83415-9

ISBN-10: 1-111-83415-6

**Wadsworth**

20 Davis Drive

Belmont, CA 94002-3098

USA

Cengage Learning is a leading provider of customized learning solutions with office locations around the globe, including Singapore, the United Kingdom, Australia, Mexico, Brazil, and Japan. Locate your local office at **www.cengage.com/global**.

Cengage Learning products are represented in Canada by Nelson Education, Ltd.

To learn more about Wadsworth visit **www.cengage.com/wadsworth**. Purchase any of our products at your local college store or at our preferred online store **www.CengageBrain.com**.

Printed in Canada

1 2 3 4 5 6 7 15 14 13 12 11

# About the Authors

**Ellen E. Pastorino** (Ph.D., Florida State University, 1990) is a developmental psychologist who established her teaching career at Gainesville State College in Georgia. As a tenured professor she created and developed the college's Teaching and Learning Center, working with faculty to promote student learning. For the past 13 years, she has been teaching at Valencia College in Orlando, Florida. Here, too, she has worked with faculty in designing learning-centered classroom practices. Ellen has won numerous teaching awards, including the University of Georgia Board of Regents Distinguished Professor, the NISOD Excellence in Teaching Award, and Valencia's Teaching and Learning Excellence Award. Ellen has published articles in *The Journal of Adolescent Research* and *Adolescence* and actively participates in many regional and national teaching conferences. However, her main passion has always been to get students excited about the field of psychology. Ellen is a member of the Association for Psychological Science (APS) and currently serves as the Discipline Coordinator of Psychological Sciences at Valencia's Osceola campus. Ellen has authored test banks, instructor manuals, and student study guides. While working as a consultant for IBM Corporation, she developed numerous educational materials for teachers and students. Her current interests include assessment, inclusion, service learning, and reaching underprepared students. Ellen strives to balance her professional responsibilities with her love of physical fitness and family life.

**Susann M. Doyle–Portillo,** a professor of psychology at Gainesville State College for the past 17 years, earned her Ph.D. in Social Cognition in 1994 from the University of Oklahoma. Prior to her doctoral program, Susann earned bachelor's degrees in engineering and psychology. This exposure to both the hard sciences and the social sciences helped to ground her firmly in the experimental tradition of psychology. She has published articles in *Social Cognition* and *Contemporary Social Psychology*, but the main focus of her career has and will always be teaching. During her tenure at Gainesville State College, Susann has earned a reputation as an excellent but challenging instructor. In 2010, she was awarded the Gainesville State College Best Practices Award for her teaching, and in 2011 she was a recipient of a Gainesville State College Foundation Innovative Teaching Grant Award. In addition, she has three times been listed in *Who's Who Among America's Teachers*. Susann is also actively engaged in student learning outside the classroom. One of her major goals is to help students learn by getting them involved in conducting original research. In addition to teaching, Susann is heavily involved in the assessment of general education at Gainesville State College. In this role, she has helped colleagues across her institution to develop and implement performance-based assessments of learning outcomes in their courses.

# Brief Contents

# Contents

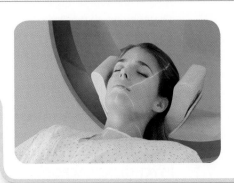

# 3  How Do We Sense and Perceive Our World?  |  78

# 4 Consciousness: Wide Awake, in a Daze, or Dreaming? | 122

# 7 Cognition, Language, and Intelligence: How Do We Think? | 240

# 8 Motivation and Emotion: What Guides Our Behavior? | 282

# 9 How Do People Grow, Change, and Develop? | 324

# 10 Social Psychology: How Do We Understand and Interact With Others? | 376

# 11  Health, Stress, and Coping: How Can You Create a Healthy Life? | 422

## 12 What Is Personality and How Do We Measure It? | 460

## 13 What are Psychological Disorders, and How Can We Understand Them? | 494

# 14 What Therapies Are Used to Treat Psychological Problems? | 538

# A How Are Statistics Used in Psychology? | 578

# B How Do We Apply Psychology in the Workplace? | 592

Together, we have over 38 years of experience teaching Introductory Psychology. We each teach four to six sections of Introductory or General Psychology each and every year—it is our bread and butter, so to speak. So, it's a good thing that Introductory Psychology is also our favorite course. Contrary to what many may think of professors teaching the same course over and over, it never grows old for us. Teaching General Psychology allows us to touch on many different aspects of our fascinating field and to work with diverse students from all walks of life, such that no two classes are ever alike.

The uniqueness of each class is just one of the challenges that keep us excited about teaching this course. There are others. General Psychology classes are often full of students who are just beginning their academic careers—some are fresh from high school, others are returning, non-traditional students who've been out of the classroom for several years. They come to us with the desire to learn about psychology, but often they face serious obstacles. Some are overworked in their personal lives. Some have lingering academic challenges. And most expect learning to be easier than we know it to be. As such, a big part of our mission is to help students overcome these obstacles and obtain success.

Getting students to read their textbook in preparation for lectures and exams is one of the biggest problems we face as instructors. Like many professors, our experience has been that few students read assigned chapters prior to lecture, and some even fail to read the chapters by the time they take exams. For years, we have tried various methods of motivating students to read—pop quizzes, reading quizzes, test questions from material in the book but not covered in lecture, and so on. None of these methods seemed to have much of an impact on students.

Students' free time is, of course, in short supply. And when they do have free time, reading a textbook doesn't always seem like an attractive option. Students often find their texts difficult to read, boring, and full of content that is far removed from the concerns of their daily lives. One of us overheard students speaking before class the second week of the semester. One student asked those sitting around him if they had read the reading assignment—most replied they had not. He then said, "I read it, but man I have no idea what they were saying in that chapter!" If we want students to read their textbooks, we will have to give them books that they will *want* to read, and that means giving them a book that they can understand and one that *they* find relevant enough to be worth the time it takes to read. That is why we've written this text. Our goal was to write a textbook that students would find interesting to read, easy to read, and memorable.

## Unlocking Curiosity in Students by Making Psychology Interesting

One of the best ways to motivate students to read is to capture their curiosity from the very beginning. Any good psychologist knows that personal relevance is one aspect of information that is very likely to capture our interest and attention. To capitalize on this, each chapter opens with the story of one of our former students who has found the information in that chapter useful in his or her work, studies, or personal life. These stories serve as testimonials from our students to our readers. If they see that their peers have found value in the material, readers may be motivated to see for themselves the ways in which psychology is relevant to their own lives.

Our *You Asked* feature also gives voice to what students actually want to know about psychology. As we were writing this text, we asked our students to share with us the questions they had about psychology. These questions then became a guide to us as we wrote each chapter. By ensuring that we address points that are of interest to students, we help encourage students to read.

## Making Psychology Relevant for All People

There is little doubt that students learn best when they become personally invested in the material they are reading and studying. However, for this to occur, students must actually find the material to be applicable to *their* lives. Given that today's college students are a diverse group of people, writing a text that is relevant to today's students means writing a text that embraces their diversity. We have written our book with this in mind.

### Psychology Across Generations

There is a growing awareness among professors that generational differences are an important type of diversity

## Enhancing Student Learning by Encouraging Active Learning and Self-Assessment

Many of our students learn best when they engage in active rather than passive learning. We have made a concerted effort to get students *involved* with the material as they read. By remaining engaged, students will be more motivated to read, and they will likely retain the information in memory much better.

### Your Turn—Active Learning

The *Your Turn—Active Learning* feature asks students to do hands-on activities to illustrate important chapter concepts. Active learning not only encourages students to see the personal relevance of the material, it also helps students elaborate the material in memory by connecting it to personal experience. Examples of *Your Turn—Active Learning* activities include having students examine their attributional biases when making judgments about celebrities (Chapter 10), illustrating the effects of elaborative rehearsal on memory for song lyrics (Chapter 6), and an activity that demonstrates the brain's predisposition to perceive faces (Chapter 9).

### Let's Review

Another feature, *Let's Review,* appears after each major section of the chapter. *Let's Review* allows students to actively assess their learning by asking them to apply the material of the preceding section to answer several multiple choice questions. Most of the *Let's Review* questions are application questions that apply the material to practical situations. For example, in Chapter 10, *Social Psychology: How Do We Understand and Interact with Others?,* we use the following question to test the student's understanding of attribution theory:

> Jasper was quick to assume that Susan was intelligent when he saw that she earned an "A" on her last psychology exam. However, when Jasper earned an "A" on his history test, he was not so quick to assume that he was intelligent. Which of the following biases in social cognition *best* explains Jasper's behavior?
>
> **a.** The fundamental attribution error
> **b.** The self-serving bias
> **c.** The social desirability bias
> **d.** The actor-observer bias

To answer this question, the student must not only understand the different attribution biases, but he or she must also be able to think analytically about them in applying these concepts to a very common student-oriented scenario.

### You Review

*What Is Psychology? Essentials,* Second Edition, also includes a *You Review* feature in each chapter that is a table that summarizes a body of content from the chapter. For example, in Chapter 11 the symptoms of sexually transmitted infections are summarized. In Chapter 7 gender differences on some cognitive tasks are highlighted.

### What Do You Know? Assess Your Understanding

In addition to the *Let's Review* questions at the end of each major section of the chapter, we have included a more extensive self-assessment for students at the end of each chapter. This assessment, *What Do You Know? Assess Your Understanding,* is a twenty-question multiple choice practice test (with the answers provided at the bottom of the page) that allows students to evaluate their retention and understanding of the entire chapter. By self-assessing, students can better judge which concepts and/or sections of the chapter they should target for further study.

### Look Back at What You've Learned

A visual summary of the chapter, entitled *Look Back at What You've Learned,* is also included in the end-of-chapter material to allow students to truly *see* the *big picture* of the chapter. In *Look Back at What You've Learned,* all the major concepts and theories of the chapter are brought together in a graphical format. This tool will be especially helpful to students who prefer to learn through visual means.

## New Content for the Second Edition— New Ways to Spark Student Curiosity

The feedback we received on the first edition of this text from students and professors alike reaffirmed our original mission to write a book that motivates students to read by capturing their interest and unlocking their curiosity. As a result, our mission in this second edition is to continue to show students that psychology is not only interesting but also practical and relevant for everyone. We also continue to encourage students to read and study the material in a manner that facilitates long-term learning and retention of the material. To help us accomplish this ongoing mission, we've made some improvements to the second edition:

- We streamlined the second edition by removing the mid-chapter visual summary of the material. This change results in a chapter that flows more smoothly and is less redundant for the reader.
- We added new *Psychology Across Generations* boxes to all chapters. These boxes highlight generational differences and similarities that are relevant to the content of the chapter. For example, in Chapter 10 we look at generational differences in destructive obedience.
- We updated roughly 25% of the *What Do You Know? Assess Your Understanding* questions in each chapter.
- We updated several of the *Neuroscience Applies to Your World* and *Psychology Applies to Your World* boxes (see the specific chapter changes below).
- We updated several of the *Your Turn—Active Learning* activities (see the specific chapter changes below.)
- Because psychology is a rapidly changing discipline, it is imperative that a text reflects the current state of the research. As such, we have added over 780 new citations to the second edition.
- We thoroughly updated the visuals in each chapter, making sure that the visual program is inclusive and diverse.

## Chapter-by-Chapter Changes to Content in the Second Edition

### CHAPTER 1: WHAT IS PSYCHOLOGY?

- Added several new key terms: positive psychology, neuroscience, stimulus, response, experimental group, control group, placebo effect, double-blind study
- Emphasized Edward Titchener's contribution to structuralism
- Moved Margaret Washburn under structuralism
- Added Gestalt psychology to the history section
- Added birth of positive psychology to the history section
- Added table on myths about behavior
- Added environmental psychology, community psychology, and positive psychology to list of specialty areas
- Updated data in figures on undergraduate degrees in psychology and work settings of psychologists in *Psychology Applies to Your World* box
- Gave more detailed information on minority contributions to psychology, adding Clark doll experiments and Inez Prosser's research
- Updated data on women and minorities in the field of psychology
- Added survey research to research methods section
- Added new box, *Psychology Across Generations: Pew Research Center: Survey on Millennials*

### CHAPTER 2: HOW DOES BIOLOGY INFLUENCE OUR BEHAVIOR?

- Added new opening case study
- Added discussion of neuroplasticity
- Added new box, *Psychology Across Generations: The Aging Brain*
- Added new box, *Neuroscience Applies to Your World: Is Fear Good for Us?*, on the function of the amygdala, containing a new case study of a woman living without a functioning amygdala
- Added new *Your Turn—Active Learning* demonstration on the patellar reflex and its relationship to inhibition and excitation

### CHAPTER 3: HOW DO WE SENSE AND PERCEIVE OUR WORLD?

- Added new box *Neuroscience Applies to Your World: Sex, Sweat, Tears,* a discussion of chemosignals/pheromones in human sexuality
- Added new box *Psychology Across Generations: Are the Youth of Today More at Risk for Hearing Loss?*
- Added update on Bem's new ESP research; made ESP a key term
- Added update on pheromone research
- Added update on feature detection theory
- Added update on colorblindness
- Umami is now listed as the fifth taste instead of a proposed fifth taste

### CHAPTER 4: CONSCIOUSNESS: WIDE AWAKE, IN A DAZE, OR DREAMING?

- Added new opening case study
- Incorporated term "slow-wave" sleep to refer to Stages III and IV
- Sleep tips now include turning off cell phone prior to sleeping
- Added table on blood alcohol concentrations and typical effects
- Added brief discussion on binge drinking
- Describe more fully the nature of crack cocaine
- Added new box *Psychology Applies to Your World: Alcohol and Caffeine: Blackout in a Can*
- Added new box *Psychology Across Generations: Generation Rx*

### CHAPTER 5: HOW DO WE LEARN?

- Replaced term *social learning* with *observational learning*
- Revised section on Real-World Classical Conditioning
- Added new key term: biological preparedness
- Added new box *Psychology Across Generations: Have Attitudes Toward Physical Punishment Changed Over Time?*

- Added new references on the effects of physical punishment on children and the European Council's commitment to reducing/eliminating the use of physical punishment in the EU
- Added new *Your Turn—Active Learning* feature on habituation

## CHAPTER 6: HOW DOES MEMORY FUNCTION?
- Added the duration of sensory memory
- Added new box *Psychology Across Generations: Is There a Generational Conflict in the Classroom?*, discussing Millennial, Gen X, and Baby Boomer expectations about college learning environments
- Restructured section on forgetting to improve readability
- Added Hermann Ebbinghaus's forgetting curves and made forgetting curve a key term
- Added discussion of autobiographical memory and its relationship to episodic memory
- Updated discussion of possible separate memory systems in the brain for episodic and semantic memory
- Added new box *Neuroscience Applies to Your World: Concussions in High School Athletes*
- Added new key terms: memory consolidation, tip of the tongue phenomenon, and misinformation effect
- Updated role of the hippocampus in memory consolidation of procedural memory

## CHAPTER 7: COGNITION, LANGUAGE, AND INTELLIGENCE: HOW DO WE THINK?
- Included brief discussion on intuition
- Added new *You Review* table on the different theoretical views on intelligence
- Added new box *Psychology Across Generations: Slang: The Changing Face of Language*
- Added information on perceptual coding of concepts
- Added new information on the WAIS-IV
- Added new information on the link between literacy skills and IQ scores

## CHAPTER 8: MOTIVATION AND EMOTION: WHAT GUIDES OUR BEHAVIOR?
- Added new opening case study
- Added new table on the liver's role in hunger
- Removed thirst from chapter to make room for new text
- Updated information on parents' prejudice against their overweight children
- Added new box *Psychology Across Generations: Sex Across the Generations*

- Added new *Your Turn—Active Learning* feature on the Sex Degrees of Separation Calculator
- Added self-determination theory to the section on incentives and motivation
- Added fraternal birth order effect and maternal immune hypothesis to theories of sexual orientation section
- Updated information on countries that allow same-sex marriage
- Added concept of display rules to the emotion discussion
- Added section on gender differences in regulation of emotion

## CHAPTER 9: HOW DO PEOPLE GROW, CHANGE, AND DEVELOP?
- Reorganized chapter to include more major heads so that each section of the chapter is shorter and more manageable
- Added new information on teenage dating
- Added discussion of emerging adulthood
- Reformatted motor milestones table for improved readability
- Added separate section on the influence of Piaget
- Added new research on analysis of gender stereotypes in television ads in 20 countries
- Added new box *Psychology Across Generations: Trends in Generational Attitudes on Marriage and Parenting*
- Made distinction between permissive-indulgent and permissive-neglectful parents

## CHAPTER 10: SOCIAL PSYCHOLOGY: HOW DO WE UNDERSTAND AND INTERACT WITH OTHERS?
- Updated information on audience variables affecting persuasion
- Added new box *Psychology Across Generations: Generational Differences in Obedience*
- Added concept of aversive racism
- Added concept of social facilitation and social loafing

## CHAPTER 11: HEALTH, STRESS, AND COPING: HOW CAN YOU CREATE A HEALTHY LIFE?
- Added discussion on potential positive effect of stressful life experiences for *some* people, referred to as *post-traumatic growth* or *benefit-finding*
- Added and defined psychoneuroimmunology as key term
- Added new box *Psychology Applies to Your World: Texting and Driving: Increasing Your Chances of Injury or Death*

- Increased coverage of health-promoting behaviors, referring to positive psychology and including detailed information on physical activity, eating healthy, and getting enough sleep
- Added new section that discusses research on the five factors that contribute to happiness and well-being
- Added new section on Gender and the Stress Response
- Added new box *Psychology Across Generations: Generations and Stress*

## CHAPTER 12: WHAT IS PERSONALITY, AND HOW DO WE MEASURE IT?

- Added new opening case study
- Added new key terms: five factor theory, emotional stability, and behavioral genetics
- Included brief coverage of the CPI
- Added new box *Psychology Across Generations: Generation Me*
- Updated sensation-seeking research
- Added discussion of genes that direct neurotransmitters as aspect of personality
- Restructured section on influence of age, gender, and culture on personality for improved readability
- Mentioned emergence of positive psychology as rebirth of humanistic perspective

## CHAPTER 13: WHAT ARE PSYCHOLOGICAL DISORDERS, AND HOW CAN WE UNDERSTAND THEM?

- Added new box *Psychology Across Generations: Millennials and Psychological Distress*
- Reorganized schizophrenia symptoms for improved flow
- Updated suicide references
- Added more headings in explaining mood disorders to foster organization and clarity
- Updated discussion of Brodmann's area 25, depression, and deep brain stimulation treatment
- Updated discussion of major stressful life events and onset of depression
- Moved dissociative and somatoform disorders so that they come after anxiety disorders for improved readability
- Discussed relation of stress and trauma to dissociative fugue disorder
- Discussed role of hormones and sociocultural factors in age of onset in schizophrenia
- Added new key terms: anhedonia, blunted affect, disorganized speech, alogia, avolition, and disorganized behavior

## CHAPTER 14: WHAT THERAPIES ARE USED TO TREAT PSYCHOLOGICAL PROBLEMS?

- Added new *You Review* table on Psychotherapy Approaches
- Added brief mention of interpersonal therapy
- Added coverage of Mary Cover Jones experiment for systematic desensitization
- More attention to culturally-sensitive therapy under ethics and effective therapy
- Added brief discussion of flooding
- Added short discussion on Eye Movement Desensitization Reprocessing (EMDR) therapy
- Added new key term psychopharmacology to biomedical section
- Added new box *Psychology Across Generations: Attitudes Toward Mental Health Services*

# Available Supplements

To access additional course materials including CourseMate, please visit **www.cengagebrain.com**. At the CengageBrain.com home page, search for the ISBN of your title (from the back cover of your book) using the search box at the top of the page. This will take you to the product page where these resources can be found.

## Instructor Resources

### Instructor's Resource Manual
ISBN: 978-1-111-83853-9

Written by Thomas Hancock, University of Oklahoma. A comprehensive resource, the Instructor's Resource Manual contains tools for each chapter of the text. The contents include lecture topics, activities, student projects, journal prompts, web links, video suggestions, and handouts.

### PowerLecture™
ISBN: 978-1-111-83841-6

The fastest, easiest way to build powerful, customized media-rich lectures, PowerLecture provides a collection of book-specific PowerPoint lecture and class tools to enhance the educational experience.

### Test Bank
ISBN: 978-1-111-83840-9

Written by Kelly Bouas Henry, Missouri Western State University. The Test Bank includes over 200 questions for each text chapter (multiple choice, true/false, and essay).

### ABC Videos: Introductory Psychology

Volume I ISBN: 978-0-495-50306-4

Volume II ISBN: 978-0-495-59637-0

Volume III ISBN: 978-0-495-60490-7

Available to adopters, these ABC videos feature short, high-interest clips about current studies and research in psychology. These videos are perfect to start discussions or to enrich lectures. Topics include brain damage, measuring IQ, sleep patterns, obsessive-compulsive disorder, obedience to authority, rules of attraction, and much more.

### WebTutor on Blackboard and WebCT

Jumpstart your course with customizable, rich, text-specific content within your Course Management System.

- Jumpstart—Simply load a WebTutor cartridge into your Course Management System.
- Customizable—Easily blend, add, edit, reorganize, or delete content.
- Content—Rich, text-specific content, media assets, quizzing, weblinks, discussion topics, interactive games and exercises, and more.

Whether you want to Web-enable your class or put an entire course online, WebTutor delivers. Visit **webtutor.cengage.com** to learn more.

## Student Supplements

### Aplia™ for *What Is Psychology? Essentials,* Second Edition

www.aplia.com

Aplia is an online interactive learning solution that improves comprehension and outcomes by increasing student effort and engagement. Aplia provides automatically graded assignments with detailed, immediate explanations on every question. Aplia presents a variety of question types to reinforce student reading and require them to demonstrate their understanding of the material in multiple ways. Short engagement activities—such as experiments, videos, and surveys—provide experiential learning opportunities while illustrating concepts, piquing students' interest, and motivating them to learn more. As students complete assignments, grades flow directly into your Aplia gradebook.

To package Aplia with each new text, contact your local Cengage representative. For a demo, visit **www .aplia.com.**

### Psychology CourseMate

Psychology CourseMate includes:

- An interactive eBook
- Interactive teaching and learning tools including:
  - Quizzes
  - Flashcards
  - Videos
  - Tools formerly found in the study guide
  - And more
- Engagement Tracker, a first-of-its-kind tool that monitors student engagement in the course

Go to **login.cengage.com** to access these resources.

### CengageNOW™

CengageNOW offers all of your teaching and learning resources in one intuitive program organized around the essential activities you perform for class—lecturing, creating assignments, grading, quizzing, and tracking student progress and performance. CengageNOW's intuitive "tabbed" design allows you to navigate to all key functions with a single click and a unique homepage tells you just what needs to be done and when. CengageNOW provides students access to an integrated eBook, interactive tutorials, videos, and animations that help them get the most out of your course.

### Writing Papers in Psychology: A Student Guide to Research Papers, Essays, Proposals, Posters, and Handouts

ISBN-13: 978-0-534-53331-1

This brief, inexpensive, and easy-to-use "how-to" manual has helped thousands of students in psychology and related fields with the task of writing term papers and reports. This best seller includes a wealth of information and has been updated to reflect the latest APA Style Manual.

### Writing With Style: APA Style Made Easy

ISBN-13: 978-0-495-09972-7

This accessible and invaluable workbook-style reference guide will help your students smoothly make the transition from writing for composition classes to writing for psychology classes. In her Third Edition of *Writing With Style,* author Lenore T. Szuchman quickly and succinctly provides the basics of style presented by the Fifth Edition of the APA's Publication Manual. Dr. Szuchman's years of experience teaching writing-intensive courses give her an inside track on the trouble spots students often encounter when writing papers and dealing with APA style. Her students play a large part in tailoring this guide's exercises to ensure an effective learning experience. This unique workbook format offers both a quick reference to APA style and interactive exercises that give students a chance to practice what they've learned.

## Challenging Your Preconceptions: Thinking Critically About Psychology
ISBN-13: 978-0-534-26739-4

This supplement supports the development of critical thinking skills necessary to success in the introductory psychology course. The chapter sequence mirrors the organization of the typical introductory psychology course. In the first chapter, the author identifies seven characteristics of critical thinkers, and in the following chapters he dissects a challenging issue in the discipline and models critical thinking for the reader. Each chapter concludes with an analysis of the process, exercises for the student, and extensive references. This useful volume supports the full semester of the course.

## Critical Thinking in Psychology: Separating Sense from Nonsense
ISBN-13: 978-0-534-63459-1

Do your students have the tools to distinguish between the true science of human thought and behavior from pop psychology? John Ruscio's book provides a tangible and compelling framework for making that distinction. Because we are inundated with "scientific" claims, the author does not merely differentiate science and pseudoscience, but goes further to teach the fundamentals of scientific reasoning on which students can base their evaluation of information.

## Cross-Cultural Perspectives in Introductory Psychology
ISBN-13: 978-0-534-54653-6

With its 27 carefully selected cross-cultural articles, this book enriches the introductory psychology course—helping students to better understand the similarities and differences among the peoples of the world as they relate to psychological principles, concepts, and issues.

## Introduction to Positive Psychology
ISBN-13: 978-0-534-64453-8

This brief paperback presents in-depth coverage of the relatively new area of positive psychology. Topically organized, it looks at how positive psychology relates to stresses and health within such traditional research areas as developmental, clinical, personality, motivational, social, and behavioral psychology.

## Acknowledgments

Writing a college textbook has been an exhausting yet rewarding experience. We are ordinary college professors who teach four to six classes every semester, so we are often writing in whatever free time we have—weekends, nights, and holidays. We do not live in a "publish or perish" environment. Instead we are valued for our contributions to student learning and service to our institutions. Yet, we have grown so much as educators and psychologists in tackling this project. This would not have been possible without the support of many people who deserve our acknowledgement.

We would like to thank Melissa Pedone at Valencia College and Pamela Elfenbein and Al Panu from Gainesville State College for their administrative support. Our deepest gratitude and thanks also go out to the great people who have helped with both the development of *What Is Psychology?*, Third Edition and this *Essentials* edition: Jaime Perkins, Kristin Makarewycz, Shannon LeMay-Finn, Kim Russell, Liz Rhoden, Nicole Lee Petel, Mary Noel, Christy Frame, Vernon Boes, Paige Leeds, Jessica Alderman, Roman Barnes, and everyone else at Cengage and Lachina Publishing Services who help make these texts the best possible learning tools for students everywhere.

We also would like to thank the following reviewers for their insightful comments and expert guidance in developing this text:

David Baskind
*Delta College*

Brenda J. Beagle
*John Tyler Community College*

Amy A. Bradshaw
*Embry-Riddle Aeronautical University*

Wendy Brooks
*College of the Desert*

Mary Cordell
*Hills College*

Adria DiBenedetto
*Quinnipiac University*

Kimberley Duff
*Cerritos College*

Jean M. Egan
*Asnuntuck Community College*

Kimberly Fairchild
*Manhattan College*

Keith D. Foust
*Shasta College*

Laura Fry
*Coconino Community College*

Terry Lyn Funston
*Sauk Valley Community College*

Andrea Goldstein
*Keiser University*

Pete Gram
*Pensacola Junior College*

Julie A. Gurner
*Community College of Philadelphia*

Jill Haasch
*Glenville State College*

Sean C. Hill
*Lewis and Clark Community College*

Bobby Hutchison
*Modesto Junior College*

Joni Jecklin
*Heartland Community College*

Michael Leffingwell
*Tarrant County College, NE Campus*

John Lu
*Concordia University Irvine*

George Martinez
*Somerset Community College*

Cheryl McGill
*Florence Darlington Technical College*

Robin P. McHaelen
*University of Connecticut, School of Social Work*

Yvonne Kim McKeithen-Franks
*Massasoit Community College*

Antoinette R. Miller
*Clayton State University*

Nancy Murray
*Vermont Technical College*

Linda Petroff
*Central Community College*

Andrea Rashtian
*California State University Northridge*

Illeana P. Rodriguez
*Triton College*

Gwendolyn Scott
*University of Houston-Downtown*

Jason S. Spiegelman
*College of Baltimore County*

Ronald W. Stoffey
*Kutztown University of Pennsylvania*

Eva Szeli
*Arizona State University*

Christopher C. Thomas
*Florence Darlington Technical College*

Jeff Wachsmuth
*Napa Valley College*

We would also like to thank our friends and colleagues at Gainesville State College and Valencia College for their support and latitude over the past decade. Special gratitude goes to the students who helped shape this text by offering their stories, insights, and curiosities about psychology to our readers: Cris Arthurs, Amber Brandt, Franco Chevalier, Diana Flores, Pamela Hunter, Edgar Lituma, Stan Roberts, Tamara Stewart, Tyler Larko, Joshua Kennedy, Carolanne Parker, Megan Arispe, Paige Redmon, Jonathan Gantes, Jean-Paul Eslava, Brooke Landers, Heather Lacis, Zach Veatch, Joseph Vickers, Jeff Wright, Cristian Caceres, Erica Breglio, Karen Arevalo, Candace Kendrick, Christie Knight, Emily Phillips, Amber Maner, Nick Tatum, Holly Sosebee, Rebecca Mboh, Erick Hernandez, Cassidy Turner, Taylor Evans, Pam Lively, Clinton Blake Roberts, Bredron Lytle, Ally Burke, Angel Rosa-Rivera, Bianca Vaughan, Brittany Bryant, Brittany Teller, Carla Belliard, Charlotte Anderson, Christian Forero, Danie Lipschutz, David Melendez, Dierdra Torres, Emmanuel Cotto, Erika Larkins, Jaelynn Packer, Jennifer Deane, Jesse Madonna, Jose Moreno, Junior Louis, Justen Carter, Katiria Mejia, Kayla Campana, Keiran Siddiqi, Kiara Suarez, Kristin MacPherson, Laura Fernandez, Lesley Manzano, Lisandra Machado, Melissa Tyndale, Michael Horsfall, Nick DeGori, Niesha Hazzard, Paola Chavez, Ramon Velez, Rebecca Cantarero, Richard Nieves, Saqib Abbas, Sarah Knych, Sheila Quinones, Susy Alvarez, Takese McKenzie, Tiffany Slowey, Victor Ocasio, Yanilsa Osoria, Michelle Lewis, Tawnya Brown, Crystal Athas Thatcher, Kaymari Invictus, and Jeff Deshommes.

We would also like to thank the thousands of other students we have worked with over the years. In your own way, each of you has helped us to become better teachers and better people. Our hope is that this book will touch many other students and foster an interest in and passion for psychology.

Finally, we would like to thank our families. Susann would like to thank her husband, Eddie, for his loving support and for selflessly allowing her to put work first on far too many occasions. Ellen would like to thank her husband, Dave, for his technical assistance, his tireless rereading of material, and his patience and support through all the frustration, deadlines, and apprehension. Love is indeed something that you do.

# 1

# What Is
# PSYCHOLOGY?

© Greg Hinsdale/Corbis

## Chapter Outline

*It was the first day* of the semester. Parking as usual was a challenge. Christian finally found a spot, parked his car, and headed toward campus. While grabbing a coffee at the college café, he ran into his friend Andrew. "Hey, man, what's up?" he asked. "Not much," Andrew replied. "Just getting coffee before I head to class." "What are you taking?" Christian asked. "Well, I've got math and music appreciation tomorrow. Today, I've got oceanography and intro to psych. I'm heading to the psych class now." Christian smiled, "Cool, I've got that psych class now too." The two students grabbed their coffees and headed toward the psychology building, continuing their conversation. "What do you think the course will be about?" Andrew asked. "Probably how you feel about things. Ought to be an easy A—like being with Dr. Phil all semester," Christian joked. Andrew laughed. "Yeah, I guess we'll see how screwed up we are and get a lot of therapy." "Speak for yourself," Christian kidded. "I figure it's just commonsense stuff, things your parents have been telling you since you were a kid. Shouldn't be too hard." Andrew nodded in agreement as they arrived at the classroom. "Let's take a seat in the back so we don't have to share our feelings too much," Christian whispered. The two found a seat in the back and waited for class to begin.

© Ellen Pastorino

*Many students hold misconceptions about the field of psychology.*

3

# What Is Psychology?

Welcome to the world of **psychology**, the scientific study of behavior and mental processes. But what exactly does that include? Behavior includes actions, feelings, and biological states such as sleeping. Mental processes include problem solving, intelligence, and memory, to name just a few. Psychology is a *science* because psychologists conduct research in accord with the **scientific method**—a systematic process used to test ideas about behavior. Psychologists analyze the behavior of humans as well as other species.

Psychology is probably one of the few disciplines in which students come to the first class believing they already know much about the topic. We see psychologists and psychiatrists on talk shows (Dr. Phil, Dr. Drew) and listen to them on the radio. We frequently see them depicted on television (*Lie to Me*, *Criminal Minds*, *Bones*) and in the movies (*Shutter Island*; *A Beautiful Mind*; *I, Robot*). Many of these portrayals are quite entertaining, but they do not always represent psychology accurately. As a result, the public image of the discipline tends to be distorted.

The purpose of this textbook is to help you develop a deeper understanding of psychology. In this chapter, we explain what psychologists do, how they think, and where they work. It is a general overview of the field of psychology, an introduction to the more specific areas of psychology discussed in subsequent chapters. We describe how psychology became a science, and what the field is like today. We also describe the goals of psychological research and how psychologists study behavior.

Each chapter begins with former students relating how psychological principles and concepts have helped them better understand their jobs, their relationships, and their world. We hope that by reading these real-life stories, you will find psychological topics easier to understand and will be better able to apply psychological principles and concepts to your own life.

## Correcting Common Misconceptions About the Field of Psychology

You are probably reading this book because you have enrolled in a general psychology course. Your expectations of what you will learn have been influenced by your general impressions of psychology. Much of the psychological information presented in the media focuses on practitioners, therapy, and helping others, and you—like the students in the opening section—may have the impression that psychology is all about how you feel and how you can feel better. Although a large proportion of psychologists counsel or otherwise treat clients, most of these professionals hold a doctorate degree in psychology, which required that they study scientific methodology and complete a considerable amount of research (Wicherski, Michalski, & Kohout, 2009).

Psychology is rooted in scientific research. The information in this book is research based. Every idea put forward in the field is subject to scientific study. You will notice that many statements in this text are followed by names and years in parentheses—for example, (Pastorino, 2012). These text citations refer to the scientific studies on which the stated conclusions are based, with the researcher name(s) and date of the study. The complete research citations can be found in the References section at the end of this book. An example of a complete research citation is shown in ■ FIGURE 1.1.

A psychologist's explanation of a particular behavior is generally presented as a theory. A **theory** is an explanation of why and how a behavior occurs. It does

**psychology** the scientific study of behavior and mental processes

**scientific method** a systematic process used by psychologists for testing hypotheses about behavior

**theory** an explanation of why and how a behavior occurs

not explain a particular behavior for all people, but it provides general guidelines that summarize facts and help us organize research on a particular subject.

We all, at times, fancy ourselves as psychologists. We interact with people all the time, we observe others' behaviors, and we have our own personal experiences. Therefore, we might naturally think that we already know a lot about psychology. People often behave the way we think they will behave, so psychology seems as though it is just common sense. However, we often overlook the examples of behavior that don't confirm our expectations or support our preexisting beliefs. Psychologists systematically test their ideas about behavior using the prescribed methods and procedures we will describe later in this chapter.

Take a look at ■ TABLE 1.1 and answer the questions about behavior. All the statements are false, yet many students have such misconceptions or believe such myths about human behavior. Psychological findings do *not* always confirm our everyday observations about behavior. Only by objectively measuring and testing our ideas and observations about behavior can we determine which ideas are more likely to stand up to scientific scrutiny. Behavior is much more complex than the simple statements in Table 1.1 suggest.

Most students entering a general psychology class, like Christian and Andrew, expect to focus on diagnosing and treating mental disorders. Although some psychologists specialize in mental illness, many others work in academic settings,

**You Asked...**

*What exactly do psychologists do, other than treat mental disorders or help people cope?*

PAOLA CHAVEZ, STUDENT

**APA Style:**

**Author, A. A., Author, B. B., & Author, C. C. (Year). Title of article:**

**Subtitle of article. *Title of Periodical or Journal, Vol #,* pages.**

Example:

Whitton, S. W., & Whisman, M. A. (2010). Relationship satisfaction instability and depression. *Journal of Family Psychology, 24,* 791–794.

**FIGURE**

# 1.1

**Reference Citations in Psychology**

The References section at the end of this book lists the complete source for each citation. Here is the APA style format for psychological references. The citation for this particular reference would appear in the text as (Whitton & Whisman, 2010).

## TABLE 1.1
## How Much Do You Know About Behavior?

| Indicate whether you believe each statement is true (T) or false (F). | | |
|---|---|---|
| 1. We are either left-brain or right-brain thinkers. | T | F |
| 2. Genes work only during prenatal development. | T | F |
| 3. No new neurons develop after infancy. | T | F |
| 4. Brain injury in children is always worse than brain injury in adults. | T | F |
| 5. Stress is caused by bad things that happen to you. | T | F |
| 6. During sleep, the brain rests. | T | F |
| 7. There are female brains and male brains. | T | F |
| 8. Males are better than females at math. | T | F |
| 9. We have only five senses. | T | F |
| 10. Legal drugs don't hurt the brain, but illegal ones do. | T | F |
| 11. Our memory works like a video recorder. | T | F |
| 12. Schizophrenia means you have multiple personalities. | T | F |

in the business world, in education, or in government agencies. Psychology is an extremely diverse field, and new specialties are appearing each year. Psychologists are interested in numerous topics, including learning, memory, aging, development, gender, motivation, emotion, sports, criminal behavior, and many other subjects. We cannot cover every area of psychology in this textbook, but we will give you an overview of the main areas of psychological research.

## Psychology Will Teach You About Critical Thinking

Because behavior is so complex, psychological theories generally don't definitively explain the behavior of all people. To think like a psychologist, you must think critically, analyzing and evaluating information. You must be able to distinguish true psychological information from **pseudopsychology**. Pseudopsychological findings sound persuasive, but they are not necessarily based on scientific procedures. Their conclusions may go far beyond the scope of their actual data. For example, have you ever heard that people use only 10% of their brains? Many college students believe this false statement despite evidence that shows it is not true (Higbee & Clay, 1998). To think like a psychologist, you must be skeptical rather than accepting about explanations of behavior.

**Critical thinking** involves analyzing and evaluating information and applying it to other situations. Critical thinking also makes you an intelligent consumer of information. You will be encouraged to practice this skill throughout the book as you read the chapter and test your mastery of the material in the *Let's Review* sections at the end of each main topic and in the *What Do You Know? Assess Your Understanding* questions at the end of each chapter.

Because we all engage in behavior, much of the information in this text will apply to your life. We all dream, remember, like or dislike others, are motivated, have high or low self-esteem, experience depression, behave aggressively, help others, learn, perceive, and use our senses. Consequently, we recommend that you apply the material in this text to your own behavior as much as possible. This connection will increase your interest in the text, and you will study more effectively.

**pseudopsychology**   psychological information or conclusions that sound scientific but that have not been systematically tested using the scientific method

**critical thinking**   thought processes used to evaluate and analyze information and apply it to other situations

# Let's
## REVIEW

In this section we defined psychology and identified some common misconceptions about the field. For a quick check of your understanding, answer these questions.

1. Which of the following statements is *true*?
   a. Psychology is just common sense.
   b. Psychologists only study abnormal behavior.
   c. Psychologists know why people behave the way that they do.
   d. Psychologists test ideas about behavior according to the scientific method.

2. Which of the following topics would a psychologist most likely study?
   a. Weather patterns in Africa
   b. Memory changes in adults
   c. Causes of the Vietnam War
   d. All of the above

3. Which of the following statements is *not* a pseudopsychology claim?
   a. Transplant organs carry personality traits that are always transferred from donors to receivers.
   b. Walking on hot coals without burning one's feet requires paranormal abilities.
   c. You can make a blood clot in your brain disappear by humming.
   d. Several studies show a relationship between academic achievement and self-esteem.

Answers 1. d; 2. b; 3. d

# The Origins of Psychology

**LEARNING OBJECTIVE**

● Describe the early schools of psychology and identify the major figures that influenced its development.

Psychology has been described as having "a long past but only a short history" (Ebbinghaus, 1910, p. 9). Although psychology did not formally become a science until the 1870s, people have always been interested in explaining behavior. The roots of psychology can be traced back to philosophy and medicine in ancient Egypt, Greece, India, and Rome. Although these issues were not considered "psychological" at the time, doctors and philosophers debated many of the same issues that concern modern psychologists.

## Early Approaches: Structuralism, Functionalism, Gestalt Psychology, and Psychoanalytic Theory

Traditionally, psychology's birth is linked with the first psychology laboratory, which was established by Wilhelm Wundt in 1879 at the University of Leipzig, in Germany. As you will see, some of the people who brought psychology into the scientific arena were trained as physicians; others were more philosophical in nature. However, these differences produced a field that was broad and complex, with many avenues of exploration.

### WILHELM WUNDT, EDWARD TITCHENER, AND STRUCTURALISM

For Wilhelm Wundt (1832–1920), the goal of psychology was to study conscious processes of the mind and the body. He wanted to know what thought processes enable us to experience the external world. In particular, Wundt attempted to detail the *structure* of our mental experiences. Like a chemist who questions what elements combine to create different substances, Wundt questioned what elements, when combined, would explain mental processes. Wundt's view that mental experiences were created by different elements is referred to as **structuralism**, a term coined not by Wundt but by his student Edward Titchener.

To identify the structure of thought, British psychologist Titchener (1867–1927) used a process known as **introspection**, a self-observation technique. Trained observers were presented with an event and asked to describe their mental processes. The observations were repeated many times. From these introspections, Titchener identified three basic elements of all conscious experiences: sensations, images, and feelings.

© Bettmann/Corbis

Wilhelm Wundt (1832–1920) wanted to know what psychological processes enable us to experience the external world.

---

© David Young-Wolf/PhotoEdit

## YOUR TURN | Active Learning

To illustrate the nature of introspection, look at the photo of the object shown here. If you were asked to describe the object, what would you say? How do you know that the object is a potato? Does the object fit your visual image or memory of a potato? That is, does it look like a potato? If it were in front of you right now, how else might you conclude it is a potato? Does it smell like a potato, taste like a potato, and feel like a potato? Using your senses, you deduce that the object before you is a potato.

Apply the technique of introspection to determine how you know what this object is.

**structuralism** an early psychological perspective concerned with identifying the basic elements of experience

**introspection** observing one's own thoughts, feelings, or sensations

Wundt's and Titchener's research went beyond introspection and structuralism to encompass a very broad view of psychology. They also conducted detailed studies on color vision, visual illusions, attention, and feelings, and influenced the field of psychology through their students, many of whom went on to establish psychology departments and laboratories in the United States. For example, Titchener's first graduate student, American Margaret Washburn (1871–1939), became the first woman to earn a doctorate in psychology. Washburn did not share Titchener's emphasis on structuralism, but instead investigated the connection between motor movement and the mind and conducted extensive research on animal behavior.

## MAX WERTHEIMER AND GESTALT PSYCHOLOGY

Like Washburn, other psychologists soon reacted against the limited view of the mind that structuralism presented, claiming that it did not adequately explain how we actively organize or *perceive* our sensations. Such disagreement gave rise to another early school of psychology called **Gestalt psychology**. The word *Gestalt* is German for "whole form." Gestalt psychology, founded by Czech/German psychologist Max Wertheimer (1880–1943) in the early 1900s, emphasized how our minds organize sensory stimuli to produce the perception of a whole form (such as perceiving a group of stars in the night sky as the Big Dipper).

## WILLIAM JAMES AND FUNCTIONALISM

American psychologist and philosopher William James (1842–1910) had visited Wundt's laboratory in Germany but did not share Wundt's focus on breaking down mental events into their smallest elements. Rather, James proposed a focus on the wholeness of an event and the impact of the environment on behavior. He emphasized *how* a mental process operates as opposed to the *structure* of a mental process. He came to believe that consciousness and thought evolved through the process of natural selection, to help the organism adapt to its environment (Nielsen & Day, 1999). *Evolution* and *natural selection* were ideas that were quite new at the time. *Evolution* refers to the development of a species—the process by which, through a series of changes over time, humans have acquired behaviors and characteristics that distinguish them from other species. For James, the question was not what elements contribute to one's experience but rather what *function* the event serves for the person or animal. How does a particular behavior help an organism adapt to its environment and thereby increase its chances of surviving and reproducing? James's perspective on psychology became known as **functionalism**.

Functionalism's focus on the adaptive value of behavior was influenced by Charles Darwin's theory of evolution. Darwin's theory speculated that certain behaviors or traits that enhance survival are *naturally selected*. For example, Darwin had collected several different types of birds in the Galapagos Islands. The birds were all about the same size but had different beaks (see photo). Through research with other scientists in London, Darwin discovered that the birds were all finches and that each species was uniquely related to a specific island. Darwin thought that the different species had been formed from a small number of common ancestors. The differences in their beaks could be attributed to adapting to different food supplies on each island. According to James,

The first woman to be awarded a doctorate in psychology was Margaret Washburn (1871–1939).

William James (1842–1910) is associated with functionalism.

**Gestalt psychology** an early psychological approach that emphasized how our minds organize sensory stimuli to produce the perception of a whole form

**functionalism** an early psychological perspective concerned with how behavior helps people adapt to their environment

Darwin's finches illustrated the interaction between genes and adaptation to the environment. The different species originated from common ancestors (genes), yet variations in their beaks arose as they adapted to different food supplies on each island.

if human behavior is naturally selected like Darwin's finches' beaks, it is important for psychologists to understand the function, or survival value, of a behavior.

Functionalism was not the whole of James's work in the young field of psychology. James suggested applications of psychology to teaching, creating the field of *educational psychology*. The James-Lange theory of emotion, formulated by James and a Danish physiologist, Carl Lange, at about the same time, describes how physical sensations give rise to emotions (more on this in Chapter 8). In addition, James published books on religious experiences and philosophy. James's open-mindedness also influenced psychology when he became intrigued by the unorthodox ideas of a Viennese physician named Sigmund Freud.

## SIGMUND FREUD AND PSYCHOANALYTIC THEORY

Sigmund Freud is probably the best known historical figure in psychology, and his ideas permeate Western culture in music, media, advertising, art, and humor—a testament to his influence and importance. Before creating theories of psychology, however, Freud (1856–1939) studied medicine, focusing on neurology and disorders of the nervous system. He began studying people with all kinds of "nervous" disorders, such as an intense fear of horses or heights or the sudden paralysis of an arm. He began asking patients to express any and every thought that occurred to them, no matter how trivial or unpleasant. Freud theorized that encouraging patients to say whatever came to mind allowed them to recall forgotten memories that seemed to underlie their problems. This process, known today as *free association*, is one element of *psychoanalysis*, a therapy that Freud developed.

From these experiences, Freud came to believe that the *unconscious* plays a crucial role in human behavior. For Freud, the unconscious was that part of the mind that includes impulses, behaviors, and desires that we are unaware of but that influence our behavior. Until this time, much of psychology had focused on conscious mental processes. Freud's focus on the unconscious was unique and led to his formulation of **psychoanalytic theory**. According to this theory, humans are similar to animals in that they possess basic sexual and aggressive instincts that motivate behavior. However, unlike animals, humans can reason and think, especially as they mature. In childhood we learn to use these conscious reasoning abilities to deal with and to suppress our basic sexual and aggressive desires so that we can be viewed approvingly by others. For Freud, the conflict between the conscious reasoning part of the mind and the unconscious instinctual one was key to understanding human behavior. Although controversial, Freud's theory dominated European psychology. However, in the early 1900s in the United States, Freud's ideas were overshadowed by another approach to understanding behavior called *behaviorism*.

Sigmund Freud's (1856–1939) focus on the unconscious was unique and led to his formulation of psychoanalytic theory.

## Behaviorism: A True Science of Psychology

In the 1920s, in the United States, functionalism was slowly being replaced by a school of thought referred to as **behaviorism**. A growing number of psychologists believed that in order for psychology to be taken seriously as a "true" science, it must focus on observable behavior and not on the mind. You can't see the mind or what a person thinks; you can only see what a person does. Behaviorists believed that only overt, observable behaviors could truly be measured consistently from person to person. One of the most vocal proponents of this school of thought was American psychologist John B. Watson (1878–1958).

**psychoanalytic theory**   Sigmund Freud's view that emphasizes the influence of unconscious desires and conflicts on behavior

**behaviorism**   a psychological perspective that emphasizes the study of observable responses and behavior

## JOHN B. WATSON'S BEHAVIORISM

Watson was influenced by Russian physiologist Ivan Pavlov's studies of digestion in dogs. While measuring and analyzing the first process of digestion (salivation), Pavlov (1849–1936) noticed that his dogs started to salivate before he gave them meat powder. When the experiments first started, the salivation had occurred only *after* the dogs were given the meat powder. To further study this curious change in response, Pavlov performed experiments to train the dogs to salivate to other non-food stimuli. (You will learn more about Pavlov's classic experiments in Chapter 5.)

Pavlov's experiments were important to Watson as examples of how behavior is the product of *stimuli* and *responses*. A **stimulus** is any object or event that is perceived by our senses. A **response** is an organism's reaction to a stimulus. To further his point, Watson and his associate, Rosalie Rayner, performed an experiment on a 9-month-old infant named Albert. Watson first presented "Little Albert" with the stimulus of a white rat. Albert played with the white rat and showed no fear of it (response). Knowing that infants fear loud noises, Watson paired the two stimuli, first presenting the rat to Albert and then presenting a loud gong sound behind Albert's head. Little Albert reacted to the loud noise with the startle, or fear, response. Over and over again, Watson repeated the procedure of pairing the two stimuli—presenting the rat followed by the loud gong. Then, when Watson presented the rat to Albert with no gong, the infant responded with the startle response. Watson had conditioned Little Albert to fear a white rat, a rat that Albert had played with earlier without fear. This demonstrated for Watson that observable stimuli and responses should be the focus of psychology. Unfortunately for Watson, a personal scandal resulted in his dismissal as the chair of the psychology department at Johns Hopkins University (Buckley, 1989).

## B. F. SKINNER AND BEHAVIORAL CONSEQUENCES

Although Watson was no longer operating within mainstream psychology, behaviorism remained strong in the United States, partially due to the work of B. F. Skinner (1904–1990). Skinner, like Watson, believed that psychology should focus on observable behavior. But Skinner added a dimension to Watson's framework: *consequences*. Skinner believed that psychologists should look not only at the stimuli in the environment that cause a particular response but also at what happens to a person or animal after the response—what Skinner called the consequences of a behavior. To illustrate consequences, let's look at Little Albert's behavior from Skinner's perspective. Once Albert was afraid of the rat, how would he act when he saw it? If Albert moved away from the rat, his behavior effectively reduced his fear. Feeling less fear or anxiety is a good (positive) consequence, or outcome. Whenever Albert saw the rat again, he probably moved away even faster. Skinner asserted that positive consequences, such as the reduction of Albert's anxiety, would lead him to engage in the same behavior again. Negative consequences, or outcomes that are not liked, would lessen Albert's desire to engage in the behavior again. We know these processes as *reinforcement* and *punishment*, topics that are explored further in Chapter 5.

## Beyond Behaviorism: Humanism, Cognitive Psychology, and the Birth of Positive Psychology

Behaviorism was a dominant force in American psychology until the 1960s. By that time, it became evident that this one theory could not account for all behaviors. Behaviors such as feelings and thoughts could not easily be reduced to stimuli and responses. This criticism, combined with the social climate of the time,

John B. Watson and Rosalie Rayner showed how stimuli and responses could be studied in their experiment on Little Albert.

Archives of the History of American Psychology. University of Akron, Akron, Ohio

B. F. Skinner's (1904–1990) behaviorism emphasized the influence of consequences on behavior.

Nina Leen/Time Life Pictures/Getty Images

**stimulus**  any object or event that is perceived by our senses

**response**  an organism's reaction to a stimulus

opened the door for other views on behavior and a willingness to explore topics previously ignored.

## THE HUMANISTS

Discontent with behaviorism and the social upheaval of the 1960s led to a growing interest in an approach toward treatment called **humanism**. Many psychologists did not accept the behaviorists' view that humans were governed by stimuli and responses, with no will of their own to change their behavior. In the 1960s, societal values were rapidly changing, and the civil rights movement and the Vietnam War sparked widespread civil disobedience. Many young Americans were endorsing women's rights, free love, and free will. Psychology was changing too, and humanists emphasized that everyone possesses inner resources for personal growth and development. The goal of humanistic therapy, therefore, would be to help people use these inner resources to make healthier choices and thus lead better lives. Humanism stressed the free will of individuals to choose their own patterns of behavior. Two well-known humanists are Abraham Maslow and Carl Rogers. You will read more about their ideas in Chapters 8 and 12.

## COGNITIVE PSYCHOLOGY

While humanism was changing how psychologists were treating clients, changes were also occurring in research psychology. Researchers were becoming disenchanted with the limits of testing stimuli, responses, and consequences in the laboratory, and there was renewed interest in the study of mental processes. Research expanded to subjects such as memory, problem solving, and decision making. However, unlike the earlier functionalism and structuralism, this new study of mental processes was based on more objective experimental methods. Acknowledging that mental processes are not directly observable to the eye, scientists believed that reasonable inferences about mental processes could be made from performance data.

For example, in studying memory processes in children, a researcher can ask children what strategies or techniques they use to remember a list of items. If children using a particular strategy (Strategy A) remember more compared to children using a different strategy (Strategy B), then one can infer that there must be something about Strategy A that facilitates memory. This conclusion is reasonable even though we can't directly see the children use the techniques. Such reasoning led to much experimental research on mental processes, or *cognition*. By the 1980s, the study of cognitive processes, or **cognitive psychology**, was a part of mainstream psychology.

## THE BIRTH OF POSITIVE PSYCHOLOGY

Focusing on *how* we think, particularly whether our thoughts are pessimistic or optimistic in nature, soon led to a growing emphasis on human strengths and on how humans attain happiness, called **positive psychology**. Led by American psychologists Martin Seligman (1942–) (Seligman & Csikszentmihalyi, 2000) and Ed Diener (1946–), positive psychology has produced an explosion of research over the past decade describing the factors that contribute to happiness, positive emotions, and well-being (Ruark, 2009; Wallis, 2005). By scientifically studying positive aspects of human behavior, the goal of positive psychology is to enable individuals, families, and communities to thrive.

**humanism**   a psychological perspective that emphasizes the personal growth and potential of humans

**cognitive psychology**   the study of mental processes such as reasoning and problem solving

**positive psychology**   the study of factors that contribute to happiness, positive emotions, and well-being

Positive psychology investigates those factors that contribute to happiness, positive emotions, and well-being.

Anne Ackermann/Getty Images

# Let's
## REVIEW

In this section we discussed early theories of psychology. For a quick check of your understanding, answer these questions.

**1.** Javier wants to know how aggression helps a person adapt to the environment. Which historical approach is Javier emphasizing?
  **a.** Structuralism     **c.** Functionalism
  **b.** Psychoanalysis     **d.** Humanism

**2.** Karena believes that elements, when combined, can explain our mental processes. Which historical approach is Karena emphasizing?
  **a.** Structuralism     **c.** Functionalism
  **b.** Psychoanalysis     **d.** Humanism

**3.** Which of the following persons would be least likely to emphasize the influence of stimuli and responses on behavior?
  **a.** John Watson     **c.** Rosalie Rayner
  **b.** Carl Rogers     **d.** B. F. Skinner

*Answers 1. c; 2. a; 3. b*

## LEARNING OBJECTIVES

- Distinguish among the seven modern perspectives of psychology and understand the nature of the eclectic approach.

- Describe the training of a psychologist and compare and contrast the different specialty areas of the profession.

- Describe how women and minorities have contributed to the field of psychology.

**biological perspective**  an approach that focuses on physical causes of behavior

**neuroscience**  a field of science that investigates the relationships between the nervous system and behavior/mental processes

**evolutionary perspective**  an approach that focuses on how evolution and natural selection influence behavior

# Psychology in the Modern World

Given the historical sketch of psychology you have just read, it is probably no surprise to learn that modern psychology is a very broad profession. Not everyone agreed on how to explain behavior then, just as many debate the causes of behavior today. Many modern perspectives are an extension of the historical schools of thought. Here we discuss seven orientations or perspectives on behavior (■ FIGURE 1.2): *biological, evolutionary, cognitive, psychodynamic, behavioral, sociocultural,* and *humanistic.*

## Modern Perspectives and the Eclectic Approach

Psychologists who adopt a **biological perspective** look for a physical cause for a particular behavior. Such psychologists examine genetic, biochemical, and nervous system (brain functioning) relationships to behavior and mental processes. The biological perspective is also a branch of science referred to as **neuroscience**. (We discuss the physical processes of the nervous system in Chapter 2.) For example, knowing how the brain monitors motor behavior has enabled neuroscientists to develop devices to assist people with severe motor deficits or spinal cord injuries, as seen in the Neuroscience Applies to Your World box (Srinivasan, Eden, Mitter, & Brown, 2007).

Closely aligned to the biological perspective is the **evolutionary perspective**. This approach is similar to the biological approach in that both see the cause of behavior as biological. However, this is where the similarity ends. The evolutionary perspective proposes that natural selection is the process at work. Behaviors that increase your chances of surviving are favored or selected over behaviors that decrease your chances of surviving. Remember James's functionalism? One could say that James was an early evolutionary psychologist. Similarly, this approach analyzes whether a particular behavior increases a person's ability to adapt to the environment, thus increasing the chances of surviving, reproducing, and passing one's genes on to future generations (Buss, 2009).

## Neuroscience Applies to Your World:

### Restoring and Enhancing Motor Movement

Using electroencephalography (EEGs) and other brain imaging and computer technology, neuroscientists have been able to measure how a person's body movements cause nerve cells in the brain to fire. They can then use this information to design neuromotor prosthetic devices, such as robotic arms, that work in much the same way. These appliances can help replace or restore lost motor functioning in people with spinal cord injuries and other severe motor deficits (Hochberg, Serruya, Friehs et al., 2006).

The Rehabilitation Institute of Chicago (RIC)

The **cognitive perspective** explains behavior with an emphasis on thoughts and interpretations based on memory, expectations, beliefs, problem solving, or decision making. A cognitive view focuses on how people process information and on how that process may influence behavior. For example, in explaining depression, a cognitive approach focuses on how people who are depressed think and perceive the world differently from people who are not depressed. You will learn more about cognitive processes in Chapters 6 and 7, when we discuss such topics as memory, problem solving, thinking, decision making, intelligence, and language.

The **psychodynamic perspective** is a collective term that refers to those assumptions about behavior originally conceived by Freud, which have been modified by his followers. The psychodynamic view focuses on internal, often unconscious mental processes, motives, and desires or childhood conflicts to explain behavior. For example, many children lie to or manipulate parents to get what they want. The psychodynamic view might suggest that such behavior is an unconscious expression of feelings of powerlessness and lack of control that all children face from time to time.

The **behavioral perspective** focuses on external causes of behavior. It looks at how stimuli in our environment and/or the rewards and punishments we receive influence our behavior and mental processes. This approach suggests that behavior is learned and is influenced by other people and events. For example, if a student studies and then aces an exam, that reward may encourage her to study again the next time. If she only gets an average score, merely passing the test may not be rewarding enough to encourage the student to study for future exams. This perspective stems from Watson's and Skinner's behaviorist views (more on this in Chapter 5).

The **sociocultural perspective** adopts a wider view of the impact of the environment on behavior and mental processes. It suggests that your society or culture influences your actions. Consider, for example, that from 1996 to 2006 the United States had a higher teen birth and abortion rate than Canada, Sweden, and England/Wales (McKay & Barrett, 2010). The sociocultural perspective would attribute this phenomenon to aspects of society that may differ in these countries, such as sexual values, contraceptive availability and use, and exposure to sex education. Sociocultural views will be evident throughout this textbook when differences due to culture, income level, or gender are highlighted.

**cognitive perspective** an approach that focuses on how mental processes influence behavior

**psychodynamic perspective** an approach that focuses on internal unconscious mental processes, motives, and desires that may explain behavior

**behavioral perspective** an approach that focuses on external, environmental influences on behavior

**sociocultural perspective** an approach that focuses on societal and cultural factors that may influence behavior

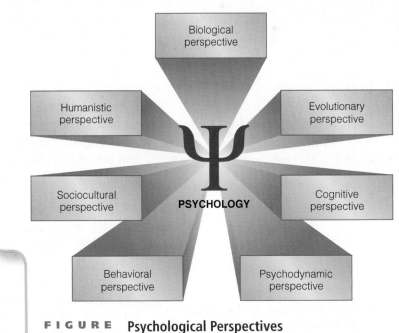

**FIGURE**

**1.2**

**Psychological Perspectives**

Just as a photograph or a piece of art can be examined from many different angles, so too can mental processes and behavior. We call these angles perspectives. Each offers a somewhat different picture of why people behave as they do. Taken as a whole, these perspectives underscore the complex nature of behavior.

The **humanistic perspective** explains behavior as stemming from your choices and free will. These choices are influenced by your *self-concept* (how you think of yourself) and by your *self-esteem* (how you feel about yourself). This view of the self and these feelings toward the self will lead you to choose certain behaviors over others. For example, if you see yourself as a low achiever in school, you may be less likely to take challenging courses or to apply yourself in the courses that you do take. Humanistic views of behavior are explored in Chapters 8, 12, and 14.

Most psychologists do not rigidly adhere to just one of these perspectives but are likely to take what is referred to as an **eclectic approach** when explaining behavior. An eclectic approach integrates or combines several perspectives to provide a more complete and complex picture of behavior. ■ YOU REVIEW 1.1 illustrates these approaches and shows how a combined approach provides a more expansive understanding of behavior than any single approach could, using anxiety as an example.

The sociocultural perspective suggests that one's culture influences behavior.

# YOU REVIEW 1.1

## Looking at Anxiety From Modern Perspectives
Psychologists can examine behavior from many different perspectives.

| PERSPECTIVE | EXPLANATION |
| --- | --- |
| Biological | Anxiety is related to chemicals in the body or to genetics (heredity). |
| Evolutionary | Anxiety is an adaptive response that prepares one to respond to potential threats in the environment. This response helps humans survive because it warns them of danger and thereby helps them avoid situations or people that may harm them. However, in modern times, these threats tend to be ongoing: traffic jams, crowding, and the hectic pace of consumerism. |
| Cognitive | Anxious people think differently than nonanxious people. Anxious people may engage in more pessimistic thinking or worry that everything will go wrong. |
| Psychodynamic | Anxiety is the product of unresolved feelings of hostility, guilt, anger, or sexual attraction experienced in childhood. |
| Behavioral | Anxiety is a learned behavior much like Albert's fear of the white rat. It is a response that is associated with a specific stimulus or a response that has been rewarded. |
| Sociocultural | Anxiety is a product of a person's culture. In the United States, more women than men report being anxious and fearful, and this gender difference results from different socialization experiences. Men in the United States are raised to believe that they must not be afraid, so they are less likely to acknowledge or report anxiety. Women do not experience this pressure to hide their fears, so they are more likely to tell others that they are anxious and to seek treatment. |
| Humanistic | Anxiety is rooted in people's dissatisfaction with their real self (how they perceive themselves) as compared to their ideal self (how they want to be). |
| Eclectic | Anxiety stems from various sources depending on the individual. One person may be prone to anxiety because many people in his family are anxious and he has learned to be anxious from several experiences. Another person may be anxious because she is dissatisfied with herself and believes that everything always goes wrong in her life. |

## Specialty Areas in Psychology

In addition to the various approaches or perspectives psychologists take, they also study different aspects of behavior, which correspond to specialty areas of psychology. A number of these specialty areas are depicted in ■ TABLE 1.2, but keep in mind that there are many more. This diversity stems from the complexity of behavior and the interrelatedness of different areas. What a developmental psychologist studies, for example, is connected to and may have an impact on the work of social, clinical, and educational psychologists.

## Gender, Ethnicity, and the Field of Psychology

In the early development of psychology, women and minorities were not allowed in many instances to receive graduate degrees despite completing all the requirements for such degrees. Despite these constraints and many other societal hurdles, several women and minority individuals contributed significantly to the field. As previously mentioned, Margaret Washburn became the first woman to be awarded a doctorate in psychology in 1894 (Furumoto, 1989). Mary Calkins (1863–1930) became the first female president of the American Psychological Association in 1905. She studied at Harvard University with William James and performed several studies on the nature of memory. Christine Ladd-Franklin (1847–1930) studied color vision in the early 1900s. Karen Horney (1885–1952) focused on environmental and cultural factors that influence personality development (see Chapter 12).

Few degrees were awarded to minority students in the early 1900s. Gilbert Haven Jones (1883–1966) was the first African American to earn a doctorate in psychology—in Germany in 1909. Francis Sumner (1895–1954) was the first African American to receive a doctorate in psychology from a university in the United States (in 1920) and is known as the father of African American psychology for his many contributions to the education of Black people. His research focused on equality between Blacks and Whites, refuting the idea that African Americans were inferior. He also helped establish an independent psychology department at Howard University, a historically Black college.

Two of Sumner's students, Kenneth Clark (1914–2005) and Mamie Phipps Clark (1917–1983), conducted research on the self-perceptions of Black children. The Clarks' experiments (Clark, 1950; Clark & Clark, 1950) found that Black children often preferred to play with White dolls over Black dolls and attributed positive descriptors such as *good* and *pretty* to the color white and negative descriptors such as *bad* and *ugly* to the color black. The Clarks' findings were noted in the landmark 1954 case, *Brown v. Board of Education of Topeka*, in which the Supreme Court ruled that segregation of public schools was unconstitutional.

Inez Prosser was the first African American woman to be awarded a doctorate in psychology, in 1933 (Benjamin, Henry, & McMahon, 2005). Her doctoral dissertation (Prosser, 1933) studied the self-perceptions of Black children. She compared the self-esteem of Black children attending a segregated school to that of Black children attending an integrated school. She found that the Black children at the segregated school fared better. The Black children at the integrated school were more likely to feel inferior and report less satisfactory school relations. Given the

Known as the father of African American psychology, in 1920 Francis Sumner (1895–1954) was the first African American to receive a doctorate from a U.S. university.

© History of American Psychology, U. of Akron, Akron, Ohio

**humanistic perspective**   an approach that focuses on how an individual's view of him- or herself and the world influences behavior

**eclectic [ee-KLECK-tic] approach**   an approach that integrates and combines several perspectives when explaining behavior

**TABLE 1.2**
## Specialty Areas in Psychology

| Specialty Area | Topics of Interest |
| --- | --- |
| Biopsychology | Researches the biological processes that underlie behavior, including genetic, biochemical, and nervous system functioning. |
| Clinical psychology | Researches, assesses, and treats children, adolescents, and adults who are experiencing difficulty in functioning or who have a serious mental health disorder such as schizophrenia. |
| Cognitive psychology | Studies mental processes such as decision making, problem solving, language, and memory. |
| Community psychology | Seeks to understand and enhance the quality of life for individuals, communities, and society. Focuses on early intervention in and prevention of individual and community problems. |
| Counseling psychology | Researches, assesses, and treats children, adolescents, and adults who are experiencing adjustment difficulties. |
| Cross-cultural psychology | Investigates cultural similarities and differences in psychological traits and behaviors. |
| Developmental psychology | Researches how we develop physically, cognitively, socially, and emotionally over the life span. |
| Educational psychology | Researches how people learn and how variables in an educational environment influence learning. May develop materials and strategies to enhance learning. |
| Envrionmental psychology | Examines the relationship between environments and human behavior. Focuses on designing, managing, protecting, and/or restoring the environment to enhance behavior. Also studies environmental attitudes, perceptions, and values to promote environmentally appropriate behavior. |
| Experimental psychology | Conducts research on sensation, perception, learning, motivation, and emotion. |
| Forensic psychology | Works with mental health issues within the context of the legal system. May study a certain type of criminal behavior such as rape or murder, or may be asked to determine a person's competence to stand trial. |
| Health psychology | Researches ways to promote health and prevent illness. May be concerned with issues such as diet and nutrition, exercise, and lifestyle choices that influence health. |
| Human factors psychology | Researches human capabilities as they apply to the design, operation, and maintenance of machines, systems, and environments to achieve optimal performance (for example, designing the most effective configuration of control knobs in airplane cockpits for pilots). |
| Industrial/organizational (I/O) psychology | Examines the relationship between people and their work environments. May study issues such as increasing job satisfaction or decreasing employee absenteeism, or focus on understanding the dynamics of workplace behavior, such as leadership styles or gender differences in management styles. |
| Personality psychology | Researches how people differ in their individual traits, how people develop personality, whether personality traits can be changed, and how these qualities can be measured. |
| Positive psychology | Seeks to discover and promote those factors that contribute to happiness, positive emotions, and well-being. |
| School psychology | Assesses students' psychoeducational abilities (academic achievement, intelligence, cognitive processing) and shares test results with teachers and parents to help them make decisions regarding the best educational placement for students. |
| Social psychology | Researches how our beliefs, feelings, and behaviors are influenced by others, whether in the classroom, on an elevator, on the beach, on a jury, or at a football game. |
| Sports psychology | Investigates the mental and emotional aspects of physical performance. |

probable prejudicial attitudes of White people at the integrated school, it is not surprising that the Black children at that school did not have positive experiences.

Have times changed for women and minorities in psychology? Women have indeed made great progress in the field of psychology. From 1920 to 1974, 23% of doctorates in psychology went to women (APA, 2000b), and from 1960 to 1999 the greatest percentage increase in science and engineering doctorates earned by women was in psychology (National Science Foundation [NSF], 2006). Currently, far more women than men earn psychology degrees. In 2007, nearly 80% of master's degrees and 73% of doctorate degrees in psychology were awarded to women (U.S. Department of Education, 2009). Educational gains have to some extent been followed by progress in the careers of women in psychology. In 2009–2010, 46% of the full-time faculty in graduate departments of psychology in the United States were women (APA Center for Workforce Studies, 2010a). However, female psychology faculty members are less likely than males to be promoted to the rank of full professor. In a faculty salaries survey conducted by the American Psychological Association (APA) in 2006–2007, women represented only 29% of full professors and 35% of tenured faculty members in U.S. psychology graduate departments (APA Center for Psychology Workforce Analysis and Research, 2007a). Thus, although psychology has become more fully open to both men and women at the educational level, inequities at the professional level still exist.

Likewise, progress also has been made in the numbers of racial and ethnic minorities in psychology. While minorities make up approximately 33% of the U.S. population (U.S. Census Bureau, 2006), 28% of newly enrolled full-time students in graduate schools in psychology were minorities in 2008–2009 (APA Center for Workforce Studies, 2010b). Between 1976 and 1993, about 8% of all doctorates in psychology were awarded to minorities (APA, 1997); by 2008, that number had increased to almost 25% (National Science Foundation, 2009). However, this means that three out of four psychology doctorates are still granted to Whites, regardless of gender.

Despite the increase in the number of advanced degrees awarded to minorities, they are still underrepresented among college faculty. In 2006–2007, minorities represented less than 9% of full professors and 10% of tenured faculty members in psychology graduate departments (APA Center for Psychology Workforce Analysis and Research Office, 2007b). To address this lack of minority representation, the APA has established several programs to attract more minorities to the field of psychology.

## Psychology Applies to Your World:

### Training to Be a Psychologist

*You Asked...*

*What do you need to do to become a psychologist?*

JOSE MORENO, STUDENT

The majority of psychologists hold a doctorate in psychology—usually a Ph.D. (Doctor of Philosophy) or a Psy.D. (Doctor of Psychology). A Ph.D. program focuses more on research, whereas the Psy.D. focuses more on clinical training. To obtain either doctorate, psychologists must first complete a bachelor's and a master's degree. The road to a doctoral degree is long, usually 4 to 7 years after the undergraduate degree. Most doctoral programs require extensive study of research methods and statistics, and most require that students do some form of research.

*(continued)*

FIGURE

## 1.3

### Undergraduate Degrees in Psychology

Psychology is a popular undergraduate degree. It ranked fifth following business, social sciences and history, education, and health professions in number of degrees awarded in 2006–2007.

*Source: Data from U.S. Department of Education, National Center for Education Statistics, 2009.*

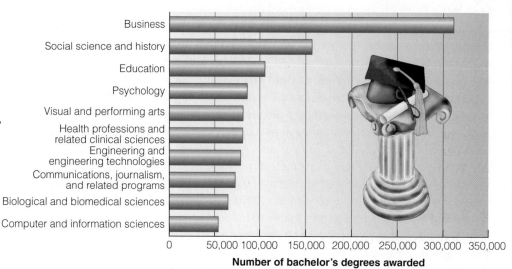

**Number of bachelor's degrees awarded**

Those who study psychology to the point of a bachelor's or master's degree aren't excluded from the profession. A bachelor's degree in psychology may qualify you to assist psychologists in mental health centers or rehabilitation and correctional programs or to serve as a research assistant. However, without additional academic training, the opportunities for advancement in the profession are limited (Appleby, 1997). As you can see in ■ FIGURE 1.3, psychology is a popular degree among undergraduate students.

A master's degree typically requires 2 to 3 years of graduate work. Master's-level psychologists may administer tests, conduct research, or counsel patients under the supervision of a doctoral-level psychologist. In a few states, they may be able to practice independently. They may teach in high schools or community colleges, work in corporate human resource departments, or work as school psychologists.

A large percentage of psychologists affiliated with colleges and universities teach and do research. Psychologists also work in school systems, hospitals, business, government, and other human services settings (APA Center for Workforce Studies, 2007; ■ FIGURE 1.4). Psychologists perform many functions in many different roles. Their job descriptions may include conducting research, counseling clients, and teaching college courses.

A related profession is *psychiatry*. A psychiatrist holds a medical degree (M.D.) and then specializes in mental health. A psychiatrist's graduate work includes a medical internship and residency, followed by training in the treatment of mental health disorders. As medical practitioners, psychiatrists have extensive training in the use of therapeutic drugs; they may dispense or prescribe medication and order medical procedures such as brain scans.

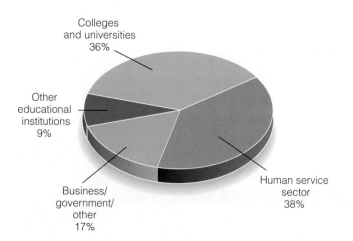

FIGURE

## 1.4

### Work Settings of Psychologists

A large percentage of psychologists affiliated with colleges and universities teach and do research. Psychologists also work in school systems, business and government, or are employed in health-related or other human services settings.

*Source: 2007 Doctorate Employment Survey. APA Center for Workforce Studies.*

# Let's
## REVIEW

In this section we discussed modern psychological perspectives, described the training needed to be a psychologist, and surveyed a number of the specialty areas of psychology. For a quick check of your understanding, answer these questions.

**1.** Which modern psychological perspective empha-sizes the importance of thought processes for understanding behavior?
  **a.** Behavioral
  **b.** Humanistic
  **c.** Sociocultural
  **d.** Cognitive

**2.** Which of the following professionals is most likely to prescribe medication for a mental health disorder?
  **a.** A clinical psychologist
  **b.** A psychiatrist
  **c.** A biopsychologist
  **d.** An experimental psychologist

**3.** A psychologist who studies individual differences in shyness is probably from which specialty area?
  **a.** Cognitive
  **b.** Social
  **c.** Developmental
  **d.** Personality

Answers 1. d; 2. b; 3. d

# Psychological Research: Goals, Hypotheses, and Methods

**LEARNING OBJECTIVES**

- Identify the four goals of psychological research.

- Outline the steps of the scientific method and distinguish between predictive and causal hypotheses.

- Describe the advantages and disadvantages of observational, survey, correlational, and experimental research methods and the types of conclusions that can be drawn from each method.

Though psychologists in various specialty areas study and emphasize different aspects of behavior, they all share similar goals. The main goals of psychology and psychological research are:

- To describe behavior
- To predict behavior
- To explain behavior
- To control or change behavior

*Description* involves observing events and describing them. Typically, descrip-tion is used to understand how events are related to one another. For example, you may notice that your health club tends to get more crowded in the months of January, February, and March. It seems you have to wait longer to use the weight machines or there are more people in the yoga classes. This observation describes an event.

If you observe that two events occur together rather reliably or with a general frequency or regularity, you can make *predictions* about or anticipate what events may occur. From your observations, you may predict that the health club will be more crowded in January. You may arrive earlier to make sure you get a parking spot or a place in the spinning class.

Although it may be known that two events regularly occur together, that doesn't tell us what *caused* a particular behavior to occur. Winter months do not cause health clubs to become crowded. These two events are related, but one event does not cause the other. Therefore, an additional goal of psychology is to *explain* or understand the causes of behavior. As stated previously, psychologists usually

**Describe Behavior**

Observe events and behaviors, then look at how events might be related.

Example: The researcher observes that the health club is more crowded in January, February, and March.

↓

**Predict Behavior**

Predict what events or behaviors may occur, based on their relationship.

Example: Colder months predict higher health club attendance.

↓

**Explain Behavior**

Suggest and test an explanation (in the form of a hypothesis).

Examples:
• The health club is full because the weather makes outdoor exercise more difficult.
• The health club is full because many people make New Year's resolutions to be physically fit, but give up by the end of March.

↓

**Control or Change Behavior**

By explaining and understanding the causes of behavior, psychologists can create programs or treatments to control or change the behaviors.

Example: If people give up on fitness after three months, develop incentives to offer during March to remain physically active. If the weather is a factor, sponsor outdoor fitness activities beginning in mid-March.

**FIGURE**

# 1.5

## Goals of Psychology

Psychologists attempt to describe, predict, explain, and ultimately control or change behavior.

**prediction**   an expected outcome of how variables will relate

**hypothesis**   an educated guess

put forth explanations of behavior in the form of theories. A *theory* is an explanation of why and how a particular behavior occurs. We introduced seven types of explanations, or perspectives, earlier in the chapter. For example, how do we explain higher health club attendance in the winter months? Is it a behavior that is influenced by the environment? Perhaps health clubs are more crowded because the weather makes outdoor exercise more difficult. Perhaps it is more influenced by motivation as many people at the start of a new year resolve to work out more. As these ideas are tested, more and more causes and predictors of behavior are discovered. Some of these explanations or theories will be modified, some will be discarded, and new ones will be developed.

The purpose behind explaining and understanding the causes of behavior is the final goal of psychology, *controlling* or *changing* behavior. It relates to the goal of explanation because one needs to understand what is causing a behavior in order to change or modify it. For example, let's say that the weather is a factor in health club attendance. Health clubs could offer outdoor fitness activities beginning in mid-March to prevent declining enrollment. Many psychologists go into the field in the hope of improving society. They may want to improve child care, create healthier work environments, or reduce discrimination in society. Such sentiments reflect the goal of control and underscore the potential impact of good research. ■ FIGURE 1.5 summarizes the goals of psychology.

## Psychologists Are Scientists: The Scientific Method

The purpose of psychological research is to test ideas about behavior. As previously stated, researchers use the *scientific method* when testing ideas about behavior. The scientific method is a set of rules for gathering and analyzing information that enables you to test an idea or hypothesis. All scientists adhere to these same steps even though they may use different techniques within each step. The decisions that scientists make at each step of the scientific method will ultimately affect the types of conclusions they can draw about behavior.

How can the scientific method be used to meet the goals of psychology? Let's say that you have an interest in understanding beer drinking among college students. You want to make some predictions (a goal of psychology) about beer drinking. You use the scientific method to test this idea, as outlined in ■ FIGURE 1.6.

1. *Define and describe the issue to be studied.* You might hypothesize that college students who buy pitchers of beer tend to drink more than college students who purchase bottles of beer (a **prediction**). You study previous research in scientific journals on alcohol consumption.

2. *Form a testable hypothesis.* Students who buy pitchers of beer tend to drink more than students who buy beer in bottles. This **hypothesis** must be phrased

in a way that can be objectively measured—that is, in such a way that another person can test the same hypothesis to verify or *replicate* your results.

3. *Choose an appropriate research strategy.* You choose a group of people to observe (college students) and a research method that allows you to measure objectively how much beer students who buy pitchers drink versus how much beer students who buy bottles drink. You decide where your study will be conducted. Will it be in the environment where the behavior naturally occurs (such as the local college bar) or in a laboratory (a more controlled setting)? You decide who you will use as *participants*. Will you use animals or humans? If using humans, how will they be selected? If using animals, what species will you use?

4. *Conduct the study to test your hypothesis.* Run the study and collect the data based on the decisions in steps 1–3.

5. *Analyze the data to support or reject your hypothesis.* Researchers usually analyze their data using statistics. If the results do not support your hypothesis, you can revise the hypothesis or pose a new one. If the results do support your hypothesis, you can make additional predictions and test them. Geller, Russ, and Altomari (1986) actually included this prediction in a larger study on beer drinking among college students and found support for the hypothesis that buying pitchers was associated with consuming larger amounts of beer.

No matter which goal of psychology you are addressing, the process is the same. The goal merely influences the decisions you make when testing an idea through the scientific method. If your goal is description or prediction, your hypothesis will state what you expect to observe or what relationships you expect to find. Your research strategy will then be designed to measure observations or relationships, and your analysis of the data will employ statistics that enable you to support or refute your hypothesis. It is in this way that the scientific method allows us to test the ideas of psychology.

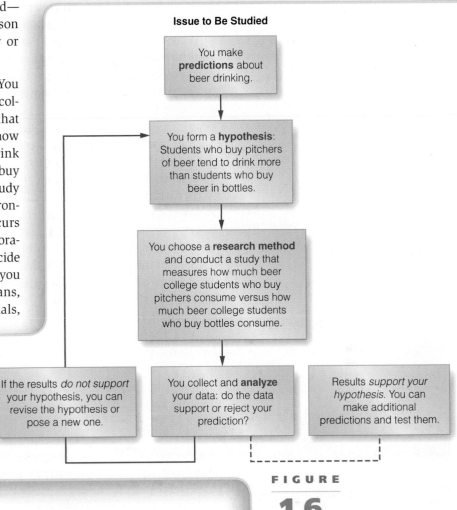

**FIGURE**

**1.6**

**The Scientific Method**

The scientific method enables researchers to test ideas about behavior.

## Psychologists Ask Questions: Hypotheses

As you have seen, one of the first steps of the scientific method is to formulate a question or hypothesis about behavior. These hypotheses generally fall into one of two categories: *predictive hypotheses* and *causal hypotheses*.

A **predictive hypothesis** makes a specific prediction or set of predictions about the relationships among variables. Such hypotheses are used to address two

**predictive hypothesis** an educated guess about the relationships among variables

goals of psychology: description and prediction. The previous example on beer drinking among college students illustrated a predictive hypothesis: The study predicted that students who buy pitchers of beer tend to drink more than students who buy beer in bottles. Predictive hypotheses are made when the researcher measures the variables of interest but does not manipulate or control the variables in the study. Because the researcher does not control the variables, conclusions of research studies that test predictive hypotheses are limited. The conclusions can only state what was observed, or what variables appear to be related to one another. They cannot be used to draw cause-and-effect conclusions; that is, one cannot conclude that buying pitchers of beer *causes* a person to drink more beer. To determine the cause, you must form and test a *causal hypothesis*.

A **causal hypothesis** specifically states how one variable will influence another variable. Causal hypotheses can be tested only when the researcher is able to control or manipulate the main variables in a study. The researcher sets up different conditions in a study and then observes whether there is a change in behavior because of the different conditions. For example, suppose a researcher has developed a new strategy to teach children how to read. The researcher hypothesizes that this program will cause greater gains in reading than the standard method for teaching reading. This is a causal hypothesis. Some students are assigned to the new reading program, and others are assigned to the standard program. The researcher then measures the children's gains in reading at the end of the year to see if there is a difference. As you will soon see, causal hypotheses can only be tested by means of an experiment. To test a causal hypothesis, a researcher must be able to conclude how one variable affects or causes a change in another variable.

## Psychologists Strategize: Research Methods

Once you have stated a hypothesis, the next step in the research process is to decide on a research strategy and a way of selecting participants. The type of hypothesis you make (predictive or causal) typically determines which research methods you can employ. You are more likely to use some research methods to test predictive hypotheses and other methods to test causal hypotheses.

*Naturalistic observations*, *case studies*, *surveys*, and *correlational research* are used to test predictive hypotheses. All of these methods are used when the researcher cannot control or manipulate the main variables in the study. Each method has its advantages and disadvantages, which we will discuss in a moment.

In a perfect world, researchers would include every person they are interested in studying. This is termed the **population of interest**. For example, for a developmental psychologist who specializes in infant development, all infants would be the population of interest. It is impossible to test everyone, however, so researchers select a portion, or subset, of the population of interest called a **sample**. Because the sample will be used to make inferences or judgments about the entire population, the sample should reflect the whole population as much as possible; that is, it should be a *representative sample*. Random sampling of participants ensures a representative sample. In a *random sample*, every member of the population has an equal chance of being selected to participate in the study; this avoids introducing *sampling bias* into the research.

**causal hypothesis**   an educated guess about how one variable will influence another variable

**population of interest**   the entire universe of animals or people that could be studied

**sample**   the portion of the population of interest that is selected for a study

The more representative the sample is, the more the results will generalize (or apply) to the population of interest. But random sampling is not always possible. Instead, psychological research often uses *samples of convenience*, or groups of people who are easily accessible to the researcher. The students in your psychology course are a sample of convenience. In fact, much psychological research relies on using college students as the sample of convenience! Only 29% of people in the United States over the age of 25 have college degrees, so samples of college students probably do not represent all types of people and groups (U.S. Census Bureau, 2008).

## NATURALISTIC OBSERVATIONS

**Naturalistic observations** are research studies that are conducted in the environment in which the behavior typically occurs. For example, Campos, Graesch, Repetti, and others (2009) wanted to investigate when and in what manner dual-earner families interact after work. The researchers measured interaction by observing and video-recording dual-earner couples and their children in their homes throughout two weekday afternoons and evenings. The researcher in a naturalistic study is a recorder or observer of behavior who then describes or makes predictions about behavior based on what he or she has observed. Because the researcher does not control events in a naturalistic study, it is not possible to pinpoint the causes of behavior. Therefore, naturalistic studies are predominately used to achieve the goals of description and prediction. In their observational study, Campos et al. found that while both mothers and fathers were likely to be greeted with positive behavior from family members, mothers spent more time with children whereas fathers spent more time alone.

While naturalistic observation can provide a picture of behavior as it normally occurs, researchers need to consider the influence of *reactivity*. Suppose you want to study childhood aggression by observing students on a school playground. What might happen if you were to simply enter the playground, sit down, and start writing about what you saw? The children might behave differently because of your presence and/or their awareness that they are being observed; as a result, your observations of aggression might not be reliable or true. When conducting a naturalistic observation, researchers attempt to minimize reactivity to ensure that they are observing the true behavior of their participants.

A school playground could be an environment for naturally observing children's behaviors.

## CASE STUDIES

A **case study** is an in-depth observation of one participant. The participant may be a person, an animal, or even a setting such as a business or a school. As with naturalistic observation, in case studies researchers do not control any variables but merely record or relate their observations. Case studies provide in-depth information on rare and unusual conditions that we might not otherwise be able to study. However, the main disadvantage of the case study method is its limited applicability to other situations. It is very difficult to take one case, especially a rare case, and say that it applies to everyone. In other words, case studies lack **generalizability**; because of this, the conclusions that are drawn from case studies are limited to the topic being studied.

**naturalistic observation**  observing behavior in the environment in which the behavior typically occurs

**case study**  an in-depth observation of one participant

**generalizability [jen-er-uh-lies-uh-BILL-uh-tee]**  how well a researcher's findings apply to other individuals and situations

## SURVEYS

Often, psychologists want to study a whole group of people but in less depth. **Surveys** can accomplish this task by asking a large group of people about their attitudes, beliefs, and/or behaviors. A large group of people can quickly respond to questions or statements in their homes, online, over the phone, or out in public.

Survey data are used to make predictions and test predictive hypotheses. For example, knowing which people are more likely to buy a product enables a company to market its products more effectively and perhaps devise new strategies to target individuals who are not buying them. Similarly, knowing which behaviors are related to a higher frequency of illness enables a psychologist to predict who is more at risk for physical or mental illness. However, *who* you ask to complete a survey and *how* you ask them are critical elements in distinguishing good survey research from biased research. Recall that a random sampling of participants minimizes sampling bias. The more representative the sample is, the more the results will generalize to the population of interest.

A second critical element of the survey method is how the questions are worded. A respondent has to be able to understand the question and interpret it in the way the researcher intended. It is important to make questions clear and precise to obtain accurate estimates of people's feelings, beliefs, and behavior. For example, differences in survey question wording have been found to have an influence on rape estimates (Fisher, 2009) and estimates of adolescent sexual behaviors (Santelli et al., 2000).

In summary, surveys are advantageous in that they allow psychologists to pose a lot of questions to a large sample of people. Accurate information can be gathered in a relatively short period of time. Yet the survey's wording, the representativeness of the sample, and whether people choose to answer the questions honestly can bias the results. The Psychology Across Generations box illustrates the survey research method.

## CORRELATIONAL STUDIES

Correlational studies test the relationship, or **correlation**, between two or more variables—television watching and violent behavior, or depression and gender, for example. The researcher does not control variables but rather measures them to see whether any reliable relationship exists between them. For example, if we were to measure your weight (one variable), what other variable might show a relationship to your weight? Your height? Your calorie consumption? Your gender? Your age? Your life expectancy? If you were to measure all these variables, you might find that all of them vary in relation to weight. These relationships are correlations.

The strength of a correlation is measured in terms of a *correlation coefficient*—a statistic that tells us how strong the relationship between two factors is. Correlation coefficients range from –1.00 to +1.00. The closer the correlation coefficient is to –1.00 or +1.00, the stronger the correlation, or the more related the two variables are. The closer the correlation coefficient is to 0, the weaker the correlation—that is, one variable does not reliably predict the other. For example, in a study on eating behaviors and weight gain in older women, Hays and Roberts (2008) found a +.25 correlation between weight gain and overeating in response to daily life circumstances. The correlation between weight gain and overeating in response to emotional states such as anxiety and depression was +.17. The higher correlation between weight gain and daily overeating opportunities suggests that ordinary environmental food cues such as television commercials, billboards, or sweets on one's food counter are a better predictor of weight gain in older women than is "emotional eating." Generally, the

**survey**   a research method that asks a large group of people about their attitudes, beliefs, and/or behaviors

**correlation [cor-ruh-LAY-shun]**   the relationship between two or more variables

## Psychology Across Generations:

### The Millennials

The Pew Research Center (2010) set out to compare the values, attitudes, and behaviors of Millennials (adults born after 1980) with those of today's older adults as well as with older adults back when they were the age that Millennials are now. Their analyses rely on the survey method, specifically a 2010 telephone survey with a nationally representative sample of 2,020 adults, including 830 participants between the ages of 18 and 29. Here we summarize just a few of their findings.

Not surprisingly, they reported differences among the groups in behaviors associated with the use of technology. For example, 83% of Millennials reported sleeping with a cell phone by their bed, compared to 68% of Generation Xers (those born between 1965 and 1980), 50% of Baby Boomers (those born between 1946 and 1964), and 20% of the Silent generation (those born before 1946). Nearly two-thirds of Millennials also admitted to texting while driving. Three quarters of Millennials have created a profile on a social networking site such as Facebook, compared with 50% of Generation Xers, 30% of Baby Boomers, and 6% of the Silent generation.

nterestingly, the Millennials appear to be the least overtly religious American generation since survey research began measuring it. Fewer Millennials reported belonging to any particular faith than older people do today, and they were less likely to be affiliated with a particular religion than previous generations were when they were 18 to 29 years of age. Millennials also reported attending religious services less often than older adults today. However, Millennials reported praying about as often as older adults did when they were 18 to 29 years old.

What accounts for these reported differences? Survey research cannot *explain* the differences; it can be used only to describe and predict behavior. However, we can generate multiple hypotheses as to why these generational differences occur. They could be due to the unique historical circumstances or social movements experienced by each generation, such as wars or technological advances. They could be due to changing social roles, longer life expectancies, or varying economic factors, to name a few, or to some combination of these factors. Also keep in mind that there are as many differences within generations as there are among them. Yet, from this survey research, we get a glimpse of the attitudes, values, and behaviors of the Millennial generation as they move into adulthood.

The Millennial generation (adults born after 1980) report more use of social networking websites.

© David J. Green/lifestyle themes/Alamy

---

stronger the correlation between two variables, the more accurate our predictions are, but perfect (+1.00 or –1.00) correlations rarely happen in psychology. Human behavior is too complex for such perfect relationships to occur.

The sign before the correlation coefficient tells us how the variables relate to one another (■ FIGURE 1.7). A **positive correlation** means that as one variable increases, the second variable also tends to increase, or as one variable decreases, the other variable tends to decrease. In both cases, the variables are changing in the *same* direction. An example of a positive correlation is marijuana use and lung cancer. As marijuana use increases, so does the likelihood of developing lung cancer (Tashkin et al., 2002).

**positive correlation**    a relationship in which increases in one variable correspond to increases in a second variable

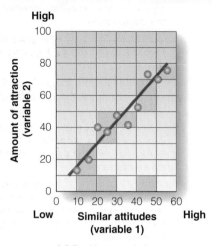

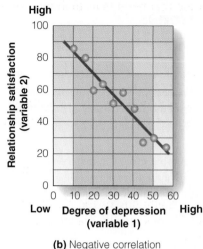

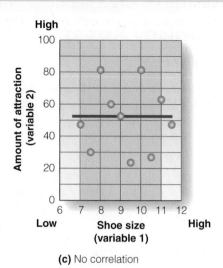

(a) Positive correlation

(b) Negative correlation

(c) No correlation

**FIGURE**

# 1.7

## Correlation

Correlation, a research method used for description and prediction, shows how two variables are related.

In a **negative correlation**, as one variable increases, the other variable tends to decrease in what is referred to as an *inverse* relationship. Notice that the variables are changing in *opposite* directions. An example of a negative correlation is video game playing and school competence. The more time children spend playing video games, the poorer their competence is at school (Hastings et al., 2009). Or consider the negative correlation between relationship satisfaction and depression. As relationship satisfaction increases, feelings of depression decrease (Whitton & Whisman, 2010).

Correlational studies enable researchers to make predictions about behavior, but they do *not* allow us to draw cause-and-effect conclusions (■ FIGURE 1.8). For example, there is a positive correlation between academic achievement and self-esteem. Students who have high academic achievement also tend to have high self-esteem. Similarly, students who have low academic achievement tend to have low self-esteem. High academic achievement may cause an increase in self-esteem. However, it is just as likely that having high self-esteem causes one to do better academically. There may be a third variable, such as the parents' educational level or genetics, which actually causes the relationship between academic

**negative correlation**  a relationship in which increases in one variable correspond to decreases in a second variable

**experiment**  a research method that is used to test causal hypotheses

**independent variable**  the variable in an experiment that is manipulated

**FIGURE**

# 1.8

## Correlation Does Not Mean Causation

When two variables are correlated or related, it does not mean that we know *why* they are related. It could be that high academic achievement causes high self-esteem. However, it is equally likely that high self-esteem causes high academic achievement. It is also possible that a third variable, such as genetics, causes both high self-esteem and high academic achievement, resulting in a relationship between the two variables. Correlation can only be used for making predictions, not for making cause-and-effect statements.

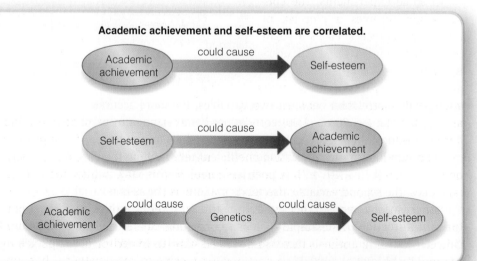

Academic achievement and self-esteem are correlated.

achievement and self-esteem. A correlational study does not tell us which of these explanations is correct. The only research method that permits us to draw cause-and-effect conclusions is the experiment.

## EXPERIMENTS

Although several types of research methods are used to test predictive hypotheses, only one research method can test a *causal* hypothesis: the **experiment**. We will discuss several features of the experiment, including its advantages and disadvantages.

Necessary Conditions for an Experiment   Two main features characterize an experiment. First, the variables in the study are controlled or manipulated. Second, participants are randomly assigned to the conditions of the study. When these two conditions have been met, causal conclusions *may* be drawn. Let's first turn our attention to the issue of experimenter control.

The point of the experiment is to manipulate one variable and see what effect this manipulation has on another variable (■ FIGURE 1.9). These variables are termed the independent and dependent variables, respectively. The **independent variable** is the variable that the experimenter manipulates; it is the *cause* in the experiment. The **dependent variable** measures any result of manipulating the independent variable; it is the *effect* in the experiment.

The typical experiment divides participants into two types of groups: the *experimental group* and the *control group*. The **experimental group** includes those participants who receive the manipulation that is being tested. The **control group** includes those participants who do not receive the manipulation that is being tested; they serve as a baseline comparison for the experimental group. Both groups are then measured on the dependent variable to see whether there is a difference *between* the groups.

In some experiments, the control group receives a *placebo*, or inactive substance such as a sugar pill, rather than being given nothing. This is to control for the *placebo effect*. The **placebo effect** occurs when participants show changes simply because they believe or expect a treatment to have certain effects. In **double-blind studies**, neither experimenters nor participants know who is receiving a placebo and who is receiving the actual treatment; they are *blind* to which group (experimental or control) a person has been assigned. In this way, neither the participant's nor the experimenter's expectations will bias the results.

Suppose, for example, that we want to study the effects of sleep deprivation. Specifically, we hypothesize that sleep deprivation causes deficits in memory. This is a causal hypothesis that can be tested with an experiment. We decide to manipulate the amount of sleep participants receive to see whether it has any

**dependent variable**   the variable in an experiment that measures any effect of the manipulation

**experimental group**   the group of participants who receive the manipulation that is being tested

**control group**   the group of participants who do not receive the manipulation that is being tested

**placebo effect**   a measurable change in participants' behavior due to the expectation or belief that a treatment will have certain effects

**double-blind study**   an experiment in which neither the experimenters nor the participants know to which group (experimental or control) participants have been assigned

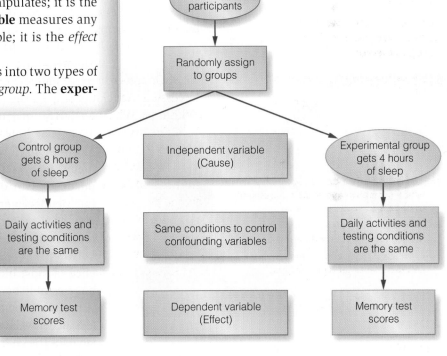

**Elements of an Experiment**

FIGURE

# 1.9

**Elements of an Experiment**

The two main ingredients of an experiment are (1) that the variables in the study are controlled or manipulated and (2) that participants are randomly assigned to the conditions of the study. When these two conditions have been met, causal conclusions *may* be drawn.

effect on memory. In this example, the amount of sleep is our independent variable. Some participants (the control group) will be allowed to sleep 8 hours per night for the week of our study. Others (the experimental group) will be allowed to sleep only 4 hours each night. The experimenter has set, or controlled, the amount of sleep (the independent variable) at two levels: 8 hours and 4 hours. Each day of our study, we measure the participants' memory (the dependent variable) by having them complete several memory tasks. At the end of the study, we compare the memory scores of those participants who received 8 hours of sleep (the control group) with those who received only 4 hours of sleep (the experimental group).

To be sure that it is the amount of sleep affecting memory and not something else, we need to be sure that we have controlled any variable (other than the independent variable) that may influence this relationship. These potentially problematic variables are called **confounding variables**. What confounding variables might we need to control? Maybe age influences one's memory or how one handles sleep deprivation. If either of these is true, we would want to control the age of our participants. We also would want to make sure that participants had not used any substances known to affect memory or the sleep cycle prior to their participation in the experiment. Consequently, we would control for this variable too.

Both groups must be treated the same except for the amount of sleep they receive, so the researcher sets the conditions of the experiment to be the same for both groups. For example, every participant should complete the memory tasks at the same time of day, and every participant should complete the same memory tasks. The criteria for scoring the memory tasks must be the same as well. The instructions for completing the tasks must be the same. The lighting, temperature, and other physical features of the room in which the participants sleep and complete the memory tasks should be the same for all participants. Our purpose is to design a study in which we manipulate the independent variable to see its effect on the dependent variable. If we control any potentially confounding variables that might influence this relationship and we find a difference between our groups on the dependent variable, that difference is most likely due to the independent variable, and we have established a cause-and-effect relationship.

If the experimenter does not control a confounding variable, we now have more than one variable that could be responsible for the change in the dependent variable: the independent variable and the confounding variable. When this occurs, the researcher is left with an alternative explanation for the results. The change in the dependent variable could have been caused by the independent variable, but it also could have been caused by the confounding variable. Consequently, causal conclusions are limited.

Let's not forget the second condition necessary for an experiment—how participants are assigned to the conditions of the independent variable. We must be sure that there are no differences in the composition of our groups of participants. Psychologists eliminate this problem through **random assignment** of participants to the conditions of the study. In our example on sleep and memory, assigning all the males in the sample to the 4-hour sleep condition and all the

By studying behavior in a lab environment, researchers are better able to control the variables in an experiment.

© Laura Dwight/PhotoEdit

**confounding variable**   any factor other than the independent variable that affects the dependent measure

**random assignment**   method of assigning participants in which they have an equal chance of being placed in any group or condition of the study

females to the 8-hour sleep condition would create a confounding variable. Gender differences might have an effect on memory scores. It may be that gender (the confounding variable) rather than sleep deprivation (the independent variable) is the cause of a difference in memory. To eliminate the influence of such confounding variables, experimenters randomly assign participants to conditions. Each participant has an equal chance of being placed in either condition. Male participants are just as likely to be assigned to the 4-hour condition as they are to the 8-hour condition, and the same is true for female participants. In this way, any participant variable that has the potential to influence the research results is just as likely to affect one group as it is the other. Without random assignment, confounding variables could affect the dependent variable. This is typically what occurs in *quasi-experiments*.

A **quasi-experiment** is in some ways like an experiment. The researcher manipulates the independent variable and sets the other conditions to be the same for both groups. However, the second requirement for an experiment—randomly assigning participants to conditions—has not been met. Quasi-experiments use existing groups of people who differ on some variable. For example, suppose you want to see if smoking cigarettes during pregnancy causes lower-birth-weight babies. For ethical reasons, you cannot assign some pregnant women to smoke and prevent others from smoking. Instead, for your smoking condition, you must select pregnant women who already smoke. These women may differ on other variables when compared to pregnant women who do not smoke. For example, their eating habits may differ. As a result, a confounding variable (the diet of the mothers) rather than smoking could cause a difference in the dependent variable (the birth weight of the offspring). Because quasi-experiments do not meet the conditions necessary for a "true" experiment, causal conclusions based on these designs should be made cautiously (Shadish, Cook, & Campbell, 2002; West, 2009).

Advantages and Disadvantages of Using Experiments   Experiments have several advantages. First, it is only through experimentation that we can approach two of the goals of psychology: explaining and changing behavior. An experiment is the only research method that enables us to determine cause-and-effect relationships. This advantage makes interpreting research results less ambiguous. In an experiment, we attempt to eliminate any confounding variables through experimenter control and random assignment of participants to groups. These techniques enable us to draw clearer conclusions from research results.

Experiments also have disadvantages. First, experiments do not address the first two goals of psychology: describing and predicting behavior. These are often the first steps in understanding behavior, and naturalistic observation, surveys, and correlational studies are quite useful for doing this. Second, in an attempt to control confounding variables, experiments conducted in laboratory settings may create an artificial atmosphere. It is then difficult to know whether the same result would occur in a more natural setting. This may be another reason to conduct naturalistic observations or correlational studies. Third, sometimes employing the experimental method is simply not possible for ethical or practical reasons. As we mentioned in the case of quasi-experimental designs, we cannot force people to be randomly assigned to a condition that would harm them (such as smoking) or that does not pertain to them (such as having high blood pressure). Psychologists must follow certain ethical guidelines and practices when conducting research. We turn our attention to this topic next.

**quasi-experiment**   a research study that is not a true experiment because participants are not randomly assigned to the different conditions

# Let's REVIEW

In this section we examined the goals of psychology, identified the steps of the scientific method, and described methods of research. For a quick check of your understanding, answer these questions.

**1.** When we know that two events regularly occur together, which goal of psychology can be met?
   a. Predicting behavior
   b. Changing behavior
   c. Understanding behavior
   d. Explaining behavior

**2.** In an experiment on attitudes, participants are given either positive or negative information about a speaker and then asked to evaluate the effectiveness of the speaker. In this experiment, which is the independent variable?
   a. The effectiveness of the speaker
   b. The type of information the participant is given
   c. Attitude change
   d. The speaker

**3.** The more hours that students work, the less successful they are academically. This is an example of what type of correlation?
   a. zero
   b. positive
   c. perfect
   d. negative

Answers 1. a; 2. b; 3. d

LEARNING OBJECTIVE

● Describe the main ethical principles that guide psychologists as they conduct research.

# Ethical Principles of Psychological Research

Generally, psychologists affiliated with universities and colleges cannot conduct research unless their research proposal has passed review by an **Institutional Review Board (IRB)**. The function of the IRB is to ensure that the research study being proposed conforms to a set of ethical standards or guidelines.

## Ethical Guidelines for Participants

The American Psychological Association (APA), one of the main professional organizations for psychologists, has taken the lead in establishing ethical guidelines, or professional behaviors that psychologists must follow. These guidelines, the "Ethical Principles of Psychologists and Code of Conduct" (APA, 2002), address a variety of issues, including general professional responsibility, clinical practice, psychological testing, and research. Here we look at the guidelines psychologists must follow when conducting research with humans and animals. The ethical duties of psychologists who treat clients are discussed in Chapter 14.

One of the main concerns of the IRB is to ensure that the proposed research has met the ethical guideline of respect and concern for the dignity and welfare of the people who participate (APA, 2002). Researchers must protect participants from any potential harm, risk, or danger as a result of their participation in a psychological study. If such effects occur, the researcher has the responsibility to remove or correct these effects.

**Institutional Review Board (IRB)**
a committee that reviews research proposals to ensure that ethical standards have been met

Another fundamental principle of ethical practice in research is **informed consent**. Researchers inform potential participants of any risks during the informed consent process, wherein the researcher establishes a clear and fair agreement with research participants prior to their participation in the research study (APA, 2002). This agreement clarifies the obligations and responsibilities of the participants and the researchers and includes the following information:

- The general purpose of the research study, including the experimental nature of any treatment
- Services that will or will not be available to the control group
- The method by which participants will be assigned to experimental and control groups
- Any aspect of the research that may influence a person's willingness to participate in the research
- Compensation for or monetary costs of participating
- Any risks or side effects that may be experienced as a result of participation in the study

Prospective participants are also informed that they may withdraw from participation in the study at any time, and they are informed of any available treatment alternatives. In addition, the researcher agrees to maintain **confidentiality**. Personal information about participants obtained by the researcher during the course of the investigation cannot be shared with others unless explicitly agreed to in advance by the participant or as required by law or court order.

It is not always possible to fully inform participants of the details of the research, as it may change their behavior. For this reason, psychologists sometimes use *deception* in their research. For example, suppose we wanted to research student cheating. If we tell participants we are studying cheating behavior, it will likely influence their behavior. If we tell participants we are investigating student–teacher behavior, we can measure student cheating more objectively. However, the use of deception must be justified by the potential value of the research results. Moreover, deception can be used only when alternative procedures that do not use deception are unavailable.

If participants have been deceived in any way during the course of a study, the researcher is obligated to *debrief* participants after the experiment ends. **Debriefing** consists of full disclosure by the researcher to inform participants of the true purpose of the research. Any misconceptions that the participant may hold about the nature of the research must be removed at this time.

Consider the following classic research study. In the 1960s, Stanley Milgram (1963) set out to determine whether the average person could be induced to hurt others in response to orders from an authority figure. (You will read more about Milgram's research in Chapter 10.) Participants were deceived into believing that they were participating in a research study on learning rather than on obedience. Participants were told that they would be playing the role of a "teacher" in the experiment. Participants were introduced to a "learner" who was then led to a separate room. The teacher's job was to administer electric shocks to the learner every time the learner made a mistake in an effort to help the learner better learn a list of words. In reality, the participant was not actually shocking the learner. The learner's responses were prerecorded on a tape, but the participants did not know this and believed that they were, indeed, shocking the learner.

**informed consent**    ethical principle that research participants be told about various aspects of the study, including any risks, before agreeing to participate

**confidentiality**    ethical principle that researchers do not reveal which data were collected from which participant

**debriefing**    ethical principle that after participating in an experiment involving deception participants be fully informed of the nature of the study

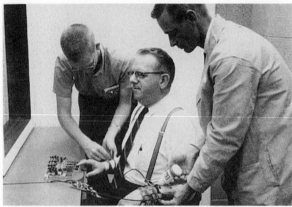

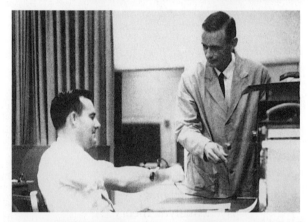

Although Stanley Milgram debriefed his participants, he still caused them psychological harm. Such a study would violate current ethical standards of psychological research.

Obedience © 1965, Stanley Milgram

Despite the fact that participants believed the learner to be ill or worse, most of them continued to follow the experimenter's orders. A full 65% of the participants shocked the learner all the way up to the highest shock level! During the procedure, Milgram's participants exhibited emotional distress. Although Milgram debriefed his participants after the study, he still violated the ethical principle of psychological harm. He was criticized for exposing participants to the trauma of the procedure itself and for not leaving the participants in at least as good a condition as they were prior to the experiment (Baumrind, 1964). Because of these ethical problems, a study such as this would not be approved today.

We should also note that for years the primary focus in research was on White males. Women and minorities were not only discouraged from becoming professionals in psychology but also were largely ignored or neglected when studying psychological issues. Many minority and female as well as male psychologists have contributed to the field of psychology by addressing these shortcomings and designing research that looks specifically at the behaviors of minorities and women.

## Ethical Guidelines for Animal Research

Animal studies have advanced our understanding of many psychological issues, including the importance of prenatal nutrition, our treatment of brain injuries, and our understanding of mental health disorders (Domjan & Purdy, 1995). Psychologists must meet certain standards and follow ethical guidelines when conducting research with animals. Psychological research using animal subjects must also be approved by an IRB. Animals must be treated humanely and in accord with all federal, state, and local laws and regulations. Researchers are responsible for the daily comfort, housing, cleaning, feeding, and health of animal subjects. Discomfort, illness, and pain must be kept at a minimum, and such procedures can only be used if alternative procedures are not available. Moreover, harmful or painful procedures used on animals must be justified in terms of the knowledge that is expected to be gained from the study. Researchers must also promote the psychological well-being of some animals that are used in research, most notably primates (APA, 2002).

In the chapters that follow, we will describe in greater detail psychological research in the main specialty areas of psychology. In the next chapter, we start with the biological processes that underlie all behavior. Each chapter will prepare you for mastering the concepts of the next chapter, and we frequently remind you of concepts presented in earlier chapters to help you connect the information. A *Look Back at What You've Learned* concludes each chapter. It will help you remember the topics and concepts that have been introduced and further your understanding of how these concepts relate to one another.

# Let's REVIEW

In this section we discussed ethical considerations in research. As a quick check of your understanding, answer these questions.

1. What is the rule for deceiving participants in a psychological study?
   a. Deception is never allowed in psychological research. It is against the law in every state.
   b. Deception is allowed only when using animals.
   c. Deception is allowed when alternative procedures are unavailable and when participants are debriefed at the end of the study.
   d. Deception can be used under any circumstances because true psychological research never harms participants.

2. Dr. Kwan is performing case study research. She should be most concerned with which of the following ethical principles?
   a. Deception
   b. Physical harm
   c. Debriefing
   d. Confidentiality

3. Which of the following is *not* an ethical guideline that psychologists must follow when conducting research?
   a. Paying participants for their participation
   b. Informed consent
   c. Freedom from harm
   d. Confidentiality

Answers 1. c; 2. d; 3. a

# Studying THE CHAPTER

## Key Terms

behavioral perspective (13)
behaviorism (9)
biological perspective (12)
case study (23)
causal hypothesis (22)
cognitive perspective (13)
cognitive psychology (11)
confidentiality (31)
confounding variable (28)
control group (27)
correlation (24)
critical thinking (6)
debriefing (31)
dependent variable (27)
double-blind study (27)
eclectic approach (14)
evolutionary perspective (12)
experiment (27)

experimental group (27)
functionalism (8)
generalizability (23)
Gestalt psychology (8)
humanism (11)
humanistic perspective (14)
hypothesis (20)
independent variable (27)
informed consent (31)
Institutional Review Board (IRB) (30)
introspection (7)
naturalistic observation (23)
negative correlation (26)
neuroscience (12)
placebo effect (27)
population of interest (22)
positive correlation (25)
positive psychology (11)

prediction (20)
predictive hypothesis (21)
pseudopsychology (6)
psychoanalytic theory (9)
psychodynamic perspective (13)
psychology (4)
quasi-experiment (29)
random assignment (28)
response (10)
sample (22)
scientific method (4)
sociocultural perspective (13)
stimulus (10)
structuralism (7)
survey (24)
theory (4)

## What Do You Know? Assess Your Understanding

Test your retention and understanding of the material by answering the following questions.

1. Which of the following is *not* true about psychology?
   a. Psychology is just common sense.
   b. Psychology is just the study of mental illness.
   c. Psychology has no connection with everyday life.
   d. All of the above are not true.

2. Which of the following topics would a psychologist have the least interest in?
   a. Learning
   b. Sexuality
   c. Weather patterns
   d. Color perception

3. The _____ perspective in psychology stresses the importance of looking at the influence of unconscious drives and motives on behavior and mental processes.
   a. functionalism
   b. structuralism
   c. psychoanalytic
   d. behaviorist

4. Dr. Babar is a psychologist who studies how people's eating habits help them adapt to and survive in their environments. Dr. Babar is emphasizing which psychological perspective?
   a. Evolutionary
   b. Structuralism
   c. Humanism
   d. Behaviorism

5. Many modern psychologists follow the _____ approach to psychology, in that they do not adhere strictly to any one psychological perspective.
   a. pragmatic
   b. functional
   c. common sense
   d. eclectic

6. Which of the following is the most likely educational attainment of the majority of psychologists?
   a. Doctorate degree
   b. Master's degree
   c. Bachelor's degree
   d. Associate's degree

7. Dr. Warren is a psychologist who studies chemicals in the brain. Dr. Warren is approaching psychology from the _____ perspective.
   a. cognitive
   b. eclectic
   c. biological
   d. sociocultural

8. Dr. Barrios is a psychologist who studies how people change over time. Dr. Barrios is most likely a _____ psychologist.
   a. cognitive
   b. biological
   c. social
   d. developmental

9. Dr. Grogan studies how psychological principles can be applied in the workplace. Dr. Grogan is most likely a(n) _____ psychologist.
   a. organizational
   b. clinical
   c. social
   d. health

10. Dr. Pi wants to test the hypothesis that smoking marijuana impairs one's ability to remember information. What type of hypothesis is Dr. Pi interested in testing?
    a. Predictive
    b. Causal
    c. Correlational
    d. Biological

11. The first African American to earn a doctorate in psychology was _____.
    a. Karen Horney
    b. Mary Calkins
    c. Gilbert Haven Jones
    d. Sidney Beckham

12. Today, who earns most of the doctorates in psychology?
    a. Men
    b. Women
    c. African Americans
    d. Asian Americans

13. Which of the following is *not* a goal of psychology?
    a. To describe behavior
    b. To change behavior
    c. To explain behavior
    d. To eliminate free will

14. Which of the following best defines the nature of a theory?
    a. An explanation of why a behavior occurs
    b. A statement of fact
    c. An untestable assumption
    d. A prediction

15. The hypothesis that the number of rapes will increase during the summer months is an example of a(n) _____ hypothesis.
    a. causal
    b. predictive
    c. untestable
    d. nonscientific

16. Dr. Vaz conducted an experiment in which she randomly assigned her participants to one of two conditions. In the first condition, the participants were shown visual images of common objects and then one hour later asked to recall as many of the objects as they could remember. In the second condition, the participants heard the names of the same objects and then one hour later were asked to recall as many of the objects as they could. Dr. Vaz then compared the number of items

recalled for these two groups of participants. In this experiment, the independent variable is _____.

a. the number of items recalled
b. whether the participants saw or heard the objects
c. the sex of the participants
d. the room in which the participants were tested

17. Dr. Ling is studying helping behavior in children. Every day, he goes to the local playground at 3 P.M., sits on the sidelines, and records the number of times one child helps another, the sex of the child who helps, and the sex of the child who is helped. Dr. Ling is using which research method in his study?

a. An experiment
b. A case study
c. A naturalistic observation
d. A quasi-experiment

18. A confounding variable _____.

a. measures the effect of the independent variable
b. is the variable that is manipulated by the experimenter
c. has no effect on the dependent variable
d. is any factor other than the independent variable that affects the dependent variable

19. The longer the commute for a student to a college campus, the less likely he or she is to complete a degree. This is an example of a _____.

a. positive correlation
b. negative correlation
c. zero correlation
d. case study

20. Dr. Eden tells potential participants of any risks they may experience prior to their participation in his research study. Dr. Eden is following the ethical guideline of _____.

a. deception
b. confidentiality
c. informed consent
d. debriefing

Answers: 1. d; 2. c; 3. c; 4. a; 5. d; 6. a; 7. c; 8. d; 9. a; 10. b; 11. c; 12. b; 13. d; 14. a; 15. b; 16. b; 17. c; 18. d; 19. b; 20. c

## Online Resources

Log in to **www.cengagebrain.com** to access the resources your instructor requires. For this book, you can access:

### Psychology CourseMate

CourseMate brings course concepts to life with interactive learning, study, and exam preparation tools that support the printed textbook. A textbook-specific website, Psychology CourseMate includes an integrated interactive eBook and other interactive learning tools including quizzes, flashcards, videos, and more.

### CENGAGENOW™

CengageNOW Personalized Study is a diagnostic study tool containing valuable text-specific resources—and because you focus on just what you don't know, you learn more in less time to get a better grade.

### WebTutor

More than just an interactive study guide, WebTutor is an anytime, anywhere customized learning solution with an eBook, keeping you connected to your textbook, instructor, and classmates.

# LOOK BACK
## AT What You've LEARNED

### How Did Psychology Become a Science?

Wilhelm Wundt

- Psychology became a distinct field of scientific study when Wilhelm Wundt established the first psychology laboratory, in Germany, in 1879. Wundt studied the elements that explained mental processes (**structuralism**).

- In the early 1900s, Max Wertheimer emphasized how our minds organize sensory stimuli to produce the perception of a whole form (**Gestalt psychology**).

- William James's focus was on how particular behaviors helped people adapt to their environment (**functionalism**).

- Sigmund Freud, one of the most famous people to influence psychology, believed the key to understanding behavior was uncovering unconscious motivations (**psychoanalytic theory**).

- John B. Watson and B. F. Skinner emphasized the need to study observable behavior and the influence of the environment on behavior (**behaviorism**).

- Carl Rogers and Abraham Maslow emphasized free will and personal growth in determining behavior (**humanism**).

- **Cognitive psychology** seeks to understand key mental processes such as memory, problem solving, and decision making.

- **Positive psychology** describes the factors that contribute to happiness, positive emotions, and well-being.

Sigmund Freud

B. F. Skinner

To think like a psychologist, you must be skeptical about explanations of behavior, rather than accepting of them. **Psychology** is:

- NOT simply giving advice
- NOT just "common sense"
- NOT limited to studying mental illness

### What Are the Goals of Psychological Research?

- To describe behavior
- To predict behavior
- To explain behavior
- To control or change behavior

# What Is PSYCHOLOGY?

## What Is Psychology Like Today?

- Psychologists typically have a doctorate in psychology, which usually involves 4–7 years of postgraduate study and research beyond the undergraduate (bachelor's) degree.
- Modern psychological perspectives include:
  - **Biological**, which examines the physiological contributions to behavior
  - **Evolutionary**, which looks at how behaviors may be genetically programmed to help us adapt better for survival
  - **Psychodynamic**, which focuses on internal, often unconscious, mental processes, motives, and desires or childhood conflicts to explain behavior
  - **Behavioral**, which focuses on external causes of behavior, such as how stimuli in the environment and/or rewards and punishments influence our behavior
  - **Cognitive**, which focuses on how people process information and on how that process may influence behavior
  - **Sociocultural**, which researches behaviors across ethnic groups and cultures
  - **Humanistic**, which explains behavior as stemming from choices and free will
- Psychologists today embrace an **eclectic approach**, which integrates several perspectives when studying and explaining behavior.
- There are numerous specialty areas in psychology, including:
  - Developmental psychology (which studies child and adult development)
  - Social psychology (which examines ways in which we are influenced by others)
  - Industrial/organizational psychology (which looks at behavior in the workplace)
  - Experimental psychology (which performs research on sensation, perception, and learning)
  - Clinical or counseling psychology (which researches and treats people who are experiencing difficulty in functioning or who have a serious mental health disorder)
- Although the numbers of women and ethnic minorities in psychology have increased, they are still underrepresented as faculty in colleges.

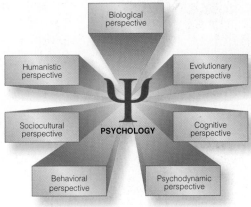

## What Research Methods Do Psychologists Use?

- Psychologists form **predictive** and **causal hypotheses** and then conduct research using the **scientific method**.
- Predictive hypotheses are tested by **naturalistic observation**, **case studies**, **surveys**, and **correlational studies**.
- Causal hypotheses are tested by **experiments** in which variables are controlled and care is taken to test a **random sample** of a **population of interest**. The **experimental group** is compared to the **control group** on the **dependent variable** to see whether the **independent variable** had an effect.
- To ensure humane conduct of experiments, the American Psychological Association has established a set of strict ethical guidelines that must be followed when researchers study animals and humans.

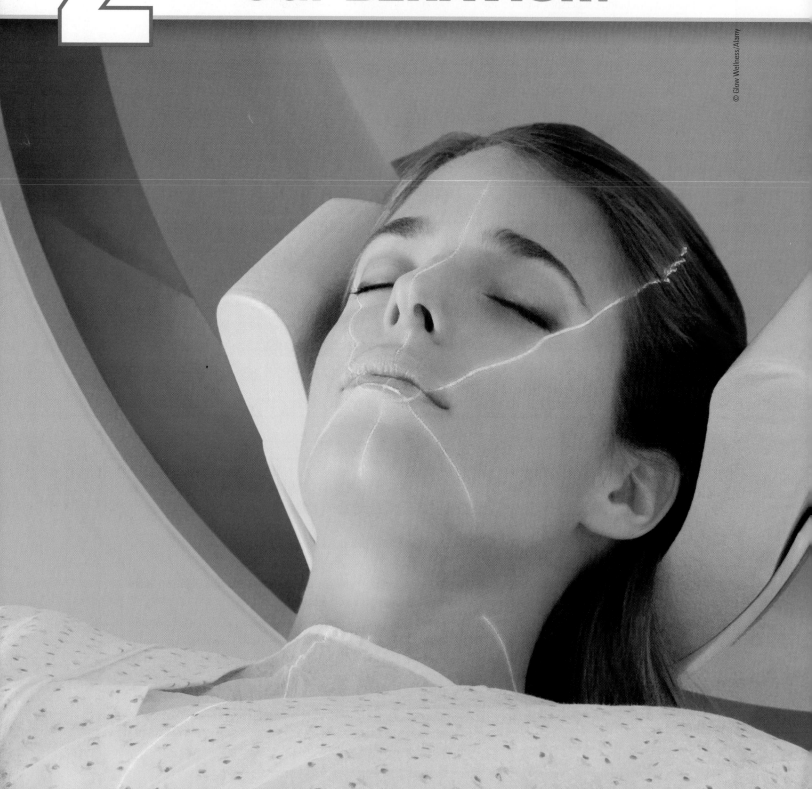

# Chapter Outline

*One of our students,* Stan Roberts, has led a remarkable life. As a child, Stan received a head injury when a truck struck the family car. After recovering, Stan was able to resume a normal childhood. But at age 14, Stan experienced another challenge when his parents abandoned him. Their marriage had disintegrated, and somehow Stan was lost in the shuffle. Later, his parents would claim that each had thought the other had taken Stan with them. The reality was that Stan had been left homeless on the streets of Southern California. For the next few years, Stan had to fend for himself on the streets, and eventually he became a ward of the state. At age 18, Stan enrolled in college but did not complete his degree.

Instead, Stan entered the business world where he found great success, eventually becoming a regional vice president with a major telecommunications company. After years of success, Stan was on the verge of being set for life, when he was involved in another serious car accident. This time, his head injuries were serious and life-altering, and Stan was unable to continue his career.

Today, Stan experiences constant double vision, and when reading or watching a movie, he often forgets what he has just seen or heard. Yet Stan is an optimist and feels blessed to now be continuing the college degree he left unfinished years ago. One of the first classes that Stan enrolled in was psychology—a course that he refers to as "a healing experience." Studying psychology gave Stan a deeper understanding of his brain injury and its effects on his behavior. He found comfort in being able to correlate the damage to areas of his brain with the changes in his behavior that others were noticing. In his words, "If you have a pain, it makes you feel better if you know where it is coming from."

© Susann Doyle-Portillo

*Learning about the brain in psychology class gave Stan Roberts insight into the effects of his own brain injury, helping him to heal and cope.*

Even if you never find yourself in a situation like Stan's, the knowledge that you gain from this chapter will give you a deeper understanding of the workings of your own brain and how it influences your behavior. We'll begin by looking at how the brain communicates information throughout our bodies.

- Describe the basic structure of a neuron, including the axon, dendrites, and synapse.
- Explain what an action potential is and how it moves down the axon and across the synapse.
- Explain the processes of excitation and inhibition at the synapse.

**neuroscience [NUR-o-SCI-ence]**  the study of how the brain and nervous system affect mental processes and behavior

**neurons [NUR-ons]**  cells in the nervous system that transmit information

**glia[GLEE-uh] cells**  brain cells that provide important support functions for the neurons and are involved in the formation of myelin

# Billions of Neurons: Communication in the Brain

> **You Asked...**
>
> *How is the brain connected to psychology?*
>
> JEAN-PAUL ESLAVA, STUDENT

Modern psychologists are very interested in **neuroscience**—the study of how the brain and nervous system affect our mental processes and our behavior. This interest is well placed because we rely on our brain and nervous system to enable us to perform all the tasks of daily life. We do not question that our brain will somehow store the information we just learned in psychology class, and that on exam day it will retrieve that information. We take for granted that we will be able to walk, to talk, to write, and to maintain a constant body temperature and a steady heart rate. But psychologists want to know how such everyday miracles are accomplished. How does your brain know when you need to eat or sleep? How does your brain tell the muscles of your arm to contract so you can hold a pencil? In short, how does the brain communicate?

The brain communicates with itself and the rest of the body over networks of specialized information-carrying cells called **neurons**. Neurons use a sophisticated communication system to conduct signals across these *neural networks*, enabling us to control our bodies. For example, when you touch a hot stove, neurons in your fingertips send information up your arm to your spinal column. In response to this possible threat, signals are sent back out from the spine to the muscles of your arm. The result is a quick, reflexive jerking of your arm away from the hot stove (■ FIGURE 2.1).

Researchers have long believed that the adult brain contains around 100 billion neurons. However, newly developed estimation techniques now suggest that the brain may contain roughly 86 billion neurons and similar numbers of another type of cell called **glia cells** (Azevedo, Carvalho, Grinberg, et al., 2009). Glia cells were once thought to provide only support functions, such as providing nutrients and removing wastes, for the neurons of the brain. However, it is more likely that glia cells also play a critical role in both neural signaling and the formation of neural networks in the brain (Eroglu & Barres, 2010; Volterra & Steinhauser, 2004).

Although scientists do not yet understand the full role of glia cells, we have abundant evidence of the importance of glia cells to normal brain functioning (Nave, 2010). For starters, glia cells help maintain the chemical environment of

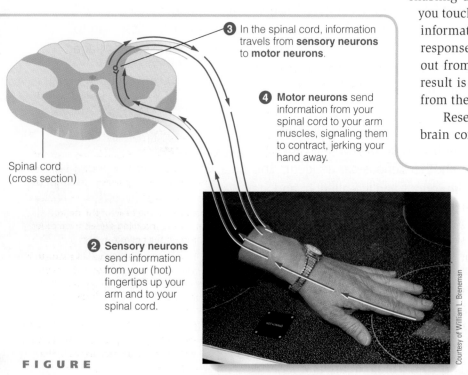

**3** In the spinal cord, information travels from **sensory neurons** to **motor neurons**.

**4** **Motor neurons** send information from your spinal cord to your arm muscles, signaling them to contract, jerking your hand away.

Spinal cord (cross section)

**2** **Sensory neurons** send information from your (hot) fingertips up your arm and to your spinal cord.

**1** You touch the hot stove; the heat registers in your skin's sensory receptors.

Courtesy of William L. Breneman

**FIGURE**

**2.1**

**The Neurons Involved in a Reflex**

When you touch a hot stove, neurons in your fingertips send information up your arm to your spinal column. In response to this possible threat, signals are sent out from the spine to the muscles of your arm. The result is a quick, reflexive jerking of your arm away from the hot stove.

the neuron, and they help repair neural damage after injuries. However, one of their most important functions is the formation of **myelin**. Myelin is a whitish, fatty, waxy substance that coats many neurons. This protective coating insulates and speeds up neural signals. Much like rubber or plastic insulation on an electrical cord, myelin helps the signal get where it is going quickly. *Myelinated* neurons can conduct signals much faster than unmyelinated neurons. To appreciate what myelin does for neural communication, let's look at what happens when myelin is lost due to illness.

Multiple sclerosis (MS) is one disease that attacks and destroys the myelin insulation on neurons (Junker, Hohlfeld, & Meinl, 2010). People with MS have difficulty controlling the actions of their body and have sensory problems, including numbness and vision loss. When myelin breaks down, neural signals are greatly slowed or halted altogether. Initially, movement becomes difficult; as the disease progresses, voluntary movement of some muscles may become impossible. Sensory systems such as vision may also fail because incoming signals from the eye do not reach the vision-processing parts of the brain. Life often becomes very challenging for people with MS as the "orders" sent to and from the brain are delayed or lost along the way.

Without myelin, our nervous system cannot function properly—our neurons cannot carry information efficiently from one point to another. As psychologists, we are particularly interested in understanding how healthy neurons send signals throughout the nervous system. Before we can examine how neurons transmit signals, however, we must first examine the anatomy of neural cells and how they connect with one another in the nervous system.

© Stephen Jaffe/AFP/Getty Images

Television personality Montel Williams has multiple sclerosis, a disease that results in the destruction of myelin. As the myelin is destroyed, patients may experience a variety of neurological symptoms, including difficulty moving and sensory loss.

## The Anatomy of the Neuron

Like any cell in the body, the neuron has a **cell body** that contains a nucleus (■ FIGURE 2.2). The cell body is somewhat similar in shape to a fried egg, with the nucleus being the yolk. Like the nucleus of any cell, the nucleus of the neuron contains **DNA** (deoxyribonucleic acid), the chemical that contains the genetic blueprint that directs the development of the neuron. Growing out of the cell body are branchlike structures called **dendrites** (from the Greek word for tree branch). The dendrites receive incoming signals from other neurons. For ease of understanding, we will refer to the dendrite end of the neuron as the *head* of the cell.

Growing out of the other end of the cell body is a long tail-like structure called an **axon**, which carries signals away from the cell body. We will refer to the axon end of the neuron as the *tail* end of the cell. When a neuron is insulated with myelin, it is the axon that is covered, or *myelinated*. As you can see in Figure 2.2, myelin does not continuously cover the entire length of a neuron's axon. Rather, the myelin covers segments of the axon with a **myelin sheath**. Axons vary in length from a few hundred micrometers to many centimeters, depending on where in the nervous system they are located. Axons in the brain are typically very short (1 millimeter or less), whereas other axons in the body, such as those that extend down the legs, can be almost a meter in length (Purves et al., 1997).

The tail end of the axon splits into separate branches (Figure 2.2). At the end of each branch is an *axon bulb* that contains small storage pouches called *vesicles* that hold **neurotransmitters**, the chemical messengers that carry signals across the synapse. A **synapse** is the junction between two neurons where the axon bulb of one neuron comes into close proximity with specialized *receptor sites* on another neuron.

The neural structure of the brain is extremely complex, and synapses can occur at several places along a neuron (e.g., dendrites, axon, or cell body). However, for

**myelin [MY-eh-lynn]** fatty, waxy substance that insulates portions of some neurons in the nervous system

**cell body** the part of the neuron that contains the nucleus and DNA

**DNA** the chemical found in the nuclei of cells that contains the genetic blueprint that guides development in the organism

**dendrites [DEN-drights]** branchlike structures on the head of the neuron that receive incoming signals from other neurons in the nervous system

**axon [AXE-on]** a long tail-like structure growing out of the cell body of a neuron that carries action potentials that convey information from the cell body to the synapse

**myelin sheath [MY-eh-lynn SHEE-th]** the discontinuous segments of myelin that cover the outside of some axons in the nervous system

**neurotransmitters [NUR-oh-TRANS-mitt-ers]** chemical messengers that carry neural signals across the synapse

**synapse [SIN-aps]** the connection formed between two neurons when the axon bulb of one neuron comes into close proximity with the dendrite of another neuron

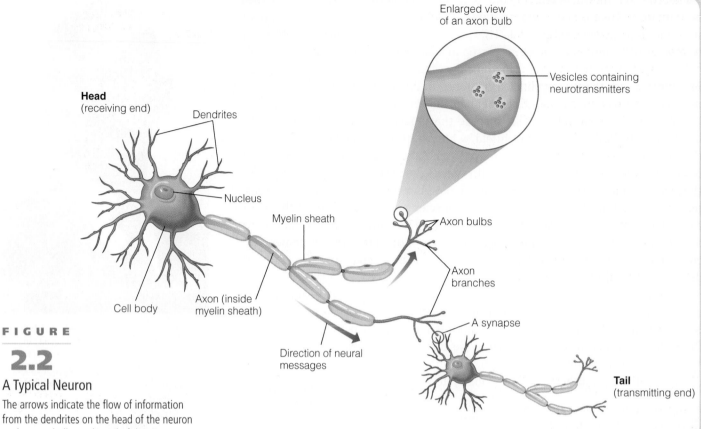

**FIGURE**

## 2.2

### A Typical Neuron

The arrows indicate the flow of information from the dendrites on the head of the neuron to the axon bulbs at the tail of the neuron. Neurons may have many dendrites and axon branches, and some neurons are insulated with myelin, which helps speed up neural signals in the neuron.

*From Gaudin and Jones,* Human Anatomy and Physiology, *Fig 11.3a, p. 263. Reprinted by permission of the author.*

simplicity's sake we will discuss only a simple *head-to-tail* synapse. In this type of synapse, the axon bulb on the tail end of the first neuron is in close proximity to specialized receptor sites on the dendrites on the head of a second neuron (■ FIGURE 2.3). You will notice that the first neuron, called the **presynaptic neuron**, does not physically touch the second neuron, called the **postsynaptic neuron**. At a synapse, there is a measurable distance, called the *synaptic gap*, between the presynaptic and postsynaptic neurons.

Humans have an extremely large number of synapses. Current estimates suggest we have more than 100 trillion synapses in our brain (Eroglu & Barres, 2010). Think about this for a moment. How is it possible for humans to have trillions of synapses but only around 86 billion neurons? It's possible because the neurons of the brain do not synapse in a one-to-one fashion. Rather, each neuron can synapse with up to 10,000 other neurons (Bloom, Nelson, & Lazerson, 2001). Look again at the neurons in Figure 2.3. Synapses can occur at any place along any of the dendrites of these neurons. The vast network of neurons that results from all of these synapses gives our nervous system the ability to generate and send the messages that are necessary to govern our bodies. Let's take a closer look at how these signals are generated within the neuron and how the signals jump across the synapse as they travel through the nervous system.

## Signals in the Brain: How Neurons Fire Up

Neural signals underlie much of the action in our bodies—breathing, movement, using our senses, and so on. To understand how these neural signals are generated within a neuron, we must first understand the chemical environment of the neuron.

**presynaptic neuron [pre-sin-AP-tic NUR-on]**   the neuron that is sending the signal at a synapse in the nervous system

**postsynaptic neuron [post-sin-AP-tic NUR-on]**   the neuron that is receiving the signal at a synapse in the nervous system

Understanding brain chemistry is important because the brain uses *electrochemical* energy that is produced by charged particles called **ions** to send neural signals. Brain tissue is made up largely of densely packed neurons and glia cells. Brain tissue is surrounded by a constant bath of body fluid that contains many different ions. Some of these ions are positively charged, whereas others carry negative charges. Of all the different ions found in our body fluids, sodium (Na+) and potassium (K+) play a particularly important role in allowing our neurons to send signals.

## THE NEURON AT REST: THE RESTING POTENTIAL

When a neuron is at rest, meaning it is not actively conducting a signal, there is an imbalance in the types of ions found inside and outside the cell walls of the neuron. This imbalance exists because openings in the axon, called *ion channels*, allow only some ions to pass into and out of the neuron. At rest, these ion channels will not allow sodium (Na+) to enter the neuron, which results in an imbalance in the type of charge that is found inside and outside of the neuron. If you look at ■ FIGURE 2.4, you'll see that at rest, the charge inside the neuron is more negative than the charge outside of the neuron.

This difference in the charges found inside and outside of the neuron is referred to as the neuron's **resting potential**. In mammals, the resting potential is about –70 millivolts (a millivolt, mv, is 1/1000 of a volt). This means that when resting, the inside of the neuron is about 70 mv more *negative* than the outside of the neuron. Although it is far less than 1 volt in magnitude, the resting potential is an important driving force in creating neural signals.

## THE NEURON IN ACTION: FIRING AN ACTION POTENTIAL

When a neuron receives input from other neurons, these incoming signals enter at the dendrites and travel across the cell body to the axon. These signals can make the inside of the cell more positive or more negative. If the incoming signals make the inside of the neuron more positive, the inside of the neuron may become positive enough to reach the neuron's **threshold of excitation** (about –55 mv in mammals). When the threshold of excitation is reached, the ion channels along the axon suddenly open and allow Na+ ions to enter the cell. As Na+ ions flood into the cell, the inside of the neuron rapidly becomes more and more positive. This is how a neuron fires. These "firings" or neural impulses within the neuron are called **action potentials** (■ FIGURE 2.5a).

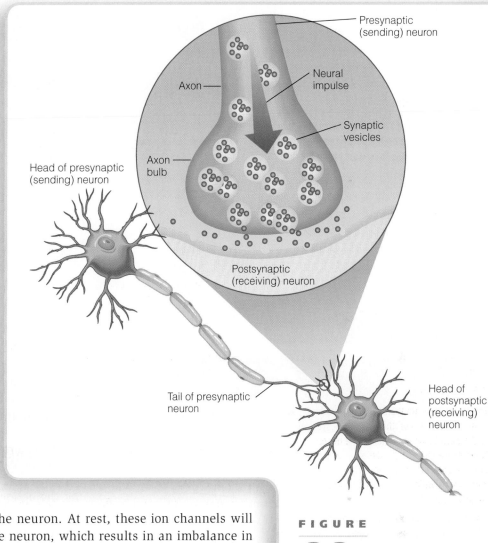

**FIGURE**

## 2.3

### Detail of a Synapse

A synapse is formed when the axon bulb of one neuron comes in close proximity to the receptors on the dendrites of the postsynaptic neuron.

**ions [EYE-ons]**    charged particles that play an important role in the firing of action potentials in the nervous system

**resting potential**    potential difference that exists in the neuron when it is resting (approximately –70 mv in mammals)

**threshold of excitation**    potential difference at which a neuron will fire an action potential (–55 mv in humans)

**action potential**    neural impulse fired by a neuron when it reaches –55 mv

# 2.4

### Resting Potential

When a neuron is at rest, the ion channels do not allow large sodium ions (Na+) to enter the cell. As a result of the high concentration of Na+, the predominant charge on the outside of the neuron is positive. The predominant charge inside the neuron is negative because of the high concentration of negatively charged ions found there. This difference in charge between the inside and the outside of the cell is called the resting potential.

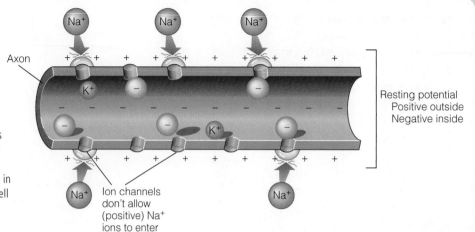

FIGURE

# 2.5

### Action Potential

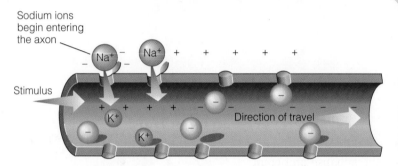

(a)

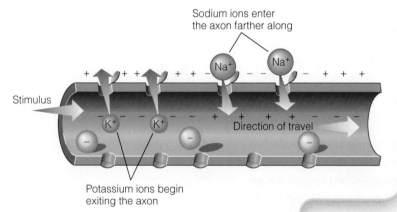

(b)

The action potential shown here (a) occurs all the way down the axon and is how we send neural signals in our nervous system. As the action potential travels down the axon (b), the sodium channels close and potassium (K+) channels open, allowing potassium to leave the cell. As the K+ leaves the cell, the inside of the cell becomes more negative. Potassium will continue to leave the cell until the neuron has returned to its resting potential.

*Source: Modified from Starr & Taggart (1989).*

All neural impulses are equally strong: If a neuron reaches threshold and fires an action potential, the neural signal will reach the synapse. A neuron firing an action potential is like firing a gun. You either shoot or you don't, and once the shot is fired, it's not going to stop in midair! Because all action potentials are equally strong and because, once fired, they will reach the synapse, action potentials are said to fire in an **all-or-none fashion**.

## RETURNING TO THE RESTING POTENTIAL: THE REFRACTORY PERIOD

As the action potential travels to the end of the axon, Na+ floods into the neuron and the inside of the axon becomes more and more positive. As the inside of the neuron becomes increasingly positive, additional ion channels open along the axon and begin to pump positive potassium ions (K+) *out* of the cell. This removal of potassium (K+) from the neuron works to once again make the inside of the neuron more negatively charged (because *positive* ions are leaving the cell). Potassium will continue to leave the neuron until the neuron's original resting potential (–70 mv) is restored (■ Figure 2.5b). As the neuron is returning to its resting potential, it will experience a very brief (a few milliseconds) **refractory period** during which it is unable to fire another action potential (■ FIGURE 2.6).

So far, we've looked at how a neural signal travels down the axon, but what happens when the action potential hits the axon bulb at the end of the axon? How does the signal get across the synapse?

## Jumping the Synapse: Synaptic Transmission

When the action potential reaches the axon bulb of the presynaptic (sending) neuron, it causes the release of neurotransmitters into

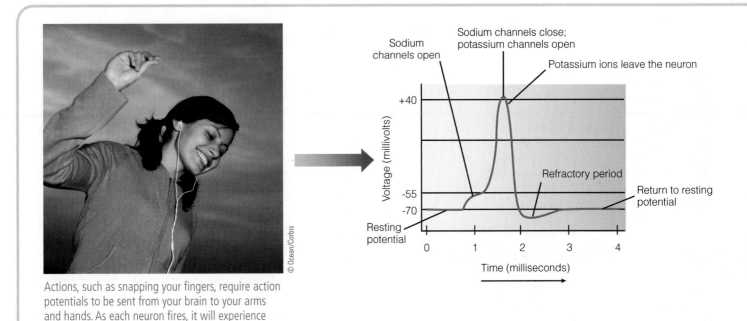

Actions, such as snapping your fingers, require action potentials to be sent from your brain to your arms and hands. As each neuron fires, it will experience changes in the electrical charges inside its axon, as depicted in the graph to the right.

© Ocean/Corbis

**FIGURE**

**2.6**

Electrical Changes in the Neuron As It Fires an Action Potential

the synapse. The neurotransmitter molecules float in the fluid-filled synapse (■ FIGURE 2.7). Some of them will quickly drift across the synapse and come into contact with the tulip-shaped receptor sites lined up on the dendrites of the postsynaptic (receiving) neuron.

Each type of neurotransmitter has a specific molecular shape, and each type of receptor site has a specific configuration. Only certain types of neurotransmitters open specific receptor sites. Just as you must have the correct key to open a lock, a particular receptor site will be activated only by a specific neurotransmitter. When a neurotransmitter finds the correct receptor site on the postsynaptic neuron, it *binds* with the receptor site and causes a change in the electrical potential inside the postsynaptic neuron (Figure 2.7).

## EXCITATION AND INHIBITION

In some instances, the neurotransmitter will cause **excitation** in the postsynaptic cell. Excitation occurs when the neurotransmitter makes the postsynaptic cell *more* likely to fire an action potential. Excitatory neurotransmitters move the postsynaptic neuron closer to its threshold of excitation by causing the postsynaptic neuron to become more positive on the inside. Excitation is very important because it ensures that messages will continue onward through the nervous system after they cross the synapse.

However, sometimes we need to stop the message from continuing onward. This process is called **inhibition**. Inhibition occurs when the neurotransmitter makes the postsynaptic cell *less* likely to fire an action potential. As you may have guessed, inhibitory neurotransmitters cause the inside of the postsynaptic cell to become more negative, moving it away from its threshold of excitation.

Because of the complexity of the brain, a single postsynaptic cell can simultaneously receive excitatory and inhibitory signals from a great number of presynaptic neurons. So, how does the postsynaptic cell know whether to fire an action potential and send the signal down the line? All the incoming signals converge

**all-or-none fashion**   all action potentials are equal in strength; once a neuron begins to fire an action potential, it fires all the way down the axon

**refractory period**   brief period of time after a neuron has fired an action potential during which the neuron is inhibited and unlikely to fire another action potential

**excitation**   when a neurotransmitter makes the postsynaptic cell more positive inside, it becomes more likely to fire an action potential

**inhibition**   when a neurotransmitter makes the postsynaptic cell more negative inside, it becomes less likely to fire an action potential

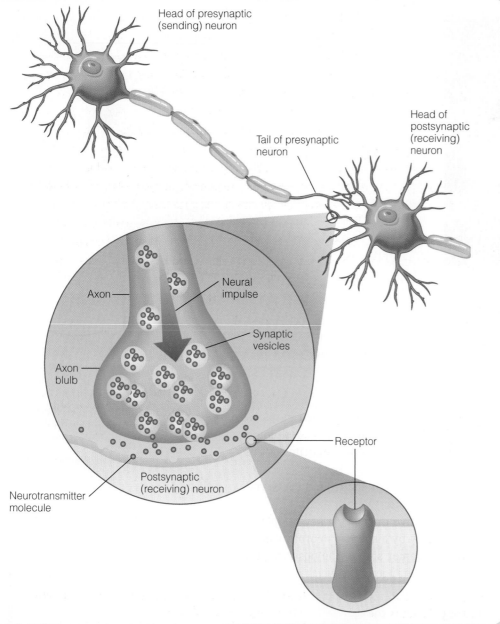

Head of presynaptic
(sending) neuron

Tail of presynaptic
neuron

Head of
postsynaptic
(receiving)
neuron

Axon

Neural
impulse

Synaptic
vesicles

Axon
blulb

Receptor

Postsynaptic
(receiving) neuron

Neurotransmitter
molecule

F I G U R E

# 2.7

**Neurotransmitters Carry the Signal Across the Synapse**

The neurotransmitter is released in the synapse from the axon bulb of the presynaptic neuron. The neurotransmitters travel across the synapse and bind with receptor sites on the postsynaptic neuron.

**reuptake**   process through which neurotransmitters are recycled back into the presynaptic neuron

on the axon, which acts like an adding machine, summing up the excitatory and inhibitory signals. Only when the sum of the signals moves the resting potential at the axon to threshold (–55 mv) will the neuron fire an action potential. If the threshold is not reached, the signal simply does not go any farther at this time.

## Cleaning Up the Synapse: Reuptake

When neurotransmitters cross the synapse to bind with postsynaptic receptor sites, not all of these floating neurotransmitters will find available receptors to bind with. What happens to the neurotransmitters left in the synapse? Neurotransmitters are removed from the synapse and returned to the presynaptic neuron by a process called **reuptake**. Reuptake accomplishes two goals. First, it resupplies the presynaptic neuron with neurotransmitters so that the next signal sent by the neuron can also jump the synapse. Second, reuptake clears the synapse of neurotransmitters, thereby ensuring that just the right amount of excitation or inhibition occurs in the postsynaptic neuron.

When neurotransmitters bind with receptor sites, they cause either excitation or inhibition. Afterward, the molecules either dislodge from the receptor site or they are broken down by specialized chemicals called *enzymes*. If reuptake did not occur, once the receptor sites were cleared out, other unattached neurotransmitters in the synapse would bind with the sites, causing further excitation or inhibition. This duplication of signals could cause confusion or dysfunction in the nervous system. Therefore, reuptake is essential to healthy functioning of our brain and nervous system.

Later in this chapter, you will see that some beneficial drugs act on the body by altering this process of reuptake. In fact, as we will see in Chapter 4, most drugs have their effect in the body at the synapse. For now, let's turn our attention to the types of neurotransmitters and their basic influence on behavior.

## YOUR TURN   Active Learning

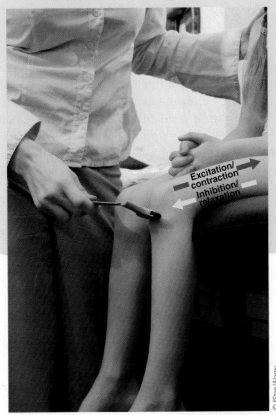

Excitation/
contraction
Inhibition/
relaxation

© rStop/Alamy

The function of excitation in the nervous system is pretty clear. Excitation starts actions in the nervous system. But why do we need inhibition in the nervous system? Simply put, inhibition is required to slow down and shut off certain processes in the nervous system. Try this demonstration: Sit on the edge of a bed or table with both legs dangling freely. Reach down with the edge of your hand and strike your left leg just below the kneecap with moderate force. If done correctly, your leg should kick forward in what's called the *patellar reflex*. This reflex results in excitatory signals being sent to contract your quadriceps muscles (top of thigh) and inhibitory signals being sent to relax your hamstring muscles (back of thigh), causing your leg to kick. If you only had the capacity for excitation, your leg would tense but not kick. The interacting inhibition and excitation seen in this reflex are also at work when we walk, helping us to balance and maintain posture.

When your knee is hit just below the kneecap, the quadricep muscles on the top of the thigh are stretched. This stretching sets off a reflex in which the quadriceps receive excitatory impulses that contract them. At the same time, the hamstring muscles on the back of the thigh receive inhibitory impulses that cause them to relax. The result is the *patellar reflex*, and the leg kicks forward. This reflex, with its combination of inhibitory and excitatory impulses, helps us to walk smoothly by automatically coordinating the contraction and relaxation of our thigh muscles.

# Let's REVIEW

For a quick check of your understanding of how neurons generate and send signals, answer these questions.

1. Suki's dentist gave her a drug that froze the sodium ion channels along Suki's neural axons. What is the likely effect of this drug?
   a. Suki's neurons will fire more action potentials than normal.
   b. Suki's neurons will fire stronger action potentials.
   c. Suki's neurons will fire weaker action potentials.
   d. Suki's neurons will fail to fire action potentials.

2. Sabrina has contracted a disease that is destroying her myelin sheath. What effect would you expect this disease to have on the functioning of Sabrina's nervous system?
   a. It will speed up the neural signals traveling through her nervous system.
   b. It will slow down the neural signals traveling through her nervous system.
   c. It won't affect the functioning of her nervous system in any measurable way.
   d. Her nervous system will speed up and slow down in a random fashion.

3. A drug that causes potassium ions to leave one's neurons is likely to produce what type of effect on the neuron?
   a. Increased firing
   b. Excitation
   c. Inhibition
   d. Both excitation and inhibition

*Answers 1. d; 2. b; 3. c*

**LEARNING OBJECTIVE**

● List the major neurotransmitters, and describe the functions they may influence.

# Neurotransmitters: Chemical Messengers in the Brain

Well over 100 different chemical compounds have been identified as neurotransmitters (Morrow et al., 2008), and researchers continue to investigate more substances that may affect neural signaling. For example, some forms of the female sex hormone *estrogen* that regulate certain aspects of reproduction in the body have recently been shown to also behave like neurotransmitters in the brain (Balthazart & Ball, 2006). A complete review of all known neurotransmitters is well beyond the scope of this text, but we will look at the ones that most influence our moods and behavior.

## Acetylcholine: Memory and Memory Loss

**Acetylcholine (ACh)** was the first neurotransmitter discovered. In the early part of the 20th century, ACh was found to inhibit the action of the heart and to excite skeletal muscles. Today, ACh is thought to play a role in awareness or consciousness and in memory (Perry et al., 1999). This hypothesized role in memory comes primarily from the discovery that during the course of their disease, people with Alzheimer's experience loss of functioning in neurons that release ACh into their synapses (Martorana et al., 2009). Because Alzheimer's disease is associated with both memory loss and the loss of ACh action in the brain, it appears that ACh *may* help the brain store and/or process memories.

## Dopamine, Serotonin, and Norepinephrine: Deepening Our Understanding of Mental Illness

**acetylcholine [uh-see-til-COE-leen] (ACh)** neurotransmitter related to muscle movement and perhaps consciousness, learning, and memory

**dopamine [DOPE-uh-mean]** neurotransmitter that plays a role in movement, motivation, learning, and attention

Another neurotransmitter, **dopamine**, appears to influence processes such as movement, learning, attention, and motivation. Dopamine may influence motivation by making some activities, such as sex and eating, very pleasurable or rewarding. The reward produced by dopamine may even play a role in the development of certain types of substance abuse (see Chapter 4; Nestler & Carlezon, 2006; Schmidt & Pierce, 2006).

Parkinson's disease is associated with the loss of neurons in an area of the brain richest in dopamine. Drugs used to treat Parkinsonian symptoms work to indirectly increase the amount of dopamine in the brain. Care must be used in administering

© Stephen Jaffe/AFP/Getty Images

Actor Michael J. Fox has Parkinson's disease, and Mohammed Ali has a related condition called *Parkinsonism*. Parkinson's is a degenerative disease that results in decreased dopamine action in the brain, which causes tremors and other neurological symptoms.

such drugs, though, because too much dopamine action in the brain produces some very troubling symptoms—in particular, symptoms similar to those of the psychiatric disorder schizophrenia (see Chapter 14), which is associated with too much dopamine action in the brain (Seeman, 2010). Drugs used to treat schizophrenia often block the action of dopamine at the synapse. Regulating brain chemistry is not simple. As you might imagine, prolonged use of dopamine-blocking drugs can cause Parkinsonian-like side effects. Think about it. Too little dopamine, and one has the symptoms of Parkinson's disease; too much dopamine, and the result is schizophrenic symptoms. It appears that healthy functioning requires just the right amount of dopamine in the brain.

## You Asked...

*What effects do serotonin and norepinephrine have on the brain?*

CRISTOFER ARTHURS, STUDENT

Mental health may depend on having proper levels of other neurotransmitters as well. The neurotransmitter **serotonin** is thought to play a role in many different behaviors, including sleep, arousal, mood, eating, and pain perception. A lack of serotonin in the brain has been linked to several mental and behavioral disorders (e.g., depression). Drugs that increase the action of serotonin at the synapse by preventing its reuptake are called *selective serotonin reuptake inhibitors* (*SSRIs*). Prozac and other SSRIs have been used to successfully treat depression, eating disorders, compulsive behavior, and pain. However, not all drugs that act on serotonin are therapeutic. The illegal drug *MDMA* (or *ecstasy*, as it is commonly known) may actually reduce serotonin action in the brain (Schenk, 2011; Xie et al., 2006). This loss of serotonin action may account for reports of depression following ecstasy highs in some users (see Chapter 4).

Also related to mental health is **norepinephrine (NOR)**, a neurotransmitter thought to play a role in regulating sleep, arousal, and mood. Some drugs that alleviate depression have an effect on NOR as well as on serotonin. NOR may also play a role in the development of synapses during childhood (Sanders et al., 2005) and recovery of functioning after brain injury (Bueno-Nava et al., 2008).

**serotonin [ser-uh-TOE-nin]**
neurotransmitter that plays a role in many different behaviors, including sleep, arousal, mood, eating, and pain perception

**norepinephrine [nor-ep-in-EF-rin] (NOR)** neurotransmitter that plays a role in regulating sleep, arousal, and mood

By inhibiting the reuptake of serotonin, Paxil increases the amount of serotonin activity in the synapse, which may reduce depressive symptoms in some patients and allow them to once again enjoy pleasurable moments of their lives.

Jose Luis Pelaez Inc./Getty Images

Joe Raedle/Getty Images

## GABA and Glutamate: Regulating Brain Activity

**Gamma amino butyric acid (GABA)** is thought to regulate arousal, our general level of energy and alertness. It is estimated that one-third of all synapses, including most inhibitory synapses, in the brain use GABA as their neurotransmitter. Therefore, it appears that GABA plays an essential role in normal brain function. Loss of GABA in the brain can produce seizures, because without GABA's inhibitory effects, arousal levels become too high. Some anticonvulsant drugs work by lessening the effects of enzymes that destroy GABA molecules (Rowlett et al., 2005). GABA may also play a role in mediating anxiety. Rats injected with drugs that increase GABA action in certain parts of the brain demonstrate fewer anxiety-related behaviors (e.g., Degroot, 2004), and drugs that increase GABA action in the brain are often used to calm and sedate humans. These drugs include benzodiazepines such as Valium, barbiturates (Phenobarbital), and alcohol (see Chapter 4). We will discuss treatment of anxiety again in Chapter 14.

Whereas GABA is the chief inhibitory neurotransmitter, **glutamate** is the chief excitatory neurotransmitter in the brain. More than 50% of all synapses in the brain use glutamate as a neurotransmitter, and without it many brain processes would not take place. Ironically, glutamate can also be a deadly force in the brain. When physical brain damage affects glutamate-bearing neurons, glutamate molecules may be released in large quantities from the damaged neuron. Large amounts of extracellular glutamate can cause brain cell death as the neurons literally become excited to death when the glutamate spreads to neighboring neurons and causes them to fire a frenzy of action potentials. It appears that in the brain too much excitation is a very bad thing!

**gamma amino butyric [GAM-ma uh-MEAN-oh bee-you-TREE-ick] acid (GABA)** the body's chief inhibitory neurotransmitter, which plays a role in regulating arousal

**glutamate [GLUE-tuh-mate]** the chief excitatory neurotransmitter in the brain, found at more than 50% of the synapses in the brain

**endorphins [in-DOOR-fins]** neurotransmitters that act as a natural painkiller

## Endorphins: Pain and Pleasure in the Brain

Have you ever heard the term *endorphin*? If you have, what was the context? If you are like most people, your first exposure to endorphins was probably in the context of exercise or physical injuries. **Endorphins** are neurotransmitters that are chemically very similar to the class of narcotic drugs called *opiates* (e.g., opium, heroin, morphine, and codeine). Endorphins are released in the central nervous system during times of stress, such as physical exertion or physical injury, to protect us from pain. Because endorphins block pain messages in the central nervous system, we feel less pain and a mild sense of euphoria when they are released. Endorphins may be one of the reasons that physical activity makes us feel physically and mentally better (Fichna, Janecka, Piestrzeniewicz, et al., 2007).

Endorphins may also play a role in making other activities, such as eating, pleasurable (Hayward et al., 2006). For example, research indicates that endorphins are released about 15 minutes after eating fat. The reward from endorphin may be one reason for the appeal of fatty foods (Mizushige, Inoue, & Fushiki, 2007).

We hope that you now have a basic understanding of the role that neurotransmitters play in allowing our neurons to communicate with one another (see ■ YOU REVIEW 2.1). Our next step is to take a look at how this neural signaling fits into the structure of the nervous system.

Exercise can lead to the release of endorphins, producing feelings of pleasure and well-being that are sometimes called a "runner's high."

© TMI/Alamy

# YOU REVIEW 2.1

**Some Neurotransmitters, Their Functions, and Related Diseases and Clinical Conditions**

| NEUROTRANSMITTER | FUNCTIONS | RELATED DISEASES AND CLINICAL CONDITIONS |
| --- | --- | --- |
| Acetylcholine | Excites skeletal muscles; inhibits heart action; memory | Alzheimer's disease |
| Dopamine | Movement; learning; attention; motivation and reward | Parkinson's disease; schizophrenia; substance abuse |
| Serotonin | Sleep; arousal; mood; eating; pain perception | Depression; obsessive compulsive disorder and other anxiety disorders; eating disorders; chronic pain |
| Norepinephrine | Sleep; arousal; mood | Depression and other mood disorders |
| GABA | Chief inhibitor; regulates arousal | Some anxiety disorders; some seizure disorders |
| Glutamate | Chief excitatory neurotransmitter; many diverse functions | Neural death following head injuries |
| Endorphins | Suppression of pain; eating; cardiovascular functioning | Some indication of a link to mood |

# Let's REVIEW

We've described some of the major neurotransmitters and the roles they may play in our functioning. For a quick check of your understanding, answer these questions.

1. Lamont developed a disease that reduces the amount of serotonin in his brain. What symptoms would you expect Lamont to have?
   a. Hallucinations
   b. Trouble with his motor skills
   c. Symptoms of depression
   d. Seizures

2. Jackson is a normal, healthy adult man. Jackson's brain likely contains more _____ than any other neurotransmitter.
   a. glutamate
   b. GABA
   c. dopamine
   d. acetylcholine

3. Sasha has been drinking an herbal tea that she believes boosts her body's ability to manufacture acetylcholine. Why do you suppose Sasha is so interested in drinking this tea?
   a. She is trying to improve her memory.
   b. She is trying to treat her depression.
   c. She is hoping it will help her have more energy.
   d. She is hoping it will help her sleep better.

Answers 1. c; 2. a; 3. a

# The Structure of the Nervous System

Our **nervous system** is the vast, interconnected network of all the neurons in our body. Every single facet of our body's functioning and our behavior is monitored and influenced by the nervous system. The nervous system is arranged in a series of interconnected subsystems, each with its own specialized tasks. At the broadest level, the nervous system is divided into the brain and spinal cord, known as the **central nervous system (CNS)**, and the remaining components of the nervous system, referred to collectively as the **peripheral nervous system (PNS)** (■ FIGURE 2.8). We will discuss the function of the CNS later when we discuss the brain, but first let's take a closer look at the PNS.

*You Asked...*

How does the brain communicate with the body?

BROOKE LANDERS, STUDENT

**nervous system**   an electrochemical system of communication within the body that uses cells called neurons to convey information

**central nervous system (CNS)**   the brain and the spinal cord

**peripheral nervous system (PNS)**   all of the nervous system except the brain and the spinal cord

**sensory neurons**   neurons that transmit information from the sense organs to the central nervous system

**motor neurons**   neurons that transmit commands from the brain to the muscles of the body

## Sensing and Reacting: The Peripheral Nervous System

The functions of the PNS are twofold. First, the PNS must ensure that the CNS is informed about what is happening inside and outside our body. To this end, the PNS is equipped with **sensory neurons** that convey information to the CNS from the outside world, such as sights and sounds, as well as information from our internal world, such as aches and pains. Once the information has reached the CNS, it is carried across *interneurons* as the brain processes the information. Then the second function of the PNS takes over as it acts out the directives of the CNS. The PNS is equipped with **motor neurons** that carry signals from the CNS to our muscles. For example, when you see a juicy apple, the sensory neurons of your eye send this information upward

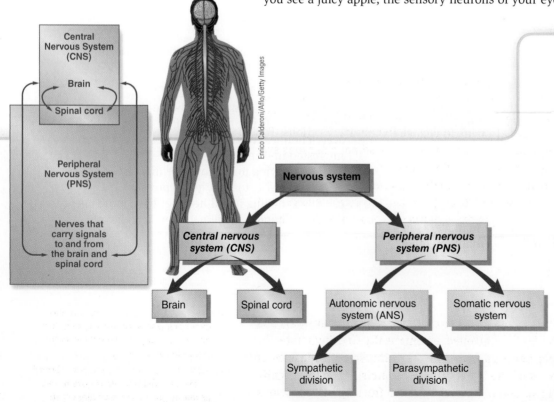

Central Nervous System (CNS)

Brain

Spinal cord

Peripheral Nervous System (PNS)

Nerves that carry signals to and from the brain and spinal cord

Enrico Calderoni/Aflo/Getty Images

**FIGURE**

# 2.8

## The Human Nervous System

The nervous system is divided into the central nervous system (CNS, shown in blue) and the peripheral nervous system (PNS, shown in red). Together the central and peripheral nervous systems affect virtually all of our bodily functions. The PNS can be further subdivided into the somatic nervous system (governs voluntary action and sensory functioning) and the autonomic nervous system (governs involuntary organ functioning). The autonomic nervous system can be further subdivided into the parasympathetic nervous system (governs organs in calm situations) and the sympathetic nervous system (governs organs during times of stress).

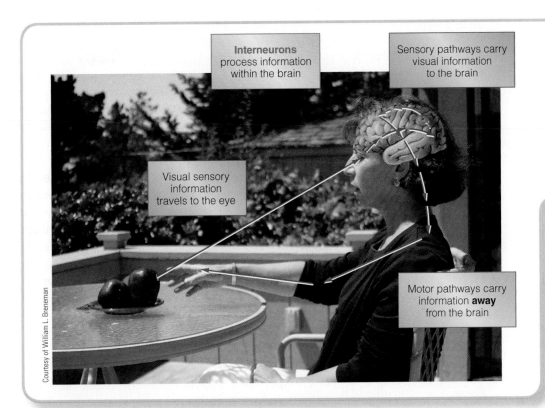

**Interneurons** process information within the brain

**Sensory pathways carry** visual information to the brain

**Visual sensory** information travels to the eye

**Motor pathways carry** information **away** from the brain

Courtesy of William L. Breneman

FIGURE

## 2.9

### Sensory and Motor Pathways

Reaching for an apple involves sensory pathways (shown in red), motor pathways (shown in blue), and interneuron pathways (shown in green).

to the part of the brain that processes visual information. Here the brain recognizes the apple, and you decide to eat the apple. The brain then sends signals downward to the motor neurons of your hand and arm, which, in turn, direct you to reach out and grasp the apple with your hand (■ FIGURE 2.9). In this fashion, the sensory pathways send sensory information *to* the spinal cord and brain, and the motor pathways carry "orders" *away* from the brain and spinal cord to the rest of the body.

## Voluntary Action: The Somatic Nervous System

Traditionally, psychologists and physiologists have further subdivided the neurons of the PNS into two subsystems: the *somatic nervous system* and the *autonomic nervous system*. The **somatic nervous system** includes those neurons that control the skeletal muscles of the body that allow us to engage in voluntary actions. For example, reaching for an apple requires the activation of the somatic nervous system. The brain makes the decision to reach for the apple, then this "order" is sent downward, across the motor neurons of the somatic nervous system that control the muscles of the arm. The arm muscles react to the orders from the CNS, and you reach for the apple. The functioning of the somatic nervous system enables us to control our bodies in a deliberate and flexible manner.

## Involuntary Actions: The Autonomic Nervous System

Although controlling body movements is important, it is equally advantageous to have some processes in the body controlled automatically and involuntarily. The neurons of the **autonomic nervous system** control the smooth muscles of the internal organs, the muscles of the heart, and the glands. By automatically regulating organ functions, the autonomic nervous system frees up our conscious resources and enables us to respond quickly and efficiently to the demands placed

**somatic nervous system**    branch of the peripheral nervous system that governs sensory and voluntary motor action in the body

**autonomic nervous system**    branch of the peripheral nervous system that primarily governs involuntary organ functioning and actions in the body

on us by the environment. Imagine how hard life would be if you had to remember to breathe, tell your heart to beat, and remind your liver to do its job! You would have little energy and attention left for thinking and learning, let alone responding quickly to threatening situations. Thankfully, we have the autonomic nervous system to regulate our organ functions, and it is equipped with separate divisions to help us survive in an ever-changing and sometimes dangerous world.

## THE PARASYMPATHETIC NERVOUS SYSTEM

The **parasympathetic nervous system** operates mainly under conditions of relative calm. As you read this page, it is very likely that your parasympathetic nervous system is primarily responsible for regulating the functions of your internal organs. When the parasympathetic nervous system is active, heart rate, blood pressure, and respiration are kept at normal levels. Blood is circulated to the digestive tract and other internal organs so that they can function properly, and your pupils are not overly dilated. Your body is calm, and everything is running smoothly. But if threat arises in the environment, this will quickly change. During times of stress, the sympathetic system takes over primary regulation of our organ functions from the parasympathetic system.

## THE SYMPATHETIC NERVOUS SYSTEM

The **sympathetic nervous system** springs into action under conditions of threat or stress. The sympathetic nervous system evolved to protect us from danger. When it is activated, heart rate increases, breathing becomes more rapid, blood pressure increases, digestion slows, muscle tissue becomes engorged with blood, the pupils dilate, and the hair on the back of the neck stands up. All of these changes help to prepare us to defend our body from threat. For this reason, the actions of the sympathetic nervous system are often referred to as the *fight or flight response.* The increased cardiovascular activity quickly pumps oxygenated blood away from internal organs and to the muscles of the arms and legs so that the animal or person can swiftly attack, defend itself, or run away. Once the danger is past, the parasympathetic system resumes control, and heart rate, respiration, blood pressure, and pupil dilation return to normal. Because the sympathetic nervous system plays an important role in our response to stress, it also plays an important role in our health. We explore this connection in Chapter 11.

**parasympathetic nervous system**
branch of the autonomic nervous system most active during times of normal functioning

**sympathetic nervous system**
branch of the autonomic nervous system most active during times of danger or stress

## REVIEW

We have described the structure of the nervous system, including the central and peripheral nervous systems. For a quick check of your understanding, answer these questions.

**1.** Juanita was hiking in the woods when she stumbled upon a rattlesnake. Immediately after she saw the snake, which division of the nervous system was most likely in control of Juanita's internal organ functions?
a. Parasympathetic    c. Endocrine
b. Sympathetic        d. Spinal

**2.** Moving your arm is an example of a behavior that is governed by which branch of the nervous system?
a. Somatic nervous system
b. Autonomic nervous system

c. Sympathetic nervous system
d. Parasympathetic nervous system

**3.** The sensory neurons in your fingertips are part of the _____ nervous system.
a. central       c. autonomic
b. peripheral    d. sympathetic

Answers 1. b; 2. a; 3. b

# The Brain and Spine: The Central Nervous System

As we have discussed, the structures of the brain are composed largely of neurons and glia cells. These structures are organized into three regions: the *hindbrain*, the *midbrain*, and the *forebrain*. The **hindbrain** sits directly above the spinal cord and is named for its position at the bottom of the brain (■ FIGURE 2.10). The hindbrain is the most "primitive" part of the brain, involved in the most basic life-sustaining functions. The hindbrain makes up a good portion of the *brainstem*, a series of brain structures that are essential for life. Even small amounts of damage to the brainstem can be life threatening.

The **forebrain** resides in the top part of the skull and regulates complex mental processes such as thinking and emotional control. It is the largest region of the brain and includes structures that regulate many emotional, motivational, and cognitive processes. Without this well-developed forebrain, humans would not have the mental abilities such as problem solving, thinking, remembering, and using language.

Between the hindbrain and the forebrain is the **midbrain**, which acts as a connection between the more basic functions of the hindbrain and the complex mental processes of the forebrain. Without the midbrain, the hindbrain could not supply the forebrain with the neural impulses it needs to remain active and to keep us conscious.

**LEARNING OBJECTIVES**

● Be able to locate the hindbrain, midbrain, and forebrain, list their parts, and explain what they do.

● Describe brain-imaging techniques and other ways we can study the brain, and explain their advantages and limitations.

**hindbrain**    primitive part of the brain that comprises the medulla, pons, and cerebellum

**forebrain**    brain structures, including the limbic system, thalamus, hypothalamus, and cortex, that govern higher-order mental processes

**midbrain**    brain structure that connects the hindbrain with the forebrain

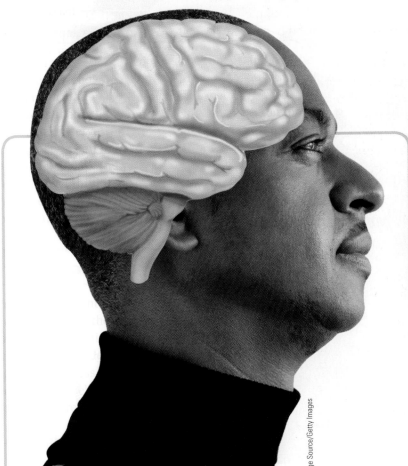

Image Source/Getty Images

**FIGURE**

## 2.10

### The Human Hindbrain, Midbrain, and Forebrain

The human hindbrain (shown in blue) governs basic and life-sustaining functions. The midbrain (shown in red) connects the lower structures of the hindbrain with the higher structures of the forebrain. The forebrain (shown in tan) governs complex processes such as cognition, sensory processing, and the planning and execution of behaviors.

FIGURE

# 2.12

### The Cerebral Hemispheres

The brain is divided into right and left hemispheres. The outside covering of the hemispheres, the cortex, is where the higher-order processing in the brain takes place.

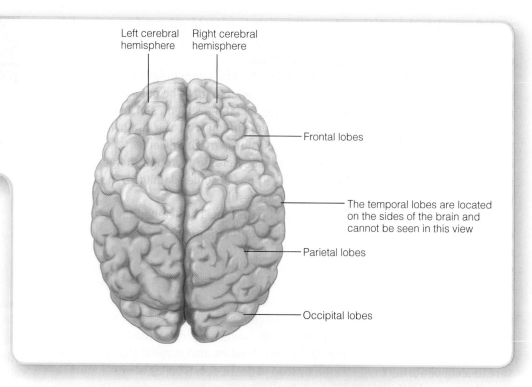

Left cerebral hemisphere

Right cerebral hemisphere

Frontal lobes

The temporal lobes are located on the sides of the brain and cannot be seen in this view

Parietal lobes

Occipital lobes

**amygdala [uh-MIG-duh-luh]**   part of the limbic system that plays a role in the emotions of fear and aggression

**hippocampus [HIP-po-CAM-puss]**   part of the brain that plays a role in the transfer of information from short- to long-term memory

The amygdala plays a role in emotions such as fear and anger.

© Masterfile

in the central region of the brain, above the hindbrain and beneath the cerebral cortex: the *amygdala* and the *hippocampus* (■ FIGURE 2.13).

The **amygdala** is an almond-shaped structure located almost directly behind the temples. The amygdala governs the emotions of fear and aggression (Sah et al., 2003). More specifically, the amygdala may play a role in the way we perceive and respond to emotion-evoking stimuli (Adolphs, 2002; Isenberg et al., 1999). Studies have found that participants with damage to their amygdala have a difficult time making accurate judgments about others' mood states by looking at their facial expressions. This is especially true when participants are making judgments about other people's level of fear and anger (Adolphs, Tranel, & Damasio, 1998; Graham, Devinsky, & LaBar, 2007).

Recently, researchers have shown that persons with *autism* or *Asperger syndrome*, psychological disorders characterized by severe deficits in social behavior, experience abnormal patterns of amygdala activation when perceiving fear in other people's faces (Ashwin et al., 2006). Studies like these suggest that the amygdala may play an essential role in helping us size up social situations and, in turn, regulate our emotional reactions to these situations. For more on what your amygdala does for you, see the Neuroscience Applies to Your World box (p. 60).

The **hippocampus**, a structure related to learning and memory, is the final structure of the limbic system that we will describe (Figure 2.13). Much of what we know about the function of the hippocampus comes from case studies of people who have had damage to their hippocampus. One of the first of these studies dates from the early 1950s. Scoville and Milner (1957) reported the case of H.M., a young man with severe, uncontrollable epilepsy. H.M.'s epilepsy did not respond to medication and threatened his health as well as his lifestyle. In a last-ditch effort to reduce the severity of his

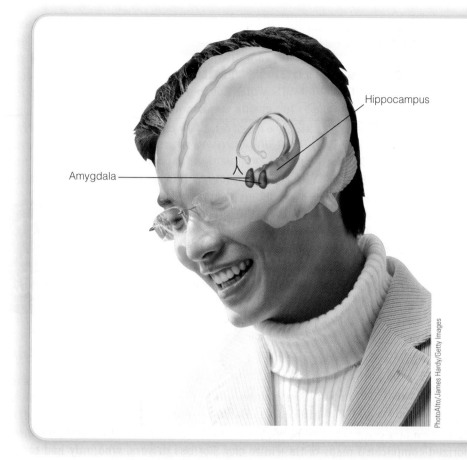

PhotoAlto/James Hardy/Getty Images

**FIGURE**

## 2.13

### The Limbic System

Limbic system structures, including the amygdala and the hippocampus, process specific aspects of emotion and memory.

seizures, doctors decided to take the drastic measure of destroying part of H.M.'s brain with surgically produced lesions. The doctors cut neurons in the limbic system, hoping to check the uncontrolled electrical current that occurs when an epileptic has a seizure. The surgery performed on H.M. destroyed his hippocampus.

The surgery did reduce the intensity of H.M.'s seizures, but it also produced some unexpected and devastating side effects. Shortly after the surgery, it became apparent that H.M. had *anterograde amnesia*, the inability to store *new* memories. He could hold information in consciousness the way we briefly hold a phone number in mind while we dial, and his memory for events that occurred prior to the surgery remained intact, but H.M. was unable to form new memories for concepts and events. He would forget conversations seconds after they occurred. He was unable to learn new facts. Oddly, though, H.M. could store new motor skills (for example, he could learn new dance steps), but later he would have no recollection of having ever executed the new skill. Imagine waking up one day and knowing how to do a dance that you don't remember ever having danced!

Since H.M.'s surgery, a large number of subsequent case studies and controlled animal experiments have supported the hypothesis that the hippocampus is important to learning and memory. For example, researchers used brain-imaging techniques to compare the hippocampi of London taxi drivers with those of London bus drivers. They found that certain areas of the hippocampus were enlarged in the taxi drivers but not in the bus drivers. Furthermore, the number of years a participant had been driving a taxi was positively correlated with the size of certain hippocampal areas. These data *suggest* that portions of the hippocampus enlarged as the taxi drivers

Researchers (Maguire, Woolett, & Spiers, 2006) found that some regions of the hippocampus in London taxi drivers were larger than the same hippocampal regions in the brains of London bus drivers. These results suggest that certain regions of the hippocampus may enlarge as a cab driver uses his or her brain to memorize complicated street maps of an entire city such as London.

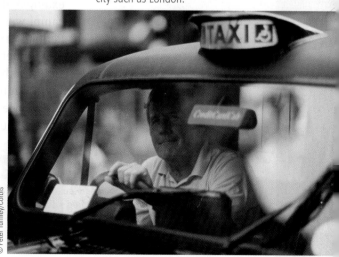

© Peter Turnley/Corbis

FIGURE

## 2.14

### FIGURE

## 2.14

### Cortex of a Human Brain and a Cat Brain

Note how much more convoluted, or folded, the human brain is compared to the cat brain. Many of the higher-order processes that humans engage in, such as language and thinking, are processed in the cortex.

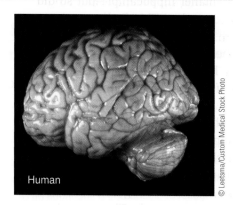

Human

© Leetsma/Custom Medical Stock Photo

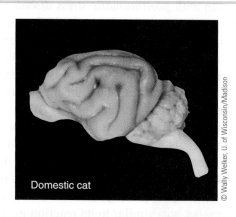

Domestic cat

© Wally Welker, U. of Wisconsin/Madison

The
the
a fu
was
Alth
pos
earl
to s
Wit
her

### FIGURE

## 2.15

### The Human Brain

(a) The lobes of the brain. (b) The language centers of the brain are generally found in the left hemisphere. Wernicke's area in the left temporal lobe allows us to comprehend speech. Broca's area in the left frontal lobe allows us to produce speech.

*From Gaudin and Jones,* Human Anatomy and Physiology, *Fig. 12.2, p. 294. Reprinted by permission of the author.*

language. It is the cortex that gives us our humanness. It is no coincidence that the human cortex is the most developed of all known creatures and that humans also have the most highly developed cognitive skills of all known species. Compare the photographs in Figure 2.14. Notice that the human cortex is very folded and convoluted, whereas the cat's cortex is much less so. The folds allow for more cortical surface area within the confines of the skull cavity. A cat has proportionately less cortical area than a human does, and this smaller cortex translates into fewer cognitive abilities for the cat.

## THE LOBES OF THE CORTEX AND LATERALIZATION IN THE BRAIN

The human cortex is divided into four distinct physical regions called *lobes*. These are the **frontal lobe**, the **parietal lobe**, the **occipital lobe**, and the **temporal lobe** (■ FIGURE 2.15a). The lobes of the cortex are structurally symmetrical in the two hemispheres of the brain, meaning that the brain has both right and left frontal

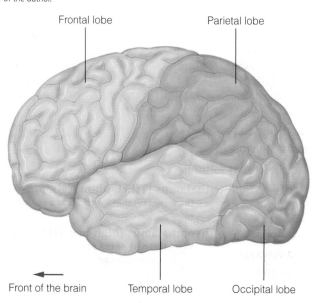

Frontal lobe        Parietal lobe

Front of the brain    Temporal lobe    Occipital lobe

**(a) Lobes of the brain (left hemisphere)**

Primary somatosensory area

Primary motor area

Broca's area

Primary auditory area    Wernicke's area    Primary visual area

**(b) Primary motor-sensory areas of the cortex**

neur
the
str

lobes, right and left temporal lobes, and so on. However, the functions of the right and left lobes are often somewhat different. Functions are *lateralized*, or found in only one hemisphere of the brain, for a couple of reasons. First, the lobes of the brain tend to be wired in a *contralateral* fashion, with the right side of the brain governing the left side of the body and the left side of the brain governing the right side of the body. Although contralateral wiring is the norm in the brain, some neural pathways carry information to and from the body to the same hemisphere of the brain.

Lateralization in the brain is also evident in that the right and left hemispheres process somewhat different types of information (Stephan et al., 2003). For example, most people process language largely in the left hemisphere. Although some people have major language centers in the right hemisphere, and some have major language centers in both hemispheres, for the average person language is located in the left hemisphere. As a result, when people incur major damage to the left hemisphere (as from a stroke), their ability to use language often suffers, a condition known as *aphasia*.

Two examples illustrate this hemispheric specialization of language. When damage is severe in **Broca's area** in the left frontal lobe (Figure 2.15b), people are unable to produce understandable speech, a condition known as **Broca's aphasia** (Geschwind, 1975; Geschwind & Levitsky, 1968). When people have damage to **Wernicke's area** in the left temporal lobe (Figure 2.15b), the resulting **Wernicke's aphasia** leaves them unable to understand spoken language. When the damage is confined to the right side of the brain, people usually remain able to understand and produce speech, but they have some difficulty processing certain types of spatial information (such as judging the distance between two objects).

Differences in the linguistic and spatial processing of the left and right hemispheres once led scientists to conclude broadly that the hemispheres of the brain processed very different categories of information: they surmised that the left hemisphere processed verbal information and the right hemisphere processed spatial information. However, more recent studies have suggested that the left and right hemispheres of the brain may not divide up their functions as neatly as once thought. For example, the right hemisphere also seems to process some of the more subtle aspects of language, such as the processing of novel metaphors (Mashal & Faust, 2008). Newer research also indicates that both hemispheres process different aspects of spatial information (Amorapanth, Widick, & Chatterjee, 2009). To sum up, we are coming to understand that the two hemispheres accomplish tasks, such as processing language and spatial information, by working together and performing complementary functions.

## THE CORPUS CALLOSUM: ARE WOMEN'S BRAINS LESS LATERALIZED THAN MEN'S?

Whether the hemispheres process different information or merely different aspects of the same information, they must have some means of coordinating the information they process. The **corpus callosum** is a dense band of neurons that sits just below the cortex along the midline of the brain (Banich & Heller, 1998; Figure 2.11). This band physically connects the right and left cortical areas and ensures that each hemisphere "knows" what the other hemisphere is doing. The corpus callosum passes information back and forth between the right and left hemispheres, allowing us to integrate these somewhat independent functions. Without the corpus callosum, the right and left cortices would function independently and in ignorance of each other.

**frontal lobe**    cortical area directly behind the forehead that plays a role in thinking, planning, decision making, language, and motor movement

**parietal [puh-RYE-it-ull] lobe**    cortical area on the top sides of the brain that play a role in touch and certain cognitive processes

**occipital [ox-SIP-it-ull] lobe**    cortical area at the back of the brain that plays a role in visual processing

**temporal [TEM-por-ull] lobe**    cortical area directly below the ears that play a role in auditory processing and language

**Broca's [BRO-kuz] area**    a region in the left frontal lobe that plays a role in the production of speech

**Broca's aphasia [ah-FAYZ-yah]**    a condition resulting from damage to Broca's area of the brain that leaves the person unable to produce speech.

**Wernicke's [WURR-neh-kees] area**    a region of the left temporal lobe that plays a role in the comprehension of speech

**Wernicke's aphasia [ah-FAYZ-yah]**    a condition resulting from damage to Wernicke's area of the brain that leaves a person unable to comprehend speech

**corpus callosum [COR-puss cal-OH-sum]**    a thick band of neurons that connects the right and left hemispheres of the brain

You Asked...

*What is different in the male's brain compared with the female's?*

ZACH VEATCH, STUDENT

Early studies suggested that certain areas of the corpus callosum may be larger in women than in men (DeLacoste-Utamsing & Holloway, 1982). Having a larger corpus callosum may allow for more connections between hemispheres, resulting in a brain that is less lateralized and more integrated (Reite et al., 1995). This interpretation is supported by the finding that at least during the performance of spatial and verbal tasks, the pattern of electrical activity in male brains tends to be more confined to one hemisphere than it is in female brains (Koles, Lind, & Flor-Henry, 2009).

Yet the idea that women have larger corpora callosa (the plural of corpus callosum) is controversial. Some researchers suggest that the differences seen may have less to do with gender than with brain size; that is, people with smaller brains may have larger corpora callosa, regardless of gender (Jäncke & Steinmetz, 2003). Still others argue that increased communication between hemispheres may actually increase lateralization in the brain (Kimura, 2000). Although a clear picture of sex differences in the corpus callosum and brain lateralization has not yet emerged, psychologists do have a much clearer understanding of what happens to the brain when the corpus callosum fails to do its job.

## THE SPLIT BRAIN

Physicians have at times willfully disrupted communication between the hemispheres by destroying the corpus callosum in the human brain. Such a drastic measure is taken in cases where people have severe, uncontrollable epilepsy. In severe epilepsy, abnormal electrical activity can build up in one hemisphere and spread across the corpus callosum to engulf the opposite hemisphere. This short-circuiting of both hemispheres produces a severe, life-threatening seizure called a *grand mal seizure*. If drugs cannot control the seizures, surgery may be performed to cut the corpus callosum and thereby contain the short-circuiting to one hemisphere only. The person still has seizures, but they are not as severe. People who have had this surgery are referred to as having **split brains** because their hemispheres are no longer connected by neural pathways. People with split brains provide scientists with an opportunity to study the lateralization of the brain.

Working with split-brain people, researchers have a chance to study the functioning of each hemisphere independent of the other. For example, split-brain research helped researchers conclude that the left hemisphere enables us to produce speech. Researcher Michael Gazzaniga (1967) briefly flashed pictures of familiar objects to the right and left visual fields of split-brain people and asked them to identify the objects (■ FIGURE 2.16). When an object is briefly presented to the right peripheral field of vision, the resulting visual information is sent directly to the left hemisphere of the brain. Because Broca's area is in the left hemisphere for most people, Gazzaniga found that the average split-brain person could verbally identify the object.

But what about an object presented to the person's left peripheral field of vision? When an object is briefly shown on the far left side, the resulting visual information is sent directly to the right hemisphere of the brain. Recall that most people do not have a Broca's area in their right hemisphere. In a normal brain, the information travels from the right hemisphere across the corpus callosum to the language centers in the left hemisphere. However, in a split-brain individual, this cannot happen. Without the corpus callosum, Gazzaniga's split-brain people

**split brain**    a brain with its corpus callosum severed; sometimes done to control the effects of epilepsy in people who do not respond to other therapies

**association cortex**    areas of the cortex involved in the association or integration of information from the motor-sensory areas of the cortex could not transmit the knowledge of what they were seeing to the language centers in their left hemisphere. The right brain knew what the objects were, but it could not inform the "speaking" left brain! Predictably, the split-brain people were unable to name the objects they saw in their left visual fields. Interestingly, in this situation, split-brain people were able to point to the objects in a drawing—provided they used their left hand (which is controlled by the right brain). Split-brain research has helped us to begin sorting out the relative contributions that the right and left hemispheres make to everyday cognitive processes.

## The Specialization of Function in the Lobes of the Cortex

Just as there is specialization in the hemispheres of the brain, there is also specialization within the different lobes of the brain. About 25% of the total surface area of the cortex is dedicated to motor and sensory functions such as vision, hearing, movement, and tactile sensation. Specific motor-sensory areas can be found in all the lobes of the brain (frontal, parietal, occipital, and temporal). The remaining 75% of the cortical area is thought to be devoted to higher-order processes that involve the integration of information, such as thinking, planning, decision making, and language. Collectively, this 75% is referred to as the **association cortex** because these areas are presumed to involve the association of information from the motor-sensory areas of the cortex.

We do not yet have a complete understanding of the functions of specific areas of the association cortex. Often, damage to the association areas produces general changes and deficits in behavior. However, stimulation of specific areas of the association cortex does not usually lead to specific, predictable physical reactions. It is thought that the association cortex plays a role in general cognition, such as planning and decision making. Where applicable, we will discuss the known functions of the association areas for the specific lobes of the brain.

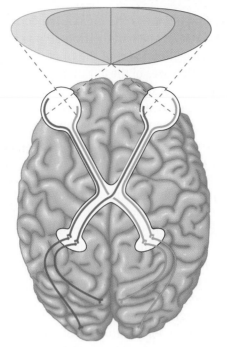

**(a) Visual pathways in the brain**

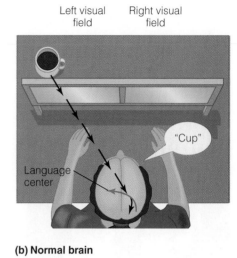

**(b) Normal brain**

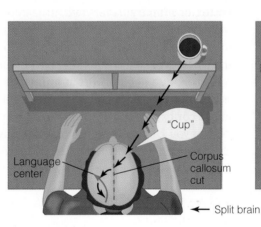

**(c) Split brain**

← Split brain →

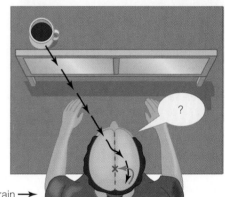

FIGURE

## 2.16

### A Typical Split-Brain Study

Visual pathways in the intact brain (a) send information to both hemispheres. As a result, when a person with an intact brain sees an object in either his right or left visual field, he will be able to name it (b). However, this is not true for people with split brains. In a typical split-brain experiment (c), an image is flashed to a split-brain person's right or left visual field, and he is asked to identify the object in the image. When the image is flashed to the person's right visual field, he is able to name it; but when it is flashed to his left visual field, he is unable to name it because the information cannot travel to the language centers in the left hemisphere.

## THE FRONTAL LOBE

The frontal lobe is the area of the cortex that lies closest to the forehead (Figure 2.15a, p. 62). Much of the frontal lobe is association cortex. We know more about the association areas of the frontal lobe than any other lobes. Broca's area in the association area of the left frontal lobe is, as previously mentioned, involved in the production of speech. It also appears that the frontal lobe association areas play a role in cognitive processes such as attention, problem solving, judgment, the planning and executing of behavior, and certain aspects of personality.

These cognitive functions are illustrated in a famous case study from the history of psychology. In 1848, a railway worker named Phineas Gage suffered severe trauma to his *prefrontal cortex* (the association area in the very front part of the frontal lobe) when a metal rod was shot through his head in an explosion. The rod entered his left cheek and shot out of the top of his head. Although he survived his injuries, they resulted in some dramatic personality changes. Whereas Gage had been a calm, responsible man prior to his injuries, he became impulsive, emotionally volatile, and irresponsible afterward. Because the prefrontal cortex is important for the regulation of emotion (Davidson, Putman, & Larson, 2000), the damage to Gage's brain robbed him of his ability to control his emotions, make good judgments, and execute planned behaviors (Damasio et al., 1994). Phineas Gage was no longer himself, but he could still move and speak because the motor-sensory areas of his frontal lobe were undamaged.

At the back of the frontal lobe (behind the prefrontal cortex) lies the **motor cortex** or *primary motor area*, a narrow band of cortex that allows us to execute motor movements. The motor cortex on the right side of the brain affects movement on the left side of the body, and vice versa. Additionally, specific points along the motor cortex correspond to particular points on the body. ■ FIGURE 2.17a is a rendering of a *homunculus*, a humorous mapping of body parts onto their appropriate motor cortical points. If stimulation were applied to these points along the motor cortex, the result would be movement of the corresponding body part.

As you can see, the frontal lobe plays several roles in our daily functioning. Curiously, the frontal lobe is also an area of the brain that experiences changes across adulthood, a topic covered in the Psychology Across Generations box, p. 68.

## THE PARIETAL LOBE

As with the frontal lobe, much of the parietal lobe is association cortex, but we know much less about the specific functions of these association areas. We do know that the motor-sensory areas of the parietal lobe play a role in sensation. A thin strip of the parietal lobe affects our sense of touch, pressure, and pain. This strip, called the **somatosensory cortex**, or *primary somatosensory area*, lies directly behind the motor cortex, along the leading edge of the parietal lobe (Figure 2.15b, p. 62). The somatosensory cortex is wired much like the motor cortex, and specific points along the somatosensory cortex correspond to particular points on the body (■ Figure 2.17b). Damage to the somatosensory cortex often results in numbness of the corresponding body part.

## THE OCCIPITAL LOBE

The occipital lobe of the brain is located at the very back of the skull, above the cerebellum. Much of the occipital lobe is dedicated to processing visual information. The **visual cortex**, or *primary visual area* (Figure 2.15b), of the occipital lobe is composed of layers of tissue that contain long axonal fibers. An action potential

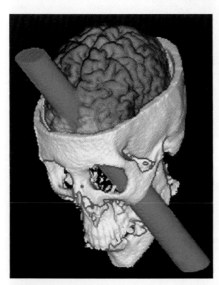

Phineas Gage was a responsible, mild-mannered worker on a railway construction crew until a rod like this one was shot through his head in a freak accident. Gage survived, but he was never the same. The damage to Gage's prefrontal cortex coincided with dramatic changes in his personality. The once calm Gage became emotionally volatile and difficult. As a result, he was unable to perform his former job with the railroad.

Reprinted with permission from Damasio, H., Grabowski, T., Frank, R., Galaburda, A. M., & Damasio, A. R. (1994). The return of Phineas Gage: The skull of a famous patient yields clues about the brain. *Science*, 264, 1102–1105. © 1994, AAAS.

**motor cortex**   a strip of cortex at the back of the frontal lobe that governs the execution of motor movement in the body

**somatosensory [so-MAT-oh-SEN-sor-ee] cortex**   a strip of cortex at the front of the parietal lobe that governs the sense of touch

**visual cortex**   a region of cortex found at the back of the occipital lobe that processes visual information in the brain

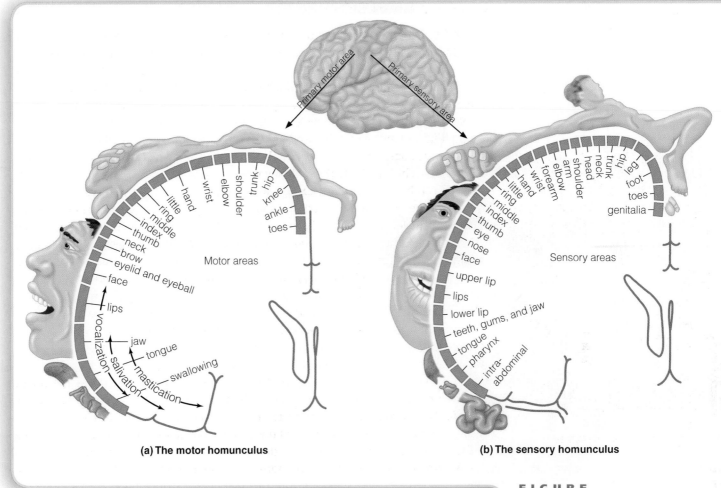

**(a) The motor homunculus**

**(b) The sensory homunculus**

FIGURE

## 2.17

**Motor and Sensory Homunculi**
Homunculi are humorous depictions of the localization of function on the cortex.

*From Penfield and Rasmussen, The Cerebral Cortex of Man, © 1950 Macmillan Library Reference. Renewed 1978 by Theodore Rasmussen. Reprinted by permission of The Gale Group.*

is stimulated in specialized cells of the visual cortex when our eyes receive specific types of visual stimuli from the outside world. For instance, some cells begin to fire only when we see lines, and other cells fire only when we see circular shapes. Like a computer, our brain integrates all the incoming neural impulses from these specialized cells in the visual cortex to enable us to perceive what we are viewing. Without the operation of the visual cortex, our brain could not make sense of what our eyes see and we would be functionally blind.

## THE TEMPORAL LOBE

The temporal lobe is in front of the occipital lobe and just below the parietal and frontal lobes—roughly behind our ears inside the skull. Not surprisingly, one of the major functions of the temporal lobe is the processing of auditory information, or hearing. The temporal lobe area devoted to hearing is the **auditory cortex**, or *primary auditory area*, located on the upper edge of the temporal lobe (Figure 2.15b). In addition to the auditory cortex, the left temporal lobe of most people contains Wernicke's area. As we've already seen, Wernicke's area is responsible for the comprehension of speech. Persons who have major damage to Wernicke's area often cannot understand the meaning of spoken words. They hear the words, but they can't make sense of them.

**auditory cortex**   a region of cortex found in the temporal lobe that governs the processing of auditory information in the brain

# Psychology Across Generations:

## The Aging Brain

Some cognitive abilities, such as the ability to learn new faces, may peak as earlier as in our 30s.

Exercise helps to maintain blood flow in the brain, and it may be one way to help us retain as many of our cognitive abilities as we can in the future.

Many studies have suggested that as we age, we tend to experience specific declines in our ability to do certain mental, or *cognitive*, tasks. For example, when compared to young adults, older adults tend to score lower on tests of *fluid intelligence*, the ability to process information rapidly and efficiently (e.g., Yu et al., 2009). Some capacities, such as the ability to learn new faces, can peak as early as our 30s (Germine, Duchaine, & Nakayama, 2010). But why do we perform more poorly as we age? What's happening in our brains?

A number of changes occur in our brains as we age. For example, certain brain structures shrink (Raz & Kennedy, 2009), lesions develop (Bohnen et al., 2009), and changes in neuronal functioning occur (Andrews-Hanna et al., 2007). Blood flow in the brain also changes as we age. Recently, researchers compared the brains of healthy people aged 20 to 80 and found that blood flow to the brain diminished about 1.38% per decade. The amount of oxygen carried in the blood also declined by about 1.4% per decade. Interestingly, some areas of the brain experienced more loss of blood flow than others did. Especially hard hit were the right frontal regions of the brain, including the prefrontal cortex (Lu et al., 2010). Unfortunately, the researchers also found that although the aging brain receives less blood flow and less oxygen, its need for oxygen actually *increases*, presenting something of a double whammy for the brain (Lu et al., 2010).

Given that blood flow to the brain is fed by the same circulatory system that feeds the body, it is reasonable to expect that keeping our cardiovascular system in good shape may also help our brain. Therefore, regular exercise may be one of our most powerful tools for protecting the aging brain (Anderson, Greenwood, & McCloskey, 2010) and maintaining our cognitive abilities (Jedrziewski et al., 2010). So, if you haven't already done so, perhaps now would be a good time to develop an exercise program. Your physician can evaluate your situation and suggest an appropriate level of activity for your age and physical condition.

Now that you have learned about the structure and function of the brain, we hope that you are suitably impressed. In this chapter we have merely begun to explore the functioning of our nervous system, and scientists are far from a complete understanding of this amazing system. As research continues, scientists learn more about how our physiology influences our thoughts and behaviors. Luckily, researchers have a great deal of modern technology to help them learn about the brain (see Psychology Applies to Your World, p. 69). These technologies have helped doctors and psychologists gain a better understanding of how the brain works to regulate and control our mental processes and behavior. Through the use of these technologies, we have learned that the human nervous system is an extremely impressive and important network. However, the nervous system is not the only communication system within the body. We turn now to the other major communication network, the endocrine system.

## Psychology Applies to Your World:

### Technologies for Studying the Brain

Recently, a friend of ours hit her head in a car accident. As a precaution, doctors ordered an MRI of her brain. An MRI, or *magnetic resonance imaging* scan, allows doctors to see a detailed picture of the brain. If our friend had serious damage from the injury, it would have shown up on the MRI. Luckily, the MRI showed no serious damage from the accident, but it did produce another surprise: It showed that despite having no troubling symptoms, she had a very large tumor growing in her brain. Without the MRI, the tumor would have gone undiagnosed until she began having serious symptoms; at that point, it might have been too late to do much for her. We are happy to report that shortly after discovering the tumor doctors were able to quickly remove most of it, and she is now recovering nicely.

### You Asked...

*How many ways are there to study the brain?*

JOSEPH VICKERS, STUDENT

Both doctors and psychologists use technologies like MRIs for studying the brain. Some of these procedures allow researchers to examine only the structure of the brain, whereas others indicate which areas of the brain are most active at a given moment. Because these techniques can be used on living brain tissue, they can give researchers important information about the specific behavioral functions that are governed by particular areas of the brain. The table to the right summarizes some of the most useful technologies available for helping us to better understand the inner workings of the brain: *CAT scans, MRIs, PET scans, fMRIs, EEGs,* and *brain stimulation.*

### Common Techniques for Studying the Brain and Examples of Their Usage

| TECHNIQUE FOR STUDYING THE BRAIN | DESCRIPTION |
|---|---|
| Computerized Axial Tomography (CAT Scan)  ©Custom Medical Stock Photo | Multiple X-ray beams are passed through the brain from different angles. A computer then analyzes the X-rays that exit the head and uses this information to build a very detailed picture of the brain and its structures. CAT scans can be used to diagnose tumors, strokes, certain diseases, and the structural features of the brain. |
| Magnetic Resonance Imaging (MRI)  S & I/Photo Researchers, Inc. | A magnetic field is used to excite the atoms in the body, and the energy emitted by these atoms is used to construct a highly detailed computer-generated picture of the brain's structure. |
| Positron Emission Tomography (PET Scan)  Tim Beddow/Photo Researchers, Inc. | Radioactive glucose (the brain's fuel source) is injected into the bloodstream. The computer measures which areas of the brain are consuming the most glucose, meaning that they are most active. |
| Functional MRI (fMRI)  © Lester Lefkowitz/ Corbis | Uses MRI technology to track which neurons in the brain are most active at a given moment by examining the energy released by hemoglobin molecules in the bloodstream. |
| Electroencephalography (EEG)  CC Studio/Photo Researchers, Inc. | Measures changes in electrical voltage at points along the scalp and yields information on gross patterns of brain activation. |
| Brain Stimulation  Nasa/Getty Images | By stimulating specific areas of the brain, researchers can see what effect this stimulation has on behavior. Doctors also use this technology to treat conditions such as depression. By implanting brain "pacemakers," doctors can stimulate areas of the brain that are not functioning properly. |

# Let's
# REVIEW

This section dealt with the structure and function of the hindbrain, midbrain, and forebrain. The hindbrain is primarily involved in life-sustaining functions, and the midbrain connects the hindbrain with the sophisticated structures of the forebrain. The function of the cortex and lateralization of the cortex were also described. For a quick check of your understanding, answer these questions.

1. Damage to which of the following brain structures would be *most* likely to cause death?
   a. Frontal lobe
   b. Amygdala
   c. Medulla
   d. Hippocampus

2. Billy had a stroke on the left side of his brain. Most of his left frontal lobe was destroyed. What symptoms would you *most* expect to see in Billy as a result of this damage?
   a. Paralysis on the right side of his body and an inability to speak
   b. Paralysis on the right side of his body and an inability to understand speech

   c. Paralysis of his left leg, partial deafness, and stuttering
   d. Paralysis on the left side of his body and an inability to understand speech

3. Juanita experienced a brain injury that left her with an inability to store new memories for events and concepts. Which part of Juanita's brain was most likely damaged?
   a. Hippocampus
   b. Hypothalamus
   c. Thalamus
   d. Midbrain

Answers 1. c; 2. a; 3. a

LEARNING OBJECTIVE

● Explain how the endocrine system works and describe the function of the endocrine glands.

# The Endocrine System: Hormones and Behavior

We have seen that because of its electrochemical nature, the nervous system is especially good at quickly conveying information within the body. It is the speed of the nervous system that enables us to react quickly to changes in our environment. Messages are sent, decisions are made, and actions are taken—all accomplished with the speed of firing action potentials. At times, however, we require communication within the body that is slower and produces more long-lasting effects. In these circumstances, the **endocrine system** is called into action.

The endocrine system is a chemical system of communication that relies on the action of specialized organs called **endocrine glands** that are located throughout the body (■ FIGURE 2.18). When stimulated, endocrine glands release chemicals called **hormones** into the bloodstream. These hormones circulate through the bloodstream until they reach other organs in the body. Our internal organs are equipped with special receptor sites to accept these hormones.

## You Asked...

*Why do our hormones affect our behavior so much?*

DIANA FLORES, STUDENT

**endocrine [EN-doe-crin] system** a chemical system of communication in the body that uses chemical messengers, called hormones, to affect organ function and behavior

**endocrine [EN-doe-crin] glands** organs of the endocrine system that produce and release hormones into the blood

**hormones** chemical messengers of the endocrine system

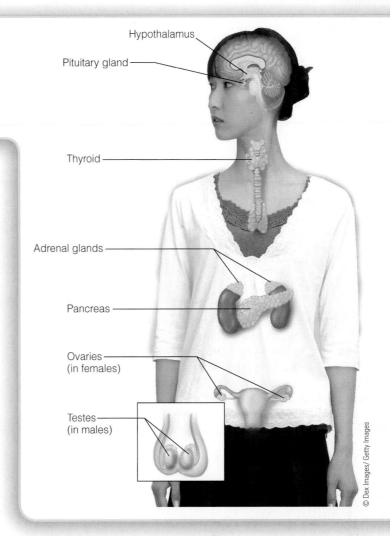

**FIGURE**

## 2.18

### Major Endocrine Glands of the Body

The glands of the endocrine system make and release hormones into the bloodstream.

The endocrine system is considerably slower than the nervous system in relaying messages because it relies on blood circulating through the veins and arteries of the cardiovascular system to transport hormones throughout the body. The stimulation created by hormones, however, tends to last longer than the stimulation caused by action potentials at the synapse. Some of the bodily processes that are heavily influenced by hormonal activity include sexual activity, eating, sleeping, general physiological arousal, and growth.

Communication between the nervous and endocrine systems takes place through the hypothalamus and its connection with the **pituitary gland**. The pituitary gland, situated in the vicinity of the limbic system under the hypothalamus (Figure 2.18), is responsible for regulating hormone release in all the other endocrine glands. When the endocrine system is called into action, the hypothalamus sends a signal to the pituitary gland. The pituitary gland then releases hormones that travel through the bloodstream to the other endocrine glands, stimulating them to release the hormones they produce into the bloodstream. These hormones circulate to their target organs, where they bring about specific changes in the functioning of these organs.

Our bodies are equipped with a great number of peripheral endocrine glands (see Figure 2.18). Probably the best known endocrine glands are the **gonads**, which are necessary for sexuality and reproduction. *Ovaries* are the female gonads, located in the abdominal cavity. Ovaries are directly responsible for the production of female eggs (ova) and the release of female sex hormones, or **estrogens**. *Testes* are the male gonads, located in the testicles. Testes produce male sex cells (sperm) and male hormones, or **androgens**.

The *adrenal glands* sit just above the kidneys in both males and females and are important for regulating arousal and sexual behavior, among many things. When the sympathetic nervous system becomes active during times of stress, the inside of the adrenal glands, or the **adrenal medulla**, releases norepinephrine and epinephrine (also known as *adrenaline*) into the body's bloodstream, where they function as hormones. The sudden flooding of the bloodstream with these hormones causes the familiar sympathetic reactions of increased heart rate, blood pressure, and respiration.

The outside of the adrenal glands, or the **adrenal cortex**, produces *adrenal androgens*, which are male sex hormones found in both males and females. These

**pituitary [peh-TOO-uh-tare-ee] gland** master gland of the endocrine system that controls the action of all other glands in the body

**gonads [go-NADS]** endocrine glands that directly affect sexual reproduction by producing sperm (testes) or eggs (ovaries)

**estrogens [ESS-tro-jens]** a class of female sex hormones that regulate many aspects of sexuality and are found in both males and females

**androgens [ANN-dro-jens]** a class of male hormones that regulate many aspects of sexuality and are found in both males and females

**adrenal [uh-DREEN-ull] medulla** center part of the adrenal gland that plays a crucial role in the functioning of the sympathetic nervous system

**adrenal cortex** outside part of the adrenal gland that plays a role in the manufacture and release of androgens, and therefore influences sexual characteristics

androgens control many aspects of our sexual characteristics and basic physiological functioning. The adrenal cortex also interacts with the immune system to help protect us from infection and disease.

Other important endocrine glands include the *thyroid*, which regulates how energy is used in our bodies; the *pancreas*, which regulates blood sugar levels in the body (see also Chapter 8); and the *pineal gland*, located in the brain, which may play a role in sexual maturation.

The nervous and endocrine systems are nothing short of amazing in their intricate structure and function. Without these systems we would not be able to control our bodies, think, feel, and interact with our environment. After studying this chapter, we hope you are impressed with the wonder of your own biology. In the next chapter, we will explore the areas of sensation and perception, the study of how we sense and perceive information from the outside world.

# Let's REVIEW

This section described the endocrine system and its relationship to the nervous system. For a quick check of your understanding, answer these questions.

1. The _____ releases male sex hormones in the body.
   a. adrenal cortex
   b. adrenal medulla
   c. hippocampus
   d. ovary

2. A malfunction in which of the following endocrine glands would be *most* disruptive to the overall functioning of the endocrine system?
   a. Ovaries/testes
   b. Thalamus
   c. Pituitary
   d. Adrenal

3. Juanita was just frightened by a snake. Which of the following endocrine glands most likely played the biggest role in her response to danger?
   a. Testes
   b. Adrenal cortex
   c. Ovaries
   d. Adrenal medulla

*Answers 1. a; 2. c; 3. d*

# Studying THE CHAPTER

## Key Terms

| | | |
|---|---|---|
| acetylcholine (ACh) (48) | autonomic nervous system (53) | corpus callosum (63) |
| action potential (43) | axon (41) | dendrites (41) |
| adrenal cortex (71) | Broca's aphasia (63) | DNA (41) |
| adrenal medulla (71) | Broca's area (63) | dopamine (48) |
| all-or-none fashion (44) | cell body (41) | endocrine glands (70) |
| amygdala (58) | central nervous system (CNS) (52) | endocrine system (70) |
| androgens (71) | cerebellum (57) | endorphins (50) |
| association cortex (65) | cerebral cortex (57) | estrogens (71) |
| auditory cortex (67) | cerebral hemispheres (57) | excitation (45) |

forebrain (55)

frontal lobe (62)

gamma amino butyric acid
    (GABA) (50)

glia cells (40)

glutamate (50)

gonads (71)

hindbrain (55)

hippocampus (58)

homeostasis (61)

hormones (70)

hypothalamus (61)

inhibition (45)

ions (43)

limbic system (57)

medulla (56)

midbrain (55)

motor cortex (66)

motor neurons (52)

myelin (41)

myelin sheath (41)

nervous system (52)

neurons (40)

neuroplasticity (60)

neuroscience (40)

neurotransmitters (41)

norepinephrine (NOR) (49)

occipital lobe (62)

parasympathetic nervous system (54)

parietal lobe (62)

peripheral nervous system (PNS) (52)

pituitary gland (71)

pons (57)

postsynaptic neuron (42)

presynaptic neuron (42)

refractory period (44)

resting potential (43)

reticular formation (57)

reuptake (46)

sensory neurons (52)

serotonin (49)

somatic nervous system (53)

somatosensory cortex (66)

split brain (64)

sympathetic nervous system (54)

synapse (41)

temporal lobe (62)

thalamus (61)

threshold of excitation (43)

visual cortex (66)

Wernicke's aphasia (63)

Wernicke's area (63)

## What Do You Know? Assess Your Understanding

Test your retention and understanding of the material by answering the following questions.

1.  The _____ system is an electrochemical system of communication in the body.
    a. nervous
    b. endocrine
    c. hormonal
    d. All of the above

2.  When the potential of a neuron hits its threshold of excitation at _____, it will fire an action potential.
    a. –55 mv
    b. +55 mv
    c. –70 mv
    d. +70 mv

3.  Neurotransmitters can be found in the _____ of the neuron.
    a. axon
    b. myelin
    c. axon bulb
    d. dendrites

4.  Sara slipped and nearly fell while walking down the stairs. The increased heart rate and blood pressure that accompanied Sara's fear at almost falling were most likely due to activation of Sara's _____ nervous system.
    a. sympathetic
    b. parasympathetic
    c. somatic
    d. voluntary

5.  There tends to be a(n) _____ of _____ in the brains of people with Alzheimer's disease.
    a. excess; dopamine
    b. lack; dopamine
    c. excess; acetylcholine
    d. lack; acetylcholine

6.  Drugs that are used to treat depression often _____ the action of _____ in the brain.
    a. increase; serotonin
    b. decrease; serotonin
    c. increase; GABA
    d. decrease; GABA

7.  The chief excitatory neurotransmitter in the brain is _____.
    a. acetylcholine
    b. dopamine
    c. GABA
    d. glutamate

8.  An inhibitory neurotransmitter makes the postsynaptic neuron _____ likely to fire an action potential by making the inside of the postsynaptic neuron more _____.
    a. more; positive
    b. less; positive
    c. more; negative
    d. less; negative

9. Rashid cut his finger while cooking. Which neurotransmitter would be most useful in alleviating his pain?
   a. Dopamine
   b. Endorphin
   c. Norepinephrine
   d. GABA

10. The frontal lobe of the brain contains the _____ cortex.
    a. somatosensory
    b. auditory
    c. motor
    d. visual

11. Our ability to detect anger and fear in others is likely influenced by which part of the brain?
    a. Hippocampus
    b. Amygdala
    c. Thalamus
    d. Hypothalamus

12. Loss of balance and coordination when drunk is most likely due to alcohol's effects on which part of the brain?
    a. Thalamus
    b. Hippocampus
    c. Cerebellum
    d. Broca's area

13. The _____ allows the right and left hemispheres of the brain to communicate.
    a. pons
    b. medulla
    c. corpus callosum
    d. limbic system

14. Yumiko was in a car accident in which she incurred massive damage to her left frontal lobe. What types of impairments would you most expect to see in Yumiko as a result of this damage?
    a. Paralysis on her right side
    b. Numbness on her right side
    c. An inability to comprehend speech
    d. Blindness in her right visual field

15. Damage to the left temporal lobe would likely produce what effect?
    a. An inability to produce speech
    b. Paralysis on the right side of the body
    c. Broca's aphasia
    d. Wernicke's aphasia

16. The master gland of the endocrine system is the _____ gland.
    a. hippocampus
    b. pituitary
    c. adrenal medulla
    d. adrenal cortex

17. During times of stress, the endocrine system is most likely to release _____.
    a. androgens
    b. estrogens
    c. adrenaline
    d. dopamine

18. Male sex hormones are called _____.
    a. estrogens
    b. androgens
    c. endorphins
    d. adrenalines

19. A split-brain operation is done to control _____.
    a. seizures
    b. depression
    c. schizophrenia
    d. pain

20. Auditory information is processed in the _____ lobe of the brain.
    a. temporal
    b. occipital
    c. parietal
    d. frontal

Answers: 1. a; 2. a; 3. c; 4. a; 5. d; 6. a; 7. d; 8. d; 9. b; 10. c; 11. b; 12. c; 13. c; 14. a; 15. d; 16. b; 17. c; 18. b; 19. a; 20. a.

## Online Resources

Log in to **www.cengagebrain.com** to access the resources your instructor requires. For this book, you can access:

### Psychology CourseMate

CourseMate brings course concepts to life with interactive learning, study, and exam preparation tools that support the printed textbook. A textbook-specific website, Psychology CourseMate includes an integrated interactive eBook and other interactive learning tools including quizzes, flashcards, videos, and more.

### CENGAGENOW™

CengageNOW Personalized Study is a diagnostic study tool containing valuable text-specific resources—and because you focus on just what you don't know, you learn more in less time to get a better grade.

### WebTutor

More than just an interactive study guide, WebTutor is an anytime, anywhere customized learning solution with an eBook, keeping you connected to your textbook, instructor, and classmates.

## How Do Neurons Communicate?

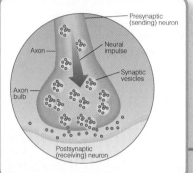

- Neurons use electrochemical energy to generate **action potentials** that travel to the end of the neuron and cause the release of **neurotransmitters**.

- Action potentials or neural signals are fired when a neuron is depolarized enough to reach its **threshold of excitation** (–55 mv).

- Neurotransmitters are chemical compounds that carry signals across neurons. Some of the key neurotransmitters are **acetylcholine**, **dopamine**, **serotonin**, **norepinephrine**, **endorphin**, **GABA**, and **glutamate**.

- Neurotransmitters play significant roles in regulating behavior and mood.

The nervous system is arranged into a hierarchy of subsystems:

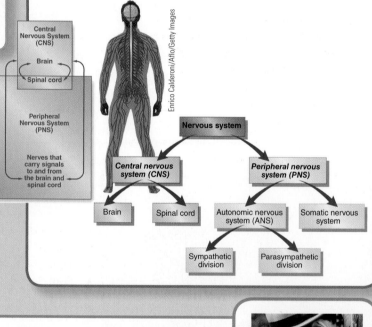

Enrico Calderoni/Aflo/Getty Images

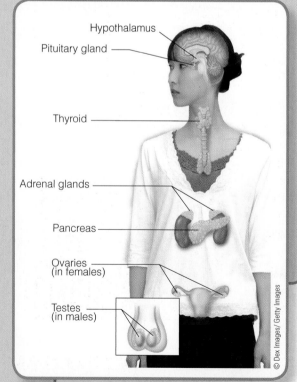

© Dex Images/ Getty Images

## What Is the Endocrine System?

The endocrine system contains glands that release chemical messengers—**hormones**—into the bloodstream. Compared to the nervous system, the endocrine system is slower and more long-lasting in its effects.

Leland Bobbe/Getty Images

## What Are the Structure and Function of the Brain?

- The brain is divided into three key regions. The **hindbrain** governs basic and life-sustaining functions in the body. The **midbrain** connects the lower structures of the hindbrain with the more sophisticated structures of the **forebrain** that regulate higher-order processes such as thinking and emotional control.

- The brain regulates motor activity, sensation and perception, emotions, our ability to learn and remember, and all the other elements of human behavior.

- The **cerebral cortex** is a thin layer of wrinkled tissue that covers the outside of the brain and is most responsible for the cognition, decision making, and language capabilities that are unique to humans.

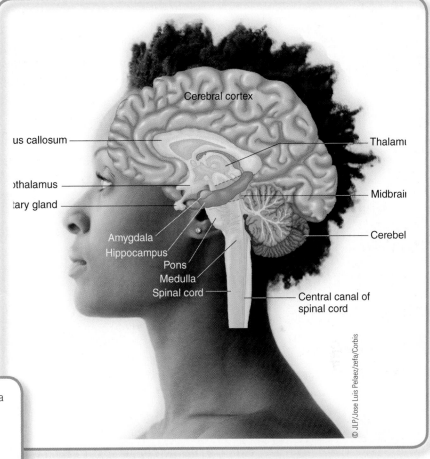

Cerebral cortex

...us callosum

...othalamus

...tary gland

Amygdala
Hippocampus
Pons
Medulla
Spinal cord

Thalam...

Midbrai...

Cerebel...

Central canal of spinal cord

© JLP/Jose Luis Pelaez/zefa/Corbis

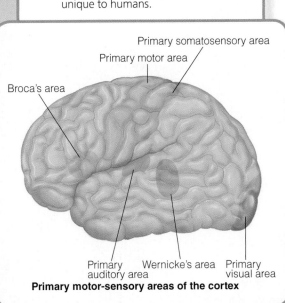

Primary somatosensory area
Primary motor area
Broca's area

Primary auditory area
Wernicke's area
Primary visual area

**Primary motor-sensory areas of the cortex**

- The brain is divided into right and left hemispheres. The left hemisphere generally governs the right side of the body, whereas the right hemisphere governs the left side of the body.

- To assist in studying the brain and its functioning, technology such as CAT scans, MRIs, fMRIs, PET scans, EEGs, and brain stimulation are all important tools.

Nasa/Getty Images

# 3 How Do We SENSE and PERCEIVE Our World?

## Chapter Outline

*Understanding how sensation* and perception occur is very useful to a number of professions. For example, one of our former students, Edgar Lituma, uses these areas of psychology on a daily basis in his work as an artist and graphic designer. Simply put, his art is about creating perceptions in people. Much of Edgar's work centers on designing elements that will be used in advertisements. One of his favorite areas is motion graphics or animated graphics such as those that you might see in videos, TV, or on the Internet. In creating graphics for ads, Edgar must understand how people sense and perceive color, texture, shape, motion, and so on. This understanding is important because being able to predict how the public will perceive an image or video is crucial to Edgar's ability to convey his client's intended message. In fact, Edgar recently told us, "If you want to get into a motion graphics department without using psychology, you won't get very far. You have to be able to predict people's reactions." Check out one of Edgar's art pieces, *Chicken Hormonia,* on page 89. As you study this chapter, you too will gain important insight into how we use our senses to experience and understand the world around us. We'll begin by looking at how psychologists measure sensation and perception.

© KB Bishi

*Edgar Lituma uses his knowledge of sensation and perception in his work as a graphic artist.*

## LEARNING OBJECTIVE

● Explain the concepts of absolute threshold, just noticeable difference (jnd), subliminal perception, and extrasensory perception.

# How Do Psychologists Measure Sensation and Perception?

To read this page, you must first focus your conscious awareness or **attention** on the page and be able to *see* the images printed on it. Seeing is an example of what psychologists call **sensation**. In sensation, sense organs of the body, such as the eyes, convert environmental energy, such as the light that is bouncing off the book page, into neural signals that the brain can then process. Sensation—in this case, seeing—is the first step to getting information into our minds. After sensation, you must *understand* what the images printed on the page mean. **Perception** occurs when you interpret the meaning of the information gathered through your senses.

> ### You Asked...
>
> *Can testing on people's senses and perceptions be that scientific, or is it just opinion?*
>
> JEFF WRIGHT, STUDENT

Psychologists who study sensation and perception are most interested in understanding how we process sensory stimuli such as sights, sounds, and smells. How does your mind interpret the color of light bouncing off the surface of an apple? What physical properties of a food make it taste sweet or bitter? Questions like these are the focus of the branch of psychology called **psychophysics**.

## The Limits of Sensation: Absolute Thresholds

One of the fundamental questions psychophysicists have sought to answer concerns the limits of human sensory capabilities. How faint a light can humans see? How soft a tone can we hear? Psychophysicists have conducted many experiments to answer these questions. These experiments typically involve presenting stimuli of gradually increasing or decreasing intensity (along with some trials on which the stimulus is not presented at all). Participants are asked to report whether they can detect the presence of the stimulus. In this way, psychophysicists establish an *absolute threshold*. **Absolute threshold** is defined as the minimum intensity of a stimulus that can be detected 50% of the time. This 50% mark is used because the level of the stimulus required for it to *just* be perceived varies from trial to trial and from person to person during an experiment. ■ TABLE 3.1 lists the approximate established absolute thresholds for our five senses, described in familiar descriptive terms.

## The Just Noticeable Difference and Weber's Law

In addition to establishing absolute thresholds for the senses, psychophysicists have tried to establish the minimum *change* in the intensity of a stimulus that can be detected 50% of the time. This barely noticeable change in the stimulus is referred to as the *difference threshold* or the **just noticeable difference (jnd)**. In the early 1800s, psychophysicist Max Weber discovered an interesting characteristic of the jnd, known as **Weber's law**. According to this law, for each of our five senses, the amount of change in the stimulus that is necessary to produce a jnd depends on the intensity at which the stimulus is *first* presented. For example, if you add one additional teaspoon of salt to a very salty pot of soup, it will probably not be noticeable. But that same teaspoon of salt added to a less salty pot of

**attention** conscious awareness; can be focused on events that are taking place in the environment or inside our minds

**sensation** the process through which our sense organs convert environmental energy such as light and sound into neural impulses

**perception** the process through which we interpret sensory information

**psychophysics** the study of how the mind interprets the physical properties of stimuli

**absolute threshold** the minimum intensity of a stimulus at which participants can identify its presence 50% of the time

**just noticeable difference (jnd)** the minimum change in intensity of a stimulus that participants can detect 50% of the time

**Weber's [VAY-bers] law** a psychological principle that states that for each of our five senses, the amount of change in the stimulus that is necessary to produce a jnd depends on the intensity at which the stimulus is first presented

soup may be very noticeable. Weber's law helps explain some of the subjectivity we experience in sensation. Under some conditions, one teaspoon of salt won't make a difference to our enjoyment of a recipe. Under other conditions, it might.

## Processing Without Awareness: Subliminal Stimulation of the Senses

Absolute thresholds and just noticeable differences describe the limits of our conscious awareness of sensations. But is sensation always a conscious experience? Or is it possible that we might be affected by sensory stimuli even when we are unaware of sensing them? **Subliminal perception**, the unconscious perception of stimuli, became a topic of many debates in the late 1950s when a man named James Vicary attempted to use subliminal messages to entice moviegoers at a public theater to buy more popcorn and soda without them knowing that they were being persuaded. Vicary flashed messages such as "Eat popcorn" and "Drink Coca-Cola" between the frames of a movie at a speed so fast that moviegoers did not have time to consciously perceive the messages. Because the messages were flashed so briefly, the moviegoers never consciously saw anything other than the movie.

Vicary reported that as a result of his "experiment," concession sales rose 18%. As it turns out, Vicary admitted in 1962 that he had not conducted a true experiment. The data that he collected were so few that they could not be used for scientific purposes (Epley, Savitsy, & Kachelski, 1999; Pratkanis, 1992). After Vicary's attempts at subliminal persuasion, researchers began to carefully examine the effects of subliminal perception both in the real world and in the laboratory. To date, most studies have failed to yield convincing evidence for the effectiveness of persuasive subliminal messages (see Pratkanis et al., 2007).

**TABLE 3.1**

### Descriptions of the Absolute Thresholds for Our Five Senses

| SENSE | | ABSOLUTE THRESHOLD |
|-------|---|--------------------|
| Vision | | A candle seen from 30 miles away on a clear, dark night. |
| Hearing | | A ticking watch that is 20 feet away in an otherwise quiet room. |
| Smell | | One drop of perfume diffused in a three-room apartment. |
| Taste | | One teaspoon of sugar dissolved in 2 gallons of water. |
| Touch | | The wing of a bumblebee failing on one's cheek from a distance of 1 centimeter. |

## Extrasensory Perception: Can Perception Occur Without Our Five Senses?

As with subliminal persuasion, scientific research casts serious doubts on the existence of **extrasensory perception (ESP)**, sometimes also referred to as *psi*. ESP is the purported ability to acquire information about the world without using the known senses—for example, the ability to read people's minds or see the

**subliminal perception** when the intensity of a stimulus is below the participant's absolute threshold and the participant is not consciously aware of the stimulus

**extrasensory perception (ESP)** also known as psi, the purported ability to acquire information about the world without using the known senses

PM Images/Getty Images

Although researchers have been searching for evidence of ESP for a century, to date compelling evidence of its existence has not been found.

future. Most of the scientific tests of ESP involve the *Ganzfeld procedure*, in which one participant acts as a *sender* who tries to send a message to another participant acting as a *receiver* in another room. Although a few of these studies have suggested that some people may be better at sending and receiving such telepathic messages, the vast majority fail to support the existence of ESP (Milton & Wiseman, 2001).

Recently, researchers have used neuroimaging to investigate whether ESP exists. Researchers Samuel Moulton and Steven Kosslyn (2008) had participants engage in a modified version of the Ganzfeld procedure. During the experiment, the receiver had to guess which of two images on a computer screen was being sent by the sender in another room. As the receivers made these judgments, their brains were scanned using fMRI technology. Moulton and Kosslyn found that the receivers guessed the correct image only about 50% of the time (no better than chance alone). Furthermore, the fMRIs showed no differences in brain functioning between the trials resulting in correct and incorrect responses. Moulton and Kosslyn interpret these results as powerful evidence against the existence of ESP.

But not everyone agrees. In 2011, one of psychology's most prestigious journals, the *Journal of Personality and Social Psychology*, published a paper by psychologist Daryl Bem (in press) in which he claims to have experimental evidence for the existence of ESP. Bem contends that his data show that his participants were able to predict events before they happened at a rate better than chance guessing. Critics contend that Bem's studies are methodologically flawed and that the statistical analyses of the data were not performed correctly. The debate over the existence of ESP seems destined to continue into the foreseeable future.

Now that we have a basic understanding of how psychologists measure the limits of our sensory abilities, we will examine how our bodies accomplish the process of sensation, starting with vision.

# Let's
## REVIEW

This section has given you a quick overview of some important aspects of measuring sensation and perception—absolute threshold, just noticeable difference, subliminal stimulation of the senses, and ESP. For a quick check of your understanding, answer these questions.

**1.** Jerry wants to sweeten his iced tea. He adds one teaspoon of sugar, but the tea does not taste sweet to him. When Jerry adds one more teaspoon of sugar, he finds that the tea now tastes sweet—but just barely. Two teaspoons of sugar seem to correspond to Jerry's _____.
   a. just noticeable difference
   b. absolute threshold
   c. k value
   d. stimulus threshold

**2.** If your tea already tastes sweet to you, the minimum amount of sugar that you would have to add to your tea to make it taste sweeter corresponds to your _____.
   a. just noticeable difference
   b. absolute threshold
   c. k value
   d. stimulus threshold

**3.** According to Weber's law, who will *most likely* notice the addition of one more teaspoon of sugar in a glass of iced tea?
   a. Joni, whose tea has no sugar in it
   b. Bill, who has two teaspoons of sugar in his tea
   c. Sarafina, who has three teaspoons of sugar in her tea
   d. All of these people will be equally likely to notice the difference.

*Answers 1. b; 2. a; 3. a*

# Vision: Seeing the World

Our eyes are at the front of our skulls, so you might assume that vision is a direct transfer from object to eye to brain. Vision is more complicated than that, however, and researchers have studied vision more than the other senses. To understand vision, we'll look at the properties of light that apply to vision, the anatomy of the eye, the layers of the retina, and how we process visual information in the brain.

## How Vision Works: Light Waves and Energy

When we see an object, what we really see are the light waves that are reflected off the surface of the object. Thus, a blue shirt appears blue because blue is the only color of light that the shirt reflects. The shirt absorbs all other colors of light. As we'll see, the specific characteristics of the shirt's color and brightness are all determined by the physical characteristics of the particular light energy that is bouncing off the shirt.

### MEASURING LIGHT: WAVELENGTH AND AMPLITUDE

■ FIGURE 3.1 depicts the electromagnetic spectrum, which includes visible light. Electromagnetic energies, including light, result from disturbances in the electrical and magnetic fields that exist in the universe. Like all electromagnetic energies, light waves are characterized by their *wavelength* and *amplitude*. The **wavelength** of light is the distance between the peaks of consecutive waves. The **amplitude** of the light wave is the height of each wave peak. These distances are typically measured in nanometers (nm).

**wavelength**   a physical property of some energies that corresponds to the distance between wave peaks

**amplitude**   a physical property of some energies that corresponds to the height of wave peaks

**F I G U R E**

# 3.1

## The Visible Spectrum of Light

The human visible spectrum comprises a narrow range of electromagnetic energies.

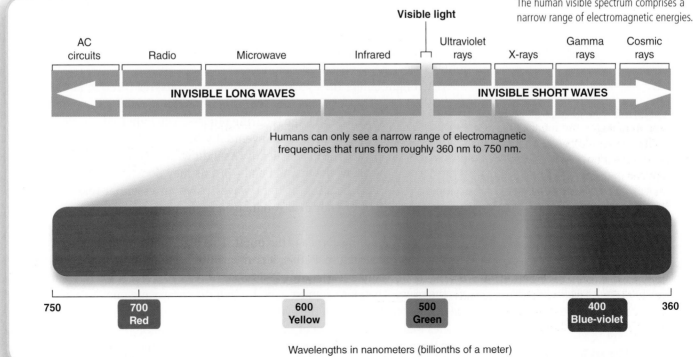

Visible light

| AC circuits | Radio | Microwave | Infrared | | Ultraviolet rays | X-rays | Gamma rays | Cosmic rays |

INVISIBLE LONG WAVES          INVISIBLE SHORT WAVES

Humans can only see a narrow range of electromagnetic frequencies that runs from roughly 360 nm to 750 nm.

750      700 Red        600 Yellow        500 Green        400 Blue-violet      360

Wavelengths in nanometers (billionths of a meter)

The human eye cannot sense all electromagnetic energy. In fact, the **visible spectrum** for humans is only a very narrow band of the electromagnetic spectrum that spans from about 360 nm to 750 nm (Figure 3.1). Other species can sense electromagnetic wavelengths that are beyond the human visible spectrum. Some snakes sense infrared rays, allowing them to sense other animals' body heat (Sinclair, 1985). Other animals, such as spiders and rats, use their ability to sense ultraviolet (UV) light during hunting (Bhaskara et al., 2009). If you are hiking through the woods, keep in mind that certain animals may be able to see you before you see them!

## PROPERTIES OF LIGHT: HUE, BRIGHTNESS, AND SATURATION

Although our eyes cannot sense much of the electromagnetic spectrum, we are capable of seeing millions of different combinations of color, richness, and brightness of light (Linhares, Pinto, & Nascimento, 2008). The wavelength of the light wave corresponds to the color or **hue** of the light we see. Shorter wavelengths correspond to cool colors such as blues and purples; longer wavelengths correspond to warmer colors such as yellows and reds (Figure 3.1). The amplitude of the light wave corresponds to its **brightness**. The higher the amplitude of the light wave, the brighter the color we perceive. One other characteristic of light, **saturation**, corresponds to the purity of the light. Light that consists of a single wavelength will produce the most saturated, or richest, color. Light that is a mixture of wavelengths produces less saturated colors. For example, pure blue light is high in saturation, but a mixture of blue and white light produces a less saturated blue light.

For vision to occur, our eyes must be able to convert the electromagnetic waves of the visible spectrum into action potentials that our brains can process. In the next section, we will look at the anatomy of the eye to get an idea of how this conversion occurs.

## The Anatomy of the Outer Eye

The process of vision begins with the parts of the eye we can readily see: the clear *cornea* that covers the iris, the colored part of your eye, and the *pupil*, the opening in the iris. From there, light is eventually focused on the retina at the back of your eye. The white part, the sclera, is a supporting structure that doesn't play a part in the processing of visual information.

When light enters the eye, the first structure it passes through is the **cornea** (■ FIGURE 3.2). The cornea is the clear, slightly bulging outer surface of the eye. It protects the eye and begins the focusing process. The light that is reflected from an object in the environment must eventually be focused on the rear surface of the eye if we are to see the object clearly. As light waves pass through the material of the cornea, they slow down and bend—just as they do when they pass through a camera lens. This bending of light waves plays an essential role in focusing images on the back of your eye. A damaged cornea can make it impossible for a person to see clearly.

Directly behind the cornea is the **pupil**. This black opening in the center of your eye is not really a structure. Rather, it is an opening, or aperture, through which light passes into the center of the eye. Light cannot pass through the white part of the eye, the *sclera*. Therefore, it must pass through the cornea and pupil to enter the eye. The *iris*, the colored part of the eye surrounding the pupil, is constructed of rings of muscles that control the size of the pupil. In dimly lit conditions, the iris relaxes to dilate the pupil, allowing the maximum amount of light into the eye. In brightly lit conditions, the iris constricts to close the pupil, thus reducing the amount of light entering the eye so as not to overwhelm the light-sensitive cells in the eye.

**visible spectrum**   the spectrum of light that humans can see

**hue**   the color of light; it corresponds to the light's wavelength

**brightness**   the intensity of light; it corresponds to the amplitude of the light waves

**saturation**   the purity of light; light that consists of a single wavelength produces the richest or most saturated color

**cornea [COR-nee-ah]**   the clear, slightly bulging outer surface of the eye that both protects the eye and begins the focusing process

**pupil**   the hole in the iris through which light enters the eye

**lens**   the part of the eye that lies behind the pupil and focuses light rays on the retina

Directly behind the iris and the pupil is the **lens** of the eye. The lens is a clear structure that is attached to the eye with strong *ciliary muscles*. The lens of the eye is rather like the lens of a camera—its job is to bring the light waves entering the eye into sharp focus on the back of the eye. The lens of the eye is somewhat soft and flexible. As the ciliary muscles stretch the lens, it changes shape, or undergoes **accommodation**, so that the image passing through it is focused properly.

© Marco Uliana/Shutterstock

Iris
Pupil
Path of light
Cornea
Lens

**Fovea.** Point of highest visual acuity; cones concentrated here.

**Retina.** Thin membrane lining back of eyeball; contains rods and cones.

Optic nerve

**Optic disk.** Point where optic nerve leaves eye; no rods or cones in this part of retina, creating a blind spot.

**FIGURE**

# 3.2

The Anatomy of the Eye

## The Retina: Light Energy to Neural Messages

Once the light waves have been focused on the back of the eye, conversion of light waves into neural impulses occurs in the **retina**, the surface that lines the inside of the back of the eyeball. In the retina, specialized cells called *rods* and *cones* convert light into neural signals. Without these cells, vision would not be possible.

### THE ANATOMY OF THE RETINA

The diagram in ■ FIGURE 3.3 shows a cross section of the layers in the human retina. The *ganglion cells* are on the surface of the retina, followed by successive layers of *amacrine*, *bipolar*, and *horizontal cells*, and finally the light-sensitive rods and cones. Look closely at Figure 3.3 and you will see that the light entering the eye must filter through all the layers of the retina before finally striking the rods and cones.

Incoming light passes unimpeded through the transparent layers of the retina to reach the rods and cones, which convert the light energy into neural impulses. These signals travel back out to the ganglion cells on the surface of the retina. Along the way, the horizontal, bipolar, and amacrine cells funnel and consolidate the neural information from the rods and cones so that we can see a unified, coherent image. The signals that reach the ganglion cells in the top layer of the retina are to some degree summaries of the visual information from the rods and cones.

### THE OPTIC NERVE AND THE BLINDSPOT

Once the neural impulses reach the ganglion cells, they exit the retina and travel to the brain via the **optic nerve**, which is composed of the axons of the ganglion cells (see Figures 3.2 and 3.3). The optic nerve actually exits the retina on the *surface* of the retina; there are no light-sensitive rods or cones at the point where the optic nerve leaves the retina. With no rods or cones at this spot, each of our eyes has a **blindspot**, which is a point in our visual field that we cannot see.

Luckily, however, our blindspots do not pose much of a problem. For one thing, the blindspot is at the side of our visual field, where we normally do not bring objects into focus in the first place (see Figure 3.2). If the blindspot were located at the *fovea* (the point directly behind the pupil), it is possible that we would be much more aware of it. Another reason is that we have two eyes. Whatever part of the world we miss seeing because of the blindspot in our left eye we see with our right eye, and vice versa.

**accommodation**   the process through which the lens is stretched or squeezed to focus light on the retina

**retina**   the structure at the back of the eye that contains cells that convert light into neural signals

**optic nerve**   the structure that conveys visual information away from the retina to the brain

**blindspot**   the point where the optic nerve leaves the retina, the optic disk, where there are no rods or cones

LWA/Getty Images

Vision problems can strike at any age. Nearsightedness, or not seeing distant objects well, is common at all ages. Another condition, presbyopia, is more common after middle age. Presbyopia occurs when, as we age, the lens of the eye becomes more rigid and the eye is less able to accommodate to close objects. Because of presbyopia, many middle-aged and older adults need reading glasses or bifocals.

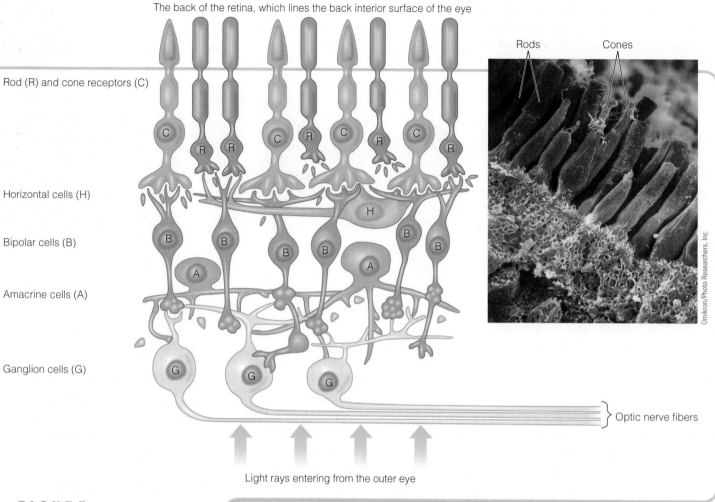

The back of the retina, which lines the back interior surface of the eye

Rods        Cones

Rod (R) and cone receptors (C)

Horizontal cells (H)

Bipolar cells (B)

Amacrine cells (A)

Ganglion cells (G)

Optic nerve fibers

Light rays entering from the outer eye

Omikron/Photo Researchers, Inc.

# FIGURE

## 3.3

### A Cross Section of the Retina

Above is a schematic of the retina with the rods shown in purple and the cones in pink. To the right is an electron micrograph of the retina showing the rods and cones.

*From "Organization of the Primate Retina," by J. E. Dowling and B. B. Boycott, in Proceedings of the Royal Society of London, 16, Series B, 80–111. Copyright © 1966 by the Royal Society.*

**rods**    the light-sensitive cells of the retina that pick up any type of light energy and convert it to neural signals

**cones**    the cells of the retina that are sensitive to specific colors of light and send information to the brain concerning the colors we are seeing

## THE RODS AND CONES

The rods and cones that line the inside layer of the retina play different roles in the process of vision. The **rods**, which are long and skinny, are sensitive to all colors of light, but they do not transmit information about color to the brain (see Figure 3.3). You can think of the rods as being black-and-white receptors. If you had only rods in your retina, you'd see everything in black and white. We see the world in color because of the cone cells in the retina. The **cones**, which are shorter and fatter than the rods, are responsible for transmitting information about color to the brain.

Relative to rods, the cones of the eye require a higher intensity of light to become activated. Because of this, we do not have good color vision in dimly lit situations. Think about driving at night. When light levels are not very intense, it may be possible to see objects in the distance, but impossible to discern their color. In each eye you have about 100 million rods but only about 5 million cones (Matlin & Foley, 1997). Having so many rods and so few cones in the retina indicates that perceiving shape and form takes precedence over perception of color. If you think about it for a minute, this arrangement makes sense. Which information would you need first: to see the shape of a car speeding toward you in the dark, or to see the color of the car? Your first concern would be seeing the car to avoid a collision!

In addition to being differentially sensitive to light energy, the rods and cones are not distributed evenly across the surface of the retina. The highest concentration of cones is at the fovea, with fewer and fewer cones toward the peripheral edges of the retina. The density of rods follows the opposite pattern, with the highest concentration at the peripheral edges of the retina and fewer and fewer rods as you move toward the fovea. This arrangement means that our best color vision is for objects placed directly in front of us, whereas our color vision for objects seen out of the corners of our eyes (in our peripheral vision) is very poor.

## TURNING LIGHT ENERGY INTO NEURAL MESSAGES

The rods and cones of the eye are able to convert light into neural impulses because they contain light-sensitive **photopigments**, chemicals that are activated by light energy. When a rod is not receiving light input, its photopigment molecules are stable. However, when light strikes the rod, this incoming light energy splits the photopigments apart (Yau & Hardie, 2009). As the photopigments break up, they set off a complex chain of chemical reactions that change the rate at which the neurons of the visual system fire action potentials. The brain uses the pattern of these action potentials to interpret what we are seeing.

## Adapting to Light and Darkness

Have you ever had to wait at the back of a dark movie theater for your eyes to adjust before you could find your seat? This type of adjustment is referred to as **dark adaptation**. It also takes our eyes a while to adapt to sudden increases in brightness, or undergo **light adaptation**.

Dark and light adaptation are accomplished, in part, by changes in pupil size. Unfortunately, the amount of dilation and constriction that our pupils can provide is limited, and they alone cannot fully account for the adaptations we experience. Another mechanism of adaptation is found in the photopigments themselves. If you were to enter a completely darkened room, no light would enter your eyes and no photopigments would break down. After remaining in these darkened conditions for a period of time, the photopigment levels in your eyes would build up because they are not being broken down by light. This is what occurs when we sleep at night. With a large store of photopigments, your eyes are very sensitive to light. If someone were to suddenly turn on the lights in the bedroom, you would experience a bright flash of light and perhaps even pain as the large number of available photopigments makes your eyes very sensitive to the light. It would take about 1 minute for your eyes to adjust to the light (Hood & Finkelstein, 1986).

The process of dark adaptation is the opposite of what occurs during light adaptation. Under normal daytime lighting conditions, we constantly use our photopigments to see our surroundings. So, at any given moment during the day, a certain percentage of our photopigments are broken down. If you suddenly enter a darkened theater after being in bright daylight, you will not have enough photopigments to be able to see well. It will take approximately 30 to 45 minutes for your photopigment levels to build up completely (Poelman & Smet, 2010). This is why you may have to stand, popcorn in hand, at the back of the darkened theater for several minutes before you can find your seat.

## How We See Color

Like the rods, the cones of the retina also contain photopigments. However, there is an important distinction between the photopigments in the rods and cones. All rods contain the same photopigment. In contrast, there are three different types of cones, each containing a slightly different photopigment. Having different types of photopigments in our cones is one reason we see color.

Jack Wild/Getty Images

When you step out of the darkness into bright light, you may experience a flash of pain as the built-up photopigment in your eyes reacts all at once to the bright light.

**photopigments**   light-sensitive chemicals that create electrical changes when they come into contact with light

**dark adaptation**   the process through which our eyes adjust to dark conditions after having been exposed to bright light

**light adaptation**   the process through which our eyes adjust to bright light after having been exposed to darkness

© Ocean/Corbis

When suddenly entering dim conditions after leaving a brightly environment, such as occurs when you enter a darkened theater, it will take more than 30 minutes for your eyes to fully adjust to the darkness. In addition, because cones require more light energy than rods, it can be difficult to discriminate among colors in dim conditions

red or green cones are not sensitive to exactly the same ranges of wavelengths as the cones found in the average person. Therefore, these men experience difficulties in distinguishing among certain hues (e.g., Baraas et al., 2006). For example, a man with abnormally insensitive green cones may have trouble distinguishing small changes in color among orange hues. These deficiencies are sometimes more detectable in a laboratory where participants are asked to view samples of color under tightly controlled conditions than they are in the real world. In the natural environment, where colors and light levels are varied and mixed, some of these color deficiencies do not seem to be as problematic (Baraas et al., 2006).

Although trichromatic theory explains certain aspects of color vision, it does not explain all aspects of vision. For example, trichromatic theory cannot explain *negative afterimages*. To understand what an afterimage is, try this demonstration.

## YOUR TURN | Active Learning

Get a blank sheet of paper and set it aside. Stare at the black dot in the center of ■ FIGURE 3.5 without blinking or moving your eyes. Continue staring for 60 to 90 seconds. Then quickly move your gaze to the blank sheet of white paper. What do you see? You should see the image of a green shamrock with a yellow border on the blank sheet of white paper. The shamrock is a negative afterimage. Notice that the colors you see in the afterimage are different from the colors in the original. Why would you see different colors in your afterimage? Simply having different types of cones cannot explain this phenomenon. So, what does explain afterimages?

## THE OPPONENT-PROCESS THEORY OF COLOR VISION

The **opponent-process theory** proposes a different type of color-sensitive cell in the visual system, a cell that is sensitive to two colors of light. There are thought to be three types of opponent-process cells in our visual system: red/green, yellow/blue, and black/white. The key to opponent-process theory is that these cells can detect the presence of only one color at a time. The colors *oppose* each other so that the opponent-process cell cannot detect the presence of both colors at the same time. For example, a red/green cell can detect either red or green light at any one time. If you shine a red light in the eye, the red/green cells tell our brain that we are seeing red. If you shine a green light in the eye, the red/green cells tell our brain that we are seeing green. But these red/green cells cannot detect red and green at the same time. Opponent-process theory is consistent with the finding that if we simultaneously shine red and green lights into your eye, you will likely see a neutral shade that is neither red nor green (Hurvich & Jameson, 1957/2000).

Opponent-process theory can explain the phenomenon of negative afterimages. Recall the demonstration you tried with Figure 3.5. After staring at the red and blue shamrock, you saw a green and yellow afterimage. Opponent-process theory proposes that as you stared at the red and blue shamrock, you were using the red and blue portions of the opponent-process cells. After a period of 60 to 90 seconds of continuous staring, you expended these cells' capacity to fire action potentials. In a sense, you temporarily "wore out" the red and blue portions of these cells. Then you looked at a blank sheet of white paper. Under normal conditions, the white light would excite *all* of the opponent-process cells. Recall that white light contains all colors of light. But, given the exhausted state of your opponent-process cells, only parts of them were capable of firing action potentials.

**FIGURE**

## 3.5

Negative Afterimages
See text for instructions.

**opponent-process theory**   the idea that we have dual-action cells beyond the level of the retina that signal the brain when we see one of a pair of colors

In this example, the green and yellow parts of the cells were ready to fire. The light reflected off the white paper could excite only the yellow and green parts of the cells, so you saw a green and yellow shamrock.

## TRICHROMATIC THEORY OR OPPONENT-PROCESS THEORY?

We've seen that trichromatic theory and opponent-process theory each explain certain aspects of color vision. So, which theory is correct? Both theories seem to have merit. It is generally believed that these two theories describe processes that operate at different places in the visual system (Hubel, 1995; Wade, 2010).

Trichromatic theory does a good job of explaining color vision at the level of the rods and cones. Opponent-process theory best explains the processing of color vision beyond the level of the rods and cones. Evidence suggests that opponent processing may occur at the level of the ganglion cells (Conway, 2009; DeValois & DeValois, 1975); the amacrine, horizontal, and bipolar cells of the retina; or even in the visual cortex (see Conway & Livingstone, 2005). In the next section, we will trace the path that visual information takes as it leaves the retina and enters the brain.

**optic chiasm**   the point in the brain where the optic nerve from the left eye crosses over the optic nerve from the right eye

## The Visual Pathways of the Brain

Once the rods and cones of the retina convert light into neural signals, this information begins its journey into the visual cortex of the brain. Along the way, visual information is continually processed and combined to ultimately give us a coherent perception of what we see in the environment. The bipolar, horizontal, and amacrine cells gather the information from the rods and cones and funnel it to the ganglion cells. The ganglion cells join together to form the optic nerve, which carries visual information into the brain.

Visual information from the right side of the body travels to the left hemisphere, and information from the left side travels to the right hemisphere. The point at which the optic nerve from the left eye and the optic nerve from the right eye cross over is called the **optic chiasm**. From the optic chiasm, most visual information travels to the *thalamus* before traveling to the visual cortex, where the meaning of the visual input is interpreted. We will discuss this interpretive process when we discuss perception later in the chapter (see ■ FIGURE 3.6).

## DO MEN AND WOMEN SEE THE WORLD DIFFERENTLY?

Evidence suggests that when it comes to processing visual information, men and women see things differently. Females tend to be better at discriminating one object from another (Overman et al., 1996), naming colors (Bornstein, 1985), and processing facial expressions accurately (Vassallo, Cooper, & Douglas, 2009). Females also tend to show a preference for using many colors and seem to prefer warm colors to cool ones. Males tend to be better at processing moving objects and the spatial aspects of

**FIGURE**

## 3.6

### The Visual Pathways in the Brain
Visual information from your right side travels to the visual cortex on the left side of the brain, and information from your left side travels to the visual cortex on the right side.

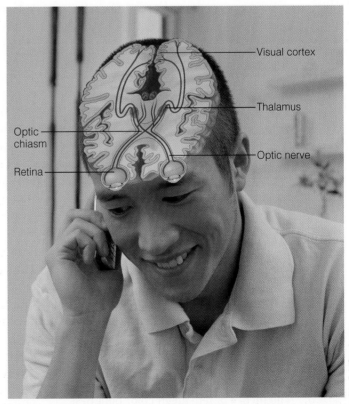

Visual cortex

Thalamus

Optic chiasm

Optic nerve

Retina

Shiva Twin/Getty Images

objects (Alexander, 2003). Differences appear at a very early age: female infants aged 3 to 8 months prefer to look at dolls, whereas male infants of the same age prefer to look at trucks (Alexander, Wilcox, & Woods, 2009).

Researcher Gerianne Alexander (2003) has argued that such gender differences in visual processing are neurological and that they have evolved to facilitate the performance of traditional male/female roles. In many societies, males have historically hunted for food, whereas women have gathered crops and nurtured children. By being able to discriminate among objects and colors well, females are well suited to gathering food. For example, good color vision allows you to see a ripe fig among the green leaves of a tree. A preference for warm colors (skin tones of all races tend to be warm) and faces may also predispose women to care for their young. On the other hand, male facility in processing movement and spatial information may have helped them perform hunting duties.

Recently, researchers have been intrigued by the finding that roughly 12% of women have a genetic condition that causes them to have four types of cones in their retinas rather than three. Does this provide evidence that at least some women have genetically superior color vision? When put to the test, color vision in these women was no better than in women with the usual three cone types (Jordan et al., 2010). So, direct evidence of Alexander's ideas on innate gender differences in color vision still awaits us.

Keep in mind that both color preference and gender roles may also be highly influenced by the particular culture in which a boy or girl is raised. For example, in many cultures, products marketed to girls are often colored with bright, warm colors. Worldwide, girls' toys often involve babies, fashion, cooking, nurturing, and other domestic themes, whereas toys marketed to boys frequently involve vehicles, weaponry, and darker, cooler colors. Thus, observed differences in gender roles and color preferences may simply reflect what we teach our children to prefer. We'll have more to say about gender roles and gender differences in Chapter 9. For now, let's turn our attention to our other senses.

**cycle**  a physical characteristic of energy defined as a wave peak and the valley that immediately follows it

**frequency**  a physical characteristic of energy defined as the number of cycles that occur in a given unit of time

**loudness**  the psychophysical property of sound that corresponds to the amplitude of a sound wave

**decibels [DESS-uh-bells] (dB)**  the unit of measurement used to determine the loudness of a sound

# Let's
## REVIEW

In this section, we discussed vision, including the physical properties of light, the anatomy of the eye and the retina, how we adapt to light and dark, how we see color, and the role of the brain in vision. For a quick check of your understanding, answer these questions.

**1.** Juan was born with no cones in his retina. How will this condition affect Juan?
   **a.** He will be blind.
   **b.** He will not be able to see black or white.
   **c.** He will see the world in shades of black and white.
   **d.** His vision will not be affected.

**2.** Which theory *best* explains why Sara would see flashes of red light after eight hours of working on a computer monitor that has a green and black screen?
   **a.** The opponent-process theory
   **b.** The trichromatic theory
   **c.** The rod-and-cone theory
   **d.** The theory of red–green color blindness

**3.** You have just returned to a darkened theater after a trip to the concession stand. Now you have a problem—you can't find your seat in the dark. Knowing what you do about vision, which of the following would *most likely* help you to find your seat?
   **a.** Stare straight ahead at the seats.
   **b.** Search for your seat out of the corner of your eye.
   **c.** Go back out into the bright light and allow your eyes to deplete their photopigments.
   **d.** Cross your eyes and search for your seat.

Answers 1. c; 2. a; 3. b

# Hearing: Listening to the World

Like vision, hearing is one of our most important senses; much of what we learn in life depends on these two senses. Additionally, hearing plays an important role in our ability to communicate with others. To understand hearing, we will describe the physical properties of sound waves, the anatomy of the ear, and how our brain processes sound.

## Vibration and Sound: A Noisy Environment Can Lead to Hearing Loss

Sounds, such as a human voice, produce waves of compressed air that our ears convert to neural impulses. Like light waves, sound waves have their own psychophysical properties. A sound wave has both peaks and valleys (■ FIGURE 3.7).

A **cycle** includes the peak of the wave and the valley that immediately follows it (Figure 3.7a). Counting the number of cycles in a given time frame allows us to determine the **frequency** of a sound wave. Traditionally, the frequency of sound waves is measured in hertz (Hz), or the number of cycles completed per second. A sound wave with a frequency of 1000 Hz would complete 1,000 cycles per second. The **loudness** of the sound we hear, measured in **decibels (dB)**, corresponds to the amplitude of a sound wave (Figure 3.7b). The higher the amplitude, the more pressure is exerted on the eardrum, and the louder the sound is.

The frequency of a sound wave corresponds to the **pitch** of the sound we perceive: the higher the frequency, the higher the pitch. The average young adult can perceive sounds that range from a low of 20 Hz to a high of 20000 Hz (Gelfand, 1981). For example, we can hear the low pitch of a foghorn and the high pitch of a mosquito's wings. We lose some of this range as we age, however, particularly our ability to hear high pitches. Some young people have capitalized on this by downloading ultra-high-pitched "mosquito" ringtones for their cell phones so that parents and other adults will be unaware of incoming calls and text messages. Tones above 16000 Hz go unheard by people as young as 24! Luckily, most of the everyday sounds we hear fall well below the 20000-Hz level. In fact, unless the gradual deterioration impairs our ability to hear sounds at 1800 Hz and below, our ability to comprehend speech should remain pretty much intact (Welford, 1987). Yet all of us would do well to protect our hearing. For more on noise-related hearing loss see the Psychology Across Generations box.

## The Anatomy and Function of the Ear

The very outside of the **outer ear** is called the *pinna* (■ FIGURE 3.8, p. 95). This is the part of the body normally referred to as the ear and earlobe. The pinna acts as a funnel to gather sound waves. After being gathered by the pinna, sound waves are channeled through the

**pitch**   the psychophysical property of sound that corresponds to the frequency of a sound wave

**outer ear**   the outermost parts of the ear, including the pinna, auditory canal, and surface of the ear drum

**FIGURE**

# 3.7

### The Amplitude and Frequency of Sound Waves

The frequency, or number of cycles per second, determines the sound's pitch. The higher the wave's frequency, the higher the sound's pitch will be (a). The height, or amplitude, of a sound wave determines its loudness. Higher amplitudes correspond to louder sounds (b).

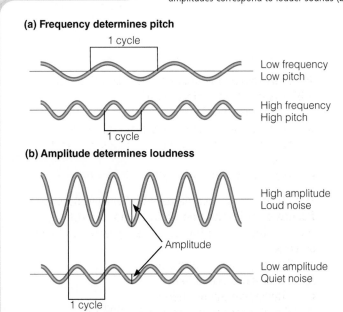

**(a) Frequency determines pitch**

1 cycle

Low frequency
Low pitch

High frequency
High pitch

1 cycle

**(b) Amplitude determines loudness**

High amplitude
Loud noise

Amplitude

1 cycle

Low amplitude
Quiet noise

## Psychology Across Generations:

### Are the Youth of Today More at Risk for Hearing Loss?

Living and working in noisy environments increase the likelihood of experiencing hearing loss as we age. For example, people living in North American urban areas experience greater age-related hearing loss than do people living in quiet rural areas of Africa (Bennett, 1990). In fact, roughly 10% of Americans between 20 and 69 have already experienced some level of permanent damage to their hearing as a result of overexposure to noise (Griest, Folmer, & Martin, 2007).

Since the industrial revolution, it seems that we have been exposed to increasing numbers of noise-producing technologies that can be damaging to our hearing (lawn mowers, power tools, MP3 players, and so on). For example, typical rock concert amplifier volumes of 120 dB can damage your hearing in as little as 15 minutes. Of particular concern today is that so many people listen to loud music on MP3 or personal listening devices (PLDs), some of which are capable of outputting more than 130 dB. Studies indicate that up to 25% of college students listen to their PLDs in violation of the so called *60–60 rule*, which states that to avoid hearing damage, one should listen to a PLD for no more than 60 minutes a day at 60% of its maximum volume (Danhauer et al., 2009).

Research shows that over the generations, people have experienced less age-related hearing loss, perhaps because they have used ear protection when working around loud machinery. Some people are concerned that young people who listen to loud music on PLDs may reverse this trend.

Because the millennial generation (those born between 1980 and the early 2000s) seems to be particularly wedded to PLDs, does this mean that Millennials are destined to experience more age-related hearing loss than those from previous generations? It's hard to say. Weihai Zhan and colleagues (2009) examined the hearing of participants aged 45 to 94 and found that for every 5-year increase in birth year, the odds of hearing impairment *decreased* 13% for men and 6% for women. Because the researchers had controlled for current age of the participants, this suggests that members of later generations had found ways to protect their hearing (most likely by avoiding overexposure to loud noises).

This study did not include millennial participants, so it remains to be seen how Millennials will fare in later life. However, if young people today take steps to protect their hearing, they may also tend to avoid later hearing loss just as the study participants did. So, wear ear protection around loud noises and follow the 60–60 rule while listening to your PLD. You'll thank yourself later!

You Asked...

How does our ear work?

CRISTIAN CACERES, STUDENT

**middle ear**   the part of the ear behind the ear drum and in front of the oval window, including the hammer, anvil, and stirrup

**inner ear**   the innermost portion of the ear that includes the cochlea

**cochlea [COCK-lee-uh]**   the curled, fluid-filled tube in the inner ear that contains the basilar membrane

*auditory canal*, where sounds are amplified and then strike the membrane at the end of the auditory canal, the *eardrum*.

The eardrum, or *tympanic membrane*, is a very thin membrane that vibrates as the incoming sound waves strike it, much as the head of a drum vibrates when a drumstick strikes it. The three bones of the **middle ear** that are directly behind the eardrum are the *hammer*, *anvil*, and *stirrup* (Figure 3.8). These very small bones mechanically amplify the vibrations coming from the eardrum and transmit them to the inner ear. The middle ear connects to the **inner ear** at the point where the stirrup rests against the *oval window* (Figure 3.8). The oval window is found on the outer end of the **cochlea**, one of the major components of the inner ear. The cochlea is a coiled, fluid-filled tube about 1.4 inches long that resembles a snail (Matlin & Foley, 1997). It is here that sound waves are turned into neural impulses.

If you were to uncoil the cochlea, you would see that it resembles a flexible tube that is closed off at the end. The inside of the tube contains a fluid-filled canal called the *cochlear duct* (■ FIGURE 3.9). The floor of the cochlear duct is lined with the **basilar membrane**. Growing out of the basilar membrane are specialized **hair cells** that convert sound wave energy into neural impulses.

Incoming sound waves cause the bones of the middle ear to vibrate (Figures 3.8 & 3.9). The vibration of the stirrup against the oval window sets up a pressure wave inside the fluid-filled cochlea. As this wave travels through the cochlea, the cochlear duct begins to ripple. Inside the cochlear duct, the traveling wave ripples across the hair cells, causing them to begin sending neural impulses.

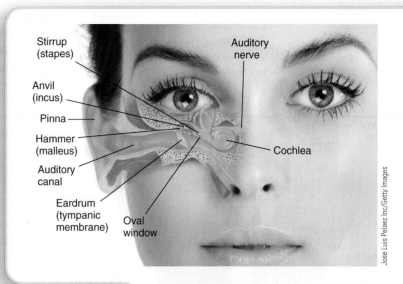

**FIGURE**

## 3.8

The Anatomy of the Ear

## The Auditory Pathways of the Brain

Once the hair cells convert sound into neural impulses, these impulses must be sent to the brain for further processing. Attached to the end of the cochlea is the **auditory nerve** (Figure 3.8). The bundled neurons of the auditory nerve gather the information from the hair cells to relay it to the brain. ■ FIGURE 3.10 shows the path that auditory information takes from the ears to the brain. Notice that auditory information from each ear reaches both sides of the brain.

The auditory cortex has the capacity to decode the meanings of the sounds we hear. Our next task is to examine how the brain perceives, or makes sense of, the auditory information it receives from the ears. We'll begin by looking at several theories that explain our ability to perceive pitch.

### PLACE THEORY OF PITCH PERCEPTION

Hermann von Helmholtz, who is credited by many with the trichromatic theory of color vision, also studied pitch perception. His **place theory** of pitch perception (1863/1930) proposes that sounds of different frequencies excite different hair cells

**basilar membrane**   the structure in the cochlear duct that contains the hair cells, which convert sound waves into action potentials

**hair cells**   neurons that grow out of the basilar membrane and convert sound waves into action potentials

**auditory nerve**   the nerve that carries information from the inner ear to the brain

**place theory**   a theory that proposes that our brain decodes pitch by noticing which region of the basilar membrane is most active

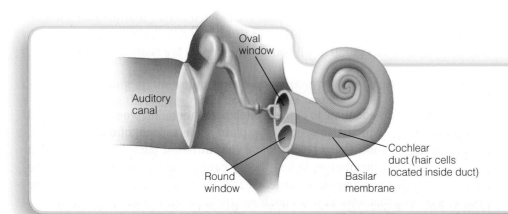

**FIGURE**

## 3.9

Enlarged Detail of the Inner Ear

# Psychology Applies to Your World:

## Why Don't We All Like the Same Foods?

Have you ever found yourself discussing where to go for dinner with your friends, only to find that everyone has a different opinion on which type of food you should have? What accounts for the wide variation in taste preferences that humans experience?

As it turns out, several factors affect our taste preferences. One of these is age. We lose some of our taste buds permanently with age. This may contribute to the diminished sense of taste that older adults often experience (Nordin et al., 2003). With fewer active taste buds, it might seem that older people would tend to prefer richly flavored foods. In fact, some people have proposed that diets enriched with intensely flavored foods may help to maintain elders' appetites. However, studies have shown that this strategy may not always work (Essed et al., 2007).

Culture is another factor in taste preferences. For example, the spouse of one of your authors is from El Salvador, where iguana meat is considered a treat enjoyed mostly by the wealthy. In the United States, iguanas are more likely to be kept as pets than eaten. Why do food preferences vary across cultures? One reason is that the availability of food sources dictates what a particular people *can* eat. Central Americans eat iguana meat today partly because their ancestors once ate the wild iguanas that roamed there. Every culture must take advantage of the food sources at its disposal, and hunger can make foods taste better, especially when those foods provide needed nutrients (Mobini, Chambers, & Yeomans, 2007).

Religious values and traditions also shape cultural food preferences. For example, observant Jews and Muslims will not eat pork, Hindus do not eat beef, and Seventh Day Adventists frown upon the use of certain spices (Grivetti, 2000). These taste preferences are passed from generation to generation as parents teach children to follow their religious values.

Our food preferences are a result of biological factors, our cultural background, and our personal experience with food.

© Catherine Karnow/Corbis

Many of our individual food preferences develop through learning—some of it very early in life. Research shows that the foods a mother eats can affect the flavor of her breast milk, and exposure to these flavors during breast-feeding can affect her child's later taste preferences (Mennella & Beauchamp, 1991). Being exposed to a variety of flavors in infancy tends to make infants more open to new and novel foods (Hausner et al., 2010).

Although the influence of learning on food preferences is strong, evidence also suggests that biological factors can affect our sense of taste. Prior to menopause, women's ability to taste fluctuates with hormone levels, and after menopause the ability to taste declines (Prutkin et al., 2000). There are also some genetic variations in the ability to taste. Some people, called *supertasters*, have a higher than average number of taste buds and are able to strongly taste a bitter compound called 6-n-propylthiocuracil (PROP). In contrast, *nontasters* perceive very little or no bitterness from PROP (Bartoshuk, 2000). Nontasters have been shown to eat a wider variety of foods (Azar, 1998; Pasquet et al., 2002) and have higher *body mass indexes* (BMI; Feeney et al., 2011) than supertasters do. Compared to nontasters, female PROP tasters tend to eat more fat and less fruit in their diets (Yackinous & Guinard, 2002). Supertasters may avoid some foods that are rich in cancer-fighting compounds but also have bitter flavors (e.g., Brussels sprouts).

Finally, our sense of taste is not influenced solely by our culture, early learning, or taste buds. Our sense of taste is also heavily dependent on our sense of smell (Shepard, 2006). If you've ever tried to taste food when you've had a bad cold, you know that your sense of smell makes a significant contribution to taste and that clogged nasal passages tend to make food taste bland.

## Smell: Aromas, Odors, and a Warning System

**Olfaction**, our sense of smell, has adaptive value. Smells can alert us to danger. The ability to smell smoke enables us to detect a fire long before we see flames. The rotten smell of spoiled food warns us not to eat it. Without such odoriferous warnings, we could easily find ourselves in harm's way.

Like the sense of taste, the sense of smell is a chemical sense. Odors come from airborne chemicals that are diffused in the air. When we inhale these molecules into our nose, we may experience smelling the substance. Compared with our other senses, our sense of smell is quite sensitive. Recall from our earlier discussion of sensory thresholds that we can detect the presence of a single drop of perfume in a three-room apartment (see Table 3.1). When it comes to discriminating between odors, we can detect roughly 500,000 different scents (Cain, 1988), and we can identify by name about 10,000 different smells (Lancet et al., 1993). Yet, despite these impressive abilities, in daily life we typically pay attention only to odors that are quite strong (Sela & Sobel, 2010). For example, we are frequently unaware of the detectable smells of other people unless they are strong (e.g., heavy cologne or strong body odor). In other words, smells have to make a big impact on us to capture our attention.

### THE MYSTERY OF SMELL

Researchers have not been able to determine precisely how our sense of smell works. Of the senses we have described to this point, smell is by far the least understood. What we do know is that we are able to smell because of a special piece of skin that lines the top of the nasal cavity (■ FIGURE 3.12). This special

The inability to smell also limits the ability to taste.

**olfaction**   the sense of smell

**FIGURE**

## 3.12

### The Anatomy of the Nose

Odors in the form of airborne chemicals are inhaled into the nasal cavity, where sensory cells in the olfactory epithelium convert them into neural signals.

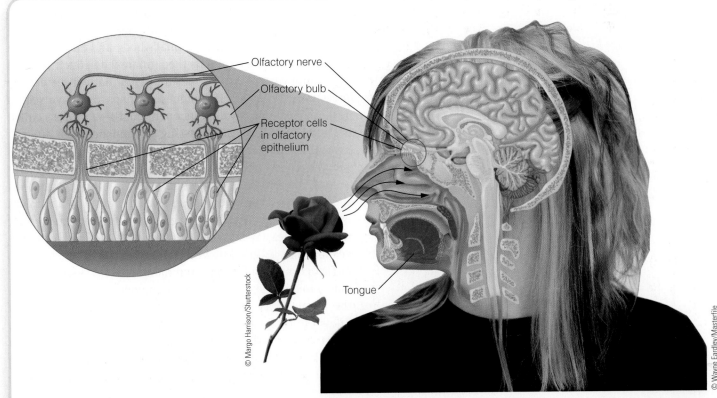

piece of skin, the **olfactory epithelium**, probably contains only a few hundred different types of odor receptors (Lancet et al., 1993). When we breathe in odor-laden air, the odor molecules reach the receptors in the olfactory epithelium and stimulate these cells. This stimulation accomplishes the conversion of odor into smell, but just how our brain understands what we smell is not well understood at this time (Matlin & Foley, 1997). One theory, **lock-and-key theory**, proposes that olfactory receptors are excited by odor molecules in much the same way that neurotransmitters excite receptor sites on the postsynaptic neuron (Amoore, 1970). According to lock-and-key theory, specific odor molecules have the power to "unlock" or excite certain olfactory receptors in the olfactory epithelium.

Once the cells of the epithelium have converted odor into neural impulses, these signals travel across the *olfactory nerve* to the *olfactory bulb* of the brain. The olfactory bulb is located just below the bottom edge of the frontal lobe of the brain (see Figure 3.12). The olfactory bulb processes incoming information before sending it on to other parts of the brain. Some olfactory information goes directly to the primary smell cortex, in the temporal lobes of the brain.

Other olfactory information is sent to both the cortex and the limbic system. Recall from Chapter 2 that the limbic system regulates emotional and motivational activity. The limbic system seems to be heavily involved in the processing of olfactory information. This may explain the strong emotional reactions we often have to certain smells. For example, the smell of one of your favorite childhood meals may conjure up beloved memories of your childhood. Are there particular smells that bring back emotionally charged memories for you?

## CHEMOSIGNALS: PHEROMONES AND THE VOMERONASAL SENSE

Some researchers believe that humans have yet another sense somewhat related to smell. This sense, the *vomeronasal sense*, is well documented in animals (Doty, 2001). Many animals communicate with each other via airborne *chemosignals* called **pheromones**. Pheromones are produced by glands in the animal's body and dispersed into the air, where other animals then inhale them. Such animals are equipped with vomeronasal organs that can detect the presence of inhaled pheromones. Perhaps you have seen a cat inhale deeply through its open mouth—a process called cat's *flehmen*. The cat is passing pheromone-laden air over special organs, called Jacobson's organs, in the roof of its mouth. These organs can detect the presence of pheromones. The presence of such an organ in humans has been the subject of controversy, but at least one study has found evidence that some people have vomeronasal organs in their nasal cavities (Won et al., 2000). There is also some suggestion that a little-known cranial nerve (cranial nerve 0, or CN0), found in humans and many other vertebrates, may play a role in the detection of pheromones. CN0 travels from the nasal cavity to the brain, including areas of the brain known to be involved in sexual behavior (see Fields, 2007). For a closer look at the role chemosignals play in human sexuality, see the Neuroscience Applies to Your World box.

**olfactory epithelium [ole-FACT-uh-ree epp-ith-THEEL-ee-um]** a special piece of skin at the top of the nasal cavity that contains the olfactory receptors

**lock-and-key theory** a theory that proposes that olfactory receptors are excited by odor molecules in a way that is similar to the way in which neurotransmitters excite receptor sites

**pheromones [FAIR-uh-moans]** airborne chemicals that are released from glands and detected by the vomeronasal organs in some animals and perhaps humans

© NaturePL/SuperStock

Many mammals use pheromones to communicate with each other. This cat is passing pheromone-laden air over vomeronasal organs in the roof of its mouth.

## Neuroscience Applies to Your World:

### Sex, Sweat, and Tears

Although the existence of human vomeronasal organs is controversial, it does seem that pheromones affect certain aspects of our behavior, particularly those related to sexuality. For example, when women are exposed to pheromones in the underarm secretions of another woman, their menstrual cycle tends to synchronize with the other woman's cycle (Larkin, 1998; Stern & McClintock, 1998). And after exposure to a pheromone that is released from men's hair follicles, women increase their social interactions with males (E. Miller, 1999). Other pheromones found in men's sweat tend to improve a woman's mood state (Monti-Bloch et al., 1998).

On the other hand, it appears that when women cry, their tears contain chemosignals that may affect the behavior of men. Recently, Shani Gelstein and colleagues (2011) collected women's tears in a vial as they watched a sad movie and later had men smell the tears without the women present. Compared to a control group that sniffed pure saline, the men who sniffed tears experienced decreased levels of testosterone (male sex hormones, see Chapter 2), and they reported lowered sexual arousal. fMRI scans of the men's brains also showed reduced brain activity in areas of the brain related to sexual arousal, such as the *hypothalamus* and the *left fusiform gyrus* (Gelstein et al., 2011). These findings suggest that men may be biologically programmed to lose interest in sex when they encounter a crying woman. More research is needed to determine the significance of this effect. Also unclear is whether chemosignals are found in the tears of men and children and what, if any, effect they may have on others.

A recent study suggests that the tears of women contain chemosignals that impact men by reducing their level of testosterone production.

© PhotoLibrary

## Touch: The Skin Sense

Touch is associated with many of life's pleasurable experiences. Feeling a friendly pat on the back can certainly enhance our social interactions. Sexual activity depends heavily on our ability to feel touch. But our ability to sense with our skin also affects our survival. Through our skin we feel touch, temperature, and pain.

> **You Asked...**
>
> *What makes us able to feel different things with our hands?*
>
> ERICA BREGLIO, STUDENT

Our keen sense of touch originates in our skin. The skin is composed of several layers that contain touch receptors. The inner layer, the **dermis**, contains most of the touch receptors (■ FIGURE 3.13). The skin's outer layer is the **epidermis**, which consists of several layers of dead skin cells. The epidermis also contains touch receptors, especially in areas of the skin that do not have hair, such as the fingertips.

We have different types of receptors for touch, temperature, and pain (Figure 3.13). We know more about the function of the touch receptors than we do about the pain and temperature receptors. Pressure on the skin pushes against the axons of the touch receptors. This causes a change in the axonal membrane's permeability to positive ions, allowing them to enter the cell (Loewenstein, 1960; Hu et al., 2010). As you recall from Chapter 2, as positive ions enter a cell, the cell becomes more likely to fire an action potential. If the touch is

**dermis**   the inner layer of the skin

**epidermis**   the outer layer of the skin

# 3.13

Anatomy of the Skin
and Its Receptors

Different types of skin receptors pick up
different types of stimulation.

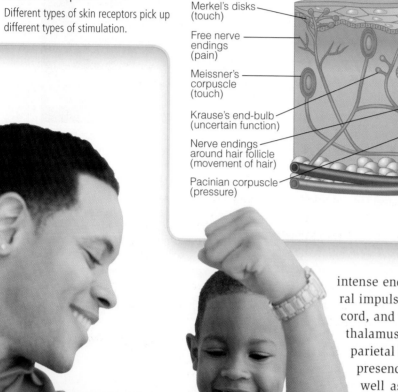

Merkel's disks
(touch)

Free nerve
endings
(pain)

Meissner's
corpuscle
(touch)

Krause's end-bulb
(uncertain function)

Nerve endings
around hair follicle
(movement of hair)

Pacinian corpuscle
(pressure)

Epidermis

Dermis

© Jose Luis Pelaez Inc/Blend Images/Corbis

intense enough to allow the receptors to reach threshold, neural impulses will be fired. These impulses travel to the spinal cord, and then to the brain. In the brain, the signals enter the thalamus and then go on to the somatosensory cortex of the parietal lobe. Some signals, particularly those indicating the presence of threatening stimuli, go to the limbic system as well as the somatosensory cortex (Coren, Ward, & Enns, 1999). Once the signals reach the somatosensory cortex, our brain interprets the sensation and directs us to take the appropriate action.

## The Body Senses: Experiencing the Physical Body in Space

So far, we have covered what are referred to as the five senses: vision, hearing, taste, smell, and touch. Do we possess other senses? The answer is "yes," but this time, we're not talking about ESP. We are referring to the body senses, the senses that help us experience our physical bodies in space: *kinesthesis* and the *vestibular sense*.

### KINESTHESIS

**Kinesthesis** is the ability to sense the position of our body parts in space and in relation to one another. As you walk, you are aware of where your arms, legs, and head are in relation to the ground. Kinesthetic sense is important to athletes, especially to gymnasts and high divers. It allows them to know where their bodies are as they execute their routines and dives. Our kinesthetic sense uses information from the muscles, tendons, skin, and joints to keep us oriented at all times. The information from these sources is processed in the somatosensory cortex and the cerebellum of the brain (see Chapter 2).

**kinesthesis [kin-ess-THEE-sis]**  the ability to sense the position of our body parts in relation to one another and in relation to space

**vestibular [ves-STIB-you-lar] sense**  the sense of balance

## THE VESTIBULAR SENSE

Another important body sense is our sense of balance, or **vestibular sense**. The vestibular system uses input from the semicircular canals and the vestibular sacs of the inner ear to keep us balanced (■ FIGURE 3.14). These structures are filled with a fluid gel that surrounds hair cells much like those in the cochlea. When your head moves in any direction, the gel inside these structures moves in the opposite direction. The movement of the gel bends the hair cells and stimulates them to send neural impulses to the brain, which then uses these signals to determine the orientation of your head. Our vestibular system allows us to do such everyday tasks as walking, driving a car, and bending over to pick up a pencil from the floor. Without our vestibular sense, we would simply topple over.

Rapid movements of your head, such as those you experience on spinning carnival rides, can overstimulate the vestibular system. Such movements can cause a violent wave action in the fluid gel of the vestibular system. When the gel crashes against the sensory cells, the result can be dizziness and nausea. People vary with respect to the degree of vestibular stimulation that they can comfortably tolerate.

You now have a working knowledge of how our sensory organs convert environmental energies into neural impulses. Our next topic is perception, or how we make sense of all of this sensory information.

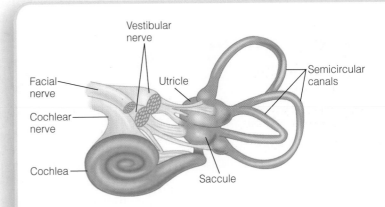

**FIGURE**

## 3.14

### The Vestibular Organs

The vestibular system helps us balance our body by monitoring the position and acceleration of our head as we move. To accomplish this, a gel-like fluid in the semicircular canals, saccule, and utricle presses against hair cells much like those found in the cochlea of the inner ear. When the hair cells of the vestibular system are moved, they signal the brain with information about the orientation of our head in three-dimensional space.

*Based on S. Iurato (1967). Submicroscopic Structure of the Inner Ear.* Pergamon Press.

Our vestibular sense keeps us balanced, and the kinesthetic sense allows this skateboarder to perform intricate moves without falling.

# Let's
# REVIEW

This section explained the chemical senses, taste and smell; touch; and the body senses, kinesthesis and the vestibular sense. For a quick check of your understanding, answer these questions.

**1.** Which of the following is *not* thought to be a taste for which your tongue has receptors?
   **a.** Salty     **c.** Acidic
   **b.** Sour     **d.** Bitter

**2.** Spinning around and around on a carnival ride is most likely to affect which of your senses?
   **a.** Taste     **c.** Smell
   **b.** Touch     **d.** Vestibular sense

**3.** Which of your senses would be *least likely* to be affected when you have a bad head cold?
   **a.** Taste     **c.** Smell
   **b.** Touch     **d.** Vestibular sense

*Answers 1. c; 2. d; 3. b*

Nick Laham/Getty Images

# Perception: How Do We Interpret Sensory Information?

At the beginning of this chapter, we defined perception as *the interpretation of sensory information.* That's it in a nutshell. When you look at your friend, light bounces off his or her face. This light strikes your retina, and the rods and cones convert the light into neural impulses. Sensation is complete. But now your brain must interpret the meaning of the neural impulses so you will recognize your friend's face. The fact that you believe you are seeing your friend and not, say, a dog or your psychology instructor, is the result of perceptual processes in your brain. But how does your brain know that you are seeing your friend's face?

## Using What We Know: Top-Down Perceptual Processing

### You Asked...

*Why can two people look at one thing and have it be different to them?*

JEAN-PAUL ESLAVA, STUDENT

**top-down perceptual processing**
perception that is guided by prior knowledge or expectations

**Top-down perceptual processing** occurs when we use previously gained knowledge to help us interpret a stimulus. Let's go back to the example of perceiving your friend's face. When you see a face that you recognize, what leads you to this recognition? Your memory helps you understand the "meaning" of the face you see. You know that faces usually contain two eyes, a nose, a mouth, and so on. Furthermore, you know how your friend's particular eyes, nose, and other features look. This stored knowledge allows you to quickly perceive the face of a friend.

Top-down perceptual processing can also fill in parts of a stimulus that are missing from our actual sensation of it. For example, look at ■ FIGURE 3.15. You cannot see this man's left leg or his feet, but you probably assume that they are there. Your knowledge of the human body tells you that the odds are slim that he is actually missing the limbs you cannot see. Consequently, in perceiving this picture, you implicitly assume that the "missing" leg and feet do, in fact, exist. This effect is so strong that later when you recall this picture, you might even remember having seen the missing limbs—right down to the type of shoes the man was "wearing."

Unfortunately, this "filling-in" of missing details can sometimes lead to mistakes in perception. Because people have different knowledge and expectations about the world, two people can witness the same event and yet perceive it differently. This can be a real problem in eyewitness accounts of crimes (see also Chapter 6). What if the correct identification of a

PM Images/Getty Images

**FIGURE**

## 3.15

### Top-Down Perceptual Processing

When you perceive the image in this photograph, your knowledge of the human body leads you to have certain expectations about the man in this picture. Because of top-down processing, you do not perceive that this man is missing his feet or parts of his legs.

suspect depended on accurately remembering what he was wearing? Or recalling the color of her eyes? In the real world, this can be a serious problem. In fact, one study showed that a majority of the falsely convicted people being studied had been mistakenly identified by eyewitnesses (Wells & Olson, 2003).

## Building a Perception "From Scratch": Bottom-Up Perceptual Processing

What do we do when we have very little or no stored knowledge to help us perceive a stimulus? We use a different perceptual process, one that does not rely on stored knowledge or expectations of the stimulus. In **bottom-up perceptual processing**, the properties of the stimulus itself are what we use to build our perception of that stimulus.

### YOUR TURN · Active Learning

Look at ■ FIGURE 3.16. What do you see? With few clues about what this stimulus is, you cannot easily use your knowledge to help you perceive it. The stimulus is too ambiguous. Without top-down processing, you are forced to use bottom-up processes to perceive the stimulus. You build your perception of the picture by piecing together your perceptions of the many different components that make up this stimulus. You perceive the lines, curves, dots, shaded areas, and shapes. You then try to fit these components together to figure out what the drawing means. Most people find it very difficult to figure out what Figure 3.16 is using only bottom-up perceptual processes!

If you are ready to give up and try top-down perceptual processing, look at ■ FIGURE 3.19 (p. 109). Now turn back to Figure 3.16. You will likely find that you can now readily perceive the image in Figure 3.16. You now have knowledge of what to look for, so perception becomes much easier. Your knowledge of what the picture is guides the way you piece together the components of the stimulus. When you switch to top-down processing, the picture becomes almost obvious.

**FIGURE**

## 3.16

**Top-Down Versus Bottom-Up Processing**

What is this picture? With no expectations to guide your perception, you are forced to rely mainly on bottom-up processes. Because the picture is ambiguous, bottom-up processes do not lead to a quick recognition of the stimulus. Now turn to Figure 3.19 (p. 109), which will enable you to engage your top-down perceptual processes. After looking at Figure 3.19, you should be able to quickly recognize the figure in this picture because you now have expectations to guide your perception.

In the course of a typical day, we probably use both top-down and bottom-up perceptual processes continually. We use bottom-up processes to piece together perceptions of ambiguous stimuli and top-down processes to tell us what we can expect to perceive in certain situations. Perception can be complicated in a three-dimensional world that is full of shapes and forms. To make perception even more complicated, our bodies do not remain stationary during perception. We move. The objects we perceive sometimes move. As a result, the information our senses receive from our world is highly variable. Our perceptual processes must be able to deal with these dynamic conditions. So how do we organize and make sense of our perceptions?

## Understanding What We Sense: Perceiving Size, Shape, and Brightness

One of the phenomena encountered in interpreting sensory data is *perceptual constancy*. When you look at a visual stimulus, the image it projects on your retina

**bottom-up perceptual processing** perception that is not guided by prior knowledge or expectations

**12.** Jonas, a retired jet engine mechanic, is 65 years old. Lately he's been experiencing some hearing loss. From what you know about hearing and exposure to loud sounds, what would you predict about Jonas's hearing loss?

a. He will have the most trouble hearing low-pitched sounds.

b. He will have the most trouble hearing medium-pitched sounds.

c. He will have the most trouble hearing high-pitched sounds.

d. He will most likely be completely deaf.

**13.** To date, the most widely accepted theory of pitch perception is _____ theory.

a. place      c. frequency

b. volley      d. duplicity

**14.** If you want to be sure to taste the *full* flavor of a piece of chocolate, where should you *avoid* placing the chocolate on as you taste it?

a. The front of the tongue

b. The center of the tongue

c. The right side of the tongue

d. The back of the tongue

**15.** Ultimately, most taste information is processed in the _____ cortex of the brain.

a. somatosenosory

b. occipital

c. temporal

d. motor

**16.** The fact that women who are exposed to the underarm secretions of other women tend to synchronize their menstrual cycles is most consistent with the notion that humans possess a(n) _____ sense.

a. vomeronasal

b. olfactory

c. vestibular

d. kinesthetic

**17.** Karina goes to a Halloween party where she meets a man who is wearing a monster mask that covers his entire face. Later, when her best friend asks her to describe the man, she describes him as being "good-looking" even though she never actually saw his face. Which of the following *best* explains Karina's perception of the man?

a. Good continuation

b. Closure

c. Bottom-up perceptual processing

d. Top-down perceptual processing

**18.** Mike was in an accident that injured his right eye. Although he'll recover, he must wear an eye patch for the next two weeks. During this time, Mike's doctor will not allow him to drive a car. Mike's doctor is most likely concerned with disturbances to Mike's _____.

a. vestibular system

b. binocular depth cues

c. monocular depth cues

d. kinesthetic system

**19.** In which of the following situations, would you be *most* likely to use bottom-up perceptual processing?

a. When viewing a piece of abstract art composed of nothing but paint splatters on a canvas.

b. When reading your best friend's bad handwriting.

c. When trying to watch a movie in a crowded theater where your view of the screen is obstructed by the people sitting in front of you.

d. When reading the daily news on the Internet.

**20.** According to your text, we experience perceptual constancies for all of the following except which one?

a. size

b. texture

c. shape

d. brightness

Answers: 1. a; 2. c; 3. a; 4. d; 5. b; 6. c; 7. b; 8. a; 9. b; 10. c; 11. a; 12. c; 13. d; 14. b; 15. a; 16. a; 17. d; 18. b; 19. a; 20. b.

## Online Resources

Log in to **www.cengagebrain.com** to access the resources your instructor requires. For this book, you can access:

### Psychology CourseMate

CourseMate brings course concepts to life with interactive learning, study, and exam preparation tools that support the printed textbook. A textbook-specific website, Psychology CourseMate includes an integrated interactive eBook and other interactive learning tools including quizzes, flashcards, videos, and more.

### CENGAGENOW™

CengageNOW Personalized Study is a diagnostic study tool containing valuable text-specific resources—and because you focus on just what you don't know, you learn more in less time to get a better grade.

### WebTutor

More than just an interactive study guide, WebTutor is an anytime, anywhere customized learning solution with an eBook, keeping you connected to your textbook, instructor, and classmates.

# LOOK BACK
## AT What You've
## LEARNED

### How Do Psychologists Measure Sensation and Perception?

- **Psychophysics** is the branch of psychology that studies how we process sensory stimuli.

- Psychophysicists conduct experiments to determine the **absolute threshold** and **just noticeable difference (jnd)** of each of the five senses.

- **Weber's law** is the relationship between the original intensity of a stimulus and the amount of change that is required to produce a jnd.

- When sensory stimuli are too weak in intensity to reach absolute threshold, the stimuli are said to be **subliminal**.

- The existence of **ESP** remains a controversial subject, however, to date there has not been convincing evidence of its existence.

### Vision: Seeing the World

- Light is electromagnetic energy, measured primarily by **wavelength** and **amplitude**. Wavelength = **hue**; amplitude = **brightness**.

- The **visible spectrum** of light is the narrow band we are able to see. Some animals are able to see a much broader spectrum.

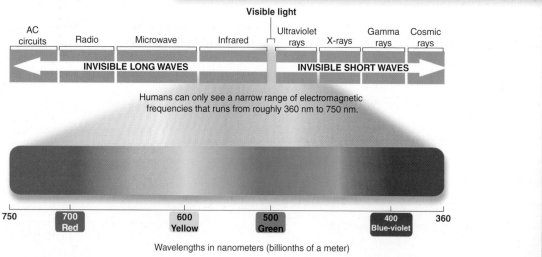

**Visible light**

| AC circuits | Radio | Microwave | Infrared | Ultraviolet rays | X-rays | Gamma rays | Cosmic rays |

**← INVISIBLE LONG WAVES**   **INVISIBLE SHORT WAVES →**

Humans can only see a narrow range of electromagnetic frequencies that runs from roughly 360 nm to 750 nm.

750   700 Red   600 Yellow   500 Green   400 Blue-violet   360

Wavelengths in nanometers (billionths of a meter)

- In the **retina** of the eye, specialized cells known as **rods** and **cones** convert light into neural impulses, which eventually travel to the brain via the **optic nerve**.

- The **trichromatic theory of color vision** and the **opponent-process theory** are both used to explain how we process color.

- **Color blindness** is the inability to see certain colors and is the result of missing cones in the retina or having cones that are sensitive to atypical ranges of light wave frequencies.

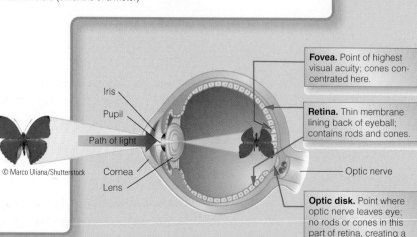

© Marco Uliana/Shutterstock

Iris
Pupil
Path of light
Cornea
Lens

**Fovea.** Point of highest visual acuity; cones concentrated here.

**Retina.** Thin membrane lining back of eyeball; contains rods and cones.

Optic nerve

**Optic disk.** Point where optic nerve leaves eye; no rods or cones in this part of retina, creating a blind spot.

# How Do We SENSE and PERCEIVE Our World?

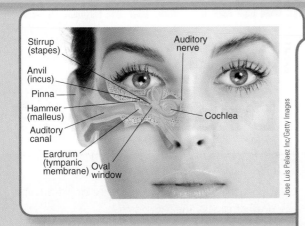

Stirrup (stapes)
Anvil (incus)
Pinna
Hammer (malleus)
Auditory canal
Eardrum (tympanic membrane)
Oval window
Auditory nerve
Cochlea

Jose Luis Pelaez Inc/Getty Images

## Hearing: Listening to the World

- Sounds are produced by waves of compressed air.

- **Frequency = pitch; amplitude = loudness**.

- The eardrum, or tympanic membrane, is a very thin membrane in the **middle ear** that vibrates to incoming sounds. It begins transmitting those sounds through the small bones to the **hair cells** of the fluid-filled **cochlea**, where neural impulses are generated.

- The **auditory nerve** carries the sounds we hear into the brain.

## The Other Senses: Taste, Smell, Touch, and the Body Senses

- Humans are sensitive to five tastes: bitter, sweet, sour, salty, and umami.

- The **taste buds**, which reside in the pits between the **papillae** on your tongue, convert the chemicals in the foods you eat into neural impulses.

- The sense of smell operates by converting odors captured by a special piece of skin, the **olfactory epithelium**, which lines the top of the nasal cavity, to neural impulses that travel via the olfactory nerve to the olfactory bulb in the brain.

- Many animals (and perhaps humans) have a vomeronasal system that allows them to communicate with other animals via airborne chemosignals known as **pheromones.** Chemosignals may impact some aspects of human sexuality.

- The sense of touch originates in the skin, with the inner layer—the **dermis**—containing most of the touch receptors.

- **Kinesthesis** is our ability to sense the position of our body parts in space and in relation to one another.

- The **vestibular sense** monitors the position of our head in space and helps us to stay balanced.

Nick Laham/Getty Images

## Perception: How Do We Interpret Sensory Information and How Accurate Are Our Perceptions?

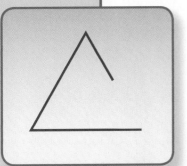

© Corbis

- **Top-down perceptual processing** refers to using previously gained knowledge to interpret a sensory stimulus.

- **Bottom-up perceptual processing** refers to using properties of the stimulus itself to form our perception of a stimulus.

- Perceptual constancies, depth cues, and **feature detection** are among the mental shortcuts we automatically employ to assist in perceiving stimuli.

- Perceptual errors can occur for a variety of reasons. They are often due to misapplied expectations that lead us to think we have seen or heard something that we have not.

# 4 CONSCIOUSNESS: WIDE AWAKE, in a DAZE, or Dreaming?

# Chapter Outline

*Altered states are relevant* to our everyday lives. Take Jeff Deshommes, a 20-year-old college student majoring in Health Services Administration. Like many students today, Jeff works full-time while also taking a full load of classes. He frequently hears students brag about how little sleep they get, and he himself used to think that the amount of sleep he got didn't have any effect on his behavior. But after learning about sleep, he now knows how important adequate sleep is for his academic and job performance. With constantly changing work shifts, Jeff had difficulty paying attention in class and while studying, and was often irritable. He noticed that when he got enough sleep, however, he was better able to prepare for exams and performed better on them—and he was also in a better mood. As he prepares for a career managing personnel in a hospital setting, he plans to be more cautious when scheduling people to varying shifts as he has personally experienced the negative effects of lack of sleep on mood, memory, and performance.

Jeff also sees the usefulness in knowing about psychoactive drugs. As a college student and full-time employee, he has often relied on energy drinks loaded with caffeine to help him stay awake and alert. At first these drinks helped, but then they seemed to have no effect and made him even more tired than before he drank them. He now realizes that drugs don't just affect his body, they affect his behavior, thoughts, and emotions too.

Like Jeff, we all experience altered states of consciousness. **Consciousness,** in psychological terms, includes the feelings, thoughts, and aroused states of which we are aware. This chapter examines the levels or gradations of consciousness—when you are not fully awake, alert, aware, or perhaps sound mind. Psychologists have done quite a bit of research in three areas: sleep, hypnosis, and the effects of various psychoactive drugs. By closely examining these states, we may better understand our behavior and the behavior of those around us. We will start with the altered state we all experience—sleep.

© Ellen Pastorino

*After learning about states of consciousness in his psychology class, Jeff Deshommes can see how important it is to get enough sleep and avoid overloading on caffeine, both for his current academic and job performance and for his future career.*

# Sleep, Dreaming, and Circadian Rhythm

## LEARNING OBJECTIVES

- Discuss why we sleep and what factors influence the amount of sleep we need.

- Describe the circadian rhythm of sleep and the role of the suprachiasmatic nucleus in controlling it, and discuss how disruptions in our circadian rhythm influence our behavior.

- Describe the stages we progress through during a typical night of sleep.

- Compare and contrast the different theories on dreaming.

- Describe and distinguish among the various sleep disorders.

Many of us never question what goes on in our bodies and minds as we sleep. But sleep offers plenty of behaviors for psychologists to explore. First, we will look at *why* we sleep and what occurs in our brains and bodies as we sleep. We will then explore the purpose of dreams and whether dreams have meaning. We will conclude by describing different types of sleep disorders. We caution you that just reading about sleep can make you drowsy!

## Functions of Sleep: Why Do We Sleep, and What If We Don't?

What would happen if you tried to stay awake indefinitely? William C. Dement, a pioneer in sleep research, actually tried this experiment on himself. Although Dement's lack of sleep made him a danger to himself and others, he was not in danger of dying from lack of sleep. Eventually, he fell asleep. In the same way that you cannot hold your breath until you die, you cannot deprive yourself of all sleep. Sleep always wins. This is because we drift into repeated *microsleeps* (Goleman, 1982). A **microsleep** is a brief (3- to 15-second) episode of sleep that occurs in the midst of a wakeful activity. We are typically unaware of its occurrence unless we are behind the wheel of a car, steering a ship, or flying a plane. In such circumstances, microsleeps could cause a disaster. In general, though, microsleeps appear to help us survive by preventing total sleep deprivation.

Sleep ensures our continued physical and mental health in several ways:

- *Sleep restores body tissues and facilitates body growth.* Sleep allows your immune system, nervous system, and organs time to replenish lost reserves and energy and to repair any cellular damage. This prepares the body for action the next day and ensures the continued health of the body. Lack of adequate sleep can affect energy levels, often making us feel drowsy and fatigued (Murphy & Delanty, 2007; Oginska & Pokorski, 2006). Sleep also activates growth hormone, which facilitates physical growth during infancy, childhood, and the teen years (Gais, Lucas, & Born, 2006; Szentirmai et al., 2007).

- *Sleep increases immunity to disease.* During sleep, the production of immune cells that fight off infection increases. Therefore, your immune system is stronger when you receive the appropriate amount of sleep (Beardsley, 1996; Lange et al., 2006; Motivala & Irwin, 2007). When you deprive your body of sleep, your natural immune responses are reduced (Irwin et al., 2003; Murphy & Delanty, 2007). This is in part why you are encouraged to sleep and rest when you are ill. This effect on immunity occurs after as few as two days of total sleep deprivation or several days of partial sleep deprivation (Heiser et al., 2000; Irwin et al., 1996; Ozturk et al., 1999; Rogers et al., 2001). For college students, this may mean you are more susceptible to colds and flu at midterm and final exam time. You are likely to sleep less at these times, thereby decreasing your immune

**consciousness [CON-shis-nus]** feelings, thoughts, and aroused states of which we are aware

**microsleep** brief episode of sleep that occurs in the midst of a wakeful activity

It is estimated that more than 24,000 deaths occur annually in accidents caused directly or in part by drowsy drivers.

Solid Web Designs LTD/Shutterstock.com

system's ability to combat illnesses. Fortunately, after a night or several nights of recovery sleep, your natural immune functions return to normal (Irwin et al., 1996; Ozturk et al., 1999). Sleeping truly is good medicine.

- *Sleep keeps your mind alert*. When people do not get enough sleep, they are more likely to be inattentive and easily distracted (Jennings, Monk, & van der Molen, 2003; Kahol et al., 2008; Kendall et al., 2006; Koslowsky & Babkoff, 1992; Murphy & Delanty, 2007). Sleep makes your body more sensitive to norepinephrine—the neurotransmitter that keeps you alert during the day (Chapter 2; Steriade & McCarley, 1990).

- *Sleep enhances your mood*. Sleep activates many chemicals that influence your emotions and mood. Consequently, if you are deprived of sleep, you are more likely to be irritable, cranky, and unhappy, in addition to being tired (Boivin et al., 1997; Durmer & Dinges, 2005; Murphy & Delanty, 2007).

- *Sleep helps learning and memory*. When you sleep, emotional experiences as well as information that you have reviewed or rehearsed are more likely to be remembered (Fogel, Smith, & Cote, 2007; Gais et al., 2006; Karni et al., 1994; Payne & Kensinger, 2010; Payne et al., 2008; Racsmany, Conway, & Demeter, 2010; Rasch & Born, 2008; Scullin & McDaniel, 2010; Stickgold & Walker, 2007; M. P. Walker, 2009; Walker & Stickgold, 2004). Chapter 6 offers an in-depth look at memory processing, but a few simple statements here will help you understand the connection between sleep and memory.

  - In order to get information into your memory, you must *encode* it, or do something to remember the information. This may mean repeating the information over and over again, visualizing the information, or associating it with a personal experience. When information is thoroughly encoded, it can be more easily transferred to long-term memory so that we can retrieve it later.

  - Sleep allows you to better store material that was actually processed (that is, encoded well enough) during studying. Information that you can't readily retrieve in the morning probably wasn't encoded well enough, and you will need to study it again. You can see the advantage of a good night's sleep before an exam.

  - Sleep's connection to memory processing may also explain why problem solving seems to improve after a night's sleep (Ellenbogen et al., 2007). You may think about a problem repeatedly during the day, frustrated by your inability to find a solution. The next day you awaken with a solution in mind. This suggests that pertinent details about the problem are processed during sleep. The phrase "sleep on it" really does have merit.

Research suggests that sleep may have evolved as a necessary behavior for humans (Hirshkowitz, Moore, & Minhoto, 1997; Webb, 1983). When humans lived in caves, it was dangerous for them to go out at night to hunt for food because they had very little night vision and were relatively small compared to other species. If they did go outside at night, they were likely to be the food for larger predators. Humans who stayed inside the cave at night were more likely to survive and produce offspring. Over time, these offspring may have adapted to the pattern of nighttime sleeping and daytime hunting and gathering.

As you can see, sleep is a necessity, not a luxury. Sleep offers many benefits to our functioning and ensures that we will be healthy, alert, and happy.

## How Much Sleep Do We Need?

Some people brag about how little sleep they need. Yet research shows that although the amount of sleep we need varies from person to person and depends on several factors, many of us are not getting enough. Here are some sleep factors and facts:

- *Age.* The older we get, the less sleep we need (■ FIGURE 4.1). Babies require a lot of sleep, between 16 and 18 hours a day. Preschoolers require less sleep, about 10 to 12 hours a day, typically including a midday nap. Teenagers and young adults need less sleep than children, but they still require 8 to 10 hours of sleep a night (McLaughlin Crabtree & Williams, 2009). However, just one in five teenagers gets an optimal 9 hours of sleep on school nights (National Sleep Foundation, 2006). People between the ages of 25 and 34 are more likely to report insufficient rest or sleep than are people over the age of 65 (McKnight-Eily et al., 2009). On average, college students sleep 6.1 hours—2 hours less than they need—each night (Maas, 1998). Adults, on average, sleep 6.7 hours a night on weekdays (National Sleep Foundation, 2009). According to sleep experts, most adults require at least 8 hours of sleep a night.

- *Lifestyle (environment).* Our cultural beliefs, lifestyle habits, and environment also influence the amount of sleep that we need or get (Giannotti & Cortesi, 2009). If you were raised in a home in which everyone was up early on the weekends to do chores, you adapted to a different sleep schedule than someone who slept until 10 A.M. or noon on weekends. In one study of college students, good sleepers were more likely to have regular bedtime and rise time schedules than poorer sleepers (Carney et al., 2006). Keep in mind, too, that stressors and responsibilities change as we get older. Living on one's own, parenting, and job responsibilities also bring about changes in our sleep schedule.

- *Genetics.* Genes may also play a role in the amount of sleep that each of us requires. For example, studies that measured the sleep patterns of identical twins compared to fraternal twins found more similar sleep needs and sleep behaviors among identical twins (de Castro, 2002; Webb & Campbell, 1983). Additional research also suggests that genes may influence our propensity to be either "night owls" or "early birds." Some people may be genetically predisposed to get up early in the morning and go to bed earlier, whereas others may prefer getting up later and going to bed later (Guthrie, Ash, & Bendapudi, 1995; Mongrain et al., 2004; Tankova, Adan, & Buela-Casal, 1994). Learn your propensity toward morningness or eveningness by completing the brief scale in Your Turn—Active Learning.

### FIGURE

# 4.1

### Age Differences in Sleep Needs

Newborns sleep an average of 16 hours a day. Preschoolers require less sleep, about 10 to 12 hours. Most teenagers and adults require 8 hours.

*From "Ontogenetic Development of Human Sleep-Dream Cycle," by H. P. Roffwarg, J. N. Muzino, and W. C. Dement, Science, 1966, 152:604–609. Copyright 1966 by the AAAS. Reprinted with permission from AAAS.*

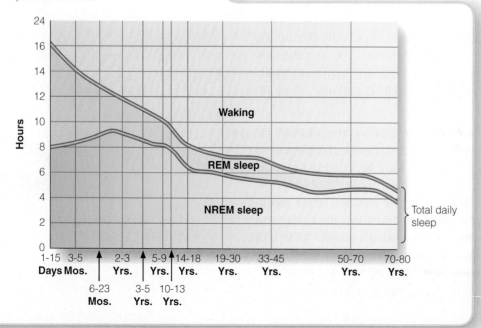

## YOUR TURN  Active Learning

Answer the following questions, then add up the values to get your total score. Compare your total score with the key at the end to get an idea of your *chronotype*.

### Morningness–Eveningness Scale

| QUESTION | ANSWER | VALUE |
|---|---|---|
| If you were entirely free to plan your evening and had no commitments the next day, at what time would you choose to go to bed? | 8 P.M.–9 P.M. | 5 |
| | 9 P.M.–10:15 P.M. | 4 |
| | 10:15 P.M.–12:30 A.M. | 3 |
| | 12:30 A.M.–1:45 A.M. | 2 |
| | 1:45 A.M.–3 A.M. | 1 |
| You have to do 2 hours of physically hard work. If you were entirely free to plan your day, in which of the following periods would you choose to do the work? | 8 A.M.–10 A.M. | 4 |
| | 11 A.M.–1 P.M. | 3 |
| | 3 P.M.–5 P.M. | 2 |
| | 7 P.M.–9 P.M. | 1 |
| For some reason you have gone to bed several hours later than normal, but there is no need to get up at a particular time the next morning. Which of the following is most likely to occur? | Will wake up at the usual time and not fall asleep again | 4 |
| | Will wake up at the usual time and doze thereafter | 3 |
| | Will wake up at the usual time but will fall asleep again | 2 |
| | Will not wake up until later than usual | 1 |
| You have a 2-hour test to take that you know will be mentally exhausting. If you were entirely free to choose, in which of the following periods would you choose to take the test? | 8 A.M.–10 A.M. | 4 |
| | 11 A.M.–1 P.M. | 3 |
| | 3 P.M.–5 P.M. | 2 |
| | 7 P.M.–9 P.M. | 1 |
| If you had no commitments the next day and were entirely free to plan your own day, what time would you get up? | 5 A.M.–6:30 A.M. | 5 |
| | 6:30 A.M.–7:45 A.M. | 4 |
| | 7:45 A.M.–9:45 A.M. | 3 |
| | 9:45 A.M.–11 A.M. | 2 |
| | 11 A.M.–12 P.M. | 1 |
| A friend has asked you to join him twice a week for a workout in the gym. The best time for him is between 10 p.m. and 11 p.m. Bearing nothing else in mind other than how you normally feel in the evening, how do you think you would perform? | Very well | 1 |
| | Reasonably well | 2 |
| | Poorly | 3 |
| | Very poorly | 4 |
| One hears about "morning" and "evening" types of people. Which of these types do you consider yourself to be? | Definitely a morning type | 6 |
| | More a morning than an evening type | 4 |
| | More an evening than a morning type | 2 |
| | Definitely an evening type | 0 |

### Morningness–Eveningness Scale

| | |
|---|---|
| Definitely morning type | 32–28 |
| Moderately morning type | 27–23 |
| Neither type | 22–16 |
| Moderately evening type | 15–11 |
| Definitely evening type | 10–6 |

*(Adapted from A Self-Assessment Questionnaire to Determine Morningness–Eveningness in Human Circadian Rhythms, by J. A. Horne and O. Ostberg, International Journal of Chronobiology, 1976, Vol. 4, 97–110. Reproduced with permission of Taylor & Francis UK LTD; permission conveyed through Copyright Clearance Center, Inc.)*

## Stages of Sleep: What Research Tells Us

You Asked...

*What happens during sleep?*

SAQIB ABBAS, STUDENT

Using electroencephalogram (EEG) technology, sleep researchers have identified five stages of sleep. Recall from Chapter 2 that EEGs examine the electrical activity of relatively large areas of the brain. These brain waves are then plotted on graph paper or a computer screen. The patterns the brain waves create give researchers an image of our brain activity when we are awake and when we are asleep (■ FIGURE 4.3).

When we are awake and alert, our brain (as measured by an EEG) emits *beta* waves. Beta brain waves are rapid, with a high number of cycles per second. This indicates frequent impulses of electrical activity in the brain. When we are awake yet relaxed, our brain emits *alpha* waves. Alpha waves are somewhat slower and less frequent than beta waves. As we sleep, our brain-wave patterns change in a predictable sequence.

If you watch someone sleep, you will notice that at times the person's eyes move under the eyelids, showing rapid eye movement (REM). At other times during sleep, such eye movement is absent. From such observations, researchers have identified two distinct sleep patterns: **non-REM sleep** and **REM sleep**. When your eyes do not move during sleep, it is referred to as non-rapid-eye-movement, or non-REM, sleep. The state in which our eyes do move is called rapid-eye-movement, or REM, sleep. During these two states of sleep, our bodies and brains are experiencing very different activities.

**non-REM sleep** relaxing state of sleep in which the person's eyes do not move

**REM sleep** active state of sleep in which the person's eyes move

### FIGURE

## 4.3

### Brain Activity During Wakefulness and the Various Stages of Sleep

Electroencephalogram technology records brain-wave activity during wakefulness and the various stages of sleep. When awake but relaxed, the brain emits alpha waves. Brain activity during non-REM sleep progressively slows from theta waves (stage I) to delta waves (stage IV). REM sleep is characterized by rapid brain waves. The brain slides also differentiate non-REM sleep, REM sleep, and wakefulness. Notice that your brain looks as though it is awake while you are in REM sleep. The brain slides labeled "awake" and "REM sleep" look very similar, whereas the portion labeled "non-REM sleep" looks quite different.

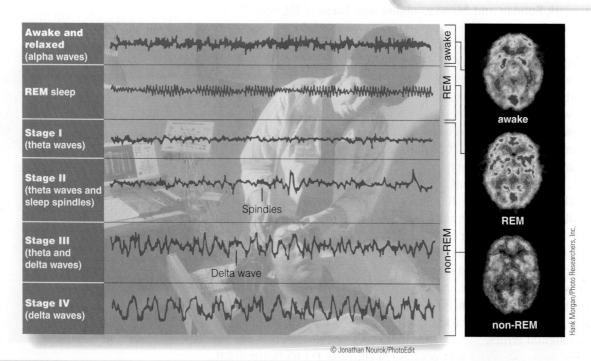

© Jonathan Nourok/PhotoEdit

Hank Morgan/Photo Researchers, Inc.

Non-REM sleep is a progressively relaxed state. In contrast, REM sleep is very active. During a night of sleep, our bodies and brains move back and forth between states of relaxation and activity until we wake up in the morning (Armitage, 1995; Dement & Kleitman, 1957). The sleep cycle begins with non-REM sleep.

## THE FOUR STAGES OF NON-REM SLEEP

When we fall asleep, our bodies and brains progress through a series of four non-REM sleep stages:

- *Stage I sleep* is a light sleep and is characterized by *theta* waves. Notice in Figure 4.3 that theta waves are slower and less frequent than beta or alpha waves. During this stage, your breathing and heart rate slow down. You may experience sensations such as falling or floating. You can easily awaken from stage I sleep, which typically lasts from 1 to 7 minutes.
- *Stage II sleep* is characterized by *sleep spindles* and lasts approximately 20 minutes. Sleep spindles (see Figure 4.3) are a pattern of slower theta waves sporadically disrupted by bursts of electrical activity. During stage II sleep, breathing, muscle tension, heart rate, and body temperature continue to decrease. You are clearly asleep and not easily awakened. Recent findings suggest that stage II sleep spindles help us process both simple and complex motor skills that we have learned (Fogel & Smith, 2006; Fogel et al., 2007; Kuriyama, Stickgold, & Walker, 2004; Tucker & Fishbein, 2009).
- *Stage III and IV sleep* are referred to as *slow-wave sleep*. In stage III sleep, you begin showing *delta* brain-wave patterns. Delta waves are large, slow brain waves. When a consistent pattern of delta waves emerges, you have entered stage IV sleep. Stage IV sleep is referred to as *deep sleep*. The body is extremely relaxed. Heart rate, respiration, body temperature, and blood flow to the brain are reduced. Growth hormone is secreted. It is believed that during this deep sleep, body maintenance and restoration occur (Dang-Vu et al., 2010; Porkka-Heiskanen et al., 1997). For example, your proportion of deep sleep increases after a day of increased physical activity (Horne & Staff, 1983). It is difficult to awaken people from deep sleep. When they are awakened, they may be disoriented or confused. Your first hour of sleep is predominately slow-wave sleep. Slow-wave sleep then progressively gets shorter the longer you sleep.

## REM SLEEP: DREAM ON

After approximately 30 to 40 minutes of slow-wave sleep, your brain and body start to speed up again. You cycle back through stage II of non-REM sleep and then enter REM (rapid-eye-movement) sleep. REM sleep is a very active stage. Your breathing rate increases, and your heart beats irregularly. Blood flow increases to the genital area and may cause erections in males (Somers et al., 1993). However, your muscle tone significantly decreases, leaving the muscles extremely relaxed and essentially paralyzed. Figure 4.3 shows that your REM brain-wave patterns are similar to your brain-wave patterns when you are awake. The brain slides labeled "awake" and "REM sleep" look almost exactly alike! You can see that the portion labeled "non-REM sleep" looks quite different.

REM sleep is intimately connected to dreaming. Although you can dream in some form in all sleep stages, dreams during REM sleep are more easily recalled. More than 80% of people awakened from REM sleep report dreaming (Hirshkowitz et al., 1997). The body paralysis that occurs during REM prevents you from acting out your dreams. However, in rare instances, people do not experience the paralysis that normally accompanies REM sleep. This condition, which mainly affects older men, is referred to as **REM behavior disorder**. People with REM behavior disorder may thrash about while in REM sleep, causing harm to themselves or others (Gugger & Wagner, 2007; Plazzi et al., 1997).

The purpose of REM sleep is constantly being questioned. Some studies indicate a connection between REM sleep and memory processing. People who are deprived of REM sleep and dreaming are less likely to recall complex information learned earlier in the day than are people who were not deprived of REM sleep (Chollar, 1989; Karni et al., 1994). REM-deprived people also report having difficulty concentrating when they awaken. These findings have led researchers to speculate that REM sleep—and perhaps dreaming—facilitates the storage of memories as well as mental strategies (Diekelmann & Born, 2010; Rauchs et al., 2004). At the same time, REM appears to help us process recent emotional experiences (Desseilles et al., in press; Walker & van der Helm, 2009) and to "discard" information that is trivial or less important to us (Crick & Mitchison, 1995; Smith, 1995). Other research shows no relationship between time spent in REM sleep and memory problems (J. M. Siegel, 2001). The exact connection between REM sleep and memory continues to be investigated (Carey, 2007).

Another curiosity of REM sleep is referred to as **REM rebound**. When people lose REM sleep because of medications, drugs, or sleep deprivation, they make up for it on subsequent nights by spending more time dreaming (Dement, 1960). Before we look at research on dreaming, let's review what happens during a typical night of sleep.

## A TYPICAL NIGHT'S SLEEP

A typical night of sleep consists of cycling through non-REM stages and REM sleep. We progress through stages I, II, III, and IV of non-REM sleep. We revisit stages III and II of non-REM sleep. We then enter REM sleep. After a brief period in REM sleep, we begin the cycle again, starting with the non-REM stages. The pattern repeats throughout the night. One complete cycle of non-REM and REM sleep takes about 90 minutes. But notice from ■ FIGURE 4.4 that as the night progresses we spend less time in slow-wave sleep and more time in REM sleep. This means that the body-restoring functions of slow-wave sleep take place early on, during the first few cycles of sleep. After these early cycles, we spend longer in REM sleep. So if you are not getting enough sleep, you will miss out on the longest period of REM sleep. On average, we spend around 20% of our total sleep time in REM sleep. If you sleep 8 hours a night, you spend roughly 90 minutes of that time in REM sleep. That means each night you spend approximately 90 minutes having REM dreams.

**REM behavior disorder**    a condition in which normal muscle paralysis does not occur, leading to violent movements during REM sleep

**REM rebound**    loss of REM sleep is recouped by spending more time in REM on subsequent nights

**FIGURE**

## 4.4

### A Typical Night of Sleep

As the night progresses, we spend less time in slow-wave sleep (stages III and IV) and more time in REM sleep.

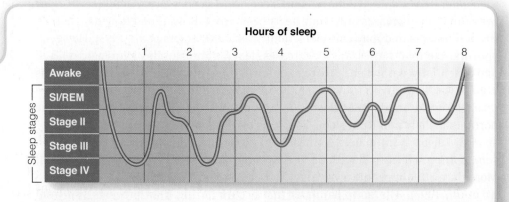

## Dreaming: The Night's Work

Although not everyone reports remembering their dreams when they awaken, everyone, regardless of culture, progresses through dream states during sleep. Dreams do show some similarities in content from one culture to another. For example, dream themes that focus on basic needs or fears (sex, aggression, and death) seem to be universal. Other content seems to be specific to its presence in a culture. For instance, today's Alaskan natives may have dreams that include snowmobiles, but their ancestors of 100 years ago obviously did not. People dream about what they know, which is influenced by the culture in which they live (Price & Crapo, 2002).

**You Asked...**

*Do dreams have meaning?*

LISANDRA MACHADO, STUDENT

### SIGMUND FREUD'S *INTERPRETATION OF DREAMS*

One of the most controversial and best-known theories of dreaming is Sigmund Freud's. In his *Interpretation of Dreams* (1900/1980), Freud called dreams "the royal road to the unconscious." According to Freud, dreams allow us to express fears and sexual and aggressive desires without the censorship of our conscious thought processes. Having straightforward dreams about these "unacceptable" desires would cause us anxiety. Instead, we dream in symbols that represent our unconscious desires. For Freud, dreams contained both **manifest content** and **latent content**. The manifest content of a dream is what you recall when you awaken. The latent, or hidden, content of the dream is the symbolic interpretation. For example, a young girl may dream of coming home from school one day to find the house deserted. She runs from room to room, looking for her parents or some sign that they will be returning soon (manifest content). Such a dream among children may signify the anxiety of being left alone, deserted, uncared for, or unprotected (latent content).

### DREAMS AS COPING, EVOLUTIONARY DEFENSE, OR JUST BIOLOGY AT WORK

Many psychologists and psychiatrists have challenged Freud's theory of dreaming and have proposed alternative explanations for why we dream. For example, the *continuity hypothesis* suggests that dreaming is a way of coping with daily problems and issues. We dream about everyday experiences and current concerns in an effort to resolve these issues (Cartwright, 1993; Pesant & Zadra, 2006; Schredl, 2009; Schredl & Erlacher, 2008). In this view, dreams are not as symbolic as Freud suggested. *Memory theory* suggests that dreams are a way to consolidate information and to get rid of trivial details in our memories (Eiser, 2005; Porte & Hobson, 1996). From this viewpoint, dreams represent a function of memory.

The **threat simulation theory (TST)** suggests an evolutionary function of dreams. TST proposes that dreaming is essentially an ancient biological defense mechanism that allows us to experience potentially threatening situations so that we can rehearse our responses to these events. Although studies do show that childhood trauma or recurrent dreams are associated with a greater number of threatening dream events, not all of our dreams involve themes of survival (Valli & Revonsuo, 2009; Valli et al., 2005; Zadra, Desjardins, & Marcotte, 2006).

A biologically based theory is the **activation-synthesis theory** (Hobson & McCarley, 1977), which suggests that dreaming is just a consequence of the highly aroused brain during REM sleep, when the brain shows activation of millions of

**manifest content**   according to Freud, what the dreamer recalls on awakening

**latent content**   according to Freud, the symbolic meaning of a dream

**threat simulation theory (TST)** suggests that dreaming is an ancient biological defense mechanism that allows us to repeatedly simulate potentially threatening situations so that we can rehearse our responses to these events

**activation-synthesis theory**   suggests that dreams do not have symbolic meaning, but are the by-product of the brain's random firing of neural impulses during REM sleep

random neural impulses. The cortex of the brain attempts to create meaning out of these neural impulses by synthesizing them into familiar images or stories based on our stored memories. These images and stories may reflect our past, our emotions, our personal perspectives, and information accessed during waking (Hobson, Pace-Schott, & Stickgold, 2000), but they have no hidden "Freudian" meaning. However, because we are the ones who integrate these images into a plot, the storyline may provide us with insights about ourselves (McCarley, 1998).

Obviously, our understanding of the purpose and meaning of dreaming is incomplete. Dreams aside, sleep research indicates that not everyone always gets a good night's sleep. Some of us exhibit sleep disturbances, our next topic of discussion.

## Sleep Disorders: Tossing and Turning—and More

It is estimated that 95% of Americans experience a **sleep disorder**, or a disturbance in the normal pattern of sleep, at some point in their lives (Dement & Vaughan, 1999). Sleep disorders also affect approximately 25% to 40% of children and adolescents (Meltzer & Mindell, 2006). Sleep disorders include *insomnia, narcolepsy, sleep apnea, sleepwalking, night terrors,* and *enuresis.*

### INSOMNIA: THERE IS HELP!

**Insomnia**, the most commonly reported sleep disorder, is the inability to get to sleep and/or stay asleep. Occasional insomnia is quite common, with more than a third of American adults reporting insomnia in the last year (Roth, 2005). Insomnia is associated with a multitude of factors, including stress, coping with the loss of a loved one, a change in sleep schedule, obesity, chronic pain, drug abuse, anxiety, or depression (Roth, Krystal, & Lieberman, 2007).

Insomnia can be treated medically using antianxiety or sedative medications such as Xanax or Ambien, or by taking over-the-counter medications such as Sominex and Nytol that contain antihistamines and pain relievers to induce sleepiness. However, long-term use of these drugs may lead to dependence and serious side effects, including memory loss, fatigue, and increased sleepiness. Chronic insomnia is best treated with a combination of taking medication for a limited time, cognitive-behavioral therapy (which focuses on changing thoughts and behaviors that interfere with restful sleep—discussed more in Chapter 14), and following several sleep guidelines that have evolved from our study of how we sleep (Bootzin & Rider, 1997; Morin et al., 2009; Riemann & Perlis, 2009; Roth, Krystal, & Lieberman, 2007):

> ### You Asked...
>
> *Are there ways to avoid insomnia? Are there ways to help it?*
>
> KAYLA CAMPANA, STUDENT

- Establish a regular sleep–wake cycle to work with your body's circadian rhythm. Go to bed at the same time every evening and wake up at the same time every morning. Even if you have difficulty falling asleep at night, continue to get up at the same time each morning.
- Avoid long naps during waking hours. Naps can disrupt your circadian rhythm. What about children who take daily naps and adults who take a "power nap" or siesta? Children's naps and siestas typically occur at the same time every day and thereby work with, rather than against, the circadian rhythm. Power naps are short periods of rest (15–20 minutes) that are relaxing and that can reenergize the body and mind; because they are short, they generally do not interfere with our sleep cycles (Milner & Cote, 2009).

**sleep disorder**   a disturbance in the normal pattern of sleeping

**insomnia**   a sleep disorder in which a person cannot get to sleep and/or stay asleep

- Don't use your bed for anything other than sleeping. For example, people with insomnia should not eat, study, work, or watch television in bed. The bed should be associated only with sleeping.
- If you can't get to sleep after 15 minutes, get up and do something that you think will make you tired enough to get to sleep, such as reading (but not in your bed). Then try again to fall asleep.
- Avoid sleeping pills, alcohol, cigarettes, and caffeine. These are all drugs that can interfere with your natural sleep cycle and disrupt REM sleep. A glass of milk before bedtime, however, may be helpful. Milk helps the body produce serotonin, a neurotransmitter that regulates sleep (see Chapter 2).
- Exercise during the day can promote good sleep. However, avoid physical workouts within an hour of bedtime. Your body should be relaxed prior to sleeping.
- Turn off your cell phone prior to sleeping. Anticipating incoming text messages or calls, as well as the vibration or sound that occurs when a message or call is received, interrupts the natural sleep cycle and makes deep sleep less likely (Van den Bulck, 2003, 2007).

## NARCOLEPSY AND CATAPLEXY

**Narcolepsy**, a rare sleep disorder that affects approximately 140,000 to 250,000 Americans, occurs when a person falls asleep during alert times of the day (Zeman et al., 2004). This is not the same as a microsleep, though. The person with narcolepsy experiences brief periods of REM sleep that may be accompanied by muscle paralysis, a condition called *cataplexy*. Cataplexy occurs in about 70% of people with narcolepsy (American Psychiatric Association, 2000a). People with narcolepsy may fall down or otherwise injure themselves during these episodes. Narcolepsy is thought to stem from a loss of neurons in the hypothalamus of the brain. These neurons are responsible for producing a chemical, called *hypocretin*, that helps to control the sleep–wake cycle (J. M. Siegel & Boehmer, 2006; Nishino, 2007; Zeitzer, Nishino, & Mignot, 2006). Those with the condition typically take *modafinil* to improve wakefulness (Becker et al., 2004; Gallopin et al., 2004; Roth, Schwartz, et al., 2007) and *sodium oxybate*, the only FDA-approved medication for cataplexy (Thorpy, 2007).

**narcolepsy [NAR-co-lep-see]**    a rare sleep disorder in which a person falls asleep during alert activities during the day

**sleep apnea [APP-nee-uh]**    a sleep disorder in which a person stops breathing during sleep

## SLEEP APNEA AND SIDS

**Sleep apnea** is a disorder in which a person stops breathing while sleeping. In an attempt to get air, people with sleep apnea often emit loud snores or snorts that may awaken them or their partners. This pattern may occur hundreds of times during the night. People afflicted may feel sluggish, tired, irritable, or unable to concentrate the next day because of the nighttime sleep disruption (Naegele et al., 1995). Obesity, being overweight, and the use of alcohol or sedatives increase one's chances of developing sleep apnea (Ball, 1997; Pillar & Lavie, 2011; Resta et al., 2001). Once diagnosed, sleep apnea may be treated in various ways. If obesity is a factor, a weight-loss program is the first treatment. In addition, a nasal mask (called a Continuous Positive Airway Pressure, or CPAP, device) that blows air into the nose to facilitate continuous breathing can be worn at night. Wearing mouth retainers can help in some cases. In severe cases, removing the tonsils or surgery to alter the position of the jaw can be

A Continuous Positive Airway Pressure, or CPAP, device blows air into the nose to facilitate continuous breathing for people who have sleep apnea.

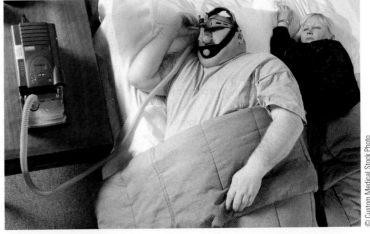

© Custom Medical Stock Photo

# Hypnosis: Real or Imagined?

> **You Asked...**
>
> *How does hypnosis work?*
>
> LAURA FERNANDEZ, STUDENT

**Hypnosis** is a method occasionally used by researchers and psychologists (and frequently by hypnotists) to create a state of heightened suggestibility in others. This section describes the experience of hypnosis, explains several theories about how hypnosis occurs, and explains what hypnosis can and cannot do for you. Note that not all psychologists are hypnotists, and not all hypnotists are psychologists.

Typically, if you are undergoing hypnosis, you are asked to focus on an object, an image, or the hypnotist's voice. For several minutes, you are told that you are getting sleepy and becoming more relaxed (Druckman & Bjork, 1994). You don't fall asleep—though EEG brain-wave patterns of hypnotized people show an increase in alpha waves—and this isn't followed by the non-REM pattern of sleep stages discussed earlier (Graffin, Ray, & Lundy, 1995). After inducing you into this relaxed hypnotic state, the hypnotist makes suggestions about what you are seeing, feeling, or perceiving. For example, one suggestion might be to lift your left arm over your head. A more complex suggestion might be that your eyelids feel as though they are glued shut and you cannot open them. Although accounts vary widely, many hypnotized people report that they feel as though they are floating or that their bodies are sinking. Under hypnosis, they remain in control of their bodies and are aware of their surroundings (Kirsch & Lynn, 1995).

**hypnosis**   a state of heightened suggestibility

## Hypnotic Susceptibility

> **You Asked...**
>
> *What kind of people does hypnosis work on?*
>
> DANIE LIPSCHUTZ, STUDENT

*Hypnotic susceptibility* is the ability to become hypnotized. Some people have a low degree of susceptibility—they cannot easily be hypnotized. Others have a high susceptibility, meaning that they can be easily hypnotized. One well-known standard test for measuring the degree to which people respond to hypnotic suggestions is the *Stanford Hypnotic Susceptibility Scale*. The scale assesses your suggestibility to certain tasks while in a state of hypnosis with a trained hypnotist. The tasks range from pulling apart your interlocked fingers to hallucinating the presence of a buzzing fly.

Contrary to what you may see on television or in the movies, research using such measures has found that not everyone can be hypnotized. The critical factor appears to be whether you want to be hypnotized, rather than the skill of the hypnotist (Kirsch & Lynn, 1995). About 10% of adults are extremely difficult to hypnotize (Hilgard, 1982).

Not everyone can be hypnotized. You have to want to be hypnotized and believe it will work for you.

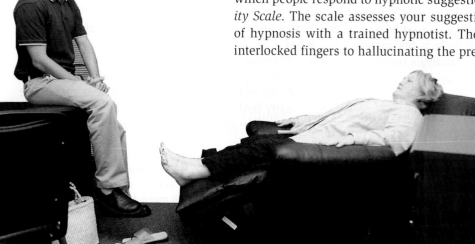

© AP Photo/News Tribune/Stephen Brooks

People who are easily hypnotized tend to be better able to focus their attention (Crawford, Brown, & Moon, 1993; Egner, Jamieson, & Gruzelier, 2005; Raz, 2005), have vivid imaginations (Silva & Kirsch, 1992; Spanos, Burnley, & Cross, 1993; Terhune, Cardena, & Lindgren, 2010), and have positive expectations about hypnosis (Bates, 1994). Neuroimaging studies even document differences in brain activation between people who are highly hypnotizable and those who are low in hypnotic susceptibility (Naish, 2010; Nash, 2005; Raz, Fan, & Posner, 2006). Hypnotic suggestibility does not appear to be related to such factors as intelligence, gender, sociability, or gullibility (Kirsch & Lynn, 1995), although in one study (Page & Green, 2007), female undergraduates did score higher than males on the Harvard Group Scale of Hypnotic Susceptibility.

## Explaining Hypnosis: Is It an Altered State?

Currently, two theories seek to explain hypnosis: *dissociation theory* and the *response set theory*. Ernest Hilgard's (1977, 1992) **dissociation theory** suggests that hypnosis is truly an altered state of consciousness: a person feels, perceives, and behaves differently than in a conscious state. To dissociate means to split or break apart. Hilgard maintains that under hypnosis, your consciousness divides into two states. One level of your consciousness voluntarily agrees to behave according to the suggestions of the hypnotist. However, at the same time, a *hidden observer* state exists. This hidden observer is aware of all that is happening.

We all engage in dissociation at times. Have you ever driven to a familiar location and realized when you arrived that you couldn't consciously remember driving there? Have you ever dissociated in a class—paying attention to the lesson while at the same time doodling or mentally organizing the rest of your day? If you have experienced any of these behaviors, then you are familiar with the concept of dissociation. Hilgard believes that hypnosis works in much the same way, allowing the person to attend to the hypnotist's suggestions while still being aware of what is happening through the hidden observer.

In a classic demonstration, Hilgard hypnotized participants and suggested that they would feel no pain. The participants were then instructed to submerge one arm in ice-cold water. When Hilgard asked them whether they felt pain, the participants replied "No." However, when they were asked to press a key with their other hand if they felt pain, the participants did so. On one level, they agreed with the hypnotist that there was no pain, while at the same time a part of them indicated that there was pain (Hilgard, Morgan, & MacDonald, 1975).

Another view, the **response set theory of hypnosis** (Kirsch, 2000; Kirsch & Lynn, 1997; Lynn, 1997), asserts that hypnosis is *not* an altered state of consciousness. Rather, hypnosis is merely a willingness to respond appropriately to suggestions. Several studies do support that people's response expectancies influence their responsiveness to hypnosis (Benham et al., 2006; Milling, Reardon, & Carosella, 2006). Highly hypnotizable people enter hypnosis with the intention of behaving as a "hypnotized person" and hold the expectation that they will succeed in following the hypnotist's suggestions. Their intentions and expectations trigger their positive response to being hypnotized. Nonhypnotized participants show behaviors similar to those of hypnotized people, such as behaving in strange ways or acting like a young child, simply because they are willing to do what the hypnotist asks them to do (Dasgupta et al., 1995; Kirsch, 1994).

**dissociation [dis-so-see-AYE-shun] theory**   Hilgard's proposal that hypnosis involves two simultaneous states: a hypnotic state and a hidden observer

**response set theory of hypnosis**   asserts that hypnosis is not an altered state of consciousness, but a cognitive set to respond appropriately to suggestions

# Psychoactive Drugs

## LEARNING OBJECTIVES

- Define tolerance, substance dependence, and substance abuse, and explain how psychoactive drugs work.

- Identify depressants, opiates, stimulants, and hallucinogens, and describe the effects these types of drugs have on behavior.

**Psychoactive drugs** are substances that influence the brain and thereby a person's behavior. Over the past 25 years, millions of teenagers and children in the United States have routinely been educated about the effects of drugs. The most popular of these programs, Drug Abuse Resistance Education, or DARE, began in 1983. Yet despite widespread education programs, many misperceptions about drugs still exist. For example, can you name the three most widely used psychoactive drugs in American society? The three drugs most commonly used by Americans over the age of 12 are alcohol, nicotine, and caffeine (see ■ FIGURE 4.5)—substances that are all legal for adults to use (SAMHSA, 2010a).

In 2009, 47% of people in the United States age 12 or older admitted to having tried an illegal substance at some time in their lives (SAMHSA, 2010a). Illicit drug use is highest among young adults between the ages of 18 and 25, and is higher in males than in females (SAMHSA, 2010a). Substance use in the United States also varies considerably by ethnic group (■ FIGURE 4.6; SAMHSA, 2010a). Multiracial and American Indian/Alaska Native groups have the highest rates of current illegal drug use, and Asians have the lowest. We will discuss the most frequently used drugs and their effects, and describe how these drugs work and how they cause damage. Increasingly, young people are also engaging in nonmedical use of prescription drugs, highlighted in the Psychology Across Generations box.

## Drug Tolerance, Substance Dependence, and Substance Abuse

In order to understand the effects of psychoactive drugs, it is important to establish the scientific meaning of three specific drug terms: *tolerance*, *substance dependence*, and *substance abuse*. Defining these terms will help you understand the effects of different psychoactive drugs.

**Tolerance** has to do with the amount of a drug required to produce its effect. After repeated use of a drug, it is usually the case that more and more of it is

**psychoactive drugs** substances that influence the brain and thereby the individual's behavior

**tolerance** a condition in which after repeated use, more of a drug is needed to achieve the same effect

**FIGURE**

## 4.5

### Drug Use in the United States, Ages 12 and Over, 2009

Caffeine, alcohol, and nicotine (the active ingredient in cigarettes) are the three most commonly used psychoactive drugs in the United States.

*Data from SAMHSA, 2010a, Results from the 2009 National Survey on Drug Use and Health.*

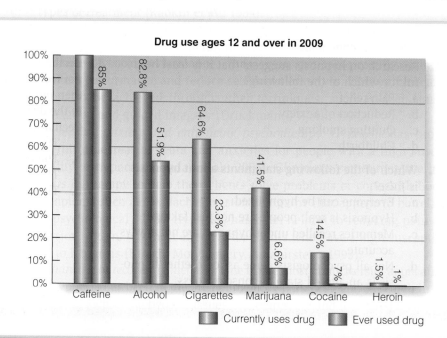

**Drug use ages 12 and over in 2009**

| Drug | Currently uses drug | Ever used drug |
|------|---------------------|----------------|
| Caffeine | 100% | 85% |
| Alcohol | 82.8% | 51.9% |
| Cigarettes | 64.6% | 23.3% |
| Marijuana | 41.5% | 6.6% |
| Cocaine | 14.5% | .7% |
| Heroin | 1.5% | .1% |

■ Currently uses drug    ■ Ever used drug

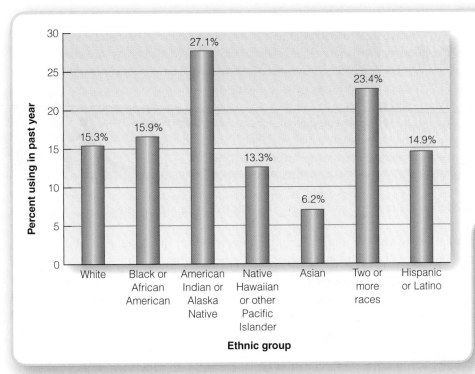

FIGURE

## 4.6

### Ethnicity and Illicit Drug Use

Substance use in the United States varies considerably by ethnic group. Multiracial and American Indian/Alaska Native groups have the highest rates of illegal substance abuse; Asians have the lowest incidence.

*Data from SAMHSA, 2010a, Results from the 2009 National Survey on Drug Use and Health.*

## Psychology Across Generations:

### Generation Rx

Have you ever heard of or been to a "pharm party"? Have you heard of recent state crackdowns on "pill mills"— pain clinics that allegedly dole out narcotic pain relievers? Have you ever taken a prescription medication such as OxyContin or Adderall for a purpose other than prescribed, or do you know of someone who has? Because more young people in the United States are using prescription drugs simply for the experience or feelings the drugs cause, the media have labeled the current generation as "Generation Rx."

Data from the National Survey on Drug Use and Health (Lessenger & Feinberg 2008; SAMHSA, 2010a) support this trend. From 2002 to 2009, the percentage of young adults ages 18 to 25 who reported nonmedical use of prescription drugs during the past month increased from 5.5% to 6.3%; those reporting nonmedical use of pain relievers increased from 4.1% to 4.8%. Intentional abuse of prescription drugs is the second most common type of illegal drug use by young people (marijuana ranks first).

The number of current nonmedical users of prescription drugs in the United States rose in 2009 to 7.0 million, or 2.8% of persons age 12 or older. For teens between the ages of 12 and 17, the rate was 3.1%; among young adults (ages 18 to 25) the rate was 6.3%, compared with 2.1% for adults 26 or older (SAMHSA, 2010a). Increases were seen in the nonmedical use of stimulants, sedatives, and pain relievers. Stimulant medications such as Adderall and Ritalin are commonly prescribed for attention deficit hyperactivity disorder (ADHD). Sedative medications are prescribed to reduce anxiety and promote sleep. They include drugs such as Xanax and Valium. Medications commonly prescribed for pain relief include OxyContin and Vicodin. When asked how they obtained the drugs they recently

*Photo by James Wojcik for New York Magazine*

*(continued)*

used, more than half of the past-year nonmedical users of prescription drugs reported getting the drugs free from a friend or relative. The majority of these respondents indicated that their friend or relative had obtained the drugs from a doctor.

Many young people hold incorrect assumptions about the nonmedical use of prescription drugs. According to the 2005 Partnership Attitude Tracking Study (PATS, 2006), 40% of teens believe that using prescription drugs is safer than using illegal drugs, 33% believe that there is "nothing wrong" with using prescription drugs without a prescription once in a while, 29% mistakenly believe that prescription pain relievers are not addictive, and almost a third believe that prescription medications have fewer side effects than street drugs. Sadly, the nonmedical use of prescription medication may result in the same negative consequences as abuse of other drugs—most notably, dependence, seizures, and death.

needed to achieve the same effect (American Psychiatric Association, 2000a). For example, when someone first drinks alcohol, he or she may have one beer or one glass of wine and get a buzz from it. However, after drinking alcohol frequently, this person will require more beers or glasses of wine to achieve the same effect. This person has increased his or her tolerance for alcohol.

However, as tolerance develops, the difference between a safe dose and a potentially harmful dose, called the *margin of safety*, narrows. Some drugs (like barbiturates) have a very narrow, or small, margin of safety; that is, their too-high, toxic dose differs only slightly from their too-low, ineffectual dose. In order to obtain the same level of intoxication, a user who has developed tolerance may raise his or her dose to a level that may result in coma or death—the too-high, toxic dose.

Related to tolerance is **substance dependence**, which occurs when someone is either physically or psychologically reliant on a drug's effects. Typically, dependence is evident when the person stops using the drug and experiences **withdrawal symptoms**. Withdrawal symptoms may include physical symptoms such as vomiting, shaking, sweating, physical pain, hallucinations, or headaches. People may also experience behavioral withdrawal symptoms when they are deprived of responses or rituals, such as injecting a drug or lighting a cigarette, that help them cope with negative emotions (Baker et al., 2006; S. Siegel, 2005). Not all drugs produce the same withdrawal symptoms. In many cases, people continue to use a drug just to ward off the unpleasantness of the withdrawal effects or emotional distress. Psychologists typically use the term **substance abuse** to indicate that someone has lost control over his or her drug use.

**substance dependence**  a condition in which a person needs a drug in order to maintain normal functioning

**withdrawal symptoms**  physical or behavioral effects that occur after a person stops using a drug

**substance abuse**  loss of control over one's drug use

## How Drugs Work: Biology, Expectations, and Culture

> **You Asked...**
>
> *What do drugs really do to humans?*
> JOSE MORENO, STUDENT

Psychoactive drugs alter your state of functioning by interfering with the normal workings of the nervous system. Some drugs slow down normal brain activity, whereas others speed it up. Typically, drugs achieve these effects by interfering with or mimicking neurotransmitters in the brain (Chapter 2).

Psychological factors also influence a drug's effect. Exposure to stress or trauma increases a person's vulnerability to drug dependence (Goeders, 2004; Rohrbach et al., 2009). Environmental stimuli such as where a drug is taken or whether drug paraphernalia are present become associated with drug taking and later trigger the craving for the drug sensation (Crombag & Robinson, 2004; S. Siegel, 2005). If you expect a drug to alter your behavior in a particular way, you are more likely to change your behavior to fit your expectations. For example, in several studies people who believed they had consumed alcohol behaved as if they

Is the behavior of these fans due to alcohol or to their expectations of alcohol?

© David Young-Wolff/PhotoEdit

had been drinking, regardless of whether they had actually consumed any alcohol (Leigh, 1989). Their behavior was influenced by their *expectations* about the effects of alcohol (Abrams & Wilson, 1983; McMillen, Smith, & Wells-Parker, 1989).

One's culture also influences drug use. For example, rates of alcohol abuse are very low in China, where traditional beliefs scorn alcohol use or being under the influence of alcohol. People in China are not only less likely to drink alcohol, they are also less likely to advertise the fact that they have been drinking. In contrast, Korean men have a high rate of alcohol abuse, and Korean Americans have higher rates of alcohol use than other Asian American subgroups (SAMHSA, 2006). Their culture encourages drinking in social situations (Helzer & Canino, 1992).

The variety of psychoactive drugs in use today can be classified into four main groups: *depressants*, *opiates*, *stimulants*, and *hallucinogens*. ■ YOU REVIEW 4.1 provides a summary comparing the effects of these drugs. We'll begin with depressants.

## YOU REVIEW 4.1

### Psychoactive Drugs and Their Effects

The four groups of substances most often leading to substance dependence are (1) depressants, (2) opiates, (3) stimulants, and (4) hallucinogens.

| SUBSTANCE | TRADE NAMES; STREET NAMES | MEDICAL USES | ROUTE OF ADMINISTRATION | MAIN EFFECTS |
|---|---|---|---|---|
| **Depressants** | | | | |
| Alcohol | Beer, wine, liquor | Antidote for methanol poisoning, antiseptic | Oral, topical | Relaxation; lowered inhibitions; impaired reflexes, motor coordination, and memory |
| Barbiturates | Nembutal, Seconal, Phenobarbital; *barbs* | Anesthetic, anticonvulsant, sedative, relief of high blood pressure | Injected, oral | Anxiety relief, euphoria, severe withdrawal symptoms |
| Benzodiazepines | Librium, Rohypnol, Valium, Xanax; *roofies, tranks* | Antianxiety, sedative, sleeping disorders | Injected, oral | Anxiety relief, irritability, confusion, depression, sleep problems |
| **Opiates** | | | | |
| Codeine | Tylenol with codeine, Fiorinal with codeine | Pain relief, antitussive | Injected, oral | Euphoria, constipation, loss of appetite |
| Heroin | *Horse, smack* | None | Injected, smoked, sniffed | Euphoria, pain control, constipation, loss of appetite |
| Methadone | Amidone, Methadose | Pain relief, treatment for opiate dependence | Injected, oral | Relief from withdrawal symptoms, constipation, loss of appetite |
| Morphine | Roxanol | Pain relief | Injected, oral, smoked | Euphoria, pain control |
| Opium | Laudanum; *Dover's powder* | Pain relief, antidiarrheal | Oral, smoked | Euphoria, pain control |

*(continued)*

| SUBSTANCE | TRADE NAMES; STREET NAMES | MEDICAL USES | ROUTE OF ADMINISTRATION | MAIN EFFECTS |
|---|---|---|---|---|
| Stimulants | | | | |
| Caffeine | Coffee, tea, soda, chocolate, energy drink | Treatment for migraine headaches | Oral | Alertness, insomnia, loss of appetite, high blood pressure |
| Nicotine | Nicorette gum, Nicotrol; *cigars, cigarettes, snuff* | Treatment for nicotine dependence | Smoked, sniffed, oral, transdermal | Alertness, calmness, loss of appetite |
| Cocaine | *Coke, crack, rock, snow, blow* | Local anesthetic; vasoconstrictor in Europe | Injected, smoked, sniffed | Increased energy, excitation, insomnia, loss of appetite, mood swings, delusions, paranoia, heart problems |
| Amphetamine | Dexedrine; *black beauties, crosses* | ADHD, obesity, narcolepsy | Injected, oral, smoked, sniffed | Increased alertness and energy, insomnia, loss of appetite, delusions, paranoia |
| Methamphetamine | *Crank, crystal, ice, meth* | ADHD, short-term aid to weight loss | Injected, oral, smoked, sniffed | Mood elevation, alertness, insomnia, loss of appetite, anxiety, paranoia |
| MDMA | *Adam, Ecstasy, XTC* | None | Oral | Increased insight and emotion, muscle tension, sleep problems, anxiety, paranoia |
| Hallucinogens | | | | |
| Marijuana | *Grass, herb, pot, reefer, weed, sinsemilla* | Glaucoma, nausea from chemotherapy | Oral, smoked | Relaxation, altered perceptions, sleep problems, paranoia, amotivation |
| Phencyclidine | PCP; *angel dust, hog* | Anesthetic (veterinary) | Injected, oral, smoked | Euphoria, unpredictable moods, hostility |
| LSD | *Acid, microdot* | None | Oral | Altered perceptions, distortion of senses, panic reactions, flashback effects |

## Alcohol and Other Depressants

**Depressant** drugs interfere with brain functioning by inhibiting or slowing normal neural functioning. In *low* doses, depressants often cause a feeling of well-being, or a "nice buzz." Anxiety is reduced when the nervous system slows down. This may be why many people mistakenly believe that alcohol is an "upper." In high dosages,

**depressants**  drugs that inhibit or slow down normal neural functioning

depressants can cause blackouts, coma, or death. The deaths of Anna Nicole Smith, Heath Ledger, and Michael Jackson were attributed in part to overdoses of depressants. Depressants are usually grouped into *alcohol*, *barbiturates*, and *sedatives*.

## HEALTH EFFECTS OF ALCOHOL

Alcohol affects the neurotransmitter GABA, which is related to anxiety levels. As noted earlier, in low dosages, alcohol may make one feel more sociable and relaxed. Alcohol also depresses the functioning of the cerebral cortex. So, in addition to feeling calm and relaxed, we are more likely to shed our inhibitions in regard to our thoughts and behaviors (Giancola et al., 2010; Koob & Bloom, 1988; Stahl, 1996). When we drink alcohol, we are more willing to be silly or aggressive, share our emotions, or engage in behaviors that we would think twice about if we were sober.

Alcohol also inhibits the functioning of the brain stem, impairing motor functioning and coordination. Reaction time and reflexes are slowed. When your tolerance is exceeded, your speech becomes slurred and your judgment is impaired. It is also harder for your brain to sustain attention, process information, and form new memories (Givens, 1995; Tsai, Gastfriend, & Coyle, 1995; Sayette, Reichle, & Schooler, 2009).

Heavy drinking on college campuses across Europe and the United States has led to a growing concern about the effects of binge drinking. *Binge drinking* is excessive alcohol use over a short period of time that brings a person's blood alcohol concentration (BAC) to 0.08 percent or above. This often happens when males consume five or more drinks and when females consume four or more drinks in two hours (National Institute of Alcohol Abuse and Alcoholism, 2004). Binge drinking is two times higher among males than females (Kanny, Liu, & Brewer, 2011) and puts one at risk for later developing an alcohol use disorder (Crabbe, Harris, & Koob, 2011). Binge drinking and alcohol use may cause *memory blackouts*—after a heavy night of drinking, you may not remember the events of the night before. Chronic alcohol use can lead to *Korsakoff's syndrome*, a memory disorder caused by a deficiency of vitamin B (thiamine). A person who is an alcoholic often substitutes alcohol for more nutritious foods, which results in numerous vitamin deficiencies. Unfortunately, these memory deficits tend to be irreversible.

Because drinking alcohol results in reduced inhibitions, people are more likely to engage in sexual activity (M. L. Cooper, 2002; Davis et al., 2009; Patrick & Maggs, 2009). However, alcohol impairs sexual performance. It makes it more difficult for a male to get and maintain an erection. The ability to achieve orgasm is also hampered by the effects of alcohol. We may think and feel that we are better lovers when under the influence of alcohol, but in reality we are not.

Because ingested alcohol crosses the placenta, women who drink alcohol heavily during pregnancy put their unborn child at risk for **fetal alcohol syndrome (FAS)**. Children born with FAS tend to have low birth weight; exhibit limb, head, and facial deformities; and suffer brain abnormalities that retard intellectual functioning and cause difficulties in learning, memory, problem solving, and attention (Ikonomidou et al., 2000; Kumada et al., 2007; Young, 1997). Because of the negative effects of alcohol on prenatal development, even moderate drinking during pregnancy is not recommended.

Does everyone experience the same effects from alcohol? No. The degree to which each of us experiences these effects depends on several factors. For example, alcohol has either more or less effect depending on

**fetal alcohol syndrome (FAS)**
a birth condition resulting from the mother's chronic use of alcohol during pregnancy; characterized by facial and limb deformities and intellectual impairment

Alcohol's effect on motor coordination can be seen in a police sobriety test.

© Corbis

your tolerance level: the higher your tolerance, the more alcohol you can consume before feeling its effects. Another factor is the rate of consumption. The faster you drink, the faster the alcohol is absorbed into the blood, increasing the alcohol's effect. Gender influences alcohol's effect as well. Metabolic and weight differences between males and females make it easier for male bodies to tolerate higher levels of alcohol (York & Welte, 1994). ■ TABLE 4.1 describes the typical effects of alcohol at increasingly higher blood concentrations.

## TABLE 4.1
### Typical Effects of Blood Alcohol Concentrations (BAC)

ALCOHOL INTOXICATION VARIES GREATLY AMONG INDIVIDUALS. SOME PEOPLE BECOME INTOXICATED AT LOWER BLOOD ALCOHOL CONCENTRATION LEVELS.

| BAC | TYPICAL EFFECTS |
| --- | --- |
| .02–.03 | Slight euphoria and loss of shyness; light-headedness. Depressant effects of alcohol are not yet apparent. |
| .04–.06 | Feelings of well-being, relaxation, and lowered inhibitions; minor impairment of reasoning and memory; lowered alertness |
| .07–.09 | Feelings of well-being; slight impairment of balance, speech, vision, reaction time, and hearing; reduced judgment and self-control; impaired reasoning and memory |
| .10–.125 | Significant impairment of motor coordination; loss of judgment; slowed thinking; slurred speech; impairment of balance, vision, reaction time, and hearing |
| .13–.15 | Gross motor impairment and lack of physical control; blurred vision and major loss of balance; severely impaired judgment. Feelings of well-being are reduced. |
| .16–.20 | Anxiety, restlessness, sadness; nausea and vomiting; feeling dazed and confused; blackouts |
| .25 | Severely impaired physical and mental abilities; increased risk of injury by falls or accidents |
| .30 | Stupor; little comprehension of whereabouts; loss of consciousness |
| .35 | Possible coma |
| .40+ | Onset of coma; possible death due to respiratory arrest |

## ALCOHOL AND GENETICS

Research suggests a possible genetic factor in alcohol's effect (Stacey, Clarke, & Schumann, 2009). Studies of twins show that if one identical twin is an alcoholic, the other twin has almost a 40% chance of developing a drinking problem. Rates for fraternal twins are much lower (Prescott et al., 1994). Research on sons of alcoholic fathers also suggests a possible genetic predisposition to alcohol dependence. The sons are likely to have an overall higher tolerance for alcohol, requiring more alcohol before feeling its effects, and are therefore at greater risk for abusing alcohol (Schuckit & Smith, 1997). More recently, researchers have located specific strands of genes that regulate the function of GABA. These genes vary across families with multiple members who have alcohol problems and may contribute to a person's vulnerability to alcoholism (Edenberg & Foroud, 2006; Krystal et al., 2006; Soyka et al., 2008).

Cultural studies also support a possible genetic link. In some ethnic groups, such as Japanese and Chinese, drinking alcohol can cause facial flushing. This sudden reddening of the face is a genetic trait that rarely occurs in Europeans. The physical and social discomfort of facial flushing tends to reduce the rate of alcohol consumption and alcoholism in these groups. People in ethnic groups that do not experience facial flushing are more likely to become alcoholics (Helzer & Canino, 1992).

However, environmental factors such as learning also play a role. Children of alcoholics have an increased risk of developing alcoholism that cannot be attributed solely to genetics. As adults, they are more likely to cope with personal or work-related stress by imitating the behavior of an alcoholic parent (Blane, 1988; Rivers, 1994). Clearly, the effects of alcohol and whether one becomes an abuser of alcohol depend on the interaction among genetic, cultural, individual, and environmental factors.

## SOCIAL COSTS OF ALCOHOL USE

Alcohol dependence is devastating to individuals, families, and society in general. According to the National Highway Transportation Safety Administration, almost 32% of all traffic deaths in the United States are alcohol-related (NHTSA, 2008). Alcohol-impaired driving is highest for people between the ages of 16 and 25 and more common for males than for females (Centers for Disease Control and Prevention, 2002; Chou et al., 2006; SAMHSA, 2010b). More than half of rapists report that they drank alcohol before committing their crime. In college campus surveys, alcohol plays a role in the majority of sexual assaults and rapes. More than half of spousal abuse incidents involve alcohol (Adler & Rosenberg, 1994; Camper, 1990; Seto & Barbaree, 1995). Millions of children who live with alcoholic parents are also seriously affected. High levels of conflict—as well as physical, emotional, and sexual abuse—are likely in these households (Mathew et al., 1993).

Alcohol abuse also has economic costs. Alcohol abuse is associated with excessive absenteeism, lost productivity at work, and higher rates of on-the-job injury. These costs tend to be significantly higher for heavy drinkers (Fisher et al., 2000; Gorsky, Schwartz, & Dennis, 1988; Jones, Casswell, & Zhang, 1995). Alcohol-related car accidents cost about $51 billion each year in the United States (Blincoe et al., 2002). Alcohol, contrary to the beer commercials, is indeed dangerous to our health and our society.

Alcohol-impaired driving tragically affects families and friends.

© AP/Jack Kustron

The combined effects of pain medications and depressant drugs were a major factor in the death of Michael Jackson.

## BARBITURATES AND SEDATIVES

Barbiturates, commonly called "downers," are a category of depressants that are typically prescribed to reduce anxiety or to induce sleep. Well-known barbiturate drugs include Nembutal and Seconal. Sedatives or tranquilizers are also prescribed to reduce anxiety. They include a class of drugs called the *benzodiazepines*, including Valium and Xanax. Both types of depressants have effects similar to alcohol. In small dosages, they slow the nervous system, promoting relaxation. In high dosages, though, they severely impair motor functioning, memory, and judgment. Like alcohol, these drugs influence the functioning of the neurotransmitter GABA (Barbee, 1993). When these drugs are taken in combination with alcohol, they are potentially lethal because they can cause suppression of those brain areas that control breathing and heart rate, which can lead to unconsciousness, coma, or death.

You may have heard of the tranquilizer called Rohypnol ("roofies"), commonly known and used as a *date rape drug*. It is placed in a woman's drink at a party or club without her knowledge or consent, and the combined effect of alcohol and Rohypnol renders her unconscious. In this state she is then sexually assaulted or raped. In the morning, because of the drugs' effects on memory, she may not recall the event (Navarro, 1995).

When used as prescribed, barbiturates and sedatives can be helpful in the short-term treatment of anxiety disorders and sleeping problems such as insomnia. However, over the long term, there is a risk of dependence. Long-term use of tranquilizers leads to memory loss and actually heightens anxiety. When the effect of the drug has worn off, the body goes into "overdrive" to overcome its depressing effects (McKim, 1997). Withdrawal from these drugs can be brutal and includes convulsions, hallucinations, and intense anxiety.

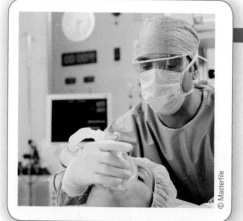

## Neuroscience Applies to Your World:

### Psychoactive Drugs and General Anesthesia

Many people who have surgery receive general anesthesia, in which a combination of barbiturate, sedative, and narcotic drugs is used to induce unconsciousness and immobility, block pain, and cause the patient to forget the surgery and the time right after it. These drugs may be administered as injections or as inhaled gases. General anesthetics affect the whole brain and the entire body. The 2007 horror movie *Awake* dramatizes a condition called *anesthesia awareness*, in which general anesthetics fail and the person can hear or feel what is happening to him or her during surgery. Anesthesia awareness is actually quite rare, affecting roughly 2 out of every 1,000 surgery patients (Pollard et al., 2007; Sebel et al., 2004). In an attempt to minimize the amount of drugs given during surgery, neuroscientists are currently investigating safer, site-specific anesthetic drugs.

## Opiates (Narcotics): Morphine, Codeine, Opium, and Heroin

The **opiates**, or narcotics, are drugs that are used to treat pain by mimicking pain-inhibiting neurotransmitters in the body such as endorphins. Opiates include morphine, codeine, opium, and heroin, although heroin and opium are not considered or prescribed as a medicine. While depressing some brain areas, these drugs create excitation in other brain areas. In addition to blocking pain, they produce a feeling of pleasure that is almost like floating on a cloud or being in a dreamlike

**opiates [OH-pee-ates]** painkilling drugs that depress some brain areas and excite others

state (Bozarth & Wise, 1984). The opiates are extremely addictive, causing dependence within a few weeks. When you take opiates, your brain recognizes an abundance of pain inhibitors in the body and decreases its own production of endorphins. So when the effect of the opiate wears off, you feel your earlier pain *and* the absence of pleasure, and will want another, larger dose (Hughes et al., 1975; Zadina et al., 1997). It is for this reason that health professionals monitor narcotic administration so closely.

Physical withdrawal symptoms related to opiate use include hot and cold flashes, cramps, sweating, and shaking. These symptoms typically last from 4 to 7 days, but they are not life-threatening. What *is* life-threatening is the risk of overdose. Street concentrations of narcotic drugs such as heroin and opium can vary widely. In addition, a person's sensitivity to opiates may fluctuate on a daily basis (Gallerani et al., 2001). The user never knows, therefore, if the concentration of drug he or she is taking will exceed the body's ability to handle it. There is an added risk of contracting HIV/AIDS and hepatitis C from using contaminated needles because opiates are often injected into a vein.

Currently, many heroin addicts are treated with the chemical *methadone* or buprenorphine. Each reduces the unpleasantness of the withdrawal symptoms yet does not produce the intense high of heroin. They are both equally effective in treating heroin dependence (Fiellin, Friedland, & Gourevitch, 2006; Payte, 1997; Vigezzi et al., 2006).

## Stimulants: Legal and Otherwise

The **stimulants** include drugs that interfere with brain functioning by speeding up normal brain activity. Five stimulant substances we will review are *caffeine*, *nicotine*, *cocaine*, *amphetamines*, and *MDMA (Ecstasy)*.

### CAFFEINE: JAVA JITTERS

Because many of us wake up each morning reaching for that cup of coffee or that can of Monster or Red Bull to get us going, we may not even consider caffeine a mind-altering drug. Yet caffeine is a psychoactive drug because of its effects on the brain. It is perhaps the most frequently used psychoactive drug in the world. Caffeine is an active ingredient in coffee, tea, sodas, some energy drinks, chocolate, migraine headache medications, and some diet pills. It stimulates the brain by blocking neurotransmitters (primarily adenosine) that slow down our nervous system and cause sleep (Julien, 1995). In small doses, caffeine gives us a boost, keeping us more alert and helping us focus. It helps problem solving and decreases reaction time (Warburton, 1995). However, in large doses, caffeine can "wire" you, causing insomnia, upset stomach, racing heartbeat, nervousness, and irritability.

Regular caffeine use can lead to dependence. If you suddenly stop drinking coffee or kick your cola habit, you will likely experience headaches, irritability, tiredness, and flu-like symptoms (Schuh & Griffiths, 1997). These withdrawal symptoms, even if they aren't severe, can last a week. Excessive caffeine use increases the risk of high blood pressure and encourages the development of fibroid cysts in women's breasts. Pregnant women in particular should reduce caffeine intake because high amounts of caffeine are associated with an increased risk of miscarriage and have been linked with birth defects (Infante-Rivard et al., 1993). Young people today often mix energy drinks high in caffeine with alcohol, as described in the Psychology Applies to Your World box.

**stimulants**   drugs that speed up normal brain functioning

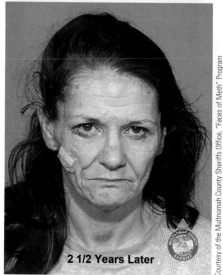

2 1/2 Years Later

Courtesy of the Multnomah County Sheriffs Office, "Faces of Meth" Program

Methamphetamine abuse can radically alter one's physical appearance as it causes skin lesions and tooth decay.

## AMPHETAMINES

Amphetamines, called "uppers" or "speed," have effects similar to those of cocaine. The high produced by these drugs is less intense but generally lasts longer (a few hours). Currently, the most abused form of amphetamine is *methamphetamine*, commonly called crystal meth, ice, chalk, or crank. According to the 2009 National Survey on Drug Use and Health (NSDUH), 5% of the U.S. population age 12 or over has used crystal meth at least once (SAMHSA, 2010a). Approximately 4.1% of college students and 8.3% of young adults between the ages of 19 and 28 have tried methamphetamine (NIDA & University of Michigan, 2006).

Methamphetamine, like cocaine, affects dopamine, serotonin, and norepinephrine levels in the brain (Volkow et al., 2001). The result is enhanced mood and pleasure, energy, alertness, and reduced appetite. Heart rate and blood pressure also increase. Like cocaine, methamphetamine leads to a crash to low energy levels, paranoia, and depressed mood when the effects of the drug have subsided. However, methamphetamine remains present in the brain longer than cocaine. It not only blocks the reuptake of dopamine but also increases the release of dopamine, leading to a more toxic effect on the central nervous system (NIDA, 2006b). Continued use results in insomnia, paranoia, agitation, confusion, violent behavior, memory loss, and dependence. Methamphetamine use can also cause strokes, cardiovascular problems, and extreme anorexia. An overdose can cause coma and death. Users who inject the drug and share needles are also at risk for acquiring HIV/AIDS and hepatitis C (Bezchlibnyk-Butler & Jeffries, 1998).

## MDMA (ECSTASY)

In its "pure" form, Ecstasy is called MDMA, but street Ecstasy, Adam, or XTC typically contains other drugs such as amphetamine, ketamine, caffeine, and ephedrine (Walters, Foy, & Castro, 2003). MDMA's use dramatically increased as a "club drug" in the 1990s and early 2000s, particularly among college students and young adults. In 2009, 5.7% of people in the United States over the age of 12 reported having used Ecstasy at some point in their lives (SAMHSA, 2010a), including 4.3% of U.S. high school seniors (Johnston et al., 2009). Use has been spreading beyond predominately European American youth to African American and Hispanic populations (Boeri, Sterk, & Elifson, 2004; Maxwell & Spence, 2003), and Ecstasy has become a popular drug among urban gay males (NIDA, 2006a).

Taken orally, usually in a tablet or a capsule, Ecstasy enhances mood and energy levels and heightens users' sensations. Users report increased self-confidence, increased feelings of love and warmth toward others, emotional openness, and lack of inhibition (Fry & Miller, 2002). The effect begins very fast, within half an hour of consumption, and lasts approximately 3 to 6 hours. Negative effects of Ecstasy use are insomnia, teeth clenching, nausea, increase in heart rate and blood pressure, fatigue, and blurred vision. Most of these negative effects subside within 24 hours. Paranoia, depression, drug craving, overheating, cardiac problems, kidney failure, seizures, strokes, and/or loss of touch with reality may also occur (Bezchlibnyk-Butler & Jeffries, 1998).

Although MDMA increases the activity of several neurotransmitters in the brain, it is the serotonin pathway that has received the most attention. Ecstasy binds to the serotonin transport protein so that the availability of free serotonin increases (Britt & McCance-Katz, 2005; Colado, O'Shea, & Green, 2004). The long-term effects of Ecstasy use on the human brain have not yet been determined (Cowan, 2007). However, disrupted sleep patterns and subtle, persistent deficits in memory have been documented (Kuypers, Wingen, & Ramaekers, 2008; McCann et al., 2009; Randall et al., 2009). It also is unclear whether Ecstasy shares properties with the hallucinogens. Users regularly report hallucinations, but it is impossible to know whether they have really been using pure MDMA or have bought low doses of LSD instead.

## Hallucinogens: Distorting Reality

**Hallucinogens** are drugs that interfere with brain functioning by simultaneously exciting and inhibiting the nervous system. These contrasting effects often cause distortions in perception, or *hallucinations*. Hallucinogenic substances include *marijuana*, *PCP*, and *LSD*.

### MARIJUANA

Marijuana, also called pot, reefer, or weed, is a mild hallucinogen. It rarely, if ever, leads to overdoses that cause death (Zimmer & Morgan, 1997). Fifteen states and the District of Columbia currently allow for its medicinal use. It has been prescribed for medical conditions such as glaucoma, chronic pain, and nausea from cancer chemotherapy and has been found moderately effective in clinical trials for muscle spasms and multiple sclerosis (Croxford, 2003; Grinspoon & Bakalar, 1995; Iverson, 2003; Klein & Newton, 2007). It is also the most widely used illegal substance in the United States, with 41.5% of people over the age of 12 reporting having tried the drug. Past-year usage is highest among 17- to 24-year-olds, and males report higher usage than females. American Indian and multiracial groups report the highest use and Asian Americans the lowest (SAMHSA, 2010a).

The active ingredient in marijuana is **THC (tetrahydrocannabinol)**. THC is absorbed by the lungs and produces a high that lasts for several hours. THC binds to the neurotransmitter called anandamide that influences learning, short-term memory, motor coordination, emotions, and appetite—behaviors that are all affected when people are high on marijuana (Matsuda et al., 1990). In low doses, THC makes users feel good and experience vivid sensations. THC also slows reaction time and impairs judgment and peripheral vision. For this reason, marijuana users are just as dangerous driving a car or operating machinery as users of other drugs. Marijuana use also interferes with memory, disrupting both the formation of memories and the recall of information (Nestor et al., 2008; Pope & Yurgelun-Todd, 1996; Ranganathan & D'Souza, 2006). Its stimulation of appetite and increased sensitivity to taste may result in an attack of the "munchies." In high doses, THC may produce hallucinations, delusions, paranoia, and distortions in time and body image (Hanson & Venturelli, 1998; Morrison et al., 2009). Long-term marijuana use can lead to dependence. Many people report mild withdrawal symptoms when marijuana use is stopped, including irritability, sleeplessness, decreased appetite, anxiety, and drug cravings (Z. D. Cooper & Haney, 2008; de Fonseca et al., 1997; Grinspoon et al., 1997; Stephens, Roffman, & Simpson, 1994; Vandrey et al., 2008; Wickelgren, 1997).

Studies on long-term users of marijuana have shown long-lasting cognitive effects including impaired attention, learning, and motor coordination (Pope & Yurgelun-Todd, 1996; Volkow et al., 1996). However, permanent structural changes in the brain have not been identified with chronic use (Quickfall & Crockford, 2006). Marijuana also has serious long-term health effects. Because it is typically smoked, users may experience respiratory problems such as bronchitis and lung damage (Tashkin, 2005).

**hallucinogens [huh-LOO-sin-no-gens]** drugs that simultaneously excite and inhibit normal neural activity, thereby causing distortions in perception

**THC (tetrahydrocannabinol) [tet-rah-high-dro-can-NAH-bin-all]** the active ingredient in marijuana that affects learning, short-term memory, coordination, emotion, and appetite

Although controversy continues over the medicinal uses of marijuana, smoking pot increases one's chances of respiratory problems and lung damage.

Uriel Sinai/Getty Images

night terrors (136)
nightmare (136)
non-REM sleep (130)
opiates (150)
psychoactive drugs (142)
REM behavior disorder (132)
REM rebound (132)

REM sleep (130)
response set theory of hypnosis (139)
sleep apnea (135)
sleep disorder (134)
sleepwalking (136)
stimulants (151)
substance abuse (144)

substance dependence (144)
suprachiasmatic nucleus (SCN) (128)
THC (tetrahydrocannabinol) (155)
threat simulation theory (TST) (133)
tolerance (142)
withdrawal symptoms (144)

## What Do You Know? Assess Your Understanding

Test your retention and understanding of the material by answering the following questions.

**1.** Which of the following is *not* a benefit of sleep?
  a. Increased alertness
  b. Memory processing
  c. Decreased immunity to disease
  d. Enhanced mood

**2.** Marco is 62 and Isaac is 22. Which of these men requires more sleep at night?
  a. Marco
  b. Isaac
  c. Both men require the same amount of sleep.
  d. Marco needs more non-REM sleep, and Isaac needs more REM sleep.

**3.** Alfred is just falling asleep. His brain waves most likely resemble _____ waves.
  a. beta          c. sleep spindle
  b. delta         d. theta

**4.** Which of the following brain waves is most likely to occur during slow-wave sleep?
  a. Beta          c. Delta
  b. Alpha         d. Theta

**5.** Benita often wakes up in the morning feeling very tired, despite sleeping 9–10 hours. Her partner has noticed that she often emits loud snores and seems to have erratic breathing while she is sleeping. Benita most likely has which sleep disorder?
  a. Narcolepsy
  b. Sleep apnea
  c. Night terrors
  d. Enuresis

**6.** Recent research suggests a relationship between the sleep spindles of stage II sleep and _____.
  a. processing of motor skills
  b. body restoration
  c. storage of memories
  d. growth hormone

**7.** Dr. Surrell believes that dreaming evolved to help us rehearse potentially harmful events. Dr. Surrell is endorsing which dream theory?
  a. Freudian theory
  b. Activation synthesis theory
  c. Continuity hypothesis
  d. Threat simulation theory

**8.** When Kaitlin wakes up in the morning, she recalls having a dream that toads were invading her room. According to Freud, Kaitlin's recall is an example of _____.
  a. latent content
  b. manifest content
  c. survival themes
  d. the continuity hypothesis

**9.** Why is melatonin referred to as the "Dracula hormone"?
  a. Because it decreases during the day
  b. Because it increases at night
  c. Both a and b
  d. Neither a nor b

**10.** EEG brain-wave patterns of people who are hypnotized show an increase in _____ waves.
  a. theta          c. beta
  b. delta          d. alpha

**11.** Which of the following is not a documented use of hypnosis?
  a. Decreasing anxiety
  b. Relieving pain
  c. Recovering memories
  d. Enhancing therapy

**12.** People who are easily hypnotized tend to have which of the following traits?
  a. Positive expectations about hypnosis
  b. Higher intelligence
  c. Higher sociability
  d. All of the above

**13.** Which of the following drugs is a depressant?

a. Cocaine    c. Caffeine

b. Nicotine    d. Alcohol

**14.** Paz now needs more alcohol to get high than she did when she first started drinking. Paz has developed _____ alcohol.

a. substance abuse for

b. tolerance to

c. withdrawal from

d. substance dependence for

**15.** Howe has been using methamphetamine for several months now. If he stops taking the drug, which of the following is he most likely to experience?

a. Paranoia

b. Enhanced mood

c. Reduced appetite

d. High energy

**16.** Which of the following variables influences a drug's effects?

a. How much of the drug is taken

b. Your tolerance to the drug

c. Your expectations about the drug's effects

d. All of the above

**17.** The feeling of well-being that results from most illicit drug use is due to the activity of which of the following neurotransmitters?

a. Dopamine    c. Acetylcholine

b. Serotonin    d. Endorphins

**18.** After taking LSD several months ago, Sven still experiences visual disturbances and dramatic mood swings. Sven is most likely experiencing _____.

a. flashbacks    c. persistent psychosis

b. twittering    d. tweaking

**19.** While at a nightclub one weekend, Aoki had a drug slipped into her drink that made her "pass out" and have no recall of the events of the evening. What type of drug was most likely put in Aoki's drink?

a. Hallucinogen    c. Stimulant

b. Sedative    d. Opiate

**20.** Which of the following drugs is most likely to be prescribed to reduce pain?

a. Stimulant    c. Hallucinogen

b. Depressant    d. Opiate

Answers: 1. c; 2. b; 3. d; 4. c; 5. b; 6. a; 7. d; 8. b; 9. c; 10. d; 11. c; 12. a; 13. d; 14. b; 15. a; 16. d; 17. a; 18. c; 19. b; 20. d

## Online Resources

Log in to **www.cengagebrain.com** to access the resources your instructor requires. For this book, you can access:

### Psychology CourseMate

CourseMate brings course concepts to life with interactive learning, study, and exam preparation tools that support the printed textbook. A textbook-specific website, Psychology CourseMate includes an integrated interactive eBook and other interactive learning tools including quizzes, flashcards, videos, and more.

### CENGAGENOW™

CengageNOW Personalized Study is a diagnostic study tool containing valuable text-specific resources—and because you focus on just what you don't know, you learn more in less time to get a better grade.

### WebTutor

More than just an interactive study guide, WebTutor is an anytime, anywhere customized learning solution with an eBook, keeping you connected to your textbook, instructor, and classmates.

# LOOK BACK
## AT What You've LEARNED

**Consciousness** includes the feelings, thoughts, and aroused states of which we are aware. Altered states of consciousness occur when we sleep, are hypnotized, or take any psychoactive drug.

## Sleep, Dreaming, and Circadian Rhythm

- When teenagers and adults get at least 8 hours of sleep, the benefits include restored body tissues, body growth, immunity to disease, an alert mind, processing of memories, and enhanced mood.

- The **circadian rhythm** of sleep is a natural rhythm of sleep and waking programmed by a group of brain cells in the hypothalamus called the **suprachiasmatic nucleus**.

- A typical night of sleep involves cycling through two states of sleep: **non-REM sleep**, which progressively relaxes the person; and **REM** (rapid-eye-movement) **sleep**, which is very active.

- Freud believed that dreams allow us to express fears and desires without conscious censorship. Many psychologists and psychiatrists dispute Freud's emphasis on sex and aggression in interpreting dreams.

- **Threat simulation theory** proposes that dreaming is an evolved defense mechanism that allows us to rehearse our responses to threatening situations.

- **Activation-synthesis theory** suggests that dreaming is just a consequence of the highly aroused brain during REM sleep.

- **Insomnia** is the inability to get to sleep or to stay asleep. It is the most common sleep disorder.

- Other sleep disorders include **sleep apnea**, in which a person stops breathing while asleep, and a rarer condition called **narcolepsy**, in which a person falls asleep during alert times of the day.

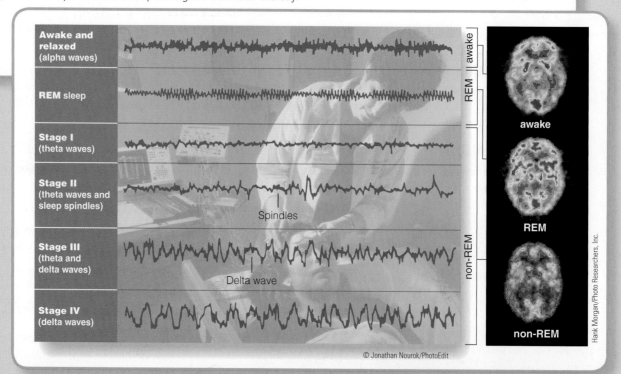

© Jonathan Nourok/PhotoEdit

Hank Morgan/Photo Researchers, Inc.

## Hypnosis: Real or Imagined?

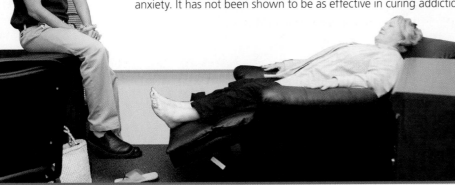

- **Hypnosis** is a technique used to create a state of heightened suggestibility. Hypnosis usually involves being asked to mentally focus on an object, image, or the hypnotist's voice, thus inducing a deeply relaxed state.

- Hypnotic susceptibility varies greatly and does not seem to be related to intelligence, gender, or sociability. People who are easily hypnotized tend to be better able to focus their attention, have vivid imaginations, and have positive expectations about hypnosis.

- Hypnosis has been shown to be effective for some people in providing pain relief and decreasing anxiety. It has not been shown to be as effective in curing addictions or recovering accurate memories.

## Psychoactive Drugs

- **Psychoactive drugs** are substances that influence the brain and therefore the behavior of a person.

- Drug **tolerance** refers to the amount of a drug required to produce its effects. After repeated use of a drug, more of it is usually needed to achieve its initial effect.

- **Substance dependence** refers to a person's need of a drug in order to function emotionally and/or physically.

- **Depressants** such as alcohol, sedatives, and barbiturate drugs interfere with brain functions by inhibiting or slowing normal neural function.

- **Opiates** such as morphine, codeine, and opium are used to treat pain by mimicking the effects of neurotransmitters such as endorphins.

- **Stimulants** are drugs such as caffeine, nicotine, cocaine, and amphetamines that interfere with brain functioning by speeding up normal brain activity.

- **Hallucinogens**, including marijuana and LSD, are drugs that interfere with brain functioning by simultaneously exciting and inhibiting normal neural activity. These contrasting effects often cause disruptions in perception or hallucinations.

# 5 How Do We LEARN?

## Chapter Outline

*Amber Brandt is an early* childhood education major who hopes one day to work with special needs children. In her present job as a supervisor of a YMCA Almost-Teens Afterschool Program, Amber puts her knowledge of psychology to work every day. Amber is responsible for leading group activities that teach pre-teens character-building skills. To help her students build their character, Amber has to find ways to combat the negative aspects of outside influences such as Facebook and the media's depiction of violence, sex, and ideal body image—all of which can affect a child's self-esteem and behavior. In managing classroom behavior, Amber must find ways to reward her students' good behavior, while at the same time ridding them of their bad behaviors. Sometimes she accomplishes this with simple interventions, such as asking an angry child to sit in a quiet place and write down the feelings he is experiencing. Other times, she places well-behaved students together in activity groups with students who are struggling, allowing the more successful students to act as role models for those who need a bit of guidance. When she works with younger children in the play center, Amber often uses enticements such as turning on the bubble machine and giving prizes to get students to clean up the playroom.

As you will see in reading this chapter, Amber's methods are applications of the learning theories developed by psychologists. After mastering this material, we bet that you too will find many ways to apply it in your personal life. Understanding how we learn is the first step to changing behavior in ourselves and others.

Amber Brandt puts her knowledge of learning into practice at her job working with Almost-Teens at the YMCA.

# Learning in Its Simplest Form: Habituation

**LEARNING OBJECTIVES**

● Define learning.

● Define and give examples of orienting reflexes, habituation, and dishabituation.

**You Asked...**

*Does everyone have the ability to learn?*

CANDACE KENDRICK, STUDENT

Our favorite definition of **learning** is *a relatively permanent change in behavior, or the potential for behavior, that results from experience.* Learning results from many experiences in life. We learn concepts and skills in school. We learn from watching others. And we learn certain skills, like riding a bike, by doing them. Learning may show up in our behavior (as when we ride a bike), or it may not (as when we get a speeding ticket even though we've learned that speeding is wrong). Learning may stay with us for years (as with riding a bike), or it may only linger for a while (as when we observe the speed limit for only a few weeks after getting a ticket).

All healthy humans have the capacity for some form of learning. In this chapter, we will look at four common types of learning, beginning with what is widely thought to be the simplest form of learning—*habituation*.

## Paying Attention and Learning to Ignore: Orienting Reflexes and Habituation

Suppose you are sitting in class, listening to your psychology professor and taking notes. All of a sudden there is a loud banging noise directly outside your classroom. What would your very *first* reaction to the unexpected noise be? If you are like most people, you would immediately stop listening to the lecture and turn your head in the direction of the noise. This very normal response is called an **orienting reflex** (Pavlov, 1927/1960). Orienting reflexes occur when we stop what we are doing to orient our sense organs in the direction of unexpected stimuli.

In our example, the stimulus was auditory, but this doesn't have to be the case. If you were standing in line to buy coffee and someone poked you in the back, you would most likely turn to see what the person wanted. If you were having dinner in a restaurant and someone started taking pictures using a flash camera, you would likely look in the direction of the flashes of light. In short, we exhibit the orienting reflex to any type of novel stimulus.

**learning** a relatively permanent change in behavior, or behavior potential, as a result of experience

**orienting reflex** the tendency of an organism to orient its senses toward unexpected stimuli

Many professors have policies discouraging lateness because when a student arrives late to class, the opening door causes everyone in the room to have an orienting reflex. As they look toward the door, their concentration is broken and learning suffers.

**YOUR TURN** Active Learning

Your course syllabus probably contains some admonishment about coming to class on time. Here's one reason why: Notice what happens to you and your classmates the next time a student comes in late to class. Does everyone automatically look toward the door as the student comes through it? This is also an orienting reflex—one that distracts from your ability to learn the course material.

© Bill Aron/PhotoEdit

Why do you think we exhibit orienting reflexes? What is the benefit of automatically paying attention to novel stimuli? If you said "self-protection," you would be correct. Orienting reflexes allow us to quickly gather information about stimuli that could potentially be threatening. For instance, that banging noise in the hallway could be a student dropping her books, or it could be a fight. In the case of a fight, you may want to take steps to ensure that the fight doesn't affect you in a negative way. By orienting your senses toward the event, you can quickly assess what, if any, action is needed to protect yourself.

The benefit of having orienting reflexes is limited, though. Suppose that after looking up at the sound of the banging, you see that it is only a worker hammering as he installs a new bulletin board in the hallway. You would likely return your attention to the psychology lecture. If the banging noise continues, your tendency to look up at the noise in the hall would steadily decrease. In other words, your orienting reflex would diminish over time. This decrease in responding to a stimulus as it is repeated over and over is called **habituation.**

After people live in these houses for a while, habituation will ensure that they barely even notice the sounds of jets like this one as they take off and land.

Despite its name, habituation does not refer to forming a habit. Instead, habituation ensures that we do not waste our energy and mental resources by responding to irrelevant stimuli. In our previous example, after you have established that the noise in the hallway is not threatening, there is no reason to keep looking. If you did keep exhibiting the orienting reflex, you would needlessly miss part of your psychology lecture and waste energy that could be spent more usefully.

Almost all creatures, including those with very simple nervous systems, seem to have the capacity for habituation (Harris, 1943). This universality implies that habituation is the simplest type of learning seen in living things (Davis & Egger, 1992). Habituation can be seen in newborn infants (Lavoie & Desrochers, 2002; Rose, 1980) and even in fetuses (Van Heteren et al., 2000). Recent studies have suggested that the cerebellum, which is part of the more primitive hindbrain (see Chapter 2), plays a role in certain instances of habituation (Frings et al., 2006). These findings seem to indicate the primitive nature of habituation.

## The Benefits of Habituation

To get a better feel for the value of habituation, imagine what life would be like if you could *not* habituate. Without habituation, you would reflexively respond to every sight, sound, touch, and smell you encountered every time you encountered it. You would not be able to ignore these stimuli. Think of how this would limit your ability to function. Every time the worker hammered the bulletin board in the hall, your attention would move away from the lecture and toward the hall. You certainly would not learn much psychology under these circumstances! With habituation, you get the best of both worlds. You can respond to novel stimuli that may pose a danger, and you can also ignore stimuli that have been checked out and deemed to be harmless. Habituation gives you flexibility in that you don't

**habituation [huh-bit-chew-AYE-shun]**
the tendency of an organism to ignore repeated stimuli

## Neuroscience Applies to Your World:

### What Causes Migraines?

Many people experience intense headaches called *migraines*. These debilitating headaches are frequently characterized by severe pain on one side of the head and can be associated with sensitivity to light, nausea, or vomiting. Some migraine sufferers also experience visual disturbances, called auras, which signal the impending onset of a migraine. In searching for the causes of migraines, researchers have uncovered some interesting information. First, having a specific genetic marker called the MTHFR C677T is correlated with a higher likelihood of having migraines, especially migraines with auras. This genetic marker is also associated with having higher levels of a chemical called homocysteine in the body (see de Tommaso et al., 2007). Second, researchers have discovered that migraine sufferers often appear to have a lessened ability to habituate to stimuli, perhaps at a neuronal level (Reyngoudt et al., 2011). For example, migraine sufferers showed less ability than non–migraine sufferers to habituate to a stressful sound (Huber, Henrich, & Gündel, 2005). This suggests that migraine suffers may have less ability to tune out stressful stimuli, which may lead to hyperactivity in the brain that results in migraine pain. In fact, when migraine sufferers are taught to increase their levels of habituation to environmental stimuli, they tend to experience fewer migraine attacks (see Kropp, Siniatchkin, & Gerber, 2002). Studies like these suggest that one function of habituation may be to protect our nervous system from sensory overload.

have to continue to respond to a stimulus. Habituation may also serve to protect our brains from overstimulation, as you can see in the Neuroscience Applies to Your World box. But does this mean that once you have habituated to a stimulus, you must ignore it forever?

## Dishabituation

Another aspect of this flexibility is that you can *stop* habituating when the circumstances warrant it. **Dishabituation** occurs when an organism begins to respond more intensely to a stimulus to which it has previously habituated. Let's return to our example of the worker in the hallway. Although you find the hammering distracting at first, you soon habituate to the sound. Then, after several minutes of ignoring the steady hammering, you hear a new sound. The worker has turned on a radio at a rather high volume. Will you ignore this sound, too? No, you likely will not. Because the quality of the stimulus has changed dramatically, you will dishabituate. You will again find yourself orienting toward the hallway. This new sound is too dissimilar to the hammering, and you have to check it out. Once you recognize that it is the worker's radio (and that it poses no threat), you will likely habituate to this new sound as well as to the hammering.

A change in the quality of the stimulus is not the only thing that can cause dishabituation. So can the passage of time. For instance, if the worker took an hour-long lunch break and then went back to hammering, you might briefly dishabituate to the hammering. This would not last long, however—after just a few bangs of the hammer, you would reenter habituation and return your attention

**dishabituation [DIS-huh-bit-chew-AYE-shun]**    re-responding to a stimulus to which one has been habituated to the lecture. As you can see, adaptive functioning is a balance of responding—habituating and dishabituating at the appropriate time.

## Practical Applications of Habituation

One practical application of habituation is the use of habituation training for people who experience chronic motion sickness, or *vertigo*. For some vertigo sufferers, simple tasks like working at a computer may be impossible. Physical therapists often use habituation techniques to help people overcome chronic motion sickness. By repeatedly exposing clients to the stimulation that produces motion sickness, the therapist can gradually train these clients to habituate, or stop responding, to some of the visual and vestibular signals that would normally cause them to feel sick (Childs, 2011; Yardley & Kirby, 2006). Similar techniques have been used to train figure skaters (Tanguy et al., 2008), pilots, and astronauts to do their jobs without experiencing motion sickness (e.g., Bagshaw, 1985).

Habituation is quite important to everyday life, but it is still a very simple type of learning. Habituation does not explain the bulk of the learning that we engage in during our lifetime, such as learning to play tennis or ride a bike. Nor does habituation explain how we come to associate certain emotions and physiological reactions with certain stimuli, such as learning to fear snakes or feeling happy when we smell Grandma's perfume. For explanations of these more complex events, we will have to turn our attention to more sophisticated and complex types of learning, discussed in the next section.

## REVIEW

This section has given you an overview of the simplest type of learning, habituation, and the related concepts of orienting reflexes and dishabituation. For a quick check of your understanding, answer these questions.

1. Which of the following is an example of habituation?
   a. Juan was teasing the family dog when it bit him. Because of the pain of the bite, Juan learned not to tease the dog again.
   b. Teresa was trying to learn to knit. At first, Teresa had to consciously think about what she was doing, but after practicing for 3 hours, Teresa could knit without thinking about it.
   c. Janel just bought a new puppy. At first, the dog's barking was distracting to Janel as she tried to watch TV, but after a while Janel did not notice the puppy's barking.
   d. Kerry loved her boyfriend very much. Now that they have broken up, every time she hears his favorite song on the radio, Kerry starts to cry.

2. Fido the puppy tilts his head up and sniffs the air as he smells his owner cooking dinner in the kitchen. Fido is exhibiting _____.
   a. habituation
   b. dishabituation
   c. an orienting reflex
   d. a & c

3. Which of the following would likely have the capacity for habituation?
   a. A 3-month-old human baby
   b. An adult monkey
   c. An adult dog
   d. All of the above

Answers 1. c; 2. c; 3. d

# Classical Conditioning: Learning Through the Association of Stimuli

The discovery of classical conditioning was something of an accident. Around the turn of the 20th century, a Russian physiologist named Ivan Pavlov (1849–1936) was doing research on the digestive processes of dogs (for which he would eventually win a Nobel Prize). Pavlov was investigating the role that salivation plays in digestion. He had surgically implanted devices in the cheeks of dogs so that he could measure how much saliva they produced. His experimental method was to place the dog in a harness, present the dog with some food, and then measure the amount of saliva the dog produced (see ■ FIGURE 5.1).

While conducting these studies, Pavlov noticed that sometimes the dogs began to salivate *before* the food was presented to them. Sometimes the mere sight of the food dish or the sound of the approaching experimenter was enough to produce salivation. So what was going on? Why would a dog start to salivate when it heard footsteps or saw an empty food bowl? Pavlov reasoned that the dog had learned to *associate* certain cues or stimuli with the presentation of food. To the dog, the approach of footsteps had come to mean that food was soon going to appear. Consequently, the dog had become *conditioned*, or taught, to respond to the footsteps the same way that it responded to the food—by salivating. Unwittingly, Pavlov had discovered a learning process, one that would become extremely influential in psychology.

Pavlov began to investigate the learning process itself. He systematically paired different stimuli with food to see which could be conditioned to produce the reflexive response of salivation. In one of these investigations, Pavlov sounded a buzzer just before he gave the dog some food. He repeated these trials several times while measuring the amount of saliva the dog produced. After repeated pairing of the buzzer and the food, the dog soon began to salivate on hearing the buzzer—even on trials in which *the food was not presented after the buzzer sounded*. The dog had become conditioned to associate the buzzer with the presentation of food. As a result, the buzzer had taken on the same power as food to cause the dog to salivate.

**FIGURE**

# 5.1

**Pavlov's Original Experiment**

The dog was held in the harness and food was placed before it. The presence of the food (unconditioned stimulus, or US) caused the dog to salivate (unconditioned response, or UR). After a while, cues in the laboratory situation (lights, sounds, or sights) became conditioned stimuli (CS) that also caused the dog to salivate (conditioned response, or CR).

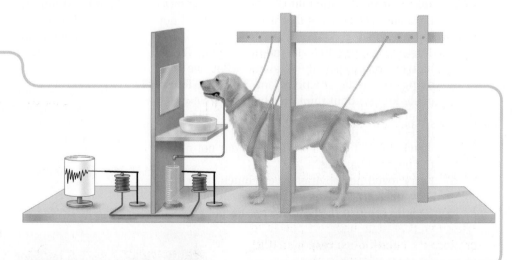

## The Elements of Classical Conditioning

The process of learning that Pavlov discovered is commonly referred to as *classical conditioning*, or *Pavlovian conditioning*. We will formally define it in a minute, but first let's look at the process that produces a conditioned response:

**1.** *The unconditioned stimulus and response.* In order to classically condition a person or animal, you must begin with a stimulus that naturally and reliably causes some response in the organism. Because this stimulus naturally causes the reflexive response, it is referred to as an **unconditioned stimulus (US)**, and the response it evokes is called an u**nconditioned response (UR)**. The term unconditioned refers to the fact that the association between the stimulus and the response is not learned. In Pavlov's case, the food was the unconditioned stimulus, and salivation was the unconditioned response. You do not need to teach a dog to salivate when food is presented. Instead, salivation occurs naturally when a dog sees food. ■ TABLE 5.1 gives some more examples of US–UR pairs that could be used in classical conditioning.

**2.** *The neutral stimulus.* The next step is the selection of a **neutral stimulus (NS)** that does *not* naturally elicit the unconditioned response. In Pavlov's case, the neutral stimulus used was a buzzer. Prior to training or conditioning, a dog would not be likely to salivate when it heard a buzzer. Therefore, the buzzer is said to be *neutral*. It has no power to naturally cause the UR.

**3.** *Pairing the neutral stimulus and the unconditioned stimulus.* The third step is to systematically pair the neutral stimulus with the unconditioned stimulus. Pavlov accomplished this by repeatedly sounding the buzzer (NS) just prior to presenting the dog with the food (US). Through this repeated association of the US and the NS, the NS eventually loses its neutrality. In Pavlov's case, the dog began to salivate when the buzzer was presented without the food. At this point, classical conditioning had occurred because the buzzer was no longer neutral. The buzzer had become a **conditioned stimulus (CS)** that had the power to produce the **conditioned response (CR)** of salivation (■ FIGURE 5.2).

**unconditioned stimulus (US)** a stimulus that naturally elicits a response in an organism

**unconditioned response (UR)** the response that is elicited by an unconditioned stimulus

**neutral stimulus (NS)** a stimulus that does not naturally elicit an unconditioned response in an organism

**conditioned stimulus (CS)** a stimulus that elicits a conditioned response in an organism

**conditioned response (CR)** the response that is elicited by a conditioned stimulus

**TABLE 5.1**
**Some Examples of US–UR Pairs**

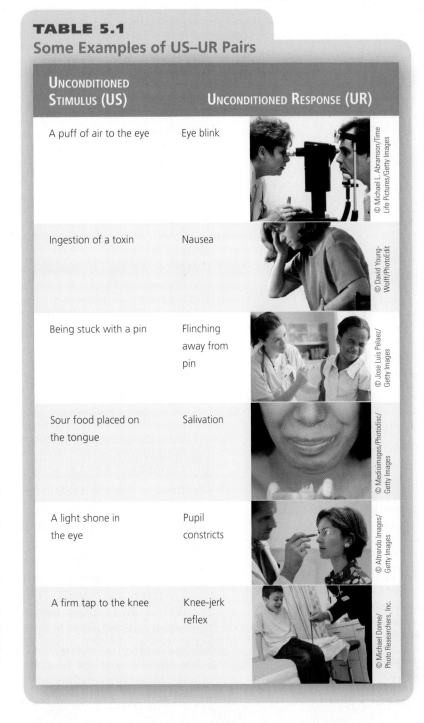

| UNCONDITIONED STIMULUS (US) | UNCONDITIONED RESPONSE (UR) |
|---|---|
| A puff of air to the eye | Eye blink |
| Ingestion of a toxin | Nausea |
| Being stuck with a pin | Flinching away from pin |
| Sour food placed on the tongue | Salivation |
| A light shone in the eye | Pupil constricts |
| A firm tap to the knee | Knee-jerk reflex |

© Michael L. Abramson/Time Life Pictures/Getty Images

© David Young-Wolff/PhotoEdit

© Jose Luis Pelaez/Getty Images

© Medioimages/Photodisc/Getty Images

© Altrendo Images/Getty Images

© Michael Donne/Photo Researchers, Inc.

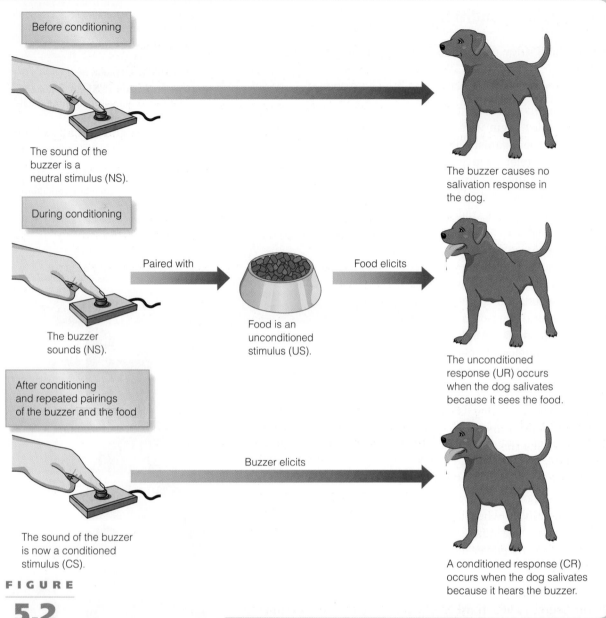

Before conditioning

The sound of the buzzer is a neutral stimulus (NS).

The buzzer causes no salivation response in the dog.

During conditioning

Paired with

The buzzer sounds (NS).

Food is an unconditioned stimulus (US).

Food elicits

The unconditioned response (UR) occurs when the dog salivates because it sees the food.

After conditioning and repeated pairings of the buzzer and the food

Buzzer elicits

The sound of the buzzer is now a conditioned stimulus (CS).

A conditioned response (CR) occurs when the dog salivates because it hears the buzzer.

FIGURE

# 5.2

### Pavlov's Classical Conditioning Procedure

Before conditioning, the neutral stimulus has no power to cause the response. After repeated pairings of the neutral stimulus with an unconditioned stimulus, which naturally elicits an unconditioned response, the neutral stimulus becomes a conditioned stimulus with the power to elicit the response—now called the conditioned response.

**classical conditioning**    learning that occurs when a neutral stimulus is repeatedly paired with an unconditioned stimulus; because of this pairing, the neutral stimulus becomes a conditioned stimulus with the same power as the unconditioned stimulus to elicit the response in the organism

Summing up classical conditioning in a nice, neat definition is a bit awkward but nonetheless extremely important. Once, when one of us asked a student to define classical conditioning, she replied, "What Pavlov did with his dogs." This isn't, of course, a definition of classical conditioning. It does reflect the student's difficulty in trying to understand the concept of classical conditioning apart from Pavlov's particular demonstration of it, however. Keep in mind that to truly understand a concept, you must be able to define it in abstract terms as well as give an example of it. So here goes.

We would define **classical conditioning** as *learning that occurs when a neutral stimulus is paired with an unconditioned stimulus that reliably causes an unconditioned response, and because of this association, the neutral stimulus loses its neutrality and takes on the same power as the unconditioned stimulus to cause the response.* This definition may seem a bit complex, but classical conditioning is actually a fairly simple process. It merely involves learning to associate two stimuli, the unconditioned stimulus and the neutral stimulus. Through this association, the neutral stimulus becomes a conditioned stimulus (■ YOU REVIEW 5.1). In the next section, we will examine some of the factors that affect the strength of the association.

# YOU REVIEW 5.1    Classical Conditioning

| Abbreviation | Term | Definition |
|---|---|---|
| US | Unconditioned stimulus | A stimulus that naturally and reliably evokes a response in the person or animal |
| UR | Unconditioned response | The response that is naturally and reliably elicited by the unconditioned stimulus |
| NS | Neutral stimulus | A stimulus that does not initially elicit the unconditioned response in the person or animal |
| CS | Conditioned stimulus | A stimulus that was once neutral but, through association with the unconditioned stimulus, now has the power to elicit the response in the animal or person |
| CR | Conditioned response | After conditioning has occurred, the response that is elicited in the person or animal by the conditioned stimulus |

## Factors Affecting Classical Conditioning

Exactly what is being learned in classical conditioning? We said that the organism learns to associate the NS/CS with the US. This is true, but what is the nature of this association? Why do these two particular stimuli become associated? Why did Pavlov's dog associate the buzzer with the food instead of associating other stimuli from the situation with the food? After training, why did the dog no longer begin to salivate when it heard the laboratory door open, or when the laboratory lights turned on? Why did it wait for the buzzer? To answer these questions, psychological researchers have experimentally examined different facets of the relationship between the NS/CS and the US.

### RELATIONSHIP IN TIME: CONTIGUITY

**Contiguity** refers to the degree to which the NS/CS and US occur close together in time. Generally speaking, for classical conditioning to occur, the NS/CS and the US must be separated by only a short period of time (Bangasser et al., 2006; Wasserman & Miller, 1997). If the interval between the presentation of the NS/CS and the US is too long, the two stimuli will not be associated, and conditioning will not occur. If Pavlov had sounded the buzzer and then 3 hours later given the dog some food, it is very unlikely that the dog would have been conditioned to salivate when it heard the buzzer.

Studies have shown that in most cases, if the US lags behind the NS/CS by more than a few seconds, conditioning will not be as strong as it could have been (Church & Black, 1958; Noble & Harding, 1963; M. C. Smith, Coleman, & Gormezano, 1969). The exact length of the optimal time interval varies depending on what response is being conditioned.

Another aspect of contiguity is the relative placement of the NS/CS and the US in time—in other words, whether the NS/CS precedes the US or follows it. Imagine if Pavlov had first given the dog the food and *then* sounded the buzzer. In that case the dog would not have been as likely to associate the food with the buzzer. ■ FIGURE 5.3 shows the five major ways to place the NS/CS and the US in classical conditioning. Of

**contiguity [con-teh-GYU-eh-tee]** the degree to which two stimuli occur close together in time

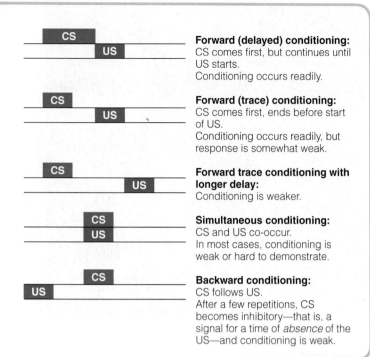

**Forward (delayed) conditioning:**
CS comes first, but continues until US starts.
Conditioning occurs readily.

**Forward (trace) conditioning:**
CS comes first, ends before start of US.
Conditioning occurs readily, but response is somewhat weak.

**Forward trace conditioning with longer delay:**
Conditioning is weaker.

**Simultaneous conditioning:**
CS and US co-occur.
In most cases, conditioning is weak or hard to demonstrate.

**Backward conditioning:**
CS follows US.
After a few repetitions, CS becomes inhibitory—that is, a signal for a time of *absence* of the US—and conditioning is weak.

FIGURE

## 5.3

**Possible Placements of the CS and the US in Classical Conditioning**

Relative positions of the CS and US are shown for five different versions of classical conditioning: forward delayed, forward trace, forward trace with longer delay, simultaneous, and backward conditioning.

**contingency [con-TINGE-en-see]**
the degree to which the presentation of one stimulus reliably predicts the presentation of the other

these placements, *forward (delayed) conditioning* produces the strongest conditioning, and *backward conditioning* produces the weakest conditioning (Klein, 1987).

## CONSISTENCY AND RELIABILITY: CONTINGENCY

Although contiguity is necessary for conditioning, it alone does not guarantee that conditioning will occur. Conditioning also requires **contingency**, which refers to the degree to which the NS/CS reliably signals that the US is going to be presented. If the NS/CS does not reliably predict the onset of the US, then conditioning will not occur (Bolles, 1972; Rescorla, 1967; for a review, see Wheeler & Miller, 2008). For example, if Pavlov had sometimes fed the dog after sounding the buzzer and other times did not feed the dog after sounding the buzzer, conditioning would have been weakened. This inconsistency would not send the dog a clear message that the buzzer meant food was coming. Therefore, the dog would be less likely to salivate on hearing the buzzer. Given that both contiguity and contingency are necessary for strong classical conditioning, the best way to ensure strong conditioning is to consistently present only one NS/CS immediately before presenting the US.

## Real-World Classical Conditioning

The process of classical conditioning seems a bit complex, doesn't it? It also seems as if it could occur only in a laboratory (where stimuli could be systematically paired)—but this is not true. Classical conditioning occurs frequently in everyday life. In fact, each of us has probably felt the effects of classical conditioning many times. For example, we have been classically conditioned to have certain emotional reactions in our lives. You may feel happy when you smell a perfume that reminds you of your mother. You may feel fear when you see a snake.

As you will recall, the starting point for classical conditioning is a preexisting US–UR relationship. Table 5.1 lists some unconditioned stimuli that naturally and reliably evoke unconditioned responses without prior training. These US-UR pairs can be used to produce an initial or *first-order* level of classical conditioning in a person. However, in the real world, sometimes classical conditioning occurs on top of preexisting classical conditioning. This is called *higher-order classical conditioning*. For example, if a snake bites you, the bite (US) may cause a fear (UR/CR) of snakes (CS). This is first-order conditioning. Later, if you see a snake (now a US) in the woods (NS), you may then fear (UR/CR) going into the woods (the new CS). This higher-order conditioning results in a conditioned fear of the woods.

Because of the nature of most unconditioned stimulus–unconditioned response relationships, the types of responses that can be classically conditioned usually fall into two categories: *emotional responses* and *physiological responses*.

## CLASSICAL CONDITIONING OF EMOTIONAL RESPONSES

The classical conditioning of emotional responses was clearly demonstrated in a famous—now infamous—set of experiments conducted by John B. Watson and his student Rosalie Rayner in the early 1900s (Watson & Rayner, 1920). Watson set out to show that classical conditioning could be used to condition fear responses in a child. Because Watson used an 11-month-old boy named Albert, the experiments are now commonly referred to as the "Little Albert" experiments.

In the Little Albert experiments, Watson classically conditioned Albert to fear a white rat. To do this, Watson first gave Albert a white lab rat and allowed him to play with it. In the beginning, the rat was an NS for Albert because it did not cause him to be afraid. A few minutes after giving Albert the rat, Watson made a very loud noise by striking a piece of metal with a hammer. As with most 11-month-olds, a loud noise such as this was a US for Albert that reliably produced the UR of frightening Albert and making him cry. Over and over, Watson repeated this sequence of presenting the rat (NS), then making the noise (US), with the result that Albert would become afraid and cry (UR).

Can you see the parallels here between what Watson and Rayner were doing to Albert and what Pavlov did with his dogs? In the same way that Pavlov conditioned his dogs to salivate at the sound of the buzzer, Watson conditioned Albert to fear a white rat by associating the rat with a frightening noise. After several trials of pairing the noise and the rat, all Watson had to do to get Albert to cry was to show him the rat. Because the rat had been paired with the noise, the rat lost its neutrality and became a CS that was able to evoke the CR of fear.

Emotional reactions such as fear are also classically conditioned outside of the laboratory. For example, one of us once had a professor who had an intense fear of bees because earlier in his life, several bees had stung him after he accidentally disturbed a beehive. In this case of classical conditioning, the multiple bee stings were a US that elicited the UR of fear. The bees were initially an NS, but because they were paired with the bee stings, they became a CS that could produce the CR of fear. From that day onward, all the professor had to do was to see a bee to feel intense fear.

In fact, the professor's fear of bees was so great that it spread to other insects as well. Not only was he afraid of bees, he was also afraid of wasps, yellow jackets, and any other flying insect that could sting. In psychological terms, his fear had undergone **stimulus generalization**, which occurs when stimuli that are similar to the CS have the same power to elicit the CR even though they have never been paired with the US. The professor had never been stung by a wasp, yet he feared them because they are similar to bees.

Stimulus generalization also occurred in the Little Albert experiments. After being conditioned to fear the rat, Albert also exhibited fear when presented with a dog, a rabbit, a fur coat, and a fake white Santa Claus beard. His fear of white rats had generalized to several *furry* things (Watson & Rayner, 1920). This may leave you wondering what happened to Little Albert. Did he suffer through life as a result of his conditioned phobias? Unfortunately, not much is known about Albert's fate. His mother withdrew him from the program and moved away before Watson and Rayner could remove the fear they had conditioned in Albert—leaving future psychologists to debate the ethics of Watson and Rayner's research.

Unlike what happened to Little Albert, all classically conditioned responses do not necessarily generalize. The opposite process, **stimulus discrimination**, often occurs. In stimulus discrimination, the conditioned response occurs in response to a particular

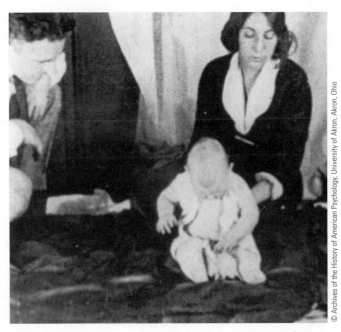

In the Little Albert experiments, John B. Watson and his assistant, Rosalie Rayner, classically conditioned Albert to fear a white lab rat.

**stimulus generalization**   responding in a like fashion to similar stimuli

**stimulus discrimination**   responding only to a particular stimulus

Phobias are classically conditioned responses. A fear-producing encounter with a dog can result in the stimulus—the dog—becoming a conditioned stimulus that elicits fear.

conditioned stimulus, but it does *not* occur in response to other stimuli that are similar to the conditioned stimulus. For instance, a woman who works in the reptile house at the zoo is probably not afraid of most snakes, but if she found herself face to face with a poisonous king cobra, she would likely feel afraid. Sometimes, knowing when to discriminate and when to generalize is important to survival!

## CLASSICAL CONDITIONING OF PHYSIOLOGICAL RESPONSES: TASTE AVERSION

Emotions are not the only responses that can be classically conditioned. Pavlov's original demonstrations of classical conditioning show a physiological response, salivation. But what other kinds of physiological responses can be classically conditioned? Table 5.1 (p. 169) lists some of the US–UR relationships that could form the basis of classical conditioning. Of these, one of the most important and common is the classical conditioning of nausea.

Have you ever eaten a food that you liked and soon after become sick to your stomach with the flu, food poisoning, motion sickness, or some other ailment? Then, after recovering from your sickness, did you find the sight, smell, or even the idea of that food nauseating? If you answered "yes" to both of these questions, you have experienced what psychologists call classically conditioned **taste aversion**.

One of the authors can vividly remember going through this type of conditioning as a child. After she ate a big dessert of peppermint ice cream, she came down with a severe case of tonsillitis that was accompanied by nausea and vomiting. After she recovered from the tonsillitis, it was *years* before she could even think about peppermint ice cream without feeling queasy. The same author regularly holds an informal contest in her classes to see who has had the longest-running taste aversion. The current record stands at more than 20 years!

> ### You Asked...
>
> *Why are some things easier to learn than others?*
>
> CHRISTIE KNIGHT, STUDENT

It seems that taste aversion is something that we learn with particular ease (Garcia & Koelling, 1966). Taste aversion is unique in two ways. First, it often occurs with only one pairing of the NS/CS and the US. Unlike most cases of classical conditioning, in taste aversion, a single pairing of the food (NS/CS) and the agent that initially causes the nausea, in this case a virus (US), is usually sufficient to cause strong conditioning. The second difference is that in taste aversion, the interval between the NS/CS and the US can be very long. Intervals as long as 24 hours can result in conditioning (Garcia, Ervin, & Koelling, 1966; Logue, 1979). Because taste aversion is an exception to some of the rules of conditioning, some psychologists believe that our genes give us a **biological preparedness** to learn taste aversion easily (Seligman, 1970).

By being biologically prepared to learn taste aversion, we are better able to avoid certain poisonous plants and substances. Once something has made us sick, we want no part of it in the future. No doubt the ability to learn taste aversion quickly, and consequently to avoid poisonous substances, has survival value. Therefore, through natural selection, genes that enabled our ancestors to learn taste aversion quickly would have been retained because animals with those genes—human and nonhuman—would have lived, whereas those with a sluggish response to taste aversion would likely die. Taste aversion is widely seen in many species of animals (Garcia, 1992).

In fact, because many other species are also susceptible to taste aversion, it can be used to help control the pesky nature of some animals. In the western United States, coyotes like to sneak into sheep pastures and kill sheep rather than hunt for food in the wild. In the past, frustrated sheep ranchers would be very tempted to either shoot the coyotes on sight or lethally poison them. But thanks to psychologists, ranchers now have a more humane and ecologically sound alternative—using

**taste aversion**    classical conditioning that occurs when an organism pairs the experience of nausea with a certain food and becomes conditioned to feel ill at the sight, smell, or idea of the food

**biological preparedness**    a genetic tendency to learn certain responses very easily

Eating a food and then becoming ill can result in a conditioned taste aversion. The food becomes a conditioned stimulus that results in the conditioned response of nausea.

© Cusp/Flirt/Masterfile

taste aversion to condition the coyotes to dislike sheep as a food source. They slaughter a few sheep and treat their carcasses with a chemical that causes nausea in coyotes. These tainted carcasses are then left out for the coyotes to eat. Because the coyotes can't pass up a free meal, they eat the sheep and get very sick to their stomachs. After they recover, they want nothing to do with sheep because of conditioned taste aversion (Gustavson & Garcia, 1974). The ranchers' problem is solved. Similarly, taste aversion can be used to control problem behaviors in humans—a topic we discuss in the Psychology Applies to Your World box (p. 176).

As you continue to read and study this chapter, keep in mind the general definition of classical conditioning and try to generate your own examples of real-world classical conditioning (perhaps even some of taste aversion). By doing this, you will increase your understanding and retention of this material—both of which will help you on exam day!

## YOUR TURN | Active Learning

You can use taste aversion to help yourself eat more healthily. Think of a food that you frequently overindulge in, but wish you wouldn't (e.g., pizza, candy). Several times a day, imagine a delicious serving of this food. While thinking of this food, also think of something disgusting such as a bunch of worms squirming on your chosen food. If you repeat this procedure for several weeks, you may find yourself less motivated to indulge in this food! In a different approach, psychologists have classically conditioned children to like healthful vegetables by pairing new vegetable flavors with the flavor of sugar to produce liking. After repeated pairings of the vegetables (NS/CS) with pleasant-tasting sugar (US), the children were conditioned to also like the vegetables (UR/CR). After conditioning, the children exhibited liking for the vegetables even when sugar was not present (Havermans & Jansen, 2007). So, initially sprinkling a little brown sugar on carrots might be just the ticket to get children to willingly eat their carrots in the future.

## Extinction of Classically Conditioned Responses

Let's assume that you had the misfortune of developing a classically conditioned taste aversion to your favorite food because you ate this food just before you became ill with the flu. Furthermore, let's assume that you wanted to be able to eat your favorite food again without feeling sick to your stomach. How would you go about ridding yourself of your acquired taste aversion?

In classical conditioning, **extinction**, or removal of the conditioned response, can be brought about by presenting the conditioned stimulus to the participant without also presenting the unconditioned stimulus. In our example, extinction would begin when you ate your favorite food (CS) and you did not have the flu (US). When the CS is presented alone, it no longer predicts the onset of the US, and the CR decreases. Years later, your author finally got over her taste aversion to peppermint ice cream after she took a job in a restaurant that sold a great deal of it. After scooping many scoops of peppermint ice cream, she found that the sight and smell of it no longer made her feel sick. It wasn't long before she was even able to eat peppermint ice cream without a problem.

### You Asked...

*Once you learn something, how long does it stick with you if you never use what you learn? Will it still last for a while, or does it fade quickly?*

TYLER LARKO, STUDENT

**extinction**   the removal of a conditioned response

## Psychology Applies to Your World:

### Using Taste Aversion to Help People

Taste aversion is applicable in several therapeutic settings. One such application is in the treatment of alcoholism. The idea behind this **aversion therapy** is to condition a taste aversion to alcohol. The client takes the drug Antabuse. If he or she then drinks alcohol, the result is intense nausea and headache, which often leads to conditioned taste aversion. One of the authors' (Doyle-Portillo's) father underwent such a treatment for his alcoholism. As a result of the treatment, the smell of any alcohol made him nauseous. Family members even had to stop wearing alcohol-based cologne in his presence for fear of making him sick!

Aversion therapy has been shown to be modestly helpful in motivating people with alcoholism to remain abstinent (J. W. Smith, Frawley, & Polissar, 1997). However, it does not represent a "cure" for alcoholism. In one study, only 20% of the people with alcoholism remained abstinent for 1 year after being treated with aversion therapy alone (Landabaso et al., 1999). So, although aversion therapy with Antabuse may be a useful part of a comprehensive treatment program, it should not be the only treatment used for alcoholism (Finn, 2003; Hunt, 2002). Recently, researchers have found a promising new use for Antabuse. Antabuse appears to intensify the negative effects of cocaine (e.g., anxiety), therefore motivating users to avoid it (Gaval-Cruz & Weinshenker, 2009).

Another application of taste aversion is in helping people undergoing chemotherapy for cancer and other diseases. Chemotherapy drugs often cause intense nausea. If a patient receiving chemotherapy experiences nausea after eating foods that he would normally eat, there is a strong possibility that he will develop a conditioned taste aversion to those foods. This could severely affect the quality of the patient's life both during and after undergoing chemotherapy as he may develop multiple taste aversions over the course of treatment. One solution to this problem is to give the patient a *novel* food prior to undergoing chemotherapy. Because novel flavors are more easily associated with feelings of illness than familiar flavors are (c.f. Batsell, 2000), novel foods can act as *scapegoats* for the patients' regularly eaten foods. For example, patients given *halva* (a Middle Eastern sweet; Andresen, Birch, & Johnson, 1990) or strongly flavored candy (Broberg & Bernstein, 1987) prior to undergoing chemotherapy later experienced less taste aversion for the foods of their regular diet. Because the novel foods eaten just prior to chemotherapy were more strongly associated with their nausea, the patients' conditioned taste aversion for the novel foods was stronger than that for the familiar foods. Because novel foods can be easily avoided, the patients should be better able to resume their normal eating patterns after chemotherapy.

Therapists can use classically conditioned taste aversion to help people with alcoholism overcome their desire to drink.

© Blue Images/Masterfile

By having chemotherapy patients consume a scapegoat food prior to undergoing chemotherapy, doctors can help ensure that the taste aversion patients experience after chemotherapy is for the scapegoat food and not for their normal diet.

© Kevin Laubacher/Getty Images

**aversion therapy**  a type of therapy that uses classical conditioning to condition people to avoid certain stimuli

**acquisition**  the process of learning a conditioned response or behavior

**spontaneous recovery**  during extinction, the tendency for a conditioned response to reappear and strengthen over a brief period of time before re-extinguishing

Pavlov's experiments with dogs also included extinction trials with the dogs. ■ FIGURE 5.4 shows the **acquisition**, or learning curve, for the CR and the extinction curve for the CR in Pavlov's experiment. As you can see from this figure, the CR of salivation to the buzzer was acquired over several trials in which the CS and the US were paired. In the extinction trials, the buzzer was sounded but no food was presented, and there was a fairly steady decrease in the CR. In other words, the dog became less and less likely to salivate when it heard the buzzer.

Does this mean that once a response has been extinguished, it is gone forever? Note that the extinction curve in Figure 5.4 does not show a completely continuous pattern of decrease in the CR. Sometimes, after a response has been extinguished, there will be a temporary increase in the CR. This phenomenon, called

**spontaneous recovery**, can occur at any point during extinction (e.g., Troisi, 2003) and may be especially likely if a response is extinguished immediately after it is originally learned (Huff et al., 2009). Let's go back to our example of taste aversion for peppermint ice cream. Today, although your author does not have an active, ongoing taste aversion for peppermint ice cream, every now and again when she thinks of peppermint ice cream, she will feel a bit sick. Thankfully, her spontaneous recovery doesn't last long. She soon reenters extinction, and she can think of peppermint ice cream and even eat it without a trace of nausea.

What do you suppose would happen if she happened to eat some peppermint ice cream on a hot day and suffered from a *small* amount of heat-induced nausea? Do you think her taste aversion to peppermint ice cream would return? It is likely that it would. In fact, responses that are extinguished are usually reacquired more easily than they were acquired in the first place. Extinction does *not* mean that we forget that there once was a connection between the CS and the US; it simply means that the CR is less likely to occur when the CS is presented.

So far, we have seen that learning can occur through habituation and classical conditioning—learning processes that both result in rather simplistic behaviors. In the next section, we'll examine how we learn more complex behaviors through reward and punishment.

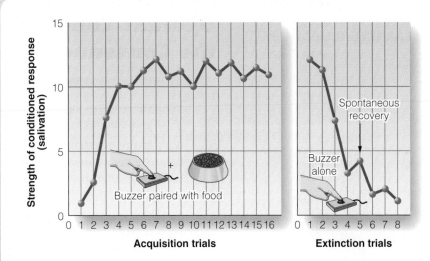

**FIGURE**

## 5.4

### The Phases of Classical Conditioning

These plots show the number of conditioning trials on the x axis and the strength of the conditioned response on the y axis. During acquisition, the response increases in strength as a function of the number of times the CS and US have been paired together. During extinction, the CS is presented without the US, which leads to a decrease in the strength of the CR. Note that during extinction, sometimes there is a temporary increase in the strength of the CR even though the CS has not been recently presented with the US. This is called spontaneous recovery.

# Let's
# REVIEW

This section has given you a brief overview of some of the important issues in classical conditioning. As a quick check of your understanding, answer these questions.

1. Which of the following is an example of classical conditioning?
   a. Damon learns to ride a bike by watching his older brother.
   b. Sally dislikes the smell of rose perfume because her crabby third-grade teacher used to wear rose perfume.
   c. After 20 minutes in the day-care center, Ralph barely notices the squealing of the children at play.
   d. Ted never speeds after receiving a $500 fine for speeding.

2. Which of the following is a US–UR pair?
   a. Receiving money–happiness
   b. An electric shock to the finger–jerking one's finger away
   c. Receiving a promotion–working overtime
   d. Seeing a snake–fear

3. Janna, a real estate agent, desperately wants to sell a home. She tells the owner to place a pan of vanilla extract in the oven and heat it just before the prospective buyers arrive to look at the house. Janna knows that the smell of vanilla in the house will increase the chance that the buyers will like the house because they have been classically conditioned to respond favorably to the smell of vanilla. In this example, what is the CR?
   a. The pleasant emotions evoked by the smell of vanilla
   b. The smell of vanilla
   c. The memory of Grandma baking cookies at Christmas
   d. The house

Answers 1. b; 2. b; 3. a.

# Operant Conditioning: Learning from the Consequences of Our Actions

Suppose you are sitting in your psychology class, listening to a lecture, when your professor asks the class a question. For some reason, you raise your hand to answer the question even though you have never made a comment in this class before. The professor calls on you, and you give the correct answer. In response to your answer, the professor smiles broadly and praises you for giving such an accurate and insightful answer.

How do you think this scenario would affect you? As a result of the professor's reaction, would you be more or less likely to raise your hand in the future when she asked a question? If you are like most people, this type of praise would encourage you to raise your hand in the future. But what would happen if, instead of praising you, she frowned and said that your answer was one of the stupidest she had ever heard. How would this reaction affect your behavior? Obviously, after such a cruel response, many of us would be very unlikely to answer any more questions in that professor's class!

Both of these examples illustrate another type of learning, called **operant conditioning**. In operant conditioning, *we learn from the consequences of our behavior.* In our example, being praised for answering a question makes one more likely to answer questions in the future; being called "stupid" makes one less likely to answer future questions. We will see that operant conditioning is a powerful means of learning that explains how we learn many of the important lessons in our lives. But first, we will begin by looking at how operant conditioning was discovered.

## E. L. Thorndike's Law of Effect

At about the same time that Ivan Pavlov was developing his theories about learning in Russia, American psychologist E. L. Thorndike (1874–1949) was busy conducting experiments on operant conditioning in New York. Thorndike was working with cats in specially constructed *puzzle boxes*. A puzzle box is a box with a lid or door that locks into place so that an animal can be placed inside. Once inside the box, the animal must activate some type of unlatching device to win its release. The device that unlatches the lid may be a rope pull, a pedal that needs to be pushed, or a switch that needs to be flipped. ■ FIGURE 5.5 shows a typical puzzle box with a foot-pedal release.

### UNLOCKING THE PUZZLE OF LEARNING

In his research, Thorndike (1898) locked a hungry cat in one of these puzzle boxes and placed some food outside the box. Then he recorded how long it took the cat to figure out how to get out of the box. Once the cat activated the device and got out of the box, Thorndike would take the cat and place it back in the puzzle box. Over and over, Thorndike repeated this procedure of imprisoning the cat and measuring the time it took the cat to win its release.

Thorndike observed in these studies that when the cat was first placed in the puzzle box, it thrashed around randomly until, by accident, it tripped the mechanism

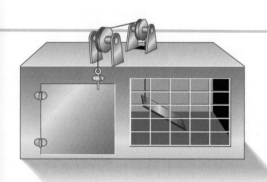

**FIGURE**

## 5.5

**Puzzle Box**

This is an example of a puzzle box like those used by Thorndike. To get out of the box, the cat would have to pull the string or step on the pedal.

and got out of the box. After several more trials, however, the cat's behavior became less random, and the time it took to get out of the box declined. This decrease in the amount of time it took the cat to get out of the box indicated to Thorndike that *learning* was taking place: The cat was learning to associate its behavior with the consequences that its behavior brought about.

Based on what he observed in his puzzle box studies, Thorndike developed a principle of learning that he called the **law of effect**. The law of effect states that *in a given situation, behaviors that lead to positive, satisfying consequences will be strengthened, such that the next time the situation occurs, the behavior is more likely to be repeated*. In addition, the law of effect also states that *in a given situation, behaviors that lead to negative, discomforting consequences will be weakened, such that the next time the situation occurs, the behavior will be less likely to be repeated* (Thorndike, 1905).

## RANDOM ACTIONS AND REINFORCEMENT

Let's examine the law of effect in terms of a hungry cat in a puzzle box. When the cat is first trapped in the box, it will likely perform many random behaviors. For instance, it may claw, hiss, bite at the bars, or meow. But none of these behaviors will open the box. The cat's early responses to being stuck in the box are random or "trial-and-error." After some time, let's say that the cat happens to step on the foot pedal that opens the puzzle box and is able to get out to where the food is waiting. This particular random behavior has led to a consequence that is far more rewarding than any of the other random behaviors the cat has tried. The law of effect states that this particular response is strengthened, or *reinforced*, because it results in a reward. This process of **reinforcement** means that the rewarded behavior will become more likely in the future. The next time the cat is locked in the box, it will be more likely to step on the pedal than to try the other behaviors that did not lead to release on prior trials. Over many trials, the law of effect results in the cat's becoming more and more likely to step on the pedal and less and less likely to use other behaviors that were not reinforced in the past. The behaviors that were not rewarded—and therefore not reinforced—are likely to die out.

## POSITIVE AND NEGATIVE REINFORCEMENT

The two types of reinforcement are *positive reinforcement* and *negative reinforcement* (see ■ YOU REVIEW 5.2). In **positive reinforcement**, the behavior leads to the *addition* of something *pleasant* to the organism's environment. For instance, Thorndike positively reinforced the cat for stepping on the pedal by giving the cat food when it got out of the puzzle box.

In **negative reinforcement**, the behavior is rewarded by the *removal* of something *unpleasant* from the organism's environment. In Thorndike's case, the cat was negatively reinforced for stepping on the pedal because this behavior led to the removal of its imprisonment in the puzzle box. (We are, of course, assuming that the hungry cat did *not* enjoy being trapped in the box.)

The difference between *punishment* and *negative reinforcement* is a point that gives many students great trouble because they tend to think that negative reinforcement is a type of punishment. This is not true! The "negative" in negative reinforcement refers to the fact that negative reinforcement *removes* something from the organism's environment; it does not refer to a negative or unpleasant consequence of the behavior. When you see the term *reinforcement*, keep in mind that reinforcement leads to an *increase* in behavior. **Punishment**, on the other hand, is an unpleasant consequence that leads to a *decrease* in behavior.

**operant conditioning**   a type of learning in which the organism learns through the consequences of its behavior

**law of effect**   a principle discovered by E. L. Thorndike, which states that behaviors that lead to positive consequences will be strengthened and behaviors that lead to negative consequences will be weakened

**reinforcement**   the strengthening of a response that occurs when the response is rewarded

**positive reinforcement**   strengthening a behavior by adding something pleasant to the environment of the organism

**negative reinforcement**   strengthening a behavior by removing something unpleasant from the environment of the organism

**punishment**   the weakening of a response that occurs when a behavior leads to an unpleasant consequence

# YOU REVIEW 5.2

## The Four Consequences of Behavior
Reinforcement increases the likelihood of a behavior; punishment decreases it.

|  | POSITIVE | NEGATIVE |
|---|---|---|
| **REINFORCEMENT**<br>*The consequence increases the behavior* | **Positive Reinforcement**<br>Something pleasant is added to the environment<br><br>Example: Your cat learns to use the cat door, so you give him a kitty treat. | **Negative Reinforcement**<br>Something unpleasant is removed from the environment<br><br>Example: Your cat, who hates to be wet, uses his new cat door to come in out of the rain. |
| **PUNISHMENT**<br>*The consequence decreases the behavior* | **Positive Punishment**<br>Something unpleasant is added to the environment<br><br>Example: Every time your cat starts to scratch your furniture, you squirt him with a water bottle. | **Negative Punishment**<br>Something pleasant is removed from the environment<br><br>Example: Your cat misbehaves, so you put him outside away from his toys. |

## POSITIVE AND NEGATIVE PUNISHMENT

As you can see from You Review 5.2, punishment also comes in two varieties. **Positive punishment** occurs when a behavior results in the *addition* of something *unpleasant* to the organism's environment. For example, a puzzle box could be rigged to electrify the floor of the cage every time the cat stepped on the pedal. The cat would then be positively punished every time it stepped on the pedal because the resulting shock would add pain to the cat's environment.

In **negative punishment**, the behavior leads to the *removal* of something *pleasant* from the organism's environment. A puzzle box could be rigged so that when the cat presses the pedal, a drape falls over the cage, and the cat can no longer see outside the cage. If the cat enjoys seeing outside the cage, then stepping on the pedal would lead to negative punishment because it leads to the loss of a pleasant privilege for the cat. The effect of punishment is to decrease a behavior, regardless of whether the punishment is positive or negative.

**positive punishment**   weakening a behavior by adding something unpleasant to the organism's environment

**negative punishment**   weakening a behavior by removing something pleasant from the organism's environment

## B. F. Skinner and the Experimental Study of Operant Conditioning

Although E. L. Thorndike is generally credited with discovering the law of effect, American psychologist B. F. Skinner (1904–1990) is more commonly associated with the scientific study of operant conditioning. Skinner began to formally study operant conditioning in the late 1920s when he was a graduate student at Harvard University. During his long career—from the 1920s through the 1980s—Skinner made many significant contributions to our understanding of operant conditioning (Schultz & Schultz, 2000). One of his most obvious contributions was to introduce new terminology and technology to the study of this type of learning.

It was Skinner who introduced the term *operant conditioning* to the study of the law of effect. Skinner felt that using the term *operant* was a good way to distinguish this type of learning from classical conditioning. Skinner wanted to emphasize the fact that in classical conditioning, the organism does not actively choose to operate on the environment to produce some consequence; rather, the response is forced from the animal. Thus, Skinner referred to classically conditioned behavior as *respondent* behavior. In contrast, Skinner wanted to emphasize that in operant conditioning, the animal makes a choice to respond to its environment in a certain way. In this type of learning, behavior *operates* on the environment to produce some consequence (Skinner, 1938).

Another of Skinner's contributions to the study of operant conditioning was the development of a new device that allows researchers to condition animals in less time than is required to condition an animal in a puzzle box. This device, now called a **Skinner box**, is a chamber large enough to house a small animal, typically a rat or a pigeon. When rats are used, the chamber contains a lever or bar that the rat can press. When the rat depresses the lever or bar, it receives reinforcement in the form of a pellet of food from an automatic feeding device attached to the chamber. When pigeons are used, the pigeon receives a reward by pecking at a disk on the side of the box.

To study operant behavior, Skinner would place a hungry rat in the Skinner box and wait for the rat to accidentally press the bar (which tends to happen rather quickly given the Skinner box's small size and simplicity). Once the rat pressed the bar, a pellet would drop into the chamber to reinforce this operant behavior. The rat was free to press the bar as often as it wanted and whenever it wanted. By recording the number of bar presses and when they occurred, Skinner could get a good picture of the acquisition of the operant behavior. Using the Skinner box, researchers have been able to learn a great deal about the different aspects of operant conditioning. This advance in the methodology and apparatus for studying animal learning is one of B. F. Skinner's major contributions to psychology.

**You Asked...**

*Why do animals learn best through repetition?*

HEATHER LACIS, STUDENT

In these operant chambers, the animals can be reinforced with food for pressing the bar or pecking the disk. Skinner boxes such as these allow researchers to efficiently gather data on operant conditioning.

## Acquisition and Extinction

Two areas that Skinner explored were *acquisition* and *extinction*. You may recall from our discussion of classical conditioning that *acquisition* refers to the conditioning of a response and *extinction* refers to the loss of a conditioned response. As in

**Skinner box** device created by B. F. Skinner to study operant behavior in a compressed time frame; in a Skinner box, an organism is automatically rewarded or punished for engaging in certain behaviors

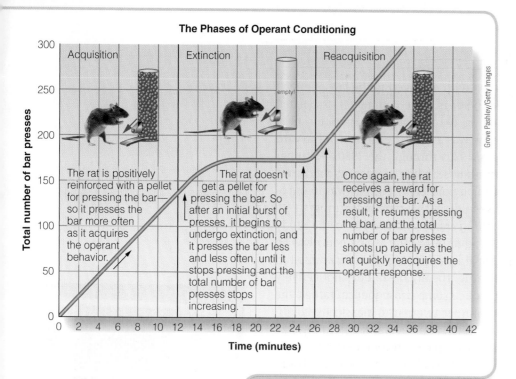

**The Phases of Operant Conditioning**

Acquisition

The rat is positively reinforced with a pellet for pressing the bar—so it presses the bar more often as it acquires the operant behavior.

Extinction

The rat doesn't get a pellet for pressing the bar. So after an initial burst of presses, it begins to undergo extinction, and it presses the bar less and less often, until it stops pressing and the total number of bar presses stops increasing.

Reacquisition

Once again, the rat receives a reward for pressing the bar. As a result, it resumes pressing the bar, and the total number of bar presses shoots up rapidly as the rat quickly reacquires the operant response.

Grove Pashley/Getty Images

*x-axis:* Time (minutes) — 0 2 4 6 8 10 12 14 16 18 20 22 24 26 28 30 32 34 36 38 40 42

*y-axis:* Total number of bar presses — 0 50 100 150 200 250 300

**FIGURE**

# 5.6

**Acquisition and Extinction in Operant Conditioning**

Just as we saw in classical conditioning, operant responses can also undergo acquisition, extinction, and reacquisition.

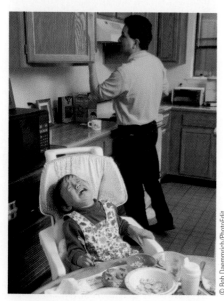

By ignoring this child's tantrum, the parent is placing the child on an extinction schedule. If the parent does not reward the child for this behavior, the behavior should be less likely to occur in the future, at least for this parent.

© Bob Daemmrich/PhotoEdit

classical conditioning, it is possible to plot acquisition and extinction curves for operantly conditioned behaviors. The rat learns that pressing the bar leads to obtaining food, and its tendency to press the bar increases. The intensity with which the rat presses the bar continues to increase until it reaches some maximum strength. For example, the rat can eat the pellets only so fast. Therefore, the number of times the rat will press the bar in a given time frame is limited by the speed at which it eats (■ FIGURE 5.6).

Extinction also occurs in operant conditioning, but it is caused by circumstances that differ from those that cause extinction in classical conditioning. In classical conditioning, extinction occurs when the CS is presented without the US. In operant conditioning, extinction occurs because the behavior is no longer reinforced (see Figure 5.6). Many of us hold jobs, and going to work is an example of an operantly conditioned response. We go to work because we expect to be reinforced for this behavior on payday. What would it take to extinguish your going-to-work behavior? The answer is simple, isn't it? All it would take is the removal of your reinforcement. If your boss stopped paying you, you would likely stop going to work! In operant conditioning, withholding the reinforcement that maintains the behavior causes the extinction of that behavior.

Like acquisition, extinction does not typically happen in one trial. Even if your boss failed to pay you on payday, you might very well return to work for a few days. In fact, you might even experience a temporary **extinction burst**, during which you worked *harder* in an attempt to obtain reward immediately after your boss withholds your pay (e.g., Galensky et al., 2001). At the very least, you probably would not entirely abandon work until it became very clear that reinforcement would no longer be forthcoming. Extinction tends to occur over a number of trials. Each time the organism emits the operant response without being reinforced, its tendency to repeat the response diminishes (see Figure 5.6).

Because extinction removes responses, it has many practical applications. One way to stop someone from engaging in an annoying behavior is to extinguish it by removing the reinforcement for that behavior. Take the example of a parent and child shopping together in a department store. The child sees a toy that he wants, but his parent refuses to buy it. At this refusal, the child begins to whine and cry, but instead of punishing the child for this behavior, the parent ignores the child. By not reinforcing the whining and crying, the parent begins to extinguish this annoying behavior. Once the child learns that crying and whining do not lead to reward, the child will stop using this behavioral strategy to get what he wants.

The trick to using extinction to reduce unwanted behaviors is figuring out what is actually reinforcing the behavior, removing that reinforcement, and then making sure that no other reinforcement of the unwanted behavior is occurring (Martin & Pear, 2007). If Dad ignores the child's tantrums when he takes the child shopping but Mom gives in and buys the child toys, then the behavior will not be completely extinguished.

## Schedules of Reinforcement

Acquisition and extinction of operant behavior seem simple enough, but numerous Skinner box studies have taught us that many factors can affect the rate at which responses are acquired or extinguished. One extremely important factor is the **schedule of reinforcement**—the timing and the consistency of the reinforcement.

### CONTINUOUS REINFORCEMENT

Conceptually, the simplest type of reinforcement schedule is **continuous reinforcement**, in which each and every instance of the desired behavior is rewarded. In a Skinner box study, every time the rat presses the bar, a pellet of food is delivered to the rat. In real life, many simple behaviors are reinforced on a continuous schedule. One example is when we reach for objects. The act of reaching is reinforced when we actually grasp the object we were trying to get. Except in unusual circumstances, such as reaching for an object on a shelf that is too high, reaching is rewarded every time we reach (Skinner, 1953). Unfortunately, continuous schedules of reinforcement are often not very helpful when using operant conditioning to modify behavior.

There are two main reasons that continuous reinforcement is often not very helpful. The first drawback is a practical one. Let's say that you were going to use continuous reinforcement to change a child's behavior. You want your child to be polite when speaking to others, so you decide to use a continuous schedule and reinforce your child with praise *every time* she is polite. Would this be feasible? We doubt it. A continuous schedule of reinforcement would mean that you would have to be around your child every time she was polite, and you would have to praise or otherwise reward her for this politeness. This just isn't practical or possible.

The second problem is that continuously reinforced behaviors are vulnerable to extinction. What happens when your children are not in your presence, and you are not there to continually reinforce their good behavior? As we have already seen, when reinforcement is withheld, behavior often starts to extinguish. The problem with using continuous schedules of reinforcement is that they lead to behaviors that extinguish very quickly once the reinforcement ceases (Nevin & Grace, 2005).

Why would this be true? When a behavior has been continuously reinforced, there is a very clear *contingency* between the behavior and the reward. The organism learns that the behavior should *always* lead to a reward. When the reinforcement stops, a clear signal is sent that the contingency no longer holds true, and extinction occurs relatively rapidly.

### PARTIAL REINFORCEMENT

However, let's say the behavior is reinforced only *some* of the time. What is likely to happen then? The child or animal is less likely to see the lack of reinforcement as a sign that the contingency is no longer operating. Schedules of reinforcement that reinforce a behavior only some of the time are called **partial reinforcement** schedules. *Ratio schedules* of partial reinforcement are based on the number of responses, whereas *interval schedules* are based on the timing of the responses.

Ratio Schedules of Reinforcement    In a **fixed ratio schedule**, a set number of responses must be emitted before a reward is given. For example, suppose every third response is rewarded. A rat in a Skinner box would have to press the bar three times to get a food pellet. In the real world, some people are paid on fixed ratio schedules. A person who works in a manufacturing plant and is paid a bonus for every 100 parts assembled is being reinforced on a fixed ratio, as are

**extinction burst** a temporary increase in a behavioral response that occurs immediately after extinction has begun

**schedule of reinforcement** the frequency and timing of the reinforcements that an organism receives

**continuous reinforcement** a schedule of reinforcement in which the organism is rewarded for every instance of the desired response

**partial reinforcement** a schedule of reinforcement in which the organism is rewarded for only some instances of the desired response

**fixed ratio schedule** a schedule of reinforcement in which the organism is rewarded for every xth instance of the desired response

# 6 How Does Memory FUNCTION?

# Chapter Outline

*One of our students,* Tamara Stewart, is living proof that understanding how your memory works can be very useful. In high school, Tamara found that she didn't need to study much. Just showing up to class and listening was enough for her to make A's and B's. However, when she went off to college, she found herself in a new and much more demanding learning environment. Instead of having a week to master a chapter, she now had one day. Overwhelmed, Tamara resorted to trying to memorize every word of the text instead of trying to truly understand the course content. This strategy did not work well, and Tamara decided to put college on hold for a while.

Tamara Stewart uses her knowledge of memory to be a more effective student.

Years later, Tamara, now a wife and mother, has returned to school to complete her degree. This time around, things are different. Tamara has learned how to work with her memory instead of against it. In class, Tamara takes good notes. She completes exercises in the student study guide. She develops outlines of the course material. She generates real-world examples to serve as memory cues for recalling the material on exam day. And, most important, she studies every day instead of cramming for exams. As you learn in this chapter about how your memory works, we hope that you too will find ways to improve your study habits and become an even more successful learner.

## LEARNING OBJECTIVES

- Explain the functions of memory.

- Explain the difference between implicit and explicit use of memory.

**encoding**   the act of inputting information into memory

**memory traces**   the stored code that represents a piece of information that has been encoded into memory

**storage**   the place where information is retained in memory

**retrieval**   the process of accessing information in memory and pulling it into consciousness

**consciousness**   an organism's awareness of its own mental processes and/or its environment

**attention**   an organism's ability to focus its consciousness on some aspect of its own mental processes and/or its environment

**explicit memory**   the conscious use of memory

**implicit memory**   the unconscious use of memory

Is the mind just like a computer?

© Rick Gomez/Masterfile

# The Functions of Memory: Encoding, Storing, and Retrieving

**You Asked...**

*How important is memory to a person's ability to learn?*

AMBER MANER, STUDENT

Many psychologists use a computer analogy to help them understand the mind. The *information-processing approach* in cognitive psychology assumes that the mind functions like a very sophisticated computer. A computer accepts input—the information you type into it—stores and processes the information, and allows you to go back and retrieve the same information. In essence, this is also what your mind does with information.

As you read this chapter, you are inputting, or **encoding**, information into your memory in the form of **memory traces**, which are stored bits of information in memory. Your mind will process this information and put it into memory **storage**. Then, on test day or some other day when the information is needed, you will use **retrieval** processes to recall and output the information from memory. Without memory, we would not be able to learn.

However, there are important differences between computers and the human mind. One difference is the human capacity for **consciousness**, the awareness of our own thoughts and the external world. When we focus our **attention** on something, we bring the stimulus into our consciousness—we become consciously aware of it. If we turn our attention inward, we become conscious of our own thoughts. If we focus our attention outward, we become conscious of the outside world. A computer does not have such awareness.

## Explicit and Implicit Memory

Psychologists define **explicit memory** as the *conscious* use of memory (Bush & Geer, 2001; Graf & Schacter, 1985). We use explicit memory when we consciously search our memory for a previously stored bit of information. For example, try to answer the following question: "What part of the brain's cortex processes visual information?" To answer, you must consciously search your memory for the information you learned in Chapter 2. We hope your search led you to the correct answer, the occipital lobe! While you were trying to answer this question, you were fully aware that you were searching your memory for the answer. In this respect, you were utilizing your memory explicitly. But do we always know what's going on inside our own memory?

Not always. Sometimes we access and retrieve memories without having consciously tried to do so. For example, have you ever pulled into your driveway, only to realize that you don't recall the last few miles of your trip home? How did you find your way home without being consciously aware of driving the car? This example illustrates the phenomenon of **implicit memory**, or the *unconscious* use of memory (Graf & Schacter, 1985; Reder, Park, & Kieffaber, 2009). During the trip home, you were using stored knowledge of how to drive your car, how to find your house, how to read street signs, and so on. The trick is that you did all of these things without conscious awareness. Every day, we execute many behaviors at the implicit level of memory. If we had to execute everything explicitly, we would literally not be able to think and walk at the same time! As we'll see in the coming sections, our cognitive resources for memory are limited. We simply can't do everything explicitly.

# Let's
## REVIEW

In this section, we discussed the functions of memory and described the difference between implicit and explicit use of memory. For a quick check of your understanding, answer these questions.

1. Printing a document from your computer is analogous to which function of memory?
   a. Encoding
   b. Storage
   c. Retrieval
   d. Forgetting

2. Which of the following *best* illustrates the use of explicit memory?
   a. Forgetting to get eggs at the grocery store
   b. Trying to remember the name of a woman you once met at a party

   c. Automatically thinking of a cat when you see a dog on TV
   d. Guessing the correct answer on a multiple-choice test

3. Which of the following *best* illustrates the use of implicit memory?
   a. Knowing the correct answer on a multiple-choice test
   b. Trying to remember where you left your car keys
   c. Forgetting where you left your car keys
   d. Tying your shoe

Answers 1. c; 2. b; 3. d

# How Do We Process New Memories?

As you may recall from Chapter 1, the study of cognition grew in psychology from the 1960s to the 1980s. As it did, the information processing approach to understanding memory also became more prominent as psychologists began to develop theories of memory that described memory using a computer analogy for the mind. In this section, we'll look at two of these models—the *three stages* and *working memory models* of memory.

## The Traditional Three Stages Model of Memory

Traditionally, memory has been explained as having three distinct stages of storage (Atkinson & Shiffrin, 1968). When information enters memory, its first stop is **sensory memory**. In sensory memory, information that comes in from our eyes, ears, and other senses is briefly stored in a sensory form, such as a sound or a visual image. If we pay attention to the information in our sensory memory, the information is sent on to the second stage, **short-term memory (STM)**, for further processing. Short-term memory functions as a temporary holding tank for a limited amount of information. We can hold information in short-term memory for only a few seconds before we must act either to send it further on in the memory system or to keep it in short-term memory by refreshing it. If we decide to further process the information, we can move it from temporary storage in short-term memory to the permanent storage system of **long-term memory (LTM)** (■ FIGURE 6.1). Let's look at each of these stages of memory in a bit more detail.

### LEARNING OBJECTIVES

● Describe the three stages model of memory, including the function and characteristics of sensory, short-term, and long-term memory.

● Describe the newer conception of working memory and how it relates to the three stages model's concept of short-term memory.

**sensory memory**   a system of memory that very briefly stores sensory impressions so that we can extract relevant information from them for further processing

**short-term memory (STM)**   a system of memory that is limited in both capacity and duration; in the three stages model of memory, short-term memory is seen as the intermediate stage between sensory memory and long-term memory

**long-term memory (LTM)**   a system of memory that works to store memories for a long time, perhaps even permanently

# FIGURE
## 6.1
### The Traditional Three Stages Model of Memory

The traditional three stages model of memory proposes that in forming new memories, information passes sequentially from sensory memory to short-term memory to long-term memory.

## SENSORY MEMORY: ICONIC AND ECHOIC MEMORY

All of the information that enters our memory from the outside world must first pass through our senses. The information we receive from our sense organs lasts for a very brief time after the sensory stimulation has ended. As noted above, this holding of sensory information after the sensory stimulus ends is sensory memory. Perhaps you have noticed your sensory memory at work. Have you ever heard a fire engine's siren and then found that you could still hear the sound of the siren in your head for a short time after you could no longer actually hear the siren? If so, you caught your sensory memory at work.

Of all our senses, sight (*iconic memory*) and hearing (*echoic memory*), the two most studied by psychologists, are also the primary means through which we acquire information. But they are not the only useful senses. We also learn through our senses of taste, smell, and touch (*haptic memory*). Psychologists assume that we have sensory memories for each of the senses.

The function of sensory memory is to hold sensory information just long enough for us to process it and send it on to short-term memory for further processing. In the case of iconic (sight) memory, the information stays in sensory memory for a fraction of a second (Massaro & Loftus, 1996). Although still very brief, the exact duration of echoic (hearing) memories seems to vary across situations (Demany & Semal, 2005). In the end, if we do not send sensory information on to short-term memory within seconds (or less), it will be lost forever as our sensory memories decay (see ■ FIGURE 6.2).

So, how do we transfer information from sensory memory to short-term memory? It's simple, actually. To transfer information from sensory memory to short-term memory, all we have to do is pay attention to the sensory information. In paying attention to a sensory stimulus, we focus our consciousness on that stimulus. For example,

Michael Caulfield/Getty Images for VH1

Asia Images/Getty Images

# FIGURE
## 6.2
### Sensory Memory

As this man watches a concert video, he stores brief sensory images of what he is seeing in his iconic memory. At the same time, he stores a brief sensory image of the sound he is hearing in his echoic memory. The resulting sensory memories may last for only a fraction of a second, but in that time he will extract the information he wants to keep and send it on into short-term memory for further processing.

as you read a phone number in a phone book, you pay attention to the number and bring it into your consciousness. As you do this, you ensure that the image of the phone number will be transferred from iconic memory into short-term memory (see ■ FIGURE 6.3a & b). If you are distracted or unmotivated, you may gaze at the page without paying attention to the number. In that case, the image will be lost as it decays from iconic memory. As you can see, if you don't pay attention to what you are reading, you are wasting your time!

**FIGURE**

# 6.3

## The Three Stages Model of Memory

(a) As Juanita looks up the phone number of a pizza shop, the information enters her visual sensory memory. (b) As she focuses her attention on the phone number, the information now moves to her short-term memory. (c) To keep the number in mind while she dials it, Juanita uses maintenance rehearsal, repeating the number over and over to herself. (d) As Juanita continues to think about the number, she engages in elaborative rehearsal by associating the number with the idea of pizza in her mind; as a result, the number is now stored in her long-term memory. (e) Later, when Juanita wants to order pizza again, she retrieves the number from long-term memory.

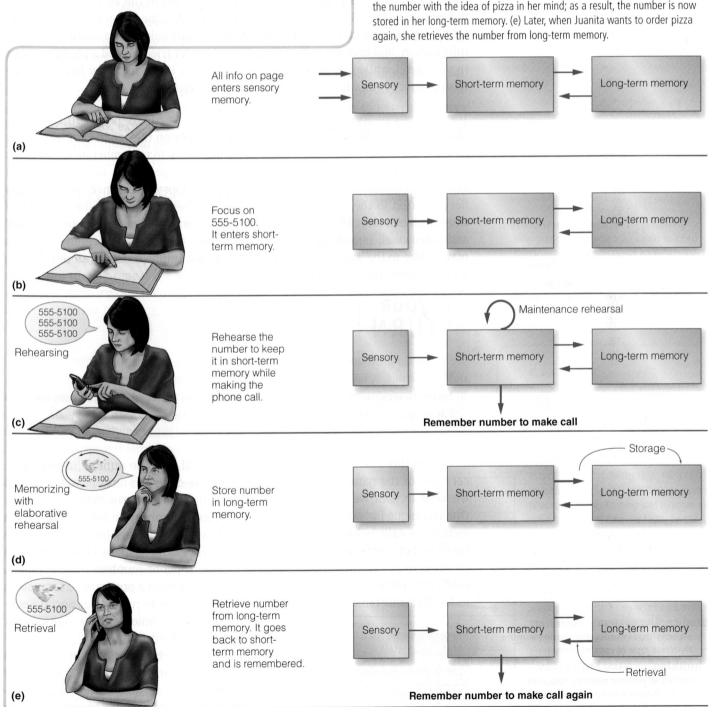

name inhibits the *newer* (correct) pronunciation in people's memory. (It's also the reason she started going by *Sue* early in childhood!)

We can also experience **retroactive interference**, in which *newer* information inhibits the retrieval of *older* information in memory. Suppose you move to a new home and work very hard to memorize your new address and phone number. Chances are, you will soon find it hard to recall your old address and phone number. This is an example of retroactive interference, because the new phone number and address interfere with your ability to retrieve the old phone number and address from long-term memory.

Unfortunately, our susceptibility to both proactive (Jacoby, Debner, & Hay, 2001) and retroactive (Hedden & Park, 2003) interference tends to increase as we age. One explanation for why interference increases with age is that our central executive function tends to decline with advancing age. As the central executive becomes less efficient, it is also less able to suppress interfering memory traces (Hedden & Yoon, 2006).

## CONTEXT AND FORGETTING

Interference theory does seem to describe one way in which we forget information, but there is reason to suspect that interference may not occur as often in the real world as it does in laboratory experiments (Slameka, 1966). **Cue-dependent forgetting** may be a better explanation of forgetting in the real world. The theory of cue-dependent forgetting (Tulving, 1974) is that the amount of information we can retrieve from long-term memory is a function of the type of cue or probe we use. If the memory cues we use are not the right ones, we may experience forgetting.

The cue-dependent forgetting theory is part of the *encoding specificity principle* developed by Endel Tulving (Wiseman & Tulving, 1976). According to this principle, we encode aspects of the context in which we learn information, later using these contextual aspects as cues to help us retrieve the information from long-term memory. If the encoding specificity principle is correct, then we should have better memory when we retrieve information in the same setting that we learned it.

In one distinctive study, researchers asked divers to learn a list of words while they were either on shore or 20 feet under water (Godden & Baddeley, 1975). Later, researchers tested the divers' recall for the words in either the context in which they had studied the words or the context in which they had not studied the words. Consistent with the encoding specificity principle, the researchers found that when the divers recalled the words in the same context in which they had learned the words, their recall was better.

Encoding specificity has also been shown to hold true for mood states and states of consciousness. People can recall information they learned while drinking alcohol better when they have been drinking (Eich et al., 1975). Information learned while smoking marijuana is better recalled while smoking marijuana (Eich, 1980). And information learned while in a bad mood is better recalled in a negative mood state than when one is happy (Teasdale & Russell, 1983). These findings do not mean that it is better to learn while in these states, however. For example, alcohol can reduce one's ability to encode information in the first place (Parker, Birnbaum, & Noble, 1976).

**retroactive interference** a type of forgetting that occurs when newer memory traces inhibit the retrieval of older memory traces

**cue-dependent forgetting** a type of forgetting that occurs when one cannot recall information in a context other than the context in which it was encoded

Studies show that we remember information best when we retrieve it in the same context in which it was learned. Godden and Baddeley (1975) found that divers who learned a list of words while under water recalled more of the words while submerged than they did on the dock. Studies like these suggest that a change in context may be one of the reasons we sometimes forget.

Nicole Duplaix/Getty Images

## REPRESSION: MOTIVATED FORGETTING

The final theory of forgetting we will discuss is Sigmund Freud's (1915, 1943) proposal that the emotional aspects of a memory can affect our ability to retrieve it. According to Freud, when we experience emotionally threatening events, we push or *repress* these memories into an inaccessible part of our mind called the *unconscious* (Chapter 1). This **repression** results in amnesia for this information.

   Repression of memories has become a very controversial subject because of its relationship to cases of childhood sexual abuse. Some people have claimed that they suddenly "remembered" abuse that had occurred many years before. After many years have passed, there is often no corroborating evidence to support such claims. Furthermore, some experiments indicate that the details of memories for past events can be incorrect, and that this may be especially true for children (Brainerd & Reyna, 2002; Howe, 2000). In one study, researchers found that preschool children could not distinguish memories for fictitious events from memories for real events after 10 weeks of thinking about the events. Even more alarming, the children were able to give detailed accounts of the fictitious events, and they seemed to really believe that the fictitious events had happened (Ceci, 1995).

   The frequent lack of corroborating evidence for recovered memories, along with experimental evidence that questions the accuracy of memory, has led some to charge that these are in fact *false memories* (Loftus & Davis, 2006). The debate is further fueled by the lack of experimental data to support the notion that repression can occur. To test the theory of repression, researchers would have to traumatize participants and then see whether they repressed their memories of the trauma. Obviously, this type of study cannot be done for ethical reasons. So, for now, psychologists cannot say for sure whether repression is one of the reasons we forget (see ■ YOU REVIEW 6.2).

**repression**   a type of forgetting proposed by Sigmund Freud in which memories for events, desires, or impulses that we find threatening are pushed into an inaccessible part of the mind called the unconscious

## YOU REVIEW 6.2    Theories of Forgetting

| THEORY | DEFINITION | EXAMPLE |
|---|---|---|
| Decay | Memory traces that are not routinely activated erode and disappear over time. | You haven't thought of your best friend from kindergarten in 15 years. When you meet him/her, you cannot recall his/her name. |
| Proactive interference | Older memory traces inhibit the retrieval of newer memory traces. | You can't seem to remember your friend's new, married name, but you can recall her maiden name. |
| Retroactive interference | Newer memory traces inhibit the retrieval of older memory traces. | You can't recall your old phone number, but you can recall your new phone number. |
| Cue-dependent forgetting | Memories are not as easily retrieved when the retrieval cues do not match the cues that were present during encoding. | You run into a classmate at the grocery store, and you can't recall her name. But you do recall her name when you see her at school. |
| Repression | Threatening memories are pushed into the inaccessible unconscious part of the mind. | You are in a horrible car accident in which other people are seriously injured. Although you are uninjured, you later cannot recall details of the accident. |

## LOOK BACK AT What You've LEARNED

### The Functions of Memory: Encoding, Storing, and Retrieving

- The human brain **encodes**, stores, and processes information. We can use memory both **explicitly** (consciously) and **implicitly** (unconsciously).

### How Do We Process New Memories?

- What is the traditional three stages model of memory?

- Many researchers today reject the rigid three stages model of memory and suggest a different type of memory, called **working memory**, that is important in moving information in and out of **long-term memory**.

© Masterfile

### Long-Term Memory: Permanent Storage

- Long-term memory is organized into **schemas**, which allow us to quickly and efficiently use our memory. In a sense, schemas are like a filing system for the library of knowledge we have stored in our long-term memory.

Susann Doyle-Portillo

**HOW IS INFORMATION STORED IN LONG-TERM MEMORY?**

**Declarative memory**          **Procedural memory**

**Semantic memory**
**+**
**Episodic/autobio-graphical memory**

*Puff-Puff*

| | |
|---|---|
| Is a: | bread |
| Contains: | flour, sugar, shortening, nutmeg, eggs, etc. |
| Method of preparation: | fried |
| Uses: | energy source; eaten with kidney bean stew |
| Appearance: | small, donut-hole sized |
| Origin: | West Africa |

# How Does Memory FUNCTION?

## Retrieval and Forgetting: Random Access Memory?

Despite our best efforts to retain information, sometimes forgetting occurs. Forgetting may be due to **decay** of memory traces, **interference**, **cue-dependent forgetting**, or perhaps even **repression**. To improve your memory:

- Pay attention to what you are trying to remember; avoid distractions.
- Do not cram for exams.
- Use **elaborative rehearsal** to reinforce retention of information.
- Use **overlearning**.
- Use **mnemonics** to make your memory mighty.
- Use the SQ3R method: Survey, Question, Read, Recite, Review.

© Bill Aron/PhotoEdit

## Is Memory Accurate?

© Steve McCurry/Magnum Photos

- **Flashbulb memories** are unusually detailed memories for emotionally charged events—memories that are quite powerful but not always accurate.
- In general, we are prone to many memory errors, including the **misinformation effect**. In cases of eyewitness testimony, these errors can have serious consequences.

## The Biology of Memory

- **Memory consolidation** is the stabilization and long-term storage of memory traces in the brain.
- Brain-imaging research shows that people who use their memory a great deal may have structural differences in their hippocampal regions. The hippocampus and frontal lobe seem to play significant roles in processing declarative memory.
- The hippocampus may also play some role in the memory consolidation of procedural memories.
- Studies suggest that procedural memory is linked to the cerebellum.

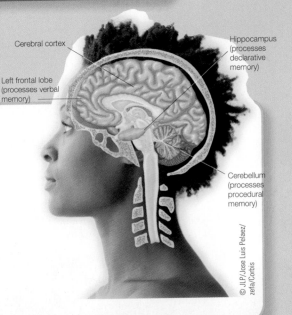

Cerebral cortex

Hippocampus (processes declarative memory)

Left frontal lobe (processes verbal memory)

Cerebellum (processes procedural memory)

© JLP/Jose Luis Pelaez/zefa/Corbis

# 7 COGNITION, LANGUAGE, and INTELLIGENCE: How Do WE THINK?

# Chapter Outline

*When one of our students,* Franco Chevalier, immigrated with his family to the United States from their native Dominican Republic, he faced many challenges. Franco had to adapt to a new culture, a new school, new friends, new customs, and so on. Most challenging was the fact that Franco came to the United States speaking Spanish and some French, but only a few words of English. In school, Franco was very anxious to make the most of his new educational opportunities, but he had difficulty understanding his English-speaking teachers. Some of Franco's classmates mistakenly assumed that his poor English meant he was unintelligent. When Franco excelled in math, a less verbal subject, they told him that the teachers gave him good grades because they felt sorry for him. However, despite the difficulty and the prejudice, Franco was determined to succeed. He knew that he was intelligent and that he could master English. In high school, he enrolled in advanced placement courses (including English!) and worked nonstop to learn.

Today, Franco speaks fluent English. He graduated in the top 5% of his high school class and is now a very successful pre-med major in college. In his college psychology course, Franco learned about how humans develop language and the role that language plays in thinking and intelligence—knowledge that no doubt gave him insight into his own experiences with language and learning. As you read about these same topics in this chapter, consider the important and intertwined roles that thinking, language, and intelligence play in your own life and the lives of others.

*Franco Chevalier*

© Susann Doyle-Portillo

# Thinking: How We Use What We Know

**cognition** the way in which we use and store information in memory

**thinking** the use of knowledge to accomplish some sort of goal

**knowledge** information stored in our long-term memory about the world and how it works

**mental representation** memory traces that represent objects, events, people, and so on that are not present at the time

FIGURE

# 7.1

## An Image-Scanning Task

In this task, participants were asked to imagine a black dot moving across the map to the points indicated by the *Xs*. The average amount of time to do this was proportionate to the distance between the starting point and the ending point on the map.

*Source: © Stephen Kosslyn 1978.*

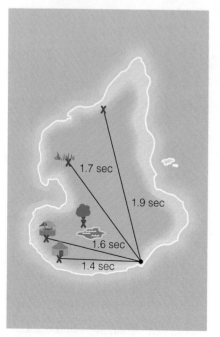

Psychologists define **cognition** as the way in which we store and use information. We engage in some sort of cognition every waking moment. Each day, we do a lot of thinking, but most of us would have difficulty defining what it is that we actually *do* when we think. Psychologists define **thinking** as the use of **knowledge**, the information we have stored in long-term memory, to accomplish some sort of goal. Thinking includes the ability to perceive and understand our world, to communicate with others, and to solve the problems we encounter in our lives (R. E. Mayer, 1983).

Thinking involves the use of all types of knowledge. We store our knowledge in long-term memory as **mental representations**—bits of memory that represent objects, events, people, and so on that are not actually present now. For instance, most of us can close our eyes and think about what our best friend looks like, the smell of her perfume, and her likes and dislikes. To do this, we call on the many mental representations of our friend that we have stored in long-term memory.

In general, thinking involves the use of two broad classes of mental representations: those based on *sensory* aspects of the object, such as its visual appearance, smell, taste, and so forth; and those based on the *meaning* of the object, such as its name, definition, and properties. We will now turn our attention to a discussion of the best-studied forms of these mental representations: *visual images* and *concepts*.

## Visual Images: How Good Is the Mental Picture?

The ability to "see" a friend's face in our mind or to visualize a map of our hometown in our head can be very useful in everyday life, but do we really store "pictures" in our memory? Over the years, psychologists have studied this question by examining how people perform on certain tasks in which they must mentally manipulate visual images (Denis & Cocude, 1999; Kosslyn, Ball, & Reiser, 1978/2004).

In a typical *image-scanning* experiment, like the one done by Stephen Kosslyn and colleagues (Kosslyn et al., 2004), participants are asked to memorize a map of a fictitious island with several objects depicted on it (see ■ FIGURE 7.1). After the participants have memorized the map, they are asked to mentally scan the path that a black dot would take as it travels from one point on the map to another. Because the points are at various distances from one another, researchers can correlate the time it takes participants to mentally scan the image with the distance between the points on the actual map. If the participants' visual images of the map are copies of the actual map, the time it takes to scan longer distances should be longer than the time it takes to scan shorter distances on the map. This is exactly what Kosslyn found: The time it took to scan distances increased proportionately with the increase in the actual distances on the map. The results of this and numerous other experiments (see Shepard, 1978, for a review) suggest that visual images may have all of the spatial properties of the real stimulus. In other words, the visual image we store is essentially a *copy* of the stimulus we see in the world.

As convincing as image-scanning experiments are in supporting the argument that visual images have spatial properties that mimic those of the actual stimulus, the question still remains: Do we actually store photographic images of the things that we see? As it turns out, there are reasons to suspect that we generally do not. For example, try the following demonstration.

## YOUR TURN · Active Learning

Let's look at your ability to answer questions about a visual stimulus that you have seen many times, a map of North America.

Which is farther east: Reno, Nevada, or San Diego, California?

Which is farther north: Montreal, Canada, or Seattle, Washington?

Which is farther west: the Atlantic or the Pacific entrance to the Panama Canal?

The answers seem obvious, but researchers have found that most people answer them incorrectly (Stevens & Coupe, 1978). The correct answers are **San Diego**, **Seattle**, and the **Atlantic entrance**. Are you surprised? Take a look at ■ FIGURE 7.2 (p. 244), which shows that these are the correct answers.

### You Asked...

*Do you actually think in a language?*

TAYLOR EVANS, STUDENT

So, where does all of this research leave us with respect to visual images? Isn't it a bit contradictory? Some studies suggest that visual images are precise mental copies of the actual stimuli (e.g., Shepard, 1978), but other studies show that visual images may deviate significantly from the actual stimuli (e.g., Boden, 1988; Chambers & Reisberg, 1992).

According to Stephen Kosslyn (1994), our mental representation of visual stimuli relies on *both* visual images and verbal knowledge. In other words, we use both types of mental representations—sensory (pictures) and meaning (words)—to fully represent visual stimuli. The pictures represent parts of the stimulus, and the words describe the stimulus and tell us how the pieces of the picture fit together. For example, when you look at a flower, you might store, among other things, a visual image of the shape of a petal, the stem, and the center, along with words describing the fact that the petals are placed around the center and the stem descends from the bottom of the flower. In Kosslyn's view, we do not store a carbon copy of the flower. Instead, we use this mixture of verbal and pictorial pieces to *construct* our visual image of the flower. Recall from Chapter 6 that memory is, after all, *constructive*. Unfortunately, the constructive nature of memory does sometimes lead to inaccuracies. So, don't feel bad if you thought Reno was east of San Diego!

## Concepts: How We Organize What We Know

As we saw in Chapter 6, we have a tendency to organize our knowledge in long-term memory. We store mental representations for related objects together in the same mental category. For example, we would store our knowledge of cats, dogs, and elephants together in the category for *animals*, and apples, oranges, and grapes together in the category for *fruits*. This tendency to organize information based on similarity shows the *conceptual* nature of human cognition. **Concepts**, the mental categories that contain related bits of knowledge, are organized

**concept**   mental category that contains related bits of knowledge

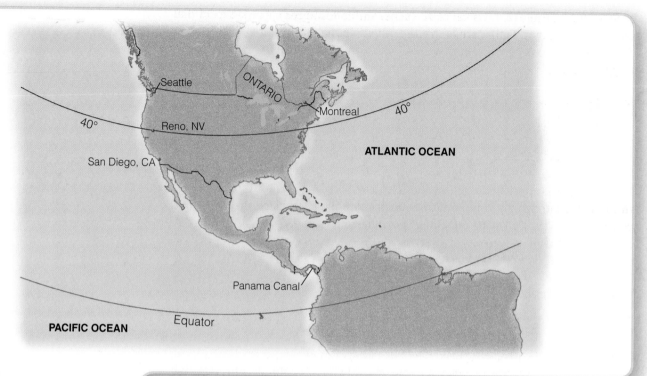

**FIGURE**

## 7.2

### A Map of North and South America

Most people answer questions about this map incorrectly even though they have seen it many times before. It is highly unlikely that we have an exact visual image of this map stored in our long-term memory.

around the *meaning* of the information they represent. For instance, *animal* is a concept. In our mind we know what it means to be an animal. Animals must be animate, but we also distinguish animals from humans.

Conceptual information is encoded in a variety of formats in long-term memory. At times, concepts are stored in a *semantic* or meaning-based form (recall Chapter 6; Collins & Quillian, 1969). For example, we may store certain facts about an orange—it's round, orange-colored, a fruit, and so on—in our memory. However, we also appear to store some of our *perceptual* experiences of objects in memory as well. When we see, smell, and taste an orange, specific patterns of neural activity arise in our brains. We capture and store information on these unique patterns of neural activity and later use this information to recreate the perceptual experience of seeing, smelling, and tasting an orange (Barsalou, 2008; Marques, 2010).

We use this stored semantic and perceptual information to perceive, think about, and deal with our world. Conceptually organizing our knowledge helps us use that knowledge more efficiently. Concepts can be viewed as a type of mental shorthand that both organizes and saves space in our cognitive system. For example, close your eyes and picture an orange in your mind's eye. Can you see it clearly? Can you describe it in detail? Most of us can do this easily for something as familiar as an orange. Now look carefully at your mental orange. Is this concept that you have stored in your mind an *actual* orange that you have seen? In other words, is this orange number 123,675 that you saw one Sunday morning at the local market? Not likely! Instead, your concept of an orange is an abstraction, or a general idea, of what an orange is. You don't have to store mental representations for each and every orange you have seen. Rather, you only need to store a generalized concept of what an orange is and what it looks like. This is a great cognitive space-saver when you think about all of the oranges you'll see in your lifetime.

## ORGANIZING CONCEPTS INTO CATEGORIES

Another benefit of mental concepts is that we can organize them into hierarchical categories (Markman & Ross, 2003). Psychologists have found that we tend to organize our knowledge into three levels of categorization (Rosch et al., 2004). The highest, most general level is called the **superordinate category**. The superordinate level contains concepts that are broad and general in their description. For example, *fruit* would be considered to be a superordinate category. The intermediate level of categorization is the **basic level category**. The basic level seems to be the level that we use most often to think about our world. For example, when we write out a shopping list, we probably list basic level concepts, such as oranges rather than fruit.

The third level in the hierarchy is the **subordinate category**. Concepts at the subordinate level are less general and more specific than those at the basic level. When speaking of oranges, the subordinate category would contain items like Valencia oranges, navel oranges, and blood oranges. Although the subordinate level is the most specific, it is not the first level that springs to mind when we think about our world. You would be much more likely to place the basic level concept—oranges—on your shopping list than you would be to place Valencia oranges. Interestingly, the basic level is also the first level of knowledge young children acquire (Quinn & Tanaka, 2007; Rosch et al., 2004).

## FORMAL AND NATURAL CATEGORIES

How do we acquire concepts in the first place? Simply put, we acquire concepts from an early age as we observe and learn from our world. We acquire **formal concepts** as we learn the rigid rules that define certain categories of things. For example, for an animal to be considered a member of the category *female*, it must possess certain attributes or characteristics. All females are genetically designed to produce either offspring or eggs. If an animal does not have this attribute, it cannot be a female.

The lines that define formal categories are very clear-cut. Unfortunately, life is not always so neat and tidy as to provide us with formal rules for everything, and much of our knowledge of the world does not fit cleanly into only one category. For example, do you consider a tomato to be a fruit or a vegetable? How do you categorize cucumbers? Many people consider tomatoes and cucumbers to be vegetables, whereas others—including botanists—categorize them as fruits. Why the confusion? Perhaps because we associate fruits with sweetness, we tend not to classify cucumbers and tomatoes as fruit even though they do contain seeds, which is a defining attribute of fruit. Most of us are aware of the rules for membership as a female but are not aware of the botanical definition of a fruit. We have organized our fruit and vegetable concepts in a less distinct and orderly fashion based on our own experiences with them.

Concepts that develop naturally as we live our lives and experience the world are referred to as **natural concepts**. We do not learn formal rules for these concepts; rather, we intuit and create the rules as we learn about our world. As a result, the boundaries defining natural concept categories are often blurry, or "fuzzy" (Rosch, 1973; Rosch et al., 2004). Our example of the tomato is a good illustration of this. You can classify the tomato as a vegetable, a fruit, or both, depending on your experience. Because many of us see tomatoes in the vegetable section of the supermarket, we include them in the vegetable category. However, botanists scientifically classify tomatoes as fruits. How do you see them?

**superordinate category**   the highest, most general level of a concept

**basic level category**   the intermediate level of categorization that seems to be the level that we use most to think about our world

**subordinate category**   the lowest level of categorization, which contains concepts that are less general and more specific than those at the basic level

**formal concept**   a concept that is based on learned, rigid rules that define certain categories of things

**natural concept**   a concept that develops naturally as we live our lives and experience the world

The basic level category *pear* falls under the superordinate category *fruit*. The label *Bosc pear* is a subordinate category of the basic level category *pear*.

Because natural concepts are a by-product of our day-to-day experience, they develop in a relatively effortless and *natural* manner as we live our lives. Curiously, when researchers try to force people to develop new natural concepts in the laboratory, people have a lot of trouble doing so (Makino & Jitsumori, 2007). In such situations, we may overthink and try to develop clear-cut rules for concepts that are inherently fuzzy. For example, if you were asked to define the criteria for identifying real-world examples of "love," you would likely find this to be a very difficult task.

## YOUR TURN  Active Learning

In the real world, we tend to do better with the fuzzy boundaries of natural concepts, but we are not perfect. The difficulty involved in deciding which items to include and which to exclude from a category varies considerably. Sometimes it's an easy task, and other times it's not. Take a look at ■ FIGURE 7.3, and answer the questions as quickly as you can. Which of the questions were you able to answer quickly? Which ones took longer? Why do you think some of them were easier than others?

FIGURE

# 7.3

## Natural Concept Categories

Answer these questions as fast as you can.

| Image | Question | Yes | No |
| --- | --- | --- | --- |
| Michael Durham/Getty Images | Is a bat a mammal? | Yes ❑ | No ❑ |
| Stephen Frink/Getty Images | Is a dolphin a mammal? | Yes ❑ | No ❑ |
| Digital Zoo/Getty Images | Is a penguin a bird? | Yes ❑ | No ❑ |
| Patricia Doyle/Getty Images | Is a cat a mammal? | Yes ❑ | No ❑ |
| © image 100/Jupiter images | Is a robin a bird? | Yes ❑ | No ❑ |
| blickwinkel/Alamy | Is a whale a mammal? | Yes ❑ | No ❑ |
| Adam Jones/Getty Images | Is an eagle a bird? | Yes ❑ | No ❑ |

All answers are "Yes."

Most people find it easier to decide that a robin is a bird than that a penguin is a bird. Why? One possibility is that a robin is a more typical example of the category *bird* than a penguin is. According to some researchers, we form what are called **prototypes** for natural concept categories, much like the mental image of the orange we discussed earlier. A prototype is our concept of the most typical member of the category—in essence, a summary of all the members of the category. When we judge whether something belongs in a natural concept category, we compare it to the prototype of the category (Minda & Smith, 2002). The more similar the object is to the prototype, the faster we judge it to be a member of the concept category.

Other researchers argue that, rather than using abstracted prototypes, we judge category membership by comparing an item to the memories we have stored for actual examples, or **exemplars**, of that concept category (Nosofsky & Zaki, 2002; Rehder & Hoffman, 2005; Vanpaemel & Storms, 2008). In this view, you would determine that the robin in your backyard is a bird by comparing this robin to the memories or exemplars of the actual birds you have seen in your lifetime. Unless you live where penguins are common, you are likely to have many more songbird exemplars than penguin exemplars available in your memory. Because robins resemble the songbird exemplars that quickly come to mind more closely than penguins do, you are quicker to decide that a robin belongs in the category of birds.

The debate over whether we use prototypes or exemplars to judge category membership is ongoing. Some argue that we may even use both (Ashby & Maddox, 2005; Storms, DeBoeck, & Ruts, 2001). Regardless of how we go about making category judgments, these judgments are crucial to our ability to think about our world. In the next section, we will see just what we can accomplish with all of our thinking. But first, take a moment to test your knowledge of this last section.

**prototype**   our concept of the most typical member of the category

**exemplar [ig-ZEM-plar]**   a mental representation of an actual instance of a member of a category

# Let's
## REVIEW

In this section, we discussed thinking and how we represent information in memory. We discussed not only the format of stored knowledge, but also its organizational structure. For a quick check of your understanding, answer these questions.

1. Which of the following is evidence indicating that our visual images contain all the properties of the actual stimulus?
   a. Memory for images is near perfect in children.
   b. The time it takes to mentally scan an image of an object is related to the actual size of the object.
   c. Most people can visualize familiar objects in great detail.
   d. Our mental maps of the world are perfect in their detail.

2. Which of the following would be a superordinate concept for the category *car*?
   a. Prius
   b. bulldozer
   c. vehicle
   d. red sports car

3. In an experiment, Dr. Kelly asks participants to name the first example of an "animal" that comes to mind. Based on what you know about concepts, which of the following would the average participant be *most* likely to name?
   a. dog
   b. caterpillar
   c. German shepherd
   d. bat

Answers 1. b; 2. c; 3. a

## Deductive and Inductive Reasoning

We engage in **reasoning** when we draw conclusions that are based on certain assumptions about the world. For example, you might reason that your friend Elva has money because she wears nice clothes. Or, based on your experiences, you might reason that studying leads to better grades. Psychologists who study reasoning have traditionally looked at two types of reasoning processes: *deductive reasoning* and *inductive reasoning*. **Deductive reasoning** involves reasoning from the *general* to the *specific*. In other words, you start with a general rule and apply it to particular cases. For example, you might *deduce* that because studying leads to good grades, your friend Melissa, who makes good grades, must study hard.

> ### You Asked...
>
> *What reasoning do we normally use to come to a decision or to solve a problem?*
>
> PAM LIVELY, STUDENT

**Inductive reasoning** is the opposite approach. When using inductive reasoning, we reason from the *specific* to the *general*. Here the object is to begin with specific instances and to discover what general rule fits all of these instances. For example, as children, we may have noticed time and time again that our classmates who did well were also those who seemed to study the most, so we reasoned that studying hard leads to good grades. We used these specific instances to help us *induce* the general rule that studying hard leads to good grades.

We hope you see the parallels between inductive reasoning and the *scientific method* that psychologists use to conduct research (see Chapter 1). When conducting studies to test theories, psychologists try to induce the general rules that explain mental processes and behavior. Once these rules have been induced, they can then be applied to individual situations to help deduce, or predict, how people and animals are likely to behave. This, of course, does not mean that reasoning is just for scientists. Deductive and inductive reasoning are equally important in everyday life. Effective reasoning can be a very important aspect of making good decisions in our lives.

## Decision Making: Outcomes and Probabilities

**Decision making** involves choosing from among several alternatives. We must first choose a course of action before we can implement a solution to a problem. Two factors that influence our decisions are the perceived *outcomes* of our decisions and the *probability* of achieving these outcomes. For example, when you consider a major, you weigh the expected outcomes of choosing that major. How interesting is the subject area to you? What kind of job will it lead to? How difficult will the course work be? What is the pay like in this field? You also temper these judgments with your perception of how likely it is that these outcomes will actually occur. There may be high-salaried jobs in your major area, but if you see little chance of actually getting one of them, then you will be less likely to choose that major.

Logically, we would seek to make decisions that we believe have a good chance of leading to favorable outcomes. However, our decision-making processes are a bit more complex than this. Another factor that affects our decisions is how the possible courses of action are presented, or *framed* (Kahneman & Tversky, 1984). For example, which of the following options would you choose? Would you choose to take a class in which you had a 60% chance of passing? Or one in which you had a 40% chance of failing? Many people would choose the first option because it is framed positively, even though the chance of succeeding in the course is the

**reasoning**   drawing conclusions about the world based on certain assumptions

**deductive reasoning**   reasoning from the general to the specific

**inductive reasoning**   reasoning from the specific to the general

**decision making**   making a choice from among a series of alternatives

same in both cases. Whether you prefer a positively framed option or a negatively framed one depends on your orientation. Sometimes we exhibit *loss aversion*, or a tendency to focus on what a certain decision could cost us in terms of potential gain—for example, worrying that your choice of major may limit your future employment opportunities. Other times, we exhibit *risk aversion*, or concern over losing what we already have—for example, worrying that the time you need to devote to your chosen major may force you to give up your current job.

## Judgments: Estimating the Likelihood of Events

**Judgment** can be seen as a type of problem solving in which we estimate the probability of an event. If you don't know what the probability of a certain event is, and you need to have this probability to make a decision, what do you do? As with all problems, you can solve this one using either an algorithm or a heuristic. An algorithm would involve somehow looking up or calculating the exact probability that a given event will occur. This is often neither possible nor practical, as in the case of trying to figure out what the stock market will do in the coming months. So, as we saw before, we tend to rely on heuristics when we make judgments.

### THE AVAILABILITY HEURISTIC

Many people are afraid to fly, even though air travel is statistically safer than traveling by car (National Safety Council, 2011). Why would people be afraid to choose a *safer* form of travel? The answer lies in the manner in which we make judgments about the frequency of events. When we estimate the frequency of events, we heuristically base our judgments on the ease with which we can recall instances of the event in memory. The more easily we can recall a memory for an event, the more frequent we estimate the event to be. This memory shortcut is called the **availability heuristic** (Tversky & Kahneman, 1974).

The availability heuristic explains the previous example of fearing air travel more than driving. Although fatal car accidents occur every day, they are not as widely covered by the media as plane crashes are. A fatal car crash may result in one or a few deaths, but a plane crash usually involves a larger number of fatalities. Therefore, when a plane goes down, the news coverage is graphic, horrifying, and prolonged. This leaves us with a strong, easily accessible memory for the plane crash. The result is that when we think of ways to travel, we more readily recall memories of plane crashes, and we may mistakenly overestimate the risk associated with air travel (Bahk, 2006). The result is that many people fear flying, when they really ought to be more afraid of traveling by car.

### THE REPRESENTATIVENESS HEURISTIC

We also make heuristic judgments when deciding whether an object, event, or person belongs in a particular category by relying on the degree to which the person or thing in question is representative of the category. This tendency, called the **representativeness heuristic**, explains some of the mistakes we make in judgment (Tversky & Kahneman, 1974).

For instance, we often ignore the true probability, or *base rate*, of events in favor of our heuristic judgments. In one experiment on the representativeness heuristic, participants were told that a group of 100 people contained 70 engineers and 30 lawyers. They were also given a description of one of the group members—a man—that included the following traits: conservative, ambitious,

**judgment** the act of estimating the probability of an event

**availability heuristic** a heuristic in which we use the ease with which we can recall instances of an event to help us estimate the frequency of the event

**representativeness heuristic** a heuristic in which we rely on the degree to which something is representative of a category, rather than the base rate, to help us judge whether or not it belongs in the category

According to the availability heuristic, the ease with which we can retrieve memories of events from long-term memory biases our judgments of how frequently the event occurs in real life. Seeing news coverage of air disasters like this one leaves us with vivid memories of plane crashes that cause us to overestimate the probability of a plane crash occurring in the future. As a result, air traffic often falls off immediately following a crash, although in general flying is still safer than driving to your destination.

Mario Tama/Getty Images

The speed and uniformity with which infants learn language across the world suggests to some that humans have a *language acquisition device* or innate knowledge of the syntax of language.

the innate nature of language also comes from cross-cultural studies on language development in hearing children. These studies show that regardless of the culture, language seems to develop in children at about the same age and in the same sequence of stages. This similarity in the developmental process, which occurs despite cultural differences, argues for some biological mechanism that underlies language.

## COOING AND BABBLING: BABY STEPS TO LEARNING ONE OR MORE LANGUAGES

Most of us acquire our first language beginning in the first couple of years of life. Research indicates that newborns from birth to 1 month are capable of perceiving vowel sounds in an adult-like manner (Aldridge, Stillman, & Bower, 2001), and by about 2 months, infants begin **cooing**. Cooing involves making vowel sounds, such as "ooo" and "ah." By 4 months, infants begin to engage in **babbling**, which adds consonant sounds to the vowel sounds they emitted during cooing. For example, an infant might repeat the sound "ka, ka, ka" over and over. Infants' first babbles are very similar across cultures, but this soon changes (Stoel-Gammon & Otomo, 1986). By 7 months, infants begin to emit babbles that contain sounds that are part of the language they have been exposed to in their environment. In this fashion, the infant's language system apparently tunes itself to the language or languages that the infant hears on a regular basis. By 1 year, children's babbling contains the sounds and intonations of their native language (Levitt & Utmann, 1992).

> ## You Asked...
>
> *Why is language easier to learn at a young age?*
>
> CLINTON BLAKE ROBERTS, STUDENT

Perhaps because the infant's language system appears to tune itself to the sounds of the language the child hears, children who grow up in *bilingual* households, where adults speak two languages to the children, tend to acquire both languages at high levels of proficiency (Petitto, 2009). But this does not mean that a child cannot learn a second language later in life. A child who is not exposed to a second language until elementary school can still develop near-native proficiency in the language (Hakuta, 1999). However, from childhood to adulthood, it seems to become steadily more difficult for us to become bilingual. For example, an adolescent who is just beginning to learn Spanish may never speak Spanish as fluently as a child who began learning Spanish in elementary school (Hakuta, Bailystok, & Wiley, 2003). Therefore, if true bilingualism is desired, it is best to begin learning the second language as early as possible.

Once a child achieves the stage of babbling the basic sounds, or **phonemes**, of her native tongue, the next step in language development is learning to communicate. At around 12 months, children begin trying to communicate in earnest with others. This communication is often based on gestures before it is based on words. For example, a child may point at a toy that he wants. When parents learn to interpret these *preverbal gestures*, communication is achieved. As they catch on to their child's preverbal gestures, parents often verbalize the meaning of the

**cooing**   the vowel sounds made by infants beginning at 2 months

**babbling**   the combinations of vowel and consonant sounds uttered by infants beginning around 4 months

**phoneme [FOE-neem]**   the smallest unit of sound in a language

gesture for the child. Parents say things like, "Oh, do you want this toy?" This verbalization of the child's intention allows the child to begin to learn **morphemes**, or the smallest sounds in a language that have meaning. As a result, by the end of the first year or so, children begin to speak their first words.

## FROM "MAMA" AND "DADA" TO FULL CONVERSATIONS

A child's first words are usually the names of familiar objects, people, actions, or situations, ones with which they have had a great deal of contact. Typically, these words are *Dada*, *Mama*, *hi*, *hot*, and the like. Between 12 to 18 months of age, children usually utter only one word at a time, and often they convey tremendous meaning with these one-word sentences. For example, the utterance "Milk!" may stand for "I want some milk, please!"

As young children begin to speak, they may exhibit **overextension** in their language, using one word to symbolize all manner of similar instances. For instance, the word *dog* may be used to symbolize any animal. During this period, the opposite problem may also occur when children exhibit **underextension** of language. In this situation, children inappropriately restrict their use of a word to a particular case, such as when a child uses the word *dog* to refer only to the family pet.

By the time children reach 20–26 months, they begin to combine words into two-word sentences in what is called **telegraphic speech**. Telegraphic speech is often ungrammatical, but it does convey meaning, such as "Doggie bad," meaning "The dog was bad." From here, children rapidly acquire both vocabulary and **grammar**, or the rules that govern sentence structure in their language, such as word order and verb tenses. From the simple subject–verb combinations of telegraphic speech, English-speaking children progress to more complex subject–verb–object sentences between ages 2 and 3. Children who speak other languages adopt the relevant grammatical patterns of their native language. As children develop throughout the preschool years, their knowledge and use of grammar becomes increasingly complex. By age 6, the average child has an impressive vocabulary of around 10,000 words and a fairly competent mastery of grammar (Tager-Flusberg, 2005).

As children develop better vocabularies and acquire the grammatical rules of language, they exercise these abilities during social interactions with others. It's during these social interactions with peers and adults that children begin to learn **pragmatics**, or the rules of conversation operating in their culture. Pragmatics may include rules about turn taking, eye contact, tone of voice, and other aspects of conversation.

These hard-earned linguistic abilities will be very valuable to the child, as they are to us all. Let's take a closer look at what, exactly, language does for us.

## The Function of Language in Culture and Perception

It is not difficult to see that language affects us in many ways. Obviously, one of language's main functions is to facilitate communication. We use language to describe our world, our thoughts, and our experiences to others. Without language, we would lead lives of social isolation. Yet language can divide us as well as unite us, a topic we explore in Psychology Across Generations (p. 258).

## LANGUAGE AND THE DEVELOPMENT OF CULTURE

Because language brings us together and allows us to share ideas and experiences, language also plays a role in the development of *culture*. Russian psychologist Lev Vygotsky (1896–1934) noted the influence of language in the

**morpheme [MORE-feem]**   the smallest unit of sound in a language that has meaning

**overextension**   when a child uses one word to symbolize all manner of similar instances (e.g., calling all birds *parakeet*)

**underextension**   when a child inappropriately restricts the use of a word to a particular case (e.g., using the word *cat* to describe only the family pet)

**telegraphic speech**   two-word sentences that children begin to utter at 20–26 months

**grammar**   the rules that govern the sentence structure in a particular language

**pragmatics**   the rules of conversation in a particular culture

## Psychology Across Generations:

### Slang—The Changing Face of Language

If someone were to say, *"That fish is a real four-flusher. He wouldn't even kick in an Abe's Cabe for some brown plaid,"* would you know what he meant? If this phrase is incomprehensible to you, don't feel bad. Most people today would not grasp its meaning. This sentence illustrates the power of *slang*, the nonstandard use of language that is often unique to a specific cultural-historical group.

© Bettmann/Corbis

The slang used by young people in the 1920s may be incomprehensible to the youth of today. The use of slang both includes and excludes people. People in the group know and use the slang while outsiders are excluded from the conversation.

Frequently, it is the youth of a culture who drive the development and spread of new slang. Slang is typically a reflection of the world in which a generation is living. For example, a Gen Xer in the workforce may use technology-oriented slang terms such as *crapplet* for a problematic Java applet (Mariotti, 1997). Or, a Millennial may say, *hit me up* (*HMU*) to encourage a friend to get in touch. Both of these terms reflect the dominance of the Internet and computing in today's world.

Some even view slang as poetic expression (Adams, 2009; Danesi, 2010). Slang words may describe the world around us in an artistic, almost musical fashion—for example, hip-hop terms such as *phat* (very good) and *grill* (face). Later, if these words are pleasing to us, they can become an enduring part of everyday language. For example, the word *hubbub* was a slang term from the era of William Shakespeare that has become common language for a noisy, bustling environment (Danesi, 2010).

Slang also serves a social need. Slang allows us to both fit in and stand apart from others (Adams, 2009). A teenager can fit in with her friends using terms like *let's bounce* (let's leave) and *toolbag* (an arrogant male) while at the same time retaining an identity that is distinct from that of her mystified parents (who think a toolbag belongs in the garage). Only those who know the slang can fully join the group. If the group is admired, it becomes "cool" to use certain slang, which further motivates people to use it in an attempt to fit in. As more people try to fit in, more people begin to use the slang. This forces the group or generation to develop new slang in an attempt to retain their unique and separate identity.

Slang is not new. It's been around for centuries. ■ TABLE 7.2 shows some examples of slang for "very good" that have been used over the years. How many of these terms have you used? Oh, and by the way, *"That fish is a real four-flusher. He wouldn't even kick in an Abe's Cabe for some brown plaid"* meant, to the young people of the 1920s, "That freshman is a cheap poser who wouldn't even chip in $5.00 for some Scotch whiskey."

### TABLE 7.2
#### Slang Used to Describe Something as Very Good or Nice Over the Decades

| 1920s | 1930s | 1940s | 1950s | 1960s | 1970s | 1980s | 1990s | 2000s |
|---|---|---|---|---|---|---|---|---|
| Cat's meow; the bee's knees | Gasser; out of this world; a riot | Dynamite; gas | Cool; a ball | A gas; groovy | Far out; neat-o; radical | Bomb; wicked; tubular; awesome | Sweet; badical; chauncy | Straight; coolio; shiznit |

*Source: Lexiteria Corporation, 2011.*

development of culture in his *sociocultural theory* (Vygotsky, 1934/1987) (see Chapter 9). According to sociocultural theory, older and more knowledgeable members of a society pass on the values, beliefs, and customs of their culture to children by telling the children stories and by engaging in conversations with them. The children store these dialogues in their memory and later use this knowledge to guide their behavior. Just as you learned from the stories of your elders, someday you too will pass down elements of your culture as you converse with younger people.

Language may facilitate the transmission of culture from generation to generation, but does the language we speak also affect the way we view the world? In the next section, we'll take a look at this interesting issue.

## LINGUISTIC RELATIVITY: THE INFLUENCE OF LANGUAGE ON THOUGHT

One of the most intriguing theories about language came from an unlikely source. Benjamin Whorf was a Connecticut fire insurance inspector whose unusual hobby was *linguistics*, or the study of language. After intensive studies of the languages of Native Americans, Whorf became convinced that one's language could directly determine or influence one's thoughts (Whorf, 1956). This notion has since come to be called the **Whorfian hypothesis** or the **linguistic relativity hypothesis** (for a review, see Tohidian, 2009).

In its strongest form, the linguistic relativity hypothesis states that one's language actually determines one's thoughts and one's perception of the world. According to this view, people who have different native languages think differently and perceive the world in a different light. For example, Whorf argued that Eskimos would understand "snow" differently than Europeans because the Eskimos' native language has more words for snow than English has. Whorf claimed that differences among languages make it impossible to express all thoughts equally in all languages. Therefore, you can think and see the world only in terms of the language that you know. According to Whorf, your language *determines* what you think and how you perceive the world.

To date, the bulk of the evidence does not support the strong form of Whorf's linguistic relativity hypothesis (see ■ TABLE 7.3). However, there is reason to think that a modified, or weaker, interpretation of the Whorfian hypothesis may hold true. The weaker version states that instead of language *determining* thought processes, language merely *influences* them. For example, a study that compared Spanish speakers to Mayan speakers found differences in their ability to remember colors. These memory differences were related to how easy it is to verbally label colors in Spanish and Mayan (Stefflre, Castillo-Vales, & Morley, 1966). It appears that how easily you can label a color in your language does affect your memory for that color.

It is also likely that language can influence our perception of the world. In one study involving the sorting of color samples, participants who spoke Setswana were more likely to group blues and greens together than were those who spoke English or Russian. This finding was attributed to the fact that in Setswana, one word describes both blue and green colors (Davies, 1998). The idea that humans do not all categorize color the same way is an important premise of the linguistic relativity hypothesis.

**Whorfian [WORE-fee-un] hypothesis, or linguistic relativity hypothesis** the theory that one's language can directly determine or influence one's thoughts

## TABLE 7.3
### Different Words for Snow
Contrary to Whorf's hypothesis, like the Eskimo, English speakers do have several words for snow.

| ESKIMO | ENGLISH |
| --- | --- |
| *qanuk*: "snowflake" | snowflake |
| *qanir*: "to snow" | snow |
| *kanevvluk*: "fine snow/rain particles" | snowfall |
| *muruaneq*: "soft deep snow" | powder |
| *pirta*: "blizzard, snowstorm" | blizzard, snowstorm |
| *nutaryuk*: "fresh snow" | powder |
| *qengaruk*: "snow bank" | snowbank |

## Psychology Applies to Your World:

### Are Humans the Only Animals to Use Language?

For centuries, humans believed that they alone had the ability to use language. It was assumed that only the advanced human mind was capable of dealing with the complexities of a language. Remarkably, this assumption has been called into question. Although it is very controversial, today some researchers believe that some other animals may possess linguistic abilities (e.g., Shanker, Savage-Rumbaugh, & Taylor, 1999).

In looking at the linguistic abilities of other species, we first have to make a distinction between *language* and *communication*. Language is a system of communication that has a set vocabulary and a set structure, or grammar. For instance, English sentences generally follow a subject–verb–object pattern. Though many languages reverse the order of the verb and the object, most of the world's languages place the subject at the beginning of the sentence—for example, *Mike ran home* (Ultan, 1969). Languages also differ with respect to the placement of adjectives and adverbs. English places the adjective before the noun, *blue dress*; Spanish places it after, *vestido azul*. As you can see, each language has its own set of rules.

In contrast to the structure and order of language, communication can be very unstructured. All that is required in a communication system is that your meaning be conveyed to others. There is little argument that animals can communicate. For example, a rooster will emit an alarm cry to warn other chickens of danger (Marler, Duffy, & Pickert, 1986) and domestic dogs respond to specific play signals of their owners (Rooney, Bradshaw, & Robinson, 2001). But does this ability of some animals to communicate mean they have the capacity for language?

Some of the best evidence for animal language comes from studies done on Bonobo chimpanzees. Bonobos, also known as pygmy chimpanzees, are perhaps our closest genetic relatives, even more closely related to us than the common chimpanzee. During the 1980s, researcher Sue Savage-Rumbaugh and others attempted to teach English to a Bonobo named Matata. Because Bonobos do not have vocal cords that produce humanlike speech, they cannot actually speak. To get around this problem, the researchers used a special computer keyboard during the language training. On the surface of the keyboard were pictures, and when a picture was pressed, a computer-generated voice spoke the name of the object in the picture. Using this keyboard, Savage-Rumbaugh tried to teach Matata the meaning of certain words, but Matata did not catch on well (Wise, 2000, p. 223). However, Matata's infant stepson, Kanzi, had been observing his mother's lessons. Although Savage-Rumbaugh and her colleagues never attempted to teach Kanzi to use the keyboard, he picked up this skill on his own (Savage-Rumbaugh et al., 1986). By age 2½, Kanzi had begun to use some of the symbols his mother was trying to learn on the keyboard. When experimenters gave up trying to teach Matata to use the keyboard, they separated her from Kanzi. The day Matata left, Kanzi approached the keyboard and began to use it to make requests and express himself. In fact, he used it a total of 120 times on that first day (Wise, 2000).

Much like a young child, Kanzi appeared to have learned some vocabulary just by observing language being used around him. Kanzi's acquisition of language seemed to occur quite naturally (Shanker et al., 1999). For example, a patch of wild strawberries grew outside of Kanzi's laboratory, and when he discovered them, Kanzi began to eat them. He overheard researchers referring to them by the word *strawberries* and soon appeared to understand what the word *strawberries* meant. After apparently learning the meaning of the word *strawberries*, Kanzi would head for the berry patch whenever he heard someone speak the word (Savage-Rumbaugh, 1987).

Overall, Kanzi's use of language is quite impressive. He uses the keyboard to make requests, such as to visit another chimpanzee named Austin. If he is told that he cannot visit because it's too cold to go outside, Kanzi modifies his request to ask to see a picture of Austin on TV (Savage-Rumbaugh, 1987). Furthermore, Kanzi seems to be able to respond to very unusual and novel requests, such as "Put the pine needles in the refrigerator" or "Put the soap on the ball."

Language abilities have been shown in species other than the Bonobos as well. Researcher Irene Pepperberg (1993, 1999) had some success in training an African grey parrot named Alex to speak some English. Unlike the Bonobo, a

As an infant, Kanzi learned to use a language keyboard like this one to communicate with humans just by watching researchers who were working with his mother, Matata.

© Michael Nichols/National Geographic Image Collection

parrot has the physical ability to produce speech as well as comprehend it. Before his death in 2007, Alex was able to speak some words in English, and identify the shape, color, and material of many objects (Pepperberg, 1991). Attempts to train other African grey parrots to use words to refer to objects have yielded mixed results (Giret et al., 2010).

Dolphins have also shown some linguistic promise. Researcher Louis Herman and his colleagues have had some success in training dolphins to understand a language that the researchers created. This created language is based on gestures, but it has a set vocabulary in which certain gestures stand for certain words, and a specific set of grammatical rules that dictate how gestures can be combined into phrases. One of the dolphins, named Phoenix, was able to follow a complex sequence of instructions delivered in this gestured language (Herman & Uyeyama, 1999). Another dolphin, Ake, seemed to notice when the grammatical laws of the language had been violated (Herman, Kuczaj, & Holder, 1993).

As impressive as the linguistic abilities of Kanzi, Alex, Ake, and Phoenix are, not everyone is convinced that animals truly have the capacity for language. Some argue that these animals are merely highly trained (Pinker, 1994). Skeptics propose that rather than actually using language, the animals are engaging in trained behaviors that they hope will lead to some reward. Certainly, Alex, Ake, and Phoenix were trained to use language, but what about Kanzi, who was never trained to use language? He learned it on his own during his early years, just as children do (Shanker et al., 1999).

Another criticism of animal language research directly questions the linguistic abilities of animals. Some argue that animal language researchers have not adequately demonstrated that animals can follow all of the grammatical and syntactical rules of human language (Kako, 1999). Animal language researchers counter that their critics have unfairly focused on the linguistic abilities that animals lack and have largely ignored the linguistic abilities that animals *do* have (Shanker et al., 1999).

You can see that this is a very passionate debate—as well it should be, for there is a great deal at stake here. If we ultimately determine that animals do have linguistic capacities, then we may have to reconsider what separates humans from the rest of the animal kingdom. This possibility brings up a whole host of ethical questions concerning animals and the manner in which we treat them in human society (Wise, 2000).

Although controversial, studies of animals like Alex, the African grey parrot, challenge the presumption that language is a solely human attribute.

© Rick Friedman/Corbis

# Let's

## REVIEW

In this section, we covered many aspects of language, including how we acquire language, what it does for us, and the debate over language as a purely human attribute. For a quick check of your understanding, answer these questions.

1. Babies begin _____ when they begin to make _____ sounds.
   a. cooing; consonant
   b. babbling; vowel
   c. cooing; vowel and consonant
   d. babbling; vowel and consonant

2. Which of the following people would be the *most* likely to agree with the statement "Language facilitates the development of culture"?
   a. Lev Vygotsky
   b. Benjamin Whorf
   c. Sue Savage-Rumbaugh
   d. Eleanor Rosch

3. One's language can influence one's _____.
   a. speech
   b. memory
   c. perception
   d. All of the above

*Answers 1. d; 2. a; 3. d*

## LEARNING OBJECTIVES

- Describe historical and modern attempts to measure intelligence, and some of the advantages and disadvantages of these methods.

- Describe the various ways that researchers have conceptualized intelligence.

- Describe the nature versus nurture debate as it applies to intelligence.

What makes a person intelligent? Is it earning good grades? Knowing how to survive in the wilderness? Having good social skills? Today, many psychologists view **intelligence** broadly as having abilities that allow you to adapt to your environment and behave in a goal-directed way. But over the years, psychologists have found that developing a precise definition of intelligence is not as easy as it may seem, and our conception of intelligence has undergone several revisions. Equally challenging has been finding ways of measuring intelligence.

### You Asked...

*What is the actual definition of intelligence?*

BREDRON LYTLE, STUDENT

## Measuring Intelligence by Abilities and IQs

One of the first people to study the measurement of intelligence was British psychologist Sir Francis Galton (1822–1911). Galton claimed that intelligence is an inherited trait that is correlated with having superior physical abilities. As such, he believed that intelligence could be measured by measuring traits like reaction time, eyesight, and so on. However, early studies failed to find much support for Galton's ideas (Schultz & Schultz, 2000), and they soon fell out of favor.

### ALFRED BINET: MEASURING INTELLIGENCE BY MEASURING COGNITIVE ABILITIES

The modern intelligence test is credited to Alfred Binet (1857–1911). In 1904, the French government appointed Alfred Binet and psychiatrist Théodore Simon to a commission charged with developing a means of measuring the intelligence of French schoolchildren so that the government could identify children who would not likely profit from traditional education.

Binet saw intelligence as the capacity to *find and maintain a purpose, adopt a strategy to reach that purpose,* and *evaluate the strategy so it can be adjusted as necessary* (Terman, 1916). In essence, Binet suggested that having intelligence makes one a good problem solver. As such, he developed an intelligence test that assessed general cognitive abilities such as the individual's attention, judgment, and reasoning skills (Binet & Simon, 1905).

Binet prepared a set of 30 tasks that measured these skills and arranged them in order of difficulty, with the easiest questions first and the hardest questions last. Not surprisingly, the brighter students could answer more of the questions than the not-so-bright students could. Also, not surprisingly, the older children tended to answer more questions correctly than the younger children. In fact, Binet noticed that the brighter younger children could sometimes answer correctly as many questions as the average child of an older age. For example, a very smart 6-year-old might be able to answer as many questions as the average 10-year-old child could. So Binet began to quantify children's intelligence in terms of **mental age**, or the age that reflects a child's mental abilities in comparison to the "average" child. In Binet's scheme, a mental age that exceeds one's chronological age indicates above-average intelligence, and a mental age that is below a

**intelligence**   abilities that enable you to adapt to your environment and behave in a goal-directed way

**mental age**   the age that reflects the child's mental abilities in comparison to the average child of the same age

child's actual age indicates a below-average level of intelligence. Binet's concept of mental age became the foundation for the IQ score, and his test became the basis for modern intelligence tests.

## LEWIS TERMAN: THE INTELLIGENCE QUOTIENT AND THE STANFORD-BINET

In 1916, Stanford psychologist Lewis Terman completed an American revision of the intelligence test that Binet and Simon had developed. He named his version of the test the Stanford Revision of the Binet-Simon Scale, which became known as the Stanford-Binet. The Stanford-Binet is an example of a **standardized test**—a test that uses a standard set of questions, procedures, and scoring methods for all test takers. In standardizing the Stanford-Binet, Terman gave the test to a large number of people and calculated the average test scores that people of different ages made on the test. These norms allowed Terman to establish mental age scores for people taking the Stanford-Binet.

Perhaps Terman's most significant contribution to the test was to popularize the use of an **intelligence quotient**, or **IQ**, as the measure of an individual's intelligence. An IQ score is calculated as follows:

$$IQ = (MA/CA) \times 100$$

where

$$MA = \text{mental age}$$

and

$$CA = \text{chronological, or actual, age}$$

Using the concept of an IQ, a person of average abilities has, by definition, an IQ of 100 or, in other words, a mental age equal to her or his actual age. IQs over 100 indicate above-average intelligence, and IQs below 100 indicate below-average intelligence.

The Stanford-Binet has undergone four major revisions since 1916 and is still in wide use today. The most recent edition, the Stanford-Binet Intelligence Scales, Fifth Edition (SB5), was released in 2003. However, a modern IQ test developed by psychologist David Wechsler (1896–1981) and first released in 1939 has greatly challenged the popularity of the Stanford-Binet.

## DAVID WECHSLER'S INTELLIGENCE SCALES

Wechsler (1939) developed his intelligence test in response to shortcomings he saw in the Stanford-Binet. Wechsler objected to the fact that the Stanford-Binet test tried to sum up intelligence in a single score. He believed that one number could not adequately express something as complex as intelligence. Furthermore, Wechsler objected to the use of the mental age concept for adults (R. M. Kaplan & Saccuzzo, 1989). After all, would you necessarily expect a 40-year-old to correctly answer more questions than a 35-year-old? The concept of mental age doesn't apply as well to adults as it does to children because adults do not change as much from year to year as children do. Therefore, mental age has little significance in adulthood.

To correct these problems, Wechsler developed an intelligence test that yields scores on individual *subscales* that measure different mental abilities. Furthermore, instead of using mental age to determine IQ, Wechsler's tests compare a participant's performance to the average person's performance to determine IQ. The Wechsler tests are standardized tests that are devised so that an average person's performance on the test results in an IQ of 100. Using this number as a benchmark, people who score above average on the test are given IQ scores above 100, and people who

**standardized test**   a test that uses a standard set of questions, procedures, and scoring methods for all test takers

**intelligence quotient (IQ)**   one's mental age divided by one's chronological age times 100

# 7.4

## The Normal Distribution of IQ Scores

IQs tend to be normally distributed across the population. This means that when a frequency distribution of IQ scores is plotted, it forms a bell-shaped curve, with most people scoring near the average of 100 on the IQ test and very few scoring extremely high or low.

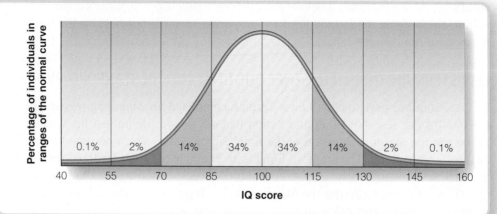

perform below average are given IQ scores below 100. Most people can expect to score near this average IQ, somewhere in the range of 85–115 (■ FIGURE 7.4).

Today there are three separate Wechsler intelligence tests. The Wechsler Preschool and Primary Scale of Intelligence, Third Edition (WPPSI-III) is administered to children ages 2½–7. The Wechsler Intelligence Scale for Children, Fourth Edition (WISC-IV) is used for children ages 6–16. And the Wechsler Adult Intelligence Scale, Fourth Edition (WAIS-IV) is used for people ages 16–90.

The WAIS-IV consists of 11 subtests that measure various verbal and performance abilities (■ TABLE 7.4). Performance on these subtests is used to calculate an overall IQ score as well as separate index scores for *verbal comprehension*, *perceptual reasoning*, *working memory*, and *processing speed*. The design of the WAIS-IV makes it flexible. Testers can administer any of the indexes alone (for example, measuring only perceptual reasoning) or all of them together to obtain an overall IQ score.

## TESTING THE TEST: WHAT MAKES A GOOD INTELLIGENCE TEST?

So far, we have looked at two widely accepted tests that psychologists and educators use to measure intelligence. These are but two of a great many tests that have been devised to measure intelligence and other psychological traits. When choosing which test to administer or when interpreting the scores yielded by these tests, we have to ask, "Is this a good test?" If psychologists never worried about the quality of their measurements, they could well find themselves making many faulty judgments about the people they measure. Think about it: How would you feel if someone gave you an IQ test and then told you that your score would determine whether you got a job? Wouldn't you want some assurance that the test actually reflected your true intellectual ability? Most of us would.

Before a test is used to make decisions about anyone's life, the test itself must be tested and evaluated. Psychologists must be assured that the test is both *reliable* and *valid* before it can be put into widespread use. The **reliability** of a test refers to the degree to which the test yields consistent measurements over time. Although intelligence can change over time, it usually does so very slowly. In general, if you are intelligent today, you will be intelligent 6 months from now. So, if we use a test to measure your IQ today and then again in 6 months, the scores should be comparable. This doesn't mean that the test has to yield *exactly* the same score, but the scores should be close.

Establishing the reliability of an intelligence test is very important, but the **validity** of the test is an equally important characteristic. Validity is the degree to which the test measures what it was designed to measure. In the case of an intelligence test, one must show that the test actually measures intelligence!

The WISC and WAIS use different types of tasks to assess IQ.

© Bob Daemmrich/The Image Works

**reliability** the degree to which a test yields consistent measurements of a trait

**validity** the degree to which a test measures the trait that it was designed to measure

## TABLE 7.4
## The Wechsler Adult Intelligence Scale (WAIS-IV) and Its Subscales

NOTE: The test items shown are examples—they do not appear in the actual test.

| CONTENT AREA | EXPLANATION OF TASKS/QUESTIONS | EXAMPLES OF POSSIBLE TASKS/QUESTIONS |
|---|---|---|
| **Verbal Comprehension** | | |
| Vocabulary | Define the meaning of the word. | What does persistent mean? <br> What does archaeology mean? |
| Information | Supply generally known information. | Who is Hillary Clinton? <br> What are six New England states? |
| Similarities | Explain how two things or concepts are similar. | In what ways are an ostrich and a penguin alike? <br> In what ways are a lamp and a heater alike? |
| **Perceptual Reasoning** | | |
| Block design | Use patterned blocks to form a design that looks identical to a design shown by the examiner. | Assemble the blocks on the left to make the design on the right. <br> |
| Matrix reasoning | Fill in the missing cell in a matrix with a picture that would logically complete the matrix. | Which of these figures would complete the logical sequence in this matrix? <br> |
| Visual puzzles | Construct a figure from a series of puzzle pieces. | Which three of these pieces go together to make this puzzle? <br> |
| **Working Memory** | | |
| Digit span | Listen to a series of digits (numbers), then repeat the numbers either forward, backward, or both. | Repeat these numbers backward: 9, 1, 8, 3, 6. |
| Arithmetic | Mental manipulation of arithmetical concepts. | How many 52-cent candy bars can you buy with a five-dollar bill? |
| **Processing Speed** | | |
| Symbol search | When given an array of symbols, find the specified symbol and circle it. | Circle the ♣ in the following array: <br> |
| Digit symbol | When given a key matching particular symbols to particular numerals, copy a sequence of symbols, transcribing from symbols to numerals, using the key. | Look carefully at the key. In the blanks, write the correct numeral for the symbol below each symbol. <br> |

# 8

## Motivation and EMOTION: What Guides Our BEHAVIOR?

© Ed Bock/Corbis

# Chapter Outline

*One of our students,* Cris, never liked school growing up. He thought it was boring, and subjects like math seemed pointless and unworthy of much effort. Unmotivated, Cris only did well in subjects that he found interesting, such as music.

Cris's motivation challenges followed him to college. After a successful first semester, Cris moved in with a friend and quickly found himself more motivated to socialize than to study. His grades plummeted. It was evident that Cris was bright, but his lack of motivation was taking its toll. He failed psychology and soon ended up on academic probation.

After a death in his family, Cris took some time off from school and moved back home. With time on his hands, he began to think about his future and some of the choices he had made. He decided to make some changes. He returned to college, re-enrolled in psychology, and began to take an interest in what he was learning. Psychology helped Cris to better understand himself and others. For example, he realized that he had *learned helplessness* (see Chapter 11; a belief that one is unable to change one's situation) when it came to math. Knowing this allowed Cris to begin reevaluating how he perceived his own behavior. For example, when he did succeed at math, he put aside his tendency to discount his success as a fluke, and he began to trust in his own abilities.

As Cris began to see the usefulness of school, he also began to believe that he could succeed. As his motivation increased, he began reading, taking notes, and studying. As a result, he got an A in psychology and passed a math course he had once thought impossible to pass. Today, Cris still has his challenges, but he is committed to doing his best, and he appears

*Our student, Cris Arthurs, had to overcome a lack of motivation to begin succeeding in college.*

to be happier than when we first met him. He now likes to say that *unmotivated* and *student* are two words that shouldn't be used in the same sentence—because they just don't work together.

In this chapter, we will explore the role that motivation and emotion play in our lives. As you read, think about how this information is relevant to your life. Like Cris, you may just find yourself even more motivated to keep reading and learning.

# How Do Psychologists View Motivation?

**You Asked...**

*What motivates us to do something?*
ERICK HERNANDEZ, STUDENT

When we are *motivated*, we are driven to engage in some form of behavior. Just as something motivated you to start reading this chapter, every day we are motivated to do many different things. For example, we are motivated to eat, drink, attend school, go to work, interact with family and friends, and so on. In psychological terms, a **motive** is the tendency to desire and seek out positive incentives or rewards and to avoid negative outcomes (Atkinson, 1958/1983; McClelland, 1987). This means that we are motivated to avoid aversive states and to seek more pleasant states. When we experience the motive of hunger, we eat to avoid this aversive feeling. We are motivated to study because we want the feelings of pride and the opportunities for advancement that accompany academic success. Because we are generally motivated to avoid pain and other aversive states, our motives often serve to protect us. Without the motivation to eat, we could experience malnutrition or even starvation. As you can see, without motivation we would not engage in many behaviors that are necessary for good health and survival.

In an attempt to better understand what motivates us, psychologists have historically viewed motivation in several different ways: as *instincts* that direct our behavior; as uncomfortable biological states called *drives* that motivate us to find ways to feel better; as the desire to maintain an optimal level of *arousal* in our body; or as *incentives* that guide us to seek reward from the world. However, none of these theories seems to fully explain all aspects of motivation. Today psychologists do not expect any single theory to explain all our motivations. Instead, we recognize that each of these theories has its strengths and weaknesses. Let's take a closer look at these different theories of motivation.

## Motivation as Instinct

**motive** a tendency to desire and seek out positive incentives or rewards and to avoid negative outcomes

**instinct** innate impulse from within a person that directs or motivates behavior

**drive reduction theory** a theory of motivation that proposes that people seek to reduce internal levels of drive

**drive** an uncomfortable internal state that motivates us to reduce this discomfort through our behavior

**primary drive** a drive that motivates us to maintain homeostasis in certain biological processes within the body

**homeostasis [hoe-mee-oh-STAY-suss]** an internal state of equilibrium in the body

**negative feedback loop** a system of feedback in the body that monitors and adjusts our motivation level so as to maintain homeostasis

**secondary drive** a learned drive that is not directly related to biological needs

One of the earliest views on motivation was one that was heavily influenced by the work of Charles Darwin and the theory of natural selection (see Chapter 7; Darwin, 1859/1936). Back in the 1800s, American psychologist William James proposed that motives are, in fact, genetically determined **instincts** that have evolved in humans because they support survival and procreation. According to James, instincts are impulses from within a person that direct or motivate that person's behavior. James proposed that we are motivated by more than 35 different innate instincts, including the impulse to love, fight, imitate, talk, and acquire things (James, 1890).

Over time, the idea that motives are inborn instincts gradually fell out of favor with psychologists. One problem with James's view was that the list of proposed instincts kept getting longer and longer, and it seemed unrealistic to argue that *all* behavior is due to instinct. Furthermore, it is impossible to determine whether many of the proposed instincts are truly inborn. Many of James's so-called instincts, such as being sympathetic or being secretive, may result from learning.

## Motivation as a Drive

Instinct theory was followed by **drive reduction theories** of motivation. According to the drive reduction approach, motivation stems from the desire to reduce an uncomfortable, internal state, called a **drive**, that results when our needs are not fulfilled (Hull, 1943). For instance, when we do not have enough food in our system, we feel the uncomfortable state of hunger, which drives us to eat until we have taken in the food that our bodies require. Then, when we have taken in enough food, the hunger drive dissipates, and we stop eating. In this fashion, our drives can help us survive by creating what psychologists call a *drive state*, which ensures that we will be motivated to meet our biological needs.

**Primary drives**, such as needing food, water, and warmth, motivate us to maintain certain bodily processes at an internal state of equilibrium, or **homeostasis**. Obviously, it would be desirable for us to take in just the right amount of food and water, to sleep just enough, and to maintain our body temperature at 98.6 degrees. Without the motivation from drives, we would not keep our bodies at homeostasis because we would not know when to eat, sleep, drink, and so on. But what causes a drive state in the first place?

Primary drives begin in the body when the brain recognizes that we are lacking in some biological need. The brain recognizes need based on the *feedback* that it receives from the body's systems and organs. One type of feedback system is called a **negative feedback loop** (■ FIGURE 8.1). Negative feedback loops are information systems in the body that monitor the level of a bodily process and adjust it up or down accordingly. A good analogy for a negative feedback loop is a thermostat. In your home, you set the thermostat at a desired level. The thermostat monitors the air temperature and compares it to that set level. If the room gets too cold, the heater turns on; if the room gets too warm, the heater turns off. Many primary drives in the body work in the same fashion.

The idea that motivation in the form of primary drives serves to maintain homeostasis makes a great deal of sense. Without primary drives, our biological needs would likely not be met, and we might not survive. But how well does the idea of drives explain some of our other motivations? For example, does drive reduction theory explain academic achievement motivation, or motivation to be loved? To help explain what motivates these kinds of behaviors, drive reduction theorists developed the notion of **secondary drives**—drives that motivate us to perform behaviors that are not directly related to biological needs.

Secondary drives are presumed to have developed through learning and experience. Back in the 1930s, Henry Murray proposed that human behavior is motivated by a host of secondary motives such as *need for achievement*, *need for affiliation* (the need to be close to others), and *need for understanding* (the need to understand one's world) (Murray, 1938). According to some psychologists, the need to

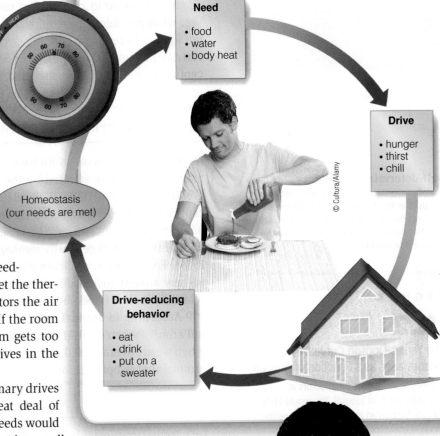

**FIGURE**

**8.1**

**Negative Feedback Loops**

Negative feedback loops maintain homeostasis in our bodies by monitoring certain physiological conditions (e.g., glucose levels and fluid levels). When levels drop too low, feedback from the body tells the brain to increase motivation (e.g., hunger or thirst). When levels are too high, feedback from the body tells the brain to decrease motivation.

**Need**
• food
• water
• body heat

**Drive**
• hunger
• thirst
• chill

**Drive-reducing behavior**
• eat
• drink
• put on a sweater

Homeostasis (our needs are met)

© Cultura/Alamy

© Ashley Cooper/Corbis

According to drive reduction theory, we are motivated to eat when our body sends feedback to the brain indicating that our energy supplies are running low. This need for fuel sets up a primary drive state, which motivates us to eat so that we can reduce our hunger.

Further clues about the role of the hypothalamus in hunger regulation come from animal studies in which surgical lesions are made in the brain. By destroying part of the hypothalamus and observing the effect that this destruction has on behavior, psychologists have uncovered some clues about the role that the different parts of the hypothalamus play in both initiating and stopping eating.

One part of the hypothalamus, the **lateral hypothalamus**, or **LH**, seems to function as an "on switch" for hunger. When the LH is destroyed in a rat, the rat stops eating. As a result, the rat loses weight and eventually dies. Without the LH, the rat simply starves to death (Teitelbaum & Stellar, 1954), which seems to indicate that the LH turns *on* hunger. However, further investigation has shown that the LH is not the only "on switch" for hunger. Curiously, if a rat is force-fed for long enough after having had its LH destroyed, the rat will eventually get some of its appetite back. Its appetite will not be as great as it was prior to losing its LH, but the rat will eat, particularly very tasty foods (Teitelbaum & Epstein, 1962).

Another bit of evidence that suggests an "on switch" for hunger outside of the LH comes from studies using **neuropeptide Y**, the most powerful hunger stimulant known (Gibbs, 1996). When an animal is injected with neuropeptide Y, its strongest effect occurs outside of the LH (Leibowitz, 1991). It stands to reason that if the LH were the primary "on switch" for hunger, then this powerful stimulant would have its strongest effect in the LH. That this does not appear to be the case suggests that there is an even more important "on switch" for hunger elsewhere in the brain.

The hypothalamus is also thought to play a role in shutting off hunger. Some evidence suggests that a part of the hypothalamus, the **ventromedial hypothalamus**, or **VMH**, plays a role in creating a feeling of *satiety*. When we are sated, we feel full and do not wish to eat more. Rats who have had their VMH destroyed will begin to eat ravenously and will gain enormous amounts of weight ( ■ FIGURE 8.4). If the VMH were the rat's only satiety center, or hunger "off switch," then destroying its VMH should make the rat eat continuously until it dies. But this doesn't happen. A rat without a VMH will eat a great deal of food and gain a great deal of weight, but after a certain amount of weight gain, its appetite will level off and the rat will then eat only enough food to maintain its new, higher weight. It's as if losing the VMH changes the rat's set point. In other words, the weight that the rat's body tries to maintain through homeostatic regulation has been shifted upward to a new, higher weight.

So, although the VMH may not be the only "off switch" for hunger, it does appear to play a role in obesity (see Levin & Routh, 1996). When the VMH is damaged, the endocrine system's control over insulin release is disturbed. The result is an increased release of insulin into the bloodstream, which produces great hunger and subsequent increases in eating (Valensi et al., 2003). Loss of the VMH doesn't remove the satiety center, but rather causes disturbances in the endocrine system that result in increased eating.

What we have learned from studies of the hunger centers in the brain is that many mechanisms turn on and shut off feelings of hunger. There does not appear to be a single "on" or "off" switch for hunger (King, 2006). Rather, hunger seems to be regulated by a complex network of feedback to the brain from various sources in the body, as well as direct signaling in the brain (Suzuki et al., 2010) (see ■ YOU REVIEW 8.1).

## OTHER CUES THAT INFLUENCE EATING: CULTURE AND CONSUMERISM

Have you ever eaten a big bag of popcorn at the movies just minutes after you finished a large meal? Have you ever consumed a fast-food meal that contained far more calories, fat, and salt than you really needed? If so, your behavior has shown that

**lateral hypothalamus (LH)**   a region of the hypothalamus once thought to be the hunger center in the brain

**neuropeptide Y**   the most powerful hunger stimulant known

**ventromedial [ven-tro-MEE-dee-al] hypothalamus (VMH)**   a region of the hypothalamus that plays an indirect role in creating a feeling of satiety

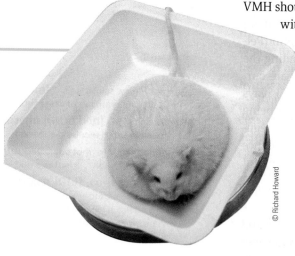

© Richard Howard

**FIGURE**

## 8.4

### A Mouse With a Lesion in the Ventromedial Hypothalamus (VMH)

This mouse had its ventromedial hypothalamus damaged. As a result, the mouse has eaten more than normal and gained a great deal of weight. But this mouse will not eat itself to death. Rather, it will now eat just enough to maintain this new, higher set point weight.

# YOU REVIEW 8.1    How Do We Decide When to Eat?

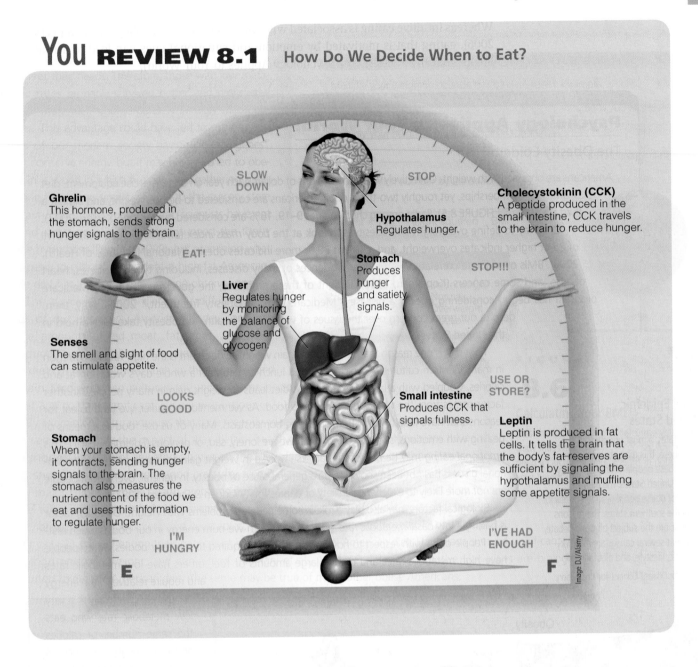

**Ghrelin**
This hormone, produced in the stomach, sends strong hunger signals to the brain.

**Senses**
The smell and sight of food can stimulate appetite.

**Stomach**
When your stomach is empty, it contracts, sending hunger signals to the brain. The stomach also measures the nutrient content of the food we eat and uses this information to regulate hunger.

**Liver**
Regulates hunger by monitoring the balance of glucose and glycogen.

**Hypothalamus**
Regulates hunger.

**Stomach**
Produces hunger and satiety signals.

**Small intestine**
Produces CCK that signals fullness.

**Cholecystokinin (CCK)**
A peptide produced in the small intestine, CCK travels to the brain to reduce hunger.

**Leptin**
Leptin is produced in fat cells. It tells the brain that the body's fat reserves are sufficient by signaling the hypothalamus and muffling some appetite signals.

SLOW DOWN   STOP   STOP!!!   EAT!   LOOKS GOOD   USE OR STORE?   I'M HUNGRY   I'VE HAD ENOUGH   E   F

Image DJ/Alamy

eating is often more than just satisfying biological needs and maintaining homeostasis in the body. Recently, psychologists have begun to discriminate between *intuitive eating*, or eating that is motivated by physiological hunger and satiety feedback, and eating that is motivated by emotional and situational cues that have little connection to energy requirements (Avalos & Tylka, 2006; Augustus-Horvath & Tylka, 2011). For example, the smell of popping popcorn at a theater can make you want to eat popcorn, even if you've just had a full meal. Or you may be tempted to indulge in a big bowl of ice cream after a stressful day.

Such eating occurs for reasons other than supplying fuel for our bodies. In many cultures, food and feasting are an integral part of cultural customs. This is especially true in the United States, where our holiday celebrations—including Christmas, Thanksgiving, Halloween, Hanukkah, Passover, Kwanzaa, and New Year's—are all associated with special foods in large quantities. The same holds true for more personal celebrations—birthdays, weddings, reunions, and even funerals. Americans and many other peoples around the world use food and eating to celebrate. This connection between joy and food can lead to eating when we do not really need to.

# LOOK BACK
## AT What You've LEARNED

A **motive** is the tendency to desire and seek out positive incentives and rewards and to avoid negative outcomes.

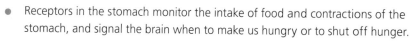

Transcendence

Self-actualization needs: to find self-fulfillment and realize one's potential

Aesthetic needs: symmetry, order, and beauty

Cognitive needs: to know, understand, and explore

Esteem needs: to achieve, be competent, and gain approval and recognition

Belongingness and love needs: to affiliate with others, be accepted, and belong

Safety needs: to feel secure and safe, out of danger

Physiological needs: hunger, thirst, and so forth

Maslow, "Hierarchy of Needs," from *Motivation and Personality*. Copyright © 1954 by Harper and Row Publishers, Inc. (Reprinted by permission of Pearson Education, Inc., Upper Saddle River, NJ.)

## How Do Psychologists View Motivation?

- William James believed that motives tend to be inborn **instincts**.

- According to the **drive reduction theory**, **primary drives** maintain **homeostasis**.

- **Arousal theories** of motivation suggest that each of us has an optimal level of arousal.

- According to **self-determination theory**, as we pursue the fulfillment of basic needs, we are motivated by both **intrinsic** and **extrinsic motives**.

- Abraham Maslow proposed a **hierarchy of needs** in which some needs take priority over others.

© Thomas Imo/Alamy

## Hunger: What Makes Us Eat?

© foodfolio/Alamy

- Receptors in the stomach monitor the intake of food and contractions of the stomach, and signal the brain when to make us hungry or to shut off hunger.

- Liver cells, hormones, fat cells, and glucoreceptors in the hypothalamus all play a role in signaling hunger or shutting it off.

- External cues such as advertisements and the sight or smell of food can also trigger hunger.

- **Obesity** can be caused by biological factors, such as a slow metabolism, as well as a number of behavioral factors, including a poor diet, excessive food intake, and emotional eating.

- **Bulimia nervosa** involves bingeing on food followed by purging or drastic reduction in caloric intake to rid the body of the extra calories.

- **Anorexia nervosa** is a serious eating disorder that involves extreme concern about gaining weight and reduction in caloric intake that leads to drastic weight loss.

- **Binge eating disorder** involves bingeing on food without compensatory measures to rid the body of extra calories.

© Envision/Corbis

© AP Photo/The Grand Island Independent, Barnett Stinson

## Sexual Motivation

Thinkstock/Getty Images

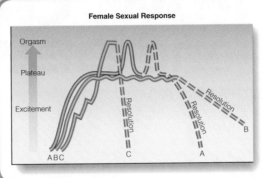

**Female Sexual Response**

Orgasm

Plateau

Excitement

A B C · C · A · B · Resolution

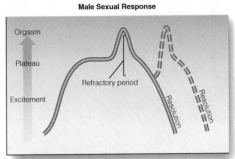

**Male Sexual Response**

Orgasm

Plateau

Refractory period

Excitement

Resolution · Resolution

- **Sexual desire** is influenced by neurotransmitters, hormones, sensory cues, and cultural attitudes about what is sexually appealing.

- Masters and Johnson's research examined the physiological changes that men and women undergo during sexual activity. Their results indicate that the sexual response cycle involves **excitement**, **plateau**, **orgasm**, and **resolution** phases.

- **Sexual orientation** is not just a matter of whether you have sex with men or women. Surveys show that some people may have some same-sex encounters but not consider themselves gay or lesbian.

- Sexual orientation falls along a continuum from **heterosexual** (attracted to the other sex) to **bisexual** (attracted to both sexes) to **homosexual** (attracted to the same sex).

- **Homophobia**, prejudice against homosexuals and bisexuals, is still a big problem in some cultures, including the United States.

## Theories and Expression of Emotion

- Components of **emotion** include physiological reactions, behavioral reactions, facial expressions, cognition, and **affective** response.

- The **James-Lange theory** of emotion proposes that emotion can be understood as a physiological response to some stimulus.

- The **Cannon-Bard theory** of emotion holds that emotion is the brain responding to some stimulus or situation, then prompting an emotional reaction.

- In the **facial feedback hypothesis**, the experience of an emotion is affected by the feedback the brain receives from muscles in the face. Thus, smiling can influence us to feel happy, and frowning can influence us to feel bad.

- The Schachter-Singer **two-factor theory of emotion** states that emotions are a product of both physiological arousal and cognitive interpretations of this arousal.

- **Cognitive-meditational theory** states that our cognitive appraisal of a situation determines what emotion we will feel in the situation; thus, different people react with different emotions in the same situation.

- **Basic emotions**, including happiness, sadness, anger, and fear, have been found to be present across cultures.

- **Display rules** determine the appropriate expression of emotion in a culture.

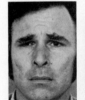

Source: Ekman & Friesen, 1984.

# 9

## How Do People GROW, CHANGE, and DEVELOP?

© Masterfile

## Chapter Outline

*At 35 years of age,* Michelle Lewis decided to leave her job in the hotel industry and take some courses at the local college. However, after a year in school, Michelle became pregnant, giving birth to Morgan, and two years later, another son, Matthew. Morgan and Matthew joined her two stepchildren Rachel and Nick, now teenagers. Michelle could no longer afford to go to school, so she returned to work at a child-care center. While at school, Michelle had enrolled in a general psychology course. Little did she know how helpful the information on child and adult development would be to her personal and professional life.

Michelle now looks at kids differently. Her knowledge of child development has enabled her to tailor activities and tasks more appropriately to a child's developmental level. She is more likely to encourage and praise the children she takes care of as well as her own, and less likely to just expect that the children will know what to do. Michelle has changed as a parent and wife too. She provides a structured environment for her two young sons and tries to be firm as a parent. She tries to communicate better with her husband by not criticizing him and accepts him for who he is.

This chapter outlines the processes of development. **Development** consists of changes in behavior and abilities. In this chapter, we will see that human development is complicated. Physical changes are occurring along with emotional, social, and mental (or cognitive) development. At the same time, social forces (such as people around us) and our environment also affect these processes. We hope that by understanding the physical, cognitive, and social aspects of development, you, like Michelle, will be able to appreciate the many forces that make each child, teenager, and adult unique.

© Ellen Pastorino

*Knowing about child and adult development has helped Michelle Lewis in her personal and professional life.*

325

# Development: How Does It All Begin?

## LEARNING OBJECTIVES

● Explain the nature–nurture issue.

● Identify and describe the three stages of prenatal development.

● Explain the importance of a positive prenatal environment.

Psychologists study development in order to understand the changes that humans experience from conception to the end of life. Because development covers such a large time span, developmental psychologists typically specialize by limiting their investigations to a particular period of life, such as infancy, childhood, adolescence, or adulthood. Within any one of these age stages, psychologists may focus on different aspects of development: physical, mental, social, or personality development. One developmental psychologist may study how language develops in infants while another may research how peer pressure affects drug use in adolescents.

Recall from Chapter 1 that psychology seeks to *describe*, *predict*, *control*, and *explain* behavior. If psychologists can accomplish these goals, then we can promote healthy development and prevent or alter maladaptive patterns of development. For example, if we understand how children think, we can then create appropriate educational environments, thus maximizing each child's potential. Understanding the dynamics of peer pressure during adolescence may suggest strategies to reduce drug use, delinquency, and teenage pregnancy. Knowing about developmental processes, therefore, has numerous real-world applications. However, as we'll read about next, explaining developmental changes is not easy, and psychologists do not always agree on what causes such changes to occur.

## Nature–Nurture Revisited: Biology and Culture

Think about all the variables that can potentially influence how a person grows and changes. In addition to a unique biological foundation (genetics), every person is also influenced by a multitude of environments: family, school, friends, neighborhoods, religion, and culture. The potential contribution of these biological and environmental factors to development has become a central issue for developmental psychologists. Recall from Chapter 7 that this is referred to as the **nature–nurture issue**. Psychologists are interested in how much one's biology, or *nature*, contributes to a person's development versus how much one's environment and culture, or *nurture*, influence this process.

Genetics or *nature* influences almost every aspect of development, from personality and physical development to cognitive processes such as language development and intelligence (Bouchard, 2004; Davis, Haworth, & Plomin, 2009; Gottlieb, Wahlsten, & Lickliter, 1998; R. J. Rose, 1995). *Nurture* is the total effect of all the external environmental events and circumstances that influence your development. It includes your family, friends, how others perceive and behave toward you, events that happen to you, television programs that you watch, music that you listen to, the customs and rituals of your ethnic background, your gender, your culture, your schooling, and so on.

Recall that it is not really a case of nature *or* nurture. Rather, it is the *interaction* of these two forces that influences behavior. Genes may moderate the influence of environmental forces; likewise, gene pathways may be altered by the environment (Champagne, 2010; Champagne & Mashoodh, 2009; Cole, 2009). As you read about the various types of development that we experience, keep this nature–nurture issue in mind, as the influences of nature and nurture seem to interact in a complex fashion.

**development**   changes in behavior or abilities or both

**nature–nurture issue**   the degree to which biology (nature) or the environment (nurture) contributes to a person's development

Both nature and nurture influence every aspect of development.

Alison Wright/Photo Researchers, Inc.

## Changes in the Prenatal Period

From the outside, all we see is a woman with a swollen belly who walks with a waddle. We may even have the opportunity to see or feel movement occurring inside her belly. Any woman who has been pregnant has experienced having some people want to touch her stomach or to treat her more delicately because of her "condition." Both tendencies speak to our fascination with the developments going on inside.

As we saw in Chapter 2, all the genetic material for development is inherited from your biological parents at the time of conception. The male sperm cell, containing 23 single chromosomes, fertilizes the female ovum, also containing 23 single chromosomes, to create a fertilized egg, called a **zygote**, that has 23 pairs

**zygote [ZIE-goat]**    a fertilized egg

**germinal stage**    the first stage of prenatal development, from conception to 14 days

**embryonic [em-bree-AH-nik] stage**    the second stage of prenatal development, lasting from the 3rd through the 8th week

**fetal stage**    the third stage of prenatal development from the 9th week through the 9th month

### You Asked...

*How does a baby develop in the mother's womb?*

MELISSA TYNDALE, STUDENT

of chromosomes. Over the next 38 to 40 weeks, the average gestation period for a human, the zygote will experience dramatic changes as it evolves into a baby. So many changes occur during this time that scientists divide the prenatal period into three stages: the *germinal* or *zygotic stage*, the *embryonic stage*, and the *fetal stage*.

The first 14 days after conception are the **germinal stage** of development. The major characteristic of this stage is cell division. Following conception, the zygote starts to replicate itself and divide. This process ensures that all the cells of the organism contain the same genetic material. The zygote divides into 2 cells, which then replicate and divide again, creating a 4-cell organism. The cells continue replicating and dividing, and around the 5th day after conception the zygote has become a 100-cell organism, called a *blastocyst*. During this process of cell division, the mass of cells also travels down the fallopian tube to the uterus. On approximately the 9th day after conception, the blastocyst implants itself in the lining of the uterine wall. Cell division continues through the 2nd week.

The **embryonic stage** covers development of the organism, now called an *embryo*, from the 3rd through the 8th week. After the blastocyst attaches to the uterine wall, its outside cells develop into the support structures: the *placenta*, *umbilical cord*, and *amniotic sac*. The inner cells become the embryo.

The major characteristic of the embryonic period is the formation and development of the major organs and systems. Cells start to specialize into bone, muscle, and body organs. All the major biological systems—the cardiovascular system, the digestive system, the skeletal system, the excretory system, the respiratory system, and the nervous system—are forming. Given the importance of these systems for survival and well-being, the embryonic stage is perhaps the most precarious stage of prenatal development. Most miscarriages and genetic defects surface during this stage. The embryo's development may also be harmed by outside environmental factors, producing devastating effects. We will return to these topics in a moment.

By the end of the embryonic stage, all basic bodily structures and systems are forming. About 4 weeks after conception, the heart is beating, the spinal cord is forming, the liver is producing red blood cells, and ovaries or testes have formed (but the embryo's sex is not apparent by ultrasound until between 12 and 18 weeks). Although only an inch long, the embryo already looks human. Facial features, such as the eyes, lips, nose, and jaw, have taken shape. Short stubs represent arms and legs, and the beginnings of fingers and toes are apparent.

The third prenatal development period, the **fetal stage**, begins the 9th week after conception. From now until birth, the organism is referred to as a *fetus*. The

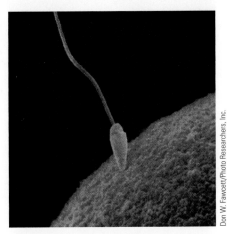

Human sperm and egg at the moment of penetration. The sperm cell fertilizes the female ovum to create a zygote.

Don W. Fawcett/Photo Researchers, Inc.

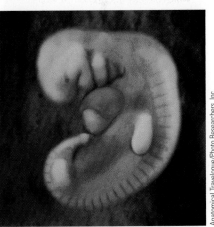

Micro-MRI, reconstructed with 3-D imagery, actual size of embryo 4.0 mm. The image depicts a human embryo during its 4th week of development. Age is calculated from the day of fertilization. In this image, the fusing tubes of the heart are highlighted in red. Early growth of the cardiovascular system begins during the 3rd week, when blood vessels form, and continues into the following weeks of development. Image from the book *From Conception to Birth: A Life Unfolds.*

Anatomical Travelogue/Photo Researchers, Inc.

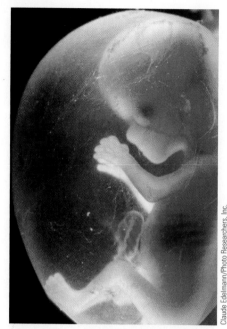

Claude Edelmann/Photo Researchers, Inc.

At 14 weeks, the fetus's lungs and external sex organs have developed.

major characteristic of the fetal stage is continued growth and maturation. The fetus grows larger and starts to move. By 14 weeks, the fetus can kick, open its mouth, swallow, and turn its head. Its lungs and external sex organs have developed. By the end of the 6th month (24 weeks), the organs are sufficiently formed that the fetus has reached *viability*—the possibility of surviving outside the womb (but only in a neonatal intensive care unit). During the last 3 months, the fetus is responsive to sound, light, and touch.

From the union of a single sperm cell and egg, the fetus has undergone significant and complex changes over the course of 40 weeks. However, not all zygotes experience these changes. About half of all fertilized eggs die and are miscarried, usually before the woman knows she is pregnant. Of pregnancies that the mother knows about (because of a missed menstrual cycle), approximately 10% to 20% end in miscarriage (Mortensen, Sever, & Oakley, 1991).

## The Importance of a Positive Prenatal Environment

The support structures of the intrauterine environment are designed to protect the developing organism. However, internal and external forces can still interfere with this natural defense system and cause birth defects.

### You Asked...

*What are some birth defects that can occur?*

NIESHA HAZZARD, STUDENT

When internal chromosomal abnormalities are present at conception, their effects typically arise during the embryonic stage. For example, **Down syndrome** results from an extra 21st chromosome. Babies with Down syndrome are characterized by distinct facial features (such as almond-shaped eyes or a flat nose) and are more likely to experience heart defects and varying degrees of intellectual disability. Medical tests can identify the presence of Down syndrome and hundreds of other inherited genetic disorders so that parents can prepare themselves or terminate the pregnancy (Painter, 1997; Rappaport, 2008). This possibility highlights the importance of regular prenatal consultations with a physician.

Birth defects may also be caused by outside environmental forces. Any environmental agent that has the potential to harm the embryo is referred to as a **teratogen**. It may be a drug that the mother takes, such as cocaine or alcohol; a disease, such as German measles (rubella); or chemicals that the mother inhales, such as certain cleaning fluids. All these substances have the potential to cause birth defects. The critical factor seems to be *when* the mother is exposed to these agents. These **sensitive periods** emphasize the complex interplay of nature and nurture on development. Certain organs and systems are more vulnerable to the effects of teratogens during particular stages of prenatal development (■ FIGURE 9.1). Notice that the most severe effects are most likely to occur during the embryonic stage of development. Because a woman usually does not discover that she is pregnant until the embryo is already formed and developing, she may unknowingly expose her developing baby to harm.

Women who use any type of drug during pregnancy can potentially affect their babies. Women who smoke during pregnancy reduce the flow of oxygen to the fetus; their babies tend to be irritable, have respiratory problems, and have lower birth weight (Lester, Andreozzi, & Appiah, 2004; Rosenblith, 1992; Shea & Steiner, 2008). Women who drink alcohol heavily during pregnancy put their unborn children at risk for **fetal alcohol syndrome (FAS)**. Children with

**Down syndrome**  a genetic birth disorder resulting from an extra 21st chromosome, characterized by distinct facial features and a greater likelihood of heart defects and intellectual disability

**teratogen [tur-RAH-tuh-jun]**  an environmental substance that has the potential to harm the developing organism

**sensitive period**  in prenatal development, a time when genetic and environmental agents are most likely to cause birth defects

**fetal alcohol syndrome (FAS)**  a birth condition resulting from the mother's chronic use of alcohol during pregnancy that is characterized by facial and limb deformities and intellectual disability

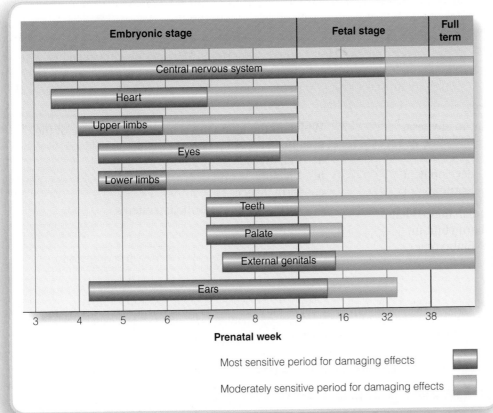

FIGURE

# 9.1

**Sensitive Periods and Effect on Prenatal Development**

The darker bars indicate the most sensitive period for certain organs and structures; the lighter bars indicate lessened vulnerability. Sensitivity is greatest during the embryonic period, although some structures remain vulnerable throughout the prenatal period.

*Adapted from K. L. Moore and T. V. N. Persaud,* Before We Are Born: Essentials of Embryology and Birth Defects. *Philadelphia: Saunders. Copyright © 1998 Elsevier Science (USA). All rights reserved. Reprinted by permission.*

FAS tend to have low birth weight, brain abnormalities, and lowered intellectual functioning, and tend to exhibit limb, head, and facial deformities (Dalen et al., 2009; Ikonomidou et al., 2000; Ornoy & Ergaz, 2010). Even moderate drinking can affect the embryo's brain development, resulting in later intellectual impairments (Kraft, 1996; Rasmussen, Soleimani, & Pei, 2011). Prenatal alcohol exposure has also been linked to an increased risk of low birth weight and poorer visual acuity in infancy (R. C. Carter et al., 2005; Mariscal et al., 2006).

Illegal drugs also produce damaging effects. If the mother is a heroin addict, the baby will be born addicted and have to undergo withdrawal. Crack or cocaine babies are often born premature, underweight, and irritable, and tend to have poor feeding habits (Gouin et al., 2011; Frank et al., 2002; Inciardi, Surratt, & Saum, 1997).

Prenatal exposure to teratogens may also have long-term effects. Children exposed to drugs during pregnancy tend to be more impulsive, less adaptable, and evidence more behavioral problems later in life than children not exposed to drugs during pregnancy (Espy, Riese, & Francis, 1997; Richardson et al., 2011). In southern Japan, adults whose mothers took in high levels of methylmercury (found in fish) during pregnancy have shown accelerated rates of aging (Newland & Rasmussen, 2003).

Prescription and over-the-counter medicines may also influence fetal development. Read the warning labels on any over-the-counter medication, and you will see that pregnant women are cautioned to seek a doctor's advice before using any medicine. Whatever the mother takes in during pregnancy or breastfeeding, so does the baby. Proper nutrition and a healthy lifestyle are paramount for a pregnant woman. They increase the chances of producing a healthy newborn who is better prepared to face the developmental and life challenges ahead. These challenges include the enormous changes that occur in infancy and childhood—our next topic of discussion.

# Let's REVIEW

In this section, we reviewed the nature–nurture issue, described prenatal development, and emphasized the importance of a positive prenatal environment. For a quick check of your understanding, answer these questions.

**1.** If identical twins are very similar in shyness, this provides evidence for the _____ side of a key developmental issue.
   **a.** nature
   **b.** nurture
   **c.** development
   **d.** learning

**2.** Loretta is in her 5th month of pregnancy. What stage of development is her unborn child in?
   **a.** Germinal
   **b.** Zygote
   **c.** Embryonic
   **d.** Fetal

**3.** Which of the following is *most* characteristic of the germinal stage of prenatal development?
   **a.** Cell division
   **b.** Viability
   **c.** Birth defects
   **d.** Formation of major body systems

*Answers 1. a; 2. d; 3. a*

LEARNING OBJECTIVES

- Describe brain changes in infancy and childhood and understand the concept of plasticity.

- Describe how reflexes prepare the infant for voluntary actions and differentiate between gross and fine motor skills.

# Physical Development in Infancy and Childhood

The average **neonate**, or newborn up to 28 days old, enters the world 20 inches long, weighing 7 pounds. One year later, the average infant is 29 inches long and will have tripled in weight, emphasizing how rapidly babies grow during infancy. Physical growth and developmental changes result from the complex interaction of the forces of nature and nurture. Our genes lay the foundation for how tall we grow and how our body fat is distributed. The environmental factors of nutrition, health care, and lifestyle also influence our height and build. A similar interplay of nature and nurture is seen in brain and motor development.

## Brain Development

What is your very first childhood memory? How old were you then? Most people do not recall events in infancy or before 3 years old. This lack of memory may be related to the development of the nervous system. At birth, an infant's brain has billions of neurons, but the connections between the neurons are very limited, and myelin (see Chapter 2) is incomplete. Experience and learning mix with heredity to shape brain development. Neural pathways grow rapidly, and by the time a child is 3 years old, 1,000 trillion synapses have formed (Garlick, 2003). A 2-month-old has very few neural connections compared to the billions a 2-year-old has. More experience plus increased activity equals more neural connections.

During childhood and early adolescence, the brain prunes and discards unnecessary connections, reducing the total number of synapses (Cook & Cook, 2005; Seeman, 1999; Thompson et al., 2000). Those connections that are used repeatedly become permanent, whereas those that are used infrequently or not at all are unlikely to survive (Greenough et al., 1993). This discovery has altered researchers' thinking on infant care and early education. Providing stimulating age-appropriate activities fosters and strengthens brain development.

**neonate** a newborn during the first 28 days of life

Impoverished environments weaken neural connections—fewer connections are made, and unexercised connections are likely to be discarded.

A young child's brain is highly *plastic*, or changeable, and very dense with neurons when compared to adults' brains. If a certain area of the brain is damaged in infancy, other areas of the brain can compensate by reorganizing neural connections (Rakic, 1991; Xiong, Mahmmod, & Chopp, 2010). However, there are individual inherited differences in this process; some brains may be better able to adapt than others (Garlick, 2002). As children age, the brain is less able to change and adapt because neural connections have already been formed, and in some cases discarded, although some plasticity remains throughout adulthood (Huttenlocher, 2002; Kelsch, Sim, & Lois, 2010). The plasticity and density of the brain ensure a child's best chance of adapting to his or her environment. This adaptation is also evident in the development of children's motor skills.

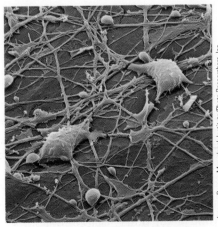

Synaptic connections proliferate during infancy and early childhood. The brain then selectively prunes and discards unused connections during childhood and early adolescence.

## Reflexes and Motor Development

Infants are born relatively helpless creatures. They cannot feed themselves and are unable to walk. Infants do have certain sensory abilities, a good set of lungs that enable them to cry, and a set of *reflexes*, all of which biologically prepare them to get the help they need to survive.

A **reflex** is an *automatic* response to a particular stimulus. Reflexes enable infants to learn about their environment, thus establishing important neural connections for *voluntary* motor behaviors. Hence, reflexes serve as the foundation for behaviors such as walking, eating, crying, smiling, and grasping. For example, infants are born with a sucking reflex. They will automatically suck on any object that touches their lips. Infants also have a *rooting reflex*. When you touch the side of infants' cheeks, they will turn in that direction and open their mouth. These two reflexes teach infants how to use their mouths to get food. Infants are also born with a grasping reflex. When an object is placed on their palm, they will automatically grasp it. From this reflex, infants learn to handle items with their hands, an ability referred to as *prehension*. Their brains and bodies learn, through grasping, the necessary skills that will later be used to write with a pen, play a musical instrument, tie their shoes, or give a parent a hug.

Infants are also biologically prepared to communicate, despite lacking formal language skills. A crying reflex—automatically crying when distressed—alerts the caretaker to the infant's needs. In a matter of weeks, the baby learns to use crying to get the caretaker's attention. Luckily, infants are also born with a smiling reflex to use when they are pleased (which also serves as positive reinforcement for their caregivers). This reflex evolves into a *social smile* during the second month of life, when the infant smiles at everybody. Infants' smiles then become more discriminating; by 6 months of age, they reserve their smiles for familiar voices and faces.

Reflexes also initiate *locomotive* ability, or the ability to move around. Crawling and stepping reflexes prepare the brain and body for motions involved in pulling oneself up, crawling, and walking. These abilities develop in much the same sequence for all infants around the world, evidence of our genetic heritage. However, experience may speed up this process, and lack of opportunities may slow it down (Thelen, 1995).

By age 2, most infants are walking, running, and getting into everything. However, motor development, the changes in a child's body activities, does not end there. As children age, *gross motor skills* become more proficient. **Gross motor skills** refer to behaviors that involve large muscle groups such as the biceps or quadriceps. These include running, walking, jumping, and hopping. This proficiency is apparent when you watch a toddler, a preschooler, and an 8-year-old run.

**reflex** an automatic response to a specific environmental stimulus

**gross motor skills** motor behaviors involving the large muscles of the body

The toddler waddles and is unsteady on her feet. The preschooler is more coordinated compared to the toddler, but less fluid and not as fast as the 8-year-old.

Similar changes occur in **fine motor skills**, which involve small muscle groups. Fine motor skills include such activities as writing, using utensils, and playing a musical instrument. Toddlers and preschoolers are less adept at tasks involving fine motor skills, but as the school years approach, children become much more proficient. ■ TABLE 9.1 shows average age ranges for specific gross and fine motor skills achieved in infancy and early childhood. Notice that the achievement of a particular task lays the foundation for attaining the subsequent, more difficult, task. In other words, babies must be able to sit up before they can crawl. Children must walk before they learn to jump rope.

Enormous changes occur in physical development through the infancy and childhood years. The same magnitude of change characterizes cognitive development, or how children think, which we'll turn to next.

**fine motor skills**    motor behaviors involving the small muscles of the body

## TABLE 9.1
## Motor Milestones in Infancy and Early Childhood

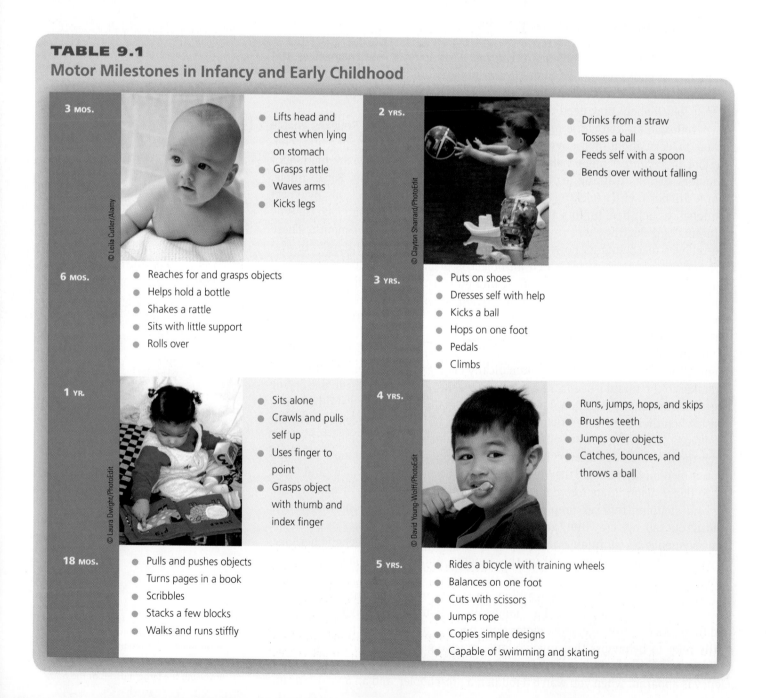

**3 mos.**
- Lifts head and chest when lying on stomach
- Grasps rattle
- Waves arms
- Kicks legs

© Leila Cutler/Alamy

**6 mos.**
- Reaches for and grasps objects
- Helps hold a bottle
- Shakes a rattle
- Sits with little support
- Rolls over

**1 yr.**
- Sits alone
- Crawls and pulls self up
- Uses finger to point
- Grasps object with thumb and index finger

© Laura Dwight/PhotoEdit

**18 mos.**
- Pulls and pushes objects
- Turns pages in a book
- Scribbles
- Stacks a few blocks
- Walks and runs stiffly

**2 yrs.**
- Drinks from a straw
- Tosses a ball
- Feeds self with a spoon
- Bends over without falling

© Clayton Sharrard/PhotoEdit

**3 yrs.**
- Puts on shoes
- Dresses self with help
- Kicks a ball
- Hops on one foot
- Pedals
- Climbs

**4 yrs.**
- Runs, jumps, hops, and skips
- Brushes teeth
- Jumps over objects
- Catches, bounces, and throws a ball

© David Young-Wolff/PhotoEdit

**5 yrs.**
- Rides a bicycle with training wheels
- Balances on one foot
- Cuts with scissors
- Jumps rope
- Copies simple designs
- Capable of swimming and skating

# Let's
## REVIEW

In this section, we described the physical development of infants and children. For a quick check of your understanding, answer these questions.

1. Which of the following infants is *most* likely to have the fewest neural connections?
   a. A 1-month-old
   b. A 2-month-old
   c. A 3-month-old
   d. A 4-month-old

2. The rooting reflex is to eating as the grasping reflex is to _____.
   a. locomotion
   b. crawling
   c. gross motor skills
   d. prehension

3. Children in preschool learn how to use scissors in order to help develop their _____ skills.
   a. gross motor
   b. fine motor
   c. reflex
   d. locomotive

Answers 1. a; 2. d; 3. b

# Cognitive Development in Infancy and Childhood

Television shows, movies, and comic strips capitalize on the unique way in which children develop mentally (their *cognitive development*). What is it about children's thinking that makes adults laugh? This section reviews psychological research into how infants first learn to conceptualize the world and how this thinking changes as they proceed through childhood. We will start with perceptual development.

## Perceptual Development

Infants are hard to study. They sleep most of the time, and they can't talk much. We can't remember what it's like to be an infant. Researchers must therefore study infants when they are awake and active, and devise clever ways to measure what infants know. The best way to gather information about what infants can and cannot perceive seems to be to measure certain behaviors and see how those behaviors change under particular conditions. For example, researchers may measure how long an infant spends looking at a stimulus or how long an infant sucks when exposed to different sounds. As researchers create more precise ways of measuring infant behavior, we are discovering that infants know a lot more than we once believed.

### VISION

Babies are very nearsighted at birth. Objects need to be close in order for babies to see them, and even then, the objects look blurry. In addition, a baby's eyes lack *convergence*, or the ability to focus both eyes on an object. This may be why newborns typically look cross-eyed in photographs. However, as the structure of the eyes and the neural connections in the brain mature, babies attain visual convergence.

Newborns show a preference for looking at complex, high-contrast stimuli. If given a choice of various complex visual stimuli, infants will spend most of their time looking at faces (Pascalis & Kelly, 2009; Turati, 2004; Turati & Simion, 2002;

**LEARNING OBJECTIVES**

- Describe the perceptual abilities of infants and how these abilities develop in the first weeks and months of life.
- Compare and contrast Piaget's and Vygotsky's theories of cognitive development.
- Compare and contrast Kohlberg's and Gilligan's theories of moral reasoning.

Valenza et al., 1996). This preference is adaptive, as it helps foster a social bond with the primary caretaker. By 3 months old, a baby can tell the difference between its primary caretaker's face and that of a stranger and more easily recognizes faces from its own race (Bar-Haim et al., 2006; Burnham, 1993; Kelly et al., 2007; Sangrigoli & de Schonen, 2004). Infants also have more difficulty processing male faces than female faces (Ramsey-Rennels & Langlois, 2006).

© Corbis

### YOUR TURN : Active Learning

Our brains are predisposed to recognize a face, and this predisposition is present in babies. Look closely at the upside-down image of Lincoln on this page before looking at it right side up. Notice anything? Even when presented with an inverted portrait, we ignore the distortions and recognize that it is a face. When you look at Lincoln's portrait right side up, you notice all the distortions.

## DEPTH PERCEPTION

During their first year, infants develop depth perception. In a classic experiment conducted in 1960, researchers Eleanor Gibson and Richard Walk created an apparatus called a "visual cliff" (■ FIGURE 9.2). They then observed at what age infants would or would not cross over the surface where it appeared to drop off. Infants as young as 6 months of age hesitated when approaching this perceived cliff. Again, we see that biology prepares us for developmental challenges. Babies acquire depth perception at about the same time they become mobile. Because depth perception and body coordination may not yet be developed in some infants, it is extremely important to never leave a baby unattended on a bed, a changing table, or any other elevated surface. Immature depth perception, as well as inadequate body control, makes it more likely that infants will fall and hurt themselves.

## HEARING

Unborn babies react to sounds in the intrauterine environment at around the 20th week. A mother's voice is one of those sounds, which may explain why babies are likely to recognize their mothers' voices soon after birth (L. S. Black et al., 2004; DeCasper & Fifer, 1980). Infants can locate the direction of sounds. They readily learn the difference between similar consonant sounds, such as /d/ and /p/, and appear to remember simple speech sounds a day after hearing them (Swain, Zelazo, & Clifton, 1993). Research suggests that these abilities to discriminate sounds and familiar voices from unfamiliar ones may also be present in fetuses (Draganova et al., 2007; Kisilevsky et al., 2003; Lecanuet, Manera, & Jacquet, 2002).

Babies prefer soft and rhythmic sounds, which explains why they enjoy lullabies so much. They prefer most to listen to voices, specifically the rising tones

### FIGURE

## 9.2

### Depth Perception in Infancy

Eleanor Gibson and Richard Walk's visual cliff apparatus tests depth perception in infants.

© Mark Richards/Photo Edit

used by women and children (Sullivan & Horowitz, 1983) and the exaggerated, high-pitched sounds typically used in baby talk. Infants do not like loud noises, which may explain why some children become classically conditioned to fear thunderstorms (see Chapter 5).

## THE OTHER SENSES

Taste, touch, and smell are other ways that infants gather meaning from their environment. Infants' taste buds are functional at birth, and infants prefer sweet tastes. Infants are also born with an acute sense of smell. As soon as 3 days after birth, breastfed infants can discriminate the smell of their own mother from that of an unfamiliar female (Cernoch & Porter, 1985; R. H. Porter, 1999).

Infants are also very responsive to touch. Touching and caressing infants stimulates their growth and can improve brain development and cognitive development (Diamond & Amso, 2008). In one study, two groups of premature infants were given the same neonatal care with one exception—half the infants were routinely massaged, and the other half were not. Those receiving the massages gained weight faster, developed faster neurologically, and were therefore able to leave the hospital sooner than those in the control group (Field et al., 1986). Today, it is standard practice to encourage parents of preterm babies to hold them often. Holding and touching infants also fosters their social development.

Infants' perceptual abilities allow them to gather much needed information from the environment—how their caretakers look, sound, and smell, where the food is, and what sounds contribute to language. From these beginnings, infants develop the abilities to know, think, and remember, a process called **cognition**. Perhaps no one has advanced our understanding of children's thinking more than Jean Piaget, whose ideas and research are presented next.

## Piaget's Theory of Cognitive Development

Swiss psychologist Jean Piaget (1896–1980) interviewed and observed infants and children, including his own, to discover and describe the changes in thinking that occur in childhood. Piaget gave children certain tasks to perform, observed their problem-solving strategies, and then asked them how they came to their conclusions.

From these observations and interviews, Piaget (1929, 1952) developed a theory about how children acquire their mental abilities. His theory traces the shifts in thinking from infants' reflexes to a teenager's reasoning abilities. He believed that cognition advances in a series of distinct stages, and that how a preschooler thinks differs dramatically from how an elementary school student thinks. Three concepts central to his theory are *schema*, *assimilation*, and *accommodation*.

### You Asked...

*How does a young mind absorb its environment?*

DIERDRA TORRES, STUDENT

## SCHEMAS, ASSIMILATION, AND ACCOMMODATION

To Piaget, any mental idea, concept, or thought is a **schema**. We form these schemas based on our experiences of the world. For example, a baby may have a sucking schema, "Is this object suckable?" or a mother schema, "Does this person fit with my cognitive framework of mother?" A preschooler may have the schema "The sun follows me wherever I go." Adults' schemas may be very simple—"A key will start a car"—or more complex, such as individual ideas of justice, morality, or love.

Piaget observed children's problem-solving strategies to discover and describe the changes in thinking that they experience.

**cognition**   the ability to know, think, and remember

**schema [SKEE-ma]**   a mental idea, concept, or thought

Hill-Soderlund & Braungart-Rieker, 2008; Rothbaum et al., 1995). Bonds with individuals other than the caretaker can compensate for insecure attachments at home. Moreover, given the number of variables that can influence attachment, an early pattern of insecure attachment does not guarantee a lifelong pattern of insecure relationships. As family circumstances improve, so too may the quality of the attachment. Similarly, social relationships *after* infancy must also be considered when we evaluate children's psychological adjustment.

## Parenting Styles

Parents' responses to their infants and children also influence the parent–child relationship. Diana Baumrind (1967, 1971) investigated these responses by observing parents' interactions with their children. From her observations, three styles of parenting emerged.

**Authoritarian parents** tend to exhibit a high level of control and a low level of affection toward their children. They set high expectations for their children but without communicating the reasons behind their expectations. "It's my way or the highway" would be a characteristic attitude of authoritarian parents. The children are not included in discussions of family issues, rules, or roles. They are to do what they are told. If they do not obey, force and physical punishment are used to ensure compliance. Baumrind found that children from authoritarian households tended to be more withdrawn, anxious, and conforming than other children.

**Authoritative parents** tend to exhibit moderate control and are warm toward their children. Authoritative parents are least likely to spank or hit their children. Rules—and the consequences for violating them—are established in a democratic manner, and children are included in family discussions. Reasonable expectations and demands are made of the children, and the children respond accordingly. Baumrind found that parents who use this style of parenting tended to have competent, happy, and self-confident children. It appears to be the most effective approach to parenting. Although Baumrind's sample was predominantly restricted to European Americans, these benefits of authoritative parenting have also been found to apply to several U.S. ethnic groups, including African Americans, Korean Americans, Chinese Americans, and Hispanic Americans (Abar, Carter, & Winsler, 2009; Cheah et al., 2009; H. Kim & Chung, 2003; Querido, Warner, & Eyberg, 2002; Steinberg et al., 1992).

**Permissive parents** have very little control over their children. Discipline is lax. Children make their own decisions even when they may not be capable of doing so. Very few demands are made of the children in terms of rules or chores. Permissive parenting includes two distinct types: indulgent and neglectful. *Permissive-indulgent* parents are very warm, affectionate, and involved with their children but still make few demands on their children, hence the name indulgent. *Permissive-neglectful* parents make few demands and show little affection or warmth toward their children; they are uninvolved with parenting and neglect the emotional needs of their children. Children of permissive-indulgent parents tend to be impulsive, disobedient, yet emotionally secure, whereas children of permissive-neglectful parents tend to have the poorest outcomes in terms of social skills, self-esteem, and academic achievement.

Do parents always *cause* children to act a certain way? Perhaps not. Recall that these are correlations, and causal connections cannot be made from correlational data. A parent–child relationship is not a one-way street. Children's temperaments influence the way parents treat them just as much as parents' responses influence the development of their children. Moreover, other variables such as the quality of the parents' relationship or the level of family functioning can influence how parents and children interact (Caldera & Lindsey, 2006; Schoppe-Sullivan et al., 2007). How a child

© Simon Marcus/Corbis

Parents who are warm and moderate in control are more likely to have competent and happy children.

**authoritarian [ah-thor-uh-TARE-ee-an] parent**   a parenting style characterized by high levels of control and low levels of affection

**authoritative [ah-thor-uh-TAY-tive] parent**   a parenting style characterized by moderate levels of control and affection

**permissive parent**   a parenting style characterized by low levels of control or discipline

develops socially and emotionally will depend in part on the *goodness of fit* between the child's temperament and his or her surrounding social relationships, including those with parents (Bradley & Corwyn, 2008; Chess & Thomas, 1984; Kochanska, 1995; Reiss, 2005; Roisman & Fraley, 2006; Stright, Gallagher, & Kelley, 2008).

## Erikson's Stages of Psychosocial Development: The Influence of Culture

After studying child-rearing practices in several cultures, Erik Erikson (1902–1994) believed that children and adults progress through eight stages, or developmental crises (Erikson, 1963, 1968, 1980). At each stage, the environment and the person's responses to the environment influence the development of either a healthy or an unhealthy personality characteristic. At each stage, the person incorporates a new quality into his or her personality. Resolving earlier stages with healthy outcomes makes it easier to resolve later stages with positive outcomes. An unhealthy resolution of a stage can have potential negative effects throughout life, although damage can sometimes be repaired at later stages. Four of Erikson's eight stages pertain to the childhood years and are discussed here. The other four stages focus on the adolescent and adult years and are discussed later in the chapter. ■ YOU REVIEW 9.2 summarizes all eight stages.

For Erikson, the child-rearing practices of a culture fulfill basic psychological and emotional needs to influence healthy personality development.

## YOU REVIEW 9.2     Erikson's Stages of Psychosocial Development

| AGE | STAGE | DEVELOPMENTAL CHALLENGE |
|---|---|---|
| Birth–1 year | Trust versus mistrust | Sense of security |
| 1–3 years | Autonomy versus shame and doubt | Independence |
| 3–6 years | Initiative versus guilt | Trying new things |
| 6–12 years | Industry versus inferiority | Sense of mastery and competence |
| Adolescence | Identity versus role confusion | Sense of self, personal values, and beliefs |
| Young adulthood | Intimacy versus isolation | Committing to a mutually loving relationship |
| Middle adulthood | Generativity versus stagnation | Contributing to society through one's work, family, or community services |
| Late adulthood | Ego integrity versus despair | Viewing one's life as satisfactory and worthwhile |

1. *Trust versus mistrust.* This stage occurs during the first year of life, when infants are totally dependent on others in their environment to meet their needs. An infant whose needs are met is more likely to develop trust in others than one whose needs are not met. Developing a sense of trust also fosters the development of a secure attachment.

2. *Autonomy versus shame and doubt.* From 1 to 3 years of age, toddlers struggle with separating from their primary caretaker. They must negotiate an appropriate balance between autonomy, or independence, and dependence. If people in the toddler's environment belittle the child's efforts at independence

Society encourages stereotypical gender schema by prescribing what are appropriate "girl" and "boy" toys, as indicated by this obviously girl-oriented display.

activities such as playing dress-up, house, and school. Parents often assign different household chores to their sons and daughters. Girls wash the dishes and do chores inside the house such as vacuuming and dusting. Boys take out the trash and do outdoor chores such as mowing the lawn, washing cars, and cleaning out the garage. Fathers are much more likely to hold to these gender stereotypes and tend to be less accepting of cross-gender behaviors, especially in their sons (Lytton & Romney, 1991; O'Bryan, Fishbein, & Ritchey, 2004).

Parents who are less likely to hold these gender expectations tend to have children who are less gender-typed (Warner & Steel, 1999; Weisner & Wilson-Mitchell, 1990; Witt, 1997). Moreover, children who *see* their parents behave in a less stereotypical fashion—moms taking out the trash or dads performing household tasks—also tend to be less gender-typed (Hupp et al., 2010; Turner & Gervai, 1995). Parents, however, are not the only ones who influence children's gender roles. Once children begin school, teachers and peers influence gender schemas as well.

Research suggests that *gender bias* exists in many classrooms (Stromquist, 2007). Gender bias is the favoring of one gender over the other because of different views of male and female roles. Boys tend to receive both more positive and more negative attention from teachers, and are called on more often (Beal, 1994; Einarsson & Granstrom, 2004; V. L. Hamilton et al., 1991; Jones & Dindia, 2004; Swinson & Harrop, 2009). Teachers are also more likely to accept wrong answers from girls, encourage boys to try harder when they make errors, and see boys as more clever (Horgan, 1995; Skelton, 2006). Teachers also tend to stereotype mathematics as a male domain even when boys and girls performed similarly (Keller, 2001; Tiedemann, 2002). When it comes to career counseling, boys are more likely to be encouraged to enter higher status professions in math and science, such as engineering, whereas girls are encouraged to pursue education, nursing, and social work (Sadker, 2000).

Children's notions about gender are also reinforced within their peer groups, starting as early as age 3. Same-sex peers praise the child for engaging in gender-appropriate behaviors. Children who engage in gender-inappropriate behavior may be teased, laughed at, and even isolated from the group. Boys are particularly critical of same-sex peers who engage in "girlish" behavior, resulting in harsher punishment for their activities (G. D. Levy, Taylor, & Gelman, 1995; A. J. Rose & Smith, 2009).

Society in general also contributes to children's gender stereotypes. Fast-food chains offer boy and girl toys with their children's meals. Some toy stores still have aisles marked "Boys" and "Girls." Many television shows still hold to traditional gender stereotypes (Aucoin, 2000). Males appear more frequently and tend to be the dominant characters. Male characters are more likely than female characters to engage in active tasks such as climbing or riding a bike. Females are more often depicted as passive, dependent, and emotional. Many of the female characters on television are not employed. When they do have jobs, they are often stereotypical ones such as teachers, nurses, and secretaries (Huston & Wright, 1998; Signorielli & Bacue, 1999).

Analyses of television advertisements in more than 20 countries paint a similar picture. Women are more likely to be the user of the product, whereas men are more often portrayed as the wise, knowledgeable expert. Women appear more often in domestic roles selling body care and household cleaning products and appear less often in occupational settings. Men are rarely shown in private residences or with children in the background (Furnham & Paltzer, 2010; Nassif & Gunter, 2008). Children who watch television frequently may adopt these gender-role stereotypes.

# Let's
## REVIEW

In this section, we described the psychosocial changes that infants and children undergo as they develop. For a quick check of your understanding, answer these questions.

1. In the strange situation procedure, a baby who clings to the mother while she is present and who shows extreme distress when the mother leaves would be exhibiting which style of attachment?
   a. Secure
   b. Avoidant
   c. Disorganized
   d. Resistant

2. Jose is a very active toddler who prefers to do things by himself. According to Erikson, Jose appears to be successfully resolving which developmental crisis?
   a. Trust versus mistrust
   b. Autonomy versus shame and doubt
   c. Initiative versus guilt
   d. Industry versus inferiority

3. Which of the following statements about gender-role development is *false*?
   a. At 3 years old, toddlers can label their gender.
   b. At 4 years old, preschoolers have gender permanence.
   c. At 6 years old, children have gender roles.
   d. At 8 years old, children have gender permanence.

*Answers 1. d; 2. b; 3. b*

# Physical Changes in Adolescence and Adulthood

## LEARNING OBJECTIVES

- Describe pubertal changes in adolescence and discuss the psychological impact of puberty on the self-image of adolescent males and females.

- Understand the changes in the brain that occur in adolescence and adulthood.

- Describe physical changes from early to later adulthood and changes in reproductive capacity during the adulthood years.

Development is not limited to the childhood years; changes continue during the adult years, too. In adulthood, however, these changes are much more variable than in childhood. In this section, we describe the physical changes that characterize adolescence and adulthood. As in childhood, both nature and nurture influence our development.

During adolescence and adulthood we both peak and decline in terms of our physical development. How much and how rapidly we decline are very much influenced by both nature and nurture. Genes affect how we age, but so do the degree to which we exercise mind and body and the experiences we have as we age. What we think of as aging is an incremental and gradual process, but growing into our sexual maturation can be abrupt and actually quite dramatic. We are referring, of course, to the onset of *puberty*.

## Puberty: Big Changes, Rapid Growth

**Puberty** is the process of sexual maturation. These developmental changes involve overall body growth and maturation of sex characteristics that enable people to sexually reproduce. Puberty generally occurs 2 years earlier in girls than in boys, with an average onset at age 10 in females and age 12 for males, but the timing of puberty varies greatly from one person to another and from one culture to another (Parent et al., 2003; Rice, 1992). Over the past 100 years, the age at which puberty begins has dropped in the United States, Western Europe, and Japan. Even within the United States, African American and Hispanic girls tend to enter puberty a year earlier, on average, than European American girls (Butts & Seifer, 2010; Kaplowitz et al., 1999).

### You Asked...

*What kinds of changes occur to the sexuality of an adolescent?*

RICHARD NIEVES, STUDENT

**puberty [PEW-bur-tee]** the process of sexual maturation

## Neuroscience Applies to Your World:

### Are Teenagers Responsible for Their Criminal Behavior?

Research on the adolescent brain has had an impact on our legal system. In some court cases, lawyers have argued that the immaturity of the prefrontal cortex may explain why teenagers' judgment and reasoning may not always be sound. However, although structural changes in the brain *correlate* with teenage behavior, that does not mean they *cause* the behavior. Brain data do not take into account other aspects of development, such as cognitive abilities and the psychosocial challenge of forming an identity. Moreover, adolescent behavior is also influenced by environmental and cultural factors, such as parenting, peer pressure, the influence of the media, and other factors that contribute to brain processing. Adolescents all over the world experience roughly the same process of brain development, yet teenagers in different cultures and environments do not all behave the same way. Attributing a teenager's criminal behavior solely to brain changes ignores the complex interaction of nature and nurture in development.

© Ron Neubauer/PhotoEdit

### You Asked...

*When is the brain fully developed or mature?*

LESLEY MANZANO, STUDENT

## FIGURE

# 9.5

### Neural Growth and Pruning

During early adolescence, new neural connections are formed. In a process called pruning, those that are used are strengthened, whereas those that are not wither away. Hence, engaging in stimulating and interesting activities during adolescence is good for our brains.

*From Time, May 10, 2004. Reprinted with permission.*

**Nerve Proliferation...**
By age 11 for girls and 12 for boys, the neurons in the front of the brain have formed thousands of new connections. Over the next few years many of these links will be pruned.

**...and Pruning**
Those that are used and reinforced—the pathways involved in language, for example—will be strengthened, while the ones that aren't used will die out.

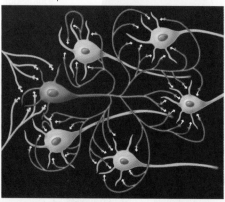

Just prior to puberty there appears to be a second wave of overproduction of cortical gray matter—the tissue that covers the outside of the cerebral hemispheres that appears gray because of the absence of myelin on the axons (Durston et al., 2001; Giedd et al., 1999; Sowell et al., 2001). The brain then prunes these connections as it did earlier in life—keeping the connections that are used while those that are not used wither away (see ■ FIGURE 9.5). This gray matter growth spurt predominates in the prefrontal cortex—the area that plays a major role in cognitive processes such as problem solving, judgment, reasoning, impulse control, and the planning and execution of behavior. This is among the latest brain areas to mature, not reaching adult dimensions until the early 20s (Casey, Giedd, & Thomas, 2000; Giedd, 2004).

Is the brain completely developed at adolescence? No. Under normal conditions, stem cells in some regions of the brain continuously generate neurons throughout life (Schmidt-Hieber, Jonas, & Bischofberger, 2004). The brain remains highly plastic—able to adapt in response to new experiences such as new jobs, marriage, divorce, children, new friends, and financial responsibilities.

## Physical Changes from Early to Later Adulthood

We hit our biological prime during early adulthood, when all major biological systems reach full maturation.

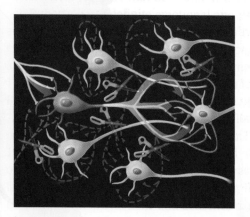

Both women and men peak during their late 20s and early 30s in terms of physical strength, stamina, coordination, dexterity, and endurance (Whitbourne, 1996). These abilities gradually decline in middle and late adulthood.

A similar process occurs in our sensory abilities. Visual acuity, or the ability to focus vision, peaks in our early 20s and remains fairly high until middle adulthood. As we age, we lose the ability to focus on close objects (*presbyopia*), so that reading glasses or bifocals may become necessary in middle or late adulthood. Age-related hearing loss is also common among older adults, especially for high-pitched tones such as a distant telephone or a doorbell. However, people's senses of taste, smell, and touch remain fairly stable until late adulthood.

We see additional signs of the aging process in people's physical appearance as they approach their 40s and 50s. The skin starts to show wrinkles, and the hair may thin and turn gray. Weight gain is likely as metabolism slows, causing noticeable "love handles" or a "pot belly." Then, as people approach their 60s, they typically begin to lose weight and muscle, which may result in a sagging of the skin (Haber, 1994). The compression of vertebrae combined with a loss of bone tissue result in a loss of height as people age.

Although many physical abilities decline over the adult years, it is not clear that these declines are inevitable. As we discuss in more detail in Chapter 11, lifestyle factors such as poor diet, smoking, drinking alcohol, and lack of exercise contribute to the decline in physical functioning for some people. Moreover, culture markedly influences the way we think about aging and our expectations of our physical abilities in middle and later adulthood. In Western cultures such as the United States, becoming old is associated with being frail, useless, and ill, so that many people attempt to push back the aging process. Yet in countries such as Brazil, China, Japan, and Russia, where older people are more valued, aging is viewed more positively and is perceived as a time to look forward to rather than to dread (Gardiner, Mutter, & Kosmitzki, 1998; Lockenhoff et al., 2009). People with positive perceptions of aging engage in more preventive health behaviors, such as exercising, and tend to live longer (B. R. Levy & Myers, 2004; B. R. Levy et al., 2002). Across the world, many older people, despite changes in physical functioning, still lead active lifestyles (Baltes, 1997). As people age, they can usually continue their daily activities by making some adjustments and allowing themselves more time.

## Gender and Reproductive Capacity

Our reproductive capacity also changes during the adulthood years. Women's fertility steadily decreases from age 15 to age 50 (McFalls, 1990; Rowe, 2006). Sometime around age 50, on average, women undergo changes associated with the process of **menopause**. Menopause signals the end of a woman's childbearing years. Her body produces less and less estrogen, affecting the number of eggs that are released from the ovaries. Eventually ovulation and menstruation stop altogether. Decreasing levels of estrogen also cause the breasts and the uterus to shrink. The vaginal walls produce less lubrication, which may make sexual intercourse somewhat painful.

Although men do not experience a "male menopause," they too undergo hormonal changes after age 60, termed *andropause* (Finch, 2001; Mohr et al., 2005; Whitbourne, 2001). They gradually produce fewer male hormones as they age, which lowers the concentration of sperm in the semen and results in hair loss on the legs and face. However, men are still capable of producing offspring into their 70s, 80s, and 90s.

Despite these reproductive changes, older adults continue to have active and satisfying sex lives (Michael et al., 1994). For example, in one national survey of

**menopause**   the period when a female stops menstruating and is no longer fertile

U.S. adults between the ages of 57 and 85, 73% of 57- to 64-year olds reported regular sexual activity, more than half of the 65- to 74-year-olds reported regular sexual activity, and 26% of the 75- to 85-year olds reported regular sexual activity (Lindau et al., 2007).

Because many cultures equate "looking old" with being unattractive, especially for women, middle age and later life may not seem very appealing. However, despite the effects of aging, almost 70% of people over 65 report being in good to excellent health (Hobbs, 1996). Although older adults may not be pleased with certain aspects of physical aging, they are no less content with their lives. Several studies show that older adults often report higher levels of well-being than do younger adults (Stawski et al., 2008; Cacioppo et al., 2008). Happiness and contentment perhaps have more to do with people's ability to adjust to these changes than with the changes themselves.

## Let's REVIEW

This section described the physical changes of adolescence and adulthood. For a quick check of your understanding, answer these questions.

**1.** Which of the following is *not* a physical change associated with puberty in males?
   **a.** Growth of the testes    **c.** Widening hips
   **b.** Voice change    **d.** Broadening shoulders

**2.** Andre, a 65-year-old man, is likely to experience all of the following as the result of aging *except* _____.
   **a.** weight loss    **c.** loss in visual acuity
   **b.** thinning of the hair    **d.** faster reaction time

**3.** Which of the following lists the brain structures in the correct order in which they change (from earliest to latest) in adolescence?
   **a.** Cerebellum, prefrontal cortex, amygdala
   **b.** Cerebellum, amygdala, prefrontal cortex
   **c.** Prefrontal cortex, cerebellum, amygdala
   **d.** Amygdala, prefrontal cortex, cerebellum

Answers 1. c; 2. d; 3. b

# Cognitive Changes in Adolescence and Adulthood

### LEARNING OBJECTIVES

- Compare and contrast formal operations and postformal thought in adolescence and adulthood.

- Describe changes in mental abilities in adulthood.

Adolescence and adulthood are also marked by changes in the way that we think. This section examines these changes in cognition. As we saw earlier in this chapter, children think and reason in ways that are qualitatively different from the thinking of adolescents and adults. Similarly, teenagers do not necessarily think like adults, but they are beginning to practice the reasoning skills and the ability to think outside themselves that characterize later cognitive development.

## Formal Operations Revisited

Recall that Piaget (1952) proposed that teenagers begin to think abstractly during the formal operations stage. This ability to reason abstractly allows them to imagine what could be and to hypothesize about future events and future outcomes. As a result, adolescents experience what they believe are—and often are—tremendous insights into how things could be rather than how they are.

This phenomenon is often labeled the *idealism of youth* (Elkind, 1998). Adolescents believe that they have the answers to problems such as world hunger or conflicts. This mental ability also helps adolescents in discovering who they are as individuals—a topic that will be discussed later in this chapter.

Formal operational thinking also allows teenagers to tackle more challenging academic subjects (science, geometry, calculus) that rely on abstract visualization and reasoning powers. It also enables adolescents to argue more effectively, a power that may not be seen positively by their parents! They are more capable of suggesting hypothetical scenarios ("What if . . .") to justify their position, making them more effective debaters (Elkind, 1998). However, along with this ability to think abstractly comes the return of *egocentrism*.

Egocentrism in adolescence involves teenagers' imagining what others must be thinking. However, teens believe that other people are concerned with the same things they are. Because adolescents' ideas focus mainly on themselves, they believe that others are equally concerned about them (Elkind & Bowen, 1979). For example, a teen with a pimple on his face may imagine that his peers and teachers are thinking only about the pimple on his face. Teenagers may not ask or answer questions in class because they are so sure that everyone is talking about them and thinking about them. They are newly and acutely aware of their own being. Because teens believe that others are focused on them, they behave as if they are on stage—playing to an audience—a phenomenon referred to as the **imaginary audience** (Elkind, 1998). They may laugh especially loudly or behave dramatically because of their belief that they are being constantly watched. Although the imaginary audience and egocentrism are most associated with the teenage years, they may still be somewhat present later in life as young adults choose clothing, jobs, or interests to impress an audience that is largely imaginary (Frankenberger, 2000; Schwartz, Maynard, & Uzelac, 2008).

Another feature of adolescents' thought that relates to egocentrism is the **personal fable** (Elkind, 1998). Teenagers develop the "personal fable" that they are special and unique, that their thoughts and feelings cannot be adequately understood by others (Elkind, 1994). Reflect back on your first love. When that relationship broke up, you may have felt as if no one in the world could identify with what you were feeling. The story you tell yourself is that this person, who is the only person in the world for you, has now gone away, and your life will never be happy again. This is one personal fable of adolescence.

Personal fables may contribute to adolescent risk taking. Because teenagers feel that they are special and unique, they often feel that their own risks are less than those of their peers. For example, they may engage in unprotected sexual intercourse, believing that they won't be the ones to contract a sexually transmitted disease or conceive a child. They may experiment with drugs, believing that they will not become addicted. In their minds, addiction happens to other people. However, recent research suggests that this *optimistic bias* is no more prevalent in adolescents than it is in adults (Reyna & Farley, 2006). Moreover, research by Vartanian (2000, 2001) suggests that both the imaginary audience and the personal fable are biased views of adolescent social cognition that have not been empirically validated.

Although formal operational thinking is often perceived as the hallmark of adolescent thinking, this does not mean that *all* adolescents think abstractly in this way. Cross-cultural research (Hollos & Richards, 1993; Rogoff & Chavajay, 1995) suggests that the development of formal

**imaginary audience**   the belief held by adolescents that everyone is watching what they do

**personal fable**   the belief held by adolescents that they are unique and special

The ability to reason abstractly allows teenagers to successfully tackle complex academic topics.

© Michael J. Doolittle/The Image Works

# 9

## LOOK BACK
### AT What You've
### LEARNED

**Development** includes changes in physical, emotional, social, and cognitive behavior and abilities over time through an interaction of **nature** (one's biology) and **nurture** (one's environment and culture).

### What Happens During Prenatal Development?

- **Germinal stage** (0–14 days): The **zygote** undergoes rapid cell division and duplication.
- **Embryonic stage** (2–8 weeks): Major organs and organ systems form.
- **Fetal stage** (week 9–birth): Body organs and systems more fully develop

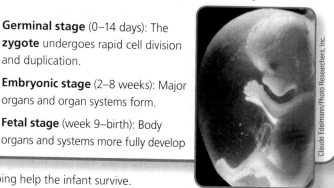

Claude Edelmann/Photo Researchers, Inc.

### How Do Infants and Children Develop Physically?

© Laura Dwight/PhotoEdit

- Infants' and children's brains are highly plastic, or changeable.
- **Reflexes** such as sucking, rooting, and grasping help the infant survive.
- **Gross motor skills** (behaviors that involve large muscle groups) develop and allow the child to run, walk, jump, and hop.
- **Fine motor skills** (involving small muscle groups) develop and aid activities such as writing, using utensils, and playing a musical instrument.

### How Do Infants and Children Develop Cognitively?

- According to Jean Piaget, infants and children apply **schemas (assimilation)** to understand their environment and adapt to change through **accommodation** when existing schemas are changed or modified in four stages of cognitive development: **sensorimotor, preoperational, concrete operations**, and **formal operations**.
- Lev Vygotsky stressed the importance of culture and social interactions in cognitive development.
- Lawrence Kohlberg's research on **moral reasoning** suggests that children's understanding of right and wrong develops progressively from a focus on the self to the external world.

© Laura Dwight/Photo Edit

### How Do Infants and Children Develop Psychosocially?

- An infant's **temperament** can influence the **attachment** or emotional tie between the infant and the primary caregiver.
- Diana Baumrind identified three styles of parenting: **authoritarian, authoritative**, and **permissive.** Permissive parenting may be indulgent or neglectful.
- Psychologist Erik Erikson proposed that the environment and the child's responses to the environment influence the development of either a healthy or an unhealthy personality.
- At a very early age, children process and develop schemas about **gender roles**, or society's expectations for how a female and a male should behave.

© Blend Images/Alamy

# How Do People GROW, CHANGE, and DEVELOP?

## How Do We Develop In Adolescence and Adulthood?

- **Puberty** involves maturation of sex characteristics that enable us to reproduce. At around age 50, women experience **menopause** and hormonal changes that eventually bring an end to reproductive capacity.

- During adolescence and throughout life, the brain remains highly plastic, allowing us to adapt to changing conditions.

- Teenagers tend to be **egocentric**, believing that others are concerned with the same things that they are.

- **Postformal thought** is characterized by **relativistic thinking**, an appreciation that the correct solution or answer may vary from situation to situation.

- Remaining cognitively active helps adults avoid steep declines in mental abilities.

- Erik Erikson considered adolescence the key stage for developing identity, but he believed adults continue to develop when they establish intimacy, generativity, and integrity.

- Adolescent and adult relationships are expressed in a wide range of lifestyles, including dating, cohabitation, marriage, divorce, and parenthood.

- Finding satisfying work and holding a job are part of adult development.

## How Do People Cope with Death and Dying?

- Death is a process rather than a point in time and is an inevitable part of our development.

- Elizabeth Kübler-Ross, a researcher on death and dying, identified five reactions that may characterize people who know they are dying: *denial*, *anger*, *bargaining*, *depression*, and *acceptance*.

# 10 SOCIAL PSYCHOLOGY:
## HOW DO WE **Understand** and INTERACT
### With OTHERS?

# Chapter Outline

*When our student* Diana Flores and her family immigrated to the United States from their native Mexico, they were the first Hispanic family to settle in their new neighborhood. At first, it appeared that they were welcomed by their new neighbors. Diana made friends at school, and her parents made new acquaintances as well. However, as time passed, Diana began to notice subtle signs indicating that they may not have been as accepted by some people as she had thought. At times, when she visited friends' homes after school, she felt as if their parents were uncomfortable with her presence. And as other Hispanic families began to move into the area, Diana began to hear some of her friends say disturbing things about "those people" and how "they" were ruining the area. Diana would quickly point out to her friends that she herself was one of "those people"—only to be told that she was different. "You're not like those people," her friends would say. "You're our friend."

Later, as Diana began to cultivate friendships with other Hispanics, she found that some of her non-Hispanic friends began to withdraw from their friendship. It was upsetting. Diana didn't understand how her friends could show so much disdain for Hispanics while at the same time professing to like her. Couldn't they see that their comments hurt Diana as well? And why did they appear to dislike Diana's Hispanic friends simply because they were Hispanic?

Possible answers to these questions lie in an understanding of the social psychological processes that guide our social behavior. As you study this chapter, you will gain insight into why people sometimes think and behave the way Diana's friends did. You will also learn about the thought processes and social pressures that influence our behavior in a variety of social situations—perhaps even gaining a deeper understanding of yourself in the process.

© Susann Doyle-Portillo

*Diana Flores's understanding of psychology helps her understand why some people discriminate against those who are different from themselves.*

# Attitudes: Changing Our Minds

**Social psychology** is the study of how we think and behave in the vast array of social situations that we experience. One area of social psychology, **social cognition**, investigates the ways in which we think (cognition) about ourselves and others—for example, studying how we develop **attitudes**, our liking or disliking for the people, places, and things in our world. We all have attitudes about a multitude of things that represent the evaluative beliefs we hold about the contents of our world (e.g., liking country music or disliking lazy people). But how do we acquire these attitudes?

## Acquiring Attitudes Through Learning

As with many of our beliefs, we *learn* to have many of the attitudes we hold. One learning process that affects our attitudes about the world is *classical conditioning*. Recall that classical conditioning is often responsible for the development of certain learned *emotional* and *physiological* responses in humans (■ FIGURE 10.1). Because classical conditioning has the power to change the way we *feel* about certain stimuli, it also has the power to influence our attitude toward these stimuli. For example, if a man is robbed by a gang member, he may be classically conditioned to fear (CR) people who wear gang colors and clothes (CS). In short, classical conditioning can often explain the gut-level emotional and physiological aspects of our attitudes (Grossman & Till, 1998).

*Operant conditioning*, or learning through the consequences of our behavior, also affects our attitudes. If you are rewarded for having certain attitudes, the attitude will be strengthened. But if you are punished for having certain attitudes, the attitude will be weakened. For example, if your friends applaud your efforts to "go green" and recycle your trash, then your pro-green attitude is likely to strengthen.

Operant conditioning can also influence our attitudes through the consequences of our direct interaction with the objects of our attitude. For example, if you try a Jamaican dish with lots of very hot peppers that burns your mouth so badly your eyes water, you might develop a negative attitude about eating hot Jamaican food. As a result, the next time you visit a Jamaican restaurant, your behavior will likely change—you'll order one of the blander dishes!

## FIGURE

# 10.1

### Classically Conditioning a Negative Attitude Toward Dogs

For a young child, a fear response in her mother (US) will naturally cause fear in the child (UR). On the other hand, the sight of a dog will not reliably elicit fear in a small child. Therefore, the dog is initially a neutral stimulus (NS). When the sight of the dog (NS) is repeatedly paired with a fear response in the mother (US), the child can easily acquire a conditioned fear of dogs (CR) that is elicited by the mere sight of a dog (CS).

US ——→ ——————→ UR    NS ——→ ——→ US ——→ ——→ UR    CS ——→ ——————→ CR

Mom shows fear.    Child is afraid.

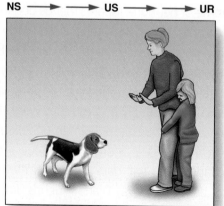

Dog+Mom shows fear.    Child is afraid.

Dog    Child is afraid.

*Is it possible to influence others without intending to do so?*

TAMARA STEWART, STUDENT

At times, we also model the attitudes of others. Recall that in *observational learning* we learn by watching the actions of others and storing mental representations of their behavior in memory. Take a minute to think about your attitudes and the attitudes of those closest to you. How do your attitudes compare to theirs? If you are like most people, you will find that overall, your attitudes are quite similar to those of your parents (Rohan & Zanna, 1996) and those around you (Kowalski, 2003). There will, of course, be some notable differences, but overall we tend to be more like those we love when it comes to attitudes. In fact, such similarity in attitudes is a factor in attraction, which we'll discuss later in this chapter.

As you can see, we learn attitudes the way that we learn everything in life—through experience. Once we form our attitudes about the world, they then have the power to affect what we know, how we feel, and how we behave toward just about everything we encounter in our lives. But is this always the case—do our attitudes always predict our behavior?

## Do Attitudes Predict Behavior?

Do you ever find yourself behaving in a manner that contradicts your attitudes? For example, have you ever laughed at a joke you didn't find very funny? Do you sometimes engage in behavior that you know is harmful to you? If so, your behavior is not unusual. We often behave in ways that go against our attitudes. This lack of *attitude–behavior consistency* has intrigued researchers because it seems so counterintuitive and illogical.

If social pressures can make it difficult for us to behave consistently with our attitudes, what factors make it *more* likely that we will behave in ways that are consistent with our attitudes? Answers to this question have great practical value in society. For instance, under what circumstances might people's positive attitudes toward safer sex actually lead them to engage in protected sex? When might political attitudes accurately predict voting behavior? And in which situations can a company assume that consumer attitudes toward their products will actually translate into sales? Researchers have been diligently trying to answer such questions. ■ TABLE 10.1 describes variables that have been shown to influence attitude–behavior consistency.

Given that our attitudes develop through experience and that once in place they influence our behavior at least part of the time, many psychologists are interested in how attitudes can be changed. This information also has great practical value. If we knew how to change attitudes, we might be able to reverse social problems such as prejudice and alcoholism. These and other pragmatic concerns have fueled a great deal of research on attitude change.

## Cognitive Consistency and Attitude Change

Throughout our lifetime, our attitudes will change as we acquire new knowledge and have different experiences. For example, a favorable attitude toward a particular restaurant may change if you read in the paper that the restaurant failed its last health inspection. In light of this new information, the old attitude may be discarded in favor of a less favorable one. In this example, the attitude change was

Whether we like it or not, we often take on the attitudes of our parents through observational learning.

**social psychology**   the branch of psychology that studies how we think and behave in social situations

**social cognition**   the area of social psychology that deals with the ways in which we think about other people and ourselves

**attitude**   an evaluative belief that we hold about something

**TABLE 10.1**
**Factors That Affect Attitude–Behavior Consistency**

| FACTOR | EXAMPLE |
|---|---|
| If your attitude about the object is low in ambivalence, the attitude will be a better predictor of behavior. | Feeling completely positive about spinach (rather than having mixed feelings about spinach) increases your chance of eating it. |
| If the cognitive and affective aspects of the attitude are both positive (or both negative), the attitude will be a better predictor of behavior. | Both enjoying spinach and knowing that it is good for you increases the chances that you will eat it. |
| Attitudes that are quickly and automatically retrieved from long-term memory are better predictors of behavior. | If the first thing you think of when ordering dinner is your love of spinach, you are more likely to order it. |
| Attitudes that have been stable over time are likely to be better predictors of behavior. | If you have loved spinach since early childhood, you are more likely to continue eating it than you would be if you only recently developed a liking for spinach. |
| Attitudes that are certain are better predictors of behavior. | If you are very sure about your love of spinach, you are more likely to eat it than you would be if you were not very certain about liking spinach. |
| Attitudes that are learned through direct experience with the attitude object are likely to be better predictors of behavior. | If you first learned to love spinach by actually eating it, you are more likely to eat it again. |

Adapted from Cooke & Sheeran (2004).

**cognitive consistency** the idea that we strive to have attitudes and behaviors that do not contradict one another

**dissonance theory** a theory that predicts that we will be motivated to change our attitudes and/or our behaviors to the extent that they cause us to feel dissonance, an uncomfortable physical state

motivated from *within* the attitude holder. The change was not the result of a concerted effort on the part of others. It was motivated more by your desire to maintain what psychologists refer to as **cognitive consistency**, or the desire to avoid contradictions in our attitudes and behaviors (Festinger, 1957). Cognitive consistency theories (Festinger, 1957; Heider, 1946) propose that humans find it uncomfortable when there is inconsistency among their attitudes or between their attitudes and their behavior. Most of us believe that we are intelligent, logical beings. This attitude about being intelligent and logical would be inconsistent with the attitude that an unhealthy restaurant is a good place to eat. So we adjust one of our attitudes (the one concerning the restaurant) to avoid such an inconsistency. But why does inconsistency make us uncomfortable and therefore motivate attitude change?

One explanation of how cognitive inconsistency motivates attitude change is **dissonance theory** (Festinger, 1957). According to dissonance theory, inconsistencies among attitudes or between attitudes and behavior cause an unpleasant physical state called *dissonance*. Think of dissonance as a state of unease much like being hungry or being anxious. It stems from the realization that we have behaved in a way that is contrary to our self-concept (Aronson, 1998). Because dissonance makes us feel bad, we are motivated to stop this unpleasant feeling, which can lead to attitude and/or behavior change (Joule & Azdia, 2003). For example, a health-conscious person who smokes is likely to experience dissonance because smoking is inconsistent with being health conscious. Once the person experiences dissonance, she will be motivated to stop the dissonance by removing the inconsistency.

In general, there are three ways to remove the inconsistencies that cause dissonance. First, she can change her behavior (stop smoking). Second, she can change her attitudes (decide that she is not health conscious after all). Or third, she can remove the inconsistency by bringing new beliefs and attitudes to bear on the situation (convince herself that smoking has never really been *proven* to cause health problems). Any of these three methods will reduce the dissonance felt by the person and restore a state of *consonance*, in which there is no inconsistency among attitudes and behavior.

Because smoking is inconsistent with being health conscious, this person is likely to experience dissonance that may lead to attitude or behavior change.

## Persuasion and Attitude Change

Dissonance theory can explain certain aspects of how we change and grow as human beings, but dissonance is not the only means through which our attitudes change. We also encounter frequent **persuasion** situations in which others directly attempt to change our attitudes. Every day we face persuasive attempts from friends, family members, politicians, the media, and advertisers. By some estimates, the average American encounters a whopping 3,000 advertisements per day (Stanton, 2004)! With all of these persuasive attempts being hurled at us on a daily basis, an understanding of how persuasion occurs becomes almost a necessity.

Obviously, not all of the persuasive attempts we are subjected to actually produce attitude change. We do not become loyal to every product we see advertised on TV. We do not vote for every political candidate we hear speak. So just what makes persuasion successful—or what makes it fail?

One very important factor in the effectiveness of persuasion is the type of *cognitive processes* that we engage in during the persuasive attempt. The degree to which we analyze persuasive arguments can influence whether those arguments are effective in changing our attitudes (Petty & Cacioppo, 1986; Wegener & Carlston, 2005). When we process on the **central route to persuasion**, we carefully and critically evaluate the logic of the persuasive arguments we encounter. When we process on the **peripheral route to persuasion**, we do not attempt to critically evaluate the arguments and are instead persuaded by superficial aspects of the arguments such as the likability of the person making them.

Other variables also affect the success of persuasion. These variables fall into three categories: variables associated with the *communicator* of the message, variables associated with the persuasive *message* itself, and variables associated with the *audience* that receives the persuasive message.

**persuasion**   a type of social influence in which someone tries to change our attitudes

**central route to persuasion**   a style of thinking in which the person carefully and critically evaluates persuasive arguments and generates counterarguments; the central route requires motivation and available cognitive resources

**peripheral route to persuasion**   a style of thinking in which the person does not carefully and critically evaluate persuasive arguments or generate counterarguments; the peripheral route ensues when one lacks motivation and/or available cognitive resources

Attractiveness of a communicator can be one factor that makes you more likely to accept an argument. This is especially true when you are processing on the peripheral route to persuasion.

## COMMUNICATOR VARIABLES

We tend to be most persuaded when the person communicating the message to us is attractive (Eagly & Chaiken, 1975), appears to be credible (Hovland & Weiss, 1951; Tormala, Briñol, & Petty, 2007), and appears to be an expert (Petty, Cacioppo, & Goldman, 1981). We are also most persuaded when the communicator does not appear to be trying to persuade us—unless he or she is attractive, in which case persuasion is still likely (Messner, Reinhard, & Sporer, 2008). This is one reason that advertisers

hire well-respected, attractive actors and actresses to sell their products. They know that we will be more likely to be persuaded because we place our trust in such people—especially if we are processing on the peripheral route (Petty et al., 1981).

## MESSAGE VARIABLES

The logic of the persuasive argument has its greatest impact when we are processing on the central route, for it is here that we can truly appreciate the goodness of the argument (see Petty & Briñol, 2008). We are more likely to be persuaded if the communicator effectively presents both the pros (why we should accept the arguments) and cons (why we might not accept the arguments) of the proposal. This is especially true when the communicator can effectively argue against objections to accepting the proposal (Crowley & Hoyer, 1994). Two-sided arguments generally work best because we tend to trust a communicator who is willing to openly discuss the drawbacks of a proposal.

## AUDIENCE VARIABLES

Effective persuasion is heavily dependent on who is being persuaded. In general, all of us are easier to persuade on the peripheral rather than the central route to persuasion. However, individual differences among us can also influence whether we are persuaded. Variables such as intelligence (Rhodes & Wood, 1992), self-esteem (Petty, Fabrigar, & Wegener, 2003), and mood (Sanaktekin & Sunar, 2008) can all affect our tendency to be persuaded. Yet, after decades of research, it is impossible to make blanket statements about the effect these variables have on persuasion because our individual differences interact in a complex fashion with other variables, such as the route we are processing on (Petty & Briñol, 2008). Under the right circumstances, either high or low levels of intelligence, self-esteem, or positive emotion can all lead to high or low persuasion.

## Let's REVIEW

In this section, we covered ways in which our attitudes can change. For a quick check of your understanding, answer these questions.

---

**1.** If Mike wishes to make the best possible decision about how to vote in the upcoming presidential election, he should watch the presidential debates while processing on the _____.
   **a.** central route
   **b.** algorithmic route
   **c.** peripheral route
   **d.** shortest route

**2.** A politician is attempting to persuade people to vote for her in an upcoming election. With which of the following types of arguments would you expect her to have the most success in winning over a skeptical audience?
   **a.** A short argument that lacks great detail
   **b.** A very long and detailed argument
   **c.** A one-sided argument explaining why voters should vote for her
   **d.** A two-sided argument explaining why voters should vote for her, as well as some concerns they may have about voting for her

**3.** Thelma recently discovered that her favorite actress supports a radical political group that Thelma despises. According to dissonance theory, what is *most* likely to happen in this situation?
   **a.** She will begin to like the actress more.
   **b.** She will begin to like the actress less.
   **c.** She will begin to dislike the political group more.
   **d.** Her attitudes toward the actress and the group will not change.

Answers 1. a; 2. d; 3. b

# Forming Impressions of Others

## You Asked...

*What gives us a perception of other people?*

JOSHUA KENNEDY, STUDENT

One of the most important aspects of social cognition is **impression formation**, or how we understand and make judgments about others. When we meet someone for the first time, we usually attempt to determine what type of person he is. Is this person kind, smart, aggressive, or untrustworthy? We want to know. Why do we want to know what other people are like? In short, if we have a good understanding of other people's traits and abilities, we can predict how they will behave in certain situations. This allows us to guide our own behavior in social situations. Without some understanding of others, social interactions would be much more awkward and uncertain.

## The Attribution Process

It appears that one of our basic social cognitive tendencies is to try to explain the behavior of ourselves and others, but how do you determine the traits and characteristics of someone you've just met? If you're thinking that we pay attention to what the person says and does, you're correct. When we judge a person, we observe his behavior, and then we attempt to determine the cause of this behavior (Heider, 1958). This process of assigning cause to behavior is called **attribution**. For example, imagine that you enter a local café and see a woman yelling at a man in the corner booth. Witnessing her outburst, you would likely try to determine why the woman is yelling. Is it because she is an aggressive person? Or did the man somehow provoke this type of outburst in an otherwise kind woman? Questions like these may pass through your mind as you watch the scene unfold.

In this example, we can attribute the woman's behavior to one of two types of causes. We can attribute the behavior to her traits, abilities, or characteristics, in which case we are making a **trait attribution**. Or we may attribute the behavior to something in the environment, in which case we are making a **situational attribution**. If we make a trait attribution about the yelling woman, we assume that she is yelling because she is an aggressive person. If we make a situational attribution, we assume that something happened in the environment that caused the woman to yell—perhaps her companion accidently spilled hot coffee in her lap. Note that when we make a situational attribution, we do *not* attribute the woman's behavior to her personality.

If you witnessed this scene, what attributions would you make about this woman's behavior? Would you assume that her behavior reflects her personality traits? Or would you assume that the situation must have elicited her behavior?

**impression formation**    the way that we understand and make judgments about others

**attribution**    the act of assigning cause to behavior

**trait attribution**    an attribution that assigns the cause of a behavior to the traits and characteristics of the person being judged

**situational attribution**    an attribution that assigns the cause of a behavior to some characteristic of the situation or environment in which the behavior occurs

## Heuristics and Biases in Attribution

Ideally, we would weigh all the available evidence before making either a trait attribution or a situational attribution. Unfortunately, the realities of the world do not always allow us to make careful, analytic attributions. Humans are *cognitive misers*, meaning that we try to conserve our cognitive resources whenever we can (Fiske & Taylor, 1991). We have seen evidence of our miserliness in earlier discussions. As we saw in Chapter 7, when we have to quickly solve a problem, we often use shortcuts, or *heuristics*, in hopes of finding a solution. Heuristics may lead to quick answers, but they do not always lead to *accurate* answers. People have been shown to employ several timesaving heuristics while making attributions, and these shortcuts often lead to errors and biases in the attribution process.

## YOUR TURN  Active Learning

Try the following demonstration. Look at the photos in ■ FIGURE 10.2 and follow the instructions. What type of personality traits did you list for these people? How confident were you in these judgments? Now ask yourself this question: What evidence do I have that these people actually possess these personality traits? If you're like most people, your perceptions of these celebrities are based on the roles they play on TV or in the movies. Most of us assume that their behavior on TV is indicative of their personality *traits* in real life. Did you? If so, what *situational* explanations for these people's TV behavior did you fail to take into account? Did you take into account that on TV, these celebrities are acting? Did you think about the fact that even "reality shows" and talk shows involve someone directing the actors' behavior and the actors are aware that they are being watched by millions of people? Probably not. The bottom line is that unless you've spent time with these celebrities in real life, you've never really seen their natural behavior; therefore, it's somewhat illogical to draw firm conclusions about their personality traits. If you did just that, don't feel bad. This tendency to rely on trait attributions and to discount situational explanations of behavior is so common that it is called the **fundamental attribution error**.

**FIGURE**

## 10.2

### What Do You Think About These Celebrities?

Take a look at these celebrities. Would you like to be friends with these people? What kind of people do you think they are? In the spaces below each photo, write down some of the traits you think this person possesses. Then rate your confidence in the accuracy of your judgments on a scale from 1 to 10, where 1 = not at all confident that your judgment is correct and 10 = very confident that your judgment is correct.

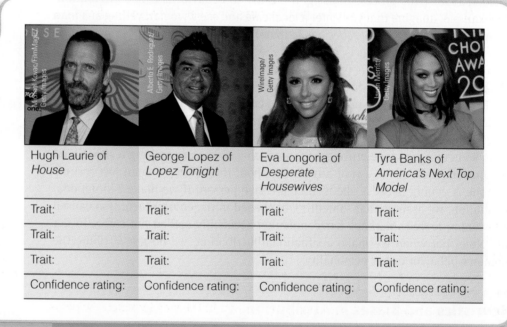

| Hugh Laurie of *House* | George Lopez of *Lopez Tonight* | Eva Longoria of *Desperate Housewives* | Tyra Banks of *America's Next Top Model* |
| --- | --- | --- | --- |
| Trait: | Trait: | Trait: | Trait: |
| Trait: | Trait: | Trait: | Trait: |
| Trait: | Trait: | Trait: | Trait: |
| Confidence rating: | Confidence rating: | Confidence rating: | Confidence rating: |

## FUNDAMENTAL ATTRIBUTION ERROR

Why we tend to engage in the fundamental attribution error is not entirely clear. Perhaps it reflects our preference to know more about a person's traits than about a person's environment. After all, the goal of forming attributions is to understand the person, not the environment (Jones, 1979). Another explanation is that when

**fundamental attribution error**
our tendency to overuse trait information when making attributions about others

we view someone in a social setting, we tend to focus our attention on the person and her behavior, paying less attention to the situation. If we don't pay much attention to the situation, we are unlikely to give situational factors much weight when making our attributions.

Engaging in the fundamental attribution error varies with the degree to which our culture emphasizes individual behavior over group behavior. Some cultures, such as those in North America and Western Europe, are **individualistic cultures**, emphasizing the behavior and success of individuals rather than groups. Some other cultures, such as those in India and Japan, are **collectivistic cultures**, emphasizing the behavior and success of groups more than individuals (Triandis, 1994). Research has shown that people from individualistic cultures are more likely to engage in the fundamental attribution error (Choi & Nesbitt, 1998). Presumably, the Western focus on the individual accounts for this difference in attribution, but more research needs to be done to pinpoint the difference between individualistic and collectivistic cultures.

## ACTOR/OBSERVER BIAS

What kind of attributions do we make when we are examining our own behavior? What if you found yourself yelling at a companion in a café? Would you be as likely to label yourself as a mean person as you would the woman in the previous example? Probably not. When we observe our own behavior, we tend to take situational factors more into account than we do for others. This tendency has been called the **actor/observer bias** because we make different attributions as *actors* than we make as *observers* of others (Choi & Nesbitt, 1998; Jones & Nesbitt, 1971). The actor/observer bias predicts that you are likely to attribute your own yelling to some situational factor. Perhaps your significant other angered you, or you had a bad day. The explanation you would likely use for others, being a mean person, would be low on your list of attributions for your own behavior.

The actor/observer bias may seem self-serving, but this is not always the case. You would also be more likely to attribute a classmate's unexpected "A" on an exam to his traits than you would your own unexpected "A." In this case, the actor/observer bias predicts that you would consider situational causes, such as an easy exam, more for yourself than for others. So why do we treat ourselves differently from others when it comes to attribution?

One potential reason for the actor/observer bias is that when we are the actor, we cannot literally see our own behavior, and our attention is generally focused outward on the environment. But when we are the observer, our attention is generally focused on the other person's behavior. Therefore, because we are relatively unaware of our own behavior and very aware of the environment, we are more likely to consider situational factors in making attributions for ourselves (Storms, 1973; Hennessy & Jakubowski, 2007).

The actor/observer bias may also stem from the different knowledge we have about ourselves and other people (Eisen, 1979). When we are making attributions about our own behavior, we are usually very aware of the way in which the environment influences it. Because we do not typically know other people's thoughts, we usually do not know how other people perceive the situation and whether it indeed influences their behavior.

## SELF-SERVING BIAS

Although the actor/observer bias does not stem from a desire to enhance one's self-esteem, this does not mean that we never seek to make ourselves look better. Often we do make self-esteem-boosting attributions. The **self-serving bias** refers to our tendency to make trait attributions for our successes and situational

**individualistic culture**   a culture, like many Western cultures, in which individual accomplishments are valued over group accomplishments

**collectivistic culture**   a culture, like many Asian cultures, in which group accomplishments are valued over individual accomplishments

**actor/observer bias**   our tendency to make the fundamental attribution error when judging others, while being less likely to do so when making attributions about ourselves

**self-serving bias**   our tendency to make attributions that preserve our own self-esteem—for example, making trait attributions for our success and situational attributions for our failures attributions for our failures (Miller & Ross, 1975). If you were to earn an "A" on your next psychology exam, you would likely attribute this grade to your ability or your study habits. However, if you were to fail your next psychology exam (and we hope that you do not!), you would be more likely to attribute your grade to some situational factor, such as your professor's teaching or the fact that your roommate interfered with your studying.

Most people, regardless of age, gender, or culture, engage in the self-serving bias (Mezulis et al., 2004). The major reason for the self-serving bias appears to be our desire to feel good about ourselves (Brown & Rogers, 1991; Trafimow, Armendariz, & Madsen, 2004). This bias helps protect our self-esteem, although it can also cause problems if we become too self-serving. For instance, not taking responsibility for our failures can lead others to like us less (Carlston & Shovar, 1983).

As we have seen in this section, we often take shortcuts, or heuristics, when making attributions about others. Heuristics may save time, but often they lead to incorrect attributions and judgments. As we will see in the next section, our tendency to use mental shortcuts can also lead to bigger problems, including prejudice and discrimination.

# Let's REVIEW

In this section, we discussed how we form impressions of ourselves and others. For a quick check of your understanding, answer these questions.

1. Our tendency to overuse trait attributions and to ignore the situational influences on behavior is known as the _____.
   a. fundamental attribution error
   b. self-serving bias
   c. social desirability bias
   d. actor/observer bias

2. Which of the following people would be *least* likely to exhibit the fundamental attribution error?
   a. Henri from Canada
   b. Kiko from Japan
   c. Lamont from the United States
   d. Greta from Germany

3. Jasper was quick to assume that Susan was intelligent when he saw that she earned an "A" on her last psychology exam. However, when Jasper earned an "A" on his history test, he was not so quick to assume that he was intelligent. Which of the following biases in social cognition best explains Jasper's behavior?
   a. The fundamental attribution error
   b. The self-serving bias
   c. The social desirability bias
   d. The actor/observer bias

Answers 1. a; 2. b; 3. d

## LEARNING OBJECTIVES

- Define and distinguish among prejudice, stereotypes, discrimination, and stereotype threat.

- Describe the processes through which prejudice develops.

- Describe ways to reduce prejudice.

# Prejudice: Why Can't We All Just Get Along?

Prejudices based on race, gender, sexual orientation, age, religion, country of origin, and other perceived differences still hamper many people's ability to live a productive and happy life. People have been harassed and belittled, lost jobs, and even been killed because of prejudice. In 2008, the FBI reported a total of 7,783 incidents of hate crimes. Most of these incidents were motivated by racial prejudice, with religious prejudice and prejudice based on sexual orientation the next most frequent motives for hate crimes (Federal Bureau of Investigation, 2009a).

Besides violent crimes and crimes against property, there are subtler forms of discrimination. For example, Hispanics are often quoted higher rents than Whites for the same property and given less help in securing mortgages for home purchases (Department of Housing and Urban Development [HUD], 2005). Real estate agents often direct African Americans to poorer, segregated minority neighborhoods (HUD, 2005). And despite gains in equal rights over the last several decades, women have still not achieved equal status in the workforce, academia, or the government (Blackwell, Snyder, & Mavriplis, 2009; Cheung & Halpern, 2010; Sanchez-Hucles & Davis, 2010). Prejudice remains a serious social problem. Because prejudice poses a threat to all of us, understanding where prejudice comes from is essential.

We can view prejudice as an extension of normal cognitive processes in that prejudices are attitudes that develop like all other attitudes. At the same time, prejudices are unique because they are especially problematic and divisive attitudes that can cause great harm to countless individuals and to society at large. As we look at the development of prejudice, we will examine the similarities between normal cognition and prejudiced thought.

Studies suggest that Hispanic people are more likely to be quoted higher rental rates than their White counterparts. These findings suggest that prejudice and discrimination are still part of our world.

## Stereotypes, Prejudice, and Discrimination

You will recall from Chapters 6 and 9 that as we acquire knowledge about the world, we store that information in generalized knowledge structures called *schemas*. Schemas reside in our long-term memory and allow us to more efficiently encode, store, and retrieve information (Fiske & Taylor, 1991). When we form a schema for a particular group of people, that schema is referred to as a **stereotype**. All of us have stereotypes for the various groups of people—such as professors, children, or females—we encounter in life. Our stereotypes allow us to make assumptions about others and to have certain expectations about how others will behave.

Although stereotypes are generally helpful to us, they are related to the prejudices that cause untold difficulties for humankind. One way to conceptualize a **prejudice** is as a stereotype gone awry. A stereotype can be thought of as the *cognitive* component of an attitude (Aronson, Wilson, & Akert, 2005) or the knowledge you have stored in memory about some group of people. Stereotypes become problematic when we generically apply them to all members of a group without regard to those individuals' unique characteristics. Furthermore, when a stereotype contains biased and negative information about a particular group of people, the stereotype begins to look like a prejudice (e.g., Chory-Assad & Tamborini, 2003). Finally, when a biased, negative stereotype becomes coupled with a negative *affective* or emotional reaction toward all (or most) people belonging to that group, a prejudice results.

In the mind of the prejudiced person, members of a particular group are disliked and labeled as having negative characteristics, regardless of their individual qualities. Additionally, prejudice can affect how the prejudiced person *behaves* toward others. All too often, prejudice motivates people to treat others poorly. **Discrimination** is the behavioral expression of a prejudice. For example, not considering a woman for a job as a forklift operator simply because she is female would be an act of discrimination.

Discrimination doesn't always take such a blatant form. It can be much more subtle. Psychologists Samuel Gaertner and John Dovidio (1986, 2005) have argued that modern-day racial prejudice in the United States takes the form of **aversive racism**. According to this theory, European Americans who outwardly support equality and fairness may still feel negative emotions in the presence of African Americans. These negative or *aversive* emotions may motivate the person to discriminate against or avoid interaction with minority members. Aversive racism may be more likely when stressful situations heighten such aversive feelings. For example, European Americans were found to be slower to help African Americans than they were to help other European Americans during a severe emergency, but equally likely to help members of either group during a minor emergency

**stereotype** a schema for a particular group of people

**prejudice** a largely negative stereotype that is unfairly applied to all members of a group regardless of their individual characteristics

**discrimination** the behavioral expression of a prejudice

**aversive racism** a proposed form of subtle racism in which European Americans feel aversive emotions around African Americans, which may lead them to discriminate against African Americans

(Kunstman & Plant, 2008). These results suggest that under stress, hidden prejudices can surface and give rise to discrimination.

## Stereotype Threat: Prejudice Can Be a Self-Fulfilling Prophecy

Like a woman seeking employment in a male-dominated field, many people live with the fear that others may harbor prejudices about them. Psychologist Claude Steele proposes that some victims of prejudice actually end up reinforcing certain aspects of the prejudices held against them because of a phenomenon called **stereotype threat**. Stereotype threat exists when a person fears that others will judge her not on her own qualities but rather on prejudicial stereotypes held about the group(s) to which she belongs (Steele, 1997). Understandably, this fear can lead to considerable anxiety in minorities because of the negative nature of the prejudices they face. For example, women often experience stereotype threat when performing mathematical and scientific tasks (Good, Woodzicka, & Wingfield, 2010). Widespread negative stereotyping of women in the workplace also leads women to expect that coworkers will give them less credit for successes and more blame for failures (e.g., Heilman & Kram, 1983).

Studies have shown that stereotype threat can actually inhibit performance on a task. For example, normally high-achieving females tend to score less well on mathematics problems but not on verbal tasks when they are asked to perform these tasks in an environment where they are outnumbered by men (Inzlicht & Ben-Zeev, 2000). In this situation, females presumably become aware of the prejudicial stereotypes that many people hold—that men are better at math—and the fear of being perceived to be mathematically inept (stereotype threat) then impairs their math performance. Females are not stereotyped as being poor at verbal tasks, so there is no stereotype threat for verbal tasks, and females exhibit no impairment in performance even when they are outnumbered by males. Stereotype threat can thus become a *self-fulfilling prophecy* in which a woman behaves in a manner that actually reinforces negative stereotypes about females (Keller & Dauenheimer, 2003).

Stereotype threat has also been shown to impair African Americans' academic performance (e.g., Steele & Aronson, 1995), and may contribute to some African Americans' experiencing *disidentification* with certain aspects of European American culture. For example, if young African Americans experience stereotype threat in school (they perceive that others expect them to fail), one way they may protect themselves emotionally is by devaluing education. If one does not feel that academic achievement is important, then if one fails at academics, it is not damaging to his or her self-esteem (Steele, 1997). Unfortunately, this not only prevents some African Americans from achieving academically, it may also place pressure on those African Americans who do wish to pursue academic success. If your friends devalue your dreams, you must either abandon your plans or distance yourself from your friends—both of which can be painful. One thing is certain: As long as negative stereotypes persist, it's a safe bet that many people will suffer as a result.

## Social Transmission of Prejudice

Like other attitudes, prejudices can develop through the processes of classical conditioning, operant conditioning, and observational learning (Duckitt, 1992). As you can see in ■ YOU REVIEW 10.1, these types of learning allow prejudices to develop and also be passed from person to person within a culture. The experiences we have with other groups of people, the models we are exposed to (Kowalski, 2003), and the rewards and punishments we receive in life all have the power to mold our stereotypes and prejudices.

**stereotype threat**    a phenomenon in which fears of being discriminated against elicit stereotype-confirming behaviors

# YOU REVIEW 10.1 The Learning of a Prejudice

| Type of Learning | Situation | Outcome |
|---|---|---|
| Classical conditioning | Marlita is robbed at knifepoint (US) by a man (CS). During the attack, she feels terror and anger (UR/CR). | After the attack, Marlita feels anger and terror when she sees men. She has been classically conditioned to feel negative emotions in response to men. |
| Operant conditioning | Bobbi makes fun of some boys at her school. She calls them "stupid crybabies" (behavior). All of Bobbi's friends laugh when they see her behaving this way (reward). | Bobbi is more likely to make fun of boys in the future because she has been rewarded for doing so. Her friends have operantly conditioned her prejudiced, discriminatory behavior. |
| Observational learning | From a young age, Jackie hears her mother frequently say that men are sloppy, stubborn, insensitive creatures. | Jackie is likely to model her mother's prejudices and adopt her mother's belief that men are sloppy, stubborn, and insensitive. |

How easily prejudices can be learned was dramatically demonstrated in one of the most famous classroom exercises ever done on prejudice. In the late 1960s, grade school teacher Jane Elliot decided to teach her third-grade class an important lesson about prejudice. She believed that her students, who were all rural White children, could benefit from learning about prejudice from both sides of the fence.

One day in class, Elliot told her students that she had recently heard that scientists had determined that brown-eyed people were inferior to blue-eyed people. She told the class that brown-eyed people were less intelligent, trustworthy, and nice than the "superior" blue-eyed people. To make the group differences very salient, Elliot had all the brown-eyed children wear brown cloth collars over their clothing so they could be immediately identified as members of the "inferior" group of students.

Within hours of her announcement concerning eye color, Elliot had created a strong prejudice in her classroom. The blue-eyed children made fun of the brown-eyed children. The blue-eyes called the brown-eyes names, ostracized them, and in general treated them cruelly. A fight even occurred on the playground as a result of the prejudice. In less than a day, Elliot turned a peaceful, egalitarian classroom into a hotbed of prejudice and discrimination (Monteith & Winters, 2002). Elliot's study showed the world how easily prejudice can be learned from others—especially when we learn it from those we look up to. What other situations contribute to the development of prejudice?

Elliot's demonstration showed how quickly prejudice can be learned. Admittedly, the environment Elliot created in her classroom was deliberately designed to create prejudice. What other types of environments may contribute to the development of prejudices? Can prejudice be developed within a family, for instance? There is some evidence to suggest that we do adopt the prejudices of our parents, but having prejudiced parents does not guarantee that we will become prejudiced. In one study that examined the match between parental values and those held by their children, it was found that children are most likely to have attitudes similar to their parents when the parents hold egalitarian beliefs. When parents hold prejudicial attitudes, the match between their values and their children's values is less strong (Rohan & Zanna, 1996).

It appears that when parents hold strong prejudices, the children may pick up these prejudices but later find that their peers do not reinforce them for holding such negative views. Because they are not reinforced and may even be punished

This child is likely to adopt the prejudices of her parents through modeling.

by their peers for holding prejudices, they experience a decline in prejudice that distances them from their parents' values. But when parents hold egalitarian values, their children may pick up these values and be reinforced by their peers for having them. Their values then remain more like those of their parents (Aronson et al., 2005). This line of research makes a powerful argument for teaching tolerance in schools and in society because if tolerance becomes prevalent in a culture, it *may* have the power to override what happens in the home.

## Intergroup Dynamics and Prejudice

We all belong to certain groups: families, schools, clubs, states, countries, religions, and races. These groups and the roles we play in them help define who we are as individuals (e.g., Gergen & Gergen, 1988). Because we tend to identify with the groups to which we belong, we also tend to prefer the groups of which we are members.

### IN-GROUP BIAS: US VS. THEM

We tend to like the people in our group a little more than we like the people who are not members. In other words, we exhibit an **in-group bias** (Hewstone, Rubin, & Willis, 2002). We tend to like our family members more than strangers. We like those who attend our school more than those who do not. We have a bias toward liking our country's citizens a little more than foreigners.

Think of the groups of spectators at a sporting event. Each group sits on its team's side, and at times the rivalry between the two sides erupts into name-calling and even violence. If these same people met under other conditions in which their team affiliations were not obvious, such as at the grocery store or library, do you think they would be as likely to call each other names and fight? Probably not. Why do we sometimes allow our group affiliations to bias how we feel about and treat others? It appears to boil down to self-esteem.

We apparently derive some of our self-esteem from the groups of which we are members. One way to enhance self-esteem is by belonging to a group we perceive as good and desirable. For example, if you perceive your religion as being the *best* religion, then belonging to this religious group increases your self-esteem. Unfortunately, one way to perceive your particular group as being good is to believe that other groups are not as good (Tajfel, 1982). When our group succeeds at something, we tend to be especially proud (Cialdini et al., 1976). In the absence of meaningful victory, we still tend to view our in-group members as superior to **out-group** members (Brewer, 1979; Molero et al., 2003; Tajfel, 1982).

### You Asked...

*Why do people have the tendency to generalize?*

DIANA FLORES, STUDENT

The in-group bias tends to make us prejudiced against those who are not part of our social groups. Further, the in-group bias tends to affect the way we *perceive* out-group members, causing us to see members of an out-group as being pretty much all alike. Researchers call this tendency the **out-group homogeneity bias** (Linville, Fischer, & Salovey, 1989). Individual characteristics are perceived not to differ much from the stereotype that defines the group. So once we have knowledge about one member of an out-group, we tend to apply it to all people in that group (Quattrone & Jones, 1980).

### INTERGROUP CONFLICT AND PREJUDICE: IT'S THEIR FAULT

**Realistic-conflict theory** (Levine & Campbell, 1972) proposes that conflict among groups for resources motivates the development of prejudice. In the United States,

**in-group bias**  our tendency to favor people who belong to the same groups that we do

**out-group**  a group that is distinct from one's own and so usually an object of more hostility or dislike than one's in-group

**out-group homogeneity [home-uh-juh-NEE-it-tee] bias**  our tendency to see out-group members as being pretty much all alike

**realistic-conflict theory**  the theory that prejudice stems from competition for scarce resources

immigrants are often the targets of prejudice because they are perceived as coming here "to steal jobs away from hard-working Americans" (Esses et al., 2001). Minority out-group members often play the role of **scapegoat**, the out-group members we blame for our problems, when times are hard (Allport, 1954/1979). In modern America, as you might expect, racial prejudice most often exists when groups are in direct competition for the same jobs (Simpson & Yinger, 1985).

Possibly the most famous study ever conducted on conflict and prejudice is Muzafer Sherif's Robber's Cave experiment (Sherif et al., 1961). Sherif and his colleagues conducted this experiment in a naturalistic setting, a summer boys' camp at Robber's Cave State Park in Oklahoma (hence the experiment's nickname). The participants were normal, healthy, middle-class, White, Protestant, 11- to 12-year-old boys who attended Boy Scout camp at the park. Prior to participation in the camp, the boys were all strangers to one another.

As they arrived at the camp, the boys were randomly assigned to one of two cabins, the Eagles' cabin or the Rattlers' cabin. The cabins were situated fairly far apart to ensure that the two groups would not have much contact with each other. The boys in each group lived together, ate together, and spent much of their time together. Under these conditions of isolation from each other, the Eagles and the Rattlers became separate, tight-knit in-groups. Once each group bonded, the experimenters placed the Eagles and Rattlers together under conditions of conflict.

In this next phase, the experimenters had the Eagles and Rattlers compete with each other in sporting events. The winning group would get prizes that 12-year-old boys find attractive, such as pocketknives. The losers got nothing for their efforts except defeat. As a result of this competition, the Eagles and the Rattlers began to call each other names, sabotage each other's cabins and belongings, and even engage in physical violence against one another. In short, the Eagles hated the Rattlers, and the Rattlers hated the Eagles. A prejudice based on the relatively meaningless distinctions of being Eagles or Rattlers was fully developed in the boys. When the prejudice between the Eagles and Rattlers reached the point of physical violence, the experimenters stopped the competition between the boys and sought ways to reduce the prejudice that had developed.

## Does Social Contact Reduce Prejudice?

One of Sherif's strategies to reduce prejudice was to increase noncompetitive contact between the Eagles and the Rattlers (e.g., watching movies together). In fact, the idea that contact between groups is enough to reduce prejudice, the so-called **contact hypothesis**, has been around for quite some time (Lee & Humphrey, 1943, cited in Allport, 1954/1979). If people from different in-groups see a lot of each other, won't they realize that the prejudices they hold about one another are unfounded and abandon them?

As Sherif found out, mere contact often does little to reduce prejudice (e.g., Poore et al., 2002). One reason contact doesn't work is that when people from different groups are thrown together, they tend to self-segregate (Binder et al., 2009). A drive through any big city illustrates this point. Neighborhoods are often well defined on the basis of ethnicity and race—even though people are legally free to live where they choose. Such segregation can prevent meaningful contact between groups from happening, precluding much chance of reducing prejudice.

To bring groups together in meaningful contact, they have to be motivated to really spend time together—not just occupy the same space. Not surprisingly, *cooperative contact*, in which the groups work together on a common task, has been shown to be more effective in reducing prejudice than merely forcing groups together (Pettigrew & Tropp, 2006).

**scapegoat**   an out-group that is blamed for many of society's problems

**contact hypothesis**   the theory that contact between groups is an effective means of reducing prejudice between them

After experimenting with increased contact between the Eagles and the Rattlers, Sherif and his colleagues (1961) tried facilitating cooperation between the two groups of boys. Sherif and his colleagues created *superordinate goals* for the Eagles and the Rattlers. A **superordinate goal** is a goal that both groups want to accomplish but cannot without the help of the other group. For instance, the researchers disrupted the water supply that both groups used by tampering with the water pipes. To reestablish water to the camp, the Eagles and Rattlers had to work together to find the source of the trouble. While they were trying to solve their mutual problem, the Eagles and Rattlers did not seem to have much time to hate one another. In another instance, a food supply truck broke down, and the two groups had to work together to push-start the truck. Without their combined efforts, both groups would have gone hungry.

After a series of such contacts, the prejudice between the groups began to dissolve, perhaps because the Eagles and Rattlers now saw themselves as part of the same group—the group that was trying to find food and water. Without clear lines between the boys, there was no basis for in-group or out-group bias or prejudice. The researchers noted that friendships began to form between individual Eagles and Rattlers, and as a whole, the Rattlers and Eagles began to cooperate, spend time together, and even share their money. The prejudice that was once so strong was dramatically reduced (Sherif, 1966).

Based in part on the results of the Robber's Cave study, researchers have attempted to outline the characteristics of the type of contact between groups that reduces prejudice. The most effective strategies are ones in which:

- The different groups need each other.
- The different groups have a common, superordinate goal that requires everyone's effort to achieve.
- The different groups work shoulder to shoulder on an equal playing field to accomplish the goal.
- The contact is hospitable, informal, and free from negative emotional interaction.
- Contact with out-group members lasts for a significant period of time.
- The norms governing the contact situation promote harmony and mutual respect.

**superordinate goal**   a goal that is shared by different groups

Superordinate goals are an effective means of reducing prejudice. These people are likely to see themselves as members of the same in-group as they work together to survive this challenge. As a result, they are likely to experience less prejudice toward one another.

© Jim West/Alamy

One practical application of these conditions is called a *jigsaw classroom* (Aronson, 2000). A jigsaw classroom is one in which students from diverse ethnic groups are asked to work together on a project in a cooperative way. Each child is responsible for a different piece of the project, which forces the children to be interdependent. Because they must rely on each other, the children begin to focus more on the tasks at hand and less on their differences. According to psychologist Elliot Aronson (2000), research on the outcomes of jigsaw classrooms over the last 25 years consistently indicates that as participants begin to identify as members of the same in-group, prejudice and hostility among the children are reduced, and self-esteem and academic performance are increased. These findings further underscore the message of the Robber's Cave experiment—that cooperation rather than competition can work to lower prejudice in the world.

We have seen that prejudices can affect the judgments we make about other people. When we attribute negative characteristics to people simply because they belong to a certain social group, we are behaving prejudicially. Our prejudices can, in turn, affect the way we treat other people.

Regardless of whether we base our impressions on a prejudice or on actual behavior, we tend to want to spend more time with people we *like*. We may decide to enter into a friendship or a romantic relationship with someone about whom we have formed a positive impression. The relationship may turn out to be wonderful, or it may fail. In the aftermath of the breakup of a relationship, we often ask ourselves, "What did I ever see in this person?" This is the question that we will tackle next as we look at what attracts us to others.

## Let's REVIEW

In this section, we discussed prejudice and ways to reduce it. As a quick check of your understanding, answer these questions.

1. Kelly is a manager at a firm that has been troubled by considerable prejudice between its male and female employees. Kelly wants to institute a program that will reduce the level of prejudice between the sexes. Which of the following plans has the best chance of working?
   a. Appoint opposite-sex managers to supervise workers.
   b. Have a "battle of the sexes" to see which sex can outperform the other on the job.
   c. Form work teams to solve company problems, and make sure that the teams contain both male and female members.
   d. Threaten to fire anyone who says or does anything prejudicial, and post this message around the workplace to ensure that everyone knows about the policy.

2. Relative to in-group members, we tend to view out-group members as being _____.
   a. less like us
   b. less favorable
   c. more homogeneous
   d. All of the above

3. Which of the following is the best example of cooperative contact?
   a. Teachers supervising students taking a math test
   b. A manager meeting with employees to discuss sales figures
   c. A police officer speaking to an elementary school class about the dangers of drugs
   d. A citizens' group meeting to find ways to reduce crime in their neighborhood

Answers 1. c; 2. d; 3. d

# The Nature of Attraction: What Draws Us to Others?

**LEARNING OBJECTIVE**

- Describe the factors affecting attraction: proximity, exposure, similarity, and physical attractiveness.

The attitudes that we form about a person determine whether or not we will be attracted to this person as a friend or as a romantic partner. The affective component of the attitudes we hold about someone is particularly important. If a person produces positive emotional reactions in us, we are much more likely to find him or her attractive. Think about the people closest to you. How do you *feel* about your best friend and your significant other? We are betting that most of you generally feel positive emotions about those you love. Most of us do. When it comes to attraction, the most important question is: What makes us feel good about another person?

## Proximity and Exposure: Attraction to Those That Are Nearby

One of the most intriguing findings in the area of attraction concerns how much exposure we have to certain people and how the exposure affects our feelings of attraction for them. Recall from Chapter 8 that the more often we see a person or

People who work in close proximity to each other are more likely to become friends and lovers.

an object, the more we tend to like it. This trend, called the *mere exposure effect* (A. Y. Lee, 2001; Zajonc, 1968), appears to be true for a variety of stimuli, including people (Zebrowitz, White, & Wieneke, 2008).

Many studies have shown that we tend to be friends and lovers with those who live and work close to us (Clarke, 1952; Festinger, 1951; Festinger, Schachter, & Back, 1950; Ineichen, 1979; Segal, 1974). The more **proximity**, or geographical closeness, we have to someone in our daily lives, the more exposure we have to them, and the more we tend to like them. For example, within an apartment building, the closer a person's apartment is to yours, the higher the probability that you will be friends with that person (Festinger, 1951). This is true even when apartments are assigned on a random basis, as you might find in university housing (Festinger et al., 1950). Attraction to those who live and work nearby seems to hold across cultures as well. Studies have found evidence supporting a relationship between proximity and liking in both Africa (Brewer & Campbell, 1976) and France (Maisonneuve, Palmade, & Fourment, 1952).

## Similarity: Having Things in Common

> ### You Asked...
> *Is it true that opposites attract?*
> CAROLANNE PARKER, STUDENT

There are two old adages about the people we tend to choose as friends or romantic partners. One says, "Birds of a feather flock together," and the other says, "Opposites attract." You probably know some couples who demonstrate both views of attraction. But what does the average person look for? Do we want someone who is similar to us, or are we looking for someone who is different to complement our personality?

Research on this issue indicates that indeed, "Birds of a feather flock together." When choosing a romantic partner, we tend to gravitate to people who are of similar age, socioeconomic status, education, intelligence, race, religion, attitudes, power, and physical attractiveness (Brehm, 1992; Browning et al., 1999; Hendrick & Hendrick, 1983). Furthermore, similarity seems to predict attraction across a variety of cultures, including Mexico, India, and Japan (Byrne et al., 1971). Similarity also seems to be a factor in the friends we choose (Kandel, 1978; Newcomb, 1961; Rubin et al., 1994).

Self-esteem may play a role in our preference for similar others. Being attracted to similar others may be motivated in part by a desire to maintain high self-esteem. After all, valuing similar others is, in a way, valuing one's self (Heine, Foster, & Spina, 2009).

It is also possible that we are attracted to similar others because finding ourselves attracted to dissimilar others might produce *dissonance* (Heider, 1958). For example, if you were attracted to someone who did not share your spiritual views, the conflict between your attitudes about the person and your attitudes about spirituality might produce dissonance. In the face of this dissonance, it might be easier to change your attitudes about the person (as opposed to your spirituality), lessening your attraction to him or her and reducing the dissonance. Overall, it is more comfortable to be attracted to those who share our attitudes.

## Physical Attractiveness: How Important Is It?

One of the first things we notice about a potential romantic partner is his or her physical attractiveness. Although standards of physical attractiveness vary across

**proximity**    physical closeness

cultures (see ■ FIGURE 10.3), it is an important factor in determining our attraction to others. In a classic study that examined physical attractiveness and attraction in a blind-date scenario, physical attractiveness was the *only* factor found to predict whether a person wanted to go out on a second date (Walster et al., 1966).

When it comes to choosing potential partners, physical attractiveness seems to be important to both men and women (Luo, 2009), but men seem to place particular emphasis on how attractive their potential romantic partners are (Jonason, 2009). This special emphasis that men place on physical attractiveness seems to hold for both homosexual and heterosexual men. Heterosexual and homosexual women, on the other hand, place more importance on the psychological traits of their potential partners. For example, heterosexual women place more emphasis on a man's social status when choosing a mate (Alterovitz & Mendelsohn, 2009). So it seems that although physical attractiveness is important to women, it is not the *most* important aspect of a partner (Deaux & Hanna, 1984).

Although we may be attracted to good-looking people, we tend to be romantically involved with people whose level of physical attractiveness is comparable to our own. This tendency, called the **matching hypothesis**, seems to be true of both dating and married couples (Zajonc et al. 1987). Matching is so pervasive that we actually expect to date people at our same level of attractiveness (Montoya, 2008).

Interestingly, the influence of physical attractiveness on romantic relationships seems to be mirrored in our same-sex friendships. The matching hypothesis predicts that our same-sex friends will be, on average, about as attractive as we

**matching hypothesis**   the theory that we are attracted to people whose level of physical attractiveness is similar to our own

FIGURE

# 10.3

**Cultural Differences in Physical Attractiveness**

Standards of physical attractiveness can vary across cultures. All of these people would be considered attractive in their respective cultures. Which of these people do you find attractive?

are (McKillip & Reidel, 1983). And although both men and women seem to choose their friends on the basis of their physical attractiveness, again men place more emphasis on this characteristic than do women (Berscheid et al., 1971; Feingold, 1988; Perlini, Bertolissi, & Lind, 1999). The importance of physical attractiveness in social relationships isn't surprising in light of findings that we tend to perceive attractive people more positively than unattractive people (Lemay, Clark, & Greenberg, 2010). For example, attractive people are perceived to be more interesting, sociable, kind, sensitive, and nurturing than unattractive people (Dion, Berscheid, & Walster, 1972). With all these *perceived* qualities, no wonder we want to be friends and lovers with attractive people!

However, there may also be another reason why we prefer attractive people. Perhaps being attracted to others is in part biological and instinctive (see Neuroscience Applies to Your World). In an interesting study, researchers found that babies as young as 2 months old looked longer at attractive faces than they did at unattractive ones (Langlois et al., 1987), indicating that they preferred the attractive faces. Because it is hard to imagine that 2-month-old babies have had time to *learn* to be biased toward attractive people, these findings suggest that we are born with an instinctive preference for good-looking people. Perhaps this instinct has evolved in humans because certain features that are found in attractive people (e.g., symmetrical facial features) indicate good health (Bronstad, Langlois, & Russell, 2008). In terms of natural selection and evolution, it makes sense for us to be sexually attracted to people who are healthy and therefore able to facilitate our ability to produce offspring.

Pure attraction is not the only reason that we are drawn to others, however. Sometimes our desire to be with others serves a purpose other than sex and reproduction. In the next section, we will further explore our social nature by examining some of the reasons we are driven to be with others in the form of social groups.

## Neuroscience Applies to Your World:

### The Chemistry of Romance

When it comes to love and romance, is there anything to the notion of "chemistry" between people? Perhaps. Neuroimaging studies suggest that many brain areas are involved in our complex feelings for our romantic partners (Acevedo et al., 2011). Furthermore, psychologists have identified three separate emotional systems involved in romantic relationships. *Lust* is our sex drive or desire for sexual gratification. *Romantic attraction* is our physical and emotional desire for a specific person. *Attachment* is companionate love, or our desire to be close with our partner. Interestingly, psychologists have discovered that each of these emotional systems seems to be related to the action of different chemicals in the body. Lust is governed by hormones—in particular, estrogens and androgens. Experiencing romantic attraction is related to increased dopamine and norepinephrine, but lowered serotonin, in the brain. Experiencing attachment or love is associated with the action of other neurotransmitters and hormones, including neuropeptides, oxytocin, and vasopressin (Fisher, 2000).

If love and romance are related to chemical action in the brain, does this mean that altering the chemical environment of the brain can affect our romantic feelings for our partner? Some researchers believe so. Psychologist Dixie Meyer suggests that antidepressant drugs such as selective serotonin reuptake inhibitors that increase serotonin action in the brain may also interfere with the brain chemicals that support romantic attraction, resulting in the person's experiencing reduced satisfaction with his/her romantic relationship (Meyer, 2007). Based on her preliminary work, Meyer suggests that therapists should be aware that satisfaction with one's romantic life is affected by many things, including perhaps one's biochemistry and the medications he or she is taking.

R1/Alamy

## Let's REVIEW

In this section, we discussed what attracts us to others. For a quick assessment of your understanding, answer these questions.

1. Based on the available psychological research, you are *most* likely to end up in a romantic relationship with _____.
   a. a neighbor who shares your values
   b. a person from another state who shares your values
   c. a fellow student who does not share your values
   d. a coworker who has opposite views

2. Attractive people are assumed to be all of the following things, *except* _____.
   a. interesting
   b. sociable
   c. nurturant
   d. proud

3. Which of the following statements is true?
   a. Women are unconcerned with physical attractiveness when choosing a romantic partner.
   b. Women and men are equally interested in physical attractiveness when choosing a romantic partner.
   c. Neither men nor women pay that much attention to physical attractiveness when choosing a romantic partner.
   d. Men pay more attention to physical attractiveness when choosing a romantic partner.

Answers 1. a; 2. d; 3. d

# Groups: How Do Others Influence Us?

Throughout our lifetime, we will belong to a multitude of groups—some of which we join and some of which we belong to by circumstance—families, communities, clubs, teams, professional organizations, and so on. For many of us, belonging to such groups is something that we value, but why? Psychologists suggest several potential explanations for why we join groups (Baumeister & Leary, 1995; Paulus, 1989). Groups may give us companionship, make us feel safe, make us feel proud, provide us with information, or help us achieve our goals in life. Regardless of why we join a group, once we do join, the group and its collective members then have the power to influence our behavior.

## LEARNING OBJECTIVES

● Describe how cohesiveness and norms function within groups.

● Describe the factors that affect our tendency to conform to the norms of a group.

● Describe how working in a group can affect both performance and decision making within the group.

## Social Forces Within Groups: Norms and Cohesiveness

Groups are characterized by the expectations and attitudes of their members. Group **norms** are the laws that guide the behavior of group members. Norms can be explicitly stated rules or unwritten expectations that members have for behavior within the group. Norms tell us how to dress, how to behave, how to interact with each other, and so on. Virtually every group has its own unique set of norms—each family, culture, workplace, and group of friends may have different expectations for how its members should behave. For an example of how norms can vary across ethnic groups in the United States, take a look at ■ TABLE 10.2.

In general, we do not like to break the norms of the groups to which we belong. When we do, we may face several unpleasant consequences. Group members may ridicule us or try to persuade us to change our behavior, or—perhaps most threatening—we might be thrown out or ostracized from the group. Recall that groups often fulfill social needs and give us a sense of security and identity. Because of these

**norm** unwritten rule or expectation for how group members should behave

## TABLE 10.2
## Some Cross-Cultural Differences in Norms Governing Conversation Within the United States

| CULTURE → / NORM ↓ | NATIVE AMERICAN CULTURE | EUROPEAN AMERICAN CULTURE | ASIAN AMERICAN CULTURE | AFRICAN AMERICAN CULTURE | HISPANIC AMERICAN CULTURE |
|---|---|---|---|---|---|
| **LEVEL OF EYE CONTACT** | Direct eye contact is seen as invasive and disrespectful. | Direct eye contact is generally expected—especially when being spoken to. | Direct eye contact that lasts more than a second or two is considered disrespectful—especially with one's superiors. | Direct eye contact is expected and prolonged during speaking, but less when listening. | Direct eye contact is often viewed as disrespectful—especially when one is being spoken to. |
| **LEVEL OF EMOTION DISPLAYED** | Conversations are often unemotional and dispassionate. | Highly emotional, animated conversation is not preferred in public settings. | Controlling one's display of emotion is very important. | Conversations are often passionate and animated. | Conversations that take place among Hispanics may be very emotional and animated. Conversations that occur in ethnically mixed settings tend to be more low-key. |
| **LEVEL OF GESTURE USE** | In daily conversation, gesture use tends to be restrained. | Moderate gesture use is typical. | Gesture use is restrained. Asian Americans tend to use fewer gestures than European Americans. | Frequent and large gestures are the norm. | Moderate to high use of gestures is typical. |

*Source: Adapted from Elliott, C. E. (1999). Cross-cultural communication styles. Available online at http://www.awesomelibrary.org/multiculturaltoolkit-patterns.html.*

---

**cohesiveness [coe-HEE-siv-ness]**
the degree to which members of a group value their group membership; cohesive groups are tight-knit groups

**conformity**   behaving in accordance with group norms

We are likely to conform to the norms of groups because we do not want to be ostracized or ridiculed.

benefits, we often value our group memberships and wish to protect them. The degree to which members wish to maintain membership in the group is referred to as **cohesiveness**. In groups whose members have very positive attitudes about their membership in the group, cohesiveness is high, and the group tends to be close-knit. When cohesiveness is high, the pressure we feel to meet group norms is also high. This means that as our attraction for certain groups increases, so does the influence these groups have over us. The more we value our membership in a group, the less willing we are to risk losing that membership. Therefore, group cohesiveness helps ensure **conformity** within a group as group members modify their behavior to avoid breaking the group's norms (Crandall, 1988; Latané & L'Herrou, 1996; Schachter, 1951).

## Conformity Within a Group

One of the most influential psychologists to formally study the process of conformity was Solomon Asch. During the 1950s, Asch conducted a series of classic experiments on conformity and the factors that make us more or less likely to conform in a given situation. Asch (1951) had male participants engage in a perceptual task with eight other men. The participants were unaware that the eight other men in the experiment were *confederates*, or actors posing as participants. Each participant, along with the eight confederates, was shown a series of lines and asked to match the length of a test line to one of three other comparison lines (■ FIGURE 10.4). The experiment was set up so that the confederates made their judgments first. The participant heard all of the confederates in turn choose—aloud—the wrong line. By the time the true participant's turn came, he had heard all the others choose what was clearly the wrong line. A norm had formed in the group, the norm of choosing the wrong line. The *dependent variable* in Asch's study was whether the participant would conform to the norm or whether he would go with his own perception and choose the correct comparison line.

What do you think Asch found? What would you have done in this situation? In fact, Asch found that 74% of his participants conformed at least once during the experiment. Apparently, many people can be easily made to conform. Only 26% of the participants consistently stood by their convictions and refused to conform.

| Test line | Comparison lines | | |
|---|---|---|---|
| 8" | 6 1/4" | 8" | 6 3/4" |

**FIGURE**

## 10.4

**The Asch Procedure for Testing Conformity**

In Asch's study, 74% of the subjects conformed and chose the 61/4-inch line as the match for the comparison line after hearing the confederates make this obviously incorrect choice.

*Source: Based on Asch, 1951.*

> ### You Asked...
>
> *Why do our peers have such a great influence on us?*
>
> MEGAN ARISPE, STUDENT

Asch also found that as the *majority group* (the number of confederates who choose the wrong line) increased, so did the participants' tendency to conform. However, Asch found that maximum conformity was reached in the participants when only three confederates were present.

Since Asch's original experiments, others have studied the factors that affect conformity in groups. Overall, the picture that emerges from the research on conformity is that we are most likely to conform if:

- We do not feel confident of our abilities.
- Cohesiveness is high in the group.
- Our responses are made public (we are not anonymous).
- The group has at least three members who are unanimous in their dedication to the norm.
- The idea that one *should* conform is itself a norm in our culture and/or we do not feel a personal need to be individuated.

**normative conformity** conformity that occurs when group members change their behavior to meet group norms but are not persuaded to change their beliefs and attitudes

## EXPLAINING CONFORMITY: THE EFFECTS OF CULTURE AND CONFIDENCE

Asch showed us that conformity is rather easy to obtain, but why are we so willing to adhere to group norms? As part of his *debriefing* at the end of his experiments, Asch asked participants why they had chosen the wrong line. Their answers were interesting.

Some participants indicated that they chose the wrong line even though they knew it was wrong. This type of conformity, involving a change of behavior to fit a norm but no real attitude change or persuasion, is called **normative conformity**. The primary motive for normative conformity seems to be a desire to fit in with the group and be liked by others. This is one reason that cohesiveness tends to increase conformity. When we like being in the group, we want others to like us as well (Sakari, 1975). Research has shown that people in cultures that value individualism (such as the United States) are less likely to conform than are people from cultures that place more value on being part of a group (such as Japan; Bond & Smith, 1996; Killen, Crystal, & Watanabe, 2002; Takano & Sogon, 2008). In cultures in which nonconformists are admired, you can expect to see less conformity.

Nonconformists seem to enjoy violating the norms of the majority group.

© Anthony Redpath/Corbis

Yet some of Asch's participants had other reasons for conforming. Some reported that they chose the wrong line because they became convinced that it was the correct choice. These participants were actually persuaded by the majority group. Recall that persuasion leads to attitude change. The way these participants perceived the lines and what they believed to be true about the lines changed as a function of the majority opinion. The majority opinion *informed* these participants of what the correct choice was. For this reason, conformity that results in actual attitude change is referred to as **informational conformity**. Informational conformity is heightened when people are unsure of their opinions and insecure about their abilities (Cacioppo & Petty, 1980).

## THE DARK SIDE OF CONFORMITY: THE STANFORD PRISON EXPERIMENT

**informational conformity** conformity that occurs when conformity pressures actually persuade group members to adopt new beliefs and/or attitudes

**deindividuation [DEE-in-dih-vid-you-AYE-shun]** a state in which a person's behavior becomes controlled more by external norms than by the person's own internal values and morals

In 1971, Stanford University psychologist Phillip Zimbardo set out to conduct an experiment on the effects of a prison setting on the behavior of prisoners and guards. Twenty-four healthy male participants were randomly assigned to play the role of either a prisoner or a guard in a mock prison set up in the basement of a campus building. All participants wore uniforms appropriate to their roles as guards or prisoners. The prisoners wore prison uniforms and were referred to by serial numbers rather than their names. The guards had dark sunglasses, wore khaki uniforms, and carried clubs.

The experiment was slated to last two weeks, with the prisoners remaining in the "prison" for the entire experiment. Within days, some very disturbing behavior began to emerge. The men assigned to play the guards became abusive toward the mock prisoners. The men assigned to play the prisoners became docile and depressed, allowing the so-called guards to abuse and manipulate them. The mock guards hooded the prisoners, called them names, and subjected them to a host of demeaning, humiliating activities. Their behavior got so out of hand that Zimbardo had to cancel the experiment before the end of the first week (Zimbardo, 1972).

Phillip Zimbardo's Stanford prison experiment shows that when we become deindividuated, we lose track of our own internal values and beliefs, and our behavior comes under the control of the group's norms. When deindividuated, we may find ourselves doing things we never thought we would do.

Why would 24 healthy young men begin to behave so abnormally in such a short time? A great deal of their behavior stemmed from the fact that they were isolated from the outside world and the norms of society. Within the prison-like setting, a new set of norms sprang up—ones that called for the guards to be abusive and the prisoners to be submissive. Another factor at work was **deindividuation**. In deindividuation, a person's behavior becomes controlled more by external norms than by the person's own internal values and morals. In short, the roles that the men were playing became stronger determinants of their behavior than their own attitudes and beliefs. Several factors aided the deindividuation process:

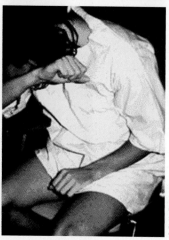

© Phillip Zimbardo

- All participants wore uniforms, which heightened their anonymity.
- All participants were "playing" an assigned *social role*. As "actors," the participants' behavior was more controlled by their roles and their ideas about how prison guards and prisoners typically behave than it was by their own internal values and beliefs.
- The guards hid behind dark glasses, which heightened their anonymity.
- The prisoners were referred to by numbers, not names, which made them seem less human.

- The experiment was conducted in a basement, away from the outside world and its norms.
- There was no strong leader who argued for fair treatment of the prisoners.

When deindividuation occurs, dangerous things can happen. All it takes is one person to begin behaving badly, and even good people may blindly conform to this new norm of behavior.

Sometimes being part of the group can be problematic, but working in a group can also enhance our performance. We'll explore both possibilities further in the next section.

## Is Working in a Group Better Than Working Alone?

Have you ever heard that "many hands make light work"? Or "two heads are better than one"? Such sayings extol the virtues of working in groups. Do we really accomplish more when we are part of a group?

In the late 1800s, psychologist Norman Triplett observed that people seem to perform tasks faster when they perform in the presence of others. For example, bicyclers seem to ride faster when riding along with other cyclists than they do when riding alone (Triplett, 1898). This enhanced performance when others are present is called **social facilitation**. Over the last century, social facilitation has been demonstrated in humans and many other species across a wide variety of situations (see Aiello & Douthitt, 2001).

But do we always perform better when others are around? Not always. For example, when we perform unfamiliar or complex tasks, having others around is likely to impede performance (Zajonc, 1965). For many of us, giving a speech is an example of an unfamiliar task that becomes more daunting when others are present. And many of us can think of times when we "choked" in front of others despite the fact that we could recite our speech perfectly when alone. Today, *social facilitation theories* seek to explain the complex interplay of situational, task, and personality factors that result in either enhanced or impaired performance in front of others (Aiello & Douthitt, 2001).

### SOCIAL LOAFING

Having an audience can affect performance, but what happens when we are working *with* others? How does working toward a common goal affect individual performance? Sometimes **social loafing** occurs, when group members fail to work as hard as they would if they were working alone (Harkins, 1987). Social loafing occurs in part because group members perceive that others will not hold them accountable for their individual performance (Pearsall, Christian, & Ellis, 2010). For example, if everyone receives the same grade for a group project, some members may be tempted to slack off in hopes that other members will pick up the slack. One way to reduce social loafing is to encourage individual effort as well as teamwork by rewarding group members for both the quality of the group's output and their individual performance (Pearsall et al., 2010).

So many hands only *sometimes* make light work. What about cognitive processes? Are two heads better than one? We often seek out others when we have important decisions to make. We form committees to set policy for organizations. We choose juries to try court cases. The assumption is that important decisions are best placed in the hands of many. Ironically, psychological research indicates that in some instances, our faith in the wisdom of groups may be misplaced. Group decisions are not necessarily better, more effective, or more logical than decisions made by individuals.

**social facilitation**  performing better on a task in the presence of others than you would if you were alone

**social loafing**  when group members exert less effort on a group task than they would if they were performing the task alone

**FIGURE**

# 10.5

**The Apparatus Used by Milgram in His Famous Obedience Studies**

How far would you go before you refused to obey?

the learner's rate of learning. In actuality, the learner was a confederate, an actor who only pretended to be shocked, but the participants did not know this until after the experiment ended.

During the procedure, the experimenter, a 31-year-old high school biology teacher dressed in a lab coat, stood slightly behind the seated teacher. Throughout the experiment, the teacher and learner communicated via an intercom system, but they did not have visual contact. The teacher was instructed to read a list of words to the learner over the intercom, and then to listen as the learner recalled the words from memory. Every time the learner made a mistake, the teacher was told to deliver a shock to the learner by flipping one of the switches on the apparatus. The procedure began with the 15-volt switch, and the teacher was instructed to move progressively up the scale toward the 450-volt switch as the learner made more and more mistakes.

Stanley Milgram was primarily interested in seeing how far up the scale the teachers would go before they refused to obey orders to shock the learner further. At the 300-volt mark, the learner began to pound on the wall as if in great pain, protesting the continued shocking. At this point, most participants began to question the experimenter as to whether they should continue to shock the learner, who was obviously in pain. The teachers began to show clear signs of distress, including shaking, stuttering, sweating, nervous laughter, and biting their lips and fingernails. The teachers often protested verbally and indicated that they didn't feel good about continuing to shock the learner.

In response to such displays and protests, the experimenter calmly prodded the participants to continue with the procedure. The experimenter never yelled. He never made verbal or physical threats. He never threatened to take away their $4.50. The experimenter merely requested that the participants continue following orders. The strongest statement by the experimenter was, "You have no other choice, you must go on" (Milgram, 1963, p. 374).

After the 315-volt mark, the learner fell completely silent and unresponsive, as if he had lost consciousness or was injured. Because the learner missed all the words on the trial by not responding, the experimenter instructed the teacher to continue delivering the shocks. At this point, it is likely that the teacher believed that he was being asked to shock an injured—or even unconscious—man! What would you do in this situation? What do you think the teachers did?

The results of Milgram's study were nothing short of shocking. A full 65% of the teachers continued to shock the learner all the way up to the 450-volt mark. Despite believing the learner to be ill or worse, most of the teachers continued to follow the experimenter's orders. Even Stanley Milgram was surprised by his findings. Prior to the experiment, Milgram had surveyed psychology students and behavioral science professionals to get a feel for how many participants they thought would go all the way to 450 volts (Milgram, 1963, 1974). Most people believed that only 1–3% would. The results showed, of course, a very different picture. Approximately 65% of the participants did go all the way to 450 volts, and no participant refused to obey before the 300-volt mark had been reached!

As you might imagine, Milgram's findings generated a great deal of skepticism. Some people questioned whether the participants in Milgram's (1963) study were abnormal in some way. To answer such skepticism and to further investigate the variables that affect the rate of obedience, Milgram repeated his procedure with different participants. He replicated the study in another town (Bridgeport, CT) and found similar results (Milgram, 1965). Milgram also conducted the study using female participants and again found high rates of obedience (Milgram, 1974).

Other researchers have since replicated Milgram's findings. High school students were found to be even *more* willing to obey orders (Rosenhan, 1969). Cross-cultural

**You Asked...**

*When others try to influence us, what factors make it more likely that we will do what they want?*

PAIGE REDMON, STUDENT

research in other Western cultures has also yielded high rates of obedience using Milgram's procedure (Triandis, 1994). However, a recent partial replication of Milgram's study (Burger, 2009) has sparked a debate over whether societal changes since the 1960s have made people less obedient. Could it be that relative to their grandparents, the young people of today would be less likely to follow orders to hurt others? For more on this debate, see the Psychology Across Generations box.

## FACTORS THAT AFFECT OBEDIENCE

Regardless of whether destructive obedience has decreased somewhat over the generations or not, it appears that Milgram's results were not flukes. Unfortunately, even today, many people seem willing to follow orders to hurt others (Burger, 2009). What accounts for this tendency?

One factor that contributed to the high rate of obedience in the Milgram studies was the presence of a perceived *authority figure*. During the procedure, the experimenter, dressed in a lab coat and looking official, stood close by the participant and issued orders to deliver the shocks. Authority figures work in two ways to ensure obedience. First, the fact that the authority figure is ultimately in charge may seem to relieve the person following orders from responsibility for his actions. A person can

## Psychology Across Generations:

### Are Millennials Less Likely to Exhibit Destructive Obedience Than Milgram's Baby Boomers Were?

Today, most institutions will not allow researchers to use Milgram's experimental procedure because of concerns over the amount of distress it would cause participants and the possibility that it might violate the ethical rule of doing no harm to research participants (see Chapter 1). Reluctance to replicate Milgram's study has largely left open the question of how people today would react when asked to obey destructive commands. Given that Millennials are thought to be more self-focused and assertive than the relatively conformist Baby Boomers, would they be more likely to assert themselves by disobeying destructive orders (Twenge, 2009)?

Recently, psychologist Jerry Burger (2009) found a way to address this question. Burger modified Milgram's procedure to reduce the amount of stress it causes participants and therefore make the procedure more ethical. In his so-called *150-volt solution*, participants are first carefully screened to eliminate those who are likely to experience psychological harm during the study; second, the participants are asked to go only to 150 volts—not the 450 volts used in Milgram's studies (Miller, 2009). Using this less stressful, more ethical procedure, Burger found that his participants were just as likely as Milgram's participants to obey at the 150-volt level (Burger, 2009).

However, Burger's sample of participants was very different from the sample Milgram used. For example, Milgram used only males in his original study. Burger had both male and female participants (Twenge, 2009). When the data were re-analyzed using only the male participants, the results showed that nearly twice as many males disobeyed in 2009 (33.3%) as did in Milgram's original study (17.5%). Although this difference did not reach statistical significance, some researchers argue that it at least suggests that obedience may be decreasing (Twenge, 2009). Clearly, more research is needed to determine whether this is true. Perhaps Burger's 150-volt solution will prove to be a valuable tool in these investigations (Miller, 2009).

Have things changed since the 1960s when Milgram conducted his original studies? Are Millennials as willing to engage in destructive obedience as their grandparents were? Today, would research participants go all the way to 450 volts?

always tell himself that he was only following orders. Second, the presence of official-looking authority figures tends to intimidate us, and we are therefore more likely to obey their orders (Bushman, 1988). Sometimes it makes sense to be intimidated by authority figures because some authority figures have true power (for example, police officers). If you perceive that authority figures can observe your behavior and that you may suffer negative consequences for disobeying, you might obey out of fear alone.

In later experiments, Milgram found that he could reduce obedience in his participants by increasing the physical distance between the experimenter and the teacher. If the experimenter was not physically present to watch the teacher's behavior, the teachers were much less likely to obey the orders to shock the participant. ■ TABLE 10.3 summarizes some of the later experimental manipulations that Milgram (1965) used to test variables that affect rates of obedience. From Table 10.3, you can see that when the experimenter telephoned his orders to the teachers, obedience dropped to 27.5%.

Another reason for the high rates of obedience in Milgram's studies is the *timing of the requests* made by the experimenter. When the participants arrived at the lab, they very quickly found themselves faced with orders from an authority figure to shock another human being. Because the orders began almost immediately after the participants arrived, they did not have much time to think about their actions. As we saw earlier, when we do not have time to think things through, we are more susceptible to persuasive attempts.

Another factor that contributed to high rates of obedience was the fact that the shock levels were increased incrementally. In essence, Milgram's procedure was a textbook example of foot-in-the-door compliance in action. The first orders were for the teachers to deliver a 15-volt shock, a mere tingle compared to the final shock level of 450 volts. Few people would have qualms about following an order to deliver an almost painless shock, so why not obey? What the participants did not know was

### TABLE 10.3
### Some Experimental Conditions in Milgram's Experiments and Their Resultant Rates of Obedience

| EXPERIMENTAL MANIPULATION | PERCENTAGE OF PARTICIPANTS WHO OBEYED ALL THE WAY TO THE 450-VOLT LEVEL |
| --- | --- |
| The learner was seated in the same room with the teacher. | 40% |
| The teacher had to hold the learner's hand down on the shock plate. | 30% |
| The experimenter delivered his orders by telephone instead of in person. | 27.5% |
| The teacher was tested with two confederates who pretended to be participants also playing the role of teacher. Halfway through the experiment, the two confederates refused to shock the learner any further. | 10% of participants continued to obey after the confederates refused to further shock the learner. |
| The teacher was tested with two confederates who pretended to be participants also playing the role of teacher. One of the confederates was the one who actually flipped the switch to shock the learner. The real participant only played an auxiliary role in shocking the learner. | 92.5% |
| Female participants played the role of teacher. | 65% |

*Source: Milgram, 1965.*

that by obeying the order to deliver the 15-volt shock, they were paving the way for their own obedience to further orders to shock the learner. Every time the participants obeyed an order to shock, it became harder for them to refuse to continue. Some have likened this type of incremental obedience to standing on a **slippery slope**. Once you begin to obey, it's like beginning to slide down the slope. The farther you go, the more momentum you gain, and the harder it is to stop obeying. If Milgram's procedure had begun with an order to deliver the potentially dangerous shock of 450 volts, it is unlikely that he would have obtained such high rates of obedience.

A final factor that affects obedience is the **psychological distance** we feel between our actions and the results of those actions. In Milgram's first experiment (Milgram, 1963), the teacher could not see the learner during the procedure. In this type of condition, psychological distance is large, meaning that it was relatively easy for the teachers to not think about the consequences of their actions. If you don't think about the consequences of your actions, then you don't have to consciously come to terms with and take responsibility for those actions. This allows you to obey even in situations in which your actions may harm others.

In one dramatic experiment, Milgram had the teacher and learner sit side by side during the procedure. In this variation of the experiment, the teacher had to reach over and hold the learner's hand down on the shock plate. As you might guess, this procedure dramatically reduced the psychological distance for the teacher. It's hard to dissociate yourself from the consequences of your actions when you're actually touching your victim. Under these conditions, only 30% of the participants delivered the maximum 450-volt shock. Note, however, that although obedience was cut in half by reducing the psychological distance, obedience was *not* eliminated. Almost one-third of participants still continued to obey the experimenter, even under these conditions.

Despite the controversy generated by Milgram's studies, his work remains one of the most powerful statements ever made about human behavior. Aside from demonstrating our obedience to authority, Milgram's work also brings up some important and perhaps frightening questions about basic human nature. For instance, how can psychologists explain the tendency of some people to behave aggressively? We will look at this issue next.

**slippery slope**   the use of foot-in-the-door compliance in an obedience situation to get people to obey increasing demands

**psychological distance**   the degree to which one can disassociate oneself from the consequences of his/her actions

# Let's
## REVIEW

In this section, we examined the social influence that occurs in compliance and obedience. As a quick check of your understanding, answer these questions.

1. You want your friend to lend you $50. If you want to use the door-in-the-face compliance technique to ensure that your friend will comply with your request, what should you do?
   a. First ask for $1,000 before asking for the $50.
   b. First ask for $10 before asking for the $50.
   c. Wash your friend's car before you ask for the $50.
   d. Tell your friend that you will pay the money back in one week.

2. In Milgram's original experiment, what percentage of participants went all the way to 450 volts when "shocking" the learner?
   a. 5%                c. 65%
   b. 35%               d. 75%

3. Which of the following compliance techniques best explains Milgram's findings in his study on obedience?
   a. Foot-in-the-door        c. Reciprocity
   b. Door-in-the-face        d. Low-balling

*Answers 1. a; 2. c; 3. a*

# Aggression: Hurting Others

Psychologists define *aggression* as an action that is intended to cause harm to another person who does not want to be harmed (Baron & Richardson, 1992; Brehm, Kassin, & Fein, 2002; Huesmann, 1994). Aggressive acts can be classified as *instrumental* or *hostile*. **Instrumental aggression** is aimed at achieving some goal. For example, a child may hit a playmate to distract her so the child can grab her toy. **Hostile aggression** is motivated solely by a desire to hurt others. For example, a bully may punch another child on the playground just to see the child cry.

Although both types of aggression are widespread in many cultures, the overall prevalence of aggression varies across cultures. Among developed countries, the United States is considered to be an aggressive society (c.f., Osterman et al., 1994). Pick up a major American metropolitan newspaper any day of the week, and you will see abundant evidence of this in the daily crime reports. In 2009, New York City, Los Angeles, and Dallas reported a combined total of 29,588 violent crimes (Federal Bureau of Investigation, 2010).

Besides the almost daily reports of violent crime in the United States, it appears that even noncriminals have aggression on their minds. Researchers surveyed 312 college students at a U.S. university about whether they had ever thought about killing someone. Fully 73% of male students and 66% of female students reported that they had (Kenrick & Sheets, 1993)! What could account for such numbers? Could aggressive feelings be more natural than we like to think?

Instrumental aggression is aimed at achieving some goal. This child is being aggressive to obtain a toy.

> ## You Asked...
>
> *What causes aggression?*
>
> JONATHAN GANTES, STUDENT

## Biological Theories of Aggression

It has been widely documented that among many species, including humans, males tend to be more aggressive than females (e.g., Sysoeva et al., 2010). In 2008, males accounted for 81.7% of those arrested for violent crimes (Federal Bureau of Investigation, 2009b). Because males have more of the hormone testosterone in their bodies, researchers have long suspected that testosterone and aggressive behavior are related. But the research on the relationship between aggression and testosterone has yielded a somewhat confusing picture. Sometimes higher levels of testosterone are associated with higher levels of aggression in animals (Wagner, Beuving, & Hutchinson, 1980), but sometimes they are not (Eaton & Resko, 1974). Likewise, human studies sometimes show a correlation between high testosterone levels and aggression (Dabbs & Morris, 1990; Van Goozen, Frijda, & de Poll, 1994), but sometimes they fail to find a clear relationship (Coccaro et al., 2007).

Even if the correlation between testosterone and aggressive behavior were more consistent in the literature, it would still be difficult to determine the actual cause(s) of aggressive behavior. Recall that *correlation* does not imply *causation*. Higher levels of testosterone are associated with muscularity and strength, which may simply give one the physical ability to be a bully. Some researchers have found that in adolescent boys, aggression is correlated with physical size but *not* correlated with levels of testosterone (Tremblay et al., 1998).

**instrumental aggression** aggression that is used to facilitate the attainment of a goal

**hostile aggression** aggression that is meant to cause harm to others

## A POSSIBLE ROLE FOR SEROTONIN

Research has suggested that another chemical, serotonin, may also play a role in regulation of aggressive behavior (Libersat & Pflueger, 2004). Researchers measured levels of the neurotransmitter serotonin in the bloodstream of three groups of people: survivors of suicide attempts, people institutionalized since childhood for aggressive behavior, and a normal control group (Marazzitti et al., 1993). They found that the suicide survivors and the aggressive patients had *lower* levels of serotonin than those in the normal control group.

Recently, researchers found that giving healthy participants an antidepressant that increases serotonin made them less likely to take action that would financially harm other players in a monetary game. This change in behavior seemed to stem from the participants becoming more empathetic and therefore more averse to harming others (Crockett et al., 2010).

Low levels of serotonin are associated with disorders such as *obsessive-compulsive disorder*, in which the person has difficulty controlling his or her behavior and feels compelled to repeat certain actions (see Chapter 13). If we extend this thinking to the relationship between serotonin and aggression, we can speculate that people with lower levels of serotonin may have difficulty in controlling their aggressive impulses toward themselves (as in suicide) and toward others (as in the institutionalized patients). However, more research is needed before any firm conclusions can be drawn about the role of serotonin in aggression.

## CHILDHOOD ABUSE AND AGGRESSION

Another connection between biology and aggression comes from research into the backgrounds of incarcerated criminals. During the 1980s and 1990s, psychiatrist Dorothy Otnow Lewis interviewed more than 100 murderers in an attempt to discover whether they had experienced physical abuse as children (Lewis, 1992). During these interviews, Lewis discovered that an overwhelming majority of these murderers had suffered extreme abuse during childhood. In particular, many had suffered severe head injuries as a result of the abuse, which led Lewis and her colleagues to hypothesize that the murderers' aggressive tendencies may have resulted from brain damage (Lewis et al., 2004).

More recent research seems to reinforce Lewis's notions. It is now thought that childhood abuse and neglect are related to the development of several brain abnormalities. Using some of the techniques for studying the brain that we discussed in Chapter 2 (such as EEG, MRI, and fMRI), researchers have found that childhood abuse and neglect correlate with having structural abnormalities in the amygdala, hippocampus, corpus callosum, left frontal lobe, left temporal lobe, and cerebellum (Teicher, 2002).

Virtually no one would disagree that an end to child abuse would be good for society. Aside from a possible link between the physical damage caused by child abuse and later aggression, psychologists have other reasons to fear the destructive influence of child abuse. An aggressive model, such as an aggressive, punitive parent or a violent TV character, can teach a child to be aggressive.

## Learning Theories of Aggression

In Chapter 5, we described Albert Bandura's *Bobo doll* experiments, in which children who watched an adult model beat up a plastic Bobo doll were likely to mimic the model's aggression when later left alone with the doll (Bandura, Ross, & Ross, 1963). After being exposed to an *aggressive model*, the children acquired new and aggressive behaviors. Many psychologists believe that aggression is often learned through this type of *observational learning*.

However, exposure to violence and aggression may promote more than just modeling of aggressive behavior. Such exposure may actually influence the cognitive, emotional, and behavioral responses we have to events in our daily lives. One model of aggression, the *cognitive neoassociation theory*, proposes that cues present during an aggressive event can become associated in memory with the thoughts and emotions experienced during that event (Anderson & Bushman, 2002; Berkowitz, 1990). For example, if you see many instances (real or televised) in which people use guns to shoot and hurt those who have humiliated them, you may begin to associate concepts from these events in your memory. You may begin to associate guns with anger, hurt, fear, and humiliation; or you may begin to associate conflict with shooting. Because these concepts become tightly linked in memory, activation of one of them can *prime* other related concepts and cause them to become active. In other words, merely seeing a gun may cause you to have aggressive thoughts. Being humiliated may activate feelings of anger and the desire to use a gun to retaliate against those who hurt you. Indeed, research participants have been shown to have aggressive thoughts after simply being shown pictures of weapons (Anderson, Benjamin, & Bartholow, 1998).

If our behavior is heavily influenced by the cues we perceive to be associated with aggression and violence, then the nature of such perceptions is very important. Given that many of our ideas about the world are influenced by the media, it is worthwhile to ask the question, does television portray violence and its consequences accurately? For a look at this issue, see the Psychology Applies to Your World box.

## Psychology Applies to Your World:

### Does Television Portray Violence Accurately?

TV has been shown to portray many aspects of life unrealistically, including marriage (Segrin & Nabi, 2002), the medical profession (Chory-Assad & Tamborini, 2001), and violence. One study reported a total of 2,126 antisocial acts in 65.5 hours of so-called reality television programming, or shows that are supposed to document real life, such as *Cops*. The problem is that these "reality shows" do not give an accurate picture of real life. They portray acts of aggression at rates that are far above the actual rates at which they occur in U.S. society (Potter et al., 1997).

And the children are watching. According to the Nielsen Company, children ages 2 to 5 watch 32 hours of television a week and children ages 6 to 11 watch 28 hours a week (Associated Press, 2009). By the time a child reaches age 18, she will have witnessed some 200,000 acts of televised violence, of which 16,000 will have been murders (APA cited in Muscari, 2002). Saturday morning children's programming exposes children to 20 to 25 acts of violence per hour (Kaiser Family Foundation, 2006). Even more disturbing is that many televised acts of aggression are ones in which the aggressor experiences no negative repercussions for his or her actions. In 1996, a report sponsored by the National Cable Television Association indicated that perpetrators go unpunished in 73% of all violent scenes on TV and that only 16% of all violent acts on TV portrayed long-term negative consequences of violence for the victim. These false impressions may increase the likelihood that children will actually model the behavior they see on TV (Bandura, 1965; Hogben, 1998).

Are these children learning to be aggressive as they watch television?

## Situations That Promote Aggressive Behavior

When are you most likely to behave aggressively? Are there circumstances in which you might behave in a physically aggressive manner toward another? What would it take?

One key factor in aggression appears to be frustration. According to the **frustration-aggression hypothesis** (Dollard et al., 1939), when we become frustrated, we activate a motive to harm other people or objects. These motives are likely to be directed at those people or objects that we perceive to be the source of our frustration. Most physically abusive parents never *intend* to threaten or harm their children. But in the heat of the moment, some parents take out their frustration on their children. A recent study of fathers with 3-year-old children found that the more parenting stress a father was under, the more likely he was to use corporal punishment on his child (S. J. Lee et al., 2011). Likewise, parents in high-stress situations—such as extreme poverty—who do not have good coping skills are most at risk for becoming abusive (Garbarino, 1997). Recall from Chapter 8 that motives drive and catalyze behavior. Consequently, when we are frustrated, our chances of behaving aggressively increase. Therefore, during stressful, frustrating situations, we have to be on guard for possible aggressive behavior in ourselves and in others.

**frustration-aggression hypothesis** the idea that frustration causes aggressive behavior

**prosocial behavior** behavior that helps others

**altruism** helping another without being motivated by self-gain

# Let's
# REVIEW

In this section, we explored the nature of aggression. As a quick check of your understanding, answer these questions.

1. Which neurotransmitter has been implicated as possibly playing a role in aggressive behavior?
   a. Testosterone
   b. Serotonin
   c. Dopamine
   d. Estrogen

2. Road rage incidents are more likely to occur in heavy traffic. This fact can *best* be explained as due to the increase in _____ that occurs among drivers in heavy traffic.
   a. frustration
   b. fatigue
   c. fear
   d. anxiety

3. Little Sabina wants to play with her sister's doll, but her sister will not let Sabina have the doll. So Sabina hits her sister and takes the doll away while her sister cries. Sabina's behavior is *best* characterized as an example of _____.
   a. hostile aggression
   b. instrumental aggression
   c. biological aggression
   d. learned aggression

Answers 1. b; 2. a; 3. b

# Prosocial Behavior: Will You or Won't You Help Others?

**LEARNING OBJECTIVES**

- Describe the steps involved in deciding whether to help another.

- Describe the factors that influence helping.

By now you might be thinking that humans are pretty rotten creatures. We seem to be easily biased against others, easily influenced by others, aggressive, and even easily convinced to do real harm to others. But it is also true that humans often engage in **prosocial behavior**, or behavior that helps others. Sometimes we even demonstrate **altruism**, or a willingness to help others without considering any possible benefit for ourselves. Just as we have the capacity for violence, we also have the capacity for kindness and compassion.

**TABLE 10.4**
**Variables That Affect Helping Behavior**

| VARIABLE | DESCRIPTION |
|---|---|
| Level of bystander's hurry | Bystanders who are in a hurry are less likely to stop and help someone in distress. |
| Bystander's relationship to other bystanders | When bystanders are friends, they are more likely to help a stranger in need. |
| Relationship between victim and bystander | A bystander who knows the victim is more likely to help. |
| Bystander's perceived ambiguity | If the situation is ambiguous, bystanders will tend to see it as a nonemergency and therefore be less likely to help. |
| Bystander's fear for own safety | If bystanders are afraid they will be harmed, they are less likely to help. |
| Bystander's prejudice against the victim or belief that the victim is an out-group member | Bystanders who are prejudiced against the victim or see the victim as an out-group member are less likely to help. |
| Victim's level of dependency | Bystanders are more likely to help a victim they perceive to be dependent—for example, a child. |
| Victim's responsibility for own plight | Bystanders are less likely to help if they perceive the emergency to be the victim's own fault. |

# Let's
# REVIEW

In this section, we discussed altruism, or helping behavior. As a quick check of your understanding, answer these questions.

**1.** What did Darley and Latané conclude about the witnesses in the Kitty Genovese murder case?
   **a.** Many of the witnesses were uncaring people, and that is why they failed to help.
   **b.** The witnesses were too busy doing other things to stop and help Kitty.
   **c.** Many of the witnesses did not help because they assumed that someone else would help.
   **d.** Fear was the best explanation for why the witnesses did not help.

**2.** Recently, one of the authors was sitting in her office when the fire alarms in her building went off. To her amazement, everyone seemed to ignore the alarms, and no one evacuated the building until security forced them to leave. Which of the following best explains their reluctance to leave the building?
   **a.** Diffusion of responsibility
   **b.** Apathy
   **c.** Pluralistic ignorance
   **d.** A lack of conformity

**3.** If you are ever the victim of an accident and there are many witnesses, what should you do to help ensure that one of the witnesses helps you?
   **a.** Scream for help.
   **b.** Remain quiet so as not to scare the witnesses.
   **c.** Single out one of the witnesses, and request that he or she help you.
   **d.** Yell "Fire!"

Answers 1. c; 2. c; 3. c

# Studying THE CHAPTER

## Key Terms

actor/observer bias (385)
altruism (413)
attitude (378)
attribution (383)
aversive racism (387)
bystander effect (414)
central route to persuasion (381)
cognitive consistency (380)
cohesiveness (398)
collectivistic culture (385)
compliance (403)
conformity (398)
contact hypothesis (391)
deindividuation (400)
destructive obedience (405)
diffusion of responsibility (415)
discrimination (387)
dissonance theory (380)
door-in-the-face compliance (404)
foot-in-the-door compliance (403)

frustration-aggression
  hypothesis (413)
fundamental attribution error (384)
groupthink (402)
helping behavior (414)
hostile aggression (410)
impression formation (383)
in-group bias (390)
individualistic culture (385)
informational conformity (400)
instrumental aggression (410)
low-balling (405)
matching hypothesis (395)
norm (397)
normative conformity (399)
obedience (403)
out-group (390)
out-group homogeneity bias (390)
peripheral route to persuasion (381)
persuasion (381)

pluralistic ignorance (415)
prejudice (387)
prosocial behavior (413)
proximity (394)
psychological distance (409)
realistic-conflict theory (390)
reciprocity (404)
scapegoat (391)
self-serving bias (385)
situational attribution (383)
slippery slope (409)
social cognition (378)
social facilitation (401)
social loafing (401)
social psychology (378)
stereotype (387)
stereotype threat (388)
superordinate goal (392)
that's-not-all (405)
trait attribution (383)

## What Do You Know? Assess Your Understanding

Test your retention and understanding of the material by answering the following questions.

1. Which of the following is not an attitude?
   a. Liking rap music
   b. Believing that honesty is the best policy
   c. Believing that Atlanta is the capital of Georgia
   d. All of the above are attitudes.

2. _____ is a direct attempt to change a person's attitudes.
   a. Dissonance          c. Conformity
   b. Persuasion          d. Compliance

3. If you are in the market for a new car, you should process television ads from car dealers on the _____ route to persuasion.
   a. central             c. cognitive
   b. peripheral          d. emotional

4. Which of the following is least likely to affect persuasion?
   a. How distracted the audience members are
   b. How intelligent the audience members are
   c. How attractive the audience members are
   d. The mood of the audience members

5. Assuming that your professor is a happy person because she was smiling today in class is most likely an example of _____.
   a. dissonance
   b. the fundamental attribution error
   c. the actor/observer bias
   d. the in-group/out-group bias

**6.** Believing that your roommate is to blame for your poor performance on your history exam is most likely an example of _____.

a. a trait attribution
b. the fundamental attribution error
c. the actor/observer bias
d. the self-serving bias

**7.** Believing that because Joe is over 70 years old, he would not be a very good waiter is an example of a _____.

a. stereotype          c. situational attribution
b. prejudice           d. All of the above

**8.** Jane Elliott's study of prejudice in brown-eyed and blue-eyed grade school students showed us that _____.

a. prejudices are already present in us
b. prejudices develop easily in us
c. prejudices develop slowly over time
d. children do not form prejudices as easily as adults do

**9.** When Mary says, "All men hate to ask for directions," she is most likely exhibiting the _____.

a. out-group homogeneity bias
b. in-group/out-group bias
c. actor-observer bias
d. fundamental attribution error

**10.** Muzafer Sherif's study of the Eagles and Rattlers indicated that _____ is the most useful way to reduce prejudice.

a. punishment
b. mere contact with out-group members
c. cooperative contact between groups
d. competition between groups

**11.** Living and working in close proximity to someone is likely to increase our liking for that person because of _____.

a. in-group/out-group bias
b. the mere exposure effect
c. similarity
d. the out-group homogeneity effect

**12.** Being in love with someone is associated with increased _____ in the brain.

a. dopamine            c. GABA
b. serotonin           d. acetylcholine

**13.** Immediately after a famous actor wears *Cooldog* brand jeans in a movie, the *Cooldog* company sees sales of its jeans increase by 500%. This sales increase is most likely the result of _____.

a. compliance          c. persuasion
b. conformity          d. obedience

**14.** Sasha loves to knit. She notices that when she knits with her knitting group, she seems to get more done than she would in the same amount of time knitting alone at home. Sasha's experience is most likely an example of _____.

a. informational conformity
b. social loafing
c. social facilitation
d. the self-serving bias

**15.** Which of the following would be *least* likely to reduce the risk of groupthink in a group?

a. Having a strong group leader
b. Allowing ample time for discussion of ideas
c. Allowing visitors to attend group meetings
d. Having low cohesiveness

**16.** The destructive obedience that Stanley Milgram demonstrated in his experiments is most closely related to which of the following social psychological phenomena?

a. Realistic conflict
b. Attribution
c. Foot-in-the door compliance
d. The frustration-aggression hypothesis

**17.** Which of the following has *not* been linked to aggressive behavior?

a. Low serotonin levels
b. High testosterone
c. Frustration
d. High norepinephrine levels

**18.** The bystander effect predicts that you are most likely to receive help from an individual when he or she _____.

a. is the only witness to your plight
b. is one of many witnesses to your plight
c. is knowledgeable about helping
d. is a compassionate person

**19.** Altruism is helping someone _____.

a. without concern for your own gain
b. because you expect a reward
c. because you are afraid you'll be sued if you fail to help
d. because other people are watching

**20.** Pluralistic ignorance prevents helping because_____.

a. everyone decides that someone else is responsible for helping
b. no one knows how to help
c. no one recognizes that help is needed
d. no one cares enough to help

Answers: 1. c; 2. b; 3. a; 4. c; 5. b; 6. d; 7. b; 8. b; 9. a; 10. c; 11. b; 12. a; 13. b; 14. c; 15. a; 16. c; 17. d; 18. a; 19. a; 20. c

## Online Resources

Log in to **www.cengagebrain.com** to access the resources your instructor requires. For this book, you can access:

### Psychology CourseMate

CourseMate brings course concepts to life with interactive learning, study, and exam preparation tools that support the printed textbook. A textbook-specific website, Psychology CourseMate includes an integrated interactive eBook and other interactive learning tools including quizzes, flashcards, videos, and more.

### CENGAGENOW™

CengageNOW Personalized Study is a diagnostic study tool containing valuable text-specific resources—and because you focus on just what you don't know, you learn more in less time to get a better grade.

### WebTutor

More than just an interactive study guide, WebTutor is an anytime, anywhere customized learning solution with an eBook, keeping you connected to your textbook, instructor, and classmates.

# 10 LOOK BACK AT What You've LEARNED

**Social psychology** is the study of how we think and behave in social situations. **Social cognition** refers to the ways in which we think about ourselves and others.

## Attitudes: Changing Our Minds

- **Attitudes** are evaluative beliefs that contain affective, behavioral, and cognitive components.

- Attitudes develop through learning processes, including classical conditioning, operant conditioning, and observational learning or modeling.

- Attitudes sometimes predict how we will behave in certain situations.

- **Dissonance** results from a lack of **cognitive consistency**; it motivates us to change either our attitudes or our behavior.

- **Persuasion** occurs when someone makes a direct attempt to change our attitudes.

- We tend to be most persuaded by people who appear to be attractive, credible, and expert.

- Typically, people are easier to persuade when they are processing on the **peripheral route** rather than the **central route**.

© Jim West/Alamy

## Forming Impressions of Others

- In forming impressions of others, we make **trait** or **situational attributions** when we assign cause to their behavior.

- The **fundamental attribution error** is the tendency to overuse trait explanations during attribution.

- The **actor/observer bias** and the **self-serving bias** are two other sources of mistaken or biased attributions.

Bloomberg via Getty Images

## Prejudice: Why Can't We All Just Get Along?

© Mark Peterson/Corbis

- **Prejudices** are negatively biased **stereotypes** that are applied to all members of a social group regardless of the members' individual characteristics.

- Like most attitudes, prejudices are learned.

- Intergroup dynamics such as **in-group bias** and **out-group homogeneity bias** often play a role in prejudice.

- The **contact hypothesis** states that mere contact between in-group and out-group members can reduce prejudice. Cooperative contact and **superordinate goals** have been shown to be more effective in reducing prejudice.

## The Nature of Attraction: What Draws Us to Others?

- Some of the factors that affect our attraction to others include **proximity**, similarity of their attitudes and characteristics to ours, physical attractiveness, and biochemicals.

© Remi Benali/Corbis

# SOCIAL PSYCHOLOGY:
### HOW DO WE **Understand**
## and INTERACT
#### With OTHERS?

## Groups: How Do Others Influence Us?

- **Conformity** is the tendency to behave in ways that are consistent with the **norms** or expectations of a group.

- In **normative conformity**, we conform just to avoid breaking norms. In **informational conformity**, we conform because we are persuaded by conformity pressure to believe the group's stance is correct.

- Conformity is influenced by such factors as majority group size, unanimity of the majority group, anonymity, group cohesion, and self-esteem.

- **Social facilitation** occurs when we perform better in the presence of others, but sometimes working with others can lead to **social loafing** as group members decrease their effort.

- **Groupthink** occurs when groups working under conditions of isolation, high **cohesiveness**, stress, and dictatorial leadership make poor decisions after failing to examine all possible solutions to a problem.

## Requests and Demands: Compliance and Obedience

- **Compliance** is giving in to a simple request.
  - In **foot-in-the-door compliance**, one is more likely to yield to a second larger request after having already complied with a first, smaller request.
  - In **door-in-the-face compliance**, one is more likely to yield to a second, smaller request after having refused an earlier large request.
  - **Reciprocity**, or feeling obligated to return others' favors, is a major reason why we comply.

- **Obedience** is giving in to a demand. Factors that make us more likely to obey orders, even when they direct us to behave destructively, include

*Obedience* © 1965, Stanley Milgram

  - the presence of an authority figure.
  - the foot-in-the door compliance of the **slippery slope**.
  - **psychological distance**.

## Aggression: Hurting Others

- Aggression is causing harm or injury to someone who does not wish to be harmed.

- **Instrumental aggression** is goal-directed aggression; **hostile aggression** is aimed solely at hurting others.

- Potential causes of aggression include high levels of testosterone, a lack of serotonin, brain damage caused by child abuse, observational learning or modeling the aggression of others, cognitive neoassociation theory, and the **frustration-aggression hypothesis**.

## Prosocial Behavior: Will You or Won't You Help Others?

- **Helping behavior**, or **altruism**, is the tendency to help others in need with little concern for our own gain.

- One of the factors affecting helping behavior is the **bystander effect**, in which **diffusion of responsibility** reduces the likelihood of obtaining help when there are many witnesses. **Pluralistic ignorance** may also prevent witnesses from perceiving the situation as an emergency.

421

# 11 HEALTH, STRESS, and COPING: HOW CAN YOU CREATE a HEALTHY LIFE?

© Kathleen Finlay/Masterfile

# Chapter Outline

*Because all of us cope* with stress on a daily basis, this chapter offers much psychological research that will be relevant to your day-to-day living, as our student Crystal Athas Thatcher discovered. Crystal, 23, lives on an Army base with her 4-year-old daughter, Nevaeh. Her husband of four years, Brian, 25, has been stationed in Iraq for the past four months. This situation has created quite a lot of stress for Crystal. However, Crystal has applied her knowledge of health psychology to cope better.

To reduce her worry and anxiety over Brian's being at war, Crystal videoconferences with Brian almost every day. Seeing him and talking to him makes her feel more connected and in control. It has also helped Nevaeh maintain a relationship with her father. When Brian first left, Nevaeh would not speak to Brian on the phone. But when she sees Brian on the video, she will speak with him. Crystal has also postponed her own education to reduce her stress level so that she can be a better mom to Nevaeh, as she is essentially raising her daughter on her own. Nevaeh asks many questions and frequently complains that she misses her daddy. Crystal copes by relying on family and friends—for advice, companionship, or a shoulder to cry on. She has an optimistic attitude and tries not to "sweat the small stuff." Although she is sometimes overwhelmed by emotions, she waits until she puts Nevaeh to bed at night before she allows herself to express them.

Lisa Athas

*Crystal Athas Thatcher does her best to cope with raising her daughter, Nevaeh, while her husband, Brian, is serving in the military.*

These strategies have by no means made Crystal stress-free. What they have done is helped her cope during a very difficult time. In this chapter, we'll explore the field of **health psychology**. Health psychologists study how a person's behavior, thoughts, personality, and attitudes influence his or her health for better and for worse. In this regard, health is seen as a result of the interaction among biological, psychological, and social forces (Brannon & Feist, 2004; S. E. Taylor, 2003). The main topics of this chapter are stress, coping, and health. We hope that, like Crystal, you will be able to apply the information in this chapter to your life and realize how some of your personal habits, thoughts, or daily actions may be unhealthy. Hopefully, this analysis will encourage you to live a healthier, longer life!

LEARNING OBJECTIVES

● Define stress, and identify the four types of stressors.

● Distinguish among the four types of conflict situations.

# What Is Stress? Stress and Stressors

You are running late for school and your car breaks down—today of all days, when you have a major project due in one class and a midterm in another. Or maybe you're a working parent, trying to get the kids off to school in the morning, when your youngest can't find her shoes and the dog just got into the garbage. Perhaps you have just fallen in love and have decided to make the relationship more serious. Or maybe you have grown dissatisfied with your relationship and are contemplating ending it. All of these situations have one thing in common. They all include *stress*, an inevitable and unavoidable fact of life.

**You Asked...**

*What causes stress?*

JUSTEN CARTER, STUDENT

**Stress** can be defined as any event or environmental stimulus (stressor) that we respond to because we perceive it as challenging or threatening. This definition implies three aspects to stress. First, we all encounter stressors—stimuli in our lives that we perceive as challenges or threats, such as traffic, an approaching midterm exam, or a hurricane. Second, our reactions to these stressors include bodily reactions. Third, by perceiving and then reacting, we cope with the challenges or threats (successfully or not, as we will see). This chapter explores these three aspects of stress.

Briefly reflect on an ordinary day in your life. There are probably many events or stimuli that you perceive as provoking or annoying: a long line at the fast-food drive-through, a confrontation with your boss, or having several errands to run in a limited amount of time. There probably have also been events in your life that you found to be particularly trying or traumatic, such as the death of a loved one, dealing with an unplanned pregnancy, or being fired from your job. Stressors come in all shapes and sizes. Psychological research classifies these stressors into four types:

● Major life events
● Catastrophes
● Daily hassles
● Conflict

Let's take a look at how each of these stressors is defined.

## Life Events: Change Is Stressful

How do we know which events in our life qualify as major, rather than minor, stressors when they all *feel* stressful? Believe it or not, psychologists have tried to measure this difference. Pioneering research by Thomas Holmes and Richard Rahe

**health psychology**   the subfield of psychology that investigates the relationship between people's behaviors and their health

**stress**   any event or environmental stimulus (stressor) that we respond to because we perceive it as challenging or threatening

in 1967 set out to measure the impact of particular stressors on people's health. They asked a large sample group to rate **life events**, or changes in one's living, both good and bad, that require us to adjust to them. In other words, which life events did the respondents perceive as more or less stressful? From these ratings, Holmes and Rahe developed the Social Readjustment Rating Scale (SRRS), reprinted in ■ TABLE 11.1.

Holmes and Rahe assigned each major life event a numerical value, referred to as a *life change unit*. The higher the number, the more stressful this life event was

**life event**   a change in one's life, good or bad, that requires readjustment

## TABLE 11.1
### Holmes & Rahe's Social Readjustment Rating Scale

| Rank | Life Event | Life Change Units | Rank | Life Event | Life Change Units |
|---|---|---|---|---|---|
| 1 | Death of spouse | 100 | 23 | Son or daughter leaving home | 29 |
| 2 | Divorce | 73 | 24 | Trouble with in-laws | 29 |
| 3 | Marital separation | 65 | 25 | Outstanding personal achievement | 28 |
| 4 | Jail term | 63 | 26 | Spouse begins or stops work | 26 |
| 5 | Death of a close family member | 63 | 27 | Begin or end school | 26 |
| 6 | Personal injury or illness | 53 | 28 | Change in living conditions | 25 |
| 7 | Marriage | 50 | 29 | Revision of personal habits | 24 |
| 8 | Fired at work | 47 | 30 | Trouble with boss | 23 |
| 9 | Marital reconciliation | 45 | 31 | Change in work hours or conditions | 20 |
| 10 | Retirement | 45 | 32 | Change in residence | 20 |
| 11 | Change in health of family member | 44 | 33 | Change in school | 20 |
| 12 | Pregnancy | 40 | 34 | Change in recreation | 19 |
| 13 | Sex difficulties | 39 | 35 | Change in church activities | 19 |
| 14 | Gain of new family member | 39 | 36 | Change in social activities | 18 |
| 15 | Business readjustment | 39 | 37 | Take out loan less than $20,000 | 17 |
| 16 | Change in financial state | 38 | 38 | Change in sleeping habits | 16 |
| 17 | Death of a close friend | 37 | 39 | Change in number of family get-togethers | 15 |
| 18 | Change to different line of work | 36 | 40 | Change in eating habits | 15 |
| 19 | Change in number of arguments with spouse | 35 | 41 | Vacation | 13 |
| 20 | Take out mortgage or loan for major purchase | 31 | 42 | Christmas | 12 |
| 21 | Foreclosure of mortgage or loan | 30 | 43 | Minor violation of the law | 11 |
| 22 | Change in responsibilities at work | 29 | | | |

Reprinted with permission from T. H. Holmes & R. H. Rahe (1967), "The Social Readjustment Rating Scale," in the Journal of Psychosomatic Research, Vol. 11, No. 2, pp. 213–218. Copyright © 1967 Elsevier Science.

Note: In Holmes and Rahe's Social Readjustment Rating Scale, each major life event is assigned a numerical value. The higher the number, the more stressful the life event is perceived to be. Add up the life change units for all those events you have experienced in the past year. Then compare your total to the standards indicated in the text.

rated by Holmes and Rahe's sample. Notice that the life events on the scale include positive as well as negative changes—for example, marriage, a new family member, and outstanding personal achievement. However, it is not just experiencing one of these events that is at issue. Rather, it is reacting to several of these events within a year that Holmes and Rahe found may influence one's health.

## YOUR TURN | Active Learning

Take a moment to look at the Social Readjustment Rating Scale (Table 11.1). Add up the life change units for all those events you have experienced in the last year. Compare your total to the standards devised by Holmes and Rahe.

| 0–150 | No significant problems |
|---|---|
| 150–199 | Mild life crisis |
| 200–299 | Moderate life crisis |
| 300 or more | Major life crisis |

Holmes and Rahe (1967) found that the higher people scored on the SRRS, the more prone they were to illness. Of those who scored within the mild life crisis range, 37% had experienced deteriorated health. This figure rose to 51% for those whose scores indicated they were experiencing a moderate life crisis, and 79% for those in the major life crisis range. Follow-up studies have supported Holmes and Rahe's findings (Gruen, 1993; Scully, Tosi, & Banning, 2000). If you scored high on the scale, you may want to consider adjusting your lifestyle in ways that reduce your chances of becoming ill. However, keep in mind that these are correlations and, as we discussed in Chapter 1, correlation does not mean causation. Life events do not directly cause illness, but they may make a person more vulnerable to illness and disease.

Life events, both good and bad, can be perceived as stressful and require us to adjust to them.

© Masterfile

Subsequent research (Pearlin, 1993) evaluating Holmes and Rahe's scale indicates that the impact of these life changes is not simply a matter of how many of them one experiences. We need to take several other variables into account, including:

- The voluntary or involuntary nature of the life change
- How desirable or undesirable the life change is perceived to be
- Whether the life change is scheduled or unscheduled

Consider as an example a couple about to break up. Typically, the partner who initiates the breakup feels less stress after she has informed her significant other of her decision. In this context, the breakup is seen as voluntary, desirable, and scheduled. At the same time, her partner may experience increased stress, as the dissolution of the relationship is involuntary (not of the partner's choosing), undesirable, and unscheduled. As this example illustrates, the amount of stress one experiences when faced with life changes may vary across people. We can consider Holmes and Rahe's scale as a rough index of how susceptible some people may be to illness, given the number of major stressors the person encounters.

You may have noticed that the scale has very few life events that are likely to be experienced by college students and younger people. The SRRS has been criticized for not adequately defining stress events among younger age groups. Yet research supports the notion that major changes, such as the breakup of a relationship, academic pressure, or even college itself, may influence the health of college students (Crandall, Preisler, & Aussprung,

1992). This is important because perceived stress also seems to predict how well students perform academically. High levels of perceived stress in college students correlate with lower grade point averages (Lloyd et al., 1980; Maville & Huerta, 1997). For example, in one survey of college students (ACHA, 2006), stress was the most frequent reason given for academic problems. You may find that the Undergraduate Stress Questionnaire (■ TABLE 11.2) includes more of the stressors that you typically face than does Holmes and Rahe's SRRS. It was specifically designed to measure life event stress in college students. Undergraduates who have experienced more of these life events are more likely to report more physical symptoms and are less likely to report a positive mood (Crandall et al., 1992). It may therefore provide a more accurate assessment of your stress level and hence your susceptibility to illness.

## Catastrophes: Natural Disasters and Wars

Unexpected traumatic events or *catastrophes* that almost all people perceive as threats also qualify as stressors. Catastrophes may affect one's physical and psychological health (Bonanno et al., 2010). After catastrophic events such as floods, earthquakes, hurricanes, tornadoes, or fires, people are generally more likely to experience depression or anxiety (Brende, 2000; Davidson, 2000; Dewaraja & Kawamura, 2006; Neria, Nandi, & Galea, 2008; Weems et al., 2007).

We have for a long time recognized the stress of war on soldiers, as evidenced by the various names we have given to the pattern of symptoms that some soldiers experience when they return. It was called *shell shock* in World War I, *battle fatigue* in World War II, and *posttraumatic stress disorder* (*PTSD*) following the Vietnam War and Operation Desert Storm. Soldiers often experience nightmares, flashbacks, and vivid memories as they relive their war experiences. They may evidence intense startle responses to loud noises and have difficulty concentrating and getting along with others. Rape victims report similar physical and psychological symptoms that may meet the criteria for what is referred to as *rape trauma syndrome*, more evidence that unexpected events may take their toll on one's health. Traumatic events and catastrophes are often involuntary, undesirable, and unscheduled, in that we typically don't have a lot of time to prepare for them; it is relatively easy to see how they might influence our health and well-being. We'll discuss PTSD in more detail in Chapter 13.

Do catastrophes or traumatic events always affect health negatively? Not necessarily. Some people exposed to disaster may show chronic dysfunction, yet many others show remarkable resilience, experiencing only temporary distress (Bonanno et al., 2010). Moreover, research has documented a potential positive effect of stressful life experiences for some people, referred to as *posttraumatic growth* or *benefit-finding*. People report that these events have changed their lives in positive ways, such as building stronger relationships with others, emphasizing enjoyment in life, and initiating positive changes in health behaviors (Bower, Moskowitz, & Epel, 2009; Updegraff, Silver, & Holman, 2008). It seems that for some people, a severe life-threatening event provides an opportunity to reevaluate their lives and prompts them to initiate positive changes.

**daily hassles**   the everyday irritations and frustrations that individuals face

Unexpected catastrophes or traumatic events also cause stress and can affect one's physical and psychological health.

© Tony Arruza/Corbis

## Daily Hassles: Little Things Add Up!

When psychologists evaluate the relationship between stress and health, they not only measure life changes and analyze the influence of catastrophes, they also evaluate the impact of everyday irritations and frustrations. These **daily hassles** also appear to play a role in our health. At times these irritants add to the stress of major life changes

# YOU REVIEW 11.1    Sexually Transmitted Infections (STIs)

| STI | TRANSMISSION MODES | SYMPTOMS | TREATMENTS |
| --- | --- | --- | --- |
| Bacterial | | | |
| Chlamydia | Vaginal, oral, or anal sexual activity, or from an infected mother to her newborn during vaginal birth | In females: frequent and painful urination, lower abdominal pain, and vaginal discharge. In males: burning or painful urination, and slight penis discharge. However, many people show no symptoms. | Antibiotics |
| Gonorrhea | Vaginal, oral, or anal sexual activity, or from an infected mother to her newborn during vaginal birth | In females: increased vaginal discharge, burning urination, or irregular menstrual bleeding (many women show no early symptoms). In males: yellowish, thick penile discharge, or burning urination. | Antibiotics |
| Syphilis | Vaginal, oral, or anal sexual activity, or by touching an infected chancre or sore | A hard, round, painless chancre or sore appears at site of infection within 2 to 4 weeks. | Penicillin or other antibiotics for penicillin-allergic patients |
| Viral | | | |
| Genital herpes | Vaginal, oral, or anal sexual activity | Painful, reddish blisters around the genitals, thighs, or buttocks, and for females on the vagina or cervix. Other symptoms may include burning urination, flu-like symptoms, or vaginal discharge in females. | No cure, although certain drugs can provide relief and help sores heal |
| HPV | Vaginal, oral, or anal sexual activity | Some strains cause painless warts to appear in the genital area or anus; other strains may cause abnormal cell changes in the cervix. | Cryotherapy (freezing), acid burning, or surgical removal of warts |
| HIV/AIDS | Sexual contact, infusion with contaminated blood, or from mother to child during pregnancy, childbirth, or breast feeding. | May develop flu-like symptoms that may disappear for many years before developing full-blown AIDS. AIDS symptoms include fever, weight loss, fatigue, diarrhea, and susceptibility to infection. | No cure; treatment includes a combination of antiretroviral drugs |
| Parasites | | | |
| Pubic lice | Sexual contact or contact with infested linens or toilet seats | Intense itching in hairy regions of the body, especially the pubic area | Prescription shampoos or nonprescription medications |
| Scabies | Sexual contact or contact with infested linens or toilet seats | Intense itching, reddish lines on skin, welts, and pus-filled blisters in affected area | Prescription shampoos |

## EATING RIGHT

Being overweight or obese is associated with a higher risk of several types of health problems such as type 2 diabetes, sleep apnea, migraine headaches, heart disease, and some cancers. It also shortens one's life span (Adams et al., 2006). Healthful eating when combined with physical activity can decrease one's risk of disease and death.

Eating right means choosing foods that are nutritious and healthy. Nutritious foods such as fruits, vegetables, and grains are high in vitamins, minerals, and fiber. Processed foods and foods high in sugar, salt, oil, or fat (like fast food) increase cholesterol, which contributes to the development of heart problems (Phelan et al., 2009). One should strive to eat well-balanced meals that meet one's nutritional needs and include a variety of foods from each of the major food groups.

Eating right also means eating breakfast. Skipping breakfast is one of the biggest nutritional mistakes that people make. Breakfast is your first chance to refuel your body to prepare it for the day's activities. Regularly eating a healthy breakfast is associated with increased attention span, less risk of chronic diseases, and living a longer life (Hoyland, Dye, & Lawton, 2009; Schoenborn, 1986). Eating a healthy breakfast also makes us less likely to overeat later in the day.

## GETTING ENOUGH SLEEP

As we saw in Chapter 4, adults and teenagers require at least 8 hours of sleep a night, yet few of us achieve this. Why is getting enough sleep so important? For one, doing so enhances your immune system (Lange et al., 2006; Motivala & Irwin, 2007). When you deprive your body of sleep, your natural immune responses are reduced (Irwin et al., 2003; Murphy & Delanty, 2007). The right amount of sleep also activates chemicals that influence your emotions and enhance mood. If you are deprived of sleep, you are more likely to be irritable, cranky, and unhappy, in addition to being tired (Durmer & Dinges, 2005; Murphy & Delanty, 2007). Sleep offers many benefits to our functioning and ensures that we will be healthy, alert, and happy.

## Happiness and Well-Being

Healthy living promotes happiness and life satisfaction. So, it is fitting to end this chapter by investigating what make makes people happy. Research typically measures happiness by asking people how satisfied they are with their lives. This is referred to as *subjective well-being*. People who score high on measures of subjective well-being live longer and healthier lives (Chida & Steptoe, 2008; Xu & Roberts, 2010). The factors that contribute to happiness nicely summarize many of the health behaviors that this chapter has explored (Diener & Biswas-Diener, 2008).

People who are happy are healthier and live longer.

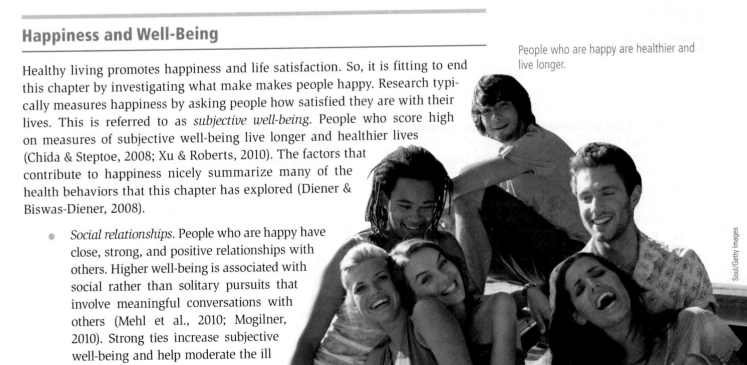

Soul/Getty Images

- *Social relationships*. People who are happy have close, strong, and positive relationships with others. Higher well-being is associated with social rather than solitary pursuits that involve meaningful conversations with others (Mehl et al., 2010; Mogilner, 2010). Strong ties increase subjective well-being and help moderate the ill effects of stress.

# LOOK BACK AT What You've LEARNED

**Health psychologists** study how people's behavior influences their health for better and for worse.

## What Is Stress? Stress and Stressors

- **Stress** is any event or environmental stimulus (stressor) that we respond to because we perceive it as challenging or threatening.

- Catastrophes and significant **life events**, such as the death of a loved one or a new job, are major stressors. Everyday frustrations—called **daily hassles**—are less serious stressors, but can have a negative effect on health.

- **Conflict** also produces stress.

© Masterfile

© Bubbles Photolibrary/Alamy

## The Stress Response: Is This Stress? How Do I React?

- If our initial interpretation or **primary appraisal** of an event is one of stress, we may view it as a threat, as harmful, or merely as a challenge.

- Our body responds to stress in a three-phase **general adaptation syndrome**:

  - The **alarm reaction** consists of those bodily responses, including the nervous system and endocrine system, that are immediately triggered when we initially appraise an event as stressful.

  - In the **resistance stage**, the body continues to cope with the stressor, but the bodily reactions are less intense than during the alarm reaction.

  - In the **exhaustion phase**, wear and tear on the body begins, causing serious damage if stress continues over an extended period of time.

- The corticosteroids and endorphins that are released into our body during the stress response dampen the activity of our immune system, making us more vulnerable to health problems.

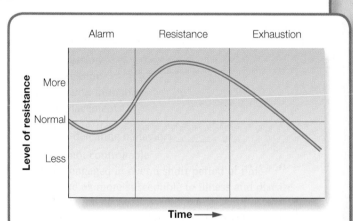

Alarm    Resistance    Exhaustion

Level of resistance

More

Normal

Less

Time ⟶

## How Can I Cope With Stress?

- **Coping** is how we manage a threatening event or stimulus..

- **Problem-focused coping** controls or alters the environment that caused the stress. It is most useful when we feel that we can do something about the stressor.

- **Emotion-focused coping** controls our internal, subjective, emotional responses to stress. We alter the way we feel or think in order to reduce stress.

- **Defense mechanisms** are unconscious coping strategies that allow us to reduce our anxiety and maintain a positive self-image and self-esteem.

- A number of strategies can be used to reduce stress in one's life, including exercise, **social support**, **guided imagery**, **meditation**, laughter, and time management.

## What Behaviors Promote Health and Well-Being?

- **Health-defeating behaviors**, such as alcohol and substance abuse, smoking, distracted driving, and unsafe sex, increase the chance of illness, disease, or death.

- **Sexually transmitted infections** are passed from one person to another primarily through sexual contact. One in four Americans will contract an STI by the age of 21. Young people are at greater risk for contracting STIs because they are more likely to engage in high-risk sexual behaviors.

- **Health-promoting behaviors** decrease the chance of illness, disease, or death. Regular physical activity, healthful eating, and getting enough sleep promote a longer and healthier life. Happiness is related to a strong social support network, an optimistic outlook, economic resources, temperament, and cultural values.

## Does Your Personality Influence Your Health?

- A person with a **Type A personality** is aggressive, competitive, and driven to achieve; a person with a **Type B personality** is relaxed, easygoing, patient, and flexible; a person with a **Type C personality** is careful and patient and suppresses negative emotions such as anger. The Type A personality trait of hostility is related to a higher incidence of heart disease.

- **Learned helplessness** results from believing that you have no control over stressful life events. You view stressors as threats, your level of stress increases, and you are more likely to develop stress-related illnesses.

- The **hardy personality** is resistant to stress; it includes characteristics such as

  - A tendency to see life as a series of challenges

  - A sense of personal commitment to self, work, family, and other values

  - A perception of control over one's life and work

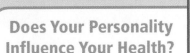

459

# 12

## WHAT IS **PERSONALITY,** and HOW DO **WE** **MEASURE** It?

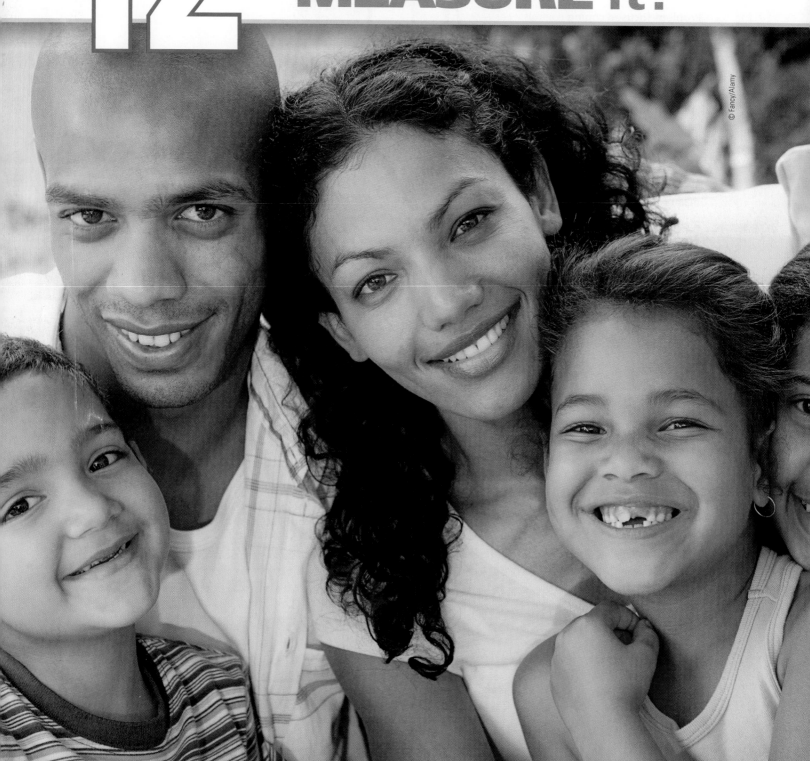

© Fancy/Alamy

# Chapter Outline

*Kaymari Invictus is a 28-year-old* student working on a bachelor's degree in elementary education. She also is the mother of four children: a 9-year-old daughter, 6-year old twin boys, and a 4-year-old daughter. After studying personality, Kaymari noticed the similarities and differences in her children's personalities and concluded that she shouldn't parent each child in the same way. Although all her children are social, she sees that her boys are more analytical and enjoy staying inside doing puzzles or drawing. Her daughters, on the other hand, love being outside and physically active, and one daughter is a tomboy while the other is more feminine. After studying personality, Kaymari knows that some of these dispositions could have been inherited, while others may be due to environmental influences. She also knows that personality unfolds in a complex manner. As a teacher, Kaymari feels it will be important to pay attention to her students' personalities so that she can best help them reach their true potentials.

Understanding the nature of personality will be beneficial in Kaymari Invictus's career as an elementary school teacher.

This chapter's topic is **personality**—the unique collection of attitudes, emotions, thoughts, habits, impulses, and behaviors that define how a person typically behaves across situations. Four dominant perspectives have emerged to explain our personalities: the *psychoanalytic approach*, the *trait approach*, the *social cognitive approach*, and the *humanistic approach*. No single approach can explain all facets of personality in all people, and each perspective has advantages and disadvantages. As we describe each approach, consider your own ideas about personality. Do you think you inherit your personality, or is it formed through experiences? Examining such ideas will allow you to connect the material to your experiences and current way of thinking, as Kaymari has done.

**personality** the unique collection of attitudes, emotions, thoughts, habits, impulses, and behaviors that define how a person typically behaves across situations

**psychoanalytic perspective [psi-co-an-uh-LIH-tic]** a personality approach developed by Sigmund Freud that sees personality as the product of driving forces within a person that are often conflicting and sometimes unconscious

The psychoanalytic perspective on personality originated with Sigmund Freud. Freud saw personality as the product of driving forces within a person that were often conflicting and sometimes unconscious.

Hulton Archive/Getty Images

# The Psychoanalytic Approach: Sigmund Freud and the Neo-Freudians

The **psychoanalytic perspective** on personality originated with Sigmund Freud (1856–1939). We introduced his approach to understanding behavior in Chapter 1. Recall that Freud practiced medicine, specializing in "nervous diseases." However, soon after beginning private practice, Freud moved away from physical explanations of nervous disorders and focused more on investigating psychological causes of these disorders. His ideas about personality were based on case studies of his patients, his reading of literature, and his own self-analysis. Freud saw personality as the product of driving forces within a person that were often conflicting and sometimes unconscious. As we saw in Chapter 4, Freud believed that dreams were one of the ways these unconscious forces expressed themselves. Freud's theory is unique in that it strongly emphasizes unconscious aspects of personality.

## Freud's Levels of Awareness

Freud (1940/1964) proposed that human personality operates at three different levels of awareness or consciousness and that each level of awareness influences behavior. Freud viewed consciousness as being like an iceberg (■ FIGURE 12.1). When we look at behavior, all we usually see is the tip of the iceberg, or the **conscious level**: the thoughts, perceptions, and explanations of behavior of which the person is aware. The major portion of the iceberg, according to Freud, is below the surface. These impulses, memories, and thoughts are unseen but have a huge impact on personality. Because so large a portion of one's personality lies below the surface of consciousness, or awareness, Freud believed, any explanation of personality and behavior must focus on these unconscious forces.

Your conscious level, as previously stated, includes any memories, thoughts, or urges of which you are currently aware. You know you want to download the new Kanye West song, or you know that it is important to read this chapter and study for the test next week. But the things you could potentially be aware of at any one time are infinite, and you cannot hold more than a couple of thoughts, urges, and memories in consciousness at any one time. So, according to Freud, it is necessary to have a holding place for easily accessible memories, thoughts, or impulses of which you could become aware. This is the role of the **preconscious level**.

The **unconscious level** contains all those thoughts, impulses, memories, and behaviors of which you are unaware. However, although you are unaware of them, they always influence your behavior. Consider the 4-year-old boy who stops his parents from hugging or inserts himself between them to prevent them from kissing. According to Freud, he is not aware that this behavior stems from a need or wish to bond with his mother, yet it is still influencing his behavior.

## Freud's Structure of Personality

To Freud (1940/1964), human personality is an energy system comprised of three major personality structures: the *id*, the *ego*, and the *superego*. At birth, all of the energy of the personality is contained within a structure called the **id**. The id is an unconscious energy force that seeks pleasure and gratification. Hungry infants cry for food or because they are wet or tired. The id operates according to the **pleasure**

## FIGURE 12.1

### Iceberg Analogy of Freud's Levels of Awareness

In Freud's "iceberg" analogy of the mind, the id and parts of the ego and superego are submerged below the water in the unconscious. Parts of the ego and superego also operate in the conscious and preconscious.

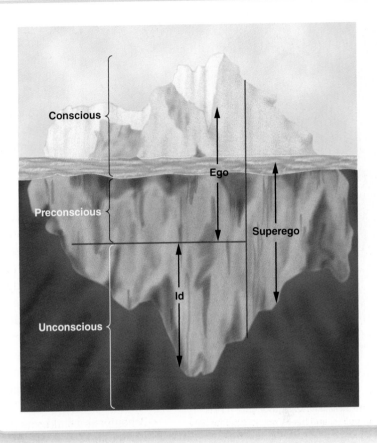

**principle**; it drives people to feel good and to maximize pleasure and gratification. Freud saw the impulses driving the id as sexual and aggressive in nature. In this way, he viewed humans as very similar to animals—unconsciously and selfishly motivated by basic sexual and aggressive instincts. Such basic instincts ensure and promote the survival of the individual, and therefore the survival of the species as a whole.

When we grow and begin to interact with our environment, we realize that our demands cannot always be immediately fulfilled. For example, when a baby's cry for food is not met every time, the baby has encountered reality. As a result, part of the energy of the id becomes directed to a second personality structure, the **ego**. The ego acts as a negotiator between the instinctual needs of the id and the demands of membership in human society. Children learn that their id demands can be fulfilled only when they behave appropriately. The ego operates according to the **reality principle**. It realizes that the desires of the id can be met only by successfully dealing with the environment, by finding appropriate or attainable means by which to fulfill id impulses. Suppose a 4-year-old wants something to eat. Does he immediately cry like a baby? Not typically. The 4-year-old with a functioning ego knows that there are more appropriate and acceptable ways of getting food. He will probably ask for something to eat and be willing to wait (at least for a little while) for his caregiver to prepare it for him. We see the ego functioning in the child's ability to delay his desire for food. But the ego's job is still to fulfill the instinctual demands of the id—the unseen force beneath the tip of the iceberg (see Figure 12.1).

As the child continues to grow, parents and other important people impart their values and standards of behavior to the child. Parents convey the right and wrong ways to feel, think, and behave. The child incorporates these standards as the energy of the personality further divides into a third personality structure. The **superego** typically emerges during the resolution of the phallic stage (discussed shortly) and represents our moral conscience. Our superego judges the rightness or wrongness of our actions. When we have the sense that we did something wrong, our superego is talking. The moral directives of the superego must also be taken into account by the ego. Just like id demands, superego demands must be met realistically by the ego in order to function in society.

The energy that these three personality components use cannot be cut apart. For Freud, personality is a dynamic, or active, process. The id, ego, and superego are not fixed entities but rather parts of our personality that serve different functions. A healthy personality will have developed a strong ego that appropriately releases and controls instinctual energy. However, problems may arise in

**conscious [CON-shus] level** the level of consciousness that holds all the thoughts, perceptions, and impulses of which we are aware

**preconscious [pre-CON-shus] level** the level of consciousness that holds thoughts, perceptions, and impulses of which we could potentially be aware

**unconscious [un-CON-shus] level** the level of awareness that contains all the thoughts, perceptions, and impulses of which we are unaware

**id** the unconscious part of the personality that seeks pleasure and gratification

**pleasure principle** the basis on which the id operates; the urge to feel good and maximize gratification

**ego** the conscious part of the personality that attempts to meet the demands of the id in a socially appropriate way

**reality principle** the basis on which the ego operates; finding socially appropriate means to fulfill id demands

**superego** the part of the personality that represents your moral conscience

According to Freud, it is a child's superego that drives feelings of guilt after wrongdoing.

**defense mechanism**  a process used to protect the ego by reducing the anxiety it feels when faced with the conflicting demands of the id and the superego

personality functioning if id energy or superego energy overwhelms the functioning of the ego.

To Freud, all adult behaviors are a reflection of the interplay among these three structures (■ FIGURE 12.2). When examining behavior, we see only the functioning of the ego, but this ego is simultaneously being influenced by the unconscious demands of the id and the superego. *Freudian slips* illustrate this interaction. A Freudian slip is the expression of an unconscious impulse from the id before the ego controls the impulse. The ego may then state that it did not mean to say something and corrects the slip to conform to socially approved behavior. For example, one might say to a rival businessperson at a meeting, "Would you like to hit in this chair?" instead of "Would you like to sit in this chair?" and then quickly correct the error. Freud would state that what "slipped out" was meant. It just hadn't yet been socially screened by the ego.

You can see that the demands of the id and the superego are often in direct opposition to one another. This internal conflict sometimes overwhelms the ego, creating anxiety. According to Freud, the ego handles this anxiety by using **defense mechanisms** (A. Freud, 1936). Defense mechanisms, discussed in Chapter 11, protect the ego by reducing the anxiety it feels when faced with the conflicting demands of the id and the superego. We all make use of these *coping mechanisms*, as they are now familiarly called. We tend to use those defense mechanisms that have been previously reinforced or that successfully reduce anxiety. For example, if you *rationalized* behavior as a child, you probably continue to use this defense mechanism as an adult.

Differences in personality, then, arise from internal energy conflicts among the id, ego, and superego (called *intrapsychic conflicts*). Freud further believed that personality is shaped by differences in how we resolve psychosexual stages of development.

**FIGURE**

# 12.2

## Freud's Personality Structures

According to Freud, adult behavior results from the interaction among the three personality structures of the id, ego, and superego.

# Freud's Psychosexual Stages of Development

*You Asked...*

*There is a common perception that we model our lives after our parents—for example, the idea that heterosexual men seek out women like their mother. Is this an accurate perspective?*

MICHAEL HORSFALL, STUDENT

According to Freud (1940/1964), personality develops through a series of five *psychosexual stages*. These stages represent a complex interaction between natural shifts of pleasure from one part of the body to another and the environmental factors that influence how we handle these sexual desires. From birth through adolescence, children must resolve numerous unconscious conflicts that arise from sexual pleasure associated with stimulation of certain body parts, or what Freud called *erogenous zones*. For example, the infant nursing (from the mother's breast or from a bottle) derives a great deal of sensual pleasure from the feel of the nipple on his or her lips, and the satisfaction of hunger the milk brings. However, the pleasure received from any erogenous zone must be balanced with parental restrictions or permissiveness placed on one's behavior. This creates an internal struggle, or "conflict," that significantly influences the resulting personality. Freud uses the term *psychosexual* to refer to the psychological significance of these sexual drives in the formation of a healthy personality. Because environmental circumstances vary in terms of how we are parented or how we respond to these socialization experiences, the result is individual differences in personality. Let's take a brief look at each of Freud's psychosexual stages.

## ORAL STAGE

The **oral stage** lasts from birth until approximately 18 months of age. The mouth, tongue, and lips are the erogenous zones, or focus of pleasure. Babies receive pleasure from sucking, licking, biting, and chewing.

## ANAL STAGE

The **anal stage** lasts from approximately 18 months to 3 years. The anus and rectum are the erogenous zones. Freud viewed production of feces as a creative act. The toddler typically feels quite proud of them, either holding them in or spreading them around. How the parent then responds to this or how the parent attempts to control this production through toilet-training practices is the key to adequately resolving this stage.

## PHALLIC STAGE

During the **phallic stage**, from 3 to 6 years of age, the genitals are the primary erogenous zones, and children receive pleasure from self-stimulation. This stage is particularly important for personality development as it represents the time when the **Oedipus complex** and the **Electra complex** occur. Freud believed that at this age, young children develop unconscious sexual urges for the parent of the other sex. The child wants to bond with the parent of the other sex as the child sees the parents bonding. Using the terms *Oedipus* and *Electra* from two ancient Greek tragedies, Freud believed that at this psychosexual stage, little boys unconsciously fall in love with their mothers and experience hostile feelings toward their fathers much as Oedipus (unknowingly) married his mother and killed his father. Like Electra, little girls unconsciously fall in love with their fathers and feel jealousy toward their mothers. Children at this age may prevent their parents from hugging or be jealous of the parents' spending time alone together. Children then resolve

**oral stage**   Freud's first psychosexual stage of development, which occurs during the first year of life, in which the handling of the child's feeding experiences affects personality development

**anal stage**   Freud's second psychosexual stage, which occurs from approximately 18 months to 3 years of age, in which the parents' regulation of the child's biological urge to expel or retain feces affects personality development

**phallic [FAH-lick] stage**   Freud's third psychosexual stage of development, which occurs between 3 and 6 years of age, in which little boys experience the Oedipus complex and little girls the Electra complex

**Oedipus [ED-uh-puss] complex**   in the male, an unconscious sexual urge for the mother that develops during the phallic psychosexual stage

**Electra complex**   in the female, an unconscious sexual urge for the father that develops during the phallic psychosexual stage

Parents' toilet-training practices influence a toddler's attempt to resolve the anal psychosexual stage, according to Freud.

Ryan McVay/Getty Images

these complexes by identifying with and behaving more like the same-sex parent. A young boy may start to imitate the way his father eats, or a young girl may mimic the way her mother brushes her hair. The child incorporates the values and standards of the same-sex parent, thus ending the rivalry. The child's psychic energy is then redirected to the growth of the superego (discussed earlier).

## LATENCY STAGE

The **latency stage** occurs from age 6 until puberty. During the latency stage, sexual impulses are pushed into the background. The child's energy focuses on other demands of the environment, most noticeably school and peer relations. Sexuality reappears at puberty as reflected in the final psychosexual stage, the genital stage.

## GENITAL STAGE

The **genital stage** begins with puberty. The genitals again become the source of pleasure, as the adolescent must revisit the sexual urges that first appeared during the phallic stage. Recall that during the phallic stage, children developed unconscious attractions to the other-sex parent. Recognizing now that the love for the parent cannot be fulfilled, the adolescent seeks resolution of the genital stage by transferring this love to an other-sex mate. Consequently, for Freud, adult heterosexual intimate relations reflect the unconscious desire to choose a mate in the image of one's other-sex parent. If during the phallic stage the child develops unconscious attractions to the same-sex parent, then during the genital stage, homosexual intimate relations arise from transferring love to a same-sex partner.

## PERSONALITY AND FIXATIONS

As Freud saw it, all children develop through these predictable stages, which are primarily sexual but are psychologically significant in forming a healthy personality. Successfully resolving these stages entails receiving an optimal amount of gratification at each stage—not too much and not too little. A child who receives too much satisfaction at one stage may be reluctant to move on to the next stage. Too little satisfaction may result in frustration for the child, who may continue to seek gratification instead of moving on. These examples of inadequate resolution of a stage result in what Freud called a *fixation*. Those who fixate at one stage remain stuck, and their personalities remain immature or underdeveloped. Part of the personality remains focused on the concerns of this stage.

For Freud, problems in adult personality reflect these unresolved issues or fixations from childhood. For example, a person whose oral urges were not adequately satisfied in infancy would develop an *oral fixation*. An oral fixation might be expressed in the adult behaviors of overeating, nail biting, constantly chewing on pens or pencils, or boasting. More serious behaviors reflecting oral fixations include smoking, alcoholism, and binge eating. Fixation at the anal stage may express itself in the adult personality as *anal-retentiveness* or *anal-expulsiveness*. Being overly neat, stingy, or orderly (anal-retentive) or being excessively sloppy, generous, or carefree (anal-expulsive) both result from inadequate resolution of the anal stage. These are just two examples of how fixations might manifest themselves in an adult personality.

**latency [LATE-an-see] stage** Freud's fourth psychosexual stage of development, which occurs from around age 6 to puberty, in which the child's sexuality is suppressed due to widening social contacts with school, peers, and family

**genital stage** Freud's final psychosexual stage of development, which begins at puberty, in which sexual energy is transferred toward peers of the other sex (heterosexual orientation) or same sex (homosexual orientation)

According to Freud, the genital stage of psychosexual development unconsciously motivates teens to interact with potential sexual partners.

© Adrian Sherratt/Alamy

## Neo-Freudians: Carl Jung, Alfred Adler, and Karen Horney

Freud's work created much controversy among professionals in the developing field of psychology. Many physicians and psychologists were initially intrigued by Freud's ideas but had their differences with aspects of his theory and eventually separated from Freud. These *neo-Freudians* agreed with Freud that unconscious conflicts were important to understanding personality, but they placed less emphasis on the role of the instinctual impulses of sex and aggression in motivating behavior. We have already introduced one neo-Freudian, Erik Erikson, whose theory of psychosocial development we discussed in Chapter 9. His eight stages described the influence of the environment on the developing ego over the life span. Three other examples of neo-Freudian theories are presented here, in the ideas of Carl Jung, Alfred Adler, and Karen Horney.

Carl Jung divided the unconscious into the personal unconscious (forgotten memories and repressed experiences) and the collective unconscious (the collected images and ideas from the earliest development of the human psyche).

### CARL JUNG AND THE COLLECTIVE UNCONSCIOUS

Carl Jung (1875–1961) was a student of Freud's who came to reject his ideas about personality, particularly the sexual aspects of his theory. Like Freud, Jung maintained that personality was a function of the interplay between conscious and unconscious processes. However, Jung (1917/1967) divided the unconscious into the *personal unconscious* and the *collective unconscious*. The **personal unconscious**, much like Freud's unconscious, consisted of forgotten memories and repressed experiences. The **collective unconscious** is universal to all people of all time periods and cultures. The collective unconscious represents the collected images and ideas from the earliest development of the human psyche.

In particular, the collective unconscious includes **archetypes**, mental representations or symbols of themes and predispositions to respond to the world in a certain way. According to Jung, two of the major archetypes of the personality are the *anima* and the *animus*, the female and male aspects of each person. Among the other archetypes Jung identified are the *persona* and the *shadow*. The persona is the appearance we present to the world, the role or character we assume when relating to others, such as the martyr, the rebel, or the teacher. The shadow includes those negative tendencies or qualities of the self that a person tries to deny or hide from the world. Jung's emphasis on the collective unconscious and his belief that spiritual and religious drives are just as important as sexual ones continue to draw attention. He also stressed the importance of enduring personality traits such as introversion and extraversion (discussed shortly).

**personal unconscious**   according to Jung, the part of the unconscious that consists of forgotten memories and repressed experiences from one's past

**collective unconscious**   according to Jung, the part of the unconscious that contains images and material universal to people of all time periods and cultures

**archetypes [ARE-kuh-types]**   according to Jung, mental representations or symbols of themes and predispositions to respond to the world in a certain way that are contained in the collective unconscious

### ALFRED ADLER AND THE INFERIORITY COMPLEX

Alfred Adler (1870–1937) also began as a student of Freud's but disagreed with his emphasis on aggressive and sexual urges as the major force in personality development. Adler (1928) believed that it is the child's desire to overcome feelings of helplessness and to master the environment that directs behavior. In the world of adults, children are small and helpless and feel inadequate and weak. Children have to be bathed by a parent and hold a parent's hand when crossing the street. These feelings of inferiority motivate the child—and later the adult—toward achievement. For Adler, personality develops from our attempts to compensate for inferiority feelings. Moderate feelings of inferiority will result in constructive achievement and creative growth, but deep feelings of inferiority will impede positive growth and development and result in an *inferiority complex*.

Adler also emphasized the importance of birth order as a factor in personality development. He argued that firstborns, middle-borns, and youngest children grow up in differing family environments and are not necessarily treated the same by

Children's small stature and dependence on parents create inferiority feelings that motivate them toward achievement, according to Adler.

parents. These different experiences are likely to affect personality development. Adler's ideas have resulted in hundreds of studies on the effects of birth order. These studies have generally not found any reliable relationships between birth order and personality (Abdel-Khalek & Lester, 2005; Harris, 2000). Yet people generally believe that birth order affects personality, which may then actually encourage those in various birth ranks to differ in their personalities (Herrera et al., 2003).

## KAREN HORNEY AND BASIC ANXIETY

Although Karen Horney (1885–1952) agreed with Freud on the significance of early childhood in personality development, she rejected his belief that this development arose from instinctual conflicts. Instead, Horney (1937, 1939) suggested that family environments and disturbances in early relationships lead to **basic anxiety**, or a feeling of helplessness in children. Children cope with this basic anxiety by pursuing love, power, prestige, or detachment. Horney further argued, in contrast to Freud, that culture plays a larger role in personality development than biology and instinct. For Horney, personality is not merely the result of psychosexual conflicts, as Freud would argue, but rather is influenced by all the events and people in the culture that make a child feel unsafe and unloved, giving rise to basic anxiety.

© Bettmann/Corbis

Karen Horney argued that culture plays a larger role in personality development than does biology and suggested that family environments and disturbances in early relationships lead to basic anxiety in children. Children cope with this basic anxiety by pursuing love, power, prestige, or detachment.

## Contributions and Criticisms of the Psychoanalytic Approach

Freud's contributions to psychology have been immense (Erwin, 2002). He is regarded as one of the most influential thinkers of the 20th century (Gedo, 2002). His presence is still felt among the general public through literature, arts, and the movies. His theory on dreams stimulated much research on the nature of sleep. His notion of defense mechanisms was extensively elaborated on by his daughter, Anna Freud, and his focus on coping and well-being sparked interest and research in health psychology. His ideas are evident in tests designed to measure personality (discussed later in this chapter) and in therapy approaches to help people with psychological problems (Chapter 14). Freud's basic notion of the unconscious influencing our behavior also has merit (Bargh & Morsella, 2008; Gedo, 2002; Greenwald & Draine, 1997; Kihlstrom, 1993; Westen, 1999). How many of us can say that we know why we have engaged in every single behavior we have ever produced? Isn't it possible that there are unconscious forces influencing our behavior?

Furthermore, Freud was one of the first to see the importance of early development in later adult behavior (Gedo, 2002). In the early 1900s, children were seen as mini-adults. People did not believe as strongly as we do now that how infants and children are treated influences their adult behavior. Although we know that infancy and childhood experiences do not *determine* adult behavior, as Freud asserted, his emphasis on the importance of these early years was a critical departure from accepted beliefs at that time. Through his psychosexual stages, Freud placed much emphasis on explaining the developmental nature of personality, probably more so than any other theorist. His views on sexuality and the impact of culture on sexuality continue to influence research (Hartmann, 2009; Person, 2005).

Freud's perspective has been criticized on several counts, however. First, many believe that Freud placed too much emphasis on sexual and aggressive instincts. His perspective shines very little light on environmental and social conditions that may affect personality functioning. We have just noted how many neo-Freudians diverged from Freud on this point, creating alternate views of the ego and personality that take our interactions with others into account (Horgan,

**basic anxiety**   according to Horney, the feeling of helplessness that develops in children from early relationships

1996). His ideas and themes have also been attacked for their focus on male development and perpetuation of the idea of male superiority (Person, 1990).

Much more problematic are Freud's methods of data collection and the fact that his theories cannot be readily tested experimentally (Crews, 1996). His theories are based almost entirely on case study research and his own self-analysis. His observations may not have been objective, and his case studies involved patients who were diagnosed with nervous disorders. What his patients told him may not have been accurate, and their statements were not corroborated by other sources. These issues make it difficult to generalize Freud's observations. Scientifically testing Freud's theoretical concepts is also quite challenging. Measuring the unconscious is difficult if participants are unaware of these impulses. It is equally difficult to measure psychosexual stages of development. For this reason, we cannot prove that Freud's theory is true, but we also cannot disprove it. Thus, it remains a possible explanation of personality functioning, though not as popular as it was in the past. Freud's ideas have not been supported by data from other cultures, possibly because his theories reflect the Western cultural value of individualism. They may not apply in collectivist cultures that emphasize the importance of the group (Matsumoto, 1994).

**trait approach**    a personality perspective that attempts to describe personality by emphasizing internal, biological aspects of personality called traits

**trait**    tendency to behave in a certain way across most situations

# Let's REVIEW

This section outlined the psychoanalytic perspective on personality. For a quick check of your understanding, answer these questions.

1. The psychoanalytic perspective emphasizes the influence of _____ on personality.
   a. unconscious desires   c. self-actualization
   b. traits                d. environmental factors

2. Maria often feels guilty when she engages in even the slightest offensive behavior. Freud would say that Maria has a strong _____.
   a. id                    c. superego
   b. ego                   d. collective unconscious

3. One of the major criticisms of Freud's theory concerns its _____.
   a. overemphasis on environmental and cognitive factors in explaining behavior
   b. difficulty in being experimentally tested and validated
   c. emphasis on the conscious
   d. assumption that all people are good

Answers 1. a; 2. c; 3. b

# The Trait Approach: Consistency and Stability in Personality

**LEARNING OBJECTIVES**

● Define traits, and compare the various trait approaches to understanding personality (Allport, Cattell, Eysenck, and the five factor theory).

● Discuss genetic contributions to personality, and address whether personality is consistent and stable over time.

● Indicate the strengths and weaknesses of the trait approach in explaining personality.

A second major perspective on personality is called the **trait approach**. The trait approach, like the psychoanalytic approach, focuses on internal aspects of personality. Whereas the psychoanalytic approach attempts to explain personality by focusing on unconscious forces, the trait perspective describes personality and emphasizes its biological aspects. Trait theory assumes that we all have internal **traits**, or tendencies to behave in a certain way across most situations. These traits remain relatively stable as we age and explain why individuals generally behave the same way across a variety of situations. Yet because people differ in the degree to which they possess various traits, we develop unique personalities. We will describe four major approaches to understanding these personality traits in the theories of Gordon Allport, Raymond Cattell, Hans Eysenck, and in the *five factor theory*.

**sensation seeker**    a person who by trait tends to seek out arousing activities

## Psychology Applies to Your World:

### Are You a Sensation Seeker?

One trait of particular interest to psychologists is that of sensation seeking. Some people seem to crave arousal, seeking out higher levels of arousal than the rest of us. In fact, sometimes they seek out levels of arousal that the rest of us would find *aversive*. These people are what psychologists call **sensation seekers**; they habitually tend to seek out high levels of physiological arousal by engaging in intensely stimulating experiences (Zuckerman, 1978, 1994). Some sensation seekers pursue daring activities such as mountain climbing, skydiving, bungee jumping, and fast driving, whereas others may be stimulated by engaging in problem behaviors such as drug use, aggression, or delinquency (Lynne-Landsman et al., 2010).

One theory that seeks to explain the causes of sensation seeking looks at biological differences in the brains of sensation seekers. Psychologist Marvin Zuckerman found that sensation seekers tend to have low levels of a substance called *monoamine oxidase*, or *MAO* (Zuckerman & Kuhlman, 2000). MAO is an enzyme that breaks down neurotransmitters like serotonin, dopamine, and norepinephrine (Chapter 2). One of these neurotransmitters, dopamine, seems to be responsible for motivating us to obtain rewards. The low level of MAO in the brains of sensation seekers may mean that they experience more dopamine activity than other people. Without MAO to break it down, the dopamine would remain in the synapse longer, continuing to stimulate the neuron. This increased dopamine action may be related to sensation seekers' motivation to experience reward from intense arousal.

Research examining brain region responses to high arousal stimuli between individuals high and low in sensation seeking supports this view. Individuals high in sensation seeking tend to show more activation in brain regions associated with reward and show less inhibition or the ability to regulate this activation compared to those low in sensation seeking (Joseph et al., 2009). What causes these brain differences? Current research suggests that multiple dopamine genes that we inherit may be at the heart of sensation-seeking behavior (Derringer et al., 2010).

Are you a sensation seeker? To get a feel for your level of sensation seeking, take the questionnaire in ■ TABLE 12.1. This questionnaire is only a brief version of the full Zuckerman Sensation Seeking Scale (Zuckerman, 1994). Therefore, your true level of sensation seeking may differ from that indicated by your test results. The questionnaire will give you some insight into your sensation-seeking tendencies, but please recognize that this test gives you only a rough idea of where you fall on this dimension.

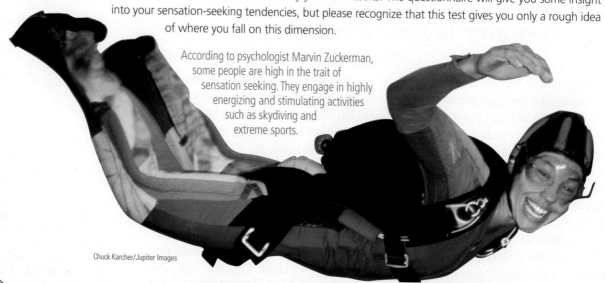

According to psychologist Marvin Zuckerman, some people are high in the trait of sensation seeking. They engage in highly energizing and stimulating activities such as skydiving and extreme sports.

Chuck Karcher/Jupiter Images

## TABLE 12.1
### Brief Sensation-Seeking Questionnaire

Answer "true" or "false" to each item listed below by circling "T" or "F." A "true" means that the item expresses your preference most of the time. A "false" means that you do not agree that the item is generally true for you. After completing the test, score your responses according to the instructions that follow the test items.

T   F   1. I would really enjoy skydiving.

T   F   2. I can imagine myself driving a sports car in a race and loving it.

T   F   3. My life is very secure and comfortable—the way I like it.

T   F   4. I usually like emotionally expressive or artistic people, even if they are sort of wild.

T   F   5. I like the idea of seeing many of the same warm, supportive faces in everyday life.

T   F   6. I like doing adventurous things and would have enjoyed being a pioneer in the early days of this country.

T   F   7. A good photograph should express peacefulness creatively.

T   F   8. The most important thing in living is fully experiencing all emotions.

T   F   9. I like creature comforts when I go on a trip or vacation.

T   F   10. Doing the same things each day really gets to me.

T   F   11. I love snuggling in front of a fire on a wintry day.

T   F   12. I would like to try several types of drugs as long as they didn't harm me permanently.

T   F   13. Drinking and being rowdy really appeals to me on weekends.

T   F   14. Rational people try to avoid dangerous situations.

T   F   15. I prefer figure A to figure B.

A

B
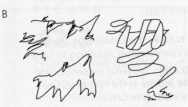

Give yourself 1 point for answering "true" to the following items: 1, 2, 4, 6, 8, 10, 12, and 13. Also give yourself 1 point for answering "false" to the following items: 3, 5, 7, 9, 11, 14, and 15. Add up your points, and compare your total to the following norms: 11–15, high sensation seeker; 6–10, moderate sensation seeker; 1–5, low sensation seeker. Bear in mind that this is a shortened version of the Sensation Seeking Scale and that it provides only a rough approximation of your status on this personality trait.

*Source: A. F. Grasha & D. S. Kirschenbaum (1986). Adjustment and competence: Concepts and applications. St. Paul, MN: West Publishing. Reprinted by permission of Anthony F. Grasha.*

## Gordon Allport's Trait Theory

Psychologist Gordon Allport (1897–1967) believed that three types of traits help us understand a person's uniqueness: *central traits*, *secondary traits*, and *cardinal traits* (Allport, 1961). **Central traits** are those tendencies we have across most situations; they are the core qualities your friends would state if they were asked to describe you. For example, if you are friendly in most situations, then friendly would be considered a central trait. We all have central traits, but the specific qualities that are considered a central trait may differ from person to person.

**Secondary traits** describe how we behave in certain situations; they are tendencies that are less consistent and more situation-specific. Many of us behave aggressively in certain situations, such as when we are frustrated or when we see others behave aggressively. Again, we all have secondary traits, but whether a specific quality is considered a secondary trait may differ from person to person.

**Cardinal traits** describe how we behave across all situations. Allport considered these a very basic and dominant element of our personalities—but he had difficulty finding cardinal traits in all people that he studied. Consequently, the validity of cardinal traits became suspect. Recall from Chapter 5 on learning and

**central traits**   according to Allport, the tendencies we have to behave in a certain way across most situations

**secondary traits**   according to Allport, the tendencies we have that are less consistent and describe how we behave in certain situations

**cardinal traits**   according to Allport, those dominant elements of our personalities that drive all of our behaviors

naïve and optimistic assumption that all people are good and are motivated toward attaining self-actualization. Critics argue that all people are not necessarily good and that humanists underestimate the capacity for evil in some individuals (Coffer & Appley, 1964; Ellis, 1959). Equally problematic is the difficulty in validating through experiments many of the humanistic concepts such as actualizing tendency, organismic valuing process, and unconditional positive regard (Burger, 2004). The major source of data for Rogers's self theory has been under scrutiny as well, as it was derived from clients' self-statements. How reliable and valid are such statements? It's possible that clients did not always present their "true" selves to Rogers and that as a listener Rogers was biased. As a result, humanistic psychology has not become as major a force in psychology as Maslow once hoped—although many consider the emergence of *positive psychology* (see Chapter 11) a rebirth of humanistic goals and its enduring legacy (Diener, Oishi, & Lucas, 2003).

# Let's REVIEW

This section presented the humanistic view of personality. For a quick check of your understanding, answer these questions.

**1.** The humanistic perspective emphasizes the influence of _____ on personality.
   a. unconscious impulses
   b. internal traits
   c. an actualizing tendency
   d. environmental and cognitive factors

**2.** Su-Ling was recently mugged. Since the mugging, she has been suspicious and paranoid. She locks her doors at night and sleeps with a night-light. Maslow would attribute Su-Ling's behavior to _____.
   a. esteem needs        c. belongingness needs
   b. safety needs        d. biological needs

**3.** Which of the following elements does Rogers believe promotes self-actualization?
   a. Unconditional positive regard
   b. Esteem
   c. Sympathy
   d. Adaptability

*Answers 1. c; 2. b; 3. a*

# Measuring Personality

## LEARNING OBJECTIVES

● Compare and contrast the advantages and disadvantages of using personality inventories, projective tests, and rating scales to measure personality.

● Describe the purpose of direct observation and the clinical interview.

We have described four different approaches to personality. Each perspective tends to employ certain tools to measure or assess personality. The results of these tests can be used in clinical settings to inform therapists about their clients' behavior, as well as in research, as the Psychology Across Generations box illustrates.

As with any tool or measuring device, it is important that the test be *reliable* and *valid*. **Reliability** refers to the consistency of a measurement tool. If we were to assess your height as an adult with a tape measure, we would want to get a consistent "reading" every time we measured your height. Personality tests also need to be reliable, or yield similar results over time. This reliability will not be perfect as we are not consistent in our behavior at all times. However, personality tests should report similar trends if they are reliable.

Measurement tools like personality tests also need to be valid. **Validity** refers to the ability of a test to measure what it says it is measuring. If a test states that it is measuring your intelligence and it does so by measuring your foot size, this test would not be valid. There is no relationship between foot size and intelligence. Notice that this test would be reliable (that is, yield a consistent measure from time to time), but it does not measure what we think of as intelligence. Therefore,

**reliability** the degree to which a test yields consistent measurements of a trait

**validity** the degree to which a test measures the trait that it was designed to measure

## Psychology Across Generations:

### Generation Me

Do you think you are a special or important person? Can you live your life any way you want to? San Diego State psychology professor Jean Twenge and her colleagues have conducted a number of studies (Twenge & Campbell, 2009; Twenge & Foster, 2008, 2010; Twenge et al., 2008a, 2008b) comparing the responses of today's college students with those of previous decades who completed personality questionnaires with statements such as these. Her analysis of 85 samples of college students between 1982 and 2009 found that today's college students are more likely to answer yes to these types of questions. Her results are part of a larger study investigating the degree to which particular personality traits have changed across generations.

Twenge's research suggests that today's young people between the ages of 18 and 25 are higher in the trait of *narcissism*, a very positive and inflated view of the self in which you believe you are important and have a high opinion of yourself. Twenge and other researchers have also found increases in traits related to narcissism, such as extraversion (Scollon & Diener, 2006; Twenge, 2001) and self-esteem (Twenge & Campbell, 2001), in today's college generation. Twenge reasons that as American society has become more individualistic and materialistic over the past few decades, it has encouraged young people to embrace these same traits in their personalities, resulting in more confidence, higher self-esteem, and more self-importance. As a result, she has titled one of her books *Generation Me* (2006).

Not everyone agrees with Twenge. Other researchers conducting surveys on large samples of high school seniors (Trzesniewski & Donnellan, 2010) and college students (Roberts, Edmonds, & Grijalva, 2010; Trzesniewski, Donnellan, & Robins, 2008) have found little evidence of increases in self-esteem and narcissism over time, or only small increases, and argue that these traits typically peak in young adulthood as a result of developmental processes and not because of cultural changes. The debate on changes in narcissism and Generation Me is sure to continue.

---

### You Asked...

*How can you tell what kind of personality a person has?*

BRITTANY BRYANT, STUDENT

personality tests should measure what we believe personality to be.

Each of the four major perspectives has developed its own way of measuring personality. These measures include *personality inventories*, *projective tests*, *rating scales*, and *clinical interviews*.

---

## Personality Inventories: Mark Which One Best Describes You

**Personality inventories** are objective paper-and-pencil or computerized self-report forms. You are typically asked to indicate how well a statement describes you or to answer true or false to a specific statement. For example, in college settings, many students have completed the *Myers-Briggs Personality Inventory*. This test assesses an individual's personality on four different dimensions. In clinical settings, the most frequently used personality inventory is the **Minnesota Multiphasic Personality Inventory (MMPI-2)**.

The MMPI-2 is a 567-item true–false questionnaire that takes about 1 hour to complete. The questions describe a wide range of behaviors (■ TABLE 12.4). The purpose

**personality inventory** an objective paper-and-pencil or computerized self-report form that measures personality on several dimensions

**Minnesota Multiphasic [mul-tee-FAZE-ick] Personality Inventory (MMPI-2)** a personality inventory that is designed to identify problem areas of functioning in an individual's personality

## TABLE 12.4
## Sample MMPI-2 Items

| | | |
|---|---|---|
| I have trouble with my bowel movements. | T | F |
| I do not sleep well. | T | F |
| At parties, I sit by myself or with one other person. | T | F |
| A lot of people have it in for me. | T | F |
| In school, I was frequently in trouble for acting up. | T | F |
| I am anxious most of the time. | T | F |
| I hear strange things that others do not hear. | T | F |
| I am a very important person. | T | F |

**projective test**   a less structured and subjective personality test in which an individual is shown an ambiguous stimulus and is asked to describe what he or she sees

**Rorschach [ROAR-shock] inkblot test**   a projective personality test consisting of 10 ambiguous inkblots in which a person is asked to describe what he or she sees; the person's responses are then coded for consistent themes and issues

**F I G U R E**

## 12.5

### Sample Rorschach Inkblot

After being shown an inkblot like this one, the person indicates what he or she sees on the card.

of the MMPI-2 is to identify problem areas of functioning in an individual's personality. It is organized into 10 groups of items, called *clinical scales*. These scales measure patterns of responses or traits associated with specific psychological disorders such as depression, paranoia, and schizophrenia. A person's response patterns are reviewed to see whether they resemble the pattern of responses from groups of people who have specific mental health disorders. Interpreting the MMPI-2 involves comparing the test taker's responses to those of the "norming" population.

As part of its construction, the MMPI-2 was given to thousands of people, called a *norming group*. Individuals in the norming group included people who had no psychological disorders and people who had particular disorders. In this way the test constructors could see how frequently someone without the disorder would respond "true" to these items and how frequently someone with the psychological disorder would respond "true." The first group established the average, or "normal," number of items for each of these clinical scales, whereas the second group gave an indication of what would be considered problematic functioning. A psychologist is interested in examining any areas of your personality that fall outside the normal range. These areas would be considered problem areas of your personality and might suggest issues for therapy.

Another widely used personality inventory is the *California Psychological Inventory (CPI)*. The CPI contains 434 true–false items, including 194 from the original MMPI. Unlike the MMPI, the CPI was developed to measure positive traits such as sociability, independence, and responsibility in healthy individuals. The CPI norming groups did not contain people who had been diagnosed with psychological problems.

One of the main problems with self-report measures such as the MMPI-2 and CPI is the test taker's honesty or truthfulness. For this reason, both the MMPI-2 and CPI contain *validity scales* to assess the truthfulness of the individual's responses.

## Projective Tests: Tell Me What You See

Another type of tool used to measure personality, the **projective test**, is less structured than the personality inventory. When taking this test, you are shown an ambiguous image and then asked to describe what you see or to tell a story about the picture. Such tests rely on the idea that whatever stories, motives, or explanations you offer reflect your own issues and concerns, projected onto the image.

One of the most famous projective tests is the **Rorschach inkblot test**. The Rorschach test consists of 10 inkblots on cards. As each card is presented, you indicate what images you see. Your responses are then coded according to specific guidelines to decrease subjectivity and enhance the validity of the results. A sample card is shown in ■ FIGURE 12.5.

Another widely used projective test is the **Thematic Apperception Test (TAT)**. In the TAT, you are shown images that are not as ambiguous as inkblots yet still allow for a variety of interpretations. You are asked to tell a story about the image, and your responses are then coded for any consistent themes, emotions, or issues. A sample TAT image is depicted in ■ FIGURE 12.6. After being shown this image, a client might relate the following story: "It's a picture of a young man who has been waiting several hours at a park for his partner to arrive. He is tired, anxious, and angry. He is hoping that nothing bad has happened to his partner. He is also hoping that he wasn't stood up."

The purpose of projective tests is similar to that of personality inventories. Psychologists want to pinpoint healthy and unhealthy areas of functioning in the individual being tested. However, unlike personality inventories, projective tests are derived from the psychoanalytic perspective; the images and stories described are thought to reflect underlying unconscious urges and desires. Because projective tests are more subject to the interpretation of the clinician than are personality inventories, coding systems have been devised to decrease variation in interpretation. However, research suggests that they are less reliable than objective tests in measuring personality (Aiken, 1996; Lilienfeld, Wood, & Garb, 2000; T. B. Rogers, 1995). Projective tests are most useful for identifying themes in a person's life or for delineating an individual's problem-solving style.

## Rating Scales and Direct Observation

A third type of tool used by psychologists to measure personality is the *rating scale*. Rating scales are formatted similarly to checklists. You check off the statements or behaviors that most apply to you. Because the person being evaluated may not answer the statements truthfully, teachers, parents, partners, and clinicians can also complete rating scales on the person being evaluated. These alternate perspectives minimize the self-distortions that are associated with self-report instruments.

Psychologists may also rely on directly observing a client's behavior and interactions with others to assess personality. Closely watching how you behave in particular situations can be helpful in determining what happens before and after your responses. Such information is particularly important to clinicians who favor a social cognitive approach and who want to understand the social or environmental factors that may be influencing problem behavior.

**FIGURE**

# 12.6

## Sample Thematic Apperception (TAT) Card

In taking the TAT, a person is asked to tell a story about a scene such as this one.

**Thematic Apperception [thee-MAT-ick ap-per-SEP-shun] Test (TAT)** a projective personality test consisting of a series of pictures in which the respondent is asked to tell a story about each scene; the responses are then coded for consistent themes and issues

---

## YOUR TURN   Active Learning

Psychologists may find rating scales on self-esteem and self-concept useful to understanding how a person perceives reality and the degree to which one's real self is congruent with one's ideal self. Take a moment to complete the self-esteem scale provided in ■ TABLE 12.5.

### TABLE 12.5
### Rosenberg Self-Esteem Scale

Below is a list of statements dealing with your general feelings about yourself. If you Strongly Agree, circle SA. If you Agree with the statement, circle A. If you Disagree, circle D. If you Strongly Disagree, circle SD.

| | | STRONGLY AGREE | AGREE | DISAGREE | STRONGLY DISAGREE |
|---|---|---|---|---|---|
| 1. | I feel that I'm a person of worth, at least on an equal plane with others. | SA | A | D | SD |
| 2. | I feel that I have a number of good qualities. | SA | A | D | SD |
| 3. | All in all, I am inclined to feel that I am a failure. | SA | A | D | SD |
| 4. | I am able to do things as well as most other people. | SA | A | D | SD |
| 5. | I feel I do not have much to be proud of. | SA | A | D | SD |

(continued)

# LOOK BACK
## AT What You've LEARNED

**12**

**Personality** is the unique collection of attitudes, emotions, thoughts, habits, impulses, and behaviors that defines how a person typically behaves across situations.

## The Psychoanalytic Approach: Sigmund Freud and the Neo-Freudians

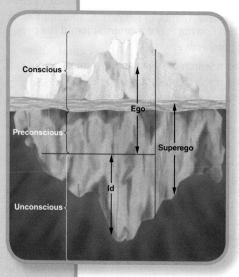

- Emphasizes unconscious aspects of personality. It proposes that personality operates at the **conscious**, **preconscious**, and **unconscious** levels.

- According to Freud, personality is comprised of the unconscious **id** that operates according to the **pleasure principle**, the conscious **ego** that operates according to the **reality principle**, and the moral directives of the **superego**.

- For Freud, personality develops through a series of five psychosexual stages (**oral, anal, phallic, latency, genital**) that represent a complex interaction between natural sexual urges and our socialization experiences.

- Neo-Freudians such as Jung, Adler, and Horney placed less emphasis on the role of the instinctual impulses in motivating behavior.

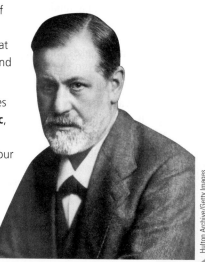

Hulton Archive/Getty Images

## The Trait Approach: Consistency and Stability in Personality

- Attempts to describe personality by identifying the internal **traits**, or tendencies that we have across most situations.

- Allport classified traits into three types: **central**, **cardinal**, and **secondary** traits.

- Cattell's factor analysis of traits yielded 16 **source traits** that could be measured in everyone. Eysenck proposed three universal traits in his PEN model: **psychoticism**, **extraversion**, and **neuroticism**.

- Costa and McCrae's **five factor theory** proposes five core universal traits: openness, conscientiousness, extraversion, agreeableness, and neuroticism (OCEAN).

- Research suggests a complex interaction between genes and the environment in producing personality. Some traits remain stable over the course of adulthood, but situational factors also influence the consistency of traits.

© Ashley Cooper/Alamy

# WHAT IS PERSONALITY, and HOW DO WE MEASURE It?

## The Social Cognitive Approach:
## The Environment and Patterns of Thought

- Evaluates environmental and cognitive factors that influence personality.

- Bandura's **reciprocal determinism** suggests that personality is due to the constant interaction between one's environment, one's behavior, and one's thoughts. A critical cognitive element is **self-efficacy**, or the expectation one has for success in a given situation.

- Rotter believes that one's **locus of control**, or one's expectations of whether the outcome of an event is due to internal or external forces, influences personality.

- The **social cognitive approach** is comprehensive, has many applications, and is easily tested experimentally.

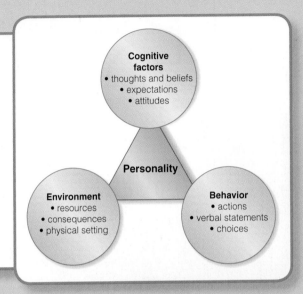

## The Humanistic Approach:
## Free Will and Self-Actualization

- Emphasizes one's drive toward uniqueness and **self-actualization**.

- Maslow believed that the pathway to self-actualization lies in fulfilling a hierarchy of needs, with physical needs at the bottom and psychological needs at the top.

- Rogers's self theory emphasizes how one's **self-concept**, or perception of self, is influenced by the standards and values of others, most notably the degree to which we perceive and receive **unconditional positive regard** from others.

- The **humanistic approach** promotes self-awareness and positive interactions with others, and its ideas have been incorporated into several therapy approaches.

© Roger Ressmeyer/Corbis

## Measuring Personality

- Tools that assess personality should be **reliable** and **valid**.

- **Personality inventories** such as the **MMPI-2** and CPI are objective paper-and-pencil or computerized self-report forms that can reliably describe a person's traits if answered honestly.

- **Projective tests** such as the **Rorschach inkblot test** and the **Thematic Apperception Test** are less structured tests in which a person is shown an ambiguous image and asked to describe it. A person's responses are believed to reflect underlying unconscious concerns, according to the psychoanalytic perspective.

- Psychologists may also use rating scales and direct observation to measure behaviors and interactions with others.

- The focus of the **clinical interview** is to identify the difficulty in functioning that a person is experiencing.

493

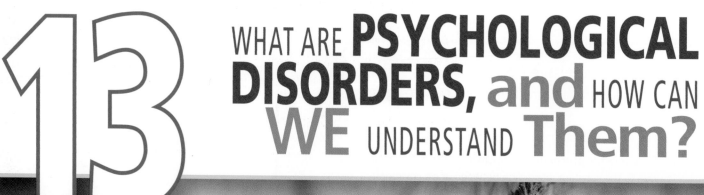

# 13 WHAT ARE **PSYCHOLOGICAL DISORDERS, and** HOW CAN **WE** UNDERSTAND **Them?**

# Chapter Outline

*After years of working at a bank,* Tawnya Brown decided to enroll in college to pursue a nursing degree. One of the first classes she took was a general psychology course. Although Tawnya could see the usefulness of some course topics such as development or biology, she didn't think that learning about psychological disorders would be of much value—it's not like she was going into psychiatry or counseling. Since then she has noticed how much she relies on this information in several areas of her life.

Tawnya serves on a hospital advisory board as an advocate for patients, many of whom have psychological disorders. By understanding the nature of these disorders, Tawnya can make sure that appropriate mental health services are included as a part of their patient care. Tawnya also volunteers as a facilitator for a women's support group in the community. Many of these women have experienced significant trauma in their lives and as a result experience depression and/or abuse drugs. Tawnya's knowledge of psychological disorders helps her better understand these women. She can now recognize the different symptoms of the psychological disorders and see the impact of negative life experiences on mental health.

This chapter outlines several major categories of psychological disorders and explains the symptoms used to diagnose particular disorders. For each type of disorder, we will consider the possible reasons why a person behaves this way. Although the research presented may seem overwhelming at times, keep in mind that these explanations are closely tied to topics with which you are already familiar. For example, many of the symptoms of mental health disorders are physical in nature, involving brain functioning, neurotransmitters, hormones, and genetics—biological factors that were introduced in Chapter 2. Many of the symptoms also relate to psychological concepts such as learning, cognition, personality, and emotions—again, topics that

*Tawnya Brown's knowledge of psychological disorders has helped her in several areas of her life.*

© Ellen Pastorino

have been addressed in previous chapters. Furthermore, we will see that certain disorders are more common among certain segments of the population. Your familiarity with previous discussions on gender, race, and culture will assist you in understanding the influence of these social factors on mental health.

## What Is Abnormal Behavior?

**LEARNING OBJECTIVES**

- Identify the criteria that psychologists use for determining abnormal behavior.

- Indicate the lifetime and annual prevalence rates of mental health disorders, and describe gender differences in the types of psychological disorders.

- Compare and contrast the varying perspectives on explaining psychological disorders, and formulate a biopsychosocial or integrated perspective to explain a particular behavior.

Autism is a childhood disorder that is marked by disordered communication.

© Michael Macor/San Francisco Chronicle/Corbis

Psychologists primarily use four main criteria when distinguishing normal from abnormal behavior:

1. *Statistical infrequency.* If we judge normal as what most people do, then one criterion that may be used to gauge abnormality is engaging in a behavior a lot less frequently than others. For example, it is considered crucial for survival to ingest a minimum amount of food per day. People who engage in this behavior a lot less than most people—as in the case of people with anorexia—would qualify as abnormal. Persons with autism engage in social communication far less than most people. As such, their behavior may be considered abnormal. Statistical infrequency can also include engaging in a behavior that most people do not. For example, believing that you are from another planet or galaxy is a thought that most people do not have. It represents an unusual, or statistically infrequent, thought and therefore may be judged as abnormal. However, there are problems with using the criterion of statistical infrequency. For example, only one person holds the record for running a mile the fastest; this person is certainly atypical but not necessarily abnormal.

2. *Violation of social norms.* Another measure of abnormality is to assess whether the behavior violates social norms of how people are supposed to behave. However, it is extremely important to emphasize that social norms vary widely across cultures, within cultures, and across historical times. What is considered socially acceptable in San Francisco may be considered unacceptable in Keokuk, Iowa. Similarly, what was deemed unacceptable in the 1950s may be considered acceptable today. For example, changing views on homosexuality in part influenced the American Psychiatric Association to remove homosexuality from its list of psychological disorders in 1973. Because social norms vary so widely, judging the abnormality of behavior on this criterion alone is especially problematic.

3. *Personal distress.* This criterion focuses on whether a behavior causes great personal distress to the individual. Often people seek treatment when a behavior causes such suffering. However, problems can also arise from judging a behavior by this criterion alone. A person may abuse one or more people and not be distressed by such behavior, although it causes great harm to others.

4. *Level of impairment.* Because each of these criteria by itself is not adequate in defining abnormality, many psychologists find that combining them and assessing whether a behavior *interferes with a person's ability to function and/or causes distress to that person or others* may best define abnormality (Wakefield, 1992).

## Prevalence of Psychological Disorders

An estimated 26% of Americans 18 and older will be diagnosed with a mental health disorder in any given year (Kessler, Chiu, et al., 2005). Lifetime prevalence estimates are quite a bit higher, with more than half of U.S. adults meeting the criteria for a mental health disorder at some time in their lives (NCS-R, 2007; see ■ FIGURE

13.1). And yet, this may be a conservative estimate (Moffitt et al., 2009). Mental health disorders are the leading cause of disability in the United States and Canada for people between the ages of 15 and 44 (World Health Organization, 2004). Although there is little overall gender difference in the lifetime risk of a psychological disorder, males and females do show differences in the types of psychological disorders they are more likely to experience (NCS-R, 2007; see ■ FIGURE 13.2). The Millennial generation in particular might be at risk for psychological distress, as the Psychology Across Generations box (p. 498) explores. Consequently, it is likely that you or someone close to you will at some time experience a mental health disorder. Being familiar with psychology's current understanding of such behavior may help you manage such a situation.

## Explaining Abnormal Behavior: Perspectives Revisited

> ### You Asked...
> What are the causes of psychological disorders?
> DAVID MELENDEZ, STUDENT

Since the beginning of recorded history, doctors and philosophers have tried to understand *why* people exhibit abnormal behavior. Today, Western cultures lean toward three main models or approaches for understanding abnormal behavior: *biological* theories, *psychological* theories, and *social* or *cultural* theories.

## BIOLOGICAL THEORIES: THE MEDICAL MODEL

Biological theories attribute abnormal behavior to some physical process: genetics, an imbalance in hormones or neurotransmitters, or some brain or bodily dysfunction.

> ### You Asked...
> What are the most common psychological disorders for men and women?
> KIARA SUAREZ, STUDENT

**FIGURE**

# 13.1

### Lifetime Prevalence of Psychological Disorders

More than half of U.S. adults will be diagnosed with a psychological disorder at some time in their lives.

*Source: National Comorbidity Survey Replication data. Table 1. Updated 2007. http://www.hcp.med.harvard.edu/ncs*

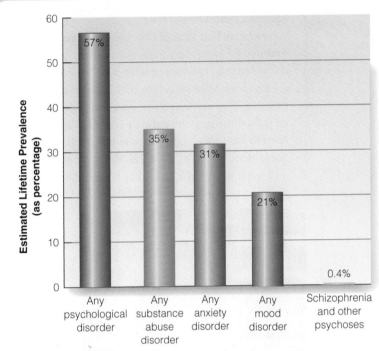

**FIGURE**

# 13.2

### Prevalence of Depression, Anxiety, Substance Abuse, and Antisocial Personality Disorder in Women and Men

Males and females differ in the types of psychological disorders they are more likely to experience.

*Source: National Comorbidity Survey Replication data. Table 1. Updated 2007. http://www.hcp.med.harvard.edu/ncs*

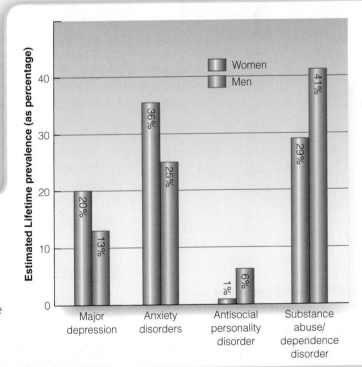

## Psychology Across Generations:

### Millennials and Psychological Distress

Rates of mental illness have risen dramatically in the last 10 to 15 years among high school and college students (Twenge, 2006). College psychological counseling is on the rise, and suicide is the third leading cause of death among those aged 15 to 24 (CDC, 2009c). In addition, 81% of college mental health service directors reported an increase in students with serious psychological problems compared with 5 years ago (Erdur-Baker et al., 2006). Self-rated emotional health for first-year college students is at its lowest level since it was first assessed 25 years ago (Pryor et al., 2010). Data from national surveys indicate that roughly 19% of females and 16% of males between the ages of 12 and 17 meet the criteria for at least one psychological disorder (Kilpatrick et al., 2003). Another national survey found that 22% of U.S. teens were likely to experience a disorder with *severe* impairment or distress at some time in their lives (Merikangas et al., 2010). Are Millennials (adults born after 1980) more likely to be psychologically distressed than previous generations? Not necessarily.

Certainly, Millennials face challenges that may be unique to their generation. During their formative years, for example, they witnessed many traumas—September 11th, Hurricane Katrina, the Virginia Tech massacre, the BP oil spill—broadcast immediately on their TVs or over the Internet. They are also more likely than previous generations to have grown up in a single-parent family (Pew Research Center, 2010). According to the Youth Risk Behavior Surveillance (Eaton et al., 2010), the number of obese or overweight teens has increased significantly since 1999, and fewer young people are physically active. Millennials are delaying marriage longer than previous generations,

which means they have more time to experience romantic failure and heartbreak (Twenge, 2006). They are also attending college in higher numbers than previous generations, increasing feelings of stress and anxiety (Pew Research Center, 2010). Meanwhile, they have high expectations for success and may be overly dependent on the opinions of parents, teachers, and other significant people in their lives (Levine, 2006). Any and all of these circumstances put an individual at risk for mental illness.

Yet much has also changed in our understanding and assessment of mental health. Public awareness of mental disorders in youth has increased, and methods for assessing mental illness in young people have improved dramatically (Costello, Egger, & Angold, 2005). Psychological services are more open to young people, and the stigma surrounding mental illness is less today than it was for previous generations, so that Millennials may be less reluctant to seek treatment. Emotional well-being also tends to improve from early to late adulthood (Carstensen et al., 2011; Turk Charles, Reynolds, & Gatz, 2001), raising the possibility that this is not a generational difference but rather a developmental difference in emotional stability. As the Millennial generation gets older, we will be able to measure if this trend in psychological distress continues.

The biological perspective is also known as the **medical model** because psychological disorders are viewed as similar to physical diseases. As such, they can be diagnosed, treated, or cured in much the same way as other physical illnesses by prescribing medications or through surgery.

## PSYCHOLOGICAL THEORIES: HUMANE TREATMENT AND PSYCHOLOGICAL PROCESSES

**medical model** perspective that views psychological disorders as similar to physical diseases; they result from biological disturbances and can be diagnosed, treated, and cured like physical illnesses

Psychological theories attribute abnormal behavior to internal or external stressors. Recall from the previous chapter on personality that four perspectives predominate:

- *The psychoanalytic perspective.* This perspective attributes abnormal behavior to unresolved unconscious conflicts. According to Freud, psychological disorders result from the conflict between the unconscious sexual and aggressive instinctual desires of the id and the outward demands of society. Newer theories, referred to as *psychodynamic* theories, developed by Freud's followers such as Alfred Adler and Karen Horney, downplay the role of sexual and aggressive instincts and instead emphasize the role of the ego and interpersonal relationships in maintaining or restoring psychological health.

- *The social learning perspective.* Learning theorists (particularly B. F. Skinner and his successors) explain abnormal behavior as a result of the same learning processes that produce normal behavior—classical conditioning, operant conditioning, and social learning. A person's responses to stimuli in the environment and the consequences of these behaviors are what lead to abnormal behavior. A person's past learning and modeling along with current experiences can explain psychological disorders.

- *The cognitive perspective.* This perspective emphasizes the role of thoughts, expectations, assumptions, and other mental processes in abnormal behavior. Think about the little voice inside of you that comments on your behavior. Does it encourage you to do well, or does it criticize you for your stupidity? Is it possible that such internal messages influence your behavior? The cognitive perspective maintains that they do.

- *The humanistic perspective.* Humanists like Carl Rogers see abnormal behavior as resulting from a distorted perception of the self and reality. When people lose touch with their personal values and their sense of self, or when they fail to fulfill their basic biological and psychological needs, they cannot attain self-actualization. Instead, they experience personal distress and are more likely to engage in maladaptive behavior.

## SOCIOCULTURAL THEORIES: THE INDIVIDUAL IN CONTEXT

Sociocultural theories emphasize social or cultural factors that may play a role in psychological disorders. Such a perspective argues that internal biological and psychological processes can be understood only in the context of the larger society and culture that shape and influence people's behavior. Abnormal behavior, therefore, can be fully understood only when social factors such as age, race, gender, social roles, and socioeconomic status are taken into account. In addition, social conditions such as poverty, discrimination, and environmental stressors must be looked at when evaluating abnormal behavior (e.g. Zvolensky et al., 2010).

## A BIOPSYCHOSOCIAL MODEL: INTEGRATING PERSPECTIVES

Despite decades of research, no single theory or perspective is correct. It is only by integrating all the perspectives that our explanations of abnormality become comprehensive. We often hear in the popular press and in television commercials that a psychological disorder such as depression or anxiety is caused by "a specific gene" or "a chemical imbalance." But such reports are too simplistic to explain the complexity of mental illness. Most psychological disorders result from a combination of biological, psychological, and social factors (hence the name of the *biopsychosocial model*); they do not have just one cause.

For example, as we will soon see, people diagnosed with major depression often show changes in brain chemistry—a biological factor. They also are likely to engage in

Poverty and adverse environments are important sociocultural factors that must be looked at when evaluating abnormal behavior.

© Owen Franken/Corbis

a negative pattern of thinking, a psychological factor. In addition, major depression is more likely to be diagnosed in women—a sociocultural factor. Current research in psychology focuses on understanding how these forces operate together, much as the pieces of a jigsaw puzzle fit together.

## Let's REVIEW

In this section, we outlined the criteria used to define abnormal behavior, indicated the prevalence of psychological disorders, and reviewed perspectives on explaining abnormal behavior. For a quick check of your understanding, answer these questions.

**1.** Susan enjoys eating garbage when she is hungry. By which criteria can Susan's behavior be considered abnormal?
   **a.** Danger to others
   **b.** Violates social norms
   **c.** Personal distress
   **d.** All of the above

**2.** What is the likelihood that you or someone close to you will be diagnosed with a psychological disorder sometime in your life?
   **a.** About 15%
   **b.** About 25%
   **c.** About 50%
   **d.** About 75%

**3.** Dr. Kwan believes that Ken's abnormal behavior has resulted from a distorted sense of self and a loss of personal values. Dr. Kwan is adopting which perspective?
   **a.** Humanistic
   **b.** Psychoanalytic
   **c.** Learning
   **d.** Cognitive

*Answers 1. b; 2. c; 3. a*

## LEARNING OBJECTIVES

- Describe the five dimensions or axes of the *DSM* model.
- Identify the strengths and weaknesses of the *DSM* model.

# The *DSM* Model for Classifying Abnormal Behavior

**You Asked...**

*What do psychologists look at in order to diagnose someone with a psychological disorder?*

CARLA BELLIARD, STUDENT

DIAGNOSTIC AND STATISTICAL MANUAL OF MENTAL DISORDERS

FOURTH EDITION

TEXT REVISION

DSM-IV-TR

AMERICAN PSYCHIATRIC ASSOCIATION

The *Diagnostic and Statistical Manual* (*DSM*) describes the specific symptoms that must be present in order for someone to be diagnosed with a specific mental health disorder.

In 1952, the American Psychiatric Association (APA) published a book listing the symptoms that must be shown in order for a person to be diagnosed with a specific psychological disorder. More than 50 years later, the **Diagnostic and Statistical Manual of Mental Disorders** (**DSM**) is in its fourth edition, published in 1994. In 2000, the APA did a text revision (TR) to clarify the diagnosis of some psychological disorders. This most recent edition, known as the *DSM-IV-TR*, lists specific and concrete criteria for diagnosing nearly 400 disorders in children, adolescents, and adults. It also indicates the length of time that a person must show these symptoms to qualify for a diagnosis. These criteria require that the symptoms interfere with the person's ability to function, adopting the maladaptive criterion that we discussed at the start of this chapter and that is accepted by many professionals today. However, the current version of the *DSM* does not speculate as to the causes of the individual's behavior—it is *atheoretical*. This atheoretical position underscores the complex nature of the causes of mental illness. The preparatory work for the next edition of the *DSM* (*DSM-5*) has begun, and it is due to be published in 2013. Here we outline the general structure of the *DSM* and describe its strengths and weaknesses.

## A Multidimensional Evaluation

With the third edition of the *DSM*, published in 1980, clinicians began to evaluate patients along five dimensions or *axes*, listed in ■ TABLE 13.1. Axis I includes 15 major categories of psychological disorders. These disorders are the focus of this chapter and are listed in ■ TABLE 13.2. The multiaxial system of the *DSM* attempts to provide as comprehensive a picture as possible of a person's behavior.

## TABLE 13.1
### *DSM-IV-TR* Diagnostic Axes

| | **Axis I** |
|---|---|
| **Clinical disorders** | Major categories of mental disorders, including depression, anxiety disorders, phobias, amnesia, substance abuse, and schizophrenia (see Table 13.2). |

| | **Axis II** |
|---|---|
| **Personality disorders; mental retardation** | Lifelong conditions that negatively affect a person's ability to function. Divided into two major classes: *mental retardation* and *personality disorders* (see Table 13.6, p. 531). |

| | **Axis III** |
|---|---|
| **General medical conditions** | Physical problems or conditions—such as cancer diagnosis and treatment, diabetes, and arthritis—that may influence a person's mental health and that must also be considered when medication is prescribed. |

| | **Axis IV** |
|---|---|
| **Psychosocial and environmental problems** | *Psychosocial* problems might include problems holding a job or staying in school, or lack of social support. *Environmental* problems might include physical or sexual abuse, or experiencing a traumatic event. |

| | **Axis V** |
|---|---|
| **Global assessment functioning** | A numerical scale for evaluating a person's level of functioning. A rating of 90 indicates a person who is functioning very well in all areas of life, has minimal symptoms, if any, and is experiencing only everyday problems. At a rating of 50, a person shows serious symptoms or one or more problems with relationships, work, or school, including possible suicidal thoughts and obsessional behavior. |

Reprinted with permission from the Diagnostic and Statistical Manual of Mental Disorders, *Fourth Edition, Text Revision, Copyright 2000. American Psychiatric Association.*

## How Good Is the *DSM* Model?

How *reliable* and *valid* is the *DSM* model? Recall from Chapter 12 that *reliability* refers to the consistency of a measurement system. We would expect two different clinicians to give a similar judgment or a consistent rating when presented with the same symptoms. Similar diagnoses should also be made when different people exhibit the same symptoms.

*Validity* refers to how well a rating system does what it was intended to do; it refers to the accuracy of the test. We would expect that the *DSM* model should be accurate in diagnosing people who are having difficulty functioning. In addition, it should be accurate in the label it applies to a person's condition. People who are depressed should be diagnosed as depressed, and people addicted to drugs should be diagnosed as having a substance abuse problem.

**Diagnostic and Statistical Manual of Mental Disorders (DSM)**
a book published by the American Psychiatric Association that lists the criteria for close to 400 mental health disorders

**TABLE 13.2**

*DSM-IV-TR* Axis I Major Categories of Clinical Disorders

| AXIS I MAJOR CATEGORY | SOME INCLUDED DISORDERS | EXAMPLES |
|---|---|---|
| Disorders usually first diagnosed in infancy, childhood, or adolescence | • Learning disorders<br>• Pervasive developmental disorders<br>• Disruptive behavior and attention deficit disorders<br>• Tic disorders<br>• Communication disorders | Attention deficit disorder, autism, enuresis (bedwetting), stuttering, difficulty in academic skills |
| Delirium, dementia, amnesia, and other cognitive disorders | • Deliria<br>• Dementias<br>• Amnesic disorders | Delirium (due to a general medical condition or substance induced), dementia (Alzheimer's), amnesia (due to a general medical condition or substance induced) |
| Substance-related disorders (see Chapter 4) | • Alcohol use disorders    • Inhalant use disorders<br>• Cocaine use disorders    • Polysubstance use disorders | Alcoholism, cocaine or crack addiction, use of inhalants (sniffing glue or paint) |
| Schizophrenia and other psychotic disorders (see Table 13.5, p. 527) | • Schizophrenia<br>• Delusional disorder<br>• Brief psychotic disorder (one major symptom of psychosis that lasts less than 1 month; often in reaction to a stressor)<br>• Psychotic disorder due to a general medical condition | Paranoid type, catatonic |
| Mood disorders | • Depressive disorders    • Substance-induced mood disorder<br>• Bipolar disorders | Major depressive disorder, dysthymic disorder, bipolar disorder, cyclothymic disorder |
| Anxiety disorders (see You Review 13.1, p. 508) | • Panic disorder<br>• Agoraphobia without history of panic disorder<br>• Specific phobia (simple phobia)<br>• Obsessive-compulsive disorder<br>• Posttraumatic stress disorder<br>• Generalized anxiety disorder | Panic disorder without agoraphobia, acrophobia |
| Somatoform disorders (see Table 13.4, p. 514) | • Conversion disorder    • Body dysmorphic disorder<br>• Hypochondriasis    • Pain disorder | |
| Dissociative disorders (see Table 13.3, p. 512) | • Dissociative amnesia    • Dissociative identity disorder<br>• Dissociative fugue disorder | |
| Sexual and gender identity disorders | • Sexual dysfunction    • Gender identity disorder<br>• Paraphilias | Sexual aversion disorder, male erectile disorder, fetishism, pedophilia |
| Eating disorders (see Chapter 8) | • Anorexia nervosa    • Bulimia nervosa | Binge eating disorder |
| Sleep disorders (see Chapter 4) | • Primary sleep disorders    • Dyssomnia not otherwise specified | Sleepwalking disorder, narcolepsy, primary insomnia |
| Factitious disorders | • Factitious disorder (deliberately faking a physical or psychological disorder) | |
| Impulse control disorders not elsewhere classified | • Kleptomania (recurrent failure to control the urge to steal things that are not needed)<br>• Pyromania (recurrent failure to control the urge to set fires)<br>• Pathological gambling | |
| Adjustment disorder | • Adjustment disorder with anxiety<br>• Adjustment disorder with disturbance of conduct (maladaptive reactions to a known stressor such as a family crisis that begins within 3 months of the stressor but does not last longer than 6 months) | |
| Other conditions that may be a focus of clinical attention | • Medication-induced movement disorders<br>• Relational problems<br>• Problems related to abuse or neglect | Parent–child relational problems, occupational problems, borderline intellectual functioning |

*Reprinted with permission from the Diagnostic and Statistical Manual of Mental Disorders, Fourth Edition, Text Revision, Copyright 2000. American Psychiatric Association.*

The numerous revisions of the *DSM* have attempted to improve its reliability and validity. As a result, the reliability and validity for many of the Axis I clinical disorders are very high (T. A. Brown et al., 2001; Hasin et al., 2006; Lahey et al., 2004). However, the reliability of Axis II personality disorders is considered extremely low, calling into question the validity of diagnosing the personality disorders (Clark, 2007; Falkum, Pedersen, & Karterud, 2009: Jablensky, 2002; Widiger, 2003; Widiger & Trull, 2007; Zanarini et al., 2000). Future revisions of the *DSM* model will need to address such inadequacies.

Having a standard system such as the *DSM* does not guarantee an accurate diagnosis. Making diagnostic judgments will always involve some subjectivity and personal bias on the part of the clinician, as people's symptoms often do not fit neatly into one category. Biases having to do with gender, race, or culture—whether conscious or unconscious—can also skew a diagnosis (Jane et al., 2007; Skodol & Bender, 2003; Widiger & Chaynes, 2003).

Critics of the *DSM* model also point out the possible negative effects of labeling someone with a psychological disorder (Baumann, 2007; Grover, 2005). A diagnostic label may serve as a *self-fulfilling prophecy*, encouraging a person to behave in a way that is consistent with the disorder. Others in the person's environment may also treat the person in a way that encourages the symptoms of the disorder. We as a society tend to treat people with any diagnostic label negatively, perhaps increasing their maladaptive functioning through prejudice and discrimination. Such negative treatment may persist even after the person's behavior returns to normal (Rosenhan, 1973; Szasz, 1987).

The *DSM* model is not perfect and can provide only a general description of the problem a person is experiencing. It does not consider the uniqueness of each individual, nor can it tell us how this person will behave in the future. Yet the DSM provides a useful framework and common language for clinicians and researchers to diagnose and study people with mental health problems. Its multiaxial system offers more information about patients than a simple diagnosis can provide to help clinicians identify appropriate treatments. Having a common language also allows researchers to more effectively study the possible underlying causes of psychological disorders. Keep in mind the advantages and criticisms of the *DSM* system as we review some of the more prevalent and more interesting mental health disorders, starting with the anxiety disorders.

## Let's REVIEW

This section presented the general structure of the *DSM* model and reviewed its strengths and weaknesses. For a quick check of your understanding, answer these questions.

---

**1.** The purpose of the *DSM* is to _____.
   a. explain the causes of psychological disorders
   b. describe the symptoms of psychological disorders
   c. indicate the frequency of psychological disorders
   d. prescribe treatment methods for psychological disorders

**2.** The *DSM* model relies mainly on which criterion of abnormality?
   a. Statistical infrequency   c. Inability to function
   b. Violation of social norms   d. Mental insanity

**3.** Which of the following is *not* information gained by using the multiaxial system of the current *DSM*?
   a. Presence of mental retardation
   b. Degree of social support
   c. Medical conditions
   d. A prediction of future behavior

*Answers 1. b; 2. c; 3. d*

# Anxiety Disorders: It's Not Just "Nerves"

We all experience anxiety from time to time. Many students are anxious when they have to make an oral presentation. Other people are nervous when they have to meet new people or fly in an airplane. In these examples, however, the anxiety tends to decrease once the situation is over. People with **anxiety disorders** are different in that they experience chronic anxiety that seriously interferes with their ability to function.

## Components of the Anxiety Disorders

Typically, anxiety disorders can be characterized by four components: *physical*, *cognitive*, *emotional*, and *behavioral*. These components interact powerfully, creating an unpleasant experience of fear or dread, although there may not be a specific fear-producing stimulus present.

The *physical* components of anxiety include dizziness, elevated heart rate and blood pressure, muscle tension, sweating palms, and dry mouth. These physical symptoms stem from the activation of the sympathetic nervous system (Chapter 2). The hormonal system is also activated as adrenalin is released into the bloodstream. Recall that this occurrence is referred to as the fight-or-flight response. This fight-or-flight response occurs every time we perceive a threat in our environment.

People with anxiety disorders have concerns that are unrealistic and out of proportion to the amount of harm that could occur. *Cognitive* components of anxiety may include worrying, fearing loss of control, exaggerating (in one's mind) the danger of a situation, exhibiting paranoia, or being extremely wary and watchful of people and events. These thoughts may lead to *emotional* reactions such as a sense of dread, terror, panic, irritability, or restlessness. These thoughts and emotions propel the person to behave in ways meant to cope with the anxiety.

Coping with abnormal anxiety may include *behaviors* such as escaping or fleeing from the situation, behaving aggressively, "freezing," which results in being unable to move, or avoiding the situation in the future. Again, these symptoms are so intense that they disrupt the quality of the person's life.

## Types of Anxiety Disorders

### You Asked...

*What are the different types of anxiety disorders?*

KAYLA CAMPANA, STUDENT

Approximately 19% of Americans over 18 years of age are diagnosed with an anxiety disorder in a given year (NCS-R, 2007). Women have consistently higher rates of anxiety disorders than do men (McLean et al., 2011). African Americans have a lower lifetime risk of anxiety disorders than European Americans and Hispanic Americans (Breslau et al., 2005). Anxiety disorders typically begin in childhood or adolescence and are highly *comorbid*, meaning that the anxiety disorder occurs along with another psychological disorder (Kessler et al., 2010). We will discuss five anxiety disorders: *generalized anxiety disorder*, *panic disorder*, *phobic disorder*, *obsessive-compulsive disorder*, and *posttraumatic stress disorder* (see ■ FIGURE 13.3).

**anxiety disorder**    a disorder marked by excessive apprehension that seriously interferes with a person's ability to function

## GENERALIZED ANXIETY DISORDER (GAD)

Some people are anxious all the time in almost all situations. These individuals may be diagnosed with **generalized anxiety disorder (GAD)**. Symptoms of GAD include excessive anxiety, worry, and difficulty in controlling such worries. The person may be easily fatigued, restless, and irritable, and may experience difficulty concentrating or sleeping (American Psychiatric Association, 2000a). People with GAD chronically worry not only about major issues, such as which car or house to buy, their children's health, or their job performance, but also about minor issues such as being late, wearing the right outfit, or what to make for dinner. It is estimated that about 3% of American adults experience GAD in any given year (Kessler, Chiu, et al., 2005). European Americans are at higher risk of GAD than African Americans and Hispanic Americans (Breslau et al., 2006).

## PANIC DISORDER

Imagine that you are attending a party given by a good friend. When you arrive at the party, a feeling of panic suddenly overwhelms you. Your heart begins to pound, you hear ringing in your ears, your skin feels tingly and numb, and it becomes harder and harder to breathe. These are common symptoms that occur during a *panic attack*, a short but intense episode of severe anxiety. As many as 30–40% of young adults in the United States report occasional panic attacks that do not interfere with their daily functioning (Ehlers, 1995; King et al., 1993). However, when panic attacks are more common, and a person begins to fear having panic attacks to the extent that it interferes with the ability to function, a diagnosis of **panic disorder** may be given (American Psychiatric Association, 2000a).

It is estimated that between 1.5% and 5% of people will develop panic disorder at some time in their lives (American Psychiatric Association, 2000a; Grant et al., 2006). It typically develops in late adolescence or early adulthood and is twice as common in women as in men (Craske & Barlow, 2001; Grant et al., 2006; Kessler, Berglund, et al., 2005). European Americans and Native Americans tend to have a higher prevalence rate of panic disorder than do African Americans, Asian Americans, and Hispanic Americans (Breslau et al., 2006; Grant et al., 2006).

People with panic disorder often feel so overwhelmed by the feelings of panic that they think they are having a heart attack or a seizure. They may believe that they are "going crazy" or going to die, and many seek medical attention to find out what is wrong with them. The panic attacks may occur frequently or only sporadically. Most people with panic disorder cannot identify any specific thing that might have triggered the attack. However, when a panic attack occurs, the same situation may then trigger a future attack.

Fear of having another panic attack may lead to **agoraphobia**, or fear of being in places from which escape may be difficult or where help may not be available if one were to experience panic. People affected with agoraphobia avoid any place—the mall, the grocery store, or the movie theater—in which they believe a panic attack may occur. Such fears can leave people housebound for years. At least 75%

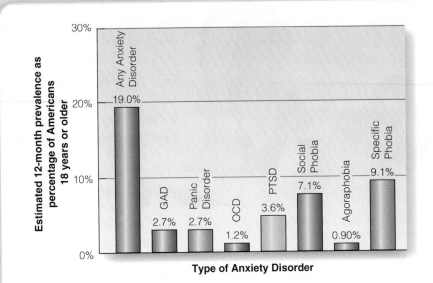

**FIGURE**

# 13.3

### Prevalence of Anxiety Disorders in a Given Year

Among adults 18 years of age or older, social and specific phobias are the most commonly diagnosed disorders in any given year because the age of onset is typically earlier for the phobias than for other anxiety disorders.

*Source: National Comorbidity Survey Replication data. Table 2. Updated 2007. http://www.hcp.med.harvard.edu/ncs*

**generalized anxiety disorder (GAD)** an anxiety disorder characterized by chronic, constant worry in almost all situations

**panic disorder** an anxiety disorder characterized by intense fear and anxiety in the absence of danger that is accompanied by strong physical symptoms

**agoraphobia [agg-or-uh-FOE-bee-uh]** an excessive fear of being in places from which escape might be difficult or where help might not be available if one were to experience panic

For many college students, taking a test is an anxiety-producing event.

of those who are diagnosed with agoraphobia are women (Barlow, 2002). Note that people without panic disorder can experience agoraphobia, which is then characterized as a *phobic disorder*, our next topic of discussion.

## PHOBIC DISORDERS

All of us have fears. Some of us get anxious when we think of or see a snake or a spider. Others may fear public speaking or eating in public. As children, we may have been afraid of the dark or the dentist. These are common fears. However, when our fears become so intense that they cause severe anxiety, possibly even panic attacks that interfere with our ability to function, then a diagnosis of **phobic disorder** is made (American Psychiatric Association, 2000a). We have already mentioned one type of phobic disorder, *agoraphobia*. Two other types of phobic disorders are *specific phobias* and *social phobias*.

**Specific phobias** involve a persistent fear and avoidance of a specific object or situation—animals, heights, bridges—or other specific stimuli. They are one of the most common disorders worldwide, affecting approximately 9% of American adults (NCS-R, 2007), 4% of the general population in Mexico (Medina-Mora et al., 2005), 2.7% in Japan (Kawakami et al., 2005), and 7.7% across several European countries (ESEMed/MHEDEA, 2004). Specific phobias typically begin in childhood (Kessler, Berglund, et al., 2005).

**Social phobias** include an irrational, persistent fear of being negatively evaluated by others in a social situation. A person with a social phobia (also called *social anxiety disorder*) may have an extreme fear of embarrassment or humiliation. This disorder may include fear of public speaking, fear of eating or undressing in front of others, or fear of using public restrooms. It is estimated that 12% of American adults will experience a social phobia at some time in their lives (Ruscio et al., 2008). Social phobias tend to develop in the early preschool years and in adolescence, and are somewhat more likely to develop in women than in men (Lang & Stein, 2001; Kessler, Berglund, et al., 2005; Turk, Heimberg, & Hope, 2001). African Americans and Hispanic Americans tend to have a lower lifetime risk of social phobias than do European Americans (Breslau et al., 2006).

People with phobic disorders typically recognize that their fears are irrational, but they cannot stop the overwhelming anxiety they feel when faced with the feared object or situation.

## OBSESSIVE-COMPULSIVE DISORDER (OCD)

**phobic [FOE-bick] disorder**
an anxiety disorder characterized by an intense fear of a specific object or situation

**specific phobia** a persistent fear and avoidance of a specific object or situation

**social phobia** an irrational, persistent fear of being negatively evaluated by others in a social situation

**obsession** a recurrent thought or image that intrudes on a person's awareness

**compulsion** repetitive behavior that a person feels a strong urge to perform

**obsessive-compulsive disorder (OCD)** an anxiety disorder involving a pattern of unwanted intrusive thoughts and the urge to engage in repetitive actions

**Obsessions** are recurrent thoughts or images that intrude on a person's consciousness or awareness. **Compulsions** are repetitive behaviors that a person feels a strong urge to perform. All of us experience intrusive thoughts and strong urges. For example, on your way to school or work, the thought pops into your head that you left the stove on, and you start worrying about a house fire. What do you do? Many of us feel compelled to turn the car around to check that everything is okay. However, what if this scenario occurred every time you got in the car, and you felt compelled to check each time? In such a case, you might be diagnosed with **obsessive-compulsive disorder (OCD)**.

Obsessive-compulsive disorder is an anxiety disorder in which a person experiences recurrent obsessions or compulsions that he or she feels cannot be controlled (American Psychiatric Association, 2000a). Obsessions often center on dirt and contamination, doing harm to oneself or others, sexual thoughts, or repeated doubts (such as having locked the house). Common compulsions include cleaning, checking, counting things, or arranging and straightening things in a particular fashion. The compulsions are often performed with the hope of preventing the obsessive thoughts or making them go away. However, performing these "rituals" provides only temporary relief. Not performing the rituals increases the person's anxiety.

Recurrent obsessions cause great personal distress, and compulsions can be time-consuming and in some cases harmful—as when a person washes his or her hands so frequently that they bleed. It is estimated that between 1% and 3% of individuals will develop OCD at some time in their lives; in the United States, the rates are higher among European Americans than among Hispanic Americans and African Americans (Hewlett, 2000; Kessler, Chiu, et al., 2005).

## POSTTRAUMATIC STRESS DISORDER (PTSD)

Another type of anxiety disorder is **posttraumatic stress disorder (PTSD)**. PTSD develops after exposure to a terrifying event or ordeal in which grave physical harm occurred or was threatened. Traumatic events may include:

© WR Publishing/Alamy

Hoarding, in which people keep large amounts of items that others consider excessive or worthless, can be a specific symptom of OCD.

- Violent personal assaults such as rape, physical abuse, or sexual abuse
- Natural or human-caused disasters such as an earthquake, a hurricane, a terrorist attack, or an outbreak of an infectious disease
- Military combat
- Events that anyone might experience—the sudden, unexpected death of a loved one or witnessing a violent crime or a deadly traffic accident

A diagnosis of PTSD requires that the person repeatedly reexperience the ordeal in the form of distressing memories, nightmares, frightening thoughts, or flashback episodes, especially when exposed to situations that are similar to the original trauma. For example, a car backfire might trigger a flashback to a combat trauma or being the victim of an armed robbery. Anniversaries of the event also can trigger symptoms. In addition, people diagnosed with PTSD may experience emotional numbness or withdrawal from themselves or others such that they lose interest in usual activities or are regarded as distant and emotionally unavailable. Finally, people with PTSD are always on guard and alert to any real or imagined potential threats in their environments—showing *hypervigilance*, having difficulty concentrating, or having difficulty sleeping (American Psychiatric Association, 2000a). They may experience depression, anxiety, irritability, or outbursts of anger; physical symptoms such as headaches, dizziness, or chest pain; or feelings of intense guilt. For some people, such symptoms can seriously disrupt the ability to work or to meet social, professional, and family obligations.

Approximately 3.5% of U.S. adults are diagnosed with PTSD in a given year (Kessler, Chiu, et al., 2005). More than twice as many females as males experience PTSD following exposure to a trauma, typically sexual assault (J. R. T. Davidson, 2000; Tolin & Foa, 2006). Women's higher PTSD risk has been attributed to a number of variables that reinforce the biopsychosocial nature of mental health disorders. For example, sex differences in the responses of the *amygdala*, the brain structure that mediates fear, have been documented (Hamann, 2005). Moreover, women are more likely to perceive threat and loss of control than men—psychological factors that may influence the risk of PTSD (Olff et al., 2007). Women are more likely to be victims of sexual abuse and experience these traumas at younger ages than men—social factors that also play a role in PTSD (Cortina & Kubiak, 2006; Olff et al., 2007; Tolin & Foa, 2006).

Soldiers (male or female) are also at high risk for developing PTSD, as military conflict is a source of trauma (Creamer et al., 2011). About 19% of Vietnam

**posttraumatic stress disorder (PTSD)** an anxiety disorder, characterized by distressing memories, emotional numbness, and hypervigilance, that develops after exposure to a traumatic event

Exposure to a trauma can lead to the development of PTSD.

veterans developed PTSD at some point after the war (Dohrenwend et al., 2006). The disorder has also been reported among Persian Gulf war veterans, with estimates running as high as 8% (Wolfe et al., 1999). After two decades of conflict in Afghanistan, 42% of Afghan participants in a national population-based survey reported PTSD symptoms (Cardozo et al., 2004). Studies of U.S. military personnel in Iraq also indicate problems in mental health, most notably PTSD (Felker et al., 2008; Hoge et al., 2004; Milliken, Auchterlonie, & Hoge, 2007).

Research on the effects of the September 11 attacks on mental health revealed a remarkable degree of PTSD, at least initially (Calderoni et al., 2006; Grieger, Fullerton, & Ursano, 2004; Lating et al., 2004). A comprehensive mental health screening of more than 11,000 rescue and recovery workers and volunteers at the World Trade Center revealed that more than 20% of the participants experienced symptoms of PTSD and 13% met the diagnostic criteria for PTSD (Centers for Disease Control and Prevention, 2004). Even non-rescue utility workers deployed to the disaster sites had risk of PTSD (Cukor et al., 2011). Years later, many of these individuals are faring better; however, people who were directly exposed to the attacks are more likely to have persistent symptoms of PTSD (Bonanno et al., 2006; Cukor et al., 2011; Laugharne, Janca, & Widiger, 2007).

■ YOU REVIEW 13.1 summarizes the anxiety disorders that we have discussed.

## YOU REVIEW 13.1   Symptoms of the Main Anxiety Disorders

| DISORDER | SYMPTOMS |
|---|---|
| Generalized anxiety disorder | Excessive worry for at least 6 months about a number of events accompanied by physical symptoms such as muscle tension, mental agitation, and irritability that impair a person's functioning. |
| Obsessive-compulsive disorder | A pattern of recurrent, persistent, intrusive thoughts or images that are followed by repetitive behaviors or mental acts that a person feels driven to perform to reduce stress or to prevent some event from happening. The thoughts or behaviors are time-consuming and interfere with the person's functioning. |
| Panic disorder | Abrupt experiences of unexpected intense fear accompanied by physical symptoms such as heart palpitations, shortness of breath, or dizziness that interfere with a person's functioning. |
| Phobic disorder | Persistent fear of a specific object or social situation that is excessive and unreasonable, and interferes with a person's ability to function. |
| Posttraumatic stress disorder | Exposure to a traumatic event during which one feels helplessness or fear followed by recurrent and intrusive memories or nightmares of the event, avoidance of stimuli associated with the event, numbing of emotions, and increased arousal that impair the person's functioning. |

## Explaining Anxiety Disorders

What causes anxiety disorders? Research on people with anxiety disorders suggests biological, psychological, and sociocultural factors that may contribute to such behavior, underscoring the biopsychosocial nature of psychological disorders presented at the beginning of the chapter.

## BIOLOGY: NEUROTRANSMITTERS, GENETICS, AND THE BRAIN

The functioning of several neurotransmitters has been linked to anxiety disorders. For example, abnormal activity of norepinephrine, serotonin, or GABA may be involved in panic attacks (Charney et al., 2000; Goddard et al., 2010). Abnormal activity of GABA has been linked to people with GAD, and problems in serotonin regulation have been suggested as a cause for OCD and PTSD (Kuzelova, Ptacek, & Milan, 2010; Mellman et al., 2009).

A genetic predisposition to an anxiety disorder also may exist. Children of parents with anxiety disorders have a greater risk for anxiety disorders than children of parents with no psychological disorders (Micco et al., 2009). Even relatives of a person (siblings, aunts, uncles) with an anxiety disorder are more likely to have one compared with relatives of someone without a disorder (Hanna, 2000). Twin and family studies have found high heritability especially for panic disorder and OCD (Grados, Walkup, & Walford, 2003; Hettema, Neale, & Kendler, 2001; Mosing et al., 2009; Nicolini et al., 2009).

Other studies have focused on specific brain areas that are involved in anxiety and fear (Lonsdorf et al., 2009; Rosen, 2004; Rosen & Donley, 2006). As stated previously, our fear response is coordinated by the amygdala, a small structure deep inside the brain that also plays a role in our emotional memories (LaBar, 2007). Neuroimaging studies on people with GAD and PTSD suggest an overactive amygdala that may contribute to their heightened level of anxiety and memory-related symptoms (Etkin et al., 2010; Kolassa & Elbert; 2007; Rauch, Shin, & Phelps, 2006; Rogers et al., 2009; Shin, Rauch, & Pitman, 2006). Abnormal functioning of a part of the forebrain called the *striatum* has been investigated as a possible factor in OCD (Choi et al., 2007). For example, in one study (Rauch et al., 1997), PET scans of individuals with OCD showed different brain activity in the striatum when performing a cognitive task than did the PET scans of people without OCD. Other research suggests that an overactive monitoring system in the brain is related to the symptoms of OCD (Gehring, Himle, & Nisenson, 2000; Ursu et al., 2003).

We may acquire fears by observing others' negative experiences either in real life or through media portrayals.

## PSYCHOLOGICAL FACTORS: LEARNING AND COGNITIONS

Psychological factors also help in explaining anxiety disorders. For example, phobias are learned in the same way that Watson and Rayner were able to condition Little Albert to fear a white rat (see Chapter 5; Field, 2006). A neutral stimulus (the phobic object) gets paired with a stimulus that naturally elicits fear. So, when a thunderstorm gets paired with a loud noise (thunder) that naturally evokes fear, we learn to be fearful of thunderstorms.

Conditioning processes also may play a role in panic disorder. Neutral stimuli that are present during an initial panic attack may then become conditioned stimuli that trigger panic symptoms on subsequent occasions. These conditioned stimuli are then thought to generalize to other neutral stimuli resulting in a variety of cues that evoke panic symptoms (Lissek et al., 2010).

Direct experience is not always necessary to develop a phobia. We may acquire fears simply by observing or hearing about others' negative experiences (Kelly & Forsyth, 2007). How many of us have come face to face with a demon? But after seeing the *Paranormal Activity* movies, we may be more fearful when we hear unexplained noises in our home. We now associate an unexpected noise with a mysterious force that is out to do us harm. We may sleep with the lights on or sleep at someone else's house to avoid these unexplainable events. Avoiding the noises reduces our anxiety but only makes us more fearful the next time anything out of the ordinary occurs in our home.

Reinforcement is a learning process that helps explain compulsions. If you engage in a certain behavior following an anxiety-provoking obsession, your anxiety is often reduced. The next time the obsession occurs, you feel more compelled to engage in the behavior so that you can reduce your anxiety (Barlow, 2002). Learning and conditioning theories have also been useful in understanding PTSD. Sights, sounds, or images of the trauma all become conditioned stimuli that trigger the fear reaction.

Cognitive research suggests that our thinking processes play a role in developing an anxiety disorder. In particular, people who perceive situations and objects as uncontrollable, unpredictable, dangerous, and disgusting are more vulnerable to anxiety disorders (Armfield, 2006; Bryant & Guthrie, 2005). People with anxiety disorders also may have the tendency to process more negative information rather than positive or neutral information about an event (Fox, Cahill, & Zougkou, 2010; Hertel & Brozovich, 2010). For example, studies show that people with panic disorder sometimes misinterpret their bodily sensations, thinking they are beginning a panic attack. Their negative and catastrophic thinking then heightens their anxiety (Barlow, 2000; Craske & Barlow, 2001). People diagnosed with GAD tend to anticipate that something bad will happen to them and that they will feel out of control. While driving in a car, they may worry that they will get lost or in an accident. These worries become constant and almost automatic in their thought processes (Beck, 1997; Riskind et al., 2000).

The shattering of common cognitive beliefs about life may bring on PTSD. An unpredictable trauma—such as a rape, an earthquake, or an automobile accident—may make us question our assumptions that the world is safe and just and that events happen for a reason. It dispels our illusion of control and invincibility, and our assumption that bad things only happen to bad people (Janoff-Bulman, 1992; Terr, 1983). Some research suggests that people with OCD are less able to turn off the intrusive, negative obsessions that we all experience from time to time (Salkovskis et al., 1997).

## SOCIOCULTURAL FACTORS: STRESS, GENDER, AND CULTURE

Sociocultural factors must also be considered when explaining anxiety disorders. For example, in cultures experiencing rapid social change or war, people are more likely to exhibit anxiety symptoms than are people in more stable countries (Compton et al., 1991). Similarly, people who have been abused as children or who have had other previous traumatic or stressful experiences are more likely to develop anxiety disorders (Green et al., 2010; Hyman & Rudorfer, 2000; McLaughlin et al., 2010). We have also seen that European Americans and women are more likely than other ethnic groups and men to be diagnosed with an anxiety disorder. More research will have to examine the role of gender and culture in anxiety disorders before we fully understand their influence.

# Let's
## REVIEW

This section described the main anxiety disorders and detailed our current understanding of what causes them. For a quick check of your understanding, answer these questions.

**1.** Marilu is anxious and nervous all the time. She constantly worries over her family, her job, and her schoolwork. Which anxiety disorder *best* describes Marilu's behavior?
    **a.** Panic disorder
    **b.** Generalized anxiety disorder
    **c.** Phobic disorder
    **d.** Obsessive-compulsive disorder

**2.** Learning theories suggest that obsessive-compulsive disorder is the result of _____.
    **a.** reinforcement processes
    **b.** faulty cognitions
    **c.** low self-esteem
    **d.** unconscious impulses

**3.** Abdul was involved in a four-car pileup on the interstate 8 months ago. Since then, he has been having nightmares and flashback episodes of the accident. He has difficulty concentrating and has withdrawn from his family and friends. Abdul would most likely be diagnosed with which anxiety disorder?
    **a.** Panic disorder
    **b.** Posttraumatic stress disorder
    **c.** Phobic disorder
    **d.** Generalized anxiety disorder

*Answers 1. b; 2. a; 3. b*

# Dissociative and Somatoform Disorders: Other Forms of Anxiety?

Dissociative and somatoform disorders are quite rare in the general population but often are of much interest to students. Here we outline the general nature of these disorders and the psychological factors that may a play a role in their development.

## Dissociative Disorders: Flight or Multiple Personalities

To *dissociate* means to break or pull apart. Thus, the **dissociative disorders** involve a loss of awareness of some part of our self, our surroundings, or what is going on around us. Mild dissociative experiences are common (Aderibigbe, Bloch, & Walker, 2001; Hunter, Sierra, & David, 2004). For instance, have you ever driven somewhere and on arrival did not remember driving there? Have you ever missed a part of a conversation but can tell from the speaker's demeanor that you appeared to have been listening the whole time? Have you ever appeared attentive in class while you were daydreaming about your plans for the weekend? All of these are common, everyday dissociative experiences.

However, when loss of awareness becomes more extreme, a diagnosis of a dissociative disorder may apply. Such extreme dissociation is typically linked to severe stress or a series of emotionally traumatic events (Isaac & Chand, 2006; Kihlstrom, 2001; Spiegel, 1997). ■ TABLE 13.3 provides a brief description of the dissociative disorders listed in the *DSM-IV-TR*. Here we will confine our discussion to two: *dissociative fugue disorder* and *dissociative identity disorder*.

### LEARNING OBJECTIVES

● Describe the nature of dissociative disorders and their link to stressful or traumatic events.

● Describe the nature of somatoform disorders and discuss their link to health anxiety.

**dissociative [dih-SO-shee-tive] disorder**   a disorder marked by a loss of awareness of some part of one's self or one's surroundings that seriously interferes with the person's ability to function

**TABLE 13.3**
## Types of Dissociative Disorders

| DISORDER | MAJOR FEATURES |
|---|---|
| Depersonalization disorder | Frequent episodes in which the person feels detached from own mental state or body. |
| Dissociative amnesia | Memory loss of important personal information, not due to organic problems or brain injury. |
| Dissociative fugue disorder | Person unexpectedly travels away from home and assumes a new identity with amnesia for previous identity. |
| Dissociative identity disorder | Separate multiple personalities in the same individual. |

## DISSOCIATIVE FUGUE DISORDER

In 2006, a 57-year-old husband and father of two left work at his New York law firm and disappeared. Six months later he was found living under a new name in a homeless shelter in Chicago. He didn't know who he was or where he came from. During the same year, another man left his Washington home to visit a friend in Canada who was dying of cancer. Four days later, he was walking around Denver asking people for help because he didn't know who he was. Both of these men were diagnosed with *dissociative fugue disorder* (Brody, 2007).

**Dissociative fugue disorder** involves one or more episodes of amnesia in which a person is unable to recall some or all of his or her past and is confused about his or her identity. A new identity may be formed in which the person suddenly and unexpectedly travels away from home (American Psychiatric Association, 2000a). In this fugue (meaning "flight") state, the person appears normal. He or she may adopt a new name, identity, and residence, and engage in normal social interactions. The fugue state may last hours, weeks, or months. However, at some point, confusion about one's identity or the return of the original identity may surface, leading to personal distress. Once the person has returned to the prefugue identity, he or she may or may not remember what happened during the fugue state, which may cause additional confusion and distress

Although no specific cause is known for dissociative fugue, its onset is typically related to a stressful or traumatic event such as a natural disaster, war experience, or unbearable stress at work or at home (Putnam, 2000). It is a relatively uncommon disorder with an estimated 0.2% prevalence in the general population (American Psychiatric Association, 2000a).

## DISSOCIATIVE IDENTITY DISORDER

**dissociative fugue [dih-SO-shee-tive FYOOG] disorder**   a disorder marked by episodes of amnesia in which a person is unable to recall some or all of his or her past and is confused about his or her identity; a new identity may be formed in which the person suddenly and unexpectedly travels away from home

**dissociative identity disorder (DID)**   a disorder in which two or more personalities coexist within the same individual; formerly called multiple personality disorder

**Dissociative identity disorder (DID)**, formerly called *multiple personality disorder*, involves the existence of two or more separate personalities in the same individual (American Psychiatric Association, 2000a). The separate personalities—referred to as *alters* (for alternate personalities)—may or may not be known to the "core," or "host," personality—the person who asks for treatment. Each personality has its own perceptions, thoughts, mannerisms, speech characteristics, and gestures. Each alter appears to have a specific function. For example, one alter may arise to deal with romantic relationships, whereas another alter deals with academic work. The alter personalities may be of different ages, gender, or ethnicities. The majority of people diagnosed with DID are women (American Psychiatric Association, 2000a).

Frequent blackouts or episodes of amnesia are common in people with dissociative identity disorder. They may notice money missing from their bank accounts that they don't remember spending, or find objects in their home that they do not recognize. Self-mutilating behavior is also common in people with this disorder. They may repeatedly burn or cut themselves and have a history of suicide attempts (Foote et al., 2008). Often they have been previously diagnosed with other disorders such as major depression, PTSD, substance abuse disorder, or schizophrenia, especially if they have reported hearing voices (Loewenstein & Putnam, 2004).

One striking similarity among people with DID is their backgrounds. Almost all have reported experiencing chronic, horrific childhood physical and/or sexual abuse at the hands of family members (Coons, 1994; Ellason, Ross, & Fuchs, 1996; Putnam et al., 1986). Many clinicians believe that in an attempt to deal with such trauma, these people defensively dissociate, developing alter personalities that can protect them from experiencing such events in life or in memory. People with DID also have a high level of hypnotic susceptibility (Kihlstrom, Glisky, & Angiulo, 1994). Thus, the ability to dissociate may have become an effective coping mechanism early in life.

Some psychologists question the validity of the dissociative identity disorder (Kihlstrom, 2005; Piper & Merskey, 2004). There has been a great increase in the number of reported cases since 1980 (American Psychiatric Association, 2000a). Only one-third of a sample of U.S. psychiatrists believe DID should have been included in the *DSM-IV* (Pope et al., 1999). Verifying the claims of amnesia and blackouts is difficult, and people with DID have often been diagnosed with other psychological disorders (Ellason & Ross, 1997; Kluft, 1999; Loewenstein & Putnam, 2004). Some believe that DID may represent an extreme form of post-traumatic stress disorder (Butler et al., 1996). Future research may help us better understand the nature of this disorder.

## Somatoform Disorders: Doctor, I'm Sure I'm Sick

*Somatic* means "related to the body." The **somatoform disorders** involve physical complaints for which there is no apparent physical cause. The physical symptoms are real to the person, but physicians can find no medical reason why the individual is experiencing such symptoms. For example, a person may complain of constant hip pain. Numerous medical tests are completed, but there is no apparent physical cause for the hip ache. Because no physical cause can be found, it is assumed that psychological distress underlies the physical problem. ■ TABLE 13.4 describes the somatoform disorders listed in the *DSM-IV-TR*. Our discussion in this section will focus on one of them, *hypochondriasis*.

In **hypochondriasis**, a person believes that he or she has a serious medical disease despite evidence to the contrary (American Psychiatric Association, 2000a). Many of us know someone who we think is a hypochondriac because that person frequently complains about physical ailments. However,

**somatoform [so-MAA-tih-form] disorder**   a disorder marked by physical complaints that have no apparent physical cause

**hypochondriasis [high-po-con-DRY-uh-sis]**   a somatoform disorder in which the person persistently worries over having a disease, without any evident physical basis

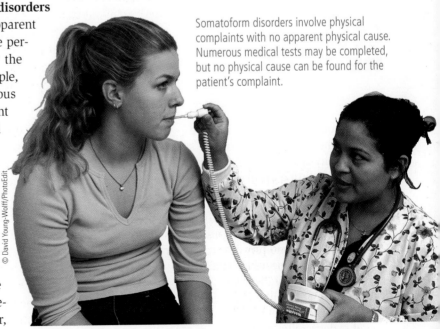

Somatoform disorders involve physical complaints with no apparent physical cause. Numerous medical tests may be completed, but no physical cause can be found for the patient's complaint.

© David Young-Wolff/PhotoEdit

**TABLE 13.4**

## Types of Somatoform Disorders

| DISORDER | MAJOR FEATURES |
|---|---|
| Conversion disorder | Loss of functioning in some part of the body, but no physical cause can be found. |
| Somatization disorder | Long history of physical complaints affecting several areas of the body. The person has sought medical attention, but no physical cause can be found. |
| Pain disorder | Long history of pain complaints. The person has sought medical attention, but no physical cause can be found. |
| Hypochondriasis | Persistent worry over having a physical disease. The person frequently seeks medical attention, but no serious physical disease can be found. |
| Body dysmorphic disorder | Extreme preoccupation and obsession with a part of the body that is believed to be defective. The person makes elaborate attempts to conceal or change the body part. |

people with hypochondriasis are convinced that they have a disease, not just one or two specific symptoms. People with hypochondriasis may undergo extensive medical testing by several doctors to confirm the existence of their disease. When a doctor suggests that they may have a psychological problem, people with hypochondriasis are likely to seek out another physician rather than seek psychological treatment (Kirmayer & Looper, 2007). People with hypochondriasis often have a family history of depression or anxiety (Escobar et al., 1998), leading some researchers to speculate that hypochondriasis is an intense form of health anxiety related to panic disorder and obsessive-compulsive disorder (Abramowitz & Moore, 2007; Braddock & Abramowitz, 2006). Hypochondriasis has an estimated prevalence between 1% and 5% in the general population (American Psychiatric Association, 2000a).

# Let's
# REVIEW

This section described the nature of the dissociative and somatoform disorders. For a quick check of your understanding, answer these questions.

**1.** Dissociative disorders involve _____.
   **a.** the disintegration of one's personality
   **b.** physical symptoms without any physical cause
   **c.** a splitting off of one's conscious mind
   **d.** a numbness or paralysis in some part of the body

**2.** Alphonsia has recurrent abdominal pain. Her doctors have conducted numerous medical tests and can find no physical cause for her symptom. Alphonsia appears to have a _____.
   **a.** personality disorder
   **b.** somatoform disorder
   **c.** dissociative disorder
   **d.** depressive disorder

**3.** What do the dissociative and somatoform disorders have in common?
   **a.** They both occur more frequently in men than in women.
   **b.** They both involve a preoccupation with the body.
   **c.** They both include a loss of identity.
   **d.** They both may represent alternate expressions of anxiety.

Answers 1. c; 2. b; 3. d

# Mood Disorders: Beyond the Blues

A third major category of disorders described in the *DSM-IV-TR* is mood disorders. **Mood disorders** involve a significant change in a person's emotional state. This change may include feeling depressed or extremely elated for an extended time. Following anxiety disorders, mood disorders are one of the more common psychological disorders, affecting approximately 9.5% of adult Americans in a given year (Kessler, Chiu, et al., 2005). Like anxiety disorders, mood disorders are also likely to have a high rate of comorbidity, or coexist with another mental health disorder.

Many of us experience sadness, but typically this period of sadness lasts only a few days. In clinical depression, the mood change is persistent and interferes significantly with a person's ability to function. Also, normal periods of sadness are usually brought on by environmental events—the loss of a loved one, the breakup of a relationship, or a disappointment in one's life. People with clinical depression are sad over a longer period, in the absence of such external events or long after most people would have adjusted to such changes.

Mood disorders can be devastating to personal relationships and to the ability to work or go to school. Many people think that the symptoms are not "real" and that the person should be able to "snap out of it." These inaccurate beliefs may cause shame, which discourages people from seeking appropriate treatment. We will discuss two basic types of mood disorders: *unipolar depression* and *bipolar depression*.

## Unipolar Depressive Disorders: A Change to Sadness

The *DSM-IV-TR* indicates two categories of unipolar depressive disorder: *major depression* and *dysthymic disorder*. A diagnosis of **major depression** requires that a person experience either extreme sadness—referred to as **dysphoria**—or loss of interest or pleasure in one's usual activities (referred to as **anhedonia**) plus at least four other symptoms of depression for a period of at least 2 weeks. These symptoms must be severe enough that they interfere with the person's ability to function but not be due to a general medical condition or the death of a loved one (American Psychiatric Association, 2000a). The other symptoms of depression may include:

### Physical and Behavioral Symptoms

- Change in sleep patterns—either sleeping too much (hypersomnia) or too little (insomnia)
- Change in appetite—either eating too much (resulting in weight gain) or too little (resulting in weight loss)
- Change in motor functioning—either moving slowly and sluggishly or appearing agitated in movement
- Fatigue, or loss of energy

### Cognitive Symptoms

- Inability to concentrate or pay attention
- Difficulty in making decisions
- Thoughts of hopelessness, pessimism, and helplessness
- Exaggerated feelings of worthlessness or guilt
- Thoughts of suicide (see Psychology Applies to Your World, p. 516)
- Delusions (believing something that is not true) and hallucinations (perceiving things that are not there) with depressing themes

**mood disorder** a disorder marked by a significant change in one's emotional state that seriously interferes with one's ability to function

**major depression** a mood disorder involving dysphoria, feelings of worthlessness, loss of interest in one's usual activities, and changes in bodily activities such as sleep and appetite that persists for at least 2 weeks

**dysphoria [dis-FOR-ee-uh]** an extreme state of sadness

**anhedonia [an-hee-DOAN-yah]** absence of pleasure from one's usual activities

## Psychology Applies to Your World:

### Suicide Facts and Misconceptions

Suicidal thoughts are one symptom of depression. Research suggests that nearly 90% of all people who commit suicide have some diagnosable mental health disorder, commonly a depressive disorder or a substance abuse disorder (National Institute of Mental Health, 2002).

In 2007, suicide was the 11th leading cause of death in the United States (higher than homicide). Among 25- to 34-year-olds, it was the second leading cause of death; among 35- to 44-year-olds, it was the fourth leading cause of death. Among 15- to 24-year-olds, suicide was the third leading cause of death. However, these rates are probably grossly underestimated given the negative stigma attached to suicide in the United States (CDC, 2009c; Heron & Smith, 2007; Kung et al., 2008; Xu, Kochanek, & Tejada-Vera, 2009). Women are two to three times more likely than men to *attempt* suicide, but four times as many men actually kill themselves, in part because of the means chosen (CDC, 2009c; Hoyert et al., 2006; Kung et al., 2008). Men tend to shoot, hang, or stab themselves. Women are more likely to choose less lethal means, such as drug overdoses. This gender difference appears in many countries across the world (Weissman et al., 1999; Welch, 2001) except China, where more women commit suicide than men (Phillips, Li, & Zhang, 2002). As seen in ■ FIGURE 13.4, in the United States, Whites and American Indian/Alaska Natives have higher rates of suicide than other ethnic groups (CDC, 2009c; Kung et al., 2008). Because many of us will encounter or already have encountered someone who is suicidal, let's take a moment to dispel some of the more common misconceptions concerning suicide.

*Misconception #1*: People who talk of suicide will not kill themselves.

Although most people who talk of suicide do not go on to attempt suicide, people who commit suicide typically have expressed their intentions at some time to family members or friends before their attempt (Ortega & Karch, 2010; Shneidman, 1987). They may have talked about "going away" or be preoccupied in general with the notion of death. Therefore, any talk of suicide should be taken seriously. A person who is suicidal should not be left alone. You may need to contact a mental health professional, call 911, or call a suicide crisis hotline in your area.

*Misconception #2*: If you ask someone who is depressed whether he or she has thoughts of suicide, it will only plant the idea of suicide in his or her head.

Asking direct questions about a person's plan for suicide is the only way to assess the person's risk for committing suicide. Bringing up the subject can also give the person an opportunity to talk about his or her problem. People who have a concrete plan in mind for when or how they will end their life are more likely to attempt suicide than those whose plans are less specific (Nock et al., 2008; SAMHSA, 2009b).

*Misconception #3*: People who have unsuccessfully attempted suicide will not try again.

In the United States from 2003 to 2007, among women aged 15 to 44 who committed suicide, 37% had a history of suicide attempts (Ortega & Karch, 2010). Similarly, among adolescents, a previous history of suicide attempts is the single best predictor of future suicide attempts and completions (Lewinsohn, Rohde, & Seeley, 1994). Therefore, a previous suicide attempt puts adolescents and young adult and middle-aged women in particular at a higher risk for future suicide attempts.

### FIGURE

# 13.4

#### U.S. Death Rates for Suicide by Gender and Ethnicity in 2006

Although women attempt suicide more often, men across all ethnic groups are more likely to commit suicide.

*Source: Centers for Disease Control and Prevention (2009c). Web-based Injury Statistics Query and Reporting System (WISQARS). Fatal Injury Reports. Atlanta, GA: National Center for Injury Prevention and Control.*

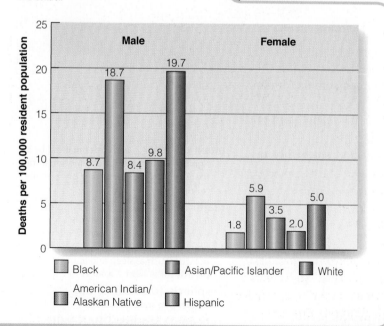

*Misconception #4*: A better mood means the risk of suicide is gone.

Suicide does not typically happen when a person is in the depths of a deep depression. Rather, suicide attempts are more likely to occur when people with depression have energy and can think more clearly and make decisions. This energy and clearer thinking make it appear to loved ones that the person is getting better and is therefore at a lower risk of suicide, when sometimes a better mood can indicate an increased risk of suicide.

*Misconception #5*: Only people who are depressed attempt suicide.

Although suicidal thoughts are a symptom of depression, people with other serious psychological disorders, including bipolar disorder, substance abuse disorder, dissociative disorders, and schizophrenia, are also at risk for suicide (Foote et al., 2008; Statham et al., 1998; Tsuang, Fleming, & Simpson, 1999). According to findings from the WHO World Mental Health Surveys, the strongest predictors of suicide attempts in developed countries are mood disorders, whereas in developing countries, they are substance use, PTSD, and impulse control disorders (Nock et al., 2009).

Though overall women attempt suicide more often, males who are depressed are especially at risk, with a rate four times higher than that for women who are depressed (National Institute of Mental Health, 2007). A number of other events and situations also increase one's risk of suicide, including economic hardship, serious illness, problems with a partner or the loss of a relationship, childhood sexual or physical abuse, and the presence of a firearm in the home (Bruffaerts et al., 2010; Enns et al., 2006; Karch et al., 2009; McHolm, MacMillan, & Jamieson, 2003; Ortega & Karch, 2010; Welch, 2001). Suicide occurs among people who have psychological disorders as well as those who face environmental stressors. The majority of suicide attempts are expressions of extreme distress and helplessness, not just "harmless" bids for attention.

Major depression may occur as a single episode or as repeated episodes over the course of years. Some episodes may be so severe that the person requires hospitalization, especially in the presence of frequent suicide attempts or delusional thinking.

**Dysthymic disorder** is a less severe but more chronic form of major depression. The person seems sad and downcast over a longer time. A diagnosis of dysthymic disorder requires the symptom of depressed mood plus at least two other symptoms of depression for a period of at least 2 years. Dysthymic disorder generally begins in childhood, adolescence, or early adulthood (American Psychiatric Association, 2000a). Typically, the symptoms of dysthymic disorder are not severe enough to require hospitalization. However, most people with dysthymic disorder eventually experience a major depressive episode (Klein, Lewinsohn, & Seeley, 2001; Klein, Shankman & Rose, 2006).

Worldwide, major depression is the leading cause of disability (World Health Organization, 2004). In the United States, 17% of adults will experience an acute episode of depression at some time in their lives, and 6% will experience more chronic depression (Kessler, Chiu, et al., 2005). Depression also appears to be related to age and gender. Although major depression can develop at any age, the average age of onset is 32 (Kessler, Berglund, et al., 2005). People between 15 and 24 years of age are at high risk for experiencing a major depressive episode, whereas 45- to 54-year-olds experience the lowest rates of major depressive episodes (Kessler et al., 2003). Women are twice as likely as men to experience both mild and more severe depression, a difference found in many different countries, ethnic groups, and across adult age groups (Bradley & Hopcroft, 2007; Ebmeier, Donaghey, & Steele, 2006; Kessler et al., 2003; Nolen-Hoeksema, 2002; D. R. Williams et al., 2007). Although African Americans and Hispanic Americans have a lower lifetime

Uygar Oze/Getty Images

Major depression is marked by physical, behavioral, and cognitive symptoms, in addition to depressed mood.

**dysthymic [dis-THIGH-mik] disorder**
a mood disorder that is a less severe but more chronic form of major depression

risk for a major depressive disorder, when they do experience one, it tends to be more chronic and severe (Breslau et al., 2005, 2006; D. R. Williams et al., 2007).

Unfortunately, many people with depression never receive treatment. In one study, only 51% of participants who met the criteria for major depression during the prior year received some type of treatment for it. African Americans and Mexican Americans were least likely to receive any care (Gonzalez et al., 2010).

## Bipolar Depressive Disorders: The Presence of Mania

A second major group of mood disorders is the bipolar depressive disorders. The *DSM-IV-TR* indicates two categories of bipolar depressive disorders: *bipolar disorder* and *cyclothymic disorder*.

**Bipolar disorder** involves a shift in mood between two states, or *poles*. One of these shifts is to a depressed state, with symptoms similar to those of major depression. The person feels sad, lacks self-worth, and may show changes in sleeping and eating over a 2-week period. The second mood change is to the opposite extreme—to a "high" or euphoric state, called **mania**. During a manic state, people feel elated and have high self-esteem, have a decreased need for sleep, are more talkative than usual, and are highly distractible. Much energy is directed at achieving goals, although many projects may be started and few finished. People in this state have an inflated sense of self, feeling confident and able to accomplish anything. This may result in delusional thinking or hallucinations. Also, their boundless energy often results in more impulsive and risk-taking behaviors. When such symptoms of mania and depression interfere with a person's ability to function, a diagnosis of bipolar disorder is appropriate (American Psychiatric Association, 2000a).

**Cyclothymic disorder** is a less severe but more chronic form of bipolar disorder. In cyclothymic disorder, a person alternates between milder periods of mania and more moderate depression for at least 2 years (American Psychiatric Association, 2000a). The person functions reasonably well during the mild mania but is likely to be more impaired during the depressive phase.

Bipolar disorders are less common than unipolar disorders, with 2.6% of adult Americans experiencing an episode of bipolar disorder at some time in their lives (Kessler, Chiu, et al., 2005; Lewinsohn, Klein, & Seeley, 2000). Men are just as likely as women to be diagnosed with bipolar disorder. The median age of onset for bipolar disorder is late adolescence and early adulthood (Angst & Sellaro, 2000; Kessler, Berglund, et al., 2005).

## Explaining Mood Disorders

What causes mood disorders? Not surprisingly, research has identified biological, psychological, and sociocultural factors that may contribute to mood disorders. Again, this highlights the biopsychosocial nature of psychological disorders.

### BIOLOGICAL FACTORS: GENES, NEUROTRANSMITTERS, STRESS HORMONES, AND BRODMANN'S AREA 25

Several biological factors have been investigated as contributing to depressive disorders: genes, neurotransmitters, stress hormones, and specific brain areas.

Genes   The evidence from family history studies and twin studies suggests that mood disorders may be genetically transmitted, especially in the case of bipolar disorder. For example, first-degree relatives (parent, child, or sibling) of persons with

© Peter Brooker/PhotoLibrary

Catherine Zeta-Jones recently sought treatment after being diagnosed with bipolar disorder.

**bipolar disorder**   a mood disorder characterized by both depression and mania

**mania**   a period of abnormally excessive energy and elation

**cyclothymic [sigh-clo-THIGH-mik] disorder**   a mood disorder that is a less severe but more chronic form of bipolar disorder

bipolar disorder are much more likely to develop the disorder than are relatives of people without the disorder (Perlis et al., 2006; Saunders et al., 2007). Similarly, if an identical twin is diagnosed as having bipolar disorder, the other identical twin has a higher probability of developing the disorder than if they were fraternal twins (McGuffin et al., 2003; Wallace, Schneider, & McGuffin, 2002). In one twin study, the heritability of bipolar disorder was estimated as high as 93% (Kieseppa et al., 2004).

The evidence for genetic factors in major depression is less clear. The trend toward genetic transmission is present, particularly in women, but it is not as strong as the evidence in bipolar disorders (Abkevich et al., 2003; Ebmeier et al., 2006; Mosing et al., 2009; Sullivan, Neale, & Kendler, 2000). Specific regions of chromosomes have been identified that may contribute to one's risk for depression and bipolar disorder, but a specific gene mechanism has not yet been identified (Duric et al., 2010; Hayden et al., 2010; Hayden & Nurnberger, 2006; Holmans et al., 2007; Kuzelova et al., 2010; Levinson et al., 2007).

**Neurotransmitters**   The malfunctioning of certain neurotransmitters has also been linked to mood disorders, specifically serotonin and norepinephrine (Carver, Johnson, & Joormann, 2009; Goddard et al., 2010; Thase, Jindal, & Howland, 2002). Antidepressant drugs that act on serotonin and norepinephrine to relieve the symptoms of depression seem to offer evidence for the role of these neurotransmitters in depression (see Neuroscience Applies to Your World). Similarly, abnormalities in the neurotransmitters norepinephrine, dopamine, and glutamate in bipolar disorder have been investigated as possible factors for bipolar disorder (Carlson et al., 2006; Cousins, Butts, & Young, 2009; Keck, McElroy, & Arnold, 2001). Dysfunction in the serotonin system may also account for the depressive phase of bipolar disorder (Oquendo et al., 2007).

**Stress Hormones**   The connection between depression and hormones has also been studied. Hormones regulate functions such as sleep, appetite, sexual desire, and pleasure. Symptoms of depression relate to these bodily functions (McClung, 2007). Of particular interest to psychologists is the link between stress hormones and depression. When stress hormones are released, they tend to inhibit the activity of brain neurotransmitters that are related to mood. Hence, repeated activation

## Neuroscience Applies to Your World:

### Let the Sun Shine In!

Sunlight helps regulate several hormones and neurotransmitters that have strong effects on mood and behavior. Two critical chemicals appear to be melatonin and serotonin. As the sun goes down, the level of sleep hormone called melatonin naturally increases, signaling the body that it is time to sleep. In the morning as the sun rises, our eyes transmit light information to the brain that signals a decrease in melatonin levels and an increase in serotonin levels. Serotonin wakes us up and keeps us in a good mood. *Seasonal affective disorder* (SAD), a type of depression that usually occurs in the fall and winter, seems to develop from inadequate bright light and the changes in brain neurochemistry that it brings. Treatment for SAD includes phototherapy (exposure to bright light 30 minutes daily), medications, and psychotherapy. Therefore, it is important to get an adequate amount of sunlight each day. Spend time outdoors during daylight hours, sit by open windows when you are unable to be outside, and use full spectrum lightbulbs in your living and work areas. Sunlight not only supplies us with Vitamin D, but it elevates our mood as well.

Stockbyte/Getty Images

unlovable. These negative attributions and cognitive distortions appear related to depressed mood (Abramson et al., 2002; Gibb et al., 2004; Moore & Fresco, 2007). Recently, Beck (2008) has suggested that early adverse experiences combined with biological vulnerabilities (genetics and neurochemistry) may influence the development of these cognitive deficits in people who are depressed. The negative cognitions then influence the interpretation and processing of future stressors as well as neurochemistry, creating a vicious cycle of biopsychosocial factors and the maintenance of depression.

## SOCIOCULTURAL FACTORS: SOCIAL STATUS, STRESS, AND GENDER

Sociocultural factors must also be considered when explaining mood disorders. Depression is more likely among people of lower social status (Blazer et al., 1994), especially those from adverse neighborhoods (Cutrona, Wallace, & Wesner, 2006). A considerable body of research also documents a consistent relationship between major stressful life events and the onset of depression, especially among people who are genetically predisposed to depression (Caspi et al., 2003; Green et al., 2010; Hammen, 2009; Monroe & Reid, 2009; Taylor et al., 2006; Wilhelm et al., 2006). Explaining such differences is further complicated by the worldwide gender difference in depression. As we have noted, women are more likely to be diagnosed with depression than men.

### You Asked...

*Why are women more likely to get depressed?*

ERIKA LARKINS, STUDENT

Biological, psychological, and social forces that are unique to women may explain their higher vulnerability to depressive disorders (see ■ FIGURE 13.5; Gorman, 2006; Mazure, Keita, & Blehar, 2002). We have already seen that the genetic risk of depression appears stronger in women than in men. Research has also investigated—over many years and many studies—the relationship between the female ovarian hormones, estrogen and progesterone, and mood in an effort to understand pathways to depression. However, it is not as simple as saying ovarian hormones *cause* depression. Symptoms of depression do not appear to correspond to changes in levels of estrogen and progesterone across the menstrual cycle (Steiner & Born, 2000). Rather, research suggests that women's estrogen and progesterone levels may influence the functioning of the neurotransmitter serotonin, which plays a central role in mood. However, researchers don't yet understand the precise actions by which estrogen and progesterone influence serotonin functioning (Hughes et al., 2009; Lu et al., 2003; Parker & Brotchie, 2004; Steiner, Dunn, & Born, 2003).

Biological differences in the stress response (see Chapter 11) may also be related to gender differences in depression (Parker & Brotchie, 2010; Young & Korszun, 2010). Psychological factors unique to women must also be considered when examining gender differences in depression. For example, females are more likely than males to engage in a ruminative coping style (Li, DiGiuseppe, & Froh, 2006; Lopez, Driscoll, & Kistner, 2009; Nolen-Hoeksema, 2001; Papadakis et al., 2006). That is, women tend to focus on how they feel and to fret about their feelings. Even co-rumination, or excessively talking about problems with friends, while offering women social support, can also amplify or increase one's depressive symptoms (Byrd-Craven et al., 2008; Rose, Carlson, & Waller, 2007). In contrast, men are more likely to engage in some activity to take their minds off their feelings, to withdraw, or to abuse drugs. As Nolen-Hoeksema and her colleagues (1999) put it, "Women think and men drink."

Women are also more likely to have an interpersonal orientation that puts them at risk for depression (Mazure et al., 2002). Relationships are more important to a woman's sense of self-worth than they are to a man's. As a result, women are

**FIGURE**

## 13.5

### Women and Depression

Biological, psychological, and sociocultural forces unique to women may explain their higher vulnerability to depressive disorders.

**Biological:** Women are genetically at risk for depression, and ovarian hormones may influence serotonin levels.

**Psychological:** Women tend to ruminate about problems, and relationships are a key part of a woman's self worth.

**Sociocultural:** Women's lower social status is a risk factor for stressors, and the female gender role encourages dependence and passivity.

© Masterfile

more likely to silence their own demands in order to maintain a positive relationship and are more likely to place their needs secondary to those of others. This relational style may also predispose women to depression.

Tied to these biological and psychological factors are the social circumstances that women face. Women are at a disadvantage in society: they earn less and have less power than men. They report less satisfaction with work and family and are more likely to be victims of violence, discrimination, sexual abuse, and poverty (Heim et al., 2009; Klonoff, Landrine, & Campbell, 2000; Koss & Kilpatrick, 2001). Negative life events such as these foster feelings of uncontrollability and helplessness, perceptions that are intimately connected to mood disorders (Browne, 1993; Fitzgerald, 1993; Ilgen & Hutchison, 2005). Traditional gender roles also discourage women from being masterful, independent, and assertive and encourage them to be dependent and passive. These prescribed roles may increase women's feelings of uncontrollability and helplessness (Barlow, 2002).

Although rates of major depression are higher in women, approximately 13% of U.S. men will experience a major depressive disorder sometime in their lives (NCS-R, 2007). We have also seen that men are at a much higher risk for committing suicide than women. Yet some men may not express the symptoms of depression in the same manner as women. Although men may report the physical symptoms of depression—fatigue, sleep problems, and loss of interest in their usual activities—men are less likely to cry and express sadness and are more likely to hide their feelings, be irritable, lash out at others, and abuse alcohol. Male gender-role socialization encourages men to be strong and in control, which may discourage men from admitting and expressing emotional distress (Cochran & Rabinowitz, 2000; Pollack, 1998).

For both men and women, depression is a complex behavior affected by biological, psychological, and sociocultural variables. Each of us probably has *some* biological vulnerability to mood disorders. However, social and psychological factors may act to protect us from such vulnerability or, alternatively, make us more likely to express this vulnerability. Research continues to explore the exact role these factors play. People's lives depend on it.

# Let's
# REVIEW

This section outlined the major types of mood disorders and described our current understanding of their causes. For a quick check of your understanding, answer these questions.

---

**1.** Maria has been sad for 3 weeks. She can't sleep, eat, or concentrate, and is constantly crying. She has lost interest in her usual activities. Maria would most likely be diagnosed with which disorder?
  a. Bipolar disorder
  b. Manic depression
  c. Major depression
  d. Cyclothymic disorder

**2.** Research on depression has found that people who are depressed are more likely to _____.
  a. engage in negative thinking
  b. engage in rumination
  c. believe they have little control over events
  d. All of the above

**3.** Which of the following statements about suicide is true?
  a. People who talk of suicide are often just looking for attention and will not kill themselves.
  b. Among adolescents, previous suicide attempts are a predictor of future attempts.
  c. A better mood means the risk of suicide is gone.
  d. Only people who are depressed commit suicide.

Answers 1. c; 2. d; 3. b

---

## LEARNING OBJECTIVES

● Describe the typical onset and prognosis for schizophrenia and its prevalence by gender and ethnicity.

● Identify and describe the symptoms of schizophrenia, and discriminate among the types of schizophrenia.

● Discuss our current understanding of the causes of schizophrenia.

# Schizophrenic Disorders: Disintegration

**Schizophrenia** is a chronic, disabling psychological disorder that affects roughly 1% to 2% of the general population worldwide (Ho, Black, & Andreasen, 2003). It involves the disintegration of one's personality.

Is schizophrenia the same thing as multiple personalities? No. Multiple personalities (now called *dissociative identity disorder*, as previously discussed) involve the existence of several *intact* personalities within a person. In schizophrenia, the one personality is no longer intact, or held together and connected. If we think of someone's personality as a related set of cognitive, emotional, perceptual, and motor behaviors, then in schizophrenia we see the disconnection among these personality elements. As these elements lose their connections with one another, the person loses his or her connection with reality. This results in impaired functioning.

## Onset, Gender, Ethnicity, and Prognosis

Symptoms of schizophrenia typically appear in adolescence or young adulthood. In some cases, the symptoms come on gradually; in others, they appear more abruptly. Schizophrenia affects men and women with equal frequency, although it typically appears earlier in men than in women. Men tend to develop the disorder in their late teens or early 20s, and women are generally affected in their 20s or early 30s (American Psychiatric Association, 2000a; Robins & Regier, 1991). This gender difference may be related to hormonal and sociocultural factors. The hormone estrogen may protect women by lessening abnormal brain development associated with schizophrenia (Canuso & Pandina, 2007). In addition, women's higher social competence and more extensive social networks may delay the onset of the disorder (Combs & Mueser, 2007; Hooley, 2010). Perhaps because of the earlier onset, men with schizophrenia tend to be more chronically impaired (Goldstein & Lewine, 2000; Ho et al., 2003).

**schizophrenia [skit-suh-FREE-nee-uh]**
a severe disorder characterized by disturbances in thought, perceptions, emotions, and behavior

Schizophrenia is diagnosed more often in African Americans and Asian Americans. However, this difference may be due to racial bias and cultural insensitivity (American Psychiatric Association, 2000a; Barnes, 2004; Bresnahan et al., 2007). Lifetime prevalence rates of schizophrenia are lower among Hispanics than among European Americans (Zhang & Snowden, 1999). Schizophrenia also is more prevalent in lower socioeconomic groups (Escobar, 1993; Kirkbride et al., 2007).

Most people with schizophrenia suffer throughout their adult lives, losing opportunities for careers and relationships (Hooley, 2010; Jobe & Harrow, 2010). Several factors contribute to this suffering: the negative stigma that a schizophrenia diagnosis brings, the lack of public understanding, and inaccurate media portrayals of people with schizophrenia as criminally violent. Most people with schizophrenia are not violent toward others but are withdrawn and prefer to be left alone (Steadman et al., 1998). Although there currently is no cure, a diagnosis of schizophrenia does not necessarily mean progressive deterioration in functioning, as most people believe. Rather, for reasons not yet understood, schizophrenic symptoms and episodes tend to decrease as a person ages, with 20% to 30% of people with schizophrenia showing only minor impairment 20 or 30 years later (Breier et al., 1991; Eaton et al., 1998; Jablensky, 2000). However, recovery is very much related to social factors such as economic and social support. Most people with schizophrenia continue to experience difficulties throughout their lives (Jobe & Harrow, 2010).

Schizophrenia is a severe psychological disorder marked by disordered thoughts, perceptions, emotions, and/or motor behavior, as depicted in this drawing by someone with schizophrenia.

## Symptoms of Schizophrenia

Schizophrenia may express itself in many forms, depending on which symptoms are present. People diagnosed with schizophrenia show two or more of the following symptoms nearly every day during a 1-month period with continued disturbance for at least 6 months. These symptoms are not due to substance use or a medical condition, and they interfere with the person's ability to function (American Psychiatric Association, 2000a). Symptoms of schizophrenia fall into two broad categories: positive and negative symptoms.

### POSITIVE SYMPTOMS OF SCHIZOPHRENIA

*Positive symptoms* of schizophrenia represent an excess or distortion of normal functions. They include *delusions, hallucinations, disorganized speech,* and *grossly disorganized* or *catatonic behavior.*

- **Delusions** are thoughts and beliefs that the person believes to be true but that have no basis in reality. For example, *persecutory delusions* involve beliefs about being followed or watched, usually by agents of authorities such as the FBI or the government. *Grandiose delusions* involve beliefs about being a famous or special person. For instance, a person with schizophrenia may believe that he is the president of France. People with schizophrenia may also hold *delusions of reference* (believing that others are talking about them) or *delusions of thought control* (believing that their thoughts are controlled by another person or force).

**delusion**  a thought or belief that a person believes to be true but in reality is not

Grunnitus Studio/Photo Researchers, Inc.

In catatonic schizophrenia, the person may remain in a "posed" position for hours on end.

- People who are diagnosed with schizophrenia also may experience **hallucinations**, in which the person sees, hears, tastes, smells, or feels something that others do not perceive. In schizophrenia, hearing voices or other sounds (called *auditory hallucinations*) is the most common altered perception, followed by *visual hallucinations* (seeing things that aren't there). The hallucinations may tell the person to perform certain acts or may be frightening in nature.

- The speech of individuals with schizophrenia is often disorganized in a variety of ways that impair effective communication (American Psychiatric Association, 2000a). **Disorganized speech** (*formal thought disorder*) involves a lack of associations between ideas and events. Because the ideas of people with schizophrenia lack connection, we refer to this disconnection as *loose associations*. Their ideas seem unrelated to one another, and their speech is often characterized as a *word salad* (words seem tossed together without any apparent syntax or organization). They may be saying a lot, but what they say is not communicating anything to the receiver.

- **Disordered behavior** may also characterize some people with schizophrenia. This may take the form of unusual, odd, or repetitive behaviors and gestures. Head banging, finger flapping, or tracing a pattern over and over again are examples. Childlike silliness, inappropriate sexual behavior (such as public masturbation), or difficulty maintaining hygiene may be present. Some people with schizophrenia may show an absence of all motor behaviors, remaining totally motionless and rigid for hours on end and resisting efforts to be moved. Such behavior is referred to as a **catatonic stupor**. Other people with schizophrenia may show **catatonic excitement**, in which they are suddenly agitated, fidgety, shouting, swearing, or moving around rapidly.

## NEGATIVE SYMPTOMS OF SCHIZOPHRENIA

*Negative symptoms* of schizophrenia represent a restriction or absence of normal functions. These include *blunted affect*, *alogia*, and *avolition* (American Psychiatric Association, 2000a). Approximately 25% of persons with schizophrenia display these symptoms (Ho et al., 2003).

- *Affect*, in psychological terms, refers to expressing emotions. Some people with schizophrenia show **blunted affect**, or a lack of emotional expression. They appear passive, with immobile facial expressions. Their vocal tone does not change even when the conversation is emotional in tone. They do not respond to events in their environment with any emotion. Their speech lacks the inflection that usually communicates a speaker's mood.

- **Alogia**, also called *poverty of speech*, refers to decreased quality and/or quantity of speech. The person with schizophrenia gives brief and empty replies.

- **Avolition** is the inability to follow through on one's plans. A person with schizophrenia may seem apathetic, sitting for long periods of time, showing little interest in his or her usual activities.

Many people with schizophrenia exhibit both positive and negative symptoms. The *DSM-IV-TR* recognizes five subtypes of schizophrenia, classified according to which symptoms are most prevalent. These five types—*paranoid, disorganized, catatonic, undifferentiated,* and *residual schizophrenia*—are described in ■ TABLE 13.5. People with schizophrenia who show predominantly positive symptoms tend to have a less severe course of schizophrenia and respond better to medication. For instance, positive symptoms predominate in *paranoid schizophrenia*, which may partly explain why people with paranoid schizophrenia tend to have a more favorable prognosis

**hallucination** perceiving something that does not exist in reality

**disorganized speech** a symptom of schizophrenia in which one's speech lacks association between one's ideas and the events that one is experiencing

**disordered behavior** a symptom of schizophrenia that includes inappropriate or unusual behavior such as silliness, catatonic excitement, or catatonic stupor

**catatonic [cat-uh-TAWN-ick] stupor** a disorder in motor behavior involving immobility

**catatonic excitement** a disorder in motor behavior involving excited agitation

**blunted affect** a lack of emotional expression

**alogia [uh-LO-jeeuh]** decreased quality and/or quantity of speech

**avolition [AA-vuh-lish-un]** the inability to follow through on one's plans

**TABLE 13.5**
*DSM-IV-TR* Types of Schizophrenia

| Type | Major Features |
|---|---|
| Catatonic schizophrenia | Extreme behavior in either direction: total unresponsiveness to the environment (stupor) or excessive motor activity (agitated excitement). |
| Disorganized schizophrenia | Speech and behavior are disorganized or difficult to understand; inappropriate emotions, such as giggling constantly for no apparent reason, and repetitive, purposeless, or silly behavior. |
| Paranoid schizophrenia | Delusions of grandeur or persecution, hallucinations that may be of a frightening nature. May exhibit anxiety and/or argumentativeness. |
| Undifferentiated schizophrenia | Schizophrenic symptoms present but does not meet criteria for other subtypes. |
| Residual schizophrenia | Only negative symptoms are present or prior positive symptoms have lessened in severity or frequency. |

*Reprinted with permission from the* Diagnostic and Statistical Manual of Mental Disorders, *Fourth Edition, Text Revision, Copyright 2000. American Psychiatric Association.*

than those with other types of schizophrenia (Fenton & McGlashan, 1994; Kendler et al., 1994). Such findings have led researchers to believe that positive symptoms of schizophrenia may have a different cause than negative symptoms.

# Explaining Schizophrenia: Genetics, the Brain, and the Environment

**You Asked...**

*If schizophrenia runs in the family, how likely is it that someone from a later generation will inherit the disorder?*

Kristin MacPherson, student

To date, biological factors account for the strongest evidence in the development of schizophrenia, although environmental factors must also be considered. It is likely that environmental conditions interact with biological factors to make a person either more or less susceptible to the illness. Biological research has focused on three main areas: genetics, brain abnormalities, and the malfunctioning of specific neurotransmitters in the brain. Environmental research has focused on prenatal and development factors, as well as the role of family and the environment.

## A STRONG GENETIC FACTOR

Family, twin, and adoption studies have routinely demonstrated a high heritability of schizophrenia (Levy et al., 2010; NIMH Genetics Workgroup, 1998; Parnas et al., 1993). As ■ FIGURE 13.6 shows, although the incidence of schizophrenia in the general population is 1% to 2%, the more genetically similar a person is to someone with schizophrenia, the more likely he or she will also develop the disorder (Cardno & Gottesman, 2000). In identical twin pairs, if one twin develops schizophrenia, the other twin has about a 48% chance of developing the disorder. However, in fraternal twins (who are not genetically identical), the probability is only 17%. Adoption studies show a similar pattern (Heston, 1966; Kety et al., 1994; Tienari et al., 2003). Adopted children who have biological parents with schizophrenia are 10 times more likely to develop the disorder than are adopted children whose biological parents are not diagnosed with schizophrenia.

LEARNING OBJECTIVE

● Describe the nature of personality disorders and give a brief description of the different types of personality disorders.

# Personality Disorders: Maladaptive Patterns of Behavior

Recall from our discussion on the *DSM* model that the **personality disorders** are represented on Axis II (see Table 13.1, p. 501). They consist of lifelong or longstanding patterns of malfunctioning. All of us have personality "quirks." Some people may be excessively neat. Others may be somewhat suspicious and mistrustful of others. However, these traits do not necessarily qualify someone for a personality disorder. In personality disorders, the person's behavior (1) is maladaptive to self or others and (2) has been stable over a long period of time and across many situations, typically since childhood or adolescence.

People with personality disorders also can be diagnosed with any of the clinical disorders previously discussed, and they typically seek treatment for these clinical disorders or because someone else has a problem with their behavior and encourages them to undergo therapy. Individuals with a personality disorder often don't see a problem with their behavior and, therefore, seldom seek treatment on their own. It is estimated that as many as 14% of adults in the United States meet the criteria for at least one personality disorder (Grant et al., 2004). The list of personality disorders is long, and space considerations prohibit a discussion of all of them, but we give a brief description of the *DSM* personality disorders in ■ TABLE 13.6. Here we will confine our discussion to two: *antisocial personality disorder* and *borderline personality disorder*.

**personality disorder**   a disorder marked by maladaptive behavior that has been stable over a long period and across many situations

**antisocial personality disorder**   a personality disorder marked by a pattern of disregard for and violation of the rights of others with no remorse or guilt for one's actions

## Antisocial Personality Disorder: Charming and Dangerous

> ### You Asked...
>
> Is ignoring the thoughts and feelings of others a symptom of a psychological disorder?
>
> VICTOR OCASIO, STUDENT

People who are impulsive and disregard the rights of others without showing any remorse or guilt are diagnosed with **antisocial personality disorder** (American Psychiatric Association, 2000a). A person with this disorder is commonly referred to as a psychopath. Antisocial in this context does not mean shy or unsociable, but rather indicates harmful acts against (anti) others (social). People who have antisocial personalities are callous and malicious, blame others for their problems, and frequently have difficulty maintaining social relationships. They can also be superficially charming and sociable, typically in order to manipulate others into doing what they want. Such antisocial or harmful behavior has often been present since childhood or adolescence (Loney et al., 2007). Serial murderers such as Charles Manson, Gary Gilmore, Andrew Cunanan, and Ted Bundy come to mind when thinking about antisocial personality disorder, as they have received much media attention. It is one of the more common personality disorders, and men are 5 times more likely than women to be diagnosed with this disorder (Cloninger, Bayon, & Przybeck, 1997; Grant et al., 2004).

People with antisocial personality disorder are more often sent to prison than to treatment. However, this does not mean that all criminals have antisocial personality disorder. Although antisocial behavior is highly correlated with criminal behavior, not all criminals are antisocial. One of the key features distinguishing the two is the lack of remorse and guilt for one's actions. A person can commit armed robbery

**WANTED BY THE FBI**
Andrew Phillip Cunanan
Unlawful Flight to Avoid Prosecution - Murder

Race: White; Sex: Male; Height: 5'9" - 5'11"; Weight: 160-185 lbs.
Date of Birth: 8/31/69; Hair: Brown (short); Eyes: Brown; Wears glasses and/or contact lenses
CAUTION: CONSIDER ARMED AND DANGEROUS
Please contact the nearest FBI office if you have any information on Andrew Phillip Cunanan.

AP Photo/FBI

Andrew Cunanan murdered famous clothes designer Gianni Versace after killing several others. He was described by many as a charming and bright young man.

## TABLE 13.6
## Types of Personality Disorders

| Disorder | Major Features |
|---|---|
| **Cluster A Disorders: Odd or Eccentric Behaviors** | |
| Paranoid personality disorder | Excessive suspicion and mistrust of others. |
| Schizoid personality disorder | Lack of desire to form close relationships with others; emotional detachment and coldness toward others. |
| Schizotypal personality disorder | Considered a mild version of schizophrenia. The person shows inappropriate social and emotional behavior, and unusual thoughts and speech. |
| **Cluster B Disorders: Dramatic, Emotional, or Erratic Behaviors** | |
| Antisocial personality disorder | Chronic pattern of impulsive behavior; violates rights of others and does not show remorse or guilt for actions. |
| Borderline personality disorder | Instability in mood, self-concept, and interpersonal relationships. |
| Histrionic personality disorder | Intense need for attention; always wants to be the center of attention; excessively dramatic behavior; rapidly changing moods. |
| Narcissistic personality disorder | Preoccupation with own sense of importance and view of self as above others; typically ignores the needs and wants of others. |
| **Cluster C Disorders: Anxious or Fearful Behaviors** | |
| Avoidant personality disorder | Intense and chronic anxiety over being negatively evaluated by others, so avoids social interactions. |
| Dependent personality disorder | Excessive need to be cared for by others; denies own thoughts and feelings and clings to others. |
| Obsessive-compulsive personality disorder | Pattern of rigid and perfectionist behavior; preoccupied with details, rules, order, and routine; experiences upset when routine is disrupted. (This is *not* the same as the anxiety disorder OCD.) |

yet afterward regret his actions. The antisocial person does not experience such regret or remorse. People with antisocial personality disorder may not be violent. They may be "con artists," and more of them may live outside of prison than in it. They may function successfully in business, politics, or entertainment (Stout, 2005).

What causes antisocial personality disorder? Some research suggests biological factors. Twin studies, adoption studies, and family studies support a genetic influence (Carey & Goldman, 1997; Hicks et al., 2004; Moffitt, 2005). For example, family members of people with antisocial personality disorder have higher rates of the disorder than the general population. Other research suggests low levels of the neurotransmitter serotonin (Moffitt et al., 1998); deficits in brain areas that control impulsivity, attention, and decision making (Henry & Moffitt, 1997; Kiehl et al., 2006; Raine, 2008); elevated levels of the hormone testosterone (van Honk & Schutter, 2007); and low arousal of the nervous system (Raine, 1997; Raine et al., 2000).

However, psychological and social variables cannot be ruled out. People with antisocial personality disorder often experience conflict-filled childhoods.

Their parents may be neglectful, inconsistent in discipline, harsh, hostile, or less warm. As a result, they often learn to expect such treatment from others and adopt a mistrustful and aggressive stance toward others (Dishion & Patterson, 1997; Feinberg et al., 2007). In all likelihood, a complex interplay between genes and environment best explains the development of antisocial personality disorder (Fowles & Dindo, 2009; Moffitt, 2005; Raine, 2008; van Goozen, Fairchild, & Harold, 2008).

## Borderline Personality Disorder: Living on Your Fault Line

**Borderline personality disorder (BPD)** is characterized by instability in moods, interpersonal relationships, self-image, and behavior (American Psychiatric Association, 2000a). This key feature of instability often disrupts people's relationships, career, and identity. Their unstable emotions result in intense bouts of anger, depression, or anxiety that may occur for hours or for a day. Their unstable self-concepts are reflected in extreme insecurity at some times and exaggerated feelings of importance at other times. This instability may prompt frequent changes in goals, jobs, friendships, and values because people with borderline personalities lack a clear definition of themselves. They have little idea of who they are. Their interpersonal relationships are also characterized by instability. They may admire, idealize, and cling to loved ones at first, but when conflict occurs, feelings of abandonment and rejection surface, and their feelings quickly turn to anger and dislike. They then seek out new friends or loved ones, and the cycle repeats itself. People with this disorder often feel unworthy, bad, or empty inside. At times of extreme insecurity and depression, self-injury and suicide attempts are common (D. W. Black et al., 2004; Paris, 2002).

People with BPD are often diagnosed with other clinical disorders such as major depression, substance abuse, or anxiety (Weissman, 1993). It is estimated that approximately 2% of the population will be diagnosed with BPD at some point in their lives, and it is diagnosed more often in young women than in men (Swartz et al., 1990). Extensive mental health services are often needed to treat people with BPD.

Research on BPD has focused on biological, psychological, and social factors. Low levels of serotonin are related to impulsive behaviors (Ni et al., 2007; Siever & Koenigsberg, 2000). Difficulty in regulating emotions may be related to abnormal brain functioning (R. J. Davidson, Jackson, & Kalin, 2000; Leichsenring et al., 2011; L. M. Williams et al., 2006). However, many people with BPD report a history of adverse life events such as abuse or neglect, making environment a probable factor (Bornovalova et al., 2006; Leichsenring et al., 2011). For example, in one study (Zanarini, 2000), a large percentage of patients with BPD had reported being sexually abused. Such social stressors may impede normal attachment patterns, identity development, and the ability to express appropriate emotions.

In this chapter, we have outlined six of the major categories of psychological disorders listed in the *DSM-IV-TR*. Each disorder meets the criterion of abnormality endorsed at the beginning of the chapter—inability to function. Although research continues into the exact origins of each disorder, we have seen that in many cases, a person's biological vulnerability appears to combine with psychological and sociocultural factors—learning experiences, thinking patterns, family interactions, cultural attitudes, gender roles—to trigger the onset of the disorder.

**borderline personality disorder (BPD)** a personality disorder marked by a pattern of instability in mood, relationships, self-image, and behavior

Many people with psychological disorders seek help in the form of therapy. So, keep the symptoms of these disorders in mind. It will assist you in mastering the material of the next chapter, where we explore the different therapies psychologists and psychiatrists use to treat psychological disorders.

# Let's REVIEW

This section described the nature of personality disorders, in particular antisocial and borderline personality disorders. As a quick check of your understanding, answer these questions.

**1.** Personality disorders are represented on which axis of the *DSM*?
  - **a.** Axis I
  - **b.** Axis II
  - **c.** Axis III
  - **d.** Axis IV

**2.** Felicia is extremely insecure and lacks a clear sense of identity. She often clings to new friends and then hates them a month later. She has an intense fear of abandonment and rejection. Felicia's behavior best fits which personality disorder?
  - **a.** Narcissistic
  - **b.** Antisocial
  - **c.** Borderline
  - **d.** Paranoid

**3.** Personality disorders _____.
  - **a.** do not coexist with clinical disorders such as depression or anxiety
  - **b.** generally appear in early or middle adulthood
  - **c.** are stable patterns of malfunctioning
  - **d.** do not pose any threat to others

*Answers 1. b; 2. c; 3. c*

# Studying THE CHAPTER

## Key Terms

agoraphobia (505)
alogia (526)
anhedonia (515)
antisocial personality disorder (530)
anxiety disorder (504)
avolition (526)
bipolar disorder (518)
blunted affect (526)
borderline personality disorder (BPD) (532)
catatonic excitement (526)
catatonic stupor (526)
cognitive distortion (521)
compulsion (506)
cyclothymic disorder (518)
delusion (525)

*Diagnostic and Statistical Manual of Mental Disorders (DSM)* (500)
disordered behavior (526)
disorganized speech (526)
dissociative disorder (511)
dissociative fugue disorder (512)
dissociative identity disorder (DID) (512)
dysphoria (515)
dysthymic disorder (517)
generalized anxiety disorder (GAD) (505)
hallucination (526)
hypochondriasis (513)
learned helplessness (520)
major depression (515)

mania (518)
medical model (498)
mood disorder (515)
obsession (506)
obsessive-compulsive disorder (OCD) (506)
panic disorder (505)
personality disorder (530)
phobic disorder (506)
posttraumatic stress disorder (PTSD) (507)
ruminative coping style (521)
schizophrenia (524)
social phobia (506)
somatoform disorder (513)
specific phobia (506)

# What Do You Know? Assess Your Understanding

Test your retention and understanding of the material by answering the following questions.

1. Allison can't help feeling sad most of the time. It upsets her that she can't be happy and seem "normal." Allison's behavior best fits which criterion of abnormality?
   a. Violation of social norms
   b. Personal distress
   c. Danger to others
   d. All of the above

2. If a person had "stage fright" or fear of public speaking to the degree that it interfered with his or her ability to function, these would be examples of which psychological disorder?
   a. Specific phobia
   b. Social phobia
   c. Major depression
   d. Agoraphobia

3. Dr. Sanchez believes that abnormal behavior is the result of irrational assumptions and negative thinking patterns. Dr. Sanchez views mental illness from a _____ perspective.
   a. social learning
   b. biological
   c. psychoanalytic
   d. cognitive

4. Julissa repeatedly complains about stomach pains and nausea. Numerous medical tests and procedures cannot find a physical cause for Julissa's symptoms. Julissa may be diagnosed with what type of psychological disorder?
   a. A mood disorder
   b. An anxiety disorder
   c. A somatoform disorder
   d. A dissociative disorder

5. Alogia and avolition represent _____ symptoms of schizophrenia.
   a. positive
   b. negative
   c. neutral
   d. undifferentiated

6. Some clinicians question the validity of dissociative identity disorder and suggest that it represents an extreme form of the anxiety disorder called _____.
   a. phobic disorder
   b. panic disorder
   c. generalized anxiety disorder
   d. posttraumatic stress disorder

7. Men are more likely than women to be diagnosed with _____.
   a. anxiety disorders
   b. substance abuse
   c. mood disorders
   d. schizophrenia

8. A young woman was picked up by police after she was found wandering the streets alone and confused. She asked the police to help her discover her identity. This woman is most likely to be diagnosed with which psychological disorder?
   a. Dissociative fugue disorder
   b. Hypochondriasis
   c. Agoraphobia
   d. Borderline personality disorder

9. Which psychological disorder is characterized by delusions, hallucinations, incoherent thought and speech, and inappropriate emotions?
   a. Dissociative identity disorder
   b. Schizophrenia
   c. Panic disorder
   d. Generalized anxiety disorder

10. For the last month, Dimitri has been dysphoric, has felt worthless, has been losing weight, can't concentrate, and constantly feels tired. Dimitri is most likely to be diagnosed with which psychological disorder?
    a. Bipolar disorder
    b. Major depression
    c. Cyclothymic disorder
    d. Manic depression

11. Jayne was shopping at the local mall when all of a sudden her chest felt tight, she couldn't catch her breath, her heart began to pound, and she felt shaky and dizzy. Since that day, Jayne has had several more episodes like this. They always strike without warning and in different types of situations. It is most likely that Jayne has _____.
    a. generalized anxiety disorder
    b. a phobic disorder
    c. panic disorder
    d. agoraphobia

12. Which of the following symptoms distinguishes bipolar disorder from major depression?
    a. Mania
    b. Dysphoria
    c. Apathy
    d. Delusions

13. Betta is always worried. She worries that her kids will get sick. She worries that she will lose her job. She worries that her husband will get cancer. Sometimes she is worried without even knowing why she is worried. Betta is most likely to be diagnosed with _____.

    a. posttraumatic stress disorder
    b. obsessive-compulsive disorder
    c. generalized anxiety disorder
    d. agoraphobia

14. Which personality disorder is characterized by instability in moods, interpersonal relationships, self-image, and behavior?

    a. Histrionic
    b. Narcissistic
    c. Antisocial
    d. Borderline

15. Which of the following information is *not* covered by the five axes of the current *DSM*?

    a. Medical conditions
    b. Causes of the disorder
    c. Personality disorders
    d. Environmental problems

16. Which brain structure is most involved in anxiety and fear?

    a. Frontal lobe
    b. Temporal lobe
    c. Hippocampus
    d. Amygdala

17. When depressed, Katelyn constantly thinks about her depression and why she is depressed. This often results in Katelyn being even more depressed. Katelyn's behavior is most consistent with _____.

    a. learned helplessness
    b. negative attributions
    c. a ruminative coping style
    d. compulsions

18. The most consistent brain abnormality found in people with schizophrenia is _____.

    a. a damaged frontal lobe
    b. enlarged ventricles
    c. less white matter
    d. larger brain size

19. Ozzie always wants to be the center of attention and is excessively dramatic. His moods rapidly change. Which personality disorder best fits Ozzie's behavior?

    a. Histrionic personality disorder
    b. Antisocial personality disorder
    c. Schizoid personality disorder
    d. Borderline personality disorder

20. Sociocultural theories emphasize the role of _____ in explaining abnormal behavior.

    a. negative thoughts
    b. unconscious conflicts
    c. unrealistic self-images
    d. environmental stressors

Answers: 1. b; 2. b; 3. d; 4. c; 5. b; 6. d; 7. b; 8. a; 9. b; 10. b; 11. c; 12. a; 13. c; 14. d; 15. b; 16. d; 17. c; 18. b; 19. a; 20. d

## Online Resources

Log in to **www.cengagebrain.com** to access the resources your instructor requires. For this book, you can access:

### Psychology CourseMate
CourseMate brings course concepts to life with interactive learning, study, and exam preparation tools that support the printed textbook. A textbook-specific website, Psychology CourseMate includes an integrated interactive eBook and other interactive learning tools including quizzes, flashcards, videos, and more.

### CENGAGENOW™
CengageNOW Personalized Study is a diagnostic study tool containing valuable text-specific resources—and because you focus on just what you don't know, you learn more in less time to get a better grade.

### WebTutor
More than just an interactive study guide, WebTutor is an anytime, anywhere customized learning solution with an eBook, keeping you connected to your textbook, instructor, and classmates.

# 13 LOOK BACK AT What You've LEARNED

Psychologists use several criteria, including *statistical infrequency*, *violation of social norms*, and *personal distress*, to define abnormal behavior. However, abnormality is best explained when a behavior *interferes with a person's ability to function*.

## How Can We Explain Abnormal Behavior? Perspectives Revisited

- Biological theories suggest that abnormal behavior is a mental illness or a disease resulting from physical causes.

- Psychological theories propose that psychological factors lead to abnormal behavior.

- Sociocultural theories suggest that environmental stressors and social factors such as age, race, gender, and culture influence abnormal behavior.

- Psychological disorders result from a combination of biological, psychological, and social factors (biopsychosocial model). They do not have just one cause.

## The *DSM* Model for Classifying Abnormal Behavior

DIAGNOSTIC AND STATISTICAL MANUAL OF MENTAL DISORDERS
FOURTH EDITION
TEXT REVISION
DSM-IV-TR

- The **Diagnostic and Statistical Manual of Mental Disorders** (**DSM**), currently in its fourth edition, is an atheoretical, multiaxial system that describes specific criteria for a diagnosis of a mental health disorder.

- Labeling someone with a psychological disorder can have negative effects because it may encourage the person to behave in a way that is consistent with the disorder.

## Anxiety Disorders: It's Not Just "Nerves"

- **Anxiety disorders** include physical, cognitive, emotional, and behavioral components.
- **Generalized anxiety disorder** is characterized by excessive anxiety, worry, and difficulty in controlling such worries.
- **Panic disorder** is characterized by recurrent panic attacks or the persistent fear of having a panic attack.
- **Phobic disorder** is a persistent fear of a specific object or social situation.
- In **obsessive-compulsive disorder**, a person experiences recurrent **obsessions** or **compulsions** that cannot be controlled.
- **Posttraumatic stress disorder** develops after exposure to a terrifying event. The person experiences distressing memories, nightmares, thoughts, or flashback episodes of the event that interfere with functioning.

- Potential causes of anxiety disorders include:

  - Biological factors such as genetics, neurotransmitter imbalances, and abnormal brain functioning

  - Psychological factors such as conditioning and maladaptive cognitions

  - Social factors such as rapid social change, stress, low social status, and gender

# WHAT ARE **PSYCHOLOGICAL DISORDERS, and** HOW CAN **WE** UNDERSTAND **Them?**

## Dissociative and Somatoform Disorders: Other Forms of Anxiety?

- **Dissociative disorders** are characterized by a loss of awareness of some part of the self.

- In **dissociative fugue disorder**, a person unexpectedly travels away from home and may assume a new identity with amnesia of the previous identity. In **dissociative identity disorder**, separate multiple personalities exist in the same person. Both disorders are believed to be related to severe stress or a series of emotionally traumatic events.

- **Somatoform disorders** are characterized by physical complaints or symptoms with no apparent physical cause, as in **hypochondriasis**. Psychological distress appears to underlie the physical complaints of these disorders.

## Schizophrenic Disorders: Disintegration

- **Schizophrenia** is a chronic mental health disorder characterized by positive symptoms (**delusions**, **hallucinations**, **disorganized speech**, **catatonic stupor**, or **catatonic excitement**), and negative symptoms (**blunted affect**, **alogia**, **avolition**).

- Types of schizophrenia include paranoid, disorganized, catatonic, undifferentiated, and residual.

- Potential causes of schizophrenia are primarily biological, including genetics, dopamine and glutamate activity, and abnormal brain functioning. However, family support and interactions or stressful living conditions may influence the course of the disorder.

Uygar Ozel/Getty Images

## Mood Disorders: Beyond the Blues

- **Mood disorders** are characterized by a significant change in one's emotional state over an extended period.

- In unipolar depression, the person experiences extreme or chronic sadness (**dysphoria**) or loss of pleasure (**anhedonia**).

- **Bipolar disorder** involves a shift in mood between two states: sadness and **mania**.

- Potential causes of mood disorders include:

  - Biological factors such as genetics, neurotransmitter imbalances, and stress hormones

  - Psychological factors such as unresolved issues of loss and rejection, **learned helplessness**, **ruminative coping style**, **cognitive distortions**, and pessimistic attributions

  - Social factors such as lower social status, stressful life events, and gender

## What Are Personality Disorders?

- The **personality disorders** consist of longstanding patterns of malfunctioning typically evident in childhood or adolescence.

- People who disregard the rights of others without showing any remorse or guilt are diagnosed with **antisocial personality disorder**.

- **Borderline personality disorder** is characterized by instability in moods, interpersonal relationships, self-image, and behavior.

- Personality disorders are related to biological factors (genetics, neurotransmitters, abnormal brain functioning) and psychosocial factors (inconsistent parenting practices, gender, conflict-filled childhood).

Grunnitus Studio/Photo Researchers, Inc.

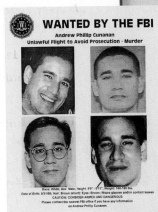

AP Photo/FBI

# 14

## WHAT **THERAPIES** ARE USED TO **TREAT** Psychological **PROBLEMS?**

# Chapter Outline

*Angel Rosa Rivera,* a 28-year-old veteran of the Marines, served two tours in the infantry before accepting a position as a combat instructor in Virginia. Now in college, Angel enrolled in a general psychology course to satisfy requirements for a nursing degree. After learning about the different types of therapy approaches, Angel can see how relevant this knowledge is to his previous military experiences.

As a section leader of enlisted men, Angel encountered many soldiers who had been diagnosed with PTSD. The soldiers had been in combat in Iraq and had witnessed ambushes, bombings, and the deaths and injuries of friends and fellow enlistees. Many had been away from loved ones for an extended period of time. Upon returning to the States, many of these men had difficulty adjusting after the stressful conditions in Iraq as they could not erase many of their combat experiences. The men saw a psychologist during group therapy sessions once a week, although some stopped going after one or two sessions. Looking back, Angel realizes that the men who continued group therapy were more likely to function better than those who were resistant to it. Often those who were resistant were more likely to get drunk or get into trouble. He also understands why the men were instructed to routinely fire off rounds from their guns—a desensitization therapy approach that you will soon learn about. Many of these men were also prescribed medications such as Zoloft and Xanax by a psychiatrist. Learning about biomedical therapies helped Angel understand what these medications do, and how they facilitate sleep and control rage responses.

*Angel Rosa Rivera can relate the various therapy approaches to his military service.*

© Ellen Pastorino

**Therapy** consists of techniques that are used to help people with psychological or interpersonal problems. All therapies attempt to change a person's behavior. However, the techniques that are used differ because each therapy approach stems from one of the main theoretical

**539**

perspectives introduced in the first chapter and explained in more detail in subsequent chapters. This chapter explores the principal approaches to therapy that are common today. We will begin by defining therapy, examining who is qualified to give it, and addressing when it is appropriate for a person to seek therapy.

# Providing Psychological Assistance

## LEARNING OBJECTIVES

● Distinguish between psychotherapy and biomedical therapy approaches.

● Describe the trained professionals who are qualified to give psychotherapy and biomedical therapy.

● Describe the four essential ethical principles that psychotherapists must follow when conducting treatment.

● Identify when a person should consider seeking therapy.

### You Asked...

*How does biomedical therapy differ from psychological therapy?*

SARAH KNYCH, STUDENT

Mental health professionals today use two broad forms of therapy to help people who are having difficulty functioning: *psychotherapy* and *biomedical therapy*. Many people, like the soldiers that Angel interacted with, receive therapy that combines both approaches.

## Psychotherapy vs. Biomedical Therapy

**Psychotherapy** is the use of psychological principles and techniques to treat the symptoms of psychological disorders, such as depression, or to treat interpersonal problems, such as troubled relationships. Psychotherapy is a general term that encompasses hundreds of different forms of therapy. However, all psychotherapies are based on the central assumption that underlying psychological factors such as emotions, cognitions, behavior, or relationships are at the root of interpersonal problems and psychological disorders.

In contrast, **biomedical therapy** uses medications or other medical interventions to treat the symptoms of mental health problems. Biomedical therapy assumes that biological factors, such as abnormal brain functioning or chemistry, are at the root of mental illness. As we saw in the previous chapter on psychological disorders, both assumptions are supported by substantial research. Indeed, American attitudes toward both psychotherapy and biomedical therapy have become more favorable over the years, as the Psychology Across Generations box highlights.

## Who Is Qualified to Give Therapy?

Trained professionals administer psychotherapy and biomedical therapy. A variety of educational and experiential backgrounds characterize psychotherapists (■ TABLE 14.1, p. 542). These include clinical psychologists, psychoanalysts, licensed counselors or social workers, and marital or family therapists. A master's degree is the minimum educational requirement for any of these professions, and some require doctorate-level degrees. Many therapists receive training in specialty areas or in specific forms of psychotherapy. For example, a psychoanalyst is trained in Freud's methods of treatment. Therapists' backgrounds often include internships in which they have been supervised in administering treatment. In addition, most states require licensing and/or certification of mental health professionals.

Only licensed psychiatrists or other medical doctors can legally administer biomedical therapies. Certification as a psychiatrist requires completion of medical school before specializing in psychiatry. In general, a psychiatrist is the only mental

**therapy**    techniques that are used to help people with psychological or interpersonal problems

**psychotherapy**    the use of psychological principles and techniques to treat mental health disorders

**biomedical therapy**    the use of medications or other medical interventions to treat mental health disorders

## Psychology Across Generations:

### Attitudes Toward Mental Health Services

How do you feel about psychotherapy? Would you seek professional help for a mental health problem? Would you feel comfortable talking to a professional about your personal problems? What are your attitudes toward biomedical therapy? Do you think there are benefits to psychiatric medications? Over the past several decades, questions such as these have been asked on surveys to measure the public's attitudes toward mental health services. The findings suggest that adult attitudes have become more accepting and favorable toward seeking psychotherapy and the benefits of psychiatric medications (biomedical therapy).

For example, Ramin Mojtabai (2007) compared data on adults' attitudes toward seeking mental health services from two large representative surveys of the U.S. population, one from 1990–1992 and one from 2001–2003. Compared to the earlier survey, participants from the more recent survey reported being more willing to seek professional help for a mental health problem, more comfortable talking with a professional about their problems, and less likely to report feeling embarrassed if others discovered they were seeking help for mental health issues. Attitudes of younger participants improved more than attitudes of middle-aged participants.

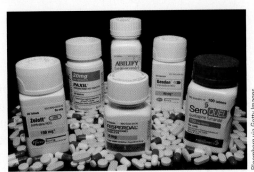

Mojtabai (2009) also assessed attitudes toward psychiatric medications by comparing data from adult participants in the U.S. General Social Survey of 1998 and of 2006. Participants in 2006 were more likely to say that medications help people deal with day-to-day stress, make it easier to deal with family and friends, and help people feel better about themselves. Participants in 2006 were also more likely to report a willingness to take medications for personal problems, depression, panic attacks, and to cope with life stresses.

Negative attitudes toward mental health services can influence a person to deny symptoms or delay treatment. Fortunately, as these studies have shown, attitudes toward psychotherapy and medications appear to be improving in the United States.

health professional who can prescribe medication. However, the right of clinical psychologists to prescribe medications is currently the subject of hot debate. For example, Louisiana and New Mexico grant prescription privileges to clinical psychologists who have completed additional training.

## Ethical Standards for Psychotherapists

In addition to being adequately trained and educated, mental health professionals are required to behave ethically and according to certain professional standards when conducting treatment. These are not legal statutes but rather standards established by the American Psychological Association (APA, 2002) indicating how psychotherapists should behave toward their clients. Violations of these standards should be reported to professional review boards that oversee the licensing of psychotherapists. Four essential ethical principles are *competent treatment, informed consent, confidentiality,* and *appropriate interactions.*

**TABLE 14.1**

## Types of Mental Health Professionals

| PROFESSION | EDUCATION | TRAINING |
|---|---|---|
| Clinical Psychologist | • College degree<br>• Graduate school in clinical psychology to earn a doctorate (PhD or PsyD; requires 5–8 years after college degree) | Supervised research and/or training in psychotherapy techniques, psychological testing, and the diagnosis of psychological disorders |
| Counseling Psychologist | • College degree<br>• Graduate school in counseling psychology or education to earn a doctorate (PhD or EdD; requires 4–6 years after college degree) | Supervised training in assessment, counseling, and therapy techniques |
| Licensed Professional Counselor | • College degree<br>• Graduate school to earn a master's degree in counseling (requires 3–5 years after college degree) | Supervised training in assessment, counseling, and therapy techniques |
| Licensed Social Worker | • College degree<br>• Graduate school in social work to receive a master's degree (MSW; requires 3–5 years after college degree) | Supervised training in a social service agency or a mental health center; may or may not include training in psychotherapy |
| Couple or Family Therapist | • College degree<br>• Graduate school to receive a master's degree in counseling, psychology, or social work (requires 3–5 years after college degree) | Supervised training in family and couple therapy; may also include training in individual psychotherapy methods |
| Psychiatrist | • College degree<br>• Medical school to receive a medical degree (MD or DO) and then specialize in psychiatry (requires 5–10 years after college degree) | Training in the diagnosis and prevention of psychological disorders with a focus on pharmaceutical treatment approaches; may include training in psychotherapy methods |

## COMPETENT TREATMENT AND INFORMED CONSENT

The primary responsibility of the clinician toward a client is to provide *appropriate and adequate treatment*. Such a guideline prevents clinicians from merely warehousing clients in a treatment center, a practice that was common in previous decades and centuries. When providing treatment, psychotherapists must get *informed consent* from their clients. This guideline involves fully informing clients of the nature of treatment and the details of their participation, including any potential side effects or consequences of treatment. These requirements are especially critical if any experimental types of treatment will be used. Additionally, clinicians must possess the necessary training to provide *culturally sensitive* and competent care to clients from diverse backgrounds including age, gender, race, ethnicity, religion, sexual orientation, disability, language, or socioeconomic status.

## CONFIDENTIALITY

Psychotherapists must respect the *confidentiality* of their communications with clients. They do not repeat to family members or friends any client discussions that occur within the context of therapy. Consultations with other professionals are permitted only when the client has agreed. Using client stories or experiences in a published work is not permitted without the express permission of the client. This ensures trust within the therapist–client relationship.

However, there are exceptions to this guideline. One exception occurs when the therapist believes that the client should be committed to a treatment facility.

In this circumstance, the therapist will have to break confidentiality to convince a court that the client is a danger to him- or herself or to others. Another exception to maintaining confidentiality occurs when others might be in danger. For example, if during therapy a client expresses violent intent toward another person, therapists are legally required to inform the potential victim of this potential harm. In addition, if a therapist suspects child abuse, partner abuse, or elder abuse, he or she is legally required to report such cases to the appropriate authorities.

## APPROPRIATE INTERACTIONS

Therapists must *interact appropriately* with clients for successful therapy to occur. For example, psychotherapists are forbidden from becoming sexually or romantically involved with any client, and are not to socialize with their clients. Psychotherapists do not drink alcohol with their clients or engage in intimate demonstrations of affection such as an arm around the waist. Psychotherapists are not to go into business with clients or establish any other form of social relationship that would impede the course of therapy. Unfortunately, when therapists are depicted in movies and on television, they often do not maintain these ethical standards. Such media portrayals confuse the public as to the appropriate behavior of therapists.

## Seeking Therapy

How do you find a therapist? Talk to family and friends for recommendations, use directories on the Internet, consult your local or state psychological association, or inquire at your community mental health center. Your church, temple, mosque, physician, or local college may also be a useful resource for finding a therapist.

### You Asked...

*What are the different types of psychotherapy?*

ALLY BURKE, STUDENT

Given the hundreds of psychotherapy approaches, which one should you choose? The next five sections of this chapter describe the main psychotherapy approaches. After reading about them, you may find that you are more comfortable with the philosophy, goals, and techniques of some over others. This information will assist you in understanding the nature of therapy, and in choosing a therapist if the need ever arises.

## Psychology Applies to Your World:

### When Does One Need to Consider Psychotherapy?

People seek psychotherapy for a variety of reasons. Many come to therapy because they are in distress from one of the many psychological disorders discussed in the previous chapter. Their behavior is maladaptive, or they are experiencing difficulty functioning in everyday life. They may be dealing with depression, extreme anxiety, or schizophrenia. Others who seek treatment have a history of mental illness and exhibit significant symptoms of a disorder. Some people are legally mandated to receive therapy by the court system. Unfortunately, people with severe mental illness are often at an economic disadvantage because they are more likely to be uninsured, so many do not receive adequate mental health care (McAlpine & Mechanic, 2000; Wang et al., 2005).

You do not have to be diagnosed with a psychological disorder in order to benefit from psychotherapy. Millions of people seek professional help to cope with other life problems. For example, couples and families in conflict may consider counseling to deal with their troubled relationships. People who have

*(continued)*

FIGURE

# 14.1

## Who Uses Therapy?

People are more likely to enter therapy if they have medical insurance and are educated. Therapy is also more likely to be used by people who are divorced or separated, people between the ages of 35 and 49, and females.

*Source: Olfson & Pincus, 1996.*

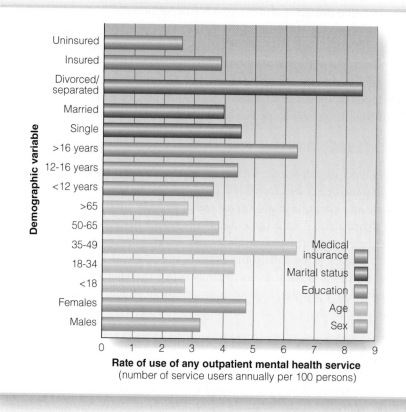

experienced major life transitions such as divorce, unemployment, retirement, or the death of a loved one may seek therapy to help them adjust to these changes. People are more likely to receive therapy if they have medical insurance and are educated. Females are also more likely than males to seek therapy (Olfson & Pincus, 1996; see ■ FIGURE 14.1).

You may want to consider therapy if you feel helpless, sad, blue, or anxious for a prolonged period or if such feelings do not improve despite several efforts to change them. You also may want to consider therapy if you are having difficulty carrying out your everyday activities. Therapy may also be useful if you want to make decisions differently, improve the functioning of important relationships, or change your life to feel more satisfied.

# Let's
# REVIEW

This section described the difference between psychotherapy and biomedical therapy, the necessary qualifications for therapists, the ethical standards that psychotherapists must follow, and when one should consider psychotherapy. As a quick check of your understanding, answer these questions.

**1.** Psychotherapy should be considered when _____.
  **a.** you get in trouble with your boss
  **b.** you are having difficulty functioning in some aspect of your life
  **c.** you have physical problems
  **d.** All of the above

**2.** Michael is seeing a social worker to help him with his interpersonal problems. Michael is undergoing _____.
  **a.** psychiatric counseling
  **b.** medical treatment
  **c.** psychotherapy
  **d.** biomedical therapy

**3.** Which of the following professionals is most likely to prescribe medication as a form of therapy?
  **a.** Clinical psychologist
  **b.** Social worker
  **c.** Biological psychologist
  **d.** Psychiatrist

Answers 1. b; 2. c; 3. d

# Psychoanalytic Therapies: Uncovering Unconscious Conflicts

As we have seen in previous chapters, Sigmund Freud originally developed the psychoanalytic approach based on his ideas about different levels of consciousness and personality formation. Recall that Freud theorized that each of us has an unconscious level that contains desires, urges, thoughts, and memories of which we are unaware or that have been repressed or hidden. These unconscious conflicts psychologically threaten the functioning of the ego by causing us distress and anxiety. Over the years, we continue to defend our ego by erecting more barriers to keep these conflicts hidden.

Freud assumed that symptoms of psychological disorders stem from these unresolved unconscious issues. Consequently, the goal of psychoanalytic therapies is to change maladaptive behavior by uncovering unconscious conflicts so that clients can gain *insight* into the real source of their problems (Wolitzky, 1995). Freud named this approach **psychoanalysis**. Professionals who administer this type of therapy are called *psychoanalysts*. Here we will describe two forms of psychoanalysis: *traditional psychoanalysis* and the more modern *psychodynamic approach*.

## Traditional Psychoanalysis

In traditional psychoanalysis as developed by Freud, the client lies down on a couch and talks about his or her concerns. It is the psychoanalyst's job to listen carefully and attentively to the client and discover what unconscious conflicts, themes, or concerns may be affecting the person. Uncovering unconscious conflicts is not an easy task. Therefore, the psychoanalyst uses several methods to help clients gain insight and uncover critical issues from their pasts (Freud, 1949). These methods include *free association*, *dream analysis*, and *interpretation*. The psychoanalyst also observes the client's behaviors for clues as to unconscious conflicts. Two examples of client behaviors that give such clues are *resistance* and *transference*.

**Free association** involves talking freely about a subject without censoring any thoughts. The client is fully awake and is asked to talk about a specific topic. The client says whatever comes to mind. The psychoanalyst makes very few comments during free association, instead focusing on important themes or issues that may be revealed.

**Dream analysis** is a tool that some psychoanalysts use to reveal unconscious conflicts (Pesant & Zadra, 2004). Dreams do not directly represent unconscious conflicts but rather are comprised of symbols that reflect these underlying unconscious impulses (see Chapter 4). It is the psychoanalyst's job to decipher the true meaning, or *latent content*, of these dreams and thereby reveal important unconscious issues.

Free association and dream content provide the psychoanalyst with information on the unconscious workings of the client's mind. The psychoanalyst can then make interpretations to the client. **Interpretations** are the psychoanalyst's views on the themes and issues that may be influencing the client's behavior. These interpretations may help the client gain insight into his or her problems.

However, if the client is not psychologically ready to deal with these issues, he or she may resist these interpretations. **Resistance** occurs when a client behaves in such a way as to deny or avoid certain topics or issues. A client may resist a psychoanalyst's interpretation because it is too close to the truth and therefore creates anxiety. Clients may miss appointments or arrive late as a way of resisting the revealing nature of the therapy session. Clients may laugh or joke about topics that are actually quite painful for them. These resistant behaviors provide the psychoanalyst an additional clue to the unconscious conflicts affecting the client.

**psychoanalysis [sigh-co-uh-NAL-uh-sis]** a method of therapy formulated by Freud that focuses on uncovering unconscious conflicts that drive maladaptive behavior

**free association** a technique in psychoanalysis in which the client says whatever comes to mind

**dream analysis** a technique in psychoanalysis in which the therapist examines the hidden symbols in a client's dreams

**interpretation** the psychoanalyst's view on the themes and issues that may be influencing the client's behavior

**resistance** a process in psychoanalysis whereby the client behaves in such a way as to deny or avoid sensitive issues

In psychoanalysis, the patient lies down on a couch away from the therapist so that the patient may freely associate and express whatever comes to mind.

© Jose Luis Pelaez, Inc./Corbis

The process of **transference** also provides a clue to a client's unconscious conflicts. Freud (1949) believed that at some point during therapy, clients would unconsciously react to the therapist as if the therapist were his or her parent, friend, sibling, or romantic partner. Freud termed this unconscious reaction *transference* because the client was unknowingly transferring feelings and emotions toward a loved one onto the therapist. The psychoanalyst can explore such instances of transference to reveal how the dynamics of clients' relationships may be influencing their behavior.

Traditional psychoanalysis was a dominant treatment approach through the 1950s. However, uncovering unconscious conflicts often took years and called for as many as five sessions per week. The long-term nature of traditional psychoanalysis made it increasingly impractical and expensive for the average person and for the growing involvement of the health insurance industry. The development of other psychotherapies as well as the advent of drug therapy (discussed later) also led to a decrease in the popularity of traditional psychoanalysis (Henry et al., 1994). Hence, psychoanalysis was forced to move in a new direction.

## Modern Psychoanalysis

Modern psychoanalysis, often referred to as **psychodynamic therapy**, or *short-term dynamic therapy*, is evident in many different forms. Such therapies are consistent with the views of Freud and the psychoanalytic approach. They continue to rely on the therapist's interpretations of the client's feelings and behavior, and on identifying instances of transference and resistance. However, modern psychoanalysis tends to focus less on the client's past. Current problems and the nature of interpersonal relationships are seen as more important in improving the client's behavior. The therapist also plays a more direct role, rapidly interviewing and questioning the client to uncover unconscious issues and themes in a shorter time. Then the therapist and client agree to focus on a limited set of problems that are seen as causing the client the most trouble. For example, in *interpersonal therapy*, extensive attention is given to the client's relationships and interpersonal behaviors that seem to be the most important in the onset and/or maintenance of depression. Modern psychoanalysis tends to be more short term, lasting no more than a few months, and appears to be effective in improving clients' symptoms (Abbass, Town, & Driessen, 2011; Blatt & Shahar, 2004; Cortina, 2010; Jakobsen et al., in press; Leichsenring & Leibing, 2007; Schottenbauer et al., 2008; Shedler, 2010; Slavin-Mulford et al., 2011).

**transference**   a process in psychoanalysis in which the client unconsciously reacts to the therapist as if the therapist were a parent, friend, sibling, or romantic partner

**psychodynamic therapy**   modern psychoanalysis delivered in a shorter time that focuses less on the client's past and more on current problems and the nature of interpersonal relationships

## Let's REVIEW

This section discussed the aim of psychoanalytic therapies and described traditional and modern psychoanalysis. As a quick check of your understanding, answer these questions.

1. The goal of psychoanalysis is to change behavior by _____.
   a. uncovering unconscious conflicts so that the client can gain insight into the source of his or her problems
   b. uncovering negative cognitive patterns that impede the client's ability to function
   c. examining environmental conditions and how they influence the client's responses
   d. providing the client with unconditional support and love so that he or she makes adaptive and healthy behavioral choices

2. Song often arrives late for her psychoanalysis appointment and sometimes forgets her appointments altogether. Her psychoanalyst might interpret Song's behavior as a sign of _____.
   a. transference          c. resistance
   b. interpretation        d. free association

3. Modern psychoanalysis differs from traditional psychoanalysis in that _____.
   a. it is shorter in duration
   b. it is focused less on the client's past and more on present relationships and issues
   c. the therapist is more direct
   d. All of the above

Answers 1. a; 2. c; 3. d

# Humanistic Therapy: Empathizing to Empower

As we have just seen, problems with psychoanalysis forced it to move in a new direction that resulted in briefer psychodynamic therapies that were still connected to the ideas of Freud. However, some psychoanalysts departed radically from these views and developed different forms of therapy. One example is *humanistic therapy*.

## The Aim of Humanistic Therapy Approaches

The *humanistic approach* focuses less on unconscious forces and more on the conscious actions we take in controlling our behavior. Humanists believe that behavior is driven not by unconscious impulses, but by how we interpret the world and our awareness of our feelings. The only way to understand a person's behavior, therefore, is to connect with and understand the person's worldview.

Humanism further assumes that people will naturally strive toward personal growth and achievement of their full potential when raised in a positive and accepting environment. When a person holds distorted perceptions or lacks self-awareness, psychological problems arise, preventing the person from becoming *self-actualized*. Yet people are capable of healing themselves, if only the right environment is provided. The therapist's role is to create this safe environment for self-exploration and facilitate the journey toward self-fulfillment (Greenberg & Rice, 1997). One of the most influential and best known of the humanistic therapies is *client-centered therapy*.

© Photofusion Picture Library/Alamy

In humanistic therapy, therapist and client sit face-to-face as they work together in solving the client's problems.

## Client-Centered Therapy

Disillusioned with the goals, methods, and assumptions of psychoanalysis, Carl Rogers (1902–1987) developed a different therapy approach that exemplifies the humanistic perspective. Whereas Freud saw the analyst as all-knowing and responsible for client change, Rogers believed that the therapist should serve more as a facilitator or coach to help move the client in the direction of change. Such a viewpoint resulted in **client-centered therapy**, or *person-centered therapy*. As the names imply, in client-centered therapy, the focus and direction of therapy comes from the person, or client. The client decides what to talk about, without interpretation or judgment from the therapist. The therapist, according to Rogers (1951, 1980, 1986), creates a positive and accepting environment to facilitate self-awareness and personal growth by providing three key characteristics: *empathy*, *genuineness*, and *unconditional positive regard*.

### EMPATHY: UNDERSTANDING THE CLIENT

Are you a good listener? Do friends and family frequently confide in you? If so, then you may possess empathy. According to Rogers, **empathy** is the ability to understand a client's feelings and thoughts without being judgmental. The therapist does not express disapproval toward the client but rather indicates understanding of the client's feelings. Conveying empathy involves actively listening to the client—making eye contact, nodding as the client speaks, and assuming an interested and attentive pose. Empathy also involves *reflection*. The therapist restates, repeats, or summarizes the thoughts and feelings that he or she hears the client express. Reflected statements communicate to the client the active attention

**client-centered therapy** a humanistic psychotherapy approach formulated by Carl Rogers that emphasizes the use of empathy, genuineness, and unconditional positive regard to help the client reach his or her potential

**empathy** the ability of a therapist to understand a client's feelings and thoughts without being judgmental

of the therapist and mirror the client's perceptions and views of reality. Consider this example of empathy and reflection from Irvin Yalom's work, *Love's Executioner and Other Tales of Psychotherapy* (1989, p. 29).

> Client: I believe he is intentionally trying to drive me to suicide. Does that sound like a crazy thought?

> Therapist: I don't know if it's crazy, but it sounds like a desperate and terribly painful thought.

Notice in this example that the therapist does not judge the client's thoughts as crazy and reflects the emotions underlying the statement of suicide. Ideally, empathy and reflection will help clients see themselves and their problems more clearly, promoting a realistic self-image and greater self-acceptance.

## GENUINENESS: SHARING THOUGHTS, FEELINGS, AND EXPERIENCES

A second key therapist quality in client-centered therapy is genuineness. **Genuineness** is the ability to openly share one's thoughts and feelings with others. The therapist expresses his or her true feelings and thoughts to the client and does not hide behind the mask of being the "professional," "doctor," or authority figure. The therapist self-discloses a fair amount to the client, which allows the client to see the therapist as a real, living person. Such disclosure also creates an open environment that promotes trust and an honest expression of thoughts and feelings. Rogers believed that such an environment would model to the client how relationships can be built on a foundation of trust and honesty.

## UNCONDITIONAL POSITIVE REGARD: VALUING THE CLIENT

The third key quality in client-centered therapy, unconditional positive regard, was introduced in the chapter on personality (Chapter 12). Recall that Rogers defined **unconditional positive regard** as the ability to accept and value a person for who he or she is, regardless of his or her faults or problems. Rogers believed that receiving unconditional positive regard in one's childhood is a key factor in healthy personality adjustment. A therapist who offers unconditional positive regard to a client does not indicate shock, dismay, or disapproval to any client statements. Instead, the therapist communicates caring and respect toward the client regardless of what the client says.

This does not mean that the therapist has to personally *agree* with everything the client states. Rather, the therapist's job is to reflect the client's feelings and thoughts in order to further the client's self-knowledge and enable the client to solve problems in his or her own way. Unconditional positive regard enables the client to believe that he or she has value and is competent at making decisions. Such attitudes foster self-confidence and self-acceptance that lead to healthier growth choices.

For Rogers, a therapist who demonstrates all three qualities—empathy, genuineness, and unconditional positive regard—establishes a positive and nurturing environment. A person feels accepted, understood, and valued. These feelings help the client self-explore a more realistic self-image and perception of the world. This in turn removes the obstacles to personal growth so that self-actualization can be realized.

Does client-centered therapy work? Compared to no-treatment control groups, people in client-centered therapy do change their behavior (Greenberg & Rice, 1997; Hill & Nakayama, 2000). Compared to more structured therapy approaches, client-centered therapy is equally effective (Greenberg, Elliot, & Lietaer, 1994; Stiles et al., 2006, 2008).

**genuineness** the ability of a therapist to openly share his or her thoughts and feelings with a client

**unconditional positive regard** the ability of a therapist to accept and value a person for who he or she is, regardless of his or her faults or problems

# Let's
# REVIEW

This section described humanistic approaches to therapy. As a quick check of your understanding, answer these questions.

**1.** The goal of humanistic therapy is to change behavior by _____.
   a. uncovering unconscious conflicts so that the client can gain insight into the source of his or her problems
   b. uncovering negative cognitive patterns that impede the client's ability to function
   c. examining environmental conditions and how they influence the client's responses
   d. providing the client with a safe environment for self-exploration and facilitating the journey toward self-fulfillment

**2.** Which of the following is *not* one of the elements used in client-centered therapy to help the client achieve self-fulfillment?
   a. Genuineness
   b. Free association
   c. Unconditional positive regard
   d. Empathy

**3.** Marcos is receiving client-centered therapy. His therapist openly shares his thoughts and feelings with Marcos, relating his own experiences that are similar to those of Marcos'. Marcos' therapist is exhibiting which quality of client-centered therapy?
   a. Genuineness
   b. Reflection
   c. Unconditional positive regard
   d. Empathy

*Answers 1. d; 2. b; 3. a*

# Behavior Therapies: Learning Healthier Behaviors

**Behavior therapy** focuses directly on changing current problem behaviors rather than delving into the client's past. Behavior therapies, also called *behavior modification*, consist of techniques and methods that use learning principles to change problem behavior. Chapter 5 described the learning processes of classical conditioning and operant conditioning. The behavioral perspective relies on these principles to modify behavior. Recall that the *behavioral perspective* assumes that behavior is a result of environmental variables such as stimuli and consequences in the environment. It further assumes that people learn maladaptive behavior in the same way that they learn adaptive behavior. So, changing behavior involves changing the environmental circumstances that seem to elicit negative behavior. Learning principles that focus on *extinction* are used to stop disruptive behaviors. Similarly, learning principles that focus on *shaping* or acquiring behaviors are used to replace undesirable behaviors with more adaptive ones.

Behavior therapy can take many forms. Here we discuss two broad categories of behavior therapy: *classical conditioning techniques* and *operant conditioning techniques*.

## LEARNING OBJECTIVES

● Describe the aim of behavior therapy approaches.

● Describe systematic desensitization, flooding, and aversion therapy, and explain how they operate through classical conditioning processes.

● Explain how operant conditioning techniques are used in therapy to modify or change problem behavior.

## Classical Conditioning Techniques

Some behavior therapies rely on the principles of classical conditioning outlined in Chapter 5. Briefly, classical conditioning occurs when stimuli in the environment become associated so that both produce the same response. For example, as a child,

**behavior therapy**   therapy that applies the principles of classical and operant conditioning to help people change maladaptive behaviors

one of the authors was bitten by a dog twice within a two-year period. In both instances, the dog was a German shepherd. Following those incidents, she developed an intense fear of large dogs. Her dog-biting experiences became associated with pain, so that now she feared pain from all large dogs and routinely avoided them. Her fear was a learned behavior. Behavior therapy would focus on having her unlearn her response to dogs. Three behavior therapy techniques that rely on classical conditioning principles are *systematic desensitization*, *flooding*, and *aversion therapy*.

## SYSTEMATIC DESENSITIZATION: RELAX AND HAVE NO FEAR

One effective tool for treating phobias and anxiety is systematic desensitization (Wolpe, 1958). **Systematic desensitization** involves replacing a fear or anxiety response with an incompatible response of relaxation and positive emotion. Anxiety and relaxation are *competing responses*. You cannot feel both at the same time; you can only feel one or the other. So the aim of systematic desensitization is to have a client learn how to relax and then slowly and systematically introduce the feared object, situation, or thought while the client maintains a positive state of pleasure or relaxation. An early example of systematic desensitization was an experiment by Mary Cover Jones (1924) in which she treated a 3-year-old's fear of rabbits. The child, Peter, sat at a distance from a caged rabbit while eating one of his favorite foods. The cage was gradually moved closer to Peter until he was able to play with the rabbit and not experience any fear. Jones had countered Peter's negative emotional reaction of fear with a positive one of pleasure from the food.

Systematic desensitization is accomplished in three basic steps. First, the client is trained in *progressive muscle relaxation*. This method involves alternately tensing and relaxing different muscle groups, beginning with the head and working down to the toes, so that the client learns to distinguish when muscles are tense and when they are relaxed.

> ### YOUR TURN : Active Learning
>
> Try progressive muscle relaxation training on your own. Close your eyes and take deep breaths for a minute. Then tighten your jaw muscles and clench your teeth. Hold the tension for a few moments and then relax and take several deep breaths. Do the same for your eyes, forehead, neck, and shoulders, alternating between tensing your muscles and then relaxing them. You will be pleasantly surprised by how a few minutes of this procedure can reduce tension.

Once the client has learned progressive relaxation, the client and therapist develop an anxiety hierarchy. An **anxiety hierarchy** (■ FIGURE 14.2) is a list of situations or items that trigger a client's anxiety or fear. The items on the hierarchy start with the least anxiety provoking situations or items and progress to the most distressing.

In the third step, progressive relaxation and the anxiety hierarchy are combined. Relaxation is paired with each item in the hierarchy. As the client becomes able to imagine a feared situation and remain relaxed, the next item in the hierarchy is addressed. Over several therapy sessions, this systematic process continues until the client has become desensitized to all items in the hierarchy.

You may be skeptical at this point, unconvinced that thinking about a feared stimulus is similar to actually encountering the object or situation. This skepticism is somewhat warranted, so once the client has mastered the mental images, behavior therapists can extend systematic desensitization to a simulated or actual environment. For many fears, this is when systematic desensitization is most effective (Antony & Barlow, 2002; Menzies & Clark, 1993). For example, flight

**systematic desensitization** [sis-tuh-MAT-ick dee-sen-sih-tuh-ZAY-shun] a behavior therapy technique that uses a gradual, step-by-step process to replace fear or anxiety with an incompatible response of relaxation and positive emotion

**anxiety hierarchy** a list that orders, according to the degree of fear, the situations or items that trigger anxiety; the list starts with the least frightening images and progresses to the most distressing

**An Anxiety Hierarchy for Systematic Desensitization**

*Degree of fear*

| | |
|---|---|
| 5 | I'm standing on the balcony of the top floor of an apartment tower. |
| 10 | I'm standing on a stepladder in the kitchen to change a light bulb. |
| 15 | I'm walking on a ridge. The edge is hidden by shrubs and treetops. |
| 20 | I'm sitting on the slope of a mountain, looking out over the horizon. |
| 25 | I'm crossing a bridge 6 feet above a creek. The bridge consists of an 18-inch-wide board with a handrail on one side. |
| 30 | I'm riding a ski lift 8 feet above the ground. |
| 35 | I'm crossing a shallow, wide creek on an 18-inch-wide board, 3 feet above water level. |
| 40 | I'm climbing a ladder outside the house to reach a second-story window. |
| 45 | I'm pulling myself up a 30-degree wet, slippery slope on a steel cable. |
| 50 | I'm scrambling up a rock, 8 feet high. |
| 55 | I'm walking 10 feet on a resilient, 18-inch-wide board which spans an 8-foot-deep gulch. |
| 60 | I'm walking on a wide plateau, 2 feet from the edge of a cliff. |
| 65 | I'm skiing an intermediate hill. The snow is packed. |
| 70 | I'm walking over a railway trestle. |
| 75 | I'm walking on the side of an embankment. The path slopes to the outside. |
| 80 | I'm riding a chair lift 15 feet above the ground. |
| 85 | I'm walking up a long, steep slope. |
| 90 | I'm walking up (or down) a 15-degree slope on a 3-foot-wide trail. On one side of the trail the terrain drops down sharply; on the other side is a steep upward slope. |
| 95 | I'm walking on a 3-foot-wide ridge. The slopes on both sides are long and more than 25 degrees steep. |
| 100 | I'm walking on a 3-foot-wide ridge. The trail slopes on one side. The drop on either side of the trail is more than 25 degrees. |

**FIGURE**

# 14.2

### Sample Anxiety Hierarchy

An anxiety hierarchy like the one shown here is used during systematic desensitization. This hierarchy was developed for a woman who had a fear of heights.

*From K. E. Rudestam,* Methods of Self Change: An ABC Primer, *© 1980 Wadsworth. Reprinted with permission of the author.*

Virtual reality exposure therapy allows clients to experience their fears in a simulated, nonthreatening environment.

simulators can be used to help desensitize people to a fear of flying. Combining systematic desensitization with the actual situation, called *in vivo exposure*, is also a very effective tool in treating a variety of anxiety disorders (Choy, Fyer, & Lipsitz, 2007; Follette & Hayes, 2000; Gould et al., 1997).

Virtual reality computer technology also can be used to simulate a feared situation. Virtual reality bridges the gap between imagining feared stimuli in a therapist's office and in vivo exposure in the field by simulating a feared situation. The client wears a head-mounted display with small video monitors and stereo earphones that integrate visual and auditory cues to immerse the client in a computer-generated virtual environment. For example, a person with a fear of flying may be exposed to stimuli that simulate sitting in a plane and hearing the plane's engines revving for takeoff. A person with a fear of public speaking may experience simulation of standing at a podium. The therapist can control the images the client receives while monitoring heart rate, respiration, and skin temperature to assess the client's fear responses during the session (Bender, 2004).

Virtual reality exposure therapy provides an effective treatment for people who have a fear of heights and of flying (Krijn et al., 2004; B. O. Rothbaum et al., 1995, 1996; Wiederhold et al., 2002). It also has had some success in treating driving phobia (Wald & Taylor, 2003), social phobia (Klinger et al., 2005), fear of public speaking (P. L. Anderson et al., 2005; Harris, Kemmerling, & North, 2002), panic disorders (Botella et al., 2004; de Carvalho, Freire, & Nardi, 2010), and posttraumatic stress disorder (J. G. Beck et al., 2007; Difede & Hoffman, 2002; McLay et al., 2010; Rothbaum, Rizzo, & Difede, 2010). It has become an increasingly common treatment for anxiety and specific phobias (Gerardi et al., 2010; Parsons & Rizzo, 2008).

## FLOODING: FACING OUR FEARS

Another form of behavior therapy that relies on classical conditioning processes is flooding. In **flooding**, the client remains exposed to the feared object, situation, or image for a prolonged period (1 to 2 hours) until his or her anxiety decreases. Recall from Chapter 5 that this is a process called *extinction* in which the CS (the feared item) is presented by itself until it no longer produces the CR of anxiety and fear. In contrast to systematic desensitization, flooding starts with the *most* feared item or situation rather than the least distressing item. In addition, instead of relaxing, the client is told to experience the fear fully and is prevented from escaping the situation or engaging in any other anxiety-avoiding behaviors. Whatever terrible consequences the client imagined would happen do not occur, and his or her anxiety decreases.

Flooding can be an effective and efficient way to reduce anxiety and fear (McNeil & Kyle, 2009; Tryon, 2005). A client's anxiety subsides rather quickly; however, relapses (return of the fear) are common (Escobar, 2008). This should not be surprising if you recall the concept of spontaneous recovery in which the conditioned response (anxiety) can reappear after it has been extinguished. For this reason, flooding is often used in combination with other therapy techniques (Corey, 2009). Because of the discomfort associated with flooding, it is ethically imperative that clients be fully informed and prepared for flooding treatment.

## AVERSION THERAPY: WE WON'T DO SOMETHING IF WE DISLIKE IT

Do you bite your nails? As a child, did you suck your thumb? Did loved ones try to get you to stop such behaviors? Many parents put a foul-tasting or spicy liquid such as Tabasco sauce on their child's nails or thumb to stop nail-biting or thumb-sucking. These parents unknowingly are performing *aversion therapy*, another example of a behavior therapy that relies on classical conditioning principles. **Aversion therapy** involves pairing an unpleasant stimulus (foul or spicy taste) with a specific undesirable behavior such as biting one's fingernails. Ideally, the aversive stimulus becomes associated with the undesirable response so that the person is less likely to engage in the response again.

Aversive conditioning occurs frequently in everyday life. Food poisoning is a prime example. If a particular food has ever made you sick, normally it will be months or even years before you touch that food again. The food (stimulus) becomes associated with being sick (response) so that you avoid it at all costs. Therapists use this knowledge to treat a variety of undesirable habits and behaviors. For example, an aversion therapy method for treating alcoholism involves taking a drug called Antabuse (Cannon & Baker, 1981). Antabuse interacts with alcohol, causing nausea and vomiting. If a person with alcohol dependence drinks while using Antabuse, it makes him or her ill. The unwanted stimulus (alcohol) becomes associated with the response of feeling ill and nauseated. The person with alcoholism learns to avoid alcohol in order to avoid the associated unpleasant response. Unfortunately, the person with alcohol dependence can also simply avoid taking the medication, thereby nullifying the effectiveness of the procedure.

In clinical trials, Antabuse has demonstrated mixed results in helping people abstain from alcohol use. When Antabuse is given under supervision and in conjunction with a drug that specifically reduces alcohol cravings, its effectiveness is improved (Barth & Malcolm, 2010; Johnson, 2008; Krampe & Ehrenreich, 2010; Suh et al., 2006).

Aversion therapy also has been effective in eliminating a variety of other undesirable behaviors, including compulsive hair pulling, gambling, smoking (tobacco, marijuana, or crack cocaine), and maladaptive sexual behaviors (Emmelkamp, 1994; Laws, 2001).

**flooding**  a behavior therapy technique in which a client is exposed to a feared object or situation for a prolonged period until his or her anxiety extinguishes

**aversion [uh-VER-shun] therapy**  a behavior therapy technique in which a specific behavior is paired with an unpleasant stimulus in order to reduce its occurrence

An alternative form of aversion therapy is called **covert sensitization therapy**. In this procedure, graphic imagery is used to create unpleasant associations with specific stimuli. For example, a person who smokes cigarettes may have to repeatedly imagine black and diseased lungs when faced with the stimulus of a cigarette. At this point, you may be disturbed by the knowledge that therapists use such unpleasant procedures in treatment. Keep in mind, though, that therapists are ethically bound to get informed consent from clients. Clients are informed of the procedure and must agree before such a method can be used.

## Operant Conditioning Techniques

Whereas systematic desensitization, flooding, and aversion therapy rely on classical conditioning principles, some behavior therapies rely on the principles of operant conditioning outlined in Chapter 5. Briefly, operant conditioning focuses on the consequences of a behavior. It assumes that reinforced behavior will be maintained and punished behavior will be extinguished. For instance, in the previous example in which your author developed a fear of large dogs, recall that following the dog-biting episodes she responded by avoiding large dogs. The consequence of this response was reinforcing—it reduced her fear. She learned that the next time she encountered a large dog, avoiding it would quickly rid her of any anxiety.

Changing undesirable behavior, therefore, involves changing the consequences of a behavior. These changes can be accomplished in a variety of ways (Thorpe & Olson, 1997).

1. *Positive Reinforcement.* Positive reinforcement is used to encourage or maintain a behavior. For example, every time a child complies with a parental request, verbal praise follows. After the child's compliance increases, verbal praise need not occur every single time.

2. *Nonreinforcement and Extinction.* To discourage unwanted behavior, any reinforcers of the behavior are removed. For instance, to discourage a child from throwing tantrums at home, the child's parents ignore the behavior so that no attention (even negative attention, such as a reprimand) reinforces the behavior. If a reinforcer does not follow a behavior, the behavior will occur less frequently. Eventually the behavior will be eliminated or extinguished. However, keep in mind that often the unwanted behavior will increase before it goes away because a person is expecting the reinforcer. The child's tantrums will initially be longer or more frequent in an attempt to get a reaction from the parents. Misbehavior may also continue because all subtle forms of reinforcers have not been eliminated. For example, consider what happens when the same child acts up in school. Although the teacher may scold or reprimand the child, the child still receives a form of attention, and therefore the behavior may not subside. Even if the teacher ignores the child's misbehavior, classmates may reinforce the behavior by laughing and paying attention to him or her.

3. *Punishment.* Sometimes punishment is used to decrease undesirable behaviors. Recall that punishment occurs when an undesired behavior is immediately followed by a negative or aversive consequence such as loss of a privilege. But also remember the side effects of punishment. It can produce negative emotions such as anger or fear, or negative behaviors, such as avoidance. For these reasons, punishment is used sparingly.

**covert sensitization [co-VERT sen-sih-tuh-ZAY-shun] therapy** a milder form of aversion therapy in which graphic imagery is used to create unpleasant associations with specific stimuli

Children's tantrums can be eliminated if their inappropriate behavior is not reinforced. However, keep in mind that the child's tantrums will initially get worse as the child attempts to get a reaction from loved ones.

© Ed Kashi/Corbis

4. *Shaping.* Recall from Chapter 5 that shaping involves positively reinforcing each successive attempt at a behavior. It is used to teach a person new, desired behaviors. For example, shaping may be used to teach children with autism how to speak. If the child makes a "t" sound to say *toy*, this attempt is rewarded. Shaping has also been successfully used to teach people with intellectual disabilities self-help skills, such as washing their face or brushing their teeth.

5. *Token Economy.* A **token economy** involves rewarding people with tokens, or symbolic rewards, for desired behavior. Because not everyone is influenced by the same reward, tokens—such as chips, points, or stars—are given each time a person engages in a desired behavior. These tokens can then be exchanged for a variety of reinforcers such as food, privileges, goods, phone time, and so on.

You may recall having had a treasure chest or goody box in elementary school. Students who had acquired a certain number of points or tokens could visit the prize box at the end of the week. Today, your consumer behavior may be unknowingly reinforced by a token economy. Many credit card companies offer points for purchases. These points can then be exchanged for a variety of merchandise. Airlines do the same thing with frequent flyer points. Their aim is to increase your consumption of their services.

The same principle can be used in hospitals, halfway houses, prisons, drug abuse treatment centers, and other institutional settings. People earn tokens for desired behavior and constructive activities, and then exchange them for passes, free time, meals, access to television, or private rooms. In some institutions, patients may lose or be charged tokens for undesired behavior such as fighting, noncompliance, or not completing their chores. A token economy can be a very effective tool for treating children with intellectual disabilities and autism, and for managing behavior in a group setting (Adams et al., 2002; Matson & Boisjoli, 2009; Mottram & Berger-Gross, 2004; Petry et al., 2004).

Although behavior therapies have been very successful in treating a variety of psychological and behavioral problems, particularly in children, they do not address the thoughts and perceptions that often accompany behavior. For this reason, behavioral strategies have been increasingly used in conjunction with cognitive therapy (Wilson, Hayes, & Gifford, 1997), our next topic of discussion.

**token economy**    a behavioral therapy technique in which people are rewarded with tokens for desired behavior; the tokens can then be exchanged for what is reinforcing to the individuals

**rational-emotive therapy**    a cognitive therapy approach created by Albert Ellis that focuses on changing the irrational beliefs that are believed to impede healthy psychological functioning

## Let's REVIEW

This section described behavior therapy approaches and the ways in which classical and operant conditioning techniques are used to change behavior. For a quick check of your understanding, answer these questions.

1. Behavior therapies change behavior by _____.
   a. uncovering unconscious conflicts so that the client can gain insight into the source of his or her problems
   b. uncovering negative cognitive patterns that impede the client's ability to function
   c. examining and then changing the environmental circumstances that seem to elicit negative behavior
   d. providing the client with a safe environment for self-exploration and facilitating the journey toward self-fulfillment

2. Celia goes to a therapist to try to reduce her fear of driving. The therapist teaches Celia how to relax and then has her imagine those aspects of driving that make her fearful while maintaining her relaxed mode. Celia is most likely undergoing _____.
   a. aversion therapy
   b. a token economy
   c. systematic desensitization
   d. client-centered therapy

3. Which of the following is a therapy approach based on the principles of classical conditioning?
   a. A token economy     c. Positive reinforcement
   b. Shaping              d. Aversion therapy

# Cognitive Therapies: Thinking Through Problems

Many psychological problems such as anxiety and depression may stem from negative and distorted thought patterns. *Cognitive therapies* focus on changing these maladaptive patterns of thinking and perceiving, and replacing them with more adaptive ways of interpreting events. Two of the most widely used cognitive therapies are Albert Ellis's *rational-emotive therapy* and Aaron Beck's *cognitive therapy*.

## Ellis's Rational-Emotive Therapy

Developed by Albert Ellis (1973, 1995), **rational-emotive therapy** is based on the premise that many psychological problems stem from how people think about and interpret events in their lives. It is not the actual event that causes the emotional upset, but rather the person's *interpretation* of the event that results in emotional distress. Specifically, rational-emotive therapy identifies the client's faulty or irrational beliefs that lead to self-defeating behaviors, anxiety, depression, anger, or other psychological problems. Several studies support Ellis's notion that people who think more irrationally experience more psychological distress (Nieuwenhuijsen et al., 2010; Solomon et al., 2003; Taghavi et al., 2006; Ziegler & Leslie, 2003; Ziegler & Smith, 2004).

Ellis identified common irrational beliefs (1991) that often impede people's functioning (see ■ TABLE 14.2). Identifying such irrational beliefs is the first step in rational-emotive therapy. For example, one client may have an excessive need for approval because she believes that she "must be loved by everyone." Another client may irrationally believe that there is a "right" solution for every problem and become frustrated or depressed because a problem recurs. Once these beliefs have been identified, the therapist challenges their validity. The therapist confronts and disputes these fallacies in a logical and persuasive manner, pushing the client to recognize that such beliefs are irrational and unhealthy. The therapist might make statements such as "What evidence do you have to support this belief?" or "In what other ways could this evidence be interpreted?" Additionally, the client may be asked "What is the worst thing that could happen?" and "If that happened, what could you do?" Asking such questions forces clients to consider alternative viewpoints, face their fears and anxieties, and explore possible problem-solving methods.

After a client's irrational beliefs have been recognized and refuted, they can then be replaced with more realistic and rational beliefs. These beliefs may be reflected in such statements as "Not everyone will like me, but that is okay and not a measure of my worth" or "There are several ways to solve a problem, and if one approach fails I can try another."

Rational-emotive therapy is a very direct and confrontational approach. Admitting that our way of thinking is irrational and unhealthy and radically changing

Albert Ellis developed rational-emotive therapy to deal with clients' faulty or irrational beliefs that lead to self-defeating behaviors such as anxiety, depression, or anger.

*Courtesy of Ellis Institute*

## TABLE 14.2
## Examples of Irrational Assumptions

1. I must be loved by or approved of by everyone.

2. I must be competent and achieving in all things I do; otherwise I am worthless.

3. Some people are bad and should be severely blamed and punished for it. I should be extremely upset over the wrongdoings of others.

4. It is awful and upsetting when things are not the way I would like them to be.

5. Unhappiness is caused by external events, and I cannot control my bad feelings and emotional reactions.

6. If something unpleasant happens, I should dwell on it.

7. Avoiding difficulties, rather than facing them, will make you happy.

8. Always rely on someone who is stronger than you.

9. Your past will always affect your present life.

10. There is a perfect solution for every problem, and it is awful and upsetting if this solution is not found.

# Let's REVIEW

This section discussed the aim of cognitive therapy approaches and described rational-emotive therapy and cognitive therapy. For a quick check of your understanding, answer these questions.

1. Svetlana goes to a therapist who focuses on her negative automatic statements. Svetlana is most likely undergoing what type of therapy?
   a. Rational-emotive therapy
   b. Cognitive therapy
   c. Systematic desensitization
   d. Client-centered therapy

2. The goal of cognitive therapy approaches is to change behavior by _____.
   a. uncovering unconscious conflicts so that the client can gain insight into the source of his or her problems
   b. uncovering negative cognitive patterns that impede the client's ability to function

   c. examining and then changing the environmental circumstances that seem to elicit negative behavior
   d. providing the client with a safe environment for self-exploration and facilitating the journey toward self-fulfillment

3. The cognitive therapies have been most effective in treating which type of disorders?
   a. Schizophrenia
   b. Personality disorders
   c. Depression
   d. Autism

Answers 1. b; 2. b; 3. c

## LEARNING OBJECTIVES

● Describe the advantages and disadvantages of group therapy.

● Identify and describe the types of group therapy.

# Group Therapy Approaches: Strength in Numbers

### You Asked...

*What types of group therapy are there?*

BIANCA VAUGHAN, STUDENT

The psychotherapies we have described so far focus on a one-to-one relationship between a client and a therapist. This is known as *individual psychotherapy*. However, therapy can be administered to many people at one time with one or more therapists, in a process called **group therapy**. Group therapy approaches are often used in psychiatric facilities, group homes, the military, addiction centers, and mental institutions. They are also frequently offered by community mental health centers and outpatient treatment programs. Group therapy often centers on one type of problem (such as addiction or depression) or is offered for a specific type of client (such as women who have been battered, teenagers, or sex offenders). Group therapy may be administered by any of the different types of professionals discussed at the beginning of this chapter.

## The Benefits of Group Therapy

Group therapy has several distinct advantages over individual therapy (Dies, 1993; Yalom & Leszcz, 2005). First, group therapy tends to be less expensive than individual therapy. The cost of one or more therapists is shared by several people. However, clients do receive less one-on-one or individualized treatment in a group therapy setting. Second, group therapy offers therapists a view into the client's social interactions with others. Because many people receive therapy to address interpersonal

**group therapy**  therapy that is administered to more than one person at a time

problems, group therapy offers a safe mini-environment in which to explore new social behaviors or to understand how our interactions with others may be impeding our psychological health.

Group therapy also enables clients to recognize that they are not the only ones struggling with difficulties. Group members can offer acceptance, trust, and support for someone who is having problems. They can offer ideas or suggestions for solving problems and can learn from one another. Studies on group therapy have found it to be generally comparable in outcomes to individual psychotherapy (Forsyth & Corazzini, 2000; Nevonen & Broberg, 2006).

Group therapy can be a less expensive alternative to individual psychotherapy.

## The Nature and Types of Group Therapy

Group therapy, like individual psychotherapy, can take many forms. Any one of the four approaches previously described can be used for treating groups of people (Alonso & Swiller, 1993). For example, group behavior therapy or group cognitive therapy can be used to reduce people's fear of flying. Group psychoanalysis or group humanistic therapy can be used to improve people's interpersonal relations. Three unique forms of group therapy are *family therapy, couple therapy,* and *self-help groups.*

### FAMILY THERAPY: THE WHOLE SYSTEM

In **family therapy**, the family unit is the group. Often families come to therapy with an "identified patient," such as a misbehaving or rebellious teenager. Yet the focus of family therapy is not on the functioning of the individual but, rather, on the functioning of the family as a whole system. The goal of family therapy is to create balance and restore harmony within the family system to improve its functioning. If one person in the family is having problems, these problems are seen as a symptom of disharmony within the family unit (Lebow & Gurman, 1995).

Think of your own family for a moment. All members of a family have roles, expectations, or labels placed on them, usually at a very young age. One member of the family may be considered "the brain." Another family member may be viewed as "the peacemaker." These roles are not spoken but rather are communicated through our interactions with our family members. If a family member does not conform to his or her assigned role, the rest of the family system will be disrupted. Many times we try to make family members behave in a way that is consistent with our expectations of their perceived roles. Do you ever feel that your family does not know the "real" you? Have you ever tried to step out of your assigned role, only to find family members so concerned or shaken by your new behavior that it is easier to just go back to your old pattern of behaving? If so, you have experienced the power of the family system.

Family therapists view the "identified patient" as merely the focus for problems in the family system. Rather than simply treating the individual, they explore and analyze the interactions and communications between family members. They address sources of conflict and note how unspoken rules or expected roles may be interfering with healthy family functioning.

**family therapy**   therapy that focuses on creating balance and restoring harmony to improve the functioning of the family as a whole system

**couple therapy**   therapy that focuses on improving communication and intimacy between two people in a committed relationship

The goal of family therapy is to improve the functioning of the family system.

### COUPLE THERAPY: IMPROVING COMMUNICATION

**Couple therapy** focuses on improving communication and intimacy between two people in a committed relationship. The unspoken rules that couples use to communicate, and the ways in which they miscommunicate, are identified and

conventional biomedical or psychological treatments. Today, psychosurgery methods are more precise, thanks to recent improvements in surgical techniques. For example, a neurosurgeon may lesion (destroy) a small target area of the brain to reduce symptoms of obsessive-compulsive disorder. Research suggests that approximately 25–30% of patients who have undergone this procedure improve significantly (Dougherty et al., 2002; Read & Greenberg, 2009; Shah et al., 2008).

Since 1993, neurosurgeons have been implanting deep brain stimulators in people who have Parkinson's disease (Benabid et al., 2001). It is the most commonly practiced surgical treatment for this disease, improving motor function by at least 60%, leading to a significant improvement in the quality of life for people with Parkinson's (Ashcan et al., 2004). Deep brain stimulation for the treatment of resistant depression and severe obsessive-compulsive disorder also shows promising results (Hamani et al., 2009; Huff et al., 2010; Mayberg et al., 2005; Read & Greenberg, 2009; Shah et al., 2008). Keep in mind, however, that such operations are performed very infrequently and only as a last resort. Psychosurgery continues to be a controversial biomedical technique (C. A. Anderson & Arciniegas, 2004).

This chapter has outlined the major types of psychotherapies and biomedical therapies. We have seen that each therapeutic approach stems from one of the main psychological perspectives introduced in the beginning of this textbook: biological, psychoanalytic, cognitive, behavioral, and humanistic. We have also seen that therapy is generally effective, regardless of the specific techniques endorsed. Of course, the effectiveness of therapy will be directly related to the characteristics of the therapist and the client.

We hope that you have enjoyed your journey through psychology. Moreover, we hope that you have found the material relevant to your life. Being aware of the complex interaction among biological, psychological, and social variables will further your understanding of not only your behavior but the behavior of those around you. Good luck!

# Let's
# REVIEW

This section described biomedical approaches to therapy, including drug therapies, electroconvulsive therapy, and psychosurgery. For a quick check of your understanding, answer these questions.

**1.** Electroconvulsive therapy is most effective for the treatment of _____.
   a. schizophrenia
   b. panic attacks
   c. severe depression
   d. bipolar disorder

**2.** Which of the following is the most serious side effect of taking conventional antipsychotic medication?
   a. Rebound anxiety
   b. Physical dependence
   c. Hallucinations
   d. Tardive dyskinesia

**3.** Prozac is what type of antidepressant drug?
   a. SSRI
   b. MAO inhibitor
   c. Tricyclic
   d. Benzodiazepine

Answers 1. c; 2. d; 3. a

# Studying THE CHAPTER

## Key Terms

antianxiety medications (565)
antidepressants (567)
antimanic medications (569)
antipsychotic medications (566)
anxiety hierarchy (550)
aversion therapy (552)
behavior therapy (549)
biomedical therapy (540)
client-centered therapy (547)
cognitive distortions (556)
cognitive therapy (556)
couple therapy (559)
covert sensitization therapy (553)
dream analysis (545)

eclectic therapy approach (561)
electroconvulsive therapy
  (ECT) (570)
empathy (547)
family therapy (559)
flooding (552)
free association (545)
genuineness (548)
group therapy (558)
interpretation (545)
lithium (569)
psychoanalysis (545)
psychodynamic therapy (546)
psychopharmacology (564)

psychosurgery (571)
psychotherapy (540)
rational-emotive therapy (555)
resistance (545)
selective serotonin reuptake
  inhibitor (SSRI) (567)
self-help group (560)
systematic desensitization (550)
tardive dyskinesia (566)
therapeutic alliance (562)
therapy (539)
token economy (554)
transference (546)
unconditional positive regard (548)

## What Do You Know? Assess Your Understanding

Test your retention and understanding of the material by answering the following questions.

1. Most psychotherapists hold at least a _____ degree and in most states hold an appropriate license or certificate.
   a. bachelor's
   b. associate's
   c. master's
   d. doctorate

2. Which of the following is *not* an ethical guideline of psychotherapists?
   a. Inform the client of the nature of the treatment
   b. Never break the confidentiality of communications with client
   c. Interact appropriately with clients
   d. Provide adequate treatment

3. _____ uses techniques such as free association and dream analysis to uncover hidden conflicts.
   a. Psychoanalysis
   b. Cognitive therapy
   c. Behavior therapy
   d. Client-centered therapy

4. Which psychotherapy would use systematic desensitization to treat a person with a phobic disorder?
   a. Psychoanalysis
   b. Cognitive therapy
   c. Behavior therapy
   d. Client-centered therapy

5. In which psychotherapy does the therapist challenge the irrational beliefs of the client?
   a. Behavior therapy
   b. Rational-emotive therapy
   c. Client-centered therapy
   d. Psychodynamic therapy

6. Dr. Ramon expresses genuineness and empathy to her client. Dr. Ramon is most likely engaging in _____.
   a. psychoanalysis
   b. cognitive therapy
   c. behavior therapy
   d. client-centered therapy

**7.** Dr. Andrews reinforces appropriate client behavior and ignores inappropriate behavior. Dr. Andrews is engaging in _____.
a. psychoanalysis
b. cognitive therapy
c. behavior therapy
d. client-centered therapy

**8.** Dr. Shu reflects her client's thoughts and feelings so that she can better understand the client's problems. Dr. Shu is engaging in _____.
a. behavior modification
b. client-centered therapy
c. rational-emotive therapy
d. free association

**9.** Which type of therapy pairs an unpleasant stimulus with the problem behavior in the hopes of reducing its occurrence?
a. Aversion therapy
b. Systematic desensitization
c. Token economy
d. Client-centered therapy

**10.** Dr. Tyler teaches his client how to recognize negative automatic thought patterns. Dr. Tyler is engaging in _____.
a. rational-emotive therapy
b. systematic desensitization
c. cognitive therapy
d. psychodynamic therapy

**11.** Which of the following is *not* a benefit of group therapy?
a. It is less expensive than individual psychotherapy.
b. Therapists can view clients' social interactions.
c. It offers more one-on-one treatment.
d. It provides social support from others experiencing the same problem.

**12.** Dr. Mendel encourages Maurice to paraphrase what his partner says to confirm that he has understood the comment. It is most likely that Maurice is engaged in _____.
a. psychoanalysis
b. family therapy
c. couple therapy
d. drug therapy

**13.** The "Dodo Bird" verdict refers to _____.
a. the effect of psychotherapy on the brain
b. how the main psychotherapy approaches are equivalent in effectiveness
c. the high relapse rates among people with psychological disorders
d. the higher effectiveness of group therapy over individual therapy

**14.** Dr. Garfield and his client have an interactive and collaborative relationship, commonly referred to as a(n) _____.
a. eclectic approach
b. therapeutic alliance
c. psychotherapeutic effect
d. transference

**15.** Which of the following is a disadvantage of cybertherapy?
a. The increased client confidentiality
b. Provides clients who live far away from therapists access to psychological services
c. Lacks the close personal contact of face-to-face interactions
d. It costs more than face-to-face therapy.

**16.** Juanita has been diagnosed with PTSD. A psychiatrist is most likely to prescribe _____ to treat Juanita's symptoms.
a. lithium
b. Xanax
c. Prozac
d. clozapine

**17.** Antipsychotic medications affect which neurotransmitter?
a. Endorphins
b. Glutamate
c. GABA
d. Dopamine

**18.** Craig has been diagnosed with schizophrenia. His psychiatrist has prescribed Thorazine to reduce Craig's delusions and hallucinations. Which of the following side effects might Craig experience from taking this medication?
a. Loss of sense of smell
b. Tardive dyskinesia
c. Fluid retention and rash
d. Kidney problems

**19.** Electroconvulsive therapy has been shown to be particularly effective for the treatment of _____.

    a. schizophrenia
    b. severe depression
    c. panic attacks
    d. obsessive-compulsive disorder

**20.** Which of the following medications has been associated with an increased risk of suicidal thoughts and behaviors in children and adolescents?

    a. Antianxiety drugs
    b. Lithium
    c. SSRI drugs
    d. Antipsychotic drugs

Answers: 1. c; 2. b; 3. a; 4. c; 5. b; 6. d; 7. c; 8. b; 9. a; 10. c; 11. c; 12. c; 13. b; 14. b; 15. c; 16. b; 17. d; 18. b; 19. b; 20. c

## Online Resources

Log in to **www.cengagebrain.com** to access the resources your instructor requires. For this book, you can access:

### Psychology ⫶CourseMate

CourseMate brings course concepts to life with interactive learning, study, and exam preparation tools that support the printed textbook. A textbook-specific website, Psychology CourseMate includes an integrated interactive eBook and other interactive learning tools including quizzes, flashcards, videos, and more.

### CENGAGENOW™

CengageNOW Personalized Study is a diagnostic study tool containing valuable text-specific resources—and because you focus on just what you don't know, you learn more in less time to get a better grade.

### WebTutor

More than just an interactive study guide, WebTutor is an anytime, anywhere customized learning solution with an eBook, keeping you connected to your textbook, instructor, and classmates.

**Therapy** consists of techniques that are used to help people with psychological or interpersonal problems.

© Nancy Sheehan/Photo Edit

## What Is the Nature of Psychotherapy?

- **Psychotherapy** is administered by clinical psychologists, licensed counselors, social workers, and therapists.

- Psychotherapists abide by ethical standards of *confidentiality*, *competent treatment* that is culturally sensitive, *informed consent*, and *appropriate interactions*.

- You should consider therapy if you feel helpless, sad, or nervous for a prolonged period of time or if such feelings do not improve despite several efforts to change them.

## What Are the Main Types of Psychotherapy?

- Traditional **psychoanalysis** has clients gain insight into the underlying source of their problems. Modern **psychodynamic therapy** also relies on the therapist's **interpretations** of the client's feelings and behaviors but places more emphasis on current problems and interpersonal relations and less on the client's past.

- Humanistic therapy such as **client-centered therapy** connects with and understands the client's worldview. The therapist offers **genuineness, empathy,** and **unconditional positive regard** to encourage self-exploration and self-fulfillment.

- **Behavior therapies** use learning principles to change maladaptive behavior.

  - Classical conditioning therapies use techniques such as **systematic desensitization**, virtual reality technology, **flooding**, and **aversion therapy** to change the client's responses to stimuli.

  - Operant conditioning therapies use techniques such as shaping, extinction, positive reinforcement, and **token economies** to change behavior.

- In cognitive therapies, maladaptive patterns of thinking and perceiving are replaced with more adaptive ways of interpreting events.

  - In **rational-emotive therapy**, the therapist confronts, questions, and challenges the validity of client's irrational beliefs.

  - In **cognitive therapy**, the therapist identifies and tracks negative automatic thoughts and has the client test the accuracy of these **cognitive distortions**.

© Photofusion Picture Library/Alamy

# WHAT **THERAPIES** ARE USED TO TREAT Psychological **PROBLEMS?**

## What Happens in Group Therapy?

- The goal of **group therapy** is to improve the functioning and interactions among individuals, couples, families, or other groups.

- Group therapy tends to be less expensive than individual therapy and offers a safe mini-environment in which to explore new social behaviors or to understand how our interactions with others may be impeding our psychological health.

## Effective Psychotherapy: What Treatments Work?

- Generally, the different psychotherapy approaches produce relatively equivalent results in terms of client improvement.

- A personalized approach to treatment is becoming more common as many therapists adopt an **eclectic therapy approach** that involves an integrated and diverse use of therapeutic methods.

- The effectiveness of modern delivery methods of therapy such as cybertherapy has not been demonstrated.

## What Are the Biomedical Therapies?

- **Biomedical therapies** are administered by psychiatrists and other medical professionals.

- The most common biomedical therapy is **psychopharmacology**, or the use of medications to treat mental health problems. Drug therapies influence brain neurotransmitters to alter behavior.

  - **Antianxiety medications** are prescribed to reduce tension and anxiety.

  - **Antipsychotic medications** are prescribed to relieve psychotic symptoms such as agitation, delusions, disordered thinking, and hallucinations.

  - **Antidepressants** are prescribed for mood and anxiety disorders, eating disorders, and substance dependence.

  - **Antimanic medications** are used primarily to treat mania.

- More controversial biomedical therapies include **electroconvulsive therapy (ECT)** and **psychosurgery**. In ECT, a seizure is created in the brain to treat severe depression. Psychosurgery involves surgically altering the brain to alleviate severe symptoms of Parkinson's disease or obsessive-compulsive disorder.

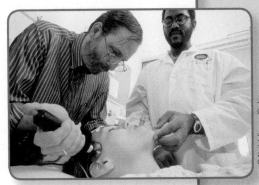

577

# How Are Statistics Used IN PSYCHOLOGY?

## Appendix Outline

## LEARNING OBJECTIVES

- Define the terms *data* and *statistics*, and explain how they are used in science.

- Describe the different types of graphs and distributions used in statistical analyses.

- Calculate and interpret the different measures of central tendency used in statistics.

- Calculate and interpret the different measures of variability used in statistics.

- Explain what a *z* score, normal distribution, and a standard normal distribution are.

- Calculate and interpret the correlation coefficient.

**data**  information gathered in scientific studies

**statistics**  a type of applied mathematics used to describe data and test hypotheses

**graph**  a visual depiction of data

## How Do Psychologists Use Statistics to Describe Data?

As you learned in Chapter 1, psychology is the scientific study of behavior and mental processes. Psychologists develop hypotheses about behavior and mental processes and then test these hypotheses using experiments, case studies, surveys, naturalistic observations, or other research methods. In the course of their research, psychologists collect a variety of information, or **data**, from their research participants.

Imagine that you are a health psychologist interested in whether the legal drinking age in a country affects the rate of underage drinking in that society. More specifically, you might ask questions like these: "Does having a lower legal drinking age encourage drinking among 15-year-olds? And if so, does the legal drinking age equally affect both male and female 15-year-olds?" To see whether such relationships exist, you must first collect data on the number of 15-year-olds who drink in particular countries along with each country's legal drinking age (see ■ TABLE A.1).

Take a moment to look at the data in Table A.1. By just looking at the table, can you tell whether a relationship exists between the percentage of 15-year-old students who drink and a country's minimum legal drinking age? If you cannot, you are in good company—it's impossible to tell from just a table whether the data support one's hypothesis. Instead, psychologists must use a type of applied mathematics, called **statistics**, to describe and analyze their data. Only then can researchers determine what the data say about their hypothesis.

### Graphs: Depicting Data Visually

Take another look at the data in Table A.1. Where would you start if you wanted to see whether the legal drinking age is related to drinking rates among 15-year-olds? Well, have you ever heard that "a picture is worth a thousand words"? One way to start would be to create a **graph**, or pictorial representation, of the data.

## TABLE A.1
### Percentage of Students Who Report Drinking Alcohol Weekly at Age 15, Selected Countries

| COUNTRY | MINIMUM LEGAL DRINKING AGE | MALES (%) | FEMALES (%) |
|---|---|---|---|
| Austria | 16 | 39 | 23 |
| Belgium | 16 | 38 | 22 |
| Canada | 18 | 22 | 17 |
| Czech Republic | 18 | 32 | 19 |
| Denmark | 15 | 46 | 38 |
| England | 18 | 47 | 36 |
| Estonia | 18* | 21 | 10 |
| Finland | 18 | 11 | 8 |
| France | 16 | 31 | 15 |
| Germany | 16 | 29 | 22 |
| Greece | 16* | 52 | 31 |
| Greenland | 18 | 13 | 10 |
| Hungary | 16 | 29 | 11 |
| Ireland | 18 | 27 | 12 |
| Israel | 18 | 26 | 10 |
| Latvia | 18 | 28 | 12 |
| Lithuania | 21 | 16 | 9 |
| Northern Ireland | 18 | 33 | 20 |
| Norway | 18 | 16 | 12 |
| Poland | 18 | 20 | 8 |
| Portugal | 16 | 29 | 9 |
| Russia | 18 | 28 | 24 |
| Scotland | 18 | 37 | 33 |
| Slovakia | 18 | 32 | 16 |
| Sweden | 18 | 17 | 11 |
| Switzerland | 16 | 19 | 9 |
| United States | 21 | 23 | 15 |
| Wales | 18 | 53 | 36 |

Source: Except where noted, data taken from Kaul, C. (2002). Statistical Handbook on the World's Children (p. 447). Westport, CT: Oryx Press.

*These data taken from http://www2.potsdam.edu/alcohol-info/LegalDrinkingAge.html#worlddrinkingages on 11/6/03

Psychologists use many different types of graphs to help analyze their data. One of the more common graphs is a **frequency distribution**. A graph of a frequency distribution is a two-dimensional illustration that plots how frequently certain events occur. For example, it might be useful to see the frequency, or rate, at which countries have set certain minimum drinking ages. This information could be depicted using several types of graphs; two of the more common ones are **frequency polygons** (a line graph) and **histograms** (a bar graph). ■ FIGURE A.1 shows the frequency distribution of legal drinking age depicted in a frequency polygon; ■ FIGURE A.2 shows the same frequency distribution using a histogram.

**frequency distribution**    a graph of data that plots the frequency of data points on the y-axis and the data points themselves on the x-axis

**frequency polygon**    a line graph that is used to illustrate a frequency distribution

**histogram**    a bar graph that is used to illustrate a frequency distribution

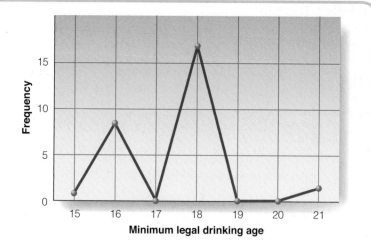

FIGURE

## A.1

### Frequency Polygon

Frequency polygon showing the frequency distribution for minimum drinking age in 28 countries (data from Table A.1).

By looking at either one of these graphs, we can see that most of these selected governments have set their minimum drinking age below 21 and that the most commonly set drinking age is 18.

An even more useful type of graph for this investigation would be a **scatter plot**. In a scatter plot, two variables are plotted as a function of each other. For example, we could plot the percentage of 15-year-old drinkers as a function of the country's minimum drinking age. ■ FIGURE A.3 shows such plots separately for males and females. By looking at the scatter plots in Figure A.3, you can get a *very crude* picture of the relationship between legal drinking age and the rate of drinking at age 15. Looking at Figure A.3, as the minimum drinking age decreases, does the rate of underage drinking increase? Do these data confirm or discount our hypothesis that lowering the drinking age encourages underage drinking? Although it is true that countries with a minimum drinking age of 16 or younger have relatively high levels of underage drinking, there are also a number of countries with a minimum drinking age of 18 that have even higher levels of underage drinking by 15-year-olds.

■ FIGURE A.4 is another scatter plot, this time relating male and female rates of drinking. It appears from this graph that as more males drink, more females also engage in drinking—but if you look closely at the scatter plot, this isn't always true. Therefore, these plots only give us a crude picture of the relationship between our variables. It's impossible to say for sure whether our hypotheses about teenage drinking have merit simply by looking at these plots. To truly examine our hypotheses, we will have to delve deeper into our statistical analysis.

**scatter plot**   a graph of data that plots pairs of data points, with one data point on the *x*-axis and the other on the *y*-axis

**descriptive statistics**   statistics that are calculated to summarize or describe certain aspects of a data set

## Measures of Central Tendency: Means, Medians, and Modes

To get to the heart of the matter, we are going to have to use **descriptive statistics**. Descriptive statistics are numerical values that are calculated to summarize and describe the data as a whole. For example, you could calculate the percentage of

FIGURE

## A.2

### Histogram

Histogram showing the frequency distribution for minimum drinking age in 28 countries (data from Table A.1).

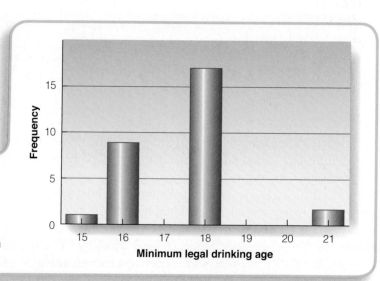

these 28 countries that have a minimum drinking age of 18 or higher. This percentage would be 19 of the 28 countries, or 67.9%. Or you could calculate the percentage of countries with a minimum drinking age under 18 in which more than 25% of their male sample indicated that they drank weekly (8 out of 9 countries, or 88.9%). Although such percentages can sometimes be helpful, there are other, better statistical methods to use in this situation.

Some of the most useful descriptive statistics are those that describe the average, or most typical, entry in a data set; in other words, a statistic that shows what a *typical* country's legal drinking age is. These measures are collectively referred to as **measures of central tendency** because they tell us something about the center of the frequency distribution (in this case, what minimum drinking age is most common, or most typical). Look again at Figures A.1 and A.2. What do you think is the most common minimum drinking age? To answer this question, we have three different measures of central tendency: the *mean*, *median*, and *mode*.

## THE MEAN

The **mean** is the average of a distribution. To calculate the mean, you add up all of the data points and then divide the total by the number of data points. This formula can be expressed with this equation:

$$\overline{X} = \Sigma X / N$$

Where

$\overline{X}$ is the symbol for the mean

$\Sigma$ is a mathematical symbol that means to sum up the items that follow it

$X$ = the individual data points in the distribution

$N$ = the total number of data points or scores in the distribution

The calculations for the average minimum drinking age and the average percentages of males and females who drink weekly at age 15 are shown in ■ TABLE A.2.

**measures of central tendency** descriptive statistics that describe the most central, or typical, data points in the frequency distribution

**mean** a descriptive statistic that describes the most average, or typical, data point in the distribution

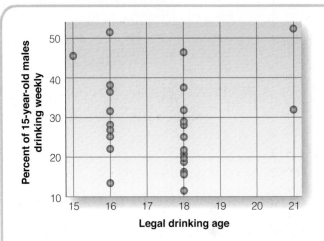

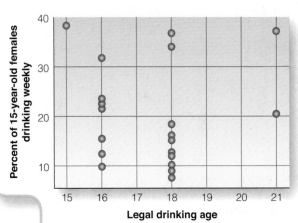

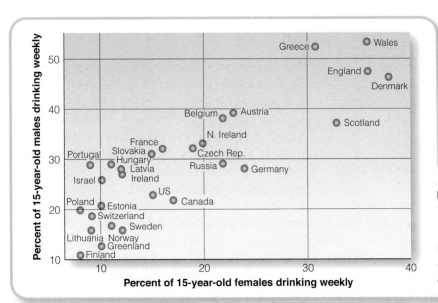

Percent of 15-year-old females drinking weekly

**FIGURE**

## A.3

Drinking at Age 15 as a Function of Minimum Legal Drinking Age

Scatter plots of the percentage of 15-year-olds who drink weekly as a function of minimum legal drinking age in 28 countries (data from Table A.1).

**FIGURE**

## A.4

Drinking at Age 15 of Males Versus Females

Scatter plot relating the percentage of 15-year-old males and females who drink alcohol weekly in 28 countries (data from Table A.1).

## TABLE A.2
### Average Minimum Drinking Age and Average Percentage of Students Who Report Drinking Alcohol Weekly at Age 15, Selected Countries

| COUNTRY | MINIMUM LEGAL DRINKING AGE | MALES | FEMALES |
|---|---|---|---|
| Austria | 16 | 39 | 23 |
| Belgium | 16 | 38 | 22 |
| Canada | 18 | 22 | 17 |
| Czech Republic | 18 | 32 | 19 |
| Denmark | 15 | 46 | 38 |
| England | 18 | 47 | 36 |
| Estonia | 18* | 21 | 10 |
| Finland | 18 | 11 | 8 |
| France | 16 | 31 | 15 |
| Germany | 16 | 29 | 22 |
| Greece | 16* | 52 | 31 |
| Greenland | 18 | 13 | 10 |
| Hungary | 16 | 29 | 11 |
| Ireland | 18 | 27 | 12 |
| Israel | 18 | 26 | 10 |
| Latvia | 18 | 28 | 12 |
| Lithuania | 21 | 16 | 9 |
| Northern Ireland | 18 | 33 | 20 |
| Norway | 18 | 16 | 12 |
| Poland | 18 | 20 | 8 |
| Portugal | 16 | 29 | 9 |
| Russia | 18 | 28 | 24 |
| Scotland | 18 | 37 | 33 |
| Slovakia | 18 | 32 | 16 |
| Sweden | 18 | 17 | 11 |
| Switzerland | 16 | 19 | 9 |
| United States | 21 | 23 | 15 |
| Wales | 18 | 53 | 36 |
| $\Sigma X$ | 491 | 814 | 498 |
| $\overline{X} = \Sigma X/N$ | 491/28 = 17.5 | 814/28 = 29.1 | 498/28 = 17.8 |

Source: Except where noted, data taken from Kaul, C. (2002). Statistical Handbook on the World's Children (p. 447). Westport, CT: Oryx Press.

*These data taken from http://www2.potsdam.edu/alcohol-info/LegalDrinkingAge .html#worlddrinkingages on 11/6/03

**median**    a descriptive statistic that identifies the center of the frequency distribution; 50% of the scores are above and 50% are below this point in the distribution

**outliers**    unusual data points that are at the extremes of the frequency distribution, either far above or far below the mean

## THE MEDIAN

Another measure of central tendency is the **median**, or the score that is at the center of a frequency distribution. To find the median, you must first list all of the scores in ascending order. Once this is done, simply find the score that is at the center of this ordered list of scores. The calculation of the median legal drinking age is shown in ■ FIGURE A.5. As you can see by comparing Figure A.5 and Table A.2, the median and the mean are not the same number. This shows one advantage of the median over the mean.

The mean is highly affected by unusual scores, or **outliers**, in the distribution. In this case, one country, Denmark, has an unusually low drinking age of 15. Although Denmark's minimum drinking age of 15 does not differ very much from the more common limit of 16, Denmark is the only country to set the age this low, and this outlying score works to lower the mean somewhat. However, because the median is simply the center score of the distribution, it is unaffected by unusual scores. So, whereas the mean drinking age is 17.5, the median drinking age is somewhat higher at 18.

When a distribution contains outliers, the median is the better choice for measuring central tendency. This is especially true for situations in which the outliers are more extreme than in our drinking-age example. For instance, assume that in a class of 10 students, 9 students score a 75 on an exam, and 1 student scores a 15. The mean for the class would be 69, but the median would be 75. That's a difference of more than half a letter grade between these two measures of central tendency, with the median more accurately reflecting how most students scored on the exam.

## THE MODE

The final measure of central tendency is the **mode**, or the most frequent score in the distribution. If you look again at Figure A.1 (or Figure A.2), you will see that the most frequent, or most common, drinking age is 18. Therefore, like the median, the mode is also 18. The mode is an especially useful measure of central tendency when the data being examined are not numerical (for example, the most typical car color in the student parking lot).

Measures of central tendency tell us something about the most representative scores at the center of the frequency distribution, but they do not tell us anything about the range, or breadth, of the scores in the distribution. To determine this characteristic of the distribution, we will have to look at *measures of variability*.

First take all of the minimum legal drinking ages for the countries and list them in ascending order:

15, 16, 16, 16, 16, 16, 16, 16, 16, 18, 18, 18, 18, 18, 18, 18, 18, 18, 18, 18, 18, 18, 18, 18, 18, 18, 21, 21

Now find the score at the center of this distribution. In this case, because there is an even number of scores ($N = 28$) the center of this distribution would be between the 14th and 15th score in the list. Therefore, to find the median or $X_{50}$, we would average the 14th and 15th score:

$$(18 + 18)/2 = 18$$

$$X_{50} = 18$$

**FIGURE**

**A.5**

Calculation of the Median Legal Drinking Age

## Measures of Variability: Analyzing the Distribution of Data

Variability refers to the degree to which the individual scores of the distribution tend to *differ* from the central tendency of the distribution. In other words, variability measures how spread out the frequency distribution is. Look back at Figure A.1. As we just saw, the mean drinking age is 17.5. As you would expect, most of the scores in the frequency distribution are clustered around 18, but that does not mean that *all* of the scores are close in value to 18. Some scores are as low as 15, and some are as high as 21. Measures of variability tell us about the degree to which these more extreme scores differ from the mean. The simplest measure of variability is the **range** of the distribution, or the difference between the highest and lowest values in the distribution. In this case, the range of drinking ages would be $21 - 15 = 6$ years.

Although the range is a measure of variability, it is fairly crude in that it doesn't really tell us how much most scores differ from the mean. Another measure of variability, called **sample variance**, takes into account the difference between the individual scores of the distribution and the mean of the distribution. The first step to calculating the sample variance is to calculate the mean of the distribution. The next step is to calculate the **sum of squares** of the distribution. Here, *squares* refers to the difference between each score in the distribution and the mean of the distribution, with this difference being taken to the second power (that is, squared, or multiplied by itself). So, the sum of squares ($SS$) can be calculated using the following equation:

$$SS = \Sigma(X - \overline{X})^2$$

Once you have calculated $SS$, to calculate the sample variance ($S^2$), simply divide by the total number of scores ($N$):

$$S^2 = \Sigma(X - \overline{X})^2/N$$

Another measure of variability is the **standard deviation** ($S$), or the square root of the sample variance:

$$S = \sqrt{\Sigma(X - \overline{X})^2/N}$$

All three measures of variability indicate the degree to which the scores in the distribution are dispersed. The higher these measures are, the more dispersion, or spread, there is among the scores. Although it may be difficult to see why you would want to know the variability of a distribution, one reason is that you can use the

**mode**   a measure of central tendency that identifies the most common, or frequent, score in the distribution

**range**   a measure of variability that is the difference between the high score and the low score of the distribution

**sample variance**   a measure of variability that shows on average how much the scores vary from the mean

**sum of squares**   the sum of the squared errors, or deviations, from the mean for the scores in the distribution; the numerator of the sample variance equation

**standard deviation**   a measure of variability equal to the square root of the sample variance; often used to gauge the degree to which an individual score deviates from the mean of a distribution

| Country<br>$N = 28$ | $X$ = Percent of<br>15-Year-Old<br>Males Drinking | $X - \bar{X} =$<br>$X - 29.1$ | $(X - \bar{X})^2 =$<br>$(X - 29.1)^2$ |
|---|---|---|---|
| Austria | 39 | 9.9 | 98.01 |
| Belgium | 38 | 8.9 | 79.21 |
| Canada | 22 | − 7.1 | 50.41 |
| Czech Republic | 32 | 2.9 | 8.41 |
| Denmark | 46 | 16.9 | 285.61 |
| England | 47 | 17.9 | 320.41 |
| Estonia | 21 | − 8.1 | 65.61 |
| Finland | 11 | −18.1 | 327.61 |
| France | 31 | 1.9 | 3.61 |
| Germany | 29 | − .1 | .01 |
| Greece | 52 | 22.9 | 524.41 |
| Greenland | 13 | −16.1 | 259.21 |
| Hungary | 29 | − .1 | .01 |
| Ireland | 27 | − 2.1 | 4.41 |
| Israel | 26 | − 3.1 | 9.61 |
| Latvia | 28 | − 1.1 | 1.21 |
| Lithuania | 16 | −13.1 | 171.61 |
| Northern Ireland | 33 | 3.9 | 15.21 |
| Norway | 16 | −13.1 | 171.61 |
| Poland | 20 | − 9.1 | 82.81 |
| Portugal | 29 | − .1 | .01 |
| Russia | 28 | − 1.1 | 1.21 |
| Scotland | 37 | 7.9 | 62.41 |
| Slovakia | 32 | 2.9 | 8.41 |
| Sweden | 17 | −12.1 | 146.41 |
| Switzerland | 19 | −10.1 | 102.01 |
| United States | 23 | − 6.1 | 37.21 |
| Wales | 53 | 23.9 | 571.21 |
| | $\sum X = 814$ | | $\sum (X - \bar{X})^2 =$<br>3407.88 |
| | $\bar{X} = \sum X / N =$<br>814/28 = 29.1 | | $S^2 = \sum (X - \bar{X})^2 / N =$<br>3407.88/28 = 121.71 |
| | | | $S = \sqrt{\sum (X - \bar{X})^2 / N} =$<br>$\sqrt{121.71} = 11.03$ |

**Legend:** $\bar{X}$ = the mean; $S^2$ = the sample variance; $S$ = the standard deviation; $\sum$ = a symbol that means sum up the items that follow; $N$ = the total number of scores or data points

FIGURE

## A.6

Calculation of the Standard Deviation for the Percentage of Males Drinking Weekly at Age 15

standard deviation as a ruler, or guideline, for judging how atypical or typical a score in the distribution is.

To see how this works, take a look at ■ FIGURE A.6. Figure A.6 shows the calculation of the standard deviation for the male drinking percentages across the 28 countries. As you can see, the standard deviation for the distribution of male drinking scores is 11.03. We can use this figure to gauge how unusual a specific score in the distribution is. Using the standard deviation and the mean of the distribution, we can calculate a **z score**. A z score expresses the degree to which an individual score differs from the mean of the distribution in terms of the standard deviation of the distribution.

$$Z = (X - \bar{X})/S$$

For example, in Germany, 29% of 15-year-old males drink weekly. This means that Germany's score would be

$$Z = (29 − 29.1)/11.03 = −.009$$

Germany's z score indicates that the percentage of German 15-year-old males who drink is far less than one standard deviation below the mean of 29.1 for all of the 28 countries. This is illustrated graphically in ■ FIGURE A.7.

On the other hand, look at the figure reported for Wales. In Wales, 53% of the 15-year-old males surveyed were drinking. Wales's z score of 2.17 indicates that its score of 53% is more than 2 standard deviations above the mean. This indicates that Wales's experience is not very typical of the average country's experience with male drinking at age 15. Wales *seems* to have a bigger problem with this issue than the average country does, but is this deviation from the mean enough of a problem to worry about? To answer this, we have to assess the probability that a given country would have a particular percentage of its young men drinking alcohol on a weekly basis. Luckily, we might be able to do this.

## Normal and Standard Normal Distributions

Many variables, such as height, weight, IQ, and so on, have a **normal distribution**. In other words, if you measured these characteristics for a very large number of people and plotted them in a frequency distribution, the resulting graph would be bell-shaped and symmetrical, like the one in Figure A.7. If we assume that drinking behavior is normally distributed, then we can also assume that if we calculated the z scores for all of the different countries and plotted them in a frequency distribution, that distribution of z scores would also be a normal distribution, with $\bar{X} = 0$ and $S = 1$.

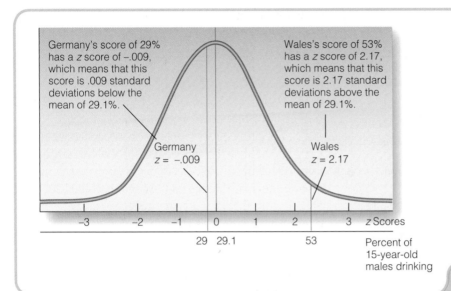

Germany's score of 29% has a *z* score of –.009, which means that this score is .009 standard deviations below the mean of 29.1%.

Wales's score of 53% has a *z* score of 2.17, which means that this score is 2.17 standard deviations above the mean of 29.1%.

Germany
*z* = –.009

Wales
*z* = 2.17

–3    –2    –1    0    1    2    3    *z* Scores

29   29.1          53    Percent of
                        15-year-old
                        males drinking

FIGURE

## A.7

### *z* Scores for Germany and Wales

The mean, or average, percentage of 15-year-old males who drank was 29.1% and the standard deviation was 11.03 across the 28 countries. This figure shows the individual *z* scores for the percentage of 15-year-old males drinking in Germany and Wales. A *z* score indicates how many standard deviations away from the mean a particular raw score falls. As you can see, Germany has a slightly below average percentage of 15-year-old male drinkers, with a raw score of 29% and a *z* score of –.009. Wales is quite a bit above average in its male underage drinking, with a raw score of 53% and a *z* score of 2.17.

When a distribution of *z* scores is normal in shape, it is referred to as the **standard normal distribution**. The great thing about the standard normal distribution is that we know exactly what percentage of the distribution falls between any two scores, as shown in ■ FIGURE A.8. As you can see, 68.26% of the *z* scores should fall within the range of *z* scores from −1 to +1, whereas only .26% of the scores will be above a *z* score of +3 or below a *z* score of −3. The probability that a country would have a *z* score of +2.17 or higher is on the order of only 1.5%. So, indeed, Wales seems to have some possible cause for concern here because the number of 15-year-old males consuming alcohol on a weekly basis is unusual compared to other countries.

**z score**   a measure of relative standing that measures the distance of a score from the mean of the distribution in standard deviation units

**normal distribution**   a bell-shaped, symmetric frequency distribution

**standard normal distribution**   a bell-shaped, symmetric distribution ($\overline{X} = 0$, $S = 1$) for which we know the exact area under the curve

## The Correlation Coefficient: Measuring Relationships

Take a look again at Figure A.4, the scatter plot for underage drinking in males versus females in the 28 countries. Do you notice anything interesting about this

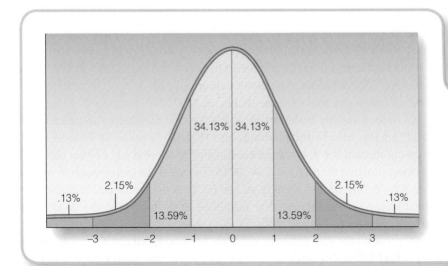

.13%    2.15%    13.59%    34.13% | 34.13%    13.59%    2.15%    .13%

–3    –2    –1    0    1    2    3

FIGURE

## A.8

### The Standard Normal Distribution of *z* Scores

The standard normal distribution is a symmetric, bell-shaped distribution of *z* scores with $\overline{X} = 0$ and $S = 1$. The *z* score is the number of standard deviations from the mean that the score is.

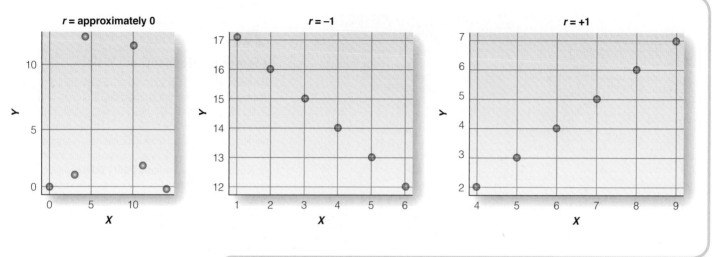

**FIGURE**

## A.9

### The Correlation Coefficient (*r*)

Graphic depictions of different values of the correlation coefficient: (a) $r$ = approximately 0; (b) $r = -1$; (c) $r = +1$.

scatter plot? Don't the data points of the scatter plot tend to fall along a line that slopes up to the right of the graph? Doesn't this seem to indicate that there might be a linear relationship between the percentage of 15-year-old males and females drinking alcohol in a country? As one sex drinks more, doesn't the other seem to generally follow suit? To examine the degree to which such a relationship might exist, psychologists would use yet another statistic to describe these data—the **correlation coefficient**. Simply put, the correlation coefficient measures the degree to which pairs of data points fall along a straight line on a scatter plot. The formula for the correlation coefficient is

$$r = (\Sigma_{z_x z_y})/N$$

Where

$r$ = the correlation coefficient

$z_x$ = the z score for one of the variables in a pair

$z_y$ = the z score for the other variable of the pair

$N$ = the total number of pairs of scores

The correlation coefficients that can be calculated with this formula have a possible range of $-1 \leq r \leq +1$. See ■ FIGURE A.9 for an interpretation of these values. As you can see, an *r* value of 0 (Figure A.9a) indicates no linear relationship between the two variables. As *r* approaches either $-1$ (Figure A.9b) or $+1$ (Figure A.9c), the linear relationship between the two variables becomes stronger. Positive *r* values indicate a *direct* relationship between the variables—as one variable increases, so does the other. Negative *r* values indicate an *inverse* relationship between the variables—as one variable increases, the other decreases.

Now let's return to our question of a relationship between the percentage of males and females in a country who at age 15 drink weekly. ■ FIGURE A.10 shows the calculation of the correlation coefficient for these data. As you can see, there is a strong positive correlation ($r = .8715$) between the percentage of males and females who drink alcohol weekly at age 15. This makes sense, because one might expect many of the factors that influence male underage drinking in a country to influence females similarly.

One might think that one of these factors would be the legal drinking age in the country—that countries with a younger drinking age would have a higher

**correlation coefficient**   the average product of z scores calculated on pairs of scores; describes the degree to which the scores in the pairs are linearly related

| Country | Percent of 15-yr-old Males Drinking | z score for Percent of Males Drinking | Percent of 15-yr-old Females Drinking | z score for Percent of Females Drinking | $z_{male}z_{female}$ |
|---|---|---|---|---|---|
| Austria | 39 | .90027 | 23 | .56263 | .50652 |
| Belgium | 38 | .80961 | 22 | .45464 | .36808 |
| Canada | 22 | −.64098 | 17 | −.08531 | .05468 |
| Czech Republic | 32 | .26564 | 19 | .13067 | .03471 |
| Denmark | 46 | 1.53490 | 38 | 2.18251 | 3.34994 |
| England | 47 | 1.62557 | 36 | 1.96652 | 3.19671 |
| Estonia | 21 | −.73164 | 10 | −.084125 | .61549 |
| Finland | 11 | −1.63826 | 8 | −1.05724 | 1.73203 |
| France | 31 | .17498 | 15 | −.30130 | −.05272 |
| Germany | 29 | −.00635 | 22 | .45464 | −.00289 |
| Greece | 52 | 2.07888 | 31 | 1.42657 | 2.96565 |
| Greenland | 13 | −1.45694 | 10 | −.84125 | 1.22565 |
| Hungary | 29 | −.00635 | 11 | −.73326 | .00465 |
| Ireland | 27 | −.18767 | 12 | −.62527 | .11734 |
| Israel | 26 | −.27833 | 10 | −.84125 | .23415 |
| Latvia | 28 | −.09701 | 12 | −.62527 | .06066 |
| Lithuania | 16 | −1.18495 | 9 | −.94924 | 1.12481 |
| Northern Ireland | 33 | .35630 | 20 | .23866 | .08504 |
| Norway | 16 | −1.18495 | 12 | −.62527 | .74091 |
| Poland | 20 | −.82230 | 8 | −1.05724 | .86937 |
| Portugal | 29 | −.00635 | 9 | −.94924 | .00602 |
| Russia | 28 | −.09701 | 24 | .67063 | −.06506 |
| Scotland | 37 | .71895 | 33 | 1.64255 | 1.18091 |
| Slovakia | 32 | .26564 | 16 | −.19330 | −.05135 |
| Sweden | 17 | −1.09429 | 11 | −.73326 | .80240 |
| Switzerland | 19 | −.91296 | 9 | −.94924 | .86663 |
| United States | 23 | −.55032 | 15 | −.30130 | .16581 |
| Wales | 53 | 2.16954 | 36 | 1.96652 | 4.26644 |

$$\Sigma\, z_{male}z_{female} = 24.403$$

$$r = \Sigma\, z_{male}z_{female}\,/\,N$$
$$= 24.403/28 = .8715$$

**Recall that the formula for a z score is:** $z = (X − \bar{X})/S$, where $\bar{X}$ = the mean and S = the standard deviation.

**FIGURE**

# A.10

Calculation of the Correlation Coefficient for the Percentage of Males and Females Who Drink Alcohol Weekly in 28 Countries

percentage of 15-year-olds drinking alcohol illegally. The data, however, do not fully support this hypothesis. In our sample, the correlation between legal drinking age and the percentage of males drinking at 15 is $r = −.412$. This moderately negative correlation indicates that countries with a lower legal drinking age tend to have higher rates of males drinking illegally at age 15. However, such a clear relationship was not found for females. Therefore, we can conclude that having a lower drinking age is *related* to higher rates of drinking at age 15 for males only.

Statistics are also used to test hypotheses about variables in the population being studied using a representative sample. When statistics are used to test hypotheses and thus to draw inferences about the population, they are referred to as inferential statistics. In testing hypotheses, researchers always set up two competing hypotheses. The null hypothesis contains a statement of what the researcher does *not* believe about the variables. The alternative hypothesis contains a statement of what the researcher believes to be true about the variables. The researcher then uses inferential statistics to test the null hypothesis.

To do this, the researcher must calculate some statistic on the data in the sample, and this statistic must be one for which we know what its distribution looks like. For instance, if the variable being studied is normally distributed in the population, then one could calculate *z* scores on the data and know that the distribution of these *z* scores in the population would be the standard normal distribution. The standard normal distribution is a bell-shaped, symmetric curve that has a mean of 0 and a standard deviation of 1. Because we know the shape, mean, and variance of the standard normal distribution, we also know exactly how much of the distribution falls between any two *z* scores. This allows us to determine the exact probability of obtaining any particular *z* score in our data.

In practice, *z* scores are not used very often to test hypotheses because psychologists frequently study more than one variable, and *z* scores can help us determine only the probability of obtaining a single data point in a sample. Therefore, psychologists often use other inferential statistics. The principle is still the same, however. You calculate an inferential statistic with a known distribution on your sample data. Next, you use the distribution to determine the probability of obtaining this particular value of the statistic, given the assumption that the null hypothesis is true. If the probability of obtaining this value of the inferential statistic when the null hypothesis is true is less than 5%, then you can safely say that, within an acceptable margin of error, it appears that the null hypothesis is not true and should be rejected in favor of the alternative hypothesis. In other words, your results are significant, and your data support your hypothesis.

In conclusion, please realize that this appendix has just skimmed the surface of what statistics is all about. All psychologists must undergo fairly extensive training in statistics before completing their degrees so that they have all the tools they need to discover the true nature of mental processes and behavior.

# Studying THE APPENDIX

## Key Terms

alternative hypothesis ($H_1$) (588)
correlation coefficient (586)
data (578)
descriptive statistics (580)
frequency distribution (579)
frequency polygon (579)
graph (578)
histogram (579)
inferential statistics (588)

mean (581)
measures of central tendency (581)
median (582)
mode (582)
normal distribution (584)
null hypothesis ($H_0$) (588)
outliers (582)
range (583)
sample variance (583)

scatter plot (580)
significant (588)
standard deviation (583)
standard normal distribution (585)
statistics (578)
sum of squares (583)
*z* score (584)

## What Do You Know? Assess Your Understanding

Test your retention and understanding of the material by answering the following questions.

1. _____ are bits of knowledge gathered in scientific studies.
   a. Statistics
   b. Data
   c. Hypotheses
   d. Correlations

2. If we want to know if a person's height is a good predictor of his shoe size, which statistic would be the most useful?
   a. The mean
   b. The mode
   c. The correlation coefficient
   d. A z score

3. If you want to describe the most common pet in America, after surveying 20,000 people to determine the type(s) of pet(s) they own, you should calculate the _____ of your data.
   a. mean                c. mode
   b. median              d. variance

4. A small company employs 10 people. At this company, three employees earn $20,000 a year, four employees earn $17,000, two employees earn $21,000, and the president earns $210,000 a year. Which of the following measures of central tendency is the most appropriate measure for accurately depicting the typical salary at this company?
   a. Mean
   b. Median
   c. Mode
   d. Variance

5. The mean of the standard normal distribution is equal to _____.
   a. 0
   b. 2
   c. 3
   d. −1

6. Which of the following statistics would be most useful for describing how the grades in a psychology course differ across the students in the class?
   a. Mean
   b. Sample variance
   c. Correlation coefficient
   d. z score

7. A z score of 2.66 means that the raw score in question is _____ the mean of the distribution.
   a. 1.33 standard deviations below
   b. 1.33 standard deviations above
   c. 2.66 standard deviations below
   d. 2.66 standard deviations above

8. Assuming that IQ scores are normally distributed, what percentage of the population can be expected to score 2 or more standard deviations above the mean on an IQ test?
   a. 2.28%
   b. 5.36%
   c. 8.77%
   d. 52.35%

9. The hypothesis that psychologists actually test is called the _____ hypothesis.
   a. true
   b. null
   c. alternative
   d. testable

10. A _____ distribution is a bell-shaped, symmetric frequency distribution.
    a. normal
    b. histogram
    c. scatter plot
    d. frequency polygon

Answers: 1. b; 2. c; 3. c; 4. b; 5. a; 6. b; 7. d; 8. a; 9. b; 10. a

Electrical workers!

Courtesy of K. Hanisch

come from your friends, other family members, school, and the media. In high school, more education and a part-time job may have given you additional details about the meaning of work. As you pursue a college degree, you may receive information about the work and jobs available in your chosen field through classes, internships, or other job or research experiences.

Work is an important part of life for many people. We often ask people we meet what they "do," which translates into "What is your job and whom do you work for?" Many people identify with their work because they spend so much of their waking lives at work. Work is important because it provides many of the things people need and value. Income from work provides us with the money necessary to satisfy our basic needs for food, shelter, and security (for example, health care or retirement income), while the "leftover" money provides us with discretionary funds to use as we see fit. These funds may be used to buy a round of golf, an iPad, or a fancy place to live; to support charities or attend athletic or fine art performances; or to save for college. Essentially, money, typically from work, provides us with a standard of living that varies from person to person depending on our income and how we choose to spend it. In addition, work provides much more. It provides a source of social interactions and friendships, independence, a sense of accomplishment, satisfaction, a reason to get up in the morning, happiness, a sense of identity, recognition, and prestige (see ■ TABLE B.1).

Although most researchers and practitioners agree that money and recognition are nearly universal motivators (R. E. Clark, 2003), many of the things we value or seek from work vary from person to person. For example, the prestige of a job may not be important to you, but it might be important to your best friend. Perhaps you will want your work to provide you with a sense of accomplishment or be a source of social interactions, while those attributes may not be valued by your friend. It is important to understand what you want from your work as well as what a job can provide.

From an employer's perspective, it is useful to determine what employees want because satisfied employees will be more likely than dissatisfied employees to work to meet organizational goals. Part of a supervisor's job is to ascertain what employees value because those values can be used to motivate employees to perform well in their jobs.

## TABLE B.1
## Jobs With the Highest and Lowest Prestige (2009)*

| Job Description | Percentage Rating Job as High Prestige |
|---|---|
| **Highest Prestige** | |
| Firefighter | 62% |
| Scientist | 57% |
| Doctor | 56% |
| Nurse | 54% |
| Teacher | 51% |
| Military Officer | 51% |
| **Lowest Prestige** | |
| Real Estate Agent/Broker | 5% |
| Accountant | 11% |
| Stockbroker | 13% |
| Actor | 15% |

*It is interesting to note that some of the professions with the highest prestige (firefighter, nurse, teacher) are not considered high-paying jobs while some of those with the least prestige (actor, stockbroker, real estate agent) are associated with fame or high earning potential or both. It appears that the polled individuals do not equate money and fame with high prestige; they appear to be unique concepts. Source: www.harrisinteractive.com.

## Types of Jobs

There are many types of work, in many types of jobs, in many different organizational settings. These settings include multinational conglomerates; public and private companies; nonprofits; federal, state, and local government organizations; and home businesses.

People in the United States work a variety of schedules, from extended workweeks (45–99 hours) to standard workweeks (35–44 hours) to part-time workweeks (fewer than 35 hours). Some people, such as police officers, medical personnel, and factory workers, because of the nature of their jobs, work shifts other than the typical 8 a.m. to 5 p.m. workday. Others are offered flexible working schedules that best fit their lives as long as they work the required number of hours and accomplish the work. Telecommuting is becoming more and more popular with the increase in appropriate technology. Some people work for virtual organizations that use communication technologies to outsource the majority of their functions.

Regardless of the type of job or your work schedule, you will likely spend most of your waking hours in some type of employment for many years. Many people spend their weekends working, too. Because work is critical to who we are and what we do, studying the psychological principles and some of the topics examined by I/O psychologists will provide you with information that may be useful to you in your future careers.

# Let's REVIEW

In this section, we provided an introduction to industrial and organizational psychology and highlighted the importance of work in our lives. As a quick check of your understanding, answer these questions.

**1.** Nearly all people value _____ and _____ from their work.
   **a.** money; prestige
   **b.** prestige; social interactions
   **c.** money; recognition
   **d.** satisfaction; prestige

**2.** Which of the following would an I/O psychologist be *least* likely to study?
   **a.** leadership
   **b.** life satisfaction
   **c.** employee selection
   **d.** performance appraisal

**3.** SAS offers many enticing work perks. CEO Jim Goodnight chooses to do this primarily because _____
   **a.** it makes inconveniences easy to deal with so employees can focus on their work
   **b.** most other companies offer these same perks
   **c.** he wanted SAS to be rated the number one company to work for in 2010
   **d.** there is a powerful employee union at SAG

Answers 1. c; 2. b; 3. a

# Selecting Employees

**LEARNING OBJECTIVE**

● Describe how employers decide which job applicants to hire.

## The Hiring Process

Industrial and organizational psychologists first became involved in the process of selecting employees when the U.S. government needed help selecting and placing officers and soldiers in World War I (Aamodt, 2010). Psychologists used mental ability tests to determine who would become officers and who would be in the infantry. The process many employers now use to hire employees is very detailed, typically consisting of five components: job analysis, testing, legal issues, recruitment, and the selection decision.

### JOB ANALYSIS

**Job analysis** is the identification of the critical elements of a job. I/O psychologists have helped devise effective strategies for determining three basic aspects of any job: (1) What tasks and behaviors are essential to the job? (2) What knowledge, skills, and abilities are needed to perform the job? (3) What are the conditions (such as stress, safety, and temperature) under which the job is performed? A

**job analysis** identification of the critical elements of a job, including tasks, skills required, and working conditions

**test** the measurement of a carefully chosen sample of behavior

**unstructured interview** informal, unplanned interview conducted by an untrained interviewer using random questions and no scoring key

**structured interview** interview conducted by a trained interviewer using standardized questions, a specific question order, and a predetermined scoring or answer key

**Title VII of the Civil Rights Act of 1964** law that prohibits discrimination based on race, color, religion, sex, and national origin

## TABLE B.2
### Typical Unstructured Interview Questions

1. What are your weaknesses?
2. Why should we hire you?
3. Why do you want to work here?
4. What are your goals?
5. Why did you leave (or why are you leaving) your job?
6. When were you most satisfied in your job?
7. What can you do for us that other candidates can't?
8. What are three positive things your last boss would say about you?
9. What salary are you seeking?
10. If you were an animal, which one would you want to be?

Source: C. Martin, 2006, Monster.com.

## TABLE B.3
### Structured Behavior-Based Interview Questions

1. Tell me in specific details about a time when you had to deal with a difficult customer.
2. Give me an example of a time when you had to make a decision without a supervisor present.
3. Give me a specific example of when you demonstrated your initiative in an employment setting.
4. Give me an example of a time when you had to work with a team.
5. Describe a time when you had to be creative at solving a problem.

Source: Adapted from The Job Centre, Niagara College Canada, 2005, http://jobs.niagarac.on.ca/.

job analysis can be conducted in many ways. An analyst (an I/O psychologist, human resources employee, manager, or outside consultant) may interview current employees, have them complete questionnaires, observe people in the job, or talk to people knowledgeable about the job (Gael, 1988).

The information from a job analysis is used in many types of personnel functions. These include employee selection, performance appraisal, training, and human resources planning. Within the hiring process, job analysis is used to write job descriptions; to determine what tests might be used to assess the relevant knowledge, skills, and abilities of job applicants; and to assist in meeting legal requirements that affect the selection process.

## TESTING

You are familiar with tests and taking tests. **Tests** are defined here as the measurement of carefully chosen samples of behavior. These include the standard paper-and-pencil tests used to measure specific skills or abilities in a class, or more general abilities as in the SAT or ACT. They also include personality assessments such as conscientiousness and honesty tests. In addition, work samples, in which applicants do a replica of the work they will be asked to do on the job, are useful tests. Tests are vital to the success of organizations. They are used to ascertain differences between people. The goal of these tests is to help employers choose the person best suited for the job and the organization. Regardless of the type of test or how it is administered, the reliability and validity of a test are very important (see Chapter 7).

Another type of test is the employee interview. Nearly all organizations use some type of interview in their selection of employees (Salgado, Viswesvaran, & Ones, 2003), even though interviews are often viewed as subjective and worthless. More than 85 years of research has provided evidence regarding when interviews are useful and when they are not.

Selection interviews can be broadly classified as unstructured and structured. **Unstructured interviews** are informal and unplanned. They are conducted by an untrained interviewer, with random questions and no scoring key. **Structured interviews** are conducted by a trained interviewer. They have standardized questions, a specific question order, and a predetermined scoring or answer key. Some typical questions asked during an unstructured interview are listed in ■ TABLE B.2. Examples of structured interview questions are listed in ■ TABLE B.3. Structured interviews, based on a job analysis, have greater reliability and validity than unstructured interviews (Huffcutt & Arthur, 1994).

## LEGAL ISSUES

One of the most important pieces of legislation regarding employment, and specifically the hiring of employees, is **Title VII of the Civil Rights Act of 1964** (Equal Employment Opportunity Commission, 2002). Title VII "prohibits discrimination based on race, color, religion, sex, and national origin," known as the "Big 5." Providing protection for people comprising the Big 5 helps to ensure that they have equal employment opportunities. Exceptions to this provision include national security, seniority systems, and bona fide occupational qualifications (BFOQs). BFOQs permit organizations to discriminate in hiring persons in a protected class if the qualification is determined to be reasonably necessary to the operation of the business. For example, women can be discriminated against when hiring someone to model men's swimwear, and vice versa. It is reasonably necessary to the marketing and selling of swimwear that organizations hire men to model male swimwear and women to model female swimwear; sex is a BFOQ. It is not reasonably necessary, however, that a secretary in a church who does secretarial work and not church or religious work believe in the same religion as the church that employs him; religion in this case could not be used as a BFOQ.

It is important for employers to abide by laws that protect people against discrimination because the costs of litigation can be very high, both monetarily and in terms of an organization's reputation. This protection applies to discrimination based not only on the Big 5, covered under the Civil Rights Act, but on other characteristics such as age (Age Discrimination in Employment Act) and disability (Americans with Disabilities Act). Employment law in the United States is meant to protect and provide equal opportunities for all individuals.

Mike Flanagan/www.cartoonstock.com

Legal issues in employment vary in different countries, however. The advertisement shown in ■ FIGURE B.1 for a bookkeeper in Johannesburg would not be legal in the United States. It specifies that the applicant must be female, which would be illegal under Title VII of the Civil Rights Act. It also specifies age 40 or older, which would be illegal in some states that protect younger individuals against age discrimination. U.S. federal law prohibits discrimination based on age once a person reaches the age of 40 (Age Discrimination in Employment Act). The employer is seeking an older woman, which is likely not related to expected job performance; people younger than 40 could perform just as well in the job of a bookkeeper.

Employment legislation offers fair treatment for people looking for a job. In the United States, organizations with several employees are required to abide by the employment laws. These laws make the U.S. job market fairer than in many other countries.

**FIGURE**

**B.1**

---

## Bookkeeper - Johannesburg East

**Expiry Date:** 2010-07-02 ▶

**Location:** Johannesburg East

**Category:** Banking and Financial Services

**Job Type:** Permanent

**Salary:** R8000.00 to R10000.00
MONTHLY
COST TO COMPANY

**Apply Now!**

**Minimum Education:**
National Diploma (NQF5)

**Required Experience:**
3 Years

**Job Details:**

We are urgently looking for a 40 year or older lady to perform full bookkeeping duties.

We will consider the candidate with an accounting degree or diploma in bookkeeping. She must have a Pastel Partner, Pastel Evolution experience and also be able to work on books to trial balance.

**Duties:**
Invoicing
Full
Creditors
Cashbook
Pettycash
Management
Reports

**Software Proficiency:**
Microsoft Excel: Intermediate
Microsoft Word: Intermediate
Pastel Partner: Intermediate
Pastel Evolution: Basic

Based on this photo, would you hire this job candidate?

# RECRUITMENT

The process organizational managers use to identify potential employees for a job is called **recruitment**. Depending on the job, a manager or owner may recruit from inside the company or seek someone outside the organization. The owner or manager may advertise on the company website or on a site for specific types of jobs. In addition, websites like monster.com and careerbuilder.com link potential employees and employers in a variety of jobs and locations. Other recruitment sources include newspapers, radio and television advertisements, trade magazines, professional publications, and employee referrals.

Research indicates that employees recruited through inside sources such as employee referrals or rehires work for the organization longer and have better job performance than those recruited through outside sources including advertisements, employment agencies, or recruiters (Zottoli & Wanous, 2000). Studies have supported the idea that those recruited using inside sources receive more accurate information about the job than those recruited through external sources (Conrad & Ashworth, 1986; McManus & Baratta, 1992). In effect, the new employees receive realistic job previews.

A survey of the 50 best small and medium organizations to work for in the United States found that 92% use employee referrals and that more than 30% of all hires were referred by a current employee (Pomeroy, 2005). Because of their effectiveness, some companies provide rewards to employees who recommend an applicant who is hired. These rewards include cash, vacations, and prizes such as televisions and free house cleaning services for a year (R. Stewart et al., 1990). Typically, the new employee must work for the organization a set period of time before the referring employee can receive the award (R. Stewart et al., 1990). SAS Canada offers a bonus up to $8,000 for a successful employee referral (http://www.eluta.ca/top-employer-sas-canada).

After applicants have submitted either a résumé or an application, someone from the organization such as the human resources manager or supervisor will determine which applicants should be considered further. In that process, he or she may make telephone inquiries of previous employers or other references and conduct criminal background checks.

A growing phenomenon is employers' use of social networking sites such as Facebook, LinkedIn, MySpace, and Twitter to learn about and even seek job candidates. In a 2009 CareerBuilder survey, 45% of employers reported that they use social networking sites in their selection process while 11% plan to start using them. On these sites employers have found promising candidates reporting on their own drug use, sexual exploits, and drinking, as well as posting inappropriate photographs and badmouthing their previous employer (Haefner, 2009). In addition to identifying risky behavior patterns, managers are using social networking sites to determine whether applicants would fit in well with the company culture and to evaluate their professionalism (Hargis, 2008). Some of the information job applicants thought would only be viewed by their peers is making its way into the public arena, with future employers and relatives viewing the information without the posters' knowledge.

## Making the Decision

When selecting employees, employers are looking for a good match between the employee and the organization. They would like to match the requirements for excellent performance in the job with the person's knowledge, skills, abilities, personality, and motivation for the job. They attempt to accomplish this by using the different types of tests discussed earlier.

**recruitment**   the process organizations use to identify potential employees for a job

Researchers have posited two groups of factors that determine an employee's performance in a job. They are the "**can-do**" and the "**will-do**" factors (Schmitt et al., 2003). "Can-do" factors suggest what an employee is capable of doing on the job if he is working to the best of his ability. Personality factors such as conscientiousness and need for achievement as well as integrity have been classified as important "will-do" factors in performance (Schmitt et al., 2003). "Will-do" factors suggest the time and effort an employee is willing to exert for the organization. A person's "can-do" and "will-do" factors may change as she moves from organization to organization. Once a person is selected, the important process of being accepted and socialized into the organization at all levels, including a work group or team, begins.

**can-do factors**    factors that determine the maximum performance an employee can exhibit

**will-do factors**    factors that determine the normal or typical performance by an employee

# Let's
## REVIEW

In this section, we discussed the process of employee selection, which consists of five components, including job analysis, testing, legal issues, recruitment, and the decision of whom to hire. As a quick check of your understanding, answer these questions.

1. Asking employees to describe their job is one way of conducting a _____.
   a. job evaluation
   c. performance appraisal
   b. job analysis
   d. job review

2. Zachary is usually a conscientious and hardworking employee, but the company has hired a new boss who is really lazy and doesn't motivate his employees. It is likely that Zachary's _____ will be compromised in this situation.
   a. try-to factors
   c. can-do factors
   b. will-do factors
   d. must-do factors

3. Alexander, a television reporter, wants access to the women's locker room right after the basketball game to conduct interviews with the team members. The women's team lets female reporters in to interview them, but wants Alexander to wait until after they have showered and changed because they think he is too critical in his reporting style. Alexander argues he needs to be treated the same as the female reporters. What would be the likely outcome if this issue goes before a court?
   a. The team would win because sex is a BFOQ in this case.
   b. The team members would win because they can discriminate against Alexander because they don't like his reporting style.
   c. Alexander would win because the team members can't discriminate against him because they don't like his reporting style.
   d. Alexander would win because sex is not a BFOQ in this case.

Answers 1. b; 2. b; 3. d

# Socializing Employees: Culture, Groups, Leadership, and Performance Appraisal

**LEARNING OBJECTIVE**

● Describe how new employees become adapted to their work and organization.

When you report for your first day of work in an organization, there will be many things you will need to learn to be successful in your job. The process of learning these things is called **organizational socialization**, which has been defined as "the process by which organizational members become a part of, or are absorbed into, the culture of the organization" (Jablin, 1982, p. 255). Organizational socialization consists of people learning how the organization operates by using information provided by management, coworkers, observation, and company handbooks or memos.

Nowadays, electronic communication is an important part of how employees are socialized (Flanagin & Waldeck, 2004). Employees communicate through e-mail, texting, company websites, chat groups, and blogs. Job applicants also use

**organizational socialization**    the process by which members of an organization become a part of, or are absorbed into, the culture of the organization

major decisions that could either make or break the organization. In his case, he created a self-managing group that had no need for external assistance from unions or other entities. As a result, Friedman demonstrated the transformational leadership approach (Bass, 1990). **Transformational leadership** is characterized by high ethical standards, inspirational motivation, intellectual stimulation, and individual consideration—all clearly evident in Arthur Friedman's leadership style.

Jim Goodnight, the CEO of SAS, has the philosophy that you should "treat employees like they make a difference and they will" (www.sas.com/jobs/corporate/index.html). Undoubtedly, his philosophy is working because SAS, even with the economic turbulence of the past several years, has continued to grow and has remained profitable. Other indicators include the company's number one ranking in 2010 by *Forbes* magazine, employee turnover of 2% in 2009 compared to the software industry average of 22%, and an employee average of only 2 sick days per year (there is no limit). Jim Goodnight wants a balanced work and personal life for his employees so they work 35-hour workweeks with many of them setting their own hours. He wants his employees to work well during their 7-hour days so his company tries to take care of inconveniences by having many services on-site (e.g., fitness center, day care, cafeteria, medical center). Employees rave about how great it is to work at SAS (Kaplan, 2010).

Leaders today must contend with information-based team environments requiring the capacity for sifting large amounts of information coming from computer networks (Avolio, Kahai, & Dodge, 2000). The widely varying working environments that result from global competition require leaders to be adaptable (Mann, 1959), capable of handling stress (Goleman, 1998), knowledgeable about competitors and products (Kirkpatrick & Locke, 1991), and able to solve complex problems quickly (Zaccaro et al., 2000). Leaders in organizations today also need to be concerned with human resources planning (the hiring and maintenance of an employee workforce) and the appropriate evaluation of employee performance to ensure their organizations will be competitive and profitable in the ensuing years.

## Performance Appraisal

**Performance appraisals** are the evaluations or reviews of employees' performance. Employees should continually be told about their job performance, both the good and the bad, by their employers. Formal employee performance appraisals are times for management to systematically evaluate employee performance and productivity on the job, set performance goals, and directly convey information about the culture of the organization (see Fletcher & Perry, 2001, for a review of research and future trends in performance appraisal). Performance reviews are important for many reasons, including (1) determining areas of employees' work needing improvement and areas to be complimented, (2) effectively managing employee raises and promotions, (3) dealing with unproductive employees in a fair and appropriate manner that may include termination, and (4) assisting in workforce planning that may be particularly important in difficult economic times, but should be done routinely to have the best employees in the organization.

Performance reviews vary in frequency, with some organizations evaluating new employees 30 or 60 days after hire while others evaluate new employees' performance 3 or 6 months after hire. Once an employee has been working for an organization for one year, most organizations formally evaluate performance annually or semi-annually (Aamodt, 2010). A typical performance review consists of some type of form that is filled out by the employee's supervisor; some organizations have both the employee and the employer fill out the same form to allow them to compare their views of the employee's performance. This is followed by

**transformational leadership** characterized by high ethical standards, inspirational motivation, intellectual stimulation, and individual consideration

**performance appraisals** the evaluations or reviews of employees' job performance

a meeting between the manager and the employee to discuss the employee's performance. This meeting should be held in a neutral, distraction-free location with an appropriate amount of time for discussion.

Because the performance review will often clearly define the most important components of employees' jobs and help shape the culture of the organization, it is recommended that employers provide performance appraisal forms to new employees when they are hired or on their first day of work. This will send a clear message to the employees about the work that is valued by the organization and about whether they will be evaluated according to criteria set by management (this may suggest a more collaborative or cooperative culture) or will be appraised relative to their coworkers (this may suggest a more competitive culture). It is in the best interest of both the employer (for performance management) and the employee (as a road map to success) that the job performance requirements be known at the time of hire. Once employees are hired who can complete the work tasks and be effective in the organization (that is, they have the ability to do the job), then their attitudes become important because their attitudes will directly influence their work behaviors.

Performance review meetings should be conducted in a distraction-free, neutral location with a prepared and trained employer.

# Let's REVIEW

In this section, we discussed employee socialization within an organization and its work groups. Leadership and the type of work group will affect employees' job performance, which should be reviewed in successful organizations. As a quick check of your understanding, answer these questions.

**1.** Spencer, a new employee of the company, has learned most of the behaviors required to do his job effectively. This would illustrate that Spencer has learned the _____ of the organization.
   a. organizational climate
   b. organizational culture
   c. transformational culture
   d. transformational climate

**2.** Performance reviews are important because they _____.
   a. help define the culture of the organization
   b. provide employees needed information on their job performance
   c. aid employers in determining the type of training needed by their employees
   d. all of the above

**3.** Carol is part of a successful self-managing team in an organization that produces handcrafted furniture. Compared to her coworkers in traditional-leader teams, Carol and her work team should have _____.
   a. better productivity, lower work quality, and a decrease in absenteeism
   b. an increase in work quality, decrease in work quantity, and better quality of life
   c. an increase in absenteeism, lower work quality, and higher work quantity
   d. better productivity, better work quality, and a better quality of life

Answers 1. b; 2. b; 3. d

# Attitudes and Behaviors at Work

One of the most important factors influencing whether you will be motivated to do a good job hinges on your attitudes at work (see Chapter 11). The causes and consequences of work attitudes have been extensively researched. Some of the outcomes of attitudes include volunteering for a project, helping out a coworker, quitting, absenteeism, tardiness, early retirement, and performance.

## LEARNING OBJECTIVE

● Describe the impact of employees' attitudes on their behaviors at work.

## Attitudes at Work

**Attitudes at work** are many and varied. In general, you can be satisfied or dissatisfied with the tasks and conditions at work, the people in your work environment, and the rewards you get from work. Employee satisfaction is important because it has been shown to be related to employee behaviors at work (Hanisch, 1995). Two of the most commonly studied work attitudes are job satisfaction and organizational commitment.

### JOB SATISFACTION

The positive or negative feelings associated with a job define **job satisfaction** (Thurstone, 1931). Some of the ways organizations can create satisfied employees include flexible working hours, professional growth opportunities, interesting work (Hackman & Oldham, 1976), autonomy, job security, a good supervisor, good benefits, competitive pay, opportunities for promotion (Cranny, Smith, & Stone, 1992), respect, recognition, and being part of something or being included. It is important to note that what makes one worker satisfied may not make another worker satisfied. For some people, interesting work is paramount. Others place higher emphasis on having coworkers they like. Still others feel that the pay and benefits they receive are most important. Virtually all employees value recognition (some acknowledgment of their work), respect, and being part of the organization. These rewards are all inexpensive and typically require very little time to implement. Just as in selection, a match between what you want and what the organization can provide will result in a successful outcome for both parties.

**attitudes at work**  satisfaction with the work itself, pay and benefits, supervision, coworkers, promotion opportunities, working conditions, and job security

**job satisfaction**  the positive or negative affect associated with a job

## YOUR TURN  Active Learning

One measure often used to assess employee work attitudes, and specifically different facets of job satisfaction, is the Job Descriptive Index (JDI; P. C. Smith, Kendall, & Hulin, 1969). This index has been improved upon based on years of research (e.g., Balzer et al., 1997; Hanisch, 1992). The JDI measures five facets of satisfaction: Work on Present Job, Supervisor, Coworkers, Present Pay, and Opportunities for Promotion. Try filling out the JDI Work on Present Job scale in ■ TABLE B.4.

### TABLE B.4
### Work on Present Job

Think of the work you do at present. How well does each of the following words or phrases describe your job? In the blank beside each word or phrase below, write:

**Y for "Yes" if it describes your work**

**N for "No" if it does *not* describe your work**

**? if you cannot decide**

| | | | |
|---|---|---|---|
| _____ 1. Fascinating | _____ 6. Creative | _____ 11. Tiring | _____ 16. Simple |
| _____ 2. Routine | _____ 7. Respected | _____ 12. Healthful | _____ 17. Repetitive |
| _____ 3. Satisfying | _____ 8. Uncomfortable | _____ 13. Challenging | _____ 18. Gives sense |
| _____ 4. Boring | _____ 9. Pleasant | _____ 14. Too much to do | of accomplishment |
| _____ 5. Good | _____ 10. Useful | _____ 15. Frustrating | |

**Scoring Key**:

| | | | |
|---|---|---|---|
| 1. Y=3, N=0, ?=1; | 6. Y=3, N=0, ?=1; | 11. Y=0, N=3, ?=1; | 16. Y=0, N=3, ?=1; |
| 2. Y=0, N=3, ?=1; | 7. Y=3, N=0, ?=1; | 12. Y=3, N=0, ?=1; | 17. Y=0, N=3, ?=1; |
| 3. Y=3, N=0, ?=1; | 8. Y=0, N=3, ?=1; | 13. Y=3, N=0, ?=1; | 18. Y=3, N=0, ?=1 |
| 4. Y=0, N=3, ?=1; | 9. Y=3, N=0, ?=1; | 14. Y=0, N=3, ?=1; | |
| 5. Y=3, N=0, ?=1; | 10. Y=3, N=0, ?=1; | 15. Y=0, N=3, ?=1; | |

To interpret your score on the work scale, 27 is considered the neutral value (Balzer et al., 1997). Values considerably higher would be evaluated as very satisfied; values considerably lower would be evaluated as very dissatisfied with the work on your present job.

A recent survey found that listening to music at work leads to higher levels of reported employee satisfaction. About one third of those participating in a Spherion Workplace Snapshot survey conducted by Harris Interactive in 2006 reported they listened to an iPod, MP3 player, or other personal music device while working (www.spherion.com). Seventy-nine percent of the participants reported that listening to music improved their job satisfaction or productivity or both at work. Allowing workers to listen to music may become more and more popular in jobs where music does not interfere with coworkers, safety, or job performance. Having happy workers contributes to an organization's success.

## ORGANIZATIONAL COMMITMENT

Employee commitment to an organization is related to employee retention within the organization. There are three types of organizational commitment: affective, normative, and continuance (Meyer & Allen, 1991). Meyer and Allen define **affective commitment** as an employee's emotional attachment to the organization that makes the employee want to stay in the organization. **Normative commitment** is based on feelings of obligation. **Continuance commitment** results when an employee remains with a company because of the high cost of losing organizational membership, including monetary (for example, pension benefits) and social (such as friendships) costs. Meyer and Herscovitch (2001) argue that employees have an organizational commitment profile at any given time in their job, with high or low values on each of the three types of commitment. In other words, an employee may have high scores on normative and continuance commitment, but be lower on affective commitment. Depending on the profile, the employee may engage in different behaviors such as quitting or helping out the organization.

Students may experience these different types of commitment to their college. Affective commitment occurs when a student feels an emotional attachment to her university because she really likes the school, including classes, the football team, and the town. Normative commitment might be evidenced by a student whose parents attended that college and who feels obligated to do the same regardless of whether it is the best school for him. Staying at a college because your friends are there and you have already paid for 2 years would typify acting under continuance commitment. The three levels of commitment could be represented as a commitment profile for a student.

Organizational commitment is related to job satisfaction. Employees who are satisfied with their job are more committed to their organization than are those who are less satisfied (Mosedeghrad, Ferlie, and Rosenberg, 2008; Mueller et al., 1994). Other correlates of organizational commitment include trust in one's supervisor and human resources practices that are supportive of employees (Arthur, 1994). The organizational commitment of Friedman's employees was very high, as evidenced by no turnover in 5 years; the low turnover at SAS also supports strong organizational commitment by its employees.

Employees report their job satisfaction and productivity increase if they are allowed privileges such as listening to music while they work.

Digital Vision/Photolibrary

## Behaviors at Work

Employers want their employees to engage in behaviors that will make them successful in the job because their success helps the organization meet its goals, including earning profits and fulfilling its mission. Employees have control over two aspects of their work: their time and their effort (Naylor, Pritchard, & Ilgen, 1980). Having employees at work instead of late or absent as well as exerting effort while at work are important to performance and productivity. Positive behaviors generally help an organization meet its goals while negative behaviors detract from goal attainment.

**affective commitment**   an employee's emotional attachment to the organization

**normative commitment**   commitment to the organization based on feelings of obligation

**continuance commitment**   remaining with an organization because of the high cost (monetary or social or both) of losing organizational membership

## ORGANIZATIONAL CITIZENSHIP BEHAVIORS

**Organizational citizenship behaviors (OCBs)**, or prosocial behaviors, are often described as extra-role behaviors because they are behaviors not specifically required by the job and not usually evaluated during performance reviews. These behaviors go beyond what is expected by the organization (C. A. Smith, Organ, & Near, 1983). Examples include staying late to finish a project, mentoring a new employee, volunteering for work, and helping a coworker. Some reasons why people engage in organizational citizenship behaviors are job satisfaction, high job autonomy, a positive organizational culture, high agreeableness (as a personality dimension; Witt et al., 2002), and high conscientiousness (Borman et al., 2001). OCBs have positive consequences for the organization and for employees in their day-to-day interactions with others in the organization.

## ORGANIZATIONAL WITHDRAWAL AND COUNTERPRODUCTIVE BEHAVIORS

Unhappy employees cause problems for organizations because they sometimes engage in behaviors that researchers refer to as **organizational withdrawal** (Hanisch, Hulin, & Roznowski, 1998) and counterproductive behaviors (Sackett & DeVore, 2001). Organizational withdrawal has been defined as behaviors employees use to avoid their work (**work withdrawal**) or their job (**job withdrawal**) (Hanisch, 1995; Hanisch & Hulin, 1990, 1991). Examples of work withdrawal are being absent from work, leaving work early, arriving to work late, missing meetings, and using work equipment for personal use without permission. Examples of job withdrawal are quitting one's job, transferring to another department within an organization, and retiring.

College students are familiar with withdrawal behaviors when it comes to certain college courses. Some classes may fail to keep your attention, and you may find yourself taking a nap in class or texting with a friend during lecture. You may even look for legitimate reasons not to attend class, such as offering to fill in for another employee at work or deciding to attend an optional session for another class.

**Counterproductive behaviors**, although similar in some ways to withdrawal behaviors, are defined as "any intentional behavior on the part of an organizational member viewed by the organization as contrary to its legitimate interests" (Sackett & DeVore, 2001). An example of a counterproductive behavior would be an intentional violation of safety procedures that puts the employee and the organization at risk. Other examples of counterproductive behavior are theft, destruction of property, unsafe behavior, poor attendance, drug use, and inappropriate physical actions such as attacking a coworker.

## Relation Between Attitude and Behavior

Organizational citizenship behaviors are positively related to job satisfaction and organizational commitment. In other words, employees with good attitudes and who feel committed to their organization are more likely to do positive things to assist the organization (LePine, Erez, & Johnson, 2002). Research indicates that those employees who demonstrate organizational citizenship behaviors are less likely to engage in counterproductive behaviors (Dalal, 2005). Researchers have found strong links between job satisfaction and specific withdrawal or counterproductive behaviors such as absenteeism (Hackett, 1989), and even stronger links with job withdrawal (Hanisch & Hulin, 1990).

Employers need to evaluate their work environment and benefit packages and make modifications where necessary to ensure that they have employees who are satisfied and committed. Art Friedman made modifications in the work environment of his organization that resulted in high satisfaction and commitment among his employees. To help with the inconvenience of going to the doctor, SAS built an

**organizational citizenship behaviors (OCBs)** employee behaviors that go beyond what is expected by the organization

**organizational withdrawal** work withdrawal or job withdrawal

**work withdrawal** behaviors employees use to avoid their work (e.g., lateness, absenteeism)

**job withdrawal** behaviors employees use to avoid their job (e.g., quitting, retiring)

**counterproductive behaviors** intentional behaviors on the part of an organizational member viewed by the organization as contrary to its legitimate interests

on-site medical center for employees and their families; there is no charge unless you fail to show up for an appointment (Kaplan, 2010). Employees need to learn how to seek out satisfying work and perks that will result in their commitment to the organization. Satisfaction and commitment facilitate OCBs and decrease withdrawal and counterproductive behaviors. Together the right employee attitudes and behaviors will lead to successful organizational functioning.

## Let's REVIEW

In this section, we discussed employee attitudes and behaviors at work, focusing on job satisfaction, organizational commitment, withdrawal, and counterproductive behaviors. As a quick check of your understanding, answer these questions.

1. Quitting one's job would be an example of _____.
   a. normative commitment
   b. job withdrawal
   c. organizational citizenship behavior
   d. work withdrawal

2. _____ would be an example of an organizational citizenship behavior while _____ would be an example of a counterproductive behavior.
   a. Mentoring a new employee; engaging in safe work practices
   b. Being late; staying late to help a coworker

   c. Missing a meeting; being late for work
   d. Volunteering to serve on a committee; physically attacking your supervisor

3. Gordon's organizational commitment has been decreasing in the last year. Which of the following is Gordon most likely to do if his organizational commitment doesn't improve soon?
   a. quit          c. ask for a raise
   b. be absent     d. steal from the organization

*Answers 1. b; 2. d; 3. a*

## Summary

This appendix has described the role of I/O psychologists in the workplace, including job analysis, employee recruitment and selection, organizational culture, performance appraisal, and the effect of employees' work attitudes on their work behaviors.

Now that you have an understanding of the process organizations use to hire successful employees, you have some of the tools necessary to help you in your search for a job. You have also learned about the appropriate matches you might strive for in seeking employment that will make your work with an organization fulfilling for both you and the company.

If you enjoyed learning about I/O psychology and think it might be a possible career for you, education and employment opportunities may interest you. Most I/O psychologists earn a master's or doctoral degree from a graduate school. This may take an additional 2 to 5 years beyond a bachelor's degree. Job opportunities are varied and often lucrative. For example, people with master's degrees in I/O psychology may work for an organization in its human resources office or conduct research on the best ways to train its employees. They may also work for the government, be employed in a consulting firm, or start their own consulting firm after obtaining some experience in the workplace. Those who earn a doctoral degree may secure the same types of jobs as those with master's degrees, but will typically be paid more for their expertise. In addition, they may work for a university or college teaching courses or conducting research on topics of their choosing, or both. I/O psychology is an excellent career choice for many students interested in business who wish to have an impact on the work lives of employees.

**association cortex** areas of the cortex involved in the association or integration of information from the motor-sensory areas of the cortex

**attachment** the emotional bond between caretaker and infant that is established by 8 or 9 months

**attention** conscious awareness; can be focused on events that are taking place in the environment or inside our minds

**attitude** an evaluative belief that we hold about something

**attitudes at work** satisfaction with the work itself, pay and benefits, supervision, coworkers, promotion opportunities, working conditions, and job security

**attribution** the act of assigning cause to behavior

**auditory cortex** a region of cortex found in the temporal lobe that governs the processing of auditory information in the brain

**auditory nerve** the nerve that carries information from the inner ear to the brain

**authoritarian [ah-thor-uh-TARE-ee-an] parent** a parenting style characterized by high levels of control and low levels of affection

**authoritative [ah-thor-uh-TAY-tive] parent** a parenting style characterized by moderate levels of control and affection

**autobiographical memory** memory for our past that gives us a sense of personal history

**autonomic nervous system** branch of the peripheral nervous system that primarily governs involuntary organ functioning and actions in the body

**availability heuristic** a heuristic in which we use the ease with which we can recall instances of an event to help us estimate the frequency of the event

**aversion [uh-VER-shun] therapy** a type of therapy that uses classical conditioning to condition people to avoid certain stimuli

**aversive racism** a proposed form of subtle racism in which European Americans feel aversive emotions around African Americans, which may lead them to discriminate against African Americans

**avoidance–avoidance conflict** a situation in which a person must choose between two undesirable events

**avolition [AA-vuh-lish-un]** the inability to follow through on one's plans

**axon [AXE-on]** a long tail-like structure growing out of the cell body of a neuron that carries action potentials that convey information from the cell body to the synapse

**babbling** the combinations of vowel and consonant sounds uttered by infants beginning around 4 months

**basal metabolic rate** the rate at which we burn energy in our bodies when resting

**basic anxiety** according to Horney, the feeling of helplessness that develops in children from early relationships

**basic emotions** a proposed set of innate emotions that are common to all humans and from which other higher-order emotions may derive

**basic level category** the intermediate level of categorization that seems to be the level that we use most to think about our world

**basilar membrane** the structure in the cochlear duct that contains the hair cells, which convert sound waves into action potentials

**behavior therapy** therapy that applies the principles of classical and operant conditioning to help people change maladaptive behaviors

**behavioral genetics** field of study that examines the influence of genetics and hereditary factors on personality traits

**behavioral perspective** an approach that focuses on external, environmental influences on behavior

**behaviorism** a psychological perspective that emphasizes the study of observable responses and behavior

**bereavement [bee-REEVE-munt]** the experience of losing a loved one

**binge eating disorder** an eating disorder characterized by recurrent episodes of binge eating, as in bulimia nervosa, but without regular use of compensatory measures to avoid weight gain

**binocular [bye-NOCK-you-lar] depth cues** depth cues that utilize information from both eyes

**biological perspective** an approach that focuses on physical causes of behavior

**biological preparedness** a genetic tendency to learn certain responses very easily

**biomedical therapy** the use of medications or other medical interventions to treat mental health disorders

**bipolar disorder** a mood disorder characterized by both depression and mania

**bisexual** one who is sexually attracted to members of both sexes

**blindspot** the point where the optic nerve leaves the retina, the optic disk, where there are no rods or cones

**blunted affect** a lack of emotional expression

**borderline personality disorder (BPD)** a personality disorder marked by a pattern of instability in mood, relationships, self-image, and behavior

**bottom-up perceptual processing** perception that is not guided by prior knowledge or expectations

**brightness** the intensity of light; it corresponds to the amplitude of the light waves

**Broca's aphasia [ah-FAYZ-yah]** a condition resulting from damage to Broca's area of the brain that leaves the person unable to produce speech.

**Broca's [BRO-kuz] area** a region in the left frontal lobe that plays a role in the production of speech

**bulimia nervosa** an eating disorder in which a person alternately binges on large quantities of food and then engages in some inappropriate compensatory behavior to avoid weight gain

**bystander effect** the idea that the more witnesses there are to an emergency, the less likely any one of them is to offer help

**can-do factors** factors that determine the maximum performance an employee can exhibit

**Cannon-Bard theory** a theory of emotion that states that emotions originate in the brain, not the body

**cardinal traits** according to Allport, those dominant elements of our personalities that drive all of our behaviors

**case study** an in-depth observation of one participant

**catatonic excitement** a disorder in motor behavior involving excited agitation

**catatonic [cat-uh-TAWN-ick] stupor** a disorder in motor behavior involving immobility

**causal hypothesis** an educated guess about how one variable will influence another variable

**cell body** the part of the neuron that contains the nucleus and DNA

**central executive** the attention-controlling component of working memory

**central nervous system (CNS)** the brain and the spinal cord

**central route to persuasion** a style of thinking in which the person carefully and critically evaluates persuasive arguments and generates counterarguments; the central route requires motivation and available cognitive resources

**central traits** according to Allport, the tendencies we have to behave in a certain way across most situations

**centration** the act of focusing on only one aspect or feature of an object

**cerebellum** hindbrain structure that plays a role in balance, muscle tone, and coordination of motor movements

**cerebral cortex** thin, wrinkled outer covering of the brain in which high-level processes such as thinking, planning, language, interpretation of sensory data, and coordination of sensory and motor information take place

**cerebral hemispheres** right and left sides of the brain that to some degree govern different functions in the body

**cholecystokinin [coe-lih-cyst-oh-KYE-nin] (CCK)** a hormone released by the small intestines that plays a role in hunger regulation

**chunking** a means of using one's limited short-term memory resources more efficiently by combining small bits of information to form larger bits of information, or chunks

**circadian rhythm [sir-KAY-dee-un RI-thum]** changes in bodily processes that occur repeatedly on approximately a 24- to 25-hour cycle

**classical conditioning** learning that occurs when a neutral stimulus is repeatedly paired with an unconditioned stimulus; because of this pairing, the neutral stimulus becomes a conditioned stimulus with the same power as the unconditioned stimulus to elicit the response in the organism

**client-centered therapy** a humanistic psychotherapy approach formulated by Carl Rogers that emphasizes the use of empathy, genuineness, and unconditional positive regard to help the client reach his or her potential

**clinical interview** the initial meeting between a client and a clinician in which the clinician asks questions to identify the difficulty in functioning that the person is experiencing

**closure** a Gestalt principle of perception that states that when we look at a stimulus, we tend to see it as a closed shape rather than lines

**cochlea [COCK-lee-uh]** the curled, fluid-filled tube in the inner ear that contains the basilar membrane

**cognition** Ch. 7: the way in which we use and store information in memory; Ch. 9: the ability to know, think, and remember

**cognitive consistency** the idea that we strive to have attitudes and behaviors that do not contradict one another

**cognitive distortion** Ch. 13: thought that tends to be pessimistic and negative; Ch. 14: distorted thinking patterns, such as overgeneralization or all-or-none thinking, that, according to Aaron Beck, lead to depression, anxiety, and low self-esteem

**cognitive map** a mental representation of the environment that is formed through observation of one's environment

**cognitive-mediational theory** a theory of emotion that states that our cognitive appraisal of a situation determines what emotion we will feel in the situation

**cognitive perspective** an approach that focuses on how mental processes influence behavior

**cognitive psychology** the study of mental processes such as reasoning and problem solving

**cognitive reappraisal [re-uh-PRAY-zull]** an active and conscious process in which we alter our interpretation of a stressful event

**cognitive therapy** a therapy created by Aaron Beck that focuses on uncovering negative automatic thought patterns that impede healthy psychological functioning

**cohesiveness [coe-HEE-siv-ness]** the degree to which members of a group value their group membership; cohesive groups are tight-knit groups

**collective unconscious** according to Jung, the part of the unconscious that contains images and material universal to people of all time periods and cultures

**collectivistic culture** a culture, like many Asian cultures, in which group accomplishments are valued over individual accomplishments

**color blindness** a condition in which a person cannot perceive one or more colors because of altered cone activity in the retina

**compliance** yielding to a simple request

**compulsion** repetitive behavior that a person feels a strong urge to perform

**concept** mental category that contains related bits of knowledge

**concrete operations** Piaget's third stage of cognitive development, characterized by logical thought

**conditioned response (CR)** the response that is elicited by a conditioned stimulus

**conditioned stimulus (CS)** a stimulus that elicits a conditioned response in an organism

**cones** the cells of the retina that are sensitive to specific colors of light and send information to the brain concerning the colors we are seeing

**confidentiality** ethical principle that researchers do not reveal which data were collected from which participant

**conflict** having to choose between two or more needs, desires, or demands

**conformity** behaving in accordance with group norms

**confounding variable** any factor other than the independent variable that affects the dependent measure

**conscious [CON-shus] level** the level of consciousness that holds all the thoughts, perceptions, and impulses of which we are aware

**consciousness [CON-shis-nus]** feelings, thoughts, and aroused states of which we are aware

**conservation** the understanding that an object retains its original properties even though it may look different

**constructive memory** memory that utilizes knowledge and expectations to fill in the missing details in retrieved memory traces

**contact hypothesis** the theory that contact between groups is an effective means of reducing prejudice between them

**contiguity [con-teh-GYU-eh-tee]** the degree to which two stimuli occur close together in time

**contingency [con-TINGE-en-see]** the degree to which the presentation of one stimulus reliably predicts the presentation of the other

**continuance commitment** remaining with an organization because of the high cost (monetary or social or both) of losing organizational membership

**continuous reinforcement** a schedule of reinforcement in which the organism is rewarded for every instance of the desired response

**control group** the group of participants who do not receive the manipulation that is being tested

**cooing** the vowel sounds made by infants beginning at 2 months

**coping** the behaviors that we engage in to manage stressors

**cornea [COR-nee-ah]** the clear, slightly bulging outer surface of the eye that both protects the eye and begins the focusing process

**corpus callosum [COR-puss cal-OH-sum]** a thick band of neurons that connects the right and left hemispheres of the brain

**correlation [cor-ruh-LAY-shun]** the relationship between two or more variables

**correlation coefficient** the average product of $z$ scores calculated on pairs of scores; describes the degree to which the scores in the pairs are linearly related

**counterproductive behaviors** intentional behaviors on the part of an organizational member viewed by the organization as contrary to its legitimate interests

**couple therapy** therapy that focuses on improving communication and intimacy between two people in a committed relationship

**covert sensitization [co-VERT sen-sih-tuh-ZAY-shun] therapy** a milder form of aversion therapy in which graphic imagery is used to create unpleasant associations with specific stimuli

**creativity** the ability to combine mental elements in new and useful ways

**critical thinking** thought processes used to evaluate and analyze information and apply it to other situations

**crystallized intelligence** abilities that rely on knowledge, expertise, and judgment

**cue-dependent forgetting** a type of forgetting that occurs when one cannot recall information in a context other than the context in which it was encoded

**cultural bias** the degree to which a test puts people from other cultures at an unfair disadvantage because of the culturally specific nature of the test items

**cycle** a physical characteristic of energy defined as a wave peak and the valley that immediately follows it

**cyclothymic [sigh-clo-THIGH-mik] disorder** a mood disorder that is a less severe but more chronic form of bipolar disorder

**daily hassles** the everyday irritations and frustrations that individuals face

**dark adaptation** the process through which our eyes adjust to dark conditions after having been exposed to bright light

**data** information gathered in scientific studies

**debriefing** ethical principle that after participating in an experiment involving deception participants be fully informed of the nature of the study

**decay theory** a theory of forgetting that proposes that memory traces that are not routinely activated in long-term memory will degrade

**decibels [DESS-uh-bells] (dB)** the unit of measurement used to determine the loudness of a sound

**decision making** making a choice from among a series of alternatives

**declarative memory** a type of long-term memory encompassing memories that are easily verbalized, including episodic and semantic memories

**deductive reasoning** reasoning from the general to the specific

**defense mechanisms** Ch. 11: unconscious, emotional strategies that are engaged in to reduce anxiety and maintain a positive self-image; Ch. 12: a process used to protect the ego by reducing the anxiety it feels when faced with the conflicting demands of the id and the superego

**deindividuation [DEE-in-dih-vid-you-AYE-shun]** a state in which a person's behavior becomes controlled more by external norms than by the person's own internal values and morals

**delusion** a thought or belief that a person believes to be true but in reality is not

**dendrites [DEN-drights]** branchlike structures on the head of the neuron that receive incoming signals from other neurons in the nervous system

**dependent variable** the variable in an experiment that measures any effect of the manipulation

**depressants** drugs that inhibit or slow down normal neural functioning

**dermis** the inner layer of the skin

**descriptive statistics** statistics that are calculated to summarize or describe certain aspects of a data set

**destructive obedience** obedience to immoral, unethical demands that cause harm to others

**development** changes in behavior or abilities or both

***Diagnostic and Statistical Manual of Mental Disorders (DSM)*** a book published by the American Psychiatric Association that lists the criteria for close to 400 mental health disorders

**diffusion of responsibility** the idea that responsibility for taking action is diffused across all the people witnessing an event

**discrimination** the behavioral expression of a prejudice

**dishabituation [DIS-huh-bit-chew-AYE-shun]** re-responding to a stimulus to which one has been habituated

**disordered behavior** a symptom of schizophrenia that includes inappropriate or unusual behavior such as silliness, catatonic excitement, or catatonic stupor

**disorganized speech** a symptom of schizophrenia in which one's speech lacks association between one's ideas and the events that one is experiencing

**display rules** cultural rules governing when it is and isn't appropriate to display certain emotions

**dissociation [dis-so-see-AYE-shun] theory** Hilgard's proposal that hypnosis involves two simultaneous states: a hypnotic state and a hidden observer

**dissociative [dih-SO-shee-tive] disorder** a disorder marked by a loss of awareness of some part of one's self or one's surroundings that seriously interferes with the person's ability to function

**dissociative fugue [dih-SO-shee-tive FYOOG] disorder** a disorder marked by episodes of amnesia in which a person is unable to recall some or all of his or her past and is confused about his or her identity; a new identity may be formed in which the person suddenly and unexpectedly travels away from home

**dissociative identity disorder (DID)** a disorder in which two or more personalities coexist within the same individual; formerly called multiple personality disorder

**dissonance theory** a theory that predicts that we will be motivated to change our attitudes and/or our behaviors to the extent that they cause us to feel dissonance, an uncomfortable physical state

**DNA** the chemical found in the nuclei of cells that contains the genetic blueprint that guides development in the organism

**door-in-the-face compliance** increasing compliance by first asking people to give in to a very large request and then, after they refuse, asking them to give in to a smaller request

**dopamine [DOPE-uh-mean]** neurotransmitter that plays a role in movement, motivation, learning, and attention

**double-blind study** an experiment in which neither the experimenters nor the participants know to which group (experimental or control) participants have been assigned

**Down syndrome** a genetic birth disorder resulting from an extra 21st chromosome, characterized by distinct facial features and a greater likelihood of heart defects and intellectual disability

**dream analysis** a technique in psychoanalysis in which the therapist examines the hidden symbols in a client's dreams

**drive** an uncomfortable internal state that motivates us to reduce this discomfort through our behavior

**drive reduction theory** a theory of motivation that proposes that people seek to reduce internal levels of drive

**dual coding system** a system of memory that encodes information in more than one type of code or format

**dualistic [do-uhl-LIS-tik] thinking** reasoning that divides situations and issues into right and wrong categories

**duplicity theory** a theory that proposes that a combination of volley and place theory explains how our brain decodes pitch

**dysphoria [dis-FOR-ee-uh]** an extreme state of sadness

**dysthymic [dis-THIGH-mik] disorder** a mood disorder that is a less severe but more chronic form of major depression

**eclectic [ee-KLECK-tic] approach** an approach that integrates and combines several perspectives when explaining behavior

**eclectic [ee-KLECK-tick] therapy approach** therapy that incorporates an integrated and diverse use of therapeutic methods

**ego** the conscious part of the personality that attempts to meet the demands of the id in a socially appropriate way

**egocentrism [ee-go-SEN-trih-zum]** the belief that everyone thinks as you do

**elaborative rehearsal** forming associations or links between information one is trying to learn and information already stored in long-term memory so as to facilitate the transfer of this new information into long-term memory

**Electra complex** in the female, an unconscious sexual urge for the father that develops during the phallic psychosexual stage

**electroconvulsive therapy (ECT)** a series of treatments in which electrical current is passed through the brain, causing a seizure; used to alleviate severe depression

**embryonic [em-bree-AH-nik] stage** the second stage of prenatal development, lasting from the 3rd through the 8th week

**emerging adulthood** the transitional period between late adolescence and the mid-20s when young people have left adolescence but have not yet assumed adult roles and responsibilities

**emotion** a complex reaction to some internal or external event that involves physiological reactions, behavioral reactions, facial expressions, cognition, and affective responses

**emotion-focused coping** behaviors aimed at controlling the internal emotional reactions to a stressor

**emotional stability** having control over one's emotions

**empathy** the ability of a therapist to understand a client's feelings and thoughts without being judgmental

**encoding** the act of inputting information into memory

**endocrine [EN-doe-crin] glands** organs of the endocrine system that produce and release hormones into the blood

**endocrine [EN-doe-crin] system** a chemical system of communication in the body that uses chemical messengers, called hormones, to affect organ function and behavior

**endorphins [in-DOOR-fins]** neurotransmitters that act as a natural painkiller

**enuresis [en-your-REE-sus]** a condition in which a person over the age of 5 shows an inability to control urination during sleep

**epidermis** the outer layer of the skin

**episodic [epp-uh-SOD-ick] memory** memory for the recent events in our lives

**erogenous [eh-ROJ-en-ous] zones** areas of the skin that are sensitive to touch

**estrogens [ESS-tro-jens]** a class of female sex hormones that regulate many aspects of sexuality and are found in both males and females

**evolutionary perspective** an approach that focuses on how evolution and natural selection influence behavior

**excitation** when a neurotransmitter makes the postsynaptic cell more positive inside, it becomes more likely to fire an action potential

**excitement phase** the first stage of the sexual response cycle, in which males get erections and females produce vaginal lubrication

**exemplar [ig-ZEM-plar]** a mental representation of an actual instance of a member of a category

**exhaustion stage** the third and final phase of the general adaptation syndrome, in which bodily resources are drained and wear and tear on the body begins

**experiment** a research method that is used to test causal hypotheses

**experimental group** the group of participants who receive the manipulation that is being tested

**explicit memory** the conscious use of memory

**extinction** the removal of a conditioned response

**extinction burst** a temporary increase in a behavioral response that occurs immediately after extinction has begun

**extrasensory perception (ESP)** also known as psi, the purported ability to acquire information about the world without using the known senses

**extraversion [ex-tra-VER-shun]** personality traits that involve energy directed outward, such as being easygoing, lively, or excitable

**extrinsic motivation** motivation that comes from outside of the person

**facial feedback hypothesis** a theory that states that our emotional state is affected by the feedback our brain gets from facial muscles

**family therapy** therapy that focuses on creating balance and restoring harmony to improve the functioning of the family as a whole system

**feature detection theory** a theory of perception that proposes that we have specialized cells in the visual cortex, feature detectors, that fire only when they receive input that indicates we are looking at a particular shape, color, angle, or other visual feature

**fetal alcohol syndrome (FAS)** a birth condition resulting from the mother's chronic use of alcohol during pregnancy that is characterized by facial and limb deformities and intellectual disability

**fetal stage** the third stage of prenatal development from the 9th week through the 9th month

**figure–ground** a Gestalt principle of perception that states that when we perceive a stimulus, we visually pull the figure part of the stimulus forward while visually pushing backward the background, or ground, part of the stimulus

**fine motor skills** motor behaviors involving the small muscles of the body

**five factor theory** Costa and McCrae's trait theory that proposes five core dimensions to personality: openness, conscientiousness, extraversion, agreeableness, and neuroticism

**fixed interval schedule** a schedule of reinforcement in which the organism is rewarded for the first desired response in an $x$th interval of time

**fixed ratio schedule** a schedule of reinforcement in which the organism is rewarded for every $x$th instance of the desired response

**flashbulb memory** an unusually detailed and seemingly accurate memory for an emotionally charged event

**flooding** a behavior therapy technique in which a client is exposed to a feared object or situation for a prolonged period until his or her anxiety extinguishes

**fluid intelligence** abilities that rely on information-processing skills such as reaction time, attention, and working memory

**foot-in-the-door compliance** increasing compliance by first asking people to give in to a small request, which then paves the way for compliance with a second, larger request

**forebrain** brain structures, including the limbic system, thalamus, hypothalamus, and cortex, that govern higher-order mental processes

**forgetting curve** a graph of the amount of learned information that is forgotten over time

**formal concept** a concept that is based on learned, rigid rules that define certain categories of things

**formal operations** Piaget's final stage of cognitive development, characterized by the ability to engage in abstract thought

**free association** a technique in psychoanalysis in which the client says whatever comes to mind

**frequency** a physical characteristic of energy defined as the number of cycles that occur in a given unit of time

**frequency distribution** a graph of data that plots the frequency of data points on the y-axis and the data points themselves on the x-axis

**frequency polygon** a line graph that is used to illustrate a frequency distribution

**frequency theory** a theory that proposes that our brain decodes pitch directly from the frequency at which the hair cells of the basilar membrane are firing

**frontal lobe** cortical area directly behind the forehead that plays a role in thinking, planning, decision making, language, and motor movement

**frustration-aggression hypothesis** the idea that frustration causes aggressive behavior

**functional fixedness** being able to see objects only in their familiar roles

**functionalism** an early psychological perspective concerned with how behavior helps people adapt to their environment

**fundamental attribution error** our tendency to overuse trait information when making attributions about others

**gamma amino butyric [GAM-ma uh-MEAN-oh bee-you-TREE-ick] acid (GABA)** the body's chief inhibitory neurotransmitter, which plays a role in regulating arousal

**gender permanence** the understanding that one's gender will not change

**gender roles** society's expectations for how males and females should behave

**gender-schema theory** the idea that gender roles are acquired through modeling and reinforcement processes that work together with a child's mental abilities

**general adaptation syndrome (GAS)** the general physical responses we experience when faced with a stressor

**general intelligence (g)** Charles Spearman's notion that there is a general level of intelligence that underlies our separate abilities

**generalizability [jen-er-uh-lies-uh-BILL-uh-tee]** how well a researcher's findings apply to other individuals and situations

**generalized anxiety disorder (GAD)** an anxiety disorder characterized by chronic, constant worry in almost all situations

**genes** strands of DNA found in the nuclei of all living cells

**genital stage** Freud's final psychosexual stage of development, which begins at puberty, in which sexual energy is transferred toward peers of the other sex (heterosexual orientation) or same sex (homosexual orientation)

**genotype [JEAN-oh-type]** inherited genetic pattern for a given trait

**genuineness** the ability of a therapist to openly share his or her thoughts and feelings with a client

**germinal stage** the first stage of prenatal development, from conception to 14 days

**Gestalt [gush-TALLT] approach** a psychological school of thought originating in Germany that proposed that the whole of a perception must be understood rather than trying to deconstruct perception into its parts

**Gestalt psychology** an early psychological approach that emphasized how our minds organize sensory stimuli to produce the perception of a whole form

**ghrelin [GRELL-in]** a hunger-stimulating hormone produced by the stomach

**glia[GLEE-uh] cells** brain cells that provide important support functions for the neurons and are involved in the formation of myelin

**glucose** the form of sugar that the body burns as fuel

**glutamate [GLUE-tuh-mate]** the chief excitatory neurotransmitter in the brain, found at more than 50% of the synapses in the brain

**glycogen [GLIE-co-jen]** a starchy molecule that is produced from excess glucose in the body; it can be thought of as the body's stored energy reserves

**gonads [go-NADS]** endocrine glands that directly affect sexual reproduction by producing sperm (testes) or eggs (ovaries)

**good continuation** a Gestalt principle of perception that states that we have a preference for perceiving stimuli that seem to follow one another as part of a continuing pattern

**grammar** the rules that govern the sentence structure in a particular language

**graph** a visual depiction of data

**grief** one's emotional reaction to the death of a loved one

**gross motor skills** motor behaviors involving the large muscles of the body

**group therapy** therapy that is administered to more than one person at a time

**groupthink** a situation in which a group fixates on one decision and members blindly assume that it is the correct decision

**guided imagery** a technique in which you focus on a pleasant, calming image to achieve a state of relaxation when you feel stressed

**loudness** the psychophysical property of sound that corresponds to the amplitude of a sound wave

**low-balling** increasing compliance by first getting the person to agree to a deal and then changing the terms of the deal to be more favorable to yourself

**maintenance rehearsal** repeating information over and over again to keep it in short-term memory for an extended period of time

**major depression** a mood disorder involving dysphoria, feelings of worthlessness, loss of interest in one's usual activities, and changes in bodily activities such as sleep and appetite that persists for at least 2 weeks

**mania** a period of abnormally excessive energy and elation

**manifest content** according to Freud, what the dreamer recalls on awakening

**matching hypothesis** the theory that we are attracted to people whose level of physical attractiveness is similar to our own

**mean** a descriptive statistic that describes the most average, or typical, data point in the distribution

**measures of central tendency** descriptive statistics that describe the most central, or typical, data points in the frequency distribution

**median** a descriptive statistic that identifies the center of the frequency distribution; 50% of the scores are above and 50% are below this point in the distribution

**medical model** perspective that views psychological disorders as similar to physical diseases; they result from biological disturbances and can be diagnosed, treated, and cured like physical illnesses

**meditation** mental exercises in which people consciously focus their attention to heighten awareness and bring their mental processes under more control

**medulla [meh-DOO-luh]** part of the hindbrain that controls basic, life-sustaining functions such as respiration, heart rate, and blood pressure

**melatonin [mel-uh-TONE-in]** hormone in the body that facilitates sleep

**memory consolidation** the stabilization and long-term storage of memory traces in the brain

**memory traces** the stored code that represents a piece of information that has been encoded into memory

**menarche [MEN-ar-kee]** a girl's first menstruation

**menopause** the period when a female stops menstruating and is no longer fertile

**mental age** the age that reflects the child's mental abilities in comparison to the average child of the same age

**mental representation** memory traces that represent objects, events, people, and so on that are not present at the time

**mental set** the tendency to habitually use methods of problem solving that have worked for you in the past

**mentoring** the pairing of a current and often long-term employee (the mentor) with a new employee

**mere exposure effect** the idea that the more one is exposed to something, the more one grows to like it

**microsleep** brief episode of sleep that occurs in the midst of a wakeful activity

**midbrain** brain structure that connects the hindbrain with the forebrain

**middle ear** the part of the ear behind the ear drum and in front of the oval window, including the hammer, anvil, and stirrup

**Minnesota Multiphasic [mul-tee-FAZE-ick] Personality Inventory (MMPI-2)** a personality inventory that is designed to identify problem areas of functioning in an individual's personality

**misinformation effect** the distortion of memory that occurs when people are exposed to misinformation

**mode** a measure of central tendency that identifies the most common, or frequent, score in the distribution

**monocular depth cues** depth cues that require information from only one eye

**mood disorder** a disorder marked by a significant change in one's emotional state that seriously interferes with one's ability to function

**moral reasoning** how you decide what is right and what is wrong

**morpheme [MORE-feem]** the smallest unit of sound in a language that has meaning

**motive** a tendency to desire and seek out positive incentives or rewards and to avoid negative outcomes

**motor cortex** a strip of cortex at the back of the frontal lobe that governs the execution of motor movement in the body

**motor neurons** neurons that transmit commands from the brain to the muscles of the body

**multiple approach–avoidance conflict** a situation that poses several alternatives that each have positive and negative features

**multiple intelligences** the idea that we possess different types of intelligence rather than a single, overall level of intelligence

**myelin [MY-eh-lynn]** fatty, waxy substance that insulates portions of some neurons in the nervous system

**myelin sheath [MY-eh-lynn SHEE-th]** the discontinuous segments of myelin that cover the outside of some axons in the nervous system

**narcolepsy [NAR-co-lep-see]** a rare sleep disorder in which a person falls asleep during alert activities during the day

**natural concept** a concept that develops naturally as we live our lives and experience the world

**natural selection** cornerstone of Darwin's theory of evolution, which states that genes for traits that allow an organism to be reproductively successful will be selected or retained in a species and genes for traits that hinder reproductive success will not be selected and therefore will die out in a species

**naturalistic observation** observing behavior in the environment in which the behavior typically occurs

**nature–nurture debate/issue** the degree to which biology (nature) or the environment (nurture) contributes to a person's development

**negative correlation** a relationship in which increases in one variable correspond to decreases in a second variable

**negative feedback loop** a system of feedback in the body that monitors and adjusts our motivation level so as to maintain homeostasis

**negative punishment** weakening a behavior by removing something pleasant from the organism's environment

**negative reinforcement** strengthening a behavior by removing something unpleasant from the environment of the organism

**neonate** a newborn during the first 28 days of life

**nervous system** an electrochemical system of communication within the body that uses cells called neurons to convey information

**neurons [NUR-ons]** cells in the nervous system that transmit information

**neuropeptide Y** the most powerful hunger stimulant known

**neuroplasticity [NUR-o-plas-TI-city]** the nervous system's ability to rewire its structures as a result of experience

**neuroscience** a field of science that investigates the relationships between the nervous system and behavior/mental processes

**neuroticism [nur-RAH-tuh-siz-um]** the degree to which one is emotionally unstable

**neurotransmitters [NUR-oh-TRANS-mitt-ers]** chemical messengers that carry neural signals across the synapse

**neutral stimulus (NS)** a stimulus that does not naturally elicit an unconditioned response in an organism

**night terrors** very frightening non-REM sleep episodes

**nightmare** a brief scary REM dream that is often remembered

**non-REM sleep** relaxing state of sleep in which the person's eyes do not move

**norepinephrine [nor-ep-in-EF-rin] (NOR)** neurotransmitter that plays a role in regulating sleep, arousal, and mood

**norm** unwritten rule or expectation for how group members should behave

**normal distribution** a bell-shaped, symmetric frequency distribution

**normative commitment** commitment to the organization based on feelings of obligation

**normative conformity** conformity that occurs when group members change their behavior to meet group norms but are not persuaded to change their beliefs and attitudes

**null hypothesis (H$_0$)** the hypothesis that contains a statement of what we do *not* believe is true about our variables in the population

**obedience** yielding to a demand

**obese** having a body mass index of 30 or over

**object permanence** the understanding that an object continues to exist even when it is not present

**observational learning** learning through observation and imitation of others' behavior

**obsession** a recurrent thought or image that intrudes on a person's awareness

**obsessive-compulsive disorder (OCD)** an anxiety disorder involving a pattern of unwanted intrusive thoughts and the urge to engage in repetitive actions

**occipital [ox-SIP-it-ull] lobe** cortical area at the back of the brain that plays a role in visual processing

**Oedipus [ED-uh-puss] complex** in the male, an unconscious sexual urge for the mother that develops during the phallic psychosexual stage

**olfaction** the sense of smell

**olfactory epithelium [ole-FACT-uh-ree epp-ith-THEEL-ee-um]** a special piece of skin at the top of the nasal cavity that contains the olfactory receptors

**operant conditioning** a type of learning in which the organism learns through the consequences of its behavior

**opiates [OH-pee-ates]** painkilling drugs that depress some brain areas and excite others

**opponent-process theory** the idea that we have dual-action cells beyond the level of the retina that signal the brain when we see one of a pair of colors

**optic chiasm** the point in the brain where the optic nerve from the left eye crosses over the optic nerve from the right eye

**optic nerve** the structure that conveys visual information away from the retina to the brain

**oral stage** Freud's first psychosexual stage of development, which occurs during the first year of life, in which the handling of the child's feeding experiences affects personality development

**organizational citizenship behaviors (OCBs)** employee behaviors that go beyond what is expected by the organization

**organizational climate** the behavioral norms of an organization

**organizational culture** the shared cognitive assumptions and beliefs of an organization

**organizational socialization** the process by which members of an organization become a part of, or are absorbed into, the culture of the organization

**organizational withdrawal** work withdrawal or job withdrawal

**orgasm phase** the third stage of the sexual response cycle, in which the pelvic and anal muscles contract

**orienting reflex** the tendency of an organism to orient its senses toward unexpected stimuli

**out-group** a group that is distinct from one's own and so usually an object of more hostility or dislike than one's in-group

**out-group homogeneity [home-uh-juh-NEE-it-tee] bias** our tendency to see out-group members as being pretty much all alike

**outer ear** the outermost parts of the ear, including the pinna, auditory canal, and surface of the ear drum

**outliers** unusual data points that are at the extremes of the frequency distribution, either far above or far below the mean

**ovaries** the organs in a female's body that produce eggs, or ova

**overextension** when a child uses one word to symbolize all manner of similar instances (e.g., calling all birds *parakeet*)

**panic disorder** an anxiety disorder characterized by intense fear and anxiety in the absence of danger that is accompanied by strong physical symptoms

**papillae [puh-PILL-ee]** bumps on the tongue that many people mistake for taste buds

**parasympathetic nervous system** branch of the autonomic nervous system most active during times of normal functioning

**parietal [puh-RYE-it-ull] lobe** cortical area on the top sides of the brain that play a role in touch and certain cognitive processes

**partial reinforcement** a schedule of reinforcement in which the organism is rewarded for only some instances of the desired response

**perception** the process through which we interpret sensory information

**performance appraisals** the evaluations or reviews of employees' job performance

**peripheral nervous system (PNS)** all of the nervous system except the brain and the spinal cord

**peripheral route to persuasion** a style of thinking in which the person does not carefully and critically evaluate persuasive arguments or generate counterarguments; the peripheral route ensues when one lacks motivation and/or available cognitive resources

**permissive parent** a parenting style characterized by low levels of control or discipline

**person–situation interaction** the influence of the situation on the stability of traits; when in the same situation, we display similar behavior, but when the situation is different, behavior may change

**personal fable** the belief held by adolescents that they are unique and special

**personal unconscious** according to Jung, the part of the unconscious that consists of forgotten memories and repressed experiences from one's past

**personality** the unique collection of attitudes, emotions, thoughts, habits, impulses, and behaviors that define how a person typically behaves across situations

**personality disorder** a disorder marked by maladaptive behavior that has been stable over a long period and across many situations

**personality inventory** an objective paper-and-pencil or computerized self-report form that measures personality on several dimensions

**persuasion** a type of social influence in which someone tries to change our attitudes

**phallic [FAH-lick] stage** Freud's third psychosexual stage of development, which occurs between 3 and 6 years of age, in which little boys experience the Oedipus complex and little girls the Electra complex

**phenotype [FEEN-oh-type]** actual characteristic that results from interaction of the genotype and environmental influences

**pheromones [FAIR-uh-moans]** airborne chemicals that are released from glands and detected by the vomeronasal organs in some animals and perhaps humans

**phobic [FOE-bick] disorder** an anxiety disorder characterized by an intense fear of a specific object or situation

**phoneme [FOE-neem]** the smallest unit of sound in a language

**photopigments** light-sensitive chemicals that create electrical changes when they come into contact with light

**pitch** the psychophysical property of sound that corresponds to the frequency of a sound wave

**pituitary [peh-TOO-uh-tare-ee] gland** master gland of the endocrine system that controls the action of all other glands in the body

**place theory** a theory that proposes that our brain decodes pitch by noticing which region of the basilar membrane is most active

**placebo effect** a measurable change in participants' behavior due to the expectation or belief that a treatment will have certain effects

**plateau phase** the second stage of the sexual response cycle, in which excitement peaks

**pleasure principle** the basis on which the id operates; the urge to feel good and maximize gratification

**pluralistic ignorance** the idea that we use the behavior of others to help us determine whether a situation is an emergency requiring our help; if no one else is helping, we may conclude that help isn't needed

**pons** hindbrain structure that plays a role in respiration, consciousness, sleep, dreaming, facial movement, sensory processes, and the transmission of neural signals from one part of the brain to another

**population of interest** the entire universe of animals or people that could be studied

**positive correlation** a relationship in which increases in one variable correspond to increases in a second variable

**positive psychology** the study of factors that contribute to happiness, positive emotions, and well-being

**positive punishment** weakening a behavior by adding something unpleasant to the organism's environment

**positive reinforcement** strengthening a behavior by adding something pleasant to the environment of the organism

**postformal thought** the idea that a correct solution (or solutions) may vary, depending on the circumstances

**postsynaptic neuron [post-sin-AP-tic NUR-on]** the neuron that is receiving the signal at a synapse in the nervous system

**posttraumatic stress disorder (PTSD)** an anxiety disorder, characterized by distressing memories, emotional numbness, and hypervigilance, that develops after exposure to a traumatic event

**pragmatics** the rules of conversation in a particular culture

**preconscious [pre-CON-shus] level** the level of consciousness that holds thoughts, perceptions, and impulses of which we could potentially be aware

**prediction** an expected outcome of how variables will relate

**predictive hypothesis** an educated guess about the relationships among variables

**prejudice** a largely negative stereotype that is unfairly applied to all members of a group regardless of their individual characteristics

**preoperational stage** Piaget's second stage of cognitive development, characterized by the use of symbols and illogical thought

**presynaptic neuron [pre-sin-AP-tic NUR-on]** the neuron that is sending the signal at a synapse in the nervous system

**primacy effect** the tendency for people to recall words from the beginning of a list better than words that appeared in the middle of the list

**primary appraisal [uh-PRAY-zull]** our initial interpretation of an event as either irrelevant, positive, or stressful

**primary drive** a drive that motivates us to maintain homeostasis in certain biological processes within the body

**primary reinforcer** a reinforcer that is reinforcing in and of itself

**private speech** Vygotsky's term describing the behavior of young children who talk to themselves to guide their own actions

**proactive interference** a type of forgetting that occurs when older memory traces inhibit the retrieval of newer memory traces

**problem-focused coping** behaviors that aim to control or alter the environment that is causing stress

**procedural memory** long-term memory for skills and behaviors

**progressive relaxation training** a stress management technique in which a person learns how to systematically tense and relax muscle groups in the body

**projective test** a less structured and subjective personality test in which an individual is shown an ambiguous stimulus and is asked to describe what he or she sees

**prosocial behavior** behavior that helps others

**prototype** our concept of the most typical member of the category

**proximity** Ch. 3: a Gestalt principle of perception that states that we tend to group close objects together during perception; Ch. 10: physical closeness

**pseudopsychology** psychological information or conclusions that sound scientific but that have not been systematically tested using the scientific method

**psychoactive drugs** substances that influence the brain and thereby the individual's behavior

**psychoanalysis [sigh-co-uh-NAL-uh-sis]** a method of therapy formulated by Freud that focuses on uncovering unconscious conflicts that drive maladaptive behavior

**psychoanalytic perspective [psi-co-an-uh-LIH-tic]** a personality approach developed by Sigmund Freud that sees personality as the product of driving forces within a person that are often conflicting and sometimes unconscious

**psychoanalytic theory** Sigmund Freud's view that emphasizes the influence of unconscious desires and conflicts on behavior

**psychodynamic perspective** an approach that focuses on internal unconscious mental processes, motives, and desires that may explain behavior

**psychodynamic therapy** modern psychoanalysis delivered in a shorter time that focuses less on the client's past and more on current problems and the nature of interpersonal relationships

**psychological distance** the degree to which one can disassociate oneself from the consequences of his/her actions

**psychology** the scientific study of behavior and mental processes

**psychoneuroimmunology [sigh-ko-nur-o-im-ya-NAH-la-gee]** field of study that investigates the connections among psychology (behaviors, thoughts, emotions), the nervous system, and immune system functioning

**psychopharmacology [sigh-co-farm-uh-KAH-lo-gee]** the use of medications to treat mental health problems

**psychophysics** the study of how the mind interprets the physical properties of stimuli

**psychosurgery** a biomedical treatment approach involving neurosurgery to alleviate symptoms in someone with a mental health disorder

**psychotherapy** the use of psychological principles and techniques to treat mental health disorders

**psychoticism [psi-COT-uh-siz-um]** the degree to which one is hostile, nonconforming, impulsive, and aggressive

**puberty [PEW-bur-tee]** the process of sexual maturation

**punishment** the weakening of a response that occurs when a behavior leads to an unpleasant consequence

**pupil** the hole in the iris through which light enters the eye

**quasi-experiment** a research study that is not a true experiment because participants are not randomly assigned to the different conditions

**random assignment** method of assigning participants in which they have an equal chance of being placed in any group or condition of the study

**range** a measure of variability that is the difference between the high score and the low score of the distribution

**rational-emotive therapy** a cognitive therapy approach created by Albert Ellis that focuses on changing the irrational beliefs that are believed to impede healthy psychological functioning

**realistic-conflict theory** the theory that prejudice stems from competition for scarce resources

**reality principle** the basis on which the ego operates; finding socially appropriate means to fulfill id demands

**reasoning** drawing conclusions about the world based on certain assumptions

**recall** a type of retrieval process in which the probe or cue does not contain much information

**recency effect** the tendency for people to recall words from the end of a list better than words that appeared in the middle of the list

**reciprocal determinism [ree-SIP-pra-cull dee-TER-min-iz-um]** according to Bandura, the constant interaction among one's behavior, thoughts, and environment determines personality

**reciprocity [reh-cih-PRAH-cih-tee]** a strong norm that states that we should treat others as they treat us

**recognition** a type of retrieval process in which the probe or cue contains a great deal of information, including the item being sought

**reconstructive memory** memory that is based on the retrieval of memory traces that contain the actual details of events we have experienced

**recruitment** the process organizations use to identify potential employees for a job

**reflex** an automatic response to a specific environmental stimulus

**refractory period** Ch. 2: brief period of time after a neuron has fired an action potential during which the neuron is inhibited and unlikely to fire another action potential; Ch. 8: a time during the resolution phase in which males are incapable of experiencing another orgasm or ejaculation

**reinforcement** the strengthening of a response that occurs when the response is rewarded

**relativistic [rell-uh-tah-VIS-tik] thinking** the idea that in many situations there is not necessarily one right or wrong answer

**reliability** the degree to which a test yields consistent measurements of a trait

**REM behavior disorder** a condition in which normal muscle paralysis does not occur, leading to violent movements during REM sleep

**REM rebound** loss of REM sleep is recouped by spending more time in REM on subsequent nights

**REM sleep** active state of sleep in which the person's eyes move

**representativeness heuristic** a heuristic in which we rely on the degree to which something is representative of a category, rather than the base rate, to help us judge whether or not it belongs in the category

**repression** a type of forgetting proposed by Sigmund Freud in which memories for events, desires, or impulses that we find threatening are pushed into an inaccessible part of the mind called the unconscious

**resistance** a process in psychoanalysis whereby the client behaves in such a way as to deny or avoid sensitive issues

**resistance stage** the second phase of the general adaptation syndrome, in which the nervous and endocrine systems continue to be activated

**resolution phase** the final stage of the sexual response cycle, in which the body returns to homeostasis

**response** an organism's reaction to a stimulus

**response set theory of hypnosis** asserts that hypnosis is not an altered state of consciousness, but a cognitive set to respond appropriately to suggestions

**resting potential** potential difference that exists in the neuron when it is resting (approximately –70 mv in mammals)

**reticular formation** part of the midbrain that regulates arousal and plays an important role in attention, sleep, and consciousness

**retina** the structure at the back of the eye that contains cells that convert light into neural signals

**retinal disparity** a binocular depth cue that uses the difference in the images projected on the right and left retinas to inform the brain about the distance of a stimulus

**retrieval** the process of accessing information in memory and pulling it into consciousness

**retroactive interference** a type of forgetting that occurs when newer memory traces inhibit the retrieval of older memory traces

**retrograde amnesia** a type of amnesia in which one is unable to retrieve previously stored memories from long-term memory

**reuptake** process through which neurotransmitters are recycled back into the presynaptic neuron

**rods** the light-sensitive cells of the retina that pick up any type of light energy and convert it to neural signals

**Rorschach [ROAR-shock] inkblot test** a projective personality test consisting of 10 ambiguous inkblots in which a person is asked to describe what he or she sees; the person's responses are then coded for consistent themes and issues

**ruminative [RUE-muh-nay-tive] coping style** the tendency to persistently focus on how one feels without attempting to do anything about one's feelings

**sample** the portion of the population of interest that is selected for a study

**sample variance** a measure of variability that shows on average how much the scores vary from the mean

**saturation** the purity of light; light that consists of a single wavelength produces the richest or most saturated color

**scaffolding [SKAH-fol-ding]** a process in which adults initially offer guidance and support in helping a child to reason, solve a problem, or master a task; as the child becomes more proficient and capable, the adult helps less and less until the child can master the task on his or her own

**scapegoat** an out-group that is blamed for many of society's problems

**scatter plot** a graph of data that plots pairs of data points, with one data point on the *x*-axis and the other on the *y*-axis

**schedule of reinforcement** the frequency and timing of the reinforcements that an organism receives

**schema [SKEE-ma]** Ch. 6: an organized, generalized knowledge structure in long-term memory; Ch. 9: a mental idea, concept, or thought

**schizophrenia [skit-suh-FREE-nee-uh]** a severe disorder characterized by disturbances in thought, perceptions, emotions, and behavior

**scientific method** a systematic process used by psychologists for testing hypotheses about behavior

**secondary appraisal** an evaluation of resources available to cope with a stressor

**secondary drive** a learned drive that is not directly related to biological needs

**secondary reinforcer** a reinforcer that is reinforcing only because it leads to a primary reinforcer

**secondary traits** according to Allport, the tendencies we have that are less consistent and describe how we behave in certain situations

**selective serotonin reuptake inhibitor (SSRI)** a type of antidepressant drug that inhibits the reuptake of the neurotransmitter serotonin, thereby improving mood

**self-actualization [self-ack-shu-lih-ZAY-shun]** the fulfillment of one's natural potential

**self-concept** one's perception or image of his or her abilities and uniqueness

**self-determination theory** a theory of motivation that proposes that as we pursue the fulfillment of basic needs, we experience different types of motivation that come from both the self and the outside world

**self-efficacy [self-EF-fuh-kah-see]** the expectation that one has for success in a given situation

**self-help group** a group comprised of people who share the same problem and meet to help one another

**self-serving bias** our tendency to make attributions that preserve our own self-esteem—for example, making trait attributions for our success and situational attributions for our failures

**semantic encoding** encoding memory traces in terms of the meaning of the information being stored

**semantic memory** long-term, declarative memory for conceptual information

**sensation** the process through which our sense organs convert environmental energy such as light and sound into neural impulses

**sensation seeker** a person who by trait tends to seek out arousing activities

**sensitive period** in prenatal development, a time when genetic and environmental agents are most likely to cause birth defects

**sensorimotor stage** Piaget's first stage of cognitive development, in which infants learn schemas through their senses and motor abilities

**sensory memory** a system of memory that very briefly stores sensory impressions so that we can extract relevant information from them for further processing

**sensory neurons** neurons that transmit information from the sense organs to the central nervous system

**separation anxiety** the fear an infant expresses when separated from the primary caretaker

**serotonin [ser-uh-TOE-nin]** neurotransmitter that plays a role in many different behaviors, including sleep, arousal, mood, eating, and pain perception

**set point** a particular weight that our body seeks to maintain

**sexual arousal** a heightened state of sexual interest and excitement

**sexual desire** one's motivation and interest in engaging in sexual activity

**sexual orientation** one's sexual attraction for members of the same and/or other sex

**sexually transmitted infection (STI)** an infection that is passed from one person to another primarily through sexual contact

**shaping** using operant conditioning to build a new behavior in an organism by rewarding successive approximations of the desired response

**short-term memory (STM)** a system of memory that is limited in both capacity and duration; in the three stages model of memory, short-term memory is seen as the intermediate stage between sensory memory and long-term memory

**significant** results are considered significant when there is a very small chance (usually less than 5%) of finding those results given the assumption that the null hypothesis is true

**similarity** a Gestalt principle of perception that states that we tend to group like objects together during perception

**situational attribution** an attribution that assigns the cause of a behavior to some characteristic of the situation or environment in which the behavior occurs

**Skinner box** device created by B. F. Skinner to study operant behavior in a compressed time frame; in a Skinner box, an organism is automatically rewarded or punished for engaging in certain behaviors

Blanchard, R. (2008). Review and theory of handedness, birth order, and homosexuality in men. *Laterality, 13,* 51–70.

Blane, H. T. (1988). Prevention issues with children of alcoholics. *British Journal of Addiction, 83*(7), 793–798.

Blatt, S. J., & Shahar, G. (2004). Psychoanalysis—with whom, for what, and how? Comparisons with psychotherapy. *Journal of the American Psychoanalysis Association, 52,* 393–447.

Blazer, D. G., Kessler, R. C., McGonagle, K. A., & Swartz, M. S. (1994). The prevalence and distribution of major depression in a national community sample: The National Comorbidity Study. *American Journal of Psychiatry, 151,* 979–986.

Bleiker, E. M., Hendriks, J. H., Otten, J. D., Verbeek, A. L., & van der Ploeg, H. M. (2008). Personality factors and breast cancer risk: A thirteen-year follow-up. *Journal of the National Cancer Institute, 100,* 213–218.

Bleiker, E. M., van der Ploeg, H. M., Hendriks, J. H., & Ader, H. J. (1996). Personality factors and breast cancer development: A prospective longitudinal study. *Journal of the National Cancer Institute, 88,* 1478–1482.

Blevins, J. E., & Baskin, D. G. (2010). Hypothalamic-brainstem circuits controlling eating. *Forum of Nutrition, 63,* 133–140.

Blincoe, L., Seay, A., Zaloshnja, E., Miller, T., Romano, E., Luchter, S., et al. (2002). *The economic impact of motor vehicle crashes, 2000.* Washington, DC: National Highway Traffic Safety Administration.

Block, J. A. (1995). A contrarian view of the five-factor approach. *Psychological Bulletin, 117,* 187–215.

Bloom, F., Nelson, C. A., & Lazerson, A. (2001). *Brain, mind and behavior* (3rd ed.). New York: Worth.

Bloom, J. W. (1998). The ethical practice of WebCounseling. *British Journal of Guidance and Counselling, 26,* 53–59.

Boden, M. (1988). *Computer models of the mind.* Cambridge, UK: Cambridge University Press.

Boeri, M. W., Sterk, C. E., & Elifson, K. W. (2004). Rolling beyond raves: Ecstasy use outside the rave setting. *Journal of Drug Issues, 34,* 831–860.

Bohnen, N. I., Muller, M. I., Kuwabara, H., Constantine, G. M., & Studenski, S. A. (2009). Age-associated leukoarasosis and cortical cholinergic deafferentation. *Neurology, 72,* 1411–1416.

Boivin, D. B., Czeisler, C. A., Kijk, D. J., Duffy, J. F., Folkard, S., Minors, D. S., et al. (1997). Complex interaction of sleep–wake cycle and circadian phase modulates mood in healthy subjects. *Archives of General Psychiatry, 54,* 145–152.

Bolles, R. C. (1972). Reinforcement, expectancy, and learning. *Psychological Review, 79,* 394–409.

Bolton, M., van der Straten, A., & Cohen, C. (2008). Probiotics: Potential to prevent HIV and sexually transmitted infections in women. *Sexually Transmitted Diseases, 35,* 214–225.

Bonanno, G. A. (2004). Loss, trauma, and human resilience. *American Psychologist, 59,* 20–28.

Bonanno, G. A., Brewin, C. R., Kaniasty, K., & La Greca, A. M. (2010). Weighing the costs of disaster: Consequences, risks, and resilience in individuals, families, and communities. *Psychological Science in the Public Interest, 11,* 1–49.

Bonanno, G. A., Galea, S., Bucciarelli, A., & Vlahov, D. (2006). Psychological resilience after disaster: New York City in the aftermath of the September 11th terrorist attack. *Psychological Science, 17,* 181–186.

Bond, R., & Smith, P. B. (1996). Culture and conformity: A meta-analysis of studies using Asch's (1952, 1956) line judgment task. *Psychological Bulletin, 119,* 111–137.

Bonne, O., Vythilingam, M., Inagaki, M., Wood, S., Neumeister, A., Nugent, A. C., et al. (2008). Reduced posterior hippocampal volume in post-traumatic stress disorder. *Journal of Clinical Psychiatry, 69,* 1087–1091.

Bonte, M. (1962). The reaction of two African societies to the Mueller-Lyer illusion. *Journal of Social Psychology, 58,* 265–268.

Booth, A., & Amato, P. R. (2001). Parental pre-divorce relations and offspring post-divorce well-being. *Journal of Marriage and the Family, 63,* 197–212.

Booth-Kewley, S., & Friedman, H. S. (1987). Psychological predictions of heart disease: A quantitative review. *Psychological Bulletin, 101,* 343–362.

Bootzin, R. R., & Rider, S. P. (1997). Behavioral techniques and biofeedback for insomnia. In M. R. Pressman & W. C. Orr (Eds.), *Understanding sleep: The evaluation and treatment of sleep disorders*

(pp. 315–338). Washington DC: American Psychological Association.

Borman, W. C., Penner, L. A., Allen, T. D., & Motowidlo, S. J. (2001). Personality predictors of citizenship performance. *International Journal of Selection and Assessment, 9,* 52–69.

Bornet, F. R., Jardy-Gennetier, A. E., Jacquet, N., & Stowell, J. (2007). Glycaemic response to foods: Impact on satiety and long-term weight regulation. *Appetite, 49,* 535–553.

Bornovalova, M. A., Gratz, K. L., Delany-Brumsey, A., Paulson, A., & Lejuez, C. W. (2006). Temperamental and environmental risk factors for borderline personality disorder among inner-city substance users in residential treatment. *Journal of Personality Disorders, 20,* 218–231.

Bornstein, M. H. (1985). On the development of color naming in young children: Data and theory. *Brain and Language, 26,* 72–93.

Bosch, J. A., de Geus, E. J., Kelder, A., Veerman, E. C., Hoogstraten, J., & Amerongen, A. V. (2001). Differential effects of active versus passive coping on secretory immunity. *Psychophysiology, 38,* 836–846.

Botella, C., Villa, H., Garcia Palacios, A., Quero, S., Banos, R. M., & Alcaniz, M. (2004). The use of VR in the treatment of panic disorders and agoraphobia. *Student Health and Technology Information, 99,* 73–90.

Bouchard, T. J. (2004). Genetic influence on human psychological traits: A survey. *Current Directions in Psychological Science, 13,* 148–151.

Bouchard, T. J., Lykken, D. T., McGue, M., Segal, N. L., & Tellegen, A. (1990). Sources of human psychological differences: The Minnesota study of twins reared apart. *Science, 250,* 223–228.

Bovin, M. J., & Marx, B. P. (2011). The importance of the peritraumatic experience in defining traumatic stress. *Psychological Bulletin, 137,* 47–67.

Bowden, C. L., Calabrese, J. R., Sachs, G., Yatham, L. N., Asghar, S. A., Hompland, M., et al. (2003). A placebo-controlled 18-month trial of lamotrigine and lithium maintenance treatment in recently manic or hypomanic patients with bipolar I disorder. *Archives of General Psychiatry, 60,* 392–400.

Bowden, C. L., Mosolov, S., Hranov, L., Chen, E., Habil, H., Kongsakon, R., et al. (2010). Efficacy of valproate versus lithium in mania or mixed mania: A randomized, open 12-week trial. *International Clinical Psychopharmacology, 25,* 60–67.

Bower, B. (2003, November 8). Forgetting to remember: Emotion robs memory while reviving it. *Science News, 164,* 293.

Bower, J. E., Moskowitz, J. T., & Epel, E. (2009). Is benefit finding good for your health? Pathways linking positive life changes after stress and physical health outcomes. *Current Directions in Psychological Science, 18,* 337–341.

Bowers, K. S., & LeBaron, S. (1986). Hypnosis and hypnotizability: Implications for clinical intervention. *Hospital and Community Psychiatry, 37,* 457–467.

Bowlby, J. (1980). *Attachment and loss: Vol. 3. Loss: Sadness and depression.* New York: Basic Books.

Bozarth, M. A., & Wise, R. A. (1984). Anatomically distinct opiate receptor fields mediate reward and physical dependence. *Science, 224,* 516–518.

Brackett, M. A., Rivers, S. E., Shiffman, S., Lerner, N., & Salovey, P. (2006). Relating emotional abilities to social functioning: A comparison of self-report and performance measures of emotional intelligence. *Journal of Personality and Social Psychology, 91,* 780–795.

Braddock, A. E., & Abramowitz, J. S. (2006). Listening to hypochondriasis and hearing health anxiety. *Expert Review of Neurotherapeutics, 6,* 1307–1312.

Bradley, D. B. & Hopcroft, R. L. (2007). The sex difference in depression across 29 countries. *Social Forces, 85,* 1483–1507.

Bradley, R. H., & Corwyn, R. F. (2008). Infant temperament, parenting, and externalizing behavior in first grade: A test of the differential susceptibility hypothesis. *Journal of Child Psychology and Psychiatry and Allied Disciplines, 49,* 124–131.

Brainerd, C. J., & Reyna, V. F. (2002). Recollection rejection: How children edit their false memories. *Developmental Psychology, 38,* 156–172.

Bramlett, M. D., & Mosher, W. D. (2002). Cohabitation, marriage, divorce, and remarriage in the United States. *Vital Health Statistics, 23*(22). Hyattsville, MD: National Center for Health Statistics.

Brannon, L., & Feist, J. (2004). *Health psychology: An introduction to behavior and health* (5th ed.) Belmont, CA: Wadsworth.

Bratberg, G. H., Nilsen, T. I., Holmen, T. L., & Vatten, L. J. (2005). Sexual maturation in early adolescence and alcohol drinking and cigarette smoking in late adolescence: A prospective study of 2,129 Norwegian girls and boys. *European Journal of Pediatrics, 164,* 621–625.

Braungart, J. M., Plomin, R., DeFries, J. C., & Fulker, D. W. (1992). Genetic influence on tester-rated infant temperament as assessed by Bayley's Infant Behavior Record. *Developmental Psychology, 28*(1), 40–47.

Brehm, S. S. (1992). *Intimate relationships* (2nd ed.). New York: McGraw-Hill.

Brehm, S. S., Kassin, S. M., & Fein, S. (2002). *Social psychology* (5th ed.). Boston: Houghton Mifflin.

Bremner, A. J., Bryant, P. E., & Mareschal, D. (2006). Object-centered spatial reference in 4-month-old infants. *Infant Behavior and Development, 29,* 1–10.

Brende, J. O. (2000). Stress effects of floods. In G. Fink (Ed.), *Encyclopedia of stress* (Vol. 2, pp. 153–157). San Diego: Academic Press.

Breslau, J., Aguilar-Gaxiola, S., Kendler, K. S., Su, M., Williams, D., & Kessler, R. C. (2006). Specifying race-ethnic differences in risk for psychiatric disorder in a USA national sample. *Psychological Medicine, 36,* 57–68.

Breslau, J., Kendler, K. S., Su, M., Gaxiola-Aguilar, S., & Kessler, R. C. (2005). Lifetime risk and persistence of psychiatric disorders across ethnic groups in the United States. *Psychological Medicine, 35,* 317–327.

Bresnahan, M., Begg, M. D., Browm, A., Schaefer, C., Sohler, N., Insel, B., et al. (2007). Race and risk of schizophrenia in a U.S. birth cohort: Another example of health disparity? *International Journal of Epidemiology, 36,* 751–758.

Brewer, M. B. (1979). In-group bias in the minimal intergroup situation: A cognitive-motivational analysis. *Psychological Bulletin, 86,* 307–324.

Brewer, M. B., & Campbell, D. T. (1976). *Ethnocentrism and intergroup attitudes: East African evidence.* New York: Halstead.

Britt, G. C., & McCance-Katz, E. F. (2005). A brief overview of the clinical pharmacology of "club drugs." *Substance Use and Misuse, 40,* 1189–1201.

Broberg, D. J., & Bernstein, I. L. (1987). Candy as a scapegoat in the prevention of food aversions in children receiving chemotherapy. *Cancer, 60,* 2344–2347.

Brody, J. E. (2007, April 17). When a brain forgets where memory is. *New York Times.* Retrieved May 13, 2008, from http://www.nytimes.com/2007/04/17/health/psychology/17brody.html

Brody, M. J., Walsh, B. T., & Devlin, M. (1994). Binge eating disorder: Reliability and validity of a new diagnostic category. *Journal of Consulting and Clinical Psychology, 62,* 381–386.

Bronstad, P. M., Langlois, J. H., & Russell, R. (2008). Computational models of facial attractiveness judgments. *Perception, 37,* 126–142.

Brown, A. S., Begg, M. D., Gravenstein, S., Schaefer, C. A., Wyatt, R. J., Brenahan, M., et al. (2004). Serological evidence of prenatal influenza in the etiology of schizophrenia. *Archives of General Psychiatry, 61,* 774–780.

Brown, B. B. (2004). Adolescents' relationship with peers. In R. Lerner & L. Steinberg (Eds.), *Handbook of adolescent psychology* (2nd ed., pp. 363–394). Hoboken, NJ: Wiley.

Brown, J. A. (1958). Some tests of the decay theory of immediate memory. *Quarterly Journal of Experimental Psychology, 10,* 12–21.

Brown, J. D., & Rogers, R. J. (1991). Self-serving attributions: The role of physiological arousal. *Personality and Social Psychology Bulletin, 17,* 501–506.

Brown, R., & Kulik, J. (1977). Flashbulb memories. *Cognition, 5,* 73–99.

Brown, S. L., Lee, G. R., & Bulanda, J. R. (2006). Cohabitation among older adults: A national portrait. *Journals of Gerontology, Series B: Psychological Sciences and Social Sciences, 61,* S71–S79.

Brown, S. L., Nesse, R. M., Vinokur, A. D., & Smith, D. M. (2003). Providing social support may be more beneficial than receiving it: Results from a prospective study of mortality. *Psychological Science, 14,* 320–327.

Brown, T. A., DiNardo, P. A., Lehman, C. L., & Campbell, L. A. (2001). Reliability of DSM-IV anxiety and mood disorders: Implications for the classification of emotional disorders. *Journal of Abnormal Psychology, 110,* 49–58.

Browne, A. (1993). Violence against women by male partners: Prevalence, outcomes, and policy implications. *American Psychologist, 48,* 1077–1087.

Brownell, K. (1988, January). Yo-yo dieting. *Psychology Today, 22,* 22–23.

Browning, J. R., Kessler, D., Hatfield, E., & Choo, P. (1999). Power, gender, and sexual behavior. *Journal of Sex Research, 36,* 342–348.

Bruffaerts, R., Demyttenaere, K., Borges, G., Haro, J. M., Chiu, W. T., Hwang, I., et al. (2010). Childhood adversities as risk factors for onset and persistence of suicidal behavior. *British Journal of Psychiatry, 197,* 20–27.

Brugman, T., & Ferguson, S. (2002). Physical exercise and improvements in mental health. *Journal of Psychosocial Nursing and Mental Health Services, 40,* 24–31.

Bryant, R. A., & Guthrie, R. M. (2005). Maladaptive appraisals as a risk factor for posttraumatic stress: A study of trainee firefighters. *Psychological Science, 16,* 749–752.

Bryman, A. S. (1996). The importance of context: Qualitative research and the study of leadership. *Leadership Quarterly, 7,* 353–370.

Brzezinski, A. (1997). Melatonin in humans. *New England Journal of Medicine, 336,* 186–195.

Buchanan, R. W., Breier, A., Kirkpatrick, B., Ball, P., & Carpenter, W. T. (1998). Positive and negative symptom response to clozapine in schizophrenic patients with and without the deficit syndrome. *American Journal of Psychiatry, 155,* 751–760.

Buckley, K. W. (1989). *Mechanical man: John Broadus Watson.* New York: Guilford Press.

Bucur, B., & Madden, D. J. (2010). Effects of adult age and blood pressure on executive function and speed of processing. *Experimental Aging Research, 36,* 153–168.

Buehler, R., Griffin, D., & Ross, M. (1994). Exploring the "planning fallacy": Why people underestimate their task completion times. *Journal of Personality and Social Psychology, 67,* 366–381.

Buehner, M., Mangels, M., Krumm, S., & Ziegler, M. (2005). Are working memory and attention related constructs? *Journal of Individual Differences, 26,* 121–131.

Bueno-Nava, A., Montes, S., DelaGarza-Montano, P., Alfaro-Rodriguez, A., Ortiz, A. & Gonzalez-Pina, R. (2008). Reversal of noradrenergic depletion and lipid peroxidation in the pons after brain injury correlates with motor function recovery in rats. *Neuroscience Letters, 443,* 32–36.

Bullock, W. A., & Gilliland, K. (1993). Eysenck's arousal theory of introversion–extraversion: A converging measures investigation. *Journal of Personality and Social Psychology, 64,* 113–123.

Bumpass, L. L., & Lu, H. H. (2000). Trends in cohabitation and implications for children's family contexts in the United States. *Population Studies, 54,* 29–41.

Burdakov, D., Luckman, S. M., & Verkhratsky, A. (2005). Glucose-sensing neurons of the hypothalamus. *Philosophical Transactions of the Royal Society of London, Series B, Biological Sciences, 360,* 2227–2235.

Burger, J. M. (1986). Increasing compliance by improving the deal: The that's-not-all technique. *Journal of Personality and Social Psychology, 51,* 277–283.

Burger, J. M. (2004). *Personality* (6th ed.). Belmont, CA: Wadsworth.

Burger, J. M. (2009). Replicating Milgram: Would people still obey today? *American Psychologist, 64,* 1–11.

Burnham, D. (1993). Visual recognition of mother by young infants: Facilitation by speech. *Perception, 22,* 1133–1153.

Burt, C. D. B., Kemp, S., & Conway, M. (2008). Ordering the components of autobiographical events. *Acta Psychological, 127,* 36–45.

Bush, S. I., & Geer, J. H. (2001). Implicit and explicit memory of neutral, negative emotional, and sexual information. *Archives of Sexual Behavior, 30,* 615–631.

Bushman, B. J. (1988). The effects of apparel on compliance: A field experiment with a female authority figure. *Personality and Social Psychology Bulletin, 14,* 459–467.

Buss, D. M. (1995). Psychological sex differences. *American Psychologist, 50,* 164–168.

Buss, D. N. (2009). The great struggles of life: Darwin and the emergence of evolutionary psychology. *American Psychologist, 64,* 140–148.

Bussey, K., & Bandura, A. (1999). Social cognitive theory of gender development and differentiation. *Psychological Review, 106,* 676–713.

Butler, L. D., Duran, R. E. F., Jasiukaitis, P., Koopman, C., & Spiegel, D. (1996). Hypnotizability and traumatic experience: A diathysis stress model of dissociative symptomatology. *American Journal of Psychiatry, 153,* 42–63.

Butow P. N., Hiller, J. E., Price, M. A., Thackway, S. V., Kricker, A., & Tennant, C. C. (2000). Epidemiological evidence for a relationship between life events, coping style, and personality factors in the development of breast cancer. *Journal of Psychosomatic Research, 49,* 169–181.

Butts, S. F., & Seifer, D. B. (2010). Racial and ethnic differences in reproductive potential across the life cycle. *Fertility and Sterility, 93,* 681–690.

Butzlaff, R. L., & Hooley, J. M. (1998). Expressed emotion and psychiatric relapse. *Archives of General Psychiatry, 55,* 547–552.

Byrd-Craven, J., Geary, D. C., Rose, A. J., & Ponzi, D. (2008). Co-ruminating increases stress hormone levels in women. *Hormones and Behavior, 53,* 489–492.

Byrne, D., Gouaux, C., Griffitt, W., Lamberth, J., Murakawa, N., Prasad, M. B., et al. (1971). The ubiquitous relationship: Attitude similarity and attraction: A cross-cultural study. *Human Relations, 24,* 201–207.

Byrne, M., Agerbo, E., Ewald, H., Eaton, W. W., & Mortensen, P. B. (2003). Parental age and risk of schizophrenia: A case-control study. *Archives of General Psychiatry, 60,* 673–678.

Cacioppo, J. T., & Petty, R. E. (1980). Sex differences in influenceability: Toward specifying the underlying processes. *Personality and Social Psychology Bulletin, 6,* 651–656.

Cacioppo, J. T., Hawkley, L. C., Kalil, A., Hughes, M. E., Waite, L., & Thisted, R. A. (2008). Happiness and the invisible threads of social connection: The Chicago Health, Aging, and Social Relations Study. In M. Eid & R. Larsen (Eds.), *The science of well-being* (pp. 195–219). New York: Guilford Press.

Cain, A. S., Epler, A. J., Steinley, D., & Sher, K. J. (2010). Stability and change in patterns of concerns related to eating, weight, and shape in young adult women: A latent transition analysis. *Journal of Abnormal Psychology, 119,* 255–267.

Cain, W. S. (1988). Olfaction. In R. C. Atkinson, R. J. Herrnstein, G. Lindzey, & R. D. Luce (Eds.), *Steven's handbook of experimental psychology* (2nd ed., Vol. 1, pp. 409–459). New York: Wiley.

Calabrese, J. R., Shelton, M. D., Rapport, D. J., Youngstrom, E. A., Jackson, K., Bilali, S., et al. (2005). A 20-month, double-blind, maintenance trial of lithium versus divalproex in rapid-cycling bipolar disorder. *American Journal of Psychiatry, 162,* 2152–2161.

Caldera, Y. M., & Lindsey, E. W. (2006). Coparenting, mother–infant interaction, and infant–parent attachment relationships in two-parent families. *Journal of Family Psychology, 20,* 275–283.

Calderoni, M. E., Alderman, E. M., Silver, E. J., & Bauman, L. J. (2006). The mental health impact of 9/11 on inner-city high school students 20 miles north of Ground Zero. *Journal of Adolescent Health, 39,* 57–65.

Calvert, H. (2003). Sexually transmitted diseases other than human immunodeficiency virus infection in older adults. *Clinical Infectious Diseases, 36,* 609–614.

Camper, J. (1990, February 7). Drop pompom squad, U. of I. rape study says. *Chicago Tribune,* p. 1.

Campos, B., Graesch, A. P., Repetti, R., Bradbury, T., & Ochs, E. (2009). Opportunity for interaction? A naturalistic observation study of dual-earner families after work and school. *Journal of Family Psychology, 23,* 798–807.

Cannon, D. S., & Baker, T. B. (1981). Emetic and electric shock alcohol aversion therapy: Assessment of conditioning. *Journal of Consulting and Clinical Psychology, 49,* 20–33.

Cannon, W. B. (1927). The James-Lange theory of emotions: A critical examination and an alternative theory. *American Journal of Psychology, 39,* 106–124.

Canova, A., & Geary, N. (1991). Intraperitoneal injections of nanogram CCK-8 doses inhibits feeding in rats. *Appetite, 17,* 221–227.

Canuso, C. M., & Pandina, G. (2007). Gender and schizophrenia. *Psychopharmacology Bulletin, 40,* 178–190.

Cardno, A. G., & Gottesman, I. I. (2000). Twin studies of schizophrenia: From bow-and-arrow concordances to Star Wars Mx and functional genomics. *American Journal of Medical Genetics, 97,* 12–17.

Cardozo, B. L., Bilukha, O. O., Crawford, C. A., Shaikh, I., Wolfe, M. I., Gerber, M., et al. (2004). Mental health, social functioning, and disability in postwar Afghanistan. *Journal of the American Medical Association, 292,* 575–584.

Carducci, B. J. (2009). *The psychology of personality: Viewpoints, research, and applications.* Malden, MA: Wiley-Blackwell.

Carey, B. (2007, October 23). An active, purposeful machine that comes out at night to play. *New York Times* [Online].

Carey, B. (2008). H.M., an unforgettable amnesiac, dies at age 82. *New York Times.* Retrieved December 14, 2009, from http://www.nytimes.com

Carey, G., & DiLalla, D. L. (1994). Personality and psychopathology: Genetic perspectives. *Journal of Abnormal Psychology, 103,* 32–43.

Carey, G., & Goldman, D. (1997). The genetics of antisocial behavior. In D. M. Stoff, J. Breiling, & J. D. Maser (Eds.), *Handbook of antisocial personality disorder* (pp. 243–254). New York: Wiley.

Carlson, P. J., Singh, J. B., Zarate, C. A., Jr., Drevets, W. C., & Manji, H. K. (2006). Neural circuitry and neuroplasticity in mood disorders: Insights for novel therapeutic targets. *NeuroRx, 3,* 22–41.

Carlston, D. E., & Shovar, N. (1983). Effects of performance attributions on others' perceptions of the attributor. *Journal of Personality and Social Psychology, 44,* 515–525.

Carney, C. E., Edinger, J. D., Meyer, B., Lindman, L., & Istre, T. (2006). Daily activities and sleep quality in college students. *Chronobiology International, 23,* 623–637.

Carrington, P. (1993). Modern forms of meditation. In P. M. Lehrer & R. L. Woolfolk (Eds.), *Principles and practice of stress management* (2nd ed., pp. 139–168). New York: Guilford Press.

Carroll, K. M., Ball, S. A., Martino, S., Nich, C., Babuscio, T. A., Nuro, K. F., et al. (2008). Computer-assisted delivery of cognitive-behavioral therapy for addiction: A randomized trial of CBT4CBT. *American Journal of Psychiatry, 165,* 793–795.

Carskadon, M. A., Acebo, C., & Jenni, O. G. (2004). Regulation of adolescent sleep: Implications for behavior. *Annals of the New York Academy of Sciences, 1021,* 276–291.

Carstensen, L. L., Turan, B., Scheibe, S., Ram, N., Ersner-Hershfield, H., Samanez-Larkin, G. R., et al. (2011). Emotional experience improves with age: Evidence based over 10 years of experience sampling. *Psychology and Aging, 26,* 21–33.

Carter, R. C., Jacobson, S. W., Molteno, C. D., Chiodo, L. M., Viljoen, D., & Jacobson, J. L. (2005). Effects of prenatal alcohol exposure on infant visual acuity. *Journal of Pediatrics, 14,* 473–479.

Carter, R. S., & Wojtkiewicz, R. A. (2000). Parental involvement with adolescents' education: Do daughters or sons get more help? *Adolescence, 35,* 29–44.

Cartwright, R. D. (1993). Who needs their dreams? The usefulness of dreams in psychotherapy. *Journal of the American Academy of Psychoanalysis, 21,* 539–547.

Carver, C. S., Harris, S. D., Lehman, J. M., Durel, L. A., Antoni, M. H., Spencer, S. M., et al. (2000). How important is the perception of personal control? Studies of early stage breast cancer patients. *Personality and Social Psychology Bulletin, 26,* 139–149.

Carver, C. S., Johnson, S. L., & Joormann, J. (2009). Two-mode models of self-regulation as a tool for conceptualizing effects of the serotonin system in normal behavior and diverse disorders. *Current Directions in Psychological Science, 18,* 195–199.

Cascio, W. F. (1995). Whither industrial and organizational psychology in a changing world of work? *American Psychologist, 50,* 928–939.

Casey, B. J., Giedd, J. N., & Thomas, K. M. (2000). Structural and functional brain development and its relation to cognitive development. *Biological Psychology, 54,* 241–257.

Caspi, A., Sugden, K., Moffitt, T. E., Taylor, A., Craig, I. W., Harrington, H., et al. (2003). Influence of life stress on depression: Moderation by a polymorphism in the 5-HTT gene. *Science, 301,* 386–389.

Castelnuovo, G., Gaggioli, A., Mantovani, F., & Riva, G. (2003). From psychotherapy to e-therapy: The integration of traditional techniques and new communication tools in clinical settings. *Cyberpsychology and Behavior, 6,* 375–382.

Cates, W., Jr. (1998). Reproductive tract infections. In R. A. Hatcher et al. (Eds.), *Contraceptive technology* (17th rev. ed., pp. 179–210). New York: Ardent Media.

Cattell, N. R. (2006). *An introduction to mind, consciousness and language.* London: Continuum.

Cui, M., & Donnellan, M. B. (2009). Trajectories of conflict over raising adolescent children and marital satisfaction. *Journal of Marriage and the Family, 71,* 478–494.

Cukor, J., Wyka, K., Jayasinghe, N., Weathers, F., Glosan, C., Leck, P., et al. (2011). Prevalence and predictors of posttraumatic stress symptoms in utility workers deployed to the World Trade Center following the attacks of September 11, 2001. *Depression and Anxiety, 28,* 210–217.

Curry, K., & Stasio, M. J. (2009). The effects of energy drinks alone and with alcohol on neuropsychological functioning. *Human Psychopharmacology, 24,* 473–481.

Cutrona, C. E., Wallace, G., & Wesner, K. A. (2006). Neighborhood characteristics and depression: An examination of stress processes. *Current Directions in Psychological Science, 15,* 188–192.

D'Augelli, A. R., Grossman, A. H., & Starks, M. T. (2006). Childhood gender atypicality, victimization, and PTSD among lesbian, gay, and bisexual youth. *Journal of Interpersonal Violence, 21,* 1462–1482.

Dabbs, J. M., Jr., & Morris, R. (1990). Testosterone, social class, and antisocial behavior in a sample of 4,462 men. *Psychological Science, 1,* 209–211.

Daiello, L. A. (2007). Atypical antipsychotics for the treatment of dementia-related behaviors: An update. *Medicine and Health, 90,* 191–194.

Dalal, R. S. (2005). A meta-analysis of the relationship between organizational citizenship behavior and counterproductive work behavior. *Journal of Applied Psychology, 90,* 1241–1255.

Dalen, K., Bruaroy, S., Wentzel-Larsen, T., & Laegreid, L.M. (2009). Cognitive functioning in children prenatally exposed to alcohol and psychotropic drugs. *Neuropediatrics, 40,* 162–167.

Dalman, C., & Allebeck, P. (2002). Paternal age and schizophrenia: Further support for an association. *American Journal of Psychiatry, 159,* 1591–1592.

Damak, S., Rong, M., Yasumatsu, K., Kokrashvii, Z., Varadarajan, V., Zou, S., et al. (2003). Detection of sweet and umami taste in the absence of taste receptor T1r3. *Science, 301,* 850–851.

Damasio, H., Grabowski, T., Frank, R., Galaburda, A. M., & Damasio, A. R. (1994). The return of Phineas Gage: Clues about the brain from the skull of a famous patient. *Science, 264,* 1102–1105.

Damjanovic, A. K., Yang, Y., Glaser, R., Kiecolt-Glaser, J. K., Huy, N., Laskowski, B., et al. (2007). Accelerated telomere erosion is associated with a declining immune function of caregivers of Alzheimer's disease patients. *Journal of Immunology, 179,* 4249–4254.

Damm, J., Eser, D., Schule, C., Obermeier, M., Moeller, H. J., Rupprecht, R., et al. (2010). Influence of age on effectiveness and tolerability of electroconvulsive therapy. *Journal of ECT, 26,* 282–288.

Damon, W. (1999). The moral development of children. *Scientific American, 281,* 73–78.

Danesi, M. (2010). The form and function of slang. *Semiotica: Journal of the International Association for Semiotic Studies, 182,* 507–517.

Dang-Vu, T.T., Schabus, M., Desseilles, M., Sterpenich, V., Bonjean, M., & Maquet, P. (2010). Functional neuroimaging insights into the physiology of human sleep. *Sleep, 33,* 1589–1603.

Danhauer, J. L., Johnson, C. E., Byrd, A., & DeGood, L., Meuel, C., Pecile, A., et al. (2009). Survey of college students on iPod and hearing health. *Journal of the American Academy of Audiology, 20,* 5–27.

Danielsdottir, S., O'Brien, K. S., & Ciao, A. (2010). Anti-fat prejudice reduction: A review of published studies. *Obesity Facts, 3,* 47–58.

Dannlowski, U., Ohrmann, P., Bauer, J., Kugel, H., Baune, B. T., Hohoff, C., et al. (2007). Serotonergic genes modulate amygdale activity in major depression. *Genes, Brain and Behavior, 6,* 672–676.

Darwin, C. (1936). *On the origin of species by means of natural selection.* New York: Random House. (Original work published 1859)

Dasen, P. R. (1994). Culture and cognitive development from a Piagetian perspective. In W. J. Lonner & R. Malpass (Eds.), *Psychology and culture* (pp. 141–150). Boston: Allyn & Bacon.

Dasgupta, A. M., Juza, D. M., White, G. M., & Maloney, J. F. (1995). Memory and hypnosis: A comparative analysis of guided memory, cognitive interviews, and hypnotic hyperamnesia. *Imagination, Cognition, and Personality, 14*(2), 117–130.

David, D., Szentagotai, A., Lupu, V., & Cosman, D. (2008). Rational emotive behavior therapy, cognitive therapy, and medication in the treatment of major depressive disorder: A randomized clinical trial, posttreatment outcomes, and six-month follow-up. *Journal of Clinical Psychology, 64,* 728–746.

Davidson, J. R. T. (2000). Trauma: The impact of posttraumatic stress disorder. *Journal of Psychopharmacology, 14,* S5–S12.

Davidson, R. J., Jackson, D. C., & Kalin, N. H. (2000). Emotion, plasticity, context, and regulation: Perspectives from affective neuroscience. *Psychological Bulletin, 126,* 873–889.

Davidson, R. J., Putnam, K. M., & Larson, C. L. (2000). Dysfunction in the neural circuitry of emotion regulation: A possible prelude to violence. *Science, 289,* 591–594.

Davies, H., Liao, P. C., Campbell, I. C., & Tchanturia, K. (2009). Multidimenional self reports as a measure of characteristics in people with eating disorders. *Eating and Weight Disorders, 14,* e84–91.

Davies, I. R. L. (1998). A study of colour grouping in three languages: A test of the linguistic relativity hypothesis. *British Journal of Psychology, 89,* 433–452.

Davis, K. C., George, W. H., Norris, J., Schacht, R. L., Stoner, S. A., Hendershot, C. S., et al. (2009). Effects of alcohol and blood alcohol concentration limb on sexual risk-taking intentions. *Journal of Studies on Alcohol and Drugs, 70,* 499–507.

Davis, M., & Egger, M. D. (1992). Habituation and sensitization in vertebrates. In L. R. Squire, J. H. Byrne, L. Nadel, H. L. Roediger, D. L. Schacter, & R. F. Thompson (Eds.), *Encylcopedia of learning and memory* (pp. 237–240). New York: Macmillan.

Davis, O. S., Haworth, C. M., & Plomin, R. (2009). Dramatic increase in heritability of cognitive development from early to middle childhood: An 8-year longitudinal study of 8,700 pairs of twins. *Psychological Science, 20,* 1301–1308.

Davis, P. J. (1999). Gender differences in autobiographical memory for childhood emotional experiences. *Journal of Personality and Social Psychology, 76,* 498–510.

Davis-Coelho, K., Waltz, J., & Davis-Coelho, B. (2000). Awareness and prevention of bias against fat clients in psychotherapy. *Professional Psychology: Research and Practice, 31,* 682–684.

De Benedittis, G., Lorenzetti, A., & Pieri, A. (1990). The role of stressful life events in the onset of chronic primary headache. *Pain, 40*(1), 65–75.

De Carvalho, M. R., Freire, R. C., & Nardi, A. E. (2010). Virtual reality as a mechanism for exposure therapy. *World Journal of Biological Psychiatry, 11,* 220–230.

de Castro, J. M. (2002). The influence of heredity on self-reported sleep patterns in free-living humans. *Physiology and Behavior, 76,* 479–486.

de Fonseca, F., Carrera, M. R. A., Navarro, M., Koob, G. F., & Weiss, F. (1997, June 27). Activation of corticotropin-releasing factor in the limbic system during cannabinoid withdrawal. *Science, 276,* 2050–2054.

De Lisi, R., & Gallagher, A. M. (1991). Understanding gender stability and constancy in Argentinean children. *Merrill-Palmer Quarterly, 37,* 483–502.

De May, J. (2006). A critical review of the March 27, 1964, *New York Times* article that first broke the story. Retrieved July 12, 2007, from http://www.oldkewgardens .com/ss-nytimes-3.html html

de Tommaso, M., Difruscolo, O., Sardaro, M., Losito, L., Serpino, C., Pietrapertosa, A., et al. (2007). Influence of MTHFR genotype on contingent negative variation and MRI abnormalities in migraine. *Headache, 47,* 253–265.

Deakin, J. F., Lees, J., McKie, S., Hallak, J. E., Williams, S. R., & Dursun, S. M. (2008). Glutamate and the neural basis of the subjective effects of ketamine: A pharmaco-magnetic resonance imaging study. *Archives of General Psychiatry, 65,* 154–164.

DeAngelis, T. (2004, January). Size-based discrimination may be hardest on children. *American Psychological Association Monitor on Psychology, 35,* 62.

Deary, I. J., Weiss, A., & Batty, G. D. (2010). Intelligence, personality, and health outcomes. *Psychological Science in the Public Interest, 11,* 53–79.

Deaux, K., & Hanna, R. (1984). Courtship in the personals column: The influence of gender and sexual orientation. *Sex Roles, 11,* 363–375.

DeCasper, A. J., & Fifer, W. P. (1980). Of human bonding: Newborns prefer their mothers' voices. *Science, 208,* 1174–1176.

DeCastro, J. M., & Elmore, D. K. (1988). Subjective hunger relationships with meal patterns in the spontaneous feeding behavior of humans: Evidence for a causal relationship. *Physiology and Behavior, 43,* 159–165.

Deci, E. L., & Ryan, R. M. (1985). *Intrinsic motivation and self-determination in human behavior.* New York: Plenum Press.

Deci, E. L., & Ryan, R. M. (2008). Self-determination theory: A macrotheory of human motivation, development, and health. *Canadian Psychology, 49,* 182–185.

Degroot, A. B. (2004). The role of the septo-hippocampal system in fear and anxiety. *Dissertation Abstracts International: Section B: The Sciences and Engineering, 65*(1-B), 475.

DeLacoste-Utamsing, C., & Holloway, R. L. (1982). Sexual dimorphism in the human corpus callosum. *Science, 216,* 1431–1432.

DeLoache, J. (2001). The symbol-mindedness of young children. In W. W. Hartup & R. A. Weinberg (Eds.), *Child psychology in retrospect and prospect* (Vol. 32, pp. 73–101). Mahwah, NJ: Erlbaum.

Demany, L., & Semal, C. (2005). The slow formation of a pitch percept beyond the ending time of a short tone burst. *Perception and Psychophysics, 67,* 1376–1383.

Dement, W. (1960). The effect of dream deprivation. *Science, 131,* 1705–1707.

Dement, W., & Kleitman, N. (1957). Cyclic variations in EEG during sleep and their relation to eye movements, body motility, and dreaming. *Electroencephalography and Clinical Neurophysiology, 9,* 673–690.

Dement, W., & Vaughan, C. (1999). *The promise of sleep: A pioneer in sleep medicine explains the vital connection between health, happiness, and a good night's sleep.* New York: Delacorte.

Denis, M., & Cocude, M. (1999). On the metric properties of visual images generated from verbal descriptions: Evidence for the robustness of the mental scanning effect. *Journal of Cognitive Psychology, 9,* 353–379.

Department of Housing and Urban Development (HUD). (2005). *Discrimination in metropolitan housing markets: National results from Phase 1, Phase 2, and Phase 3 of the housing discrimination study (HDS).* Retrieved May 20, 2011, from http://www.huduser.org/publications/hsgfin/hds.html

Depression and Bipolar Support Alliance (DBSA). (2002). *National DMDA support groups: An important step on the road to wellness.* Chicago: Author.

Derringer, J., Krueger, R. F., Dick, D. M., Saccone, S., Grucza, R. A., Agrawal, A., Lin, P., et al. (2010). Predicting sensation seeking from dopamine genes: A candidate-systems approach. *Psychological Science, 21,* 1282–1290.

Desseilles, M., Dabg-Vu, T. T., Sterpenich, V., & Schwartz, S. (in press). Cognitive and emotional processes during dreaming: A neuroimaging view. *Consciousness and Cognition.* doi:10.1016/j.concog.2010.10.005

Deutsch, F. M. (2001). Equally shared parenting. *Current Directions in Psychological Science, 10,* 25–28.

Deutsch, J. A. (1990). Food intake. In E. M. Stricker (Ed.), *Handbook of behavioral neurobiology: Vol. 10. Neurobiology of food and fluid intake* (pp. 151–182). New York: Plenum Press.

DeValois, R. L., & DeValois, K. K. (1975). Neural coding of color. In E. C. Carterette & M. P. Friedman (Eds.), *Handbook of perception* (pp. 117–166). New York: Academic Press.

Dewaraja, R., & Kawamura, N. (2006). Trauma intensity and posttraumatic stress: Implications of the tsunami experience in Sri Lanka for the management of future disasters. *International Congress Series, 1287,* 69–73.

Dhabhar, F. S., Miller, A. H., McEwen, B. S., & Spencer, R. L. (1995). Effects of stress on immune cell distribution. Dynamics and hormonal mechanisms. *Journal of Immunology, 154*(10), 5511–5527.

Diamond, A., & Amso, D. (2008). Contributions of neuroscience to our understanding of cognitive development. *Current Directions in Psychological Science, 17,* 136–141.

Diaz, R. M., & Berk, L. E. (Eds.). (1992). *Private speech: From social interaction to self-regulation.* Hillsdale, NJ: Erlbaum.

Dickens, W. T., & Flynn, J. R. (2006). Black Americans reduce the racial IQ gap. Evidence from standardization samples. *Psychological Science, 17,* 913–920.

Diekelmann, S., & Born, J. (2010). The memory function of sleep. *Nature Reviews: Neuroscience, 11,* 114–126.

Diener, C., Kuehner, C., Brusniak, W., Struve, M., & Flor, H. (2009). Effects of stressor controllability on psychophysiological, cognitive, and behavioral responses in patients with major depression and dysthymia. *Psychological Medicine, 39,* 77–86.

Diener, E., & Biswas-Diener, R. (2008). *Happiness: Unlocking the mysteries of psychological wealth.* Malden, MA: Blackwell.

Diener, E., Oishi, S., & Lucas, R. E. (2003). Personality, culture, and subjective well-being: Emotional and cognitive evaluations of life. *Annual Review of Psychology, 54*, 403–425.

Diener, E., & Seligman, M. E. (2004). Beyond money: Toward an economy of well-being. *Psychological Science in the Public Interest, 5*, 1–31.

Dies, R. R. (1993). Research on group psychotherapy: Overview and clinical applications. In A. Alonso & H. I. Swiller (Eds.), *Group therapy in clinical practice* (pp. 473–518). Washington, DC: American Psychiatric Press.

Difede, J., & Hoffman, H. G. (2002). Virtual reality exposure therapy for World Trade Center post-traumatic stress disorder: A case report. *Cyberpsychology and Behavior, 5*, 529–535.

Digman, J. M. (1997). Higher-order factors of the Big Five. *Journal of Personality and Social Psychology, 73*, 1246–1256.

Dillon, S. (2009, August 11). Disabled students are spanked more. *New York Times* (New York Edition), A10.

Dingfelder, S. F. (2010). How artists see. *Monitor on Psychology, 41*, p. 40.

Dion, K. K., Berscheid, E., & Walster, E. (1972). What is beautiful is good. *Journal of Personality and Social Psychology, 24*, 285–290.

Dishion, T. J., & Patterson, G. R. (1997). The timing and severity of antisocial behavior: Three hypotheses within an ecological framework. In D. M. Stoff, J. Breiling, & J. D. Maser (Eds.), *Handbook of antisocial personality disorder* (pp. 205–217). New York: Wiley

Distefan, J. M., Pierce, J. P., & Gilpin, E. A. (2004). Do favorite movie stars influence adolescent smoking initiation? *American Journal of Public Health, 94*, 1239–1244.

Dixon, J. F., & Hokin, L. E. (1998). Lithium acutely inhibits and chronically up-regulates and stabilizes glutamate uptake by presynaptic nerve endings on mouse cerebral cortex. *Neurobiology, 95*, 8363–8368.

Dobbs, D. (2006). Turning off depression. *Scientific American, 17*, 26–31.

Dobson, K. S., Backs-Dermott, B. J., & Dozois, D. J. A. (2000). Cognitive and cognitive-behavioral therapies. In C. R. Snyder & R. E. Ingram (Eds.), *Handbook of psychological change: Psychotherapy processes and practices for the 21st century* (pp. 409–428). New York: Wiley.

Doctor, R. M., & Doctor, J. N. (1994). Stress. *Encyclopedia of human behavior* (Vol. 4). San Diego, CA: Academic Press.

Dohrenwend, B. P., Turner, J. B., Turse, N. A., Adams, B. G., Koen, K. C., & Marshall, R. (2006). The psychological risk of Vietnam for U.S. veterans: A revisit with new data and methods. *Science, 313*, 979–982.

Dolbier, C. L., Cocke, R. R., Leiferman, J. A., Steinhardt, M. A., Schapiro, S. J., Nehete, P. N., et al. (2001). Differences in functional immune responses of high vs. low hardy healthy individuals. *Journal of Behavioral Medicine, 24*, 219–229.

Dollard, J., Doob, L., Miller, N., Mowrer, O. H., & Sears, R. R. (1939). *Frustration and aggression*. New Haven, CT: Yale University Press.

Dominowski, R. L., & Dallob, P. (1995). Insight and problem solving. In R. J. Sternberg & J. E. Davidson (Eds.), *The nature of insight* (pp. 33–62). Cambridge, MA: MIT Press.

Domjan, M., & Purdy, J. E. (1995). Animal research in psychology: More than meets the eye of the general psychology student. *American Psychologist, 50*, 496–503.

Doty, R. L. (2001). Olfaction. *Annual Review of Psychology, 52*, 423–452.

Dougherty, D. D., Baer, L., Cosgrove, G. R., Cassem, E. H., Price, B. H., Nirenberg, A. A., et al. (2002). Prospective long-term follow-up of 44 patients who received cingulotomy for treatment of refractory obsessive-compulsive disorder. *American Journal of Psychiatry, 159*, 269–275.

Draganova, R., Eswaran, H., Murphy, P., Lowery, C., & Preissi, H. (2007). Serial magnetoencephalographic study of fetal and newborn auditory discriminative evoked responses. *Early Human Development, 83*, 199–207.

Draguns, J. G. (2002). Universal and cultural aspects of counseling and psychotherapy. In P. B. Pedersen, J. G. Draguns, W. J. Lonner, & J. E. Trimble (Eds.), *Counseling across cultures* (5th ed., pp. 29–50). Thousand Oaks, CA: Sage.

Drea, C. M. (2009). Endocrine mediators of masculinization in female mammals. *Current Directions in Psychological Science, 18*, 221–226.

Drevets, W.C., Savitz, J., & Trimble, M. (2008). The subgenual anterior cingulated cortex in mood disorders. *CNS Spectrums, 13*, 663–681.

Drews, F. A., Yazdani, H., Godfrey, C. N., Cooper, J. M., & Strayer, D. L. (2009). Text messaging during simulated driving. *Human Factors, 51*, 762–770.

Druckman, D., & Bjork, R. A. (1994). *Learning, remembering, believing: Enhancing human performance*. Washington, DC: National Academy Press.

Duan, X., Dai, Q., Gong, Q., & Chen, H. (2010). Neural mechanism of unconscious perception of surprised facial expression. *Neuroimage*. doi:10.1016/j.neuroimage.2010.04.021

Duckitt, J. (1992). Psychology and prejudice: A historical analysis and integrative framework. *American Psychologist, 47*, 1182–1193.

Duric, V., Banasr, M., Licznerski, P., Schmidt, H. D., Stockmeier, C. A., Simen, A. A., et al. (2010). A negative regulator of MAP kinase causes depressive behavior. *Nature Medicine, 16*, 1328–1332.

Durmer, J. S., & Dinges, D. F. (2005). Neurocognitive consequences of sleep deprivation. *Seminars in Neurology, 25*, 117–129.

Durrence, H. H., & Lichstein, K. L. (2006). The sleep of African Americans: A comparative review. *Behavioral Sleep Medicine, 4*, 29–44.

Durston, S., Hulshoff Pol, H. E., Casey, B. J., Giedd, J. N., Buitelaar, J. K., & van Engeland, H. (2001). Anatomical MRI of the developing human brain: What have we learned? *Journal of the American Academy of Child and Adolescent Psychiatry, 40*, 1012–1020.

Dweck, C. (2008). Can personality be changed? The role of beliefs in personality and change. *Current Directions in Psychological Science, 17*, 391–394.

Dweck, C. S., Chiu, C., & Hong, Y. (1995). Implicit theories and their role in judgments and reactions: A world from two perspectives. *Psychological Inquiry, 6*, 267–285.

Eagly, A. H., & Chaiken, S. (1975). An attribution analysis of communicator characteristics on opinion change: The case of communicator attractiveness. *Journal of Personality and Social Psychology, 32*, 136–144.

Eaton, A. H., & Resko, J. A. (1974). Plasma testosterone and male dominance in a Japanese macaque (Macca fuscata) troop compared with repeated measures of testosterone in laboratory males. *Hormones and Behavior, 5*, 251–259.

Eaton, D. K., Kann, L., Kinchen, S., Shanklin, S., Ross, J., Hawkins, J., et al. (2010). Youth risk behavior surveillance—United States, 2009. *Morbidity & Mortality Weekly, 59*, 1–148.

Ebbinghaus, H. (1910). *Abriss der psychologie*. Leipzig: Veit & Comp.

Ebbinghaus, H. (1913). *Memory: A contribution to experimental psychology* (H. Ruyer & C. E. Bussenius, Trans.). New York: Teachers College, Columbia University. (Original work published 1885)

Ebmeier, K. P., Donaghey, C., & Steele, J. D. (2006). Recent developments and current controversies in depression. *Lancet, 367*, 153–167.

Ebstein, R. P., Zohar, A. H., Benjamin, J., & Belmaker, R. H. (2002). An update on molecular genetic studies of human personality traits. *Applied Bioinformatics, 1*, 57–68.

Edelman, B. (1981). Binge eating in normal and overweight individuals. *Psychological Reports, 49*, 739–746.

Edenberg, H. J., & Foroud, T. (2006). The genetics of alcoholism: Identifying specific genes through family studies. *Addiction Biology, 11*, 386–396.

Egner, T., Jamieson, G., & Gruzelier, J. (2005). Hypnosis decouples cognitive control from conflict monitoring processes of the frontal lobe. *Neuroimaging, 27*, 969–978.

Egner, T., Monti, J. M., & Summerfield, C. (2010). Expectation and surprise determine neural population responses in the ventral visual stream. *Journal of Neuroscicence, 49*, 16601–16608.

Ehlers, A. (1995). A 1-year prospective study of panic attacks: Clinical course and factors associated with maintenance. *Journal of Abnormal Psychology, 104*, 164–172.

Eich, J. E. (1980). The cue-dependent nature of state-dependent retrieval. *Memory and Cognition, 8*, 157–173.

Eich, J. E., Weingartner, H., Stillman, R. C., & Gillin, J. C. (1975). State-dependent accessibility of retrieval cues in the retention of a categorized list. *Journal of Verbal Learning and Verbal Behavior, 14*, 408–417.

Einarsson, C., & Granstrom, K. (2004). Gender-biased interaction in the classroom: The influence of gender and age in the relationship between teacher and pupil. *Scandinavian Journal of Educational Research, 46*, 117–127.

Eisen, S. V. (1979). Actor-observer differences in information inference and causal attribution. *Journal of Personality and Social Psychology, 37*, 261–272.

Eisenberger, N. I., Taylor, S. E., Gable, S. L., Hilmert, C. J., & Liberman, M. D. (2007). Neural pathways link social support to attenuated neuroendocrine stress responses. *NeuroImage, 35*, 1601–1612.

Eiser, A. S. (2005). Physiology and psychology of dreams. *Seminars in Neurology, 25*, 97–105.

Ekman, P. (1973). Cross-cultural studies of facial expression. In P. Ekman (Ed.), *Darwin and facial expression* (pp. 169–222). New York: Academic Press.

Ekman, P., & Friesen, W. V. (1984). *Unmasking the face* (2nd ed.). Palo Alto, CA: Consulting Psychologists Press.

El Khoury, D., El-Rassi, R., Azar, S., & Hwalla, N. (2010). Postprandial ghrelin and PYY responses of male subjects on low carbohydrate meals to varied balancing proportions of proteins and fats. *European Journal of Nutrition*. doi:10.1007/s00394-010-0108-9

Elfenbein, H. A., Beaupre, M., Levesque, M., & Hess, U. (2007). Toward a dialect theory: Cultural differences in the expression and recognition of posed facial expressions. *Emotion, 7*, 131–146.

Elicker, J., Englund, M., & Sroufe, L. A. (1992). Predicting peer competence and peer relationships in childhood from early parent–child relationships. In R. D. Parke & G. W. Ladd (Eds.), *Family–peer relationships: Modes of linkage* (pp. 77–107). Hillsdale, NJ: Erlbaum.

Elkind, D. (1994). *A sympathetic understanding of the child: Birth to sixteen* (3rd ed.). Boston: Allyn & Bacon.

Elkind, D. (1998). *All grown up and no place to go* (Rev. ed.). Reading, MA: Perseus Books.

Elkind, D., & Bowen, R. (1979). Imaginary audience behavior in children and adolescents. *Developmental Psychology, 15*, 38–44.

Ellason, J. W., & Ross, C. A. (1997). Two-year follow up of inpatients with dissociative identity disorder. *American Journal of Psychiatry, 154*, 832–839.

Ellason, J. W., Ross, C. A., & Fuchs, D. L. (1996). Lifetime Axis I and II comorbidity and childhood trauma history in dissociative identity disorder. *Psychiatry, 59*, 255–266.

Ellenbogen, J. M., Hu, P. T., Payne, J. D., Titone, D., & Walker, M. P. (2007). Human relational memory requires time and sleep. *Proceedings of the National Academy of Science, U.S.A., 104*, 7723–7728.

Ellis, A. (1959). Requisite conditions for basic personality change. *Journal of Consulting Psychology, 23*, 538–540.

Ellis, A. (1973, February). The no cop-out therapy. *Psychology Today, 7*, 56–60, 62.

Ellis, A. (1991). *Reason and emotion in psychotherapy*. New York: Carol Publishing.

Ellis, A. (1995). Changing rational-emotive therapy (RET) to rational emotive behavior therapy (REBT). *Journal of Rational-Emotive and Cognitive Behavior Therapy, 13*, 85–89.

El-Matary, A., Kemball, G., & Feteha, H. (2006). Loss of libido in postmenopausal women. *Journal of Obstetrics and Gynaecology, 26*, 495–500.

Emmelkamp, P. M. (1994). Behavior therapy with adults. In A. E. Bergin & S. L. Garfield (Eds.), *Handbook of psychotherapy and behavior change* (4th ed., pp. 379–427). New York: Wiley.

Eng, T. R., & Butler, W. T. (1997). *The hidden epidemic: Confronting sexually transmitted diseases*. Washington, DC: National Academy Press.

Engels, G. I., Garnefski, N., & Diekstra, R. F. W. (1993). Efficacy of rational-emotive therapy: A quantitative analysis. *Journal of Consulting and Clinical Psychology, 61*, 1083–1090.

Enns, M. W., Cox, B. J., Afifi, T. O., De Graaf, R., Ten Have, M., & Sareen, J. (2006). Childhood adversities and risk for suicidal ideation and attempts: A longitudinal population-based study. *Psychological Medicine, 36*, 1769–1778.

Epley, N., Savitsy, K., & Kachelski, R. A. (1999). What every skeptic should know about subliminal persuasion. *Skeptical Inquirer, 23*, 40–45.

Germine, L. T., Duchaine, B., & Nakayama, K. (2010). Where cognitive development and aging meet: Face learning ability peaks after age 30. *Cognition.* doi:10.1016/j.cognition.2010.11.002

Gernsbacher, M. A. (1985). Surface information and loss in comprehension. *Cognitive Psychology, 17,* 324–363.

Gershoff, E. T. (2002). Corporal punishment by parents and associated child behaviors and experiences: A meta-analytic and theoretical review. *Psychological Bulletin, 128,* 539–579.

Gershoff, E. T. (2010). More harm than good: A summary of scientific research on the intended and unintended effects of corporal punishment on children. *Law and Contemporary Problems, 73,* 31–56.

Geschwind, N. (1975). The apraxias: Neural mechanisms of disorders of learned movements. *American Scientist, 63,* 188–195.

Geschwind, N., & Levitsky, W. (1968). Human brain: Left-right asymmetries in temporal speech region. *Science, 161,* 186–187.

Gheysen, F., Van Opstal, F., Roggeman, C., Van Waelvelde, H., & Fias, W. (2010). Hippocampal contribution to early and later stages of implicit motor sequence learning. *Experimental Brain Research.* doi:10.1007/s00221-010-2186-6

Giancola, P. R., Josephs, R. A., Parrott, D. J., & Duke, A. A. (2010). Alcohol myopia revisited: Clarifying aggression and other acts of disinhibition through a distorted lens. *Perspectives on Psychological Science, 5,* 265–278.

Giannotti, F., & Cortesi, F. (2009). Family and cultural influences on sleep development. *Child and Adolescent Psychiatric Clinics of North America, 18,* 849–861.

Gibb, B. E., Alloy, L. B., Abramson, L. Y., Beevers, C. G., & Miller, I. W. (2004). Cognitive vulnerability to depression: A taxometric analysis. *Journal of Abnormal Psychology, 113,* 81–89.

Gibbons, C. J., Fournier, J. C., Stirman, S. W., Derubeis, R. J., Crits-Christoph, P., & Beck, A. T. (2010). The clinical effectiveness of cognitive therapy for depression in an outpatient clinic. *Journal of Affective Disorders, 125,* 169–176.

Gibbs, W. W. (1996). Gaining on fat. *Scientific American, 275,* 88–94.

Gibson, H. B. (1995, April). Recovered memories. *The Psychologist,* pp. 153–154.

Giedd, J. N. (2004). Structural magnetic resonance imaging of the adolescent brain. *Annals of the New York Academy of Sciences, 1021,* 77–85.

Giedd, J. N., Blumentahl, J., Jeffries, N. O., Castellanos, F. X., Liu, H., Zijdenbos, A., et al. (1999). Brain development during childhood and adolescence: A longitudinal MRI study. *Nature Neuroscience, 2,* 861–863.

Gilbert, D. G., Stunkard, M. E., Jensen, R. A., & Detwiler, F. R. J. (1996). Effects of exam stress on mood, cortisol, and immune functioning. *Personality and Individual Differences, 21*(2), 235–246.

Gilbertson, M. W., Shenton, M. E., Ciszewski, A., Kasai, K., Lasko, N. B., Orr, S. P., et al. (2002). Smaller hippocampal volume predicts pathologic vulnerability to psychological trauma. *Nature Neuroscience, 5,* 1242–1247.

Gildea, K. M., Schneider, T. R., & Shebilske, W. I. (2007). Appraisals and training performance on a complex laboratory task. *Human Factors, 49,* 745–758.

Gillam, B. (1980). Geometrical illusions. *Scientific American, 242,* 102–111.

Gillespie, C. F., & Nemeroff, C. B. (2007). Corticotropin-releasing factor and the psychobiology of early-life stress. *Current Directions in Psychological Science, 16,* 85–89.

Gilligan, C. F. (1982). *In a different voice.* Cambridge, MA: Harvard University Press.

Gillund, G., & Shiffrin, R. M. (1984). A retrieval model for both recognition and recall. *Psychological Review, 91,* 1–67.

Gilson, R. J., & Mindel, A. (2001). Sexually transmitted infections. *British Medical Journal, 322*(729S), 1135–1137.

Girandola, F. (2002). Sequential requests and organ donation. *Journal of Social Psychology, 142,* 171–178.

Girdler, S. S., Jamner, L. D., & Shapiro, D. (1997). Hostility, testosterone and vascular reactivity to stress: Effects of sex. *International Journal of Behavioral Medicine, 4,* 242–263.

Giret, N., Péron, F., Lindová, J., Tichotová, L., Nagle, L., Kreutzer, M., et al. (2010). Referential learning of French and Czech labels in African grey parrots (Psittacus erithacus): Different methods yield contrasting results. *Behavioural Processes, 85,* 90–98.

Gitelson, I. B., & McDermott, D. (2006). Parents and their young adult children: Transitions to adulthood. *Child Welfare League of America, 85,* 853–866.

Givens, B. (1995). Low doses of ethanol impair spatial working memory and reduce hippocampal theta activity. *Alcoholism: Clinical and Experimental Research, 19*(3), 763–767.

Gladwell, M. (2004, September 20). Annals of psychology: Personality plus. *New Yorker,* pp. 42–48.

Glanzer, M., & Cunitz, A. R. (1966). Two storage mechanisms in free recall. *Journal of Verbal Learning and Verbal Behavior, 5,* 351–360.

Glenberg, A. M., Smith, S. M., & Green, C. (1977). Type I rehearsal: Maintenance and more. *Journal of Verbal Learning and Verbal Behavior, 16,* 339–352.

Glynn, M., & Rhodes, P. (2005). *Estimated HIV prevalence in the United States at the end of 2003.* National HIV Prevention Conference, Atlanta, GA. Abstract T1-Bll01.

Goddard, A. W., Ball, S. G., Martinez, J., Robinson, M. J., Yang, C. R., Russell, J. M., et al. (2010). Current perspectives of the roles of the central norepinephrine system in anxiety and depression. *Depression and Anxiety, 27,* 339–350.

Godden, D. R., & Baddeley, A. D. (1975). Context dependent memory in two natural environments: On land and underwater. *British Journal of Psychology, 66,* 325–332.

Goeders, N. E. (2004). Stress, motivation, and drug addiction. *Current Directions in Psychological Science, 13,* 33–35.

Gold, M. S. (1994). The epidemiology, attitudes, and pharmacology of LSD use in the 1990's. *Psychiatric Annals, 24*(3), 124–126.

Goldberg, J. F. (2007). What psychotherapists should know about pharmacotherapies for bipolar disorder. *Journal of Clinical Psychology, 63,* 475–490.

Goldstein, J. M., & Lewine, R. R. J. (2000). Overview of sex differences in schizophrenia: Where have we been and where do we go from here? In D. J. Castle, J. McGrath, & J. Kulkarni (Eds.), *Women and schizophrenia* (pp. 111–141). Cambridge, UK: Cambridge University Press.

Goleman, D. (1982, March). Staying up: The rebellion against sleep's gentle tyranny. *Psychology Today,* pp. 24–35.

Goleman, D. (1995). *Emotional intelligence.* New York: Bantam.

Goleman, D. (1998). *Working with emotional intelligence.* London: Bloomsbury

Goleman, D., Boyatzis, R. E., & McKee, A. (2002). *Primal leadership: Realizing the power of emotional intelligence.* Boston: Harvard Business School Press.

Gonzalez, H. M., Vega, W. A., Williams, D. R., Tarraf, W., West, B. T., & Neighbors, H. W. (2010). Depression care in the United States: Too little for too few. *Archives of General Psychiatry, 67,* 37–46.

Good, J. J., Woodzicka, J. A., & Wingfield, L. C. (2010). The effects of gender stereotypic and counter-stereotypic textbook images on science performance. *Journal of Social Psychology, 150,* 132–147.

Goodnick, P. J. (2000). The use of nimodipine in the treatment of mood disorders. *Bipolar Disorders, 2*(3 Pt. 1), 165–173.

Goodwin, F. K., & Goldstein, M. A. (2003). Optimizing lithium treatment in bipolar disorder: A review of the literature and clinical recommendations. *Journal of Psychiatric Practice, 9,* 333–343.

Gorchoff, S. M., John, O. P., & Helson, R. (2008). Contextualizing change in marital satisfaction during middle age. *Psychological Science, 19,* 1194–1200.

Gorman, J. M. (2006). Gender differences in depression and response to psychotropic medication. *Gender Medicine, 3,* 93–109.

Gorsky, R. D., Schwartz, E., & Dennis, D. (1988). The mortality, morbidity, and economic costs of alcohol abuse: New Hampshire. *Preventative Medicine, 17,* 736–745.

Gotlib, I. H., & Hamilton, J. P. (2008). Neuroimaging and depression: Current status and unresolved issues. *Current Directions in Psychological Science, 17,* 159–163.

Gottlieb, G., Wahlsten, D., & Lickliter, R. (1998). The significance of biology for human development: A developmental psychobiological systems view. In W. Damon & R. M. Lerner (Eds.), *Handbook of child psychology* (Vol. 1, pp. 233–273). New York: Wiley.

Gottman, J. (1999a). *The marriage clinic.* New York: Norton.

Gottman, J. (1999b). *The seven principles of making marriage work.* New York: Crown.

Gouin, K., Murphy, K., & Shah, P. S. (2011). Effects of cocaine use during pregnancy on low birthweight and preterm birth: Systematic review and metaanalyses. *American Journal of Obstetrics and Gynecology, 204,* 340.e1-340.e12.

Gould, R. A., Otto, M. W., Pollack, M. H., & Yap, L. (1997). Cognitive behavioral and pharmacological treatment of generalized anxiety disorder: A preliminary meta-analysis. *Behavior Therapy, 28,* 285–305.

Graber, J. A., Brooks-Gunn, J., & Warren, M. P. (2006). Pubertal effects on adjustment in girls: Moving from demonstrating effects to identifying pathways. *Journal of Youth and Adolescence, 35,* 413–423.

Graber, J. A., Seeley, J. R., Brooks-Gunn, J., & Lewinsohn, P. M. (2004). Is pubertal timing associated with psychopathology in young adulthood? *Journal of the American Academy of Child and Adolescent Psychiatry, 43,* 718–726.

Grace, A. A. (2010). Ventral hippocampus, interneurons, and schizophrenia: A new understanding of the pathophysiology of schizophrenia and its implications for treatment and prevention. *Current Directions in Psychological Science, 19,* 232–237.

Grados, M. A., Walkup, J., & Walford, S. (2003). Genetics of obsessive-compulsive disorders: New findings and challenges. *Brain Development, 25,* S55–S61.

Graf, P., & Schacter, D. L. (1985). Implicit and explicit memory for new associations in normal and amnesiac subjects. *Journal of Experimental Psychology: Learning, Memory, and Cognition, 11,* 501–518.

Graffin, N. F., Ray, W. J., & Lundy, R. (1995). EEG concomitants of hypnosis and hypnotic susceptibility. *Journal of Abnormal Psychology, 104,* 123–131.

Graham, K. S., Simons, J. S., Pratt, K. H., Patterson, K., & Hodges, J. R. (2000). Insights from semantic dementia on the relationship between episodic and semantic memory. *Neurpsychologia, 38,* 313–324.

Graham, R., Devinsky, O., & LaBar, K. S. (2007). Quantifying deficits in the perception of fear and anger in morphed facial expressions after bilateral amygdale damage. *Neuropsychologia, 45,* 42–54.

Grant, B. F., Hasin, D. S., Stinson, F. S., Dawson, D. A., Chou, S. P., Ruan, W. J., et al. (2004). Prevalence, correlates, and disability of personality disorders in the United States: Results from the National Epidemiologic Survey on alcohol and related conditions. *Journal of Clinical Psychiatry, 65,* 948–958.

Grant, B. F., Hasin, D. S., Stinson, F. S., Dawson, D. A., Goldstein, R. B., Smith, S., et al. (2006). The epidemiology of DSM-IV panic disorder and agoraphobia in the United States: Results from the National Epidemiologic Survey on Alcohol and Related Conditions. *Journal of Clinical Psychiatry, 67,* 363–374.

Grant, J. E., & Phillips, K. A. (2004). Is anorexia nervosa a subtype of body dysmorphic disorder? Probably not, but read on. . . . *Harvard Review of Psychiatry, 12,* 123–126.

Green, J. G., McLaughlin, K. A., Berglund, P. A., Gruber, M. J., Sampson, N. A., Zaslavsky, A. M., et al. (2010). Childhood adversities and adult psychiatric disorders in the National Comorbidity Survey Replication I: Associations with first onset of DSM-IV disorders. *Archives of General Psychiatry, 67,* 113–123.

Green, J. P., & Lynn, S. J. (2000). Hypnosis and suggestion-based approaches to smoking cessation: An examination of the evidence. *International Journal of Clinical and Experimental Hypnosis, 48,* 195–224.

Greenberg, L. S., Elliot, R., & Lietaer, G. (1994). Research on humanistic and experiential psychotherapies. In A. Bergin & S. Garfield (Eds.), *Handbook of psychotherapy and behavior change* (4th ed., pp. 509–542). New York: Wiley.

Greenberg, L. S., & Rice, L. N. (1997). Humanistic approaches to psychotherapy. In P. L. Wachtel & S. B. Messer (Eds.), *Theories of psychotherapy: Origins and Evolution* (pp. 97–129). Washington DC: American Psychological Association.

Greenblatt, D., Harmatz, J., & Shader, R. I. (1993). Plasma alprazolam concentrations: Relation to efficacy and side effects in the treatment of panic disorder. *Archives of General Psychiatry, 50,* 715–732.

Greenfield, P. (1997). You can't take it with you: Why ability assessments don't cross cultures. *American Psychologist, 52,* 1115–1124.

Greenhaus, J. H. (2003). Career dynamics. In W. C. Borman, D. R. Ilgen, & R. J. Klimoski (Eds.), *Handbook of psychology: Industrial and organizational psychology* (Vol. 12, pp. 519–540). New York: Wiley.

Greenough, W. T., Wallace, C. S., Alcantara, A. A., Anderson, B. J., Hawrylak, N., Sirevaag, A. M., et al. (1993). Experience affects the structure of neurons, glia, and blood vessels. In N. J. Anastasiow & S. Harel (Eds.), *At-risk infants: Interventions, family, and research* (pp.175–185). Baltimore: Paul H. Brookes.

Greenwald, A. G., & Draine, S. C. (1997). Do subliminal stimuli enter the mind unnoticed? Tests with a new method. In J. D. Cohen & J. W. Schooler (Eds.), *Scientific approaches to consciousness: Carnegie Mellon Symposia on cognition* (pp. 83–108). Mahwah, NJ: Erlbaum.

Grieger, T. A., Fullerton, C. S., & Ursano, R. J. (2004). Posttraumatic stress disorder, depression, and perceived safety 13 months after September 11th. *Psychiatric Services, 55*, 1061–1063.

Griest, S. E., Folmer, R. L., & Martin, W. H. (2007). Effectiveness of "Dangerous Decibels," a school-based hearing loss prevention program. *American Journal of Audiology, 16*, S165–S181.

Griffiths, K. M., Calear, A. L., & Banfield, M. (2009). Systematic review on Internet Support Groups (ISGs) and depression: Do ISGs reduce depressive symptoms? *Journal of Medical Internet Research, 11*, e40.

Grinspoon, L., & Bakalar, J. B. (1995). Marijuana as medicine: A plea for reconsideration. *Journal of the American Medical Association, 273*(23), 1875–1876.

Grinspoon, L., Bakalar, J. B., Zimmer, L., & Morgan, J. P. (1997). Marijuana addiction. *Science, 277*, 751–752.

Grivetti, L. E. (2000). Food prejudices and taboos. In K. E. Kipple & K. C. Ornelas (Eds.), *The Cambridge world history of food* (Vol. 1, pp. 1495–1513). Cambridge, UK: Cambridge University Press.

Grossman, M. I., & Stein, L. F. (1948). Vagotomy and the hunger-producing action of insulin in man. *Journal of Applied Physiology, 1*, 263–269.

Grossman, P., Niemann, L., Schmidt, S., & Walach, H. (2004). Mindfulness-based stress reduction and health benefits: A meta-analysis. *Journal of Psychosomatic Research, 57*, 35–43.

Grossman, R. P., & Till, B. D. (1998). The persistence of classically conditioned brand attitudes. *Journal of Advertising, 27*, 23–31.

Grover, S. (2005). Reification of psychiatric diagnoses as defamatory: Implications for ethical clinical practice. *Ethical Human Psychology and Psychiatry, 7*, 77–86.

Gruen, R. J. (1993). Stress and depression: Toward the development of integrative models. In L. Goldberger & S. Breznitz (Eds.), *Handbook of stress: Theoretical and clinical aspects* (pp. 550–569). New York: Free Press.

Grysman, A., & Hudson, J. A. (2010). Abstracting and extracting: Causal coherence and the development of the life story. *Memory, 18*, 565–580.

Gugger, J. J., & Wagner, M. L. (2007). Rapid eye movement sleep behavior disorder. *Annals of Pharmacotherapy, 41*, 1833–1841.

Guilford, J. P. (1967). *The nature of human intelligence.* New York: McGraw-Hill.

Guilleminault, C., Palombini, L., Pelayo, R., & Chervin, R. D. (2003). Sleepwalking and sleep terrors in prepubertal children: What triggers them? *Pediatrics, 111*, e17–25.

Guisinger, S. (2003). Adapted to flee famine: Adding an evolutionary perspective on anorexia nervosa. *Psychological Review, 110*, 745–761.

Gurman, A. S., & Jacobson, N. S. (Eds.). (2002). *Clinical handbook of couple therapy* (3rd ed.). New York: Guilford Press.

Gustavson, C. R., & Garcia, J. (1974, August). Pulling a gag on the wily coyote. *Psychology Today,* pp. 68–72.

Guthrie, J. P., Ash, R. A., & Bendapudi, V. (1995). Additional validity evidence for a measure of morningness. *Journal of Applied Psychology, 80*, 186–190.

Ha, T., Overbeek, G., & Engels, R. C. (2010). Effects of attractiveness and social status on dating desire in heterosexual adolescents: An experimental study. *Archives of Sexual Behavior, 39*, 1063–1071.

Haack, L. J., Metalsky, G. I., Dykman, B. M., & Abramson, L. Y. (1996). Use of current situational information and causal inference: Do dysphoric individuals make "unwarranted" causal inferences? *Cognitive Therapy and Research, 20*, 309–331.

Haber, D. (1994). *Health promotion and aging.* New York: Springer.

Hackett, R. D. (1989). Work attitudes and employee absenteeism: A synthesis of the literature. *Journal of Occupational Psychology, 62*(3), 235–248.

Hackman, J. R., & Oldham, G. R. (1976). Motivation through the design of work: A test of a theory. *Organizational Behavior and Human Performance, 16*(2), 250–279.

Haefner, R. (2009, June). More employers screening candidates via social networking sites. Careerbuilder.com

Haidt, J. (2008). Morality. *Perspectives on Psychological Science, 1*, 65–72.

Haie, L., & Do, D. P. (2007). Racial differences in self-reports of sleep duration in a population-based study. *Sleep, 30*, 1096–1103.

Haith, M. M., & Benson, J. B. (1998). Infant cognition. In W. Damon & R. M. Lerner (Eds.), *Handbook of child psychology* (Vol. 1, pp. 235–246). New York: Wiley.

Hakuta, K. (1999). The debate on bilingual education. *Developmental and Behavioral Pediatrics, 20*, 36–37.

Hakuta, K., Bailystok, E., & Wiley, E. (2003). Critical evidence: A test of the critical-period hypothesis for second-language acquisitions. *Psychological Science, 14*, 31–38.

Hall, D. T., & Nougaim, K. E. (1968). An examination of Maslow's need hierarchy in an organizational setting. *Organizational Behavior and Human Performance, 3*, 12–35.

Halpern, D. F. (1996). Public policy implications of sex differences in cognitive abilities. *Psychology, Public Policy and Law, 2*(3/4), 564.

Halpern, D. F., & LeMay, M. L. (2000). The smarter sex: A critical review of sex-differences in intelligence. *Educational Psychology Review, 12*, 229–246.

Halpern, J. H., & Pope, H. G., Jr. (2003). Hallucinogen persisting perception disorder: What do we know after 50 years? *Drug and Alcohol Dependence, 69*, 109–119.

Hamani, C., Mayberg, H., Snyder, B., Giacobbe, P., Kennedy, S., & Lozano, A. M. (2009). Deep brain stimulation of the subcallosal cingulated gyrus for depression: Anatomical location of active contacts in clinical responders and a suggested guideline for targeting. *Journal of Neurosurgery, 111*, 1209–1215.

Hamann, S. (2005). Sex differences in the responses of the human amygdala. *Neuroscientist, 11*, 288–293.

Hamel, R., & Elshout, J. (2000). On the development of knowledge during problem solving. *Journal of Cognitive Psychology, 12*, 289–322.

Hamer, D. (2002). Genetics. Rethinking behavior genetics. *Science, 298*, 71–72.

Hamilton, C. E. (2000). Continuity and discontinuity of attachment from infancy through adolescence. *Child Development, 71*, 690–694.

Hamilton, V. L., Blumenfeld, P. C., Akoh, H., & Miura, K. (1991). Group and gender in Japanese and American elementary classrooms. *Journal of Cross-Cultural Psychology, 22*, 317–346.

Hammen, C. (2005). Stress and depression. *Annual Review of Clinical Psychology, 1*, 293–319.

Hammen, C. (2009). Adolescent depression: Stressful interpersonal contexts and risk for recurrence. *Current Directions in Psychological Science, 18*, 200–204.

Hampson, S. E., & Goldberg, L. R. (2006). A first large cohort study of personality trait stability over the 40 years between elementary school and midlife. *Journal of Personality and Social Psychology, 91*, 763–779.

Hanisch, K. A. (1992). The Job Descriptive Index revisited: Questions about the question mark. *Journal of Applied Psychology, 77*, 377–382.

Hanisch, K. A. (1995). Behavioral families and multiple causes: Matching the complexity of responses to the complexity of antecedents. *Current Directions in Psychological Science, 4*(5), 156–162.

Hanisch, K. A., & Hulin, C. L. (1990). Job attitudes and organizational withdrawal: An examination of retirement and other voluntary withdrawal behaviors. *Journal of Vocational Behavior, 37*(1), 60–78.

Hanisch, K. A., & Hulin, C. L. (1991). General attitudes and organizational withdrawal: An evaluation of a causal model. *Journal of Vocational Behavior, 39*, 110–128.

Hanisch, K. A., Hulin, C. L., & Roznowski, M. A. (1998). The importance of individuals' repertoires of behaviors: The scientific appropriateness of studying multiple behaviors and general attitudes. *Journal of Organizational Behavior, 19*, 463–480.

Hanna, G. H. (2000). Clinical and family-genetic studies of childhood obsessive-compulsive disorder. In W. K. Goodman, M. V. Rudofer, & J. D. Maser (Eds.), *Obsessive-compulsive disorder: Contemporary issues in treatment* (pp. 87–103). Mahwah, NJ: Erlbaum.

Hanson, G., & Venturelli, P. J. (1998). *Drugs and society* (5th ed.). Boston: Jones and Bartlett.

Hargis, M. (2008, November 5). Social networking sites dos and don'ts. *CNN.com.* http://www.cnn.com/2008/LIVING/worklife/11/05/cb.social.networking/index.html

Harkins, S. G. (1987). Social loafing and social facilitation. *Journal of Experimental Social Psychology, 23*, 1–18.

Harlow, H. F., & Zimmerman, R. (1959). Affectional responses in the infant monkey. *Science, 130*, 421–432.

Harold, G. T., Fincham, F. D., Osborne, L. N., & Conger, R. D. (1997). Mom and Dad are at it again: Adolescent perceptions of marital conflict and adolescent psychological distress. *Developmental Psychology, 33*, 335–350.

Harris, J. D. (1943). Habituatory response decrement in the intact organism. *Psychological Bulletin, 40*, 385–422.

Harris, J. R. (2000). Context-specific learning, personality, and birth order. *Current Directions in Psychological Science, 9*, 174–177.

Harris, S. R., Kemmerling, R. L., & North, M. M. (2002). Brief virtual reality therapy for public speaking. *Cyberpsychology and Behavior, 5*, 543–550.

Hartmann, E. (1981, April). The strangest sleep disorder. *Psychology Today,* pp. 14, 16, 18.

Hartmann, U. (2009). Sigmund Freud and his impact on our understanding of male sexual dysfunction. *Journal of Sexual Medicine, 6*, 2332–2339.

Hasin, D., Hatzenbuehler, M. L., Keyes, K., & Ogburn, E. (2006). Substance use disorders: Diagnostic and Statistical Manual of Mental Disorders, fourth edition (DSM-IV) and International Classification of Diseases, tenth edition (ICD-10). *Addiction, 101*(Suppl. 1), 59–75.

Hassett, J. M., Siebert, E. R., & Wallen, K. (2008). Sex differences in rhesus monkey toy preferences parallel those of children. *Hormones and Behavior, 54*, 359–364.

Hastings, E. C., Karas, T. L., Winsler, A., Way, E., Madigan, A., & Tyler, S. (2009). Young children's video/computer game use: Relations with school performance and behavior. *Issues in Mental Health Nursing, 30*, 638–649.

Hatcher, R., Trussell, J., Stewart, F., Stewart, G., Kowal, D., Guest, E., et al. (1994). *Contraceptive technology* (16th ed.). New York: Irvington.

Haus, E., & Smolensky, M. (2006). Biological clocks and shift work: Circadian dysregulation and potential long-term effects. *Cancer Causes and Control, 17*, 489–500.

Hausner, H., Nicklaus, S., Issanchou, S., Mølgaard, C., & Møller, P. (2010). Breastfeeding facilitates acceptance of a novel dietary flavor compound. *Clinical Nutrition, 29*, 141–148.

Havermans, R. C., & Jansen, A. (2007). Increasing children's liking of vegetables through flavour–flavour learning. *Appetite, 48*, 259–262.

Hawkley, L. C., & Cacioppo, J. T. (2007). Aging and loneliness: Downhill quickly? *Current Directions in Psychological Science, 16*, 187–191.

Hawkley, L. C., & Cacioppo, J. T. (2010). Loneliness matters: A theoretical and empirical review of consequences and mechanisms. *Annals of Behavioral Medicine, 40*, 218–227.

Hawks, S. R., Hull, M. L., Thalman, R. L., & Richins, P. M. (1995). Review of spiritual health: Definition, role, and intervention strategies in health promotion. *American Journal of Health Promotion, 9*, 371–378.

Hayden, E. P., Dougherty, L. R., Maloney, B., Emily Durbin, C., Olino, T. M., Nurnberger, J. I., et al. (2007). Temperamental fearfulness in childhood and the serotonin transporter promoter region polymorphism: A multimethod association study. *Psychiatric Genetics, 17*, 135–142.

Hayden, E. P., Klein, D. N., Dougherty, L. R., Olino, T. M., Dyson, M. W., Durbin, C. E., et al. (2010). The role of brain-derived neurotrophic factor genotype, parental depression, and relationship discord in predicting early-emerging negative emotionality. *Psychological Science, 21*, 1678–1685.

Hayden, E. P., & Nurnberger, J. I., Jr. (2006). Molecular genetics of bipolar disorder. *Genes, Brain and Behavior, 5*, 85–95.

Hayes, E. R., & Plowfield, L. A. (2007). Smoking too young: Students' decisions about tobacco use. *American Journal of Maternal Child Nursing, 32*, 112–116.

Hayes, J. R. (1989). *The complete problem solver* (2nd ed.). Hillsdale, NJ: Erlbaum.

Hayne, H., & Rovee-Collier, C. (1995). The organization of reactivated memory in infancy. *Child Development, 66*(3), 893–906.

Kirsch, I., Montgomery, G., & Sapirstein, G. (1995). Hypnosis as an adjunct to cognitive behavioral psychotherapy: A meta-analysis. *Journal of Consulting and Clinical Psychology, 63,* 214–220.

Kisilevsky, B. S., Hains, S. M., Lee, K., Xie, X., Huang, H., Ye, H. H., et al. (2003). Effects of experience on fetal voice recognition. *Psychological Science, 14,* 220–224.

Kito, S., Hasegawa, T., & Koga, Y. (2011). Neuroanatomical correlates of therapeutic efficacy of low-frequency right prefrontal transcranial magnetic stimulation in treatment-resistant depression. *Psychiatry and Clinical Neurosciences, 65,* 175–182.

Klass, D. (1993). Solace and immortality: Bereaved parents' continuing bond with their children. *Death Studies, 17,* 343–368.

Klein, B., Mitchell, J., Abbott, J., Shandley, K., Austin, D., Gilson, K., et al. (2010). A therapist-assisted cognitive behavior therapy internet intervention for posttraumatic stress disorder: Pre-, post- and 3-month follow-up results from an open trial. *Journal of Anxiety Disorders, 24,* 635–644.

Klein, D. N., Lewinsohn, P. M., & Seeley, J. R. (2001). A family study of major depressive disorder in a community sample of adolescents. *Archives of General Psychiatry, 58,* 13–21.

Klein, D. N., Shankman, S. A., & Rose, S. (2006). Ten-year prospective follow-up study of the naturalistic course of dysthymic disorder and double depression. *American Journal of Psychiatry, 163,* 872–880.

Klein, S. B. (1987). *Learning.* New York: McGraw-Hill.

Klein, T. W., & Newton, C. A. (2007). Therapeutic potential of cannabinoid-based drugs. *Advances in Experimental Medicine and Biology, 601,* 395–413.

Klinger, E., Bouchard, S., Legeron, P., Roy, S., Lauer, F., Chemin, I., et al. (2005). Virtual reality therapy versus cognitive behavior therapy for social phobia: A preliminary controlled study. *Cyberpsychology and Behavior, 8,* 76–88.

Klonoff, E. A., Landrine, H., & Campbell, R. (2000). Sexist discrimination may account for well-known gender differences in psychiatric symptoms. *Psychology of Women Quarterly, 24,* 93–99.

Kluft, R. P. (1999). Current issues in dissociative identity disorder. *Journal of Practical Psychology and Behavioral Health, 5,* 3–19.

Kobasa, S. C. (1982). Commitment and coping in stress resistance among lawyers. *Journal of Personality and Social Psychology, 42,* 707–717.

Kochanska, G. (1995). Children's temperament, mothers' discipline, and security of attachment: Multiple pathways to emerging internalization. *Child Development, 66,* 597–615.

Koff, E., & Rierdan, J. (1995). Early adolescent girls' understanding of menstruation. *Women and Health, 22,* 1–19.

Kogan, A., Impett, E. A., Oveis, C., Hui, B., Gordon, A. M., & Keltner, D. (2010). When giving feels good: The intrinsic benefits of sacrifice in romantic relationships for the communally motivated. *Psychological Science, 21,* 1918–1924.

Koh, K. B., Choe, E., Song, J. E., & Lee, E. H. (2006). Effect of coping on endocrinoimmune functions in different stress situations. *Psychiatry Research, 143,* 223–234.

Kohlberg, L. (1969). Stage and sequence: The cognitive-developmental approach to socialization. In D. A. Goslin (Ed.), *Handbook of socialization theory and research* (pp. 347–480). Chicago: Rand McNally.

Kohlberg, L., Levine, C., & Hewer, A. (1983). *Moral stages: A current formulation and a response to critics.* Basel, Switzerland: Karger.

Köhler, W. (1925). *The mentality of apes.* New York: Harcourt Brace.

Kohn, P. M., & Macdonald, J. E. (1992). The survey of recent life experiences: A decontaminated hassles scales for adults. *Journal of Behavioral Medicine, 15,* 221–236.

Kolassa, I. T., & Elbert, T. (2007). Structural and functional neuroplasticity in relation to traumatic stress. *Current Directions in Psychological Science, 16,* 321–325.

Koles, Z. J., Lind, J. C., & Flor-Henry, P. (2009). Gender differences in brain functional organization during verbal and spatial cognitive challenges. *Brain Topography.* doi:10.1007/s10548-009-0119-0

Konkol, R. J., Murphey, L. J., Ferriero, D. M., Dempsey, D. A., & Olsen, G. D. (1994). Cocaine metabolites in the neonate: Potential for toxicity. *Journal of Child Neurology, 9*(3), 242–248.

Koob, G. F., & Bloom, F. E. (1988). Cellular and molecular mechanisms of drug dependence. *Science, 242,* 715–723.

Kopelman, P. G. (2000). Obesity as a medical problem. *Nature, 404,* 635–643.

Kopta, S. M., Lueger, R. J., Saunders, S. M., & Howard, K. I. (1999). Individual psychotherapy outcome and process research: Challenges leading to greater turmoil or a positive transition? *Annual Review of Psychology, 50,* 441–469.

Koslowsky, M., & Babkoff, H. (1992). Meta-analysis of the relationship between total sleep deprivation and performance. *Chronobiology International, 9,* 132–136.

Koss, M. P., & Kilpatrick, D. G. (2001). Rape and sexual assault. In E. Gerrity (Ed.), *The mental health consequences of torture* (pp. 177–193). New York: Kluwer Academic/Plenum Press.

Kosslyn, S. M. (1994). *Image and brain: The resolution of the imagery debate.* Cambridge, MA: MIT Press.

Kosslyn, S. M., Ball, T. M., & Reiser, B. J. (2004). Visual images preserve metric spatial information: Evidence from studies of image scanning. In D. A. Balota & E. J. Marsh (Eds.), *Cognitive psychology: Key readings* (pp. 239–253). New York: Psychology Press. (Original work published 1978)

Koughan, M. (1975, February 23). Arthur Friedman's outrage: Employees decide their pay. *Washington Post.*

Kowalski, K. (2003). The emergence of ethnic and racial attitudes in preschool-aged children. *Journal of Social Psychology, 143,* 677–690.

Kozart, M. F. (2002). Understanding efficacy in psychotherapy. *American Journal of Orthopsychiatry, 72,* 217–231.

Kozlowski, S. W., & Bell, B. S. (2003). Work groups and teams in organizations. In W. C. Borman, D. R. Ilgen, & R. J. Klimoski (Eds.), *Handbook of psychology: Industrial and organizational psychology* (Vol. 12, pp. 333–375). New York: Wiley.

Kraft, J. B., Peters, E. J., Slager, S. L., Jenkins, G. D., Reinalda, M. S., McGrath, P. J., et al. (2007). Analysis of association between the serotonin transporter and antidepressant response in a large clinical sample. *Biological Psychiatry, 61,* 734–742.

Kraft, J. M. (1996). Prenatal alcohol consumption and outcomes for children: A review of the literature. In R. L. Parrott & C. M. Condit (Eds.), *Evaluating women's health messages: A resource book* (pp. 175–189). Thousand Oaks, CA: Sage.

Kraha, A., & Boals, A. (2011). Parents and vehicle purchases for their children: A surprising source of weight bias. *Obesity, 19,* 541–545.

Krampe, H., & Ehrenreich, H. (2010). Supervised disulfiram as adjunct to psychotherapy in alcoholism treatment. *Current Pharmaceutical Design, 16,* 2076–2090.

Krantz, D. S., & McCeney, M. K. (2002). Effects of psychological and social factors on organic disease: A critical assessment of research on coronary heart disease. *Annual Reviews of Psychology, 53,* 341–369.

Kraut, R. E. (1982). Social presence, facial feedback, and emotion. *Journal of Personality and Social Psychology, 42,* 853–863.

Kreibig, S. D. (2010). Autonomic nervous system activity in emotion: A review. *Biological Psychology.* doi:10.1016/j.biopsycho.2010.03.010

Kreider, R. M., (2005). Number, timing, and duration of marriages and divorces: 2001. *Current Population Reports, P70–97.* Washington, DC: U.S. Census Bureau.

Kremer, I., Bachner-Melman, R., Reshef, A., Broude, L., Nemanov, L., Gritsenko, I., et al. (2005). Association of the serotonin transporter gene with smoking behavior. *American Journal of Psychiatry, 162,* 924–930.

Krijn, M., Emmelkamp, P. M., Olafsson, R. P., & Biemond, R. (2004). Virtual reality exposure therapy of anxiety disorders: A review. *Clinical Psychology Review, 24,* 259–281.

Kropp, P., Siniatchkin, M., & Gerber, W.-D. (2002). On the pathophysiology of migraine—Links for "empirically based treatment" with neurofeedback. *Applied Psychophysiology and Biofeedback, 27,* 203–213.

Krystal, J. H., Staley, J., Mason, G., Petrakis, I. L., Kaufman, J., Harris, R. A., et al. (2006). Gamma-aminobutyric acid type A receptors and alcoholism: Intoxication, dependence, vulnerability, and treatment. *Archives of General Psychiatry, 63,* 957–968.

Kübler-Ross, E. (1969). *On death and dying.* New York: Macmillan.

Kübler-Ross, E. (1974). *Questions and answers on death and dying.* New York: Macmillan.

Kudielka, B. M., & Kirschbaum, C. (2005). Sex differences in HPA axis responses to stress: A review. *Biological Psychology, 69,* 113–132.

Kumada, T., Jiang, Y., Cameron, D. B., & Komuro, H. (2007). How does alcohol impair neuronal migration? *Journal of Neuroscience Research, 85,* 465–470.

Kumari, V., ffytche, D. H., Williams, S. C., & Gray, J. A. (2004). Personality predicts brain responses to cognitive demands. *Journal of Neuroscience, 24,* 10636–10641.

Kung, H. S., Hoyert, D. L., Xu, J., & Murphy, S. L. (2008). Deaths: Final data for 2005. *National Vital Statistics Reports, 56*(10).

Kunstman, J. W., & Plant, E. A. (2008). Racing to help: Racial bias in high emergency helping situations. *Journal of Personality and Social Psychology, 95,* 1499–1510.

Kunugi, H., Hori, H., Adachi, N., & Numakawa, T. (2010). Interface between hypothalamic-pituitary-adrenal axis and brain-derived neurotrophic factor in depression. *Psychiatry and Clinical Neurosciences, 64,* 447–459.

Kurdek, L. A. (1999). The nature and predictors of the trajectory of change in marital quality for husbands and wives over the first 10 years of marriage. *Developmental Psychology, 35,* 1283–1296.

Kuriyama, K., Stickgold, R., & Walker, M. P. (2004). Sleep-dependent learning and motor-skill complexity. *Learning and Memory, 11,* 705–713.

Kuypers, K. P., Wingen, M., & Ramaekers, J. G. (2008). Memory and mood during the night and in the morning after repeated evening doses of MDMA. *Journal of Psychopharmacology, 22,* 895–903.

Kuzelova, H., Ptacek, R., & Milan, M. (2010). The serotonin transporter gene (5-HTT) variant and psychiatric disorders: Review of current literature. *Neuroendocrinology Letters, 31,* 5.

Kwan, B. M., Dimidjian, S., & Rizvi, S. L. (2010). Treatment preference, engagement, and clinical improvement in pharmacotherapy versus psychotherapy for depression. *Behaviour Research and Therapy, 48,* 799–804.

LaBar, K. S. (2007). Beyond fear: Emotional memory mechanisms in the human brain. *Current Directions in Psychological Science, 16,* 173–177.

Lacayo, A. (1995). Neurologic and psychiatric complications of cocaine abuse. *Neuropsychiatry, Neuropsychology, and Behavioral Neurology, 8*(1), 53–60.

Lahey, B. B., Pelham, W. E., Loney, J., Kipp, H., Ehrhardt, A., Lee, S. S., et al. (2004). Three-year predictive validity of DSM-IV attention deficit hyperactivity disorder in children diagnosed at 4–6 years of age. *American Journal of Psychiatry, 161,* 2014–2020.

Lambert, M. J., & Bergen, A. E. (1994). The effectiveness of psychotherapy. In A. E. Bergen & S. L. Garfield (Eds.), *Handbook of psychotherapy and behavior change* (4th ed., pp. 143–189). New York: Wiley.

Lambeth, G. S., & Hallett, M. (2002). Promoting healthy decision making in relationships: Developmental interventions with young adults on college and university campuses. In C. L. & D. R. Atkinson (Eds.), *Counseling across the lifespan: Prevention and treatment* (pp. 209–226). Thousand Oaks, CA: Sage.

Lancet, D. Ben-Arie, N., Cohen, S., Gat, U., Gross-Isseroff, R., Horn-Saban, S., et al. (1993). Olfactory receptors: Transduction diversity, human psychophysics and genome analysis. In D. Chadwick, J. Marsh, & J. Goode (Eds.), *The molecular basis of smell and taste transduction* (pp. 131–146). New York: Wiley.

Landabaso, M. A., Iraurgi, I., Sanz, J., Calle, R., Ruiz de Apodaka, J., Jimenez-Lerma, J. M., et al. (1999). Naltrexone in the treatment of alcoholism: Two-year follow up results. *European Journal of Psychiatry, 13,* 97–105.

Lang, A. J., & Stein, M. B. (2001). Social phobia: Prevalence and diagnostic threshold. *Journal of Clinical Psychiatry, 62*(Suppl. 1), 5–10.

Lang, R., Mahoney, R., El Zein, F., Delaune, E., & Amidon, M. (2011). Evidence to practice: Treatment of anxiety in individuals with autism spectrum disorders. *Neuropsychiatric Disease and Treatment, 7,* 27–30.

Lange, T., Dimitrov, S., Fehm, H. L., Westermann, J., & Born, J. (2006). Shift of monocyte function toward cellular immunity during sleep. *Archives of Internal Medicine, 166,* 1695–1700.

Langlois, J. H., Roggman, L. A., Casey, R. J., Ritter, J. M., Rieser-Danner, L. A., & Jenkins, V. Y. (1987). Infant preferences for attractive faces: Rudiments of a stereotype? *Developmental Psychology, 23,* 363–369.

Langreth, R. (2000, May 1). Every little bit helps: How even moderate exercise can have a big impact on your health. *Wall Street Journal,* p. R5.

Lansford, J. E. (2009). Parental divorce and children's adjustment. *Perspectives on Psychological Science, 4,* 140–152.

Largo-Wight, E., Peterson, P. M., & Chen, W. W. (2005). Perceived problem solving, stress, and health among college students. *American Journal of Health Behavior, 29,* 360–370.

Larkin, M. (1998). On the trail of human pheromones. *Lancet, 351,* 809.

Lassman, D. J., McKie, S., Gregory, L. J., Lal, S., D'Amato, M., Steele, I., et al. (2010). Defining the role of cholecystokinin in the lipid-induced human brain activation matrix. *Gastroenterology, 138,* 1514–1524.

Latané, B., & Darley, J. (1969). Bystander "apathy." *American Scientist, 57,* 244–268.

Latané, B., & L'Herrou, T. (1996). Spatial clustering in the conformity game: Dynamic social impact in electronic groups. *Journal of Personality and Social Psychology, 70,* 1218–1230.

Lating, J. M., Sherman, M. F., Everly, G. S., Jr., Lowry, J. L., & Peragine, T. F. (2004). PTSD reactions and functioning of American Airlines flight attendants in the wake of September 11. *Journal of Nervous and Mental Disorders, 192,* 435–441.

Laubmeier, K. K., Zakowski, S. G., & Bair, J. P. (2004). The role of spirituality in the psychological adjustment to cancer. A test of the transactional model of stress and coping. *International Journal of Behavioral Medicine, 11,* 48–55.

Laugharne, J., Janca, A., & Widiger, T. (2007). Post-traumatic stress disorder and terrorism: Five years after 9/11. *Current Opinion in Psychiatry, 20,* 36–41.

Lavner, J. A., & Bradbury, T. N. (2010). Patterns of change in marital satisfaction over the newlywed years. *Journal of Marriage and the Family, 72,* 1171–1187.

Lavoie, C., & Desrochers, S. (2002). Visual habituation at five months: Short-term reliability of measures obtained with a new polynomial regression criterion. *Journal of Genetic Psychology, 163,* 261–271.

Laws, D. R. (2001). Olfactory aversion: Notes on procedure, with speculations on its mechanism of effect. *Sex Abuse, 13,* 275–287.

Lazarus, R. S. (1990). Theory-based stress measurement. *Psychological Inquiry, 1,* 3–13.

Lazarus, R. S. (1991). Cognition and motivation in emotion. *American Psychologist, 46,* 352–367.

Lazarus, R. S. (1993). From psychological stress to the emotions: A history of changing outlooks. *Annual Review of Psychology, 44,* 1–21.

Lazarus, R. S. (1995). Vexing research problems inherent in cognitive-mediational theories of emotion—and some solutions. *Psychological Inquiry, 6,* 183–197.

Lazarus, R. S., & Folkman, S. (1984). *Stress, appraisal, and coping.* New York: Springer.

Leaper, C., & Friedman, C. K. (2007). The socialization of gender. In J. E. Grusec & P. D. Hastings (Eds.), *Handbook of socialization: Theory and research* (pp. 561–587). New York: Guilford Press.

Leary, C., Kelley, M., Morrow, J., & Mikulka, P. (2008). Parental use of physical punishment as related to family environment, psychological well-being, and personality in undergraduates. *Journal of Family Violence, 23,* 1–7.

LeBlanc, J., Ducharme, M. B., & Thompson, M. (2004). Study on the correlation of the autonomic nervous system response to a stressor of high discomfort with personality traits. *Physiology of Behavior, 82,* 647–652.

Lebovits, A. (2007). Cognitive-behavioral approaches to chronic pain. *Primary Psychiatry, 14,* 48–54.

Lebow, J. L., & Gurman, A. S. (1995). Research assessing couple and family therapy. *Annual Review of Psychology, 46,* 27–57.

Lecanuet, J.-P., Manera, S., & Jacquet, A.-Y. (2002, April). *Fetal cardiac responses to maternal sentences, to playback of these sentences, and to their recordings by another woman's voice.* Paper presented at the XIII International Conference on Infant Studies, Toronto, Ontario, Canada.

Lee, A. Y. (2001). The mere exposure effect: An uncertainty reduction explanation revisited. *Personality and Social Psychology Bulletin, 27,* 1255–1266.

Lee, D. C., Sui, X., Ortega, F. B., Kim, Y. S., Church, T. S., Winett, R. A., et al. (2011). Comparisons of leisure-time physical activity and cardiorespiratory fitness as predictors of all-cause mortality in men and women. *British Journal of Sports Medicine, 45,* 504-510.

Lee, S. J., Perron, B. E., Taylor, C. A., & Guterman, N. B. (2011). Parental psychosocial characteristics and corporal punishment in their 3-year-old children. *Journal of Interpersonal Violence, 26,* 71–87.

Lefcourt, H. M. (2001). The humor solution. In C. R. Snyder (Ed.), *Coping with stress: Effective people and processes* (pp. 68–92). New York: Oxford University Press.

Lefcourt, H. M., & Davidson-Katz, K. (1991). The role of humor and the self. In C. R. Synder & D. R. Forsyth (Eds.), *Handbook of social and clinical psychology: The health perspective* (pp. 41–56). New York: Pergamon Press.

Lehto, U. S., Ojanen, M., Dyba, T., Aromaa, A., & Kellokumpu-Lehtinen, P. (2006). Baseline psychosocial predictors of survival in localized breast cancer. *British Journal of Cancer, 94,* 1245–1252.

Leibowitz, S. F. (1991). Brain neuropeptide Y: An integrator of endocrine, metabolic, and behavioral processes. *Brain Research Bulletin, 27,* 333–337.

Leichsenring, F., & Leibing, E. (2007). Psychodynamic psychotherapy: A systematic review of techniques, indications and empirical evidence. *Psychology and Psychotherapy, 80*(Pt. 2), 217–228.

Leichsenring, F., Leibing, E., Kruse, J., New, A. S., & Leweke, F. (2011). Borderline personality disorder. *Lancet, 377,* 74–84.

Leigh, B. C. (1989). In search of the seven dwarves: Issues of measurement and meaning in alcohol expectancy research. *Psychological Bulletin, 105,* 361–373.

Lemay, E. P., Clark, M. S., & Greenberg, A. (2010). What is beautiful is good because what is beautiful is desired: Physical attractiveness stereotyping as projection of interpersonal goals. *Personality and Social Psychology Bulletin, 36,* 339–353.

Lenox, R. H., & Manji, H. K. (1995). Lithium. In A. F. Schatzberg & C. B. Nemeroff (Eds.), *The American Psychiatric Press textbook of psychopharmacology* (pp. 303–349). Washington, DC: American Psychiatric Press.

Lenze, E. J., Rollman, B. L., Shear, M. K., Dew, M. A., Pollock, B. G., Ciliberti, C., et al. (2009). Escitalopram for older adults with generalized anxiety disorder: A randomized controlled trial. *Journal of the American Medical Association, 301,* 295–303.

Leon, S. C., Kopta, S. M., Howard, K. I., & Lutz, W. (1999). Predicting patients' responses to psychotherapy: Are some more predictable than others? *Journal of Consulting and Clinical Psychology, 67,* 698–704.

LePine, J. A., Erez, A., & Johnston, D. E. (2002). The nature and dimensionality of organizational citizenship behavior: A critical review and a meta-analysis. *Journal of Applied Psychology, 87*(1), 52–65.

Lepper, M. R., Corpus, J. H., & Iyengar, S. S. (2005). Intrinsic and extrinsic motivational orientations in the classroom: Age differences and academic correlates. *Journal of Educational Psychology, 97,* 184–196.

Lessenger, J. E., & Feinberg, S. D. (2008). Abuse of prescription and over-the-counter medications. *Journal of the American Board of Family Medicine, 21,* 175.

Lester, B. M., Andreozzi, L., & Appiah, L. (2004). Substance use during pregnancy: Time for policy to catch up with research. *Harm Reduction Journal, 1,* 5–49.

Lester, B. M., Corwin, M. J., Sepkoski, C., Seifer, R., Peucker, M., McLaughlin, S., et al. (1991). Neurobehavioral syndromes in cocaine-exposed newborn infants. *Child Development, 62,* 694–705.

Leuchter, A. F., Lesser, I. M., Trivedi, M. H., Rush, A. J., Morris, D. W., Warden, D., et al. (2008). An open pilot study of the combination of escitalopram and bupropion-SR for outpatients with major depressive disorder. *Journal of Psychiatric Practice, 14,* 271–280.

LeVay, S. (1996). *Queer science: The use and abuse of research into homosexuality.* Cambridge, MA: MIT Press.

Levenson, R. W., Carstensen, L. L., & Gottman, J. M. (1993). Long-term marriage: Age, gender, and satisfaction. *Psychology and Aging, 8,* 301–313.

Levenson, R. W., Ekman, P., & Friesen, W. V. (1990). Voluntary facial action generates emotion-specific nervous system activity. *Psychophysiology, 27,* 363–384.

Levin, B. E., & Routh, V. H. (1996). Role of the brain in energy balance and obesity. *The American Journal of Physiology, 271,* R491–500.

Levine, B., Turner, G. R., Tisserand, D., Hevenor, S. J., Graham, S. J., & McIntosh, A. R. (2004). The functional neuroanatomy of episodic and semantic autobiographical remembering: A prospective functional MRI study. *Journal of Cognitive Neuroscience, 16,* 1633–1646.

Levine, M. (2006). *The price of privilege: How parental pressure and material advantage are creating a generation of disconnected and unhappy kids.* New York: Harper Collins.

Levine, R. A., & Campbell, D. T. (1972). *Ethnocentrism: Theories of conflict, ethnic attitudes, and group behavior.* New York: Wiley.

Levinson, D. F., Evgrafov, O. V., Knowles, J. A., Potash, J. B., Weissman, M. M., Scheftner, W. A., et al. (2007). Genetics of recurrent early-onset major depression (GenRED): Significant linkage on chromosome 15q25–q26 after fine mapping with single nucleotide polymorphism markers. *American Journal of Psychiatry, 164,* 259–264.

Levitt, A. G., & Utmann, J. G. A. (1992). From babbling towards the sound systems of English and French: A longitudinal two-case study. *Journal of Child Language, 19,* 19–40.

Levy, B. R., & Myers, L. M. (2004). Preventive health behaviors influenced by self-perceptions of aging. *Preventive Medicine, 39,* 625–629.

Levy, B. R., Slade, M. D., Kunkel, S. R., & Kasl, S. V. (2002). Longevity increased by positive self-perceptions of aging. *Journal of Personality and Social Psychology, 83,* 261–270.

Levy, D. L., Coleman, M. J., Sung, H., Ji, F., Matthysse, S., Mendell, N. R., et al. (2010). The genetic basis of thought disorder and language and communication disturbances in schizophrenia. *Journal of Neurolinguistics, 23,* 176.

Levy, G. D., Taylor, M. G., & Gelman, S. A. (1995). Traditional and evaluative aspects of flexibility in gender roles, social conventions, moral rules, and physical laws. *Child Development, 66,* 515–531.

Levy, N. A., & Janicak, P. G. (2000). Calcium channel antagonists for the treatment of bipolar disorder. *Bipolar Disorders, 2,* 108–119.

Levy-Shiff, R. (1994). Individual and contextual correlates of marital change across the transition to parenthood. *Developmental Psychology, 30,* 591–601.

Lewinsohn, P. M., Clark, G. N., Hops, H., & Andrews, J. (1990). Cognitive-behavioral treatment for depressed adolescents. *Behavior Therapy, 21,* 385–401.

Lewinsohn, P. M., Klein, D. N., & Seeley, J. R. (2000). Bipolar disorder during adolescence and young adulthood in a community sample. *Bipolar Disorders, 2,* 281–293.

Lewinsohn, P. M., Rohde, P., & Seeley, J. R. (1994). Psychosocial risk factors for future adolescent suicide attempts. *Journal of Consulting and Clinical Psychology, 62,* 297–305.

Lewis, D. O. (1992). From abuse to violence: Psychophysiological consequences of maltreatment. *Journal of the American Academy of Child and Adolescent Psychiatry, 31,* 383–391.

Lewis, D. O., Yeager, C. A., Blake, P., Bard, B., & Strenziok, M. (2004). Ethics questions raised by the neuropsychiatric, neuropsychological, educational, developmental, and family characteristics of 18 juveniles awaiting execution in Texas. *Journal of the American Academy of Psychiatry and the Law, 32,* 408–429.

Lexiteria Corporation. (2011). *Alphadictionary.com.* Retrieved April 17, 2011, from http://www.alphadictionary.com/index.shtml

Li, C. E., DiGiuseppe, R., & Froh, J. (2006). The roles of sex, gender, and coping in adolescent depression. *Adolescence, 41,* 409–415.

Li, S., Lindenberger, U., Hommel, B., Aschersleben, G., Prinz, W., & Baltes, P. B. (2004). Transformations in the couplings among intellectual abilities and constituent cognitive processes across the life span. *Psychological Science, 15,* 155–163.

Libersat, F., & Pflueger, H.-J. (2004). Monoamines and the orchestration of behavior. *BioScience, 54,* 17–25.

Lichter, D. T., Qian, Z., & Mellott, L. M. (2006). Marriage or dissolution? Union transitions among poor cohabiting women. *Demography, 43,* 223–240.

Lieberman, J., Chakos, M., Wu, H., Alvir, J., Hoffman, E., Robinson, D., et al. (2001). Longitudinal study of brain morphology in first episode schizophrenia. *Biological Psychiatry, 49,* 487–499.

McLaughlin Crabtree, V., & Williams, N. A. (2009). Normal sleep in children and adolescents. *Child and Adolescent Psychiatric Clinics of North America, 18,* 799–811.

McLay, R. N., McBrien, C., Wiederhold, M. D., & Wiederhold, B. K. (2010). Exposure therapy with and without virtual reality to treat PTSD while in the combat theater: A parallel case series. *Cyberpsychology, Behavior, and Social Networking, 13,* 37–42.

McLean, C. P., Asnaani, A., Litz, B. T., & Hofmann, S. G. (in press). Gender differences in anxiety disorders: Prevalence, course of illness, comorbidity and burden of illness. *Journal of Psychiatric Research.*

McManus, M. A., & Baratta, J. E. (1992). *The relationship of recruiting source to performance and survival.* Paper presented at the annual meeting of the Society for Industrial and Organizational Psychology, Montreal.

McMillen, D. L., Smith, S. M., & Wells-Parker, E. (1989). The effects of alcohol, expectancy, and sensation seeking on driving risk taking. *Addictive Behaviors, 14,* 477–483.

McNeil, D. W., & Kyle, B. N. (2009). Exposure strategies. In S. Cormier, P. S. Nurius, & C. J. Osborn, *Interviewing and change strategies for helpers: Fundamental skills and cognitive behavioral interventions* (6th ed., pp. 486–516). Belmont, CA: Brooks/Cole.

McNeill, B., Prieto, L., Niemann, Y., Pizarro, M., Vera, E., & Gomez, S. (2001). Current directions in Chicana/o psychology. *Counseling Psychologist, 29,* 5–17.

McRae, K., Ochsner, K. N., Mauss, I. B., Gabrieli, J. J. D., & Gross, J. J. (2008). Gender differences in emotion regulation: An fMRI study of cognitive reappraisal. *Group Processes & Intergroup Relations, 11,* 143–162.

Medicare to fund obesity treatment. (2004, July 16). *CBS News.* Available online at http://www.cbsnews.com/stories/2004/07/16/health/main630141.shtml?tag=mncol;lst;1

Medina-Mora, M. E., Borges, G., Lara, C., Benjet, C., Blanco, J., Fleiz, C., et al. (2005). Prevalence, service use, and demographic correlates of 12-month DSM-IV psychiatric disorders in Mexico: Results from the Mexican National Comorbidity Survey. *Psychological Medicine, 35,* 1773–1783.

Mehl, M. R., Vazire, S., Holleran, S. E., & Clark, C. S. (2010). Eavesdropping on happiness: Well-being is related to having less small talk and more substantive conversations. *Psychological Science, 21,* 539–541.

Mellman, T. A., Alim, T., Brown, D. D., Gorodetsky, E., Buzas, B., Lawson, W. B., et al. (2009). Serotonin polymorphisms and posttraumatic stress disorder in a trauma exposed African American population. *Depression and Anxiety, 26,* 993–997.

Meltzer, L. J., & Mindell, J. A. (2006). Sleep and sleep disorders in children and adolescents. *Psychiatric Clinics of North America, 29,* 1059–1076.

Mennella, J. A., & Beauchamp, G. K. (1991). Maternal diet alters the sensory qualities of human milk and nursling's behavior. *Pediatrics, 88,* 737–744.

Menzies, R. G., & Clark, J. C. (1993). A comparison of *in vivo* and vicarious exposure in the treatment of childhood water phobia. *Behaviour Research and Therapy, 31,* 9–15.

Merikangas, K. R., He, J. P., Burstein, M., Swanson, S. A., Avenevoli, S., Cui, L., et al. (2010). Lifetime prevalence of mental disorder in U.S. adolescents: Results from the National Comorbidity Survey Replication—Adolescent Supplement (NCS-A). *Journal of the American Academy of Child and Adolescent Psychiatry, 49,* 980–989.

Merkl, A., Heuser, I., & Bajbouj, M. (2009). Antidepressant electroconvulsive therapy: Mechanism of action, recent advances and limitations. *Experimental Neurology, 219,* 20–26.

Messner, M., Reinhard, M., & Sporer, S. L. (2008). Compliance through direct persuasive appeals: The moderating role of communicator's attractiveness in interpersonal persuasion. *Social Influence, 3,* 67–83.

Meyer, D. (2007). Selective serotonin reuptake inhibitors and their effects on relationship satisfaction. *Family Journal, 15,* 392–397.

Meyer, J. P., & Allen, N. J. (1991). A three-component conceptualization of organizational commitment. *Human Resource Management Review, 1,* 61–89.

Meyer, J. P., & Herscovitch, L. (2001). Commitment in the workplace: Toward a general model. *Human Resource Management Review, 11,* 299–326.

Meyer, L. (1999). Hostile classrooms. *The Advocate, 32*(1), 33–35.

Mezulis, A. H., Abramson, L. Y., Hyde, J. S., & Hankin, B. L. (2004). Is there a universal positivity bias in attributions? A meta-analytic review of individual, developmental, and cultural differences in the self-serving attributional bias. *Psychological Bulletin, 130,* 711–747.

Micco, J. A., Henin, A., Mick, E., Kim, S., Hopkins, C. A., Biederman, J., et al. (2009). Anxiety and depressive disorders in offspring at high risk for anxiety: A meta-analysis. *Journal of Anxiety Disorders, 23,* 1158–1164.

Michael, G. A., Boucart, M., Degreef, J. F., & Goefroy, O. (2001). The thalamus interrupts top-down attentional control for permitting exploratory shiftings to sensory signals. *Neuroreport, 12,* 2041–2048.

Michael, R. T., Gagnon, J. H., Laumann, E. O., & Kolata, G. (1994). *Sex in America: A definitive survey.* Boston: Little, Brown.

Michelson, D., Bancroft, J., Targum, S., Kim, Y., & Tepner, R. (2000). Female sexual dysfunction associated with antidepressant administration: A randomized, placebo-controlled study of pharmacological intervention. *American Journal of Psychiatry, 157,* 239–243.

Migliore, M., Novara, G., & Tegolo, D. (2008). Single neuron binding properties and the magical number 7. *Hippocampus, 18,* 1122–1130.

Milgram, S. (1963). Behavioral study of obedience. *Journal of Abnormal and Social Psychology, 67,* 371–378.

Milgram, S. (1965). Some conditions of obedience and disobedience to authority. *Human Relations, 18,* 57–76.

Milgram, S. (1974). *Obedience to authority: An experimental view.* New York: Harper & Row.

Millar, M. (2002). The effectiveness of the door-in-the-face compliance strategy on friends and strangers. *Journal of Social Psychology, 142,* 295–305.

Miller, A. G. (2009). Reflections on "Replicating Milgram." *American Psychologist, 64,* 20–27.

Miller, B. C., & Benson, B. (1999). Romantic and sexual relationship development during adolescence. In W. Furman, B. B. Brown, & C. Feiring (Eds.), *The development of romantic relationships in adolescence* (pp. 99–121). New York: Cambridge University Press.

Miller, D. T., & Ross, M. (1975). Self-serving biases in the attribution of causality: Fact or fiction? *Psychological Bulletin, 82,* 213–225.

Miller, E. (1999). The pheromone androsterol: Evolutionary considerations. *Mankind Quarterly, 39,* 455–466.

Miller, G. A. (1956). The magical number seven, plus or minus two: Some limits on our capacity for processing information. *Psychological Review, 63,* 81–97.

Miller, G. E., & Blackwell, E. (2006). Turning up the heat: Inflammation as a mechanism linking chronic stress, depression, and heart disease. *Current Directions in Psychological Science, 15,* 269–272.

Miller, I. J., Jr., & Bartoshuk, L. M. (1991). Taste perception, taste bud distribution, and spatial relationships. In T. V. Gethell, R. L. Doty, L. M. Bartoshuk, & J. B. Snow, Jr. (Eds.), *Smell and taste in health and disease* (pp. 205–233). New York: Raven.

Miller, N. S., & Gold, M. S. (1994). LSD and Ecstasy: Pharmacology, phenomenology, and treatment. *Psychiatric Annals, 24,* 131–133.

Miller, S., & Maner, J. K. (2010). Scent of a woman: Men's testosterone responses to olfactory ovulation cues. *Psychological Science, 21,* 276–283.

Miller, T. Q., Smith, T. W., Turner, C. W., Guijarro, M. L., & Hallet, A. J. (1996). A meta-analytic review of research on hostility and physical health. *Psychological Bulletin, 119,* 322–348.

Miller, T. Q., Turner, C. W., Tindale, R. S., Posavac, E. J., & Dugoni, B. L. (1991). Reasons for the trend toward null findings in research on Type A behavior. *Psychological Bulletin, 110,* 469–485.

Miller, W. R., & Seligman, M. E. P. (1975). Depression and learned helplessness in man. *Journal of Abnormal Psychology, 84,* 228–238.

Miller, W. R., & Thoresen, C. E. (2003). Spirituality, religion, and health. An emerging research field. *American Psychologist, 58,* 24–35.

Milliken, C. S., Auchterlonie, J. L., & Hoge, C. W. (2007). Longitudinal assessment of mental health problems among active and reserve component soldiers returning from the Iraq war. *Journal of the American Medical Association, 298,* 2141–2148.

Milling, L. S., Reardon, J. M., & Carosella, G. M. (2006). Mediation and moderation of psychological pain treatments: Response expectancies and hypnotic suggestibility. *Journal of Consulting and Clinical Psychology, 74,* 253–262.

Milner, C. E., & Cote, K. A. (2009). Benefits of napping in healthy adults: Impact of nap length, time of day, age, and experience with napping. *Journal of Sleep Research, 18,* 272–281.

Milton, J., & Wiseman, R. (2001). Does psi exist? Reply to Storm and Ertel (2001). *Psychological Bulletin, 127,* 434–438.

Minda, J. P., & Smith, J. D. (2002). Comparing prototype-based and exemplar-based accounts of category learning and attentional allocation. *Journal of Experimental Psychology: Learning, Memory, and Cognition, 28,* 275–292.

Mischel, W., & Shoda, Y. (1995). A cognitive-affective system theory of personality: Reconceptualizing situations, dispositions, dynamics, and invariance of personality structure. *Psychological Review, 102,* 246–268.

Miselis, R. R., & Epstein, A. N. (1970). Feeding induced by 2-deoxy-D-glucose injections into the lateral ventrical of the rat. *Physiologist, 13,* 262.

Miskovic, V., Moscovitch, D. A., Santesso, D. L., McCabe, R. E., Antony, M. M., & Schmidt, L. A. (2011). Changes in EEG cross-frequency coupling during cognitive behavioral therapy for social anxiety disorder. *Psychological Science, 22,* 507–516.

Mitelman, S. A., Buchsbaum, M. S., Brickman, A. M., & Shihabuddin, L. (2005). Cortical intercorrelations of frontal area volumes in schizophrenia. *Neuroimage, 27,* 753–770.

Miyauchi, S., Misaki, M., Kan, S., Fukunaga, T., & Koike, T. (2009). Human brain activity time-locked to rapid eye movements during REM sleep. *Experimental Brain Research, 192,* 657–667.

Mizushige, T., Inoue, K., & Fushiki, T. (2007). Why is fat so tasty? Chemical reception of fatty acid on the tongue. *Journal of Nutritional Science and Vitaminology, 53,* 1–4.

Mobini, S., Chambers, L. C., & Yeomans, M. R. (2007). Effects of hunger state on flavour pleasantness conditioning at home: Flavour–nutrient learning vs. flavour–flavour learning. *Appetite, 48,* 20–28.

Moffitt, T. E. (2005). The new look of behavioral genetics in developmental psychopathology: Gene-environment interplay in antisocial behaviors. *Psychological Bulletin, 131,* 533–554.

Moffitt, T. E., Brammer, G. L., Caspi, A., Fawcet, J. P., Raleigh, M., Yuwiler, A., et al. (1998). Whole blood serotonin relates to violence in an epidemiological study. *Biological Psychiatry, 43,* 446–457.

Moffitt, T. E., Caspi, A., Taylor, A., Kokaua, J., Milne, B. J., Polanczyk, G., et al. (2009). How common are common mental disorders? Evidence that lifetime prevalence rates are doubled by prospective versus retrospective ascertainment. *Psychological Medicine.* Published online by Cambridge University Press 01 Sep. doi:10.1017/S0033291709991036

Mogilner, C. (2010). The pursuit of happiness: Time, money, and social connection. *Psychological Science, 21,* 1348–1354.

Mohr, B. A., Guay, A. T., O'Donnell, A. B., & McKinlay, J. B. (2005). Normal, bound and nonbound testosterone levels in normally ageing men: Results from the Massachusetts Male Ageing Study. *Clinical Endocrinology, 62,* 64–73.

Mohr, C. (1964, March 28). Apathy is puzzle in Queens killing. *New York Times,* pp. 21, 40.

Mojtabai, R. (2007). Americans' attitudes toward mental health treatment seeking: 1990–2003. *Psychiatric Services, 58,* 642–651.

Mojtabai, R. (2009). Americans' attitudes toward psychiatric medications: 1998–2006. *Psychiatric Services, 60,* 1015–1023.

Mokhber, N., Azarpazhooh, M. R., Khajehdaluee, M., Velayati, A., & Hopwood, M. (2010). Randomized, single-blind, trial of sertraline and buspirone for treatment of elderly patients with generalized anxiety disorder. *Psychiatry and Clinical Neurosciences, 64,* 128–133.

Molero, F., Navas, M. S., Gonzalez, J. L., Aleman, P., & Cuadrado, I. (2003). Paupers or riches: The perception of immigrants, tourists and ingroup members in a sample of Spanish children. *Journal of Ethnic and Migration Studies, 29,* 501–517.

Monaco, M., & Martin, M. (2007). The millennial student: A new generation of learners. *Athletic Training Education Journal, 2,* 42–46.

Mongrain, V., Lavoie, S., Selmaoui, B., Paquet, J., & Dumont, M. (2004). Phase relationships between sleep–wake cycle and underlying circadian rhythms in Morningness–Eveningness. *Journal of Biological Rhythms, 19*, 248–257.

Monroe, S. M., & Reid, M. W. (2009). Life stress and major depression. *Current Directions in Psychological Science, 18*, 68–72.

Monteith, M., & Winters, J. (2002, May–June). Why we hate. *Psychology Today, 35*, 44–51.

Monti-Bloch, L., Diaz-Sanchez, V., Jennings-White, C., & Berliner, D. L. (1998). Modulation of serum testosterone and autonomic function through stimuluation of the male human vomeronasal organ (VNO) with pregna-4, 20-diene-3, 6-dione. *Journal of Steroid Biochemistry and Molecular Biology, 65*, 237–242.

Montoya, M. R. (2008). I'm hot, so I'd say you're not: The influence of objective physical attractiveness on mate selection. *Personality and Social Psychology Bulletin, 34*, 1315–1331.

Moore, E. G. J. (1986). Family socialization and the IQ test performance of traditionally and transracially adopted black children. *Developmental Psychology, 22*, 317–326.

Moore, M. T., & Fresco, D. M. (2007). Depressive realism and attributional style: Implications for individuals at risk for depression. *Behavior Therapy, 38*, 144–154.

Moore, S. M. (1995). Girls' understanding and social constructions of menarche. *Journal of Adolescence, 18*, 87–104.

Moreno-Walton, L., Brunett, P., Akhtar, S., & DeBlieux, P. M. (2009). Teaching across the generation gap: A consensus from the Council of Emergency Medicine Residency Directors 2009 Academic Assembly. *Academic Emergency Medicine. Special Issue: CORD Educational Advances Supplement, 16*, s19–s24.

Morgenstern, H., & Glazer, W. M. (1993). Identifying risk factors for tardive dyskinesia among long-term outpatients maintained with neuroleptic medications: Results of the Yale Tardive Dyskinesia Study. *Archives of General Psychiatry, 50*, 723–733.

Morin, C. M., Vallieres, A., Guay, B., Ivers, H., Savard, J., Merette, C., et al. (2009). Cognitive behavioral therapy, singly and combined with medication, for persistent insomnia: A randomized controlled trial. *Journal of the American Medical Association, 301*, 2005–2015.

Morisse, D., Batra, L., Hess, L., & Silverman, R. (1996). A demonstration of a token economy for the real world. *Applied and Preventive Psychology, 5*, 41–46.

Morland, L. A., Greene, C. J., Grubbs, K., Kloezeman, K., Mackintosh, M. A., Rosen, C., et al. (2011). Therapist adherence to manualized cognitive-behavioral therapy for anger management delivered to veterans with PTSD via videoconferencing. *Journal of Clinical Psychology, 67*, 629–638.

Morlock, R. J., Tan, M., & Mitchell, D. Y. (2006). Patient characteristics and patterns of drug use for sleep complaints in the United States: Analysis of National Ambulatory Medical Survey data, 1997–2002. *Clinical Therapeutics, 28*, 1044–1053.

Morrison, P. D., Zois, V., McKeown, D. A., Lee, T. D., Holt, D. W., Powell, J. F., et al. (2009). The acute effects of synthetic intravenous Delta9-tetrahydrocannabinol on psychosis, mood and cognitive functioning. *Psychological Medicine, 39*, 1607–1616.

Morrow, E. M., Roffman, J. L., Wolf, D. H., & Coyle, J. T. (2008). Psychiatric neuroscience: Incorporating pathophysiology into clinical case formulation. In T. A. Stern, J. F. Rosenbaum, M. Fava, J. Biederman, & S. L. Rauch (Eds.), *Massachusetts General Hospital comprehensive clinical psychiatry.* Philadelphia: Mosby-Elsevier.

Mortensen, M. E., Sever, L. E., & Oakley, G. P. (1991). Teratology and the epidemiology of birth defects. In S. G. Gabbe, J. R. Niebyl, & J. L. Simpson (Eds.), *Obstetrics: Normal and problem pregnancies* (pp. 233–268). New York: Churchill Livingstone.

Mosedeghrad, A., Ferlie, E., & Rosenberg, D. (2008). A study of the relationship between job satisfaction, organizational commitment and turnover intention among hospital employees. *Health Services Management Research, 21*, 211–227.

Mosing, M. A., Gordon, S. D., Medland, S. E., Statham, D. J., Nelson, E. C., Heath, A. C., et al. (2009). Genetic and environmental influences on the co-morbidity between depression, panic disorder, agoraphobia, and social phobia: A twin study. *Depression and Anxiety, 26*, 1004–1011.

Motivala, S. J., & Irwin, M. R. (2007). Sleep and immunity: Cytokine pathways linking sleep and health outcomes. *Current Directions in Psychological Science, 16*, 21–25.

Mottram, L., & Berger-Gross, P. (2004). An intervention to reduce disruptive behaviors in children with brain injury. *Pediatric Rehabilitation, 7*, 133–143.

Moulton, S., & Kosslyn, S. (2008). Using neuroimaging to resolve the psi debate. *Journal of Cognitive Neuroscience, 20*, 182–192.

Mowen, J. C., & Cialdini, R. B. (1980). On implementing the door-in-the-face compliance technique in a business context. *Journal of Marketing Research, 17*, 253–258.

Mroczek, D. K., & Spiro, A., III. (2003). Modeling intra-individual change in personality traits: Findings from the Normative Aging Study. *Journal of Gerontology: Psychological Sciences, 58B*, P153–P165.

Mrug, S., Elliott, M., Gilliland, M. J., Grunbaum, J. A., Tortolero, S. R., Cuccaro, P., et al. (2008). Positive parenting and early puberty in girls: Protective effects against aggressive behavior. *Archives of Pediatrics and Adolescent Medicine, 162*, 781–786.

Mueller, C. W., Boyer, E. M., Price, J. L., & Iverson, R. D. (1994). Employee attachment and noncoercive conditions of work: The case of dental hygienists. *Work and Occupations, 21*, 179–212.

Mulrow, C. D., Willaims, J. W., Jr., Chiquette, E., Aguilar, C., Hitchcock-Noel, P., Lee, S., et al. (2000). Efficacy of newer medications for treating depression in primary care patients. *American Journal of Medicine, 108*, 54–64.

Mumford, M. D. (2003). Where have we been, where are we going? Taking stock in creativity research. *Creativity Research Journal, 15*, 107–120.

Mumme, D. L., & Fernald, A. (2003). The infant as onlooker: Learning from emotional reactions observed in a television scenario. *Child Development, 74*, 221–237.

Munafo, M. R., Yalcin, B., Willis-Owen, S. A., & Flint, J. (2008). Association of the dopamine D4 receptor (DRD4) gene and approach-related personality traits: Meta-analysis and new data. *Biological Psychiatry, 63*, 197–206.

Munch, M., Knoblauch, V., Blatter, K., Schroder, C., Schnitzler, C., Krauchi, K., et al. (2005). Age-related attenuation of the evening circadian arousal signal in humans. *Neurobiology of Aging, 26*, 1307–1319.

Murdoch, B. B., Jr. (1962). The serial position effect of free recall. *Journal of Experimental Psychology, 64*, 482–488.

Murillo-Rodriquez, E., Arais-Carrion, O., Sanguino-Rodriguez, K., Gonzalez-Arias, M., & Haro, R. (2009). Mechanisms of sleep-wake cycle modulation. *CNS Neurological Disorders Drug Treatment, 8*, 245–253.

Murphy, K., & Delanty, N. (2007). Sleep deprivation: A clinical perspective. *Sleep and Biological Rhythms, 5*, 2–14.

Murray, H. A. (1938). *Explorations in personality.* New York: Oxford University Press.

Murray, S. O., Olshausen, B. A., & Woods, D. L. (2003). Processing shape, motion, and three-dimensional shape-from-motion in the human cortex. *Cerebral Cortex, 13*, 508–516.

Muscari, M. (2002). Media violence: Advice for parents. *Pediatric Nursing, 28*, 585–591.

Muurahainen, N. E., Kisileff, H. R., Lachaussee, J., & Pi-Sunyer, F. X. (1991). Effect of a soup preload on reduction of food intake by cholecystokinin in humans. *American Journal of Physiology, 260*, R672–R680.

Myers, D. G. (2000). The funds, friends, and faith of happy people. *American Psychologist, 55*, 56–67.

Naegele, B., Thouvard, V., Pepin, J. L., Levy, P., Bonnet, C., Perret, J. E., et al. (1995). Deficits of cognitive functions in patients with sleep apnea syndrome. *Sleep, 18*(1), 43–52.

Nairne, J. S. (2002). Remembering over the short term: The case against the standard model. *Annual Review of Psychology, 53*, 53–81.

Naish, P. L. (2010). Hypnosis and hemispheric asymmetry. *Consciousness and Cognition, 19*, 230–234.

Nardi, A. E., Freire, R. C., Valenca, A. M., Amrein, R., de Cerqueira, A. C., Lopes, F. L., et al. (2010). Tapering clonazepam in patients with panic disorder after at least 3 years of treatment. *Journal of Clinical Psychopharmacology, 30*, 290–293.

Narvaez, D. (2010). Moral complexity: The fatal attraction of truthiness and the importance of mature moral functioning. *Perspectives on Psychological Science, 5*, 163–181.

Nash, J. M., & Thebarge, R. W. (2006). Understanding psychological stress, its biological processes, and impact on primary headache. *Headache, 46*, 1377–1386.

Nash, M. (1987). What, if anything, is regressed about hypnotic age regression? A review of the empirical literature. *Psychological Bulletin, 102*, 42–52.

Nash, M. (2005). Salient findings: A potentially ground-breaking study on the neuroscience of hypnotizability, a critical review of hypnosis' efficacy, and the neurophysiology of conversion disorder. *International Journal of Clinical and Experimental Hypnosis, 53*, 87–93.

Nassif, A., & Gunter, B. (2008). Gender representation in television advertisements in Britain and Saudi Arabia. *Sex Roles, 58*, 752–760.

Nathan, P. E., Stuart, S. P., & Dolan, S. L. (2000). Research on psychotherapy efficacy and effectiveness: Between Scylla and Charybdis? *Psychological Bulletin, 126*, 964–981.

National Comorbidity Survey Replication (NCS-R). (2007). http://www.hcp.med.harvard.edu/ncs

National Gay and Lesbian Task Force. (2007). *Hate crime laws in the U. S.* Retrieved June 25, 2007, from http://www.thetaskforce .org/downloads/reports/issue_maps/hate_crimes_5_07.pdf

National Highway Traffic Safety Administration (NHTSA). (2008). *Traffic safety facts, 2008.* Washington, DC: U.S. Department of Transportation.

National Highway Traffic Safety Administration (NHTSA). (2009). *Traffic safety facts: An examination of driver distraction as recorded in NHTSA databases.* Washington, DC: NHTSA's Center for Statistics and Analysis.

National Institute of Alcohol Abuse and Alcoholism. (2004). NIAAA council approves definition of binge drinking. *NIAAA Newsletter, 3*, 3.

National Institute of Mental Health. (2002). *Suicide facts.* Retrieved from http://www.nimh.nih.gov/research/suifact.htm

National Institute of Mental Health. (2007). *Suicide in the U.S.: Statistics and prevention* (NIH Publication No. 06–4594). Washington, DC: National Institutes of Health, U.S. Department of Health and Human Services.

National Institute on Drug Abuse (NIDA). (2001). *Research report series: Hallucinogens and dissociative drugs.* NIH Publication Number 01-4209.

National Institute on Drug Abuse (NIDA). (2006a). *Research report series: MDMA (Ecstasy) abuse.* NIH Publication Number 06-4728.

National Institute on Drug Abuse (NIDA). (2006b). *Research report series: Methamphetamine abuse and addiction.* NIH Publication Number 06-4210.

National Institute on Drug Abuse (NIDA) & University of Michigan. (2006). *Monitoring the Future national survey results on drug use, 1975–2005: Volume 11. College students and adults ages 19–45.*

National Institutes of Health. (2000). *The practical guide: Identification, evaluation, and treatment of overweight and obesity in adults* (NIH Publication No. 00-4084). Washington, DC: Author.

National Safety Council. (2011). *Injury Fact Book, 2011 Edition.* Retrieved April, 17, 2011, from http://www.nsc.org/NSC%20Picture%20Library/News/web_graphics/Injury_Facts_37.pdf

National Science Foundation (NSF). (2006). *U.S. doctorates in the 20th century.* NSF 06-319. Arlington, VA: Author.

National Science Foundation (NSF), Division of Science Resources Statistics. (2009). *Doctorate recipients from U.S. universities: Summary report 2007–08.* Special Report NSF 10-309. Arlington, VA. Available at http://www.nsf.gov/statistics/nsf10309

National Sleep Foundation. (2004). *Summary findings: 2004 Sleep in America poll.* Washington, DC: Author.

National Sleep Foundation. (2005). *Summary findings: 2005 Sleep in America poll.* Washington, DC: Author.

National Sleep Foundation. (2006). *Summary findings: 2006 Sleep in America poll.* Washington, DC: Author.

National Sleep Foundation. (2009). *Summary findings: 2009 Sleep in America poll.* Washington, DC: Author.

National Sleep Foundation. (2010). *Summary findings: 2010 Sleep in America poll.* Washington, DC: Author.

Navarro, M. (1995, December 9). Drug sold abroad by prescription becomes widely abused in U.S. *New York Times*, pp. 1, 9.

Nave, K. A. (2010). Myelination and support of axonal integrity by glia. *Nature, 468*, 244–252.

Naylor, J. C., Pritchard, R. D., & Ilgen, D. R. (1980). *A theory of behavior in organizations.* New York: Academic Press.

Neher, A. (1991). Maslow's theory of motivation: A critique. *Journal of Humanistic Psychology, 31*, 89–112.

Nemeroff, C. B. (2007). The burden of severe depression: A review of diagnostic challenges and treatment alternatives. *Journal of Psychiatric Research, 41*, 189–206.

Neria, Y., Nandi, A., & Galea, S. (2008). Post-traumatic stress disorder following disasters: A systematic review. *Psychological Medicine, 38*, 467–480.

Nestler, E. J., & Carlezon, W. A., Jr. (2006). The mesolimbic dopamine reward circuit in depression. *Biological Psychiatry, 59*, 1151–1159.

Nestor, L., Roberts, G., Garavan, H., & Hester, R. (2008). Deficits in learning and memory: Parahippocampal hyperactivity and frontocortical hypoactivity in cannabis users. *NeuroImage, 40*, 1328–1339.

Nevin, J. A., & Grace, R. C. (2005). Resistance to extinction in the steady state and in the transition. *Journal of Experimental Psychology: Animal Behavior Processes, 31*, 199–212.

Nevonen, L., & Broberg, A. G. (2006). A comparison of sequenced individual and group psychotherapy for patients with bulimia nervosa. *International Journal of Eating Disorders, 39*, 117–127.

Newcomb, T. M. (1961). *The acquaintance process.* New York: Holt, Rinehart & Winston.

Newland M. C., & Rasmussen, E. B. (2003). Behavior in adulthood and during aging is affected by contaminant exposure in utero. *Current Directions in Psychological Science, 12*, 212–217.

Ni, X., Sicard, T., Bulgin, N., Bismil, R., Chan, K., McMain, S., et al. (2007). Monoamine oxidase A gene is associated with borderline personality disorder. *Psychiatric Genetics, 17*, 153–157.

Nicodemus, K. K., Callicott, J. H., Higier, R. G., Luna, A., Nixon, D. C., Lipska, B. K., et al. (2010). Evidence of statistical epistasis between DISC1, CIT and NDEL1 impacting risk for schizophrenia: Biological validation with functional neuroimaging. *Human Genetics, 127*, 441–452.

Nicoletti, A., & Merriman, W. (2007). Teaching millennial generation students. *Momentum, 38*, 28–31.

Nicolini, H., Arnold, P., Nestadt, G., Lanzagorta, N., & Kennedy, J. L. (2009). Overview of genetics and obsessive-compulsive disorder. *Psychiatry Research, 170*, 7–14.

Niedzwienska, A. (2003). Gender differences in vivid memories. *Sex Roles: A Journal of Research, 49*, 321–331.

Nielsen, M., & Day, R. H. (1999). William James and the evolution of consciousness. *Journal of Theoretical and Philosophical Psychology, 19*, 90–113.

Nieuwenhuijsen, K., Verbeek, J. H., de Boer, A. G., Blonk, R. W., & van Dijk, F. J. (2010). Irrational beliefs in employees with an adjustment, a depressive, or an anxiety disorder: A prospective cohort study. *Journal of Rational-Emotive and Cognitive-Behavior Therapy, 28*, 57–72.

NIMH Genetics Workgroup. (1998). *Genetics and mental disorders* (NIH Publication No. 98-4268). Rockville, MD: National Institute of Mental Health.

Nisbett, R. (1995). Race, IQ, and scientism. In Steven Fraser (Ed.), *The bell curve wars: Race, intelligence, and the future of America* (pp. 36–57). New York: Basic Books.

Nishino, S. (2007). Narcolepsy: Pathophysiology and pharmacology. *Journal of Clinical Psychiatry, 68*, 9–15.

Nivoli, A. M., Murru, A., & Vieta, E. (2010). Lithium: Still a cornerstone in the long-term treatment in bipolar disorder? *Neuropsychobiology, 62*, 27–35.

Noah, T., & Robinson, L. (1997, March 3). OK, OK, cigarettes do kill. *U.S. News & World Report*, pp. 29, 32.

Noble, M., & Harding, G. E. (1963). Conditioning of rhesus monkeys as a function of the interval between CS and US. *Journal of Comparative and Physiological Psychology, 56*, 220–224.

Nock, M. K., Borges, G., Bromet, E. J., Cha, C. B., Kessler, R. C., & Lee, S. (2008). Suicide and suicidal behavior. *Epidemiologic Reviews, 30*, 133–154.

Nock, M. K., Hwang, I., Sampson, N., Kessler, R. C., Angermeyer, M., Beautrais, A., et al. (2009). Cross-national analysis of the associations among mental disorders and suicidal behavior: Findings from the WHO World Mental Health Surveys. *PLoS Medicine, 6*, e1000123.

Nolan, R. P., Spanos, N. P., Hayward, A. A., & Scott, H. A. (1995). The efficacy of hypnotic and nonhypnotic response-based imagery for self-managing recurrent headache. *Imagination, Cognition, and Personality, 14*(3), 183–201.

Nolen-Hoeksema, S. (2001). Gender differences in depression. *Current Directions in Psychological Science, 10*, 173–176.

Nolen-Hoeksema, S. (2002). Gender differences in depression. In I. H. Gotlib & C. L. Hammen (Eds.), *Handbook of depression* (pp. 492–509). New York: Guilford Press.

Nolen-Hoeksema, S., Larson, J., & Grayson, C. (1999). Explaining the gender difference in depressive symptoms. *Journal of Personality and Social Psychology, 77*, 1061–1072.

Nolen-Hoeksema, S., Stice, E., Wade, E., & Bohon, C. (2007). Reciprocal relations between rumination and bulimic, substance abuse, and depressive symptoms in female adolescents. *Journal of Abnormal Psychology, 116*, 198–207.

Nolen-Hoeksema, S., Wisco, B. E., & Lyubomirsky, S. (2008). Rethinking rumination. *Perspectives on Psychological Science, 3*, 400–424.

Norcross, J. C., & Wampold, B. E. (2011). Evidence-based therapy relationships: Research conclusions and clinical practices. *Psychotherapy, 48*, 98–102.

Nordin, S., Razani, J. L., Markison, S., & Murphy, C. (2003). Age-associated increases in intensity discrimination for taste. *Experimental Aging Research, 29*, 371–381.

Norman, R. M., & Malla, A. K. (1993). Stressful life events and schizophrenia: II. Conceptual and methodological issues. *British Journal of Psychiatry, 162*, 166–174.

Norton, P. J., & Price, E. C. (2007). A meta-analytic review of adult cognitive-behavioral treatment outcome across the anxiety disorders. *Journal of Nervous and Mental Disease, 195*, 521–531.

Nosofsky, R. M., & Zaki, S. R. (2002). Exemplar and prototype models revisited: Response strategies, selective attention, and stimulus generalization. *Journal of Experimental Psychology: Learning, Memory, and Cognition, 28*, 924–940.

Nottelmann, E. D., Inoff-Germain, G., Susman, E. J., & Chrousos, G. P. (1990). Hormones and behavior at puberty. In J. Bancroft & J. M. Reinisch (Eds.), *Adolescence and puberty* (pp. 88–123). New York: Oxford University Press.

Nunes, J., Jean-Louis, G., Zizi, F., Vasimir, G. J., von Gizycki, H., Brown, C. D., et al. (2008). Sleep duration among black and white Americans: Results of the National Health Interview Survey. *Journal of the National Medical Association, 100*, 317–322.

Nyberg, L., Marklund, P., Persson, J., Cabeza, R., Forkstam, C., Petersson, K. M., et al. (2003). Common prefrontal activations during working memory, episodic memory, and semantic memory. *Neuropsychologia, 41*, 371–377.

Nyer, P. U., & Dellande, S. (2010). Public commitment as a motivator for weight loss. *Psychology and Marketing, 27*, 1–12.

O'Brien, A., Terry, D. J., & Jimmieson, N. L. (2008). Negative affectivity and responses to work stressors: An experimental study. *Anxiety, Stress, and Coping, 21*, 55–83.

O'Brien, M. (1996). Child-rearing difficulties reported by parents of infants and toddlers. *Journal of Pediatric Psychology, 21*, 433–446.

O'Brien, M. C., McCoy, T. P., Rhodes, S. D., Wagoner, A., & Wolfson, M. (2008). Caffeinated cocktails: Energy drink consumption, high-risk drinking, and alcohol-related consequences among college students. *Academic Emergency Medicine, 15*, 453–460.

O'Bryan, M., Fishbein, H. D., & Ritchey, P. N. (2004). Intergenerational transmission of prejudice, sex role stereotyping, and intolerance. *Adolescence, 39*, 407–426.

O'Connor, D. B., Jones, F., Conner, M., McMillan, B., & Ferguson, E. (2008). Effects of daily hassles and eating style on eating behavior. *Health Psychology, 27*, S20–S31.

O'Keefe, D. J., & Figge, M. (1997). A guilt-based explanation of the door-in-the-face influence strategy. *Human Communication Research, 24*, 64–81.

Oginska, H., & Pokorski, J. (2006). Fatigue and mood correlates of sleep length in three age-social groups: School children, students, and employees. *Chronobiology International, 23*, 1317–1328.

Olff, M., Langeland, W., Draijer, N., & Gersons, B. P. (2007). Gender differences in posttraumatic stress disorder. *Psychological Bulletin, 133*, 183–204.

Olfson, M., & Pincus, H. A. (1996). Outpatient mental health care in nonhospital settings: Distribution of patients across provider groups. *American Journal of Psychiatry, 153*, 1353–1356.

Omar, H., McElderry, D., & Zakharia, R. (2003). Educating adolescents about puberty: What are we missing? *International Journal of Adolescent Medicine and Health, 15*, 79–83.

Ondersma, S. J., & Walker, C. E. (1998). Elimination disorders. In T. H. Ollendick & M. Hersen (Eds.), *Handbook of child psychopathology* (pp. 355–380). New York: Plenum Press.

Oosthuizen, P. P., Emsley, R. A., Maritz, J. S., Turner, J. A., & Keyter, N. (2003). Incidence of tardive dyskinesia in first-episode psychosis patients treated with low-dose haloperidol. *Journal of Clinical Psychiatry, 64*, 1075–1080.

Oquendo, M. A., Hastings, R. S., Huang, Y. Y., Simpson, N., Ogden, R. T., Hu, X. Z., et al. (2007). Brain serotonin transporter binding in depressed patients with bipolar disorder using positron emission tomography. *Archives of General Psychiatry, 64*, 201–208.

Ornoy, A., & Ergaz, Z. (2010). Alcohol abuse in pregnant women: Effects on the fetus and newborn, mode of action and maternal treatment. *International Journal of Environmental Research and Public Health, 7*, 364–379.

Ornstein, S., & Isabella, L. (1990). Age vs. stage models of career attitudes of women: A partial replication and extension. *Journal of Vocational Behavior, 36*, 1–19.

Ortega, L. A., & Karch, D. (2010). Precipitating circumstances of suicide among women of reproductive age in 16 U.S. states, 2003–2007. *Journal of Women's Health, 19*, 5–7.

Ortony, A., & Turner, T. J. (1990). What's basic about basic emotions? *Psychological Review, 97*, 315–331.

Osborne, R. H., Sali, A., Aaronson, N. K., Elsworth, G. R., Mdzewski, B., & Sinclair, A. J. (2004). Immune function and adjustment style: Do they predict survival in breast cancer? *Psychooncology, 13*, 199–210.

Ostelo, R. W. J. G., van Tulder, M. W., Vlaeyen, J. W. S., Linton, S. J., Morley, S. J., & Assendelft, W. J. J. (2007). Behavioural treatment for chronic low-back pain. *Cochrane Database of Systematic Reviews*, Cochrane AN: CD002014.

Osterman, K., Bjorkqvist, K., Lagerspertz, K. M. J., Kaukiainen, A., Huesmann, L. R., & Fraczek, A. (1994). Peer and self-estimated aggression and victimization in 8-year-old children from five ethnic groups. *Aggressive Behavior, 20*, 411–428.

Ostroff, C., Kinicki, A. J., & Tamkins, M. M. (2003). Organizational culture and climate. In W. C. Borman, D. R. Ilgen, & R. J. Klimoski (Eds.), *Handbook of psychology: Industrial and organizational psychology* (Vol. 12, pp. 565–593). New York: Wiley.

Oteri, A., Salvo, F., Caputi, A. P., & Calapai, G. (2007). Intake of energy drinks in association with alcoholic beverages in a cohort of students of the School of Medicine of the University of Messina. *Alcoholism, Clinical, and Experimental Research, 31*, 1677–1680.

Overman, W. H., Bachevalier, J., Schuhmann, E., & Ryan, P. (1996). Cognitive gender differences in very young children parallel biologically based cognitive gender differences in monkeys. *Behavioral Neuroscience, 110*, 673–684.

Overmier, J. B. (2002). On learned helplessness. *Integrative Physiological and Behavioral Science, 37*, 4–8.

Overmier, J. B., & Seligman, M. E. (1967). Effects of inescapable shock upon subsequent escape and avoidance responding. *Journal of Comparative and Physiological Psychology, 63*, 28–33.

Ozturk, L., Pelin, Z., Karadeniz, D., Kaynak, H., Cakar, L., & Gozukirmizi, E. (1999). Effects of 48 hours sleep deprivation on human immune profile. *Sleep Research Online, 2*, 107–111.

Packer, D. J. (2009). Avoiding groupthink: Whereas weakly identified members remain silent, strongly identified members dissent about collective problems. *Psychological Science, 20*, 546–548.

Page, R. A., & Green, J. P. (2007). An update on age, hypnotic suggestibility, and gender: A brief report. *American Journal of Clinical Hypnosis, 49*, 283–287.

Painter, K. (1997, August 15–17). Doctors have prenatal test for 450 genetic diseases. *USA Today.*

Paivio, A. (1982). The empirical case for dual coding. In J. Yuille (Ed.), *Imagery, cognition, and memory* (pp. 307–332). Hillsdale, NJ: Erlbaum.

Paivio, A. (1986). *Mental representations: A dual coding approach.* New York: Oxford University Press.

Pallier, G. (March, 2003). Gender differences in the self-assessment of accuracy on cognitive tasks. *Sex Roles: A Journal of Research, 48*(5/6), 265–276.

Papadakis, A. A., Prince, R. P., Jones, N. P., & Strauman, T. J. (2006). Self-regulation, rumination, and vulnerability to depression in adolescent girls. *Development and Psychopathology, 18*, 815–829.

Parent, A. S., Teilmann, G., Juul, A., Skakkebaek, N. E., Toppari, J., & Bourguignon, J. P. (2003). The timing of normal puberty and the age limits of sexual precocity: Variations around the world, secular trends, and changes after migration. *Endocrine Reviews, 24*, 668–693.

Paris, J. (2002). Chronic suicidality among patients with borderline personality disorder. *Psychiatric Services, 53*, 738–742.

Parker, E. S., Birnbaum, I. M., & Noble, E. P. (1976). Alcohol and memory: Storage and state dependency. *Journal of Verbal Learning and Verbal Behavior, 15*, 691–702.

Parker, G. B., & Brotchie, H. L. (2004). From diathesis to dimorphism: The biology of gender differences in depression. *Journal of Nervous and Mental Disorders, 192*, 210–216.

Parker, G. B., & Brotchie, H. L. (2010). Gender differences in depression. *International Review of Psychiatry, 22*, 429–436.

Parker, G. B., Roy, K., Wilhelm, K., & Mitchell, P. (2001). Assessing the comparative effectiveness of antidepressant therapies: A prospective clinical practice study. *Journal of Clinical Psychiatry, 62*, 117–125.

Parker-Pope, T. (2002, August 27). A new reason for teens to avoid sex: It could be harmful to their health. *Wall Street Journal*, D1.

Parkes, C. M. (1986). *Bereavement: Studies of grief in adult life* (2nd ed.). London: Tavistock.

Parkes, C. M. (1991). Attachment, bonding, and psychiatric problems after bereavement in adult life. In C. M. Parkes, J. Stevenson-Hinde, & P. Marris (Eds.), *Attachment across the life cycle* (pp. 268–292). London: Tavistock/Routledge.

Parkin, A. J., & Leng, N. R. C. (1993). *Neuropsychology of the amnesic syndrome.* Hove, UK: Psychology Press.

Parnas, J., Cannon, T., Jacobsen, B., Schulsinger, H., Schulsinger, F., & Mednick, S. (1993). Lifetime DSM-III-R diagnostic outcomes in the offspring of schizophrenic mothers. *Archives of General Psychiatry, 50*, 707–714.

Parsons, T. D., & Rizzo, A. A. (2008). Affective outcomes of virtual reality exposure therapy for anxiety and specific phobias: A meta-analysis. *Journal of Behavior Therapy and Experimental Psychiatry, 39*, 250–261.

The Partnership Attitude Tracking Study (PATS). (2006). *The Partnership for a Drug-Free America: Teens in grades 7 through 12 2005.* Retrieved January 9, 2011, from http://www.drugfree.org/Files/Full_Teen_Report

Pascalis, O., & Kelly, D. J. (2009). The origins of face processing in humans: Phylogeny and ontogeny. *Perspectives on Psychological Science, 4*, 200–209.

Pasquet, P., Obeerti, B., El Ati, J., & Hladik, C. M. (2002). Relationships between threshold-based PROP sensitivity and food preferences of Tunisians. *Appetite, 39*, 167–173.

Patrick, M. E., & Maggs, J. L. (2009). Does drinking lead to sex? Daily alcohol-sex behaviors and expectancies among college students. *Psychology of Addictive Behaviors, 23*, 472–481.

Patterson, C. J. (2006). Children of lesbian and gay parents. *Current Directions in Psychological Science, 15*, 241–244.

Paul, G., Elam, B., & Verhulst, S. J. (2007). A longitudinal study of students' perceptions of using deep breathing meditation to reduce testing stresses. *Teaching and Learning in Medicine, 19*, 287–292.

Paulson, S. E., & Sputa, C. L. (1996). Patterns of parenting during adolescence: Perceptions of adolescents and parents. *Adolescence, 31*, 369–381.

Paulus, P. B. (Ed.). (1989). *Psychology of group influence* (2nd ed.). Hillsdale, NJ: Erlbaum.

Payne, J. D., & Kensinger, E. A. (2010). Sleep's role in the consolidation of emotional episodic memories. *Current Directions in Psychological Science, 19*, 290–295.

Payne, J. D., Stickgold, R., Swanberg, K., & Kensinger, E. A. (2008). Sleep preferentially enhances memory for emotional components of scenes. *Psychological Science, 8*, 781–788.

Payte, J. T. (1997). Methadone maintenance treatment: The first thirty years. *Journal of Psychoactive Drugs, 29*, 149–153.

Pearlin, L. I. (1993). The social contexts of stress. In L. Goldberger & S. Breznitz (Eds.), *Handbook of stress: Theoretical and clinical aspects* (2nd ed., pp. 303–315). New York: Free Press.

Pearsall, M. J., Christian, M. S., & Ellis, A. P. (2010). Motivating interdependent teams: Individual rewards, shared rewards, or something in between? *Journal of Applied Psychology, 95*, 183–191.

Pedersen, D. M., & Wheeler, J. (1983). The Müller-Lyer illusion among Navajos. *Journal of Social Psychology, 121*, 3–6.

Pedersen, P. B. (2002). Ethics, competence, and other professional issues in culture-centered counseling. In P. B. Pedersen, J. G. Draguns, W. J. Lonner, & J. E. Trimble (Eds.), *Counseling across cultures* (5th ed., pp. 3–28). Thousand Oaks, CA: Sage.

Peelen, M. V., Glaser, B., Vuilleumier, P., & Eliez, S. (2009). Differential development of selectivity for faces and bodies in the fusiform gyrus. *Developmental Science, 12*, F16–F25.

Pelleymounter, M. A., Cullen, M. J., Baker, M. B., Hecht, R., Winters, D., Boone, T., et al. (1995). Effects of the obese gene product on body weight regulation in ob/ob mice. *Science, 269*, 540–543.

Penley, J. A., Tomaka, J., & Wiebe, J. S. (2002). The association of coping to physical and psychological health outcomes: A meta-analytic review. *Journal of Behavioral Medicine, 25*, 551–603.

Pepperberg, I. M. (1991). A communicative approach to animal cognition: A study of conceptual abilities of an African gray parrot. In C. A. Ristau (Ed.), *Cognitive ethology* (pp. 153–186). Hillsdale, NJ: Erlbaum.

Pepperberg, I. M. (1993). Cognition and communication in an African gray parrot (*Psittacus erithacus*): Studies on a nonhuman, nonprimate, nonmammilian, subject. In H. L. Roitblat, L. M. Herman, & P. E. Nachtigall (Eds.), *Language and communication: Comparative perspectives.* Hillsdale, NJ: Erlbaum.

Pepperberg, I. M. (1999). Rethinking syntax: A commentary on E. Kako's "Elements of syntax in the systems of three language-trained animals." *Animal Learning and Behavior, 27*, 15–17.

Perez, M., Joiner, T. E., Jr., & Lewisohn, P. M. (2004). Is major depressive disorder or dysthymia more strongly associated with bulimia nervosa? *International Journal of Eating Disorders, 36*, 55–61.

Perina, K. (2002). Hot on the trail of flashbulb memory. *Psychology Today, 35*, 15–16.

Perlini, A. H., Bertolissi, S., & Lind, D. L. (1999). The effects of women's age and physical appearance on evaluations of attractiveness and social desirability. *Journal of Social Psychology, 139*, 343–344.

Perlis, R. H., Brown, E., Baker, R. W., & Nierenberg, A. A. (2006). Clinical features of bipolar depression versus major depressive disorder in large multi-center trials. *American Journal of Psychiatry, 163*, 225–231.

Perry, C. (1997). Admissibility and per se exclusion of hypnotically elicited recall in American courts of law. *International Journal of Clinical and Experimental Hypnosis, 45*, 266–279.

Perry, E., Walker, M., Grace, J., & Perry, R. (1999). Acetylcholine in mind: A neurotransmitter correlate of consciousness? *Trends in Neurosciences, 22*, 273–280.

Perry, W. G., Jr. (1981). Cognitive and ethical growth. In A. Chickering (Ed.), *The modern American college* (pp.76–116). San Francisco: Jossey-Bass.

Person, E. S. (1990). The influence of values in psychoanalysis: The case of female psychology. In C. Zanardi (Ed.), *Essential papers in psychoanalysis* (pp. 305–325). New York: University Press.

Person, E. S. (2005). As the wheel turns: A centennial reflection on Freud's *Three Essays on the Theory of Sexuality. Journal of the American Psychoanalytic Association, 53*, 1257–1282.

Pesant, N., & Zadra, A. (2004). Working with dreams in therapy: What do we know and what should we do? *Clinical Psychology Review, 24*, 489–512.

Pesant, N., & Zadra, A. (2006). Dream content and psychological well-being: A longitudinal study of the continuity hypothesis. *Journal of Clinical Psychology, 62*, 111–121.

Peterson, B. E., & Duncan, L. E. (2007). Midlife women's generativity and authoritarianism: Marriage, motherhood, and 10 years of aging. *Psychology and Aging, 22*, 411–419.

Peterson, C. (2000). The future of optimism. *American Psychologist, 55*, 44–55.

Peterson, C., & Bossio, L. M. (2001). Optimism and physical well-being. In E. C. Chang (Ed.), *Optimism and pessimism: Implications for theory, research, and practice* (pp. 127–146). Washington, DC: American Psychological Association.

Peterson, C., Maier, S. F., & Seligman, M. E. P. (1993). *Learned helplessness: A theory for the age of personal control.* New York: Oxford University Press.

Peterson, C., & Seligman, M. E. (1984). Causal explanations as a risk factor for depression: Theory and evidence. *Psychological Review, 91*, 347–374.

Peterson, L. R., & Peterson, M. J. (1959). Short-term retention of individual verbal items. *Journal of Experimental Psychology, 58*, 193–198.

Petitto, L. (2009). New discoveries from the bilingual brain and mind across the lifespan: Implications for education. *Mind, Brain, and Education, 3*, 185–197.

Petrides, K. V., Furnham, A., & Martin, G. N. (2004). Estimates of emotional and psychometric intelligence: Evidence for gender-based stereotypes. *Journal of Social Psychology, 144*, 149–162.

Petry, N. M., Tedford, J., Austin, M., Nich, C., Carroll, K. M., & Rounsaville, B. J. (2004). Prize reinforcement contingency management for treating cocaine users: How low can we go, and with whom? *Addiction, 99*, 349–360.

Pettigrew, T. F. & Tropp, L. R. (2006). A meta-analytic test of intergroup contact theory. *Journal of Personality and Social Psychology, 90*, 751–783.

Petty, R. E., & Briñol, P. (2008). Persuasion: From single to multiple to metacognitive processes. *Perspectives on Psychological Science, 3*, 137–147.

Petty, R. E., & Cacioppo, J. T. (1986). *Communication and persuasion: Central and peripheral routes to attitude change.* New York: Springer-Verlag.

Petty, R. E., Cacioppo, J. T., & Goldman, R. (1981). Personal involvement as a determinant of argument-based persuasion. *Journal of Personality and Social Psychology, 41*, 847–855.

Petty, R. E., Fabrigar, L. R., & Wegener, D. T. (2003). Emotional factors in attitudes and persuasion. In R. J. Davidson, K. R. Scherer, & H. H. Goldsmith (Eds.), *Handbook of affective sciences* (pp. 752–772). Oxford, UK: Oxford University Press.

Pew Research Center. (2010). *Millennials: A portrait of generation next.* Retrieved March 16, 2011, from http://pewsocialtrends.org/files/2010/10/millennials-confident-connected-open-to-change.pdf

Pfaus, J. G. (2009). Pathways of sexual desire. *Journal of Sexual Medicine, 6*, 1506–1533.

Phares, E. J. (1991). *Introduction to personality* (3rd ed.). New York: HarperCollins.

Phelan, S., Nallari, M., Daroch, F. E., & Wing, R. R. (2009). What do physicians recommend to their overweight and obese patients? *Journal of the American Board of Family Medicine, 22*, 115–122.

Phillips, M. R., Li, X., & Zhang, Y. (2002). Suicide rates in China, 1995–99. *Lancet, 359*, 835–840.

Piaget, J. (1929). *The child's conception of the world.* New York: Harcourt Brace.

Piaget, J. (1952). *The origins of intelligence in children.* New York: International Universities Press.

Pidoplichko, V. I., DeBiasi, M., Williams, J. T., & Dani, J. A. (1997). Nicotine activates and desensitizes midbrain dopamine neurons. *Nature, 390*, 401–404.

Pierce, J. P. (2005). Influence of movie stars on the initiation of adolescent smoking. *Pediatric Dentistry, 27*, 149.

Pike, K. M., Devlin, M. J., & Loeb, C. (2004). Cognitive-behavioral therapy in the treatment of anorexia nervosa, and binge eating disorder. In J. K. Thompson (Ed.), *Handbook of eating disorders and obesity* (pp.130–162). New York: Wiley.

Pillar, G., & Lavie, P. (2011). Obstructive sleep apnea: Diagnosis, risk factors, and pathophysiology. *Handbook of Clinical Neurology, 98*, 383–399.

Pillemer, D. B., Wink, P., DiDonato, T. E., & Sanborn, R. L. (2003). Gender differences in autobiographical memory styles of older adults. *Memory, 11,* 525–532.

Pinedo, V. A. (2010). *Swinging '60s had nothing on the '90s—Sex study.* Retrieved April 22, 2011, from http://www.reuters.com/assests/print?aid=USTRE62F23J20100316

Pinker, S. (1994). *The language instinct: How the mind creates language.* New York: Morrow.

Pinnell, C. M., & Covino, N. A. (2000). Empirical findings on the use of hypnosis in medicine: A critical review. *International Journal of Clinical and Experimental Hypnosis, 48,* 170–194.

Piper, A., & Merskey, H. (2004). The persistence of folly: A critical examination of dissociative identity disorder: Part I. The excesses of an improbable concept. *Canadian Journal of Psychiatry, 49,* 592–600.

Pirrallo, R. G., Loomis, C. C., Levine, R., & Woodson, B. T. (in press). The prevalence of sleep problems in emergency medical technicians. *Sleep & Breathing.* doi:10.1007/s11325-010-0467-8

Plazzi, B., Corsini, R., Provini, R., Pierangeli, G., Martinelli, P., Montagna, P., et al. (1997). REM sleep behavior disorders in multiple system atrophy. *Neurology, 48,* 1094–1097.

Pleis, J. R., & Lethbridge-Ceiku, M. (2007). Summary health statistics for U.S. adults: National health interview survey, 2006. *Vital Health Statistics, 10,* No. 235.

Plomin, R., DeFries, J. C., McClearn, G. E., & Rutter, M. (2008). *Behavioral genetics* (5th ed.). New York: Freeman.

Plutchik, R. (1984). Emotions: A general psychoevolutionary theory. In K. R. Scherer & P. Ekman (Eds.), *Approaches to emotion* (pp. 197–219). Hillsdale, NJ: Erlbaum.

Poelman, D., & Smet, P. F. (2010). Photometry in the dark: Time dependent visibility of low intensity light sources. *Optics Express, 18,* 26293–26299.

Pogue-Geile, M. F., & Yokley, J. L. (2010). Current research on the genetic contributors to schizophrenia. *Current Directions in Psychological Science, 19,* 214–219.

Pollack, W. (1998). Mourning, melancholia, and masculinity: Recognizing and treating depression in men. In W. Pollack & R. Levant (Eds.), *New psychotherapy for men* (pp. 147–166). New York: Wiley.

Pollard, R. J., Coyle, J. P., Gilbert, R. L., & Beck, J. E. (2007). Intraoperative awareness in a regional medical system: A review of 3 years' data. *Anesthesiology, 106,* 269–274.

Polmin, R. (1994). The Emanuel Miller Memorial Lecture 1993: Genetic research and identification of environmental influences. *Journal of Child Psychology and Psychiatry, 35,* 817–834.

Polotsky, V. Y., & O'Donnell, C. P. (2007). Genomics of sleep-disordered breathing. *Proceedings of the American Thoracic Society, 4,* 121–126.

Pomeroy, A. (2005). 50 best small and medium places to work: Money talks. *HR Magazine, 50*(7), 44–65.

Pomeroy, W. (1965, May). Why we tolerate lesbians. *Sexology,* 652–654.

Ponniah, K., & Hollon, S. D. (2009). Empirically supported psychological treatments for adult acute stress disorder and posttraumatic stress disorder: A review. *Depression and Anxiety, 26,* 1086–1109.

Poore, A. G., Gagne, F., Barlow, K. M., Lydon, J. E., Taylor, D. M., & Wright, S. C. (2002). Contact and the personal/group discrimination discrepancy in an Inuit community. *Journal of Psychology, 136,* 371–382.

Pope, H. D., Jr., Oliva, P. S., Hudson, J. I., Bodkin, J. A., & Gruber, A. J. (1999). Attitudes toward DSM-IV dissociative disorders diagnoses among board-certified American psychiatrists. *American Journal of Psychiatry, 156,* 321–323.

Pope, H. G., & Yurgelun-Todd, D. (1996). The residual cognitive effects of heavy marijuana use in college students. *Journal of the American Medical Association, 275*(7), 521–527.

Porkka-Heiskanen, T., Strecker, R. E., Thakkar, M., Bjorkum, A. A., Greene, R. W., & McCarley, R. W. (1997). Adenosine: A mediator of the sleep-inducing effects of prolonged wakefulness. *Science, 276,* 1265–1268.

Porte, H. S., & Hobson, J. A. (1996). Physical motion in dreams: One measure of three theories. *Journal of Abnormal Psychology, 105,* 329–335.

Porter, J. N., Collins, P. F., Muetzel, R. L., Lim, K. O., & Luciana, M. (2011). Associations between cortical thickness and verbal fluency in childhood, adolescence, and young adulthood. *NeuroImage, 55,* 1865–1877.

Porter, R. H. (1999). Olfaction and human kin recognition. *Genetica, 104,* 259–263.

Post, R., Frye, M., Denicoff, K. Leverich, G., Kimbrell, T., & Dunn, R. (1998). Beyond lithium in the treatment of bipolar illness. *Neuropsychopharmacology, 19,* 206–219.

Potter, W. J., Warren, R., Vaughan, M., Howley, K., Land, A., & Hagemeyer, J. (1997). Antisocial acts in reality programming on television. *Journal of Broadcasting and Electronic Media, 41,* 69–89.

Powell, L. H., Calvin, J. E., III, & Calvin, J. E., Jr. (2007). Effective obesity treatments. *American Psychologist, 62,* 234–246.

Powell, L. H., Shahabi, L., & Thoresen, C. E. (2003). Religion and spirituality: Linkages to physical health. *American Psychologist, 58,* 36–52.

Powell, T. J., Silk, K. R., & Albeck, J. H. (2000). Psychiatrists' referrals to self-help groups for people with mood disorders. *Psychiatric Services, 51,* 809–811.

Pratkanis, A. R. (1992). The cargo-cult science of subliminal persuasion. *The Skeptical Inquirer, 16,* 260–272.

Pratkanis, A. R., Epley, N., Savitsky, K., & Kachelski, R. A. (2007). Issue 12: Is subliminal persuasion a myth? In J. A. Nier (Ed.), *Taking sides: Clashing views in social psychology* (2nd ed., pp. 230–255). New York: McGraw-Hill.

Prentice, A. M. (2009). Obesity in emerging nations: Evolutionary origins and the impact of rapid nutrition transition. Nestle Nutrition Workshop Series. *Paediatric Programme, 63,* 47–54.

Prescott, C. A., Hewitt, J. K., Truett, K. R., Heath, A. C., Neale, M. C., & Eaves, L. J. (1994). Genetic and environmental influences on alcohol-related problems in a volunteer sample of older twins. *Journal of Studies on Alcohol, 55,* 184–202.

Pressman, S. D., Cohen, S., Miller, G. E., Barkin, A., Rabin, B. S., & Treanor, J. J. (2005). Loneliness, social network size, and immune response to influenza vaccination in college freshman. *Health Psychology, 24,* 297–306.

Preston, J. A. (2005, June). *Delaying a life: The consequences of career development for the Radcliffe class of 1950.* Paper presented at the IWPR's Eighth International Women's Policy Research Conference.

Price, C. A., & Balaswamy, S. (2009). Beyond health and wealth: Predictors of women's retirement satisfaction. *International Journal of Aging and Human Development, 68,* 195–214.

Price, W. F., & Crapo, R. H. (2002). *Cross-cultural perspectives in introductory psychology.* Belmont, CA: Wadsworth.

Pritchard, M. E., Wilson, G. S., & Yamnitz, B. (2007). What predicts adjustment among college students? A longitudinal panel study. *Journal of American College Health, 56,* 15–21.

Prosser, I. B. (1933). *Non-academic development of Negro children in mixed and segregated schools.* Unpublished Doctoral Dissertation, University of Cincinnati.

Proudfoot, J. G. (2004). Computer-based treatment for anxiety and depression: Is it feasible? Is it effective? *Neuroscience Biobehavior Review, 28,* 353–363.

Prutkin, J., Duffy, V. B., Etter, L., Fast, K., Gardner, E., Lucchina, L. A., et al. (2000). Genetic variation and inferences about perceived taste intensity in mice and men. *Physiology and Behavior, 69,* 161–173.

Pryor, J. H., Hurtado, S., DeAngelo, L., PaluckiBlake, L., & Tran, S. (2010). *The American freshman: National norms fall 2010.* Los Angeles: Higher Education Research Institute, UCLA.

Ptacek, J. T., Smith, R. E., & Dodge, K. L. (1994). Gender differences in coping with stress: When stressor and appraisals do not differ. *Personality & Social Psychology Bulletin, 20,* 421–430.

Purves, D., Augustine, G. J., Fitzpatrick, D., Katz, L., LaMantia, A. S., & McNamara, J. O. (1997). *Neuroscience.* Sunderland, MA: Sinauer.

Putnam, F. W. (2000). Dissociative disorders. In A. Sameroff, M. Lewis, & S. Miller (Eds.), *Handbook of developmental psychopathology* (2nd ed., pp. 739–754). New York: Kluwer Academic/Plenum.

Putnam, F. W., Guroff, J. J., Silberman, E. K., & Barban, L. (1986). The clinical phenomenology of multiple personality disorder: Review of 100 recent cases. *Journal of Clinical Psychiatry, 47,* 285–293.

Pyke, K., & Johnson, D. (2003). Asian American women and racialized femininities: "Doing" gender across cultural worlds. *Gender and Society, 17,* 33–53.

Qiu, J., Li, H., Jou, J., Liu, J., Luo, Y., Feng, T., et al. (2010). Neural correlates of the "aha" experiences: Evidence from an fMRI study of insight problem solving. *Cortex: A Journal Devoted to the Study of the Nervous System and Behavior, 46,* 397–403.

Quattrone, G. A., & Jones, E. E. (1980). The perception of variability within ingroups and outgroups: Implications for the law of small number. *Journal of Personality and Social Psychology, 38,* 141–152.

Querido, J. G., Warner, T. D., & Eyberg, S. M. (2002). Parenting styles and child behavior in African American families of preschool children. *Journal of Clinical Child and Adolescent Psychology, 31,* 272–277.

Quickfall, J., & Crockford, D. (2006). Brain neuroimaging in cannabis use: A review. *Journal of Neuropsychiatry and Clinical Neurosciences, 18,* 318–332.

Quinn, P. C., & Tanaka, J. W. (2007). Early development of perceptual expertise: Within-basic-level categorization experience facilitates the formation of subordinate-level category representations in 6- to 7-month-old infants. *Memory & Cognition, 35,* 1422–1431.

Rabkin, S. W., Boyko, E., Shane, F., & Kaufert, J. (1984). A randomized trial comparing smoking cessation programs utilizing behavior modification, health education, or hypnosis. *Addictive Behaviors, 9,* 157–173.

Racsmany, M., Conway, M. A., & Demeter, G. (2010). Consolidation of episodic memories during sleep: Long-term effects of retrieval practice. *Psychological Science, 21,* 80–85.

Rahman, Q. (2005). The neurodevelopment of human sexual orientation. *Neuroscience and Biobehavioral Reviews, 29,* 1057–1066.

Raine, A. (1997). Antisocial behavior and psychophysiology: A biological perspective. In D. M. Stoff, J. Breiling, & J. D. Maser (Eds.), *Handbook of antisocial personality disorder* (pp. 289–304). New York: Wiley.

Raine, A. (2008). From genes to brain to antisocial behavior. *Current Directions in Psychological Science, 17,* 323–328.

Raine, A., Lencz, T., Bihrle, S., LaCasse, L., & Colletti, P. (2000). Reduced prefrontal gray matter volume and reduced autonomic activity in antisocial personality disorder. *Archives of General Psychiatry, 57,* 119–127.

Rainville, P., Duncan, G. H., Price, D. D., Carrier, B., & Bushnell, M. C. (1997). Pain affect encoded in human anterior cingulate but not somatosensory cortex. *Science, 277,* 968–971.

Rainville, P., & Price, D. D. (2003). Hypnosis phenomenology and the neurobiology of consciousness. *International Journal of Clinical and Experimental Hypnosis, 51,* 105–129.

Rakic, P. (1991). Plasticity of cortical development. In S. E. Brauth, W. S. Hall, & R. J. Dooling (Eds.), *Plasticity of Development* (pp. 127–161). Cambridge, MA: Bradford/MIT Press.

Ramsey-Rennels, J. L., & Langlois, J. H. (2006). Infants' differential processing of female and male faces. *Current Directions in Psychological Science, 15,* 59–62.

Randall, S., Johanson, C. E., Tancer, M., & Roehrs, T. (2009). Effects of acute 3, 4 methylenedioxymethamphetamine on sleep and daytime sleepiness in MDMA users: A preliminary study. *Sleep, 32,* 1513–1519.

Rando, T. A. (1995). Grief and mourning: Accommodating to loss. In H. Wass & R. A. Neimeyer (Eds.), *Dying: Facing the facts* (3rd ed., pp. 211–241). Washington DC: Taylor & Francis.

Ranganathan, M., & D'Souza, D. C. (2006). The acute effects of cannabinoids on memory in humans: A review. *Psychopharmacology* (Berlin), *188,* 425–444.

Rank, M. R. (2000). Poverty and economic hardship in families. In D. H. Demo, K. R. Allen, & M. A. Fine (Eds.), *Handbook of family diversity* (pp. 293–315). New York: Oxford University Press.

Rao, H., Hillihan, S. J., Wang, J., Korczykowski, M., Sankoorikal, G. M., Kaercher, K. A., et al. (2007). Genetic variation in serotonin transporter alters resting brain function in healthy individuals. *Biological Psychiatry, 62,* 600–606.

Rapoport, J. L., Addington, A. M., Frangou, S., & Psych, M. R. (2005). The neurodevelopmental model of schizophrenia: Update 2005. *Molecular Psychiatry, 10*, 434–449.

Rappaport, V. J. (2008). Prenatal diagnosis and genetic screening: Integration into prenatal care. *Obstetrics and Gynecology Clinics of North America, 35*, 435–458.

Rasch, B., & Born, J. (2008). Reactivation and consolidation of memory during sleep. *Current Directions in Psychological Science, 17*, 188–192.

Rasmussen, C., Soleimani, M., & Pei, J. (2011). Executive functioning and working memory deficits on the CANTAB among children with prenatal alcohol exposure. *Journal of Population Therapeutics and Clinical Pharmacology, 18*, e44–e53.

Rauch, S. L., Savage, C. R., Alpert, N. M., Dougherty, D., Kendrick, A., Curran, T., et al. (1997). Probing striatal function in obsessive-compulsive disorder: A PET study of implicit sequence learning. *Journal of Neuropsychiatry and Clinical Neuroscience, 9*, 568–573.

Rauch, S. L., Shin, L. M., & Phelps, E. A. (2006). Neurocircuitry models of posttraumatic stress disorder and extinction: Human neuroimaging research—past, present, and future. *Biological Psychiatry, 60*, 376–382.

Rauchs, G., Bertran, F., Guillery-Girard, B., Desgranges, B., Kerrouche, N., Denise, P., et al. (2004). Consolidation of strictly episodic memories mainly requires rapid eye movement sleep. *Sleep, 27*, 395–401.

Ravenna, H., Jones, C., & Kwan, V. S. (2002). Personality change over 40 years of adulthood: Hierarchical linear modeling analyses of two longitudinal samples. *Journal of Personality and Social Psychology, 83*, 752–766.

Ray, R. D., Wilhelm, F. H., & Gross, J. J. (2008). All in the mind's eye? Anger rumination and reappraisal. *Journal of Personality and Social Psychology, 94*, 133–145.

Raz, A. (2005). Attention and hypnosis: Neural substrates and genetic associations of two converging processes. *International Journal of Clinical and Experimental Hypnosis, 53*, 237–258.

Raz, A., Fan, J., & Posner, M. I. (2006). Neuroimaging and genetic associations of attentional and hypnotic processes. *Journal of Physiology* (Paris), *99*, 483–491.

Raz, N., & Kennedy, K. M. (2009). A systems approach to age-related change: Neuroanatomical changes, their modifiers, and cognitive correlates. In W. Jagust & M. D'Esposito (Eds.), *Imaging the aging brain* (pp. 43–70). New York: Oxford University Press.

Raz, N., Rodrigue, K. M., Kennedy, K. M., & Acker, J. D. (2007). Vascular health and longitudinal changes in brain and cognition in middle-aged and older adults. *Neuropsychology, 21*, 149–157.

Read, C. N., & Greenberg, B. D. (2009). Psychiatric neurosurgery 2009: Review and perspective. *Seminars in Neurology, 29*, 256–265.

Read, S., & Grundy, E. (2011). Mental health among older married couples: The role of gender and family life. *Social Psychiatry and Psychiatric Epidemiology, 46*, 331-341.

Reder, L. M., Park, H., & Kieffaber, P. D. (2009). Memory systems do not divide on consciousness: Reinterpreting memory in terms of activation and binding. *Psychological Bulletin, 135*, 23–49.

Reece, M., Herbenick, D., Schick, V., Sanders, S., Dodge, B., & Fortenberry, J. D. (2010). Condom use rates in a national probability sample of males and females ages 14 to 94 in the United States. *Journal of Sexual Medicine, 7* (Suppl. 5), 266–276.

Rehder, B., & Hoffman, A. B. (2005). Thirty-something categorization results explained: Selective attention, eyetracking, and models of category learning. *Journal of Experimental Psychology: Learning, Memory, and Cognition, 31*, 811–829.

Reid, P., & Bing, V. (2000). Sexual roles of girls and women: An ethnocultural lifespan perspective. In C. Travis & J. White (Eds.), *Sexuality, society, and feminism* (pp. 141–166). Washington, DC: American Psychological Association.

Reinisch, J. M. (1991). *The Kinsey Institute new report on sex: What you must know to be sexually literate.* New York: St. Martin's Press.

Reisenzein, R. (1983). The Schachter theory of emotion: Two decades later. *Psychological Bulletin, 94*, 239–264.

Reiss, D. (2005). The interplay between genotypes and family relationships: Reframing concepts of development and prevention. *Current Directions in Psychological Science, 14*, 139–143.

Reite, M., Sheeder, J., Teale, P., Richardson, D., Adams, M., & Simon, J. (1995). MEG based brain laterality: Sex differences in normal adults. *Neuropsychologia, 33*, 1607–1616.

Reitzes, D. C., & Mutran, E. J. (2004). The transition to retirement: Stages and factors that influence retirement adjustment. *International Journal of Aging and Human Development, 59*, 63–84.

Repetti, R., Wang, S., & Saxbe, D. (2009). Bringing it all back home: How outside stressors shape families' everyday lives. *Current Directions in Psychological Science, 18*, 106–111.

Repovs, G., & Baddeley, A. (2006). The multi-component model of working memory: Explorations in experimental cognitive psychology. *Neuroscience, 139*, 5–21.

Rescorla, R. A. (1967). Pavlovian conditioning and its proper control procedures. *Psychological Review, 74*, 71–80.

Resick, P. A., Nishith, P., Weaver, T. L., Astin, M. C., & Feuer, C. A. (2002). A comparison of cognitive-processing therapy with prolonged exposure and a waiting condition for the treatment of chronic posttraumatic stress disorder in female rape victims. *Journal of Consulting and Clinical Psychology, 70*, 867–879.

Resta, O., Foschino-Barbaro, M. P., Legari, G., Talamo, S., Bonfitto, P., Palumbo, A., et al. (2001). Sleep-related breathing disorders, loud snoring and excessive daytime sleepiness in obese subjects. *International Journal of Obesity and Related Metabolic Disorders, 25*, 669–675.

Reyna, V. F., & Farley, F. (2006). Risk and rationality in adolescent decision making. *Psychological Science in the Public Interest, 7*, 1–44.

Reyngoudt, H., Paemeleire, K., Dierickx, A., Descamps, B., Vandemaele, P., De Deene, Y., et al. (2011). Does visual cortex lactate increase following photic stimulation in migraine without aura patients? A functional (1)H-MRS study. *Journal of Headache Pain.* doi:10.1007/s10194-011-0295-7

Reynolds, C. R., & Brown, R. T. (Eds.). (1984). *Perspectives on bias in mental testing.* New York: Plenum Press.

Reynolds, J. R., & Burge, S. W. (2008). Educational expectations and the rise in women's post-secondary attainments. *Social Science Research, 37*, 485–499.

Reynolds, P., Hurley, S., Torres, M., Jackson, J., Boyd, P., & Chen, V.W. (2000). Use of coping strategies and breast cancer survival: Results from the Black/White Cancer Survival Study. *American Journal of Epidemiology, 152*, 940–949.

Rhodes, N., & Wood, W. (1992). Self-esteem and intelligence affect influencability: The mediating role of message reception. *Psychological Bulletin, 111*, 156–171.

Ricca, V., Castellini, G., Mannucci, E., Lo Sauro, C., Ravaldi, C., Rotella, C. M., et al. (2010). Comparison of individual and group cognitive behavioral therapy for binge eating disorder: A randomized, three-year follow-up study. *Appetite, 55*, 656–665.

Rice, F. P. (1992). *Intimate relationships, marriages, and families.* Mountain View, CA: Mayfield.

Rice, V. H. (Ed.). (2000). *Handbook of stress, coping and health.* Thousand Oaks, CA: Sage.

Richards, J., Klein, B., & Carlbring, P. (2003). Internet-based treatment for panic disorder. *Cognitive Behaviour Therapy, 32*, 125–135.

Richardson, G. A., Goldschmidt, L., Leech, S., & Willford, J. (2011). Prenatal cocaine exposure: Effects on mother- and teacher-rated behavior problems and growth in school-age children. *Neurotoxicology and Teratology, 33*, 69–77.

Rickels, K., DeMartinis, N., Garcia-Espana, F., Greenblatt, D. J., Mandos, L.A., & Rynn, M. (2000). Imipramine and buspirone in treatment of patients with generalized anxiety disorder who are discontinuing long-term benzodiazepine therapy. *American Journal of Psychiatry, 157*, 1973–1979.

Rieger, G., Gygax, L., & Bailey, J. M. (2008). Sexual orientation and childhood gender non-conformity: Evidence from home videos. *Developmental Psychology, 44*, 46–58.

Riemann, D., & Perlis, M. L. (2009). The treatments of chronic insomnia: A review of benzodiazepine receptor agonists and psychological and behavioral therapies. *Sleep Medicine Reviews, 13*, 205–214.

Rinsky, J. R., & Henshaw, S. P. (2011). Linkages between childhood executive functioning and adolescent social functioning and psychopathology in girls with ADHD. *Child Neuropsychology, 4*, 1–23.

Rishi, M. A., Shetty, M., Wolff, A., Amoateng-Adjepong, Y., & Manthous, C. A. (2010). Atypical antipsychotic medications are independently associated with severe obstructive sleep apnea. *Clinical Neuropharmacology, 33*, 109–113.

Riskind, J. H., Williams, N. L., Gessner, T. L., Chrosniak, L. D., & Cortina, J. M. (2000). The looming maladaptive style: Anxiety, danger, and schematic processing. *Journal of Personality and Social Psychology, 79*, 837–852.

Rivers, P. C. (1994). *Alcohol and human behavior.* Englewood Cliffs, NJ: Wiley.

Roberts, B. W., Caspi, A., & Moffitt, T. E. (2001). The kids are alright: Growth and stability in personality development from adolescence to adulthood. *Journal of Personality and Social Psychology, 81*, 670–683.

Roberts, B. W., & DelVecchio, W. F. (2000). The rank-order consistency of personality traits from childhood to old age: A quantitative review of longitudinal studies. *Psychological Bulletin, 126*, 3–25.

Roberts, B. W., Edmonds, G., & Grijalva, E. (2010). It is Developmental Me, not Generation Me: Developmental changes are more important than generational changes in narcissism: Commentary on Trzesniewski & Donnellan (2010). *Perspectives on Psychological Science, 5*, 97–102.

Roberts, B. W., Kuncel, N. R., Shiner, R., Caspi, A., & Goldberg, L. R. (2007). The power of personality: The comparative validity of personality traits, socioeconomic status, and cognitive ability for predicting important life outcomes. *Perspectives on Psychological Science, 2*, 313–345.

Roberts, B. W., & Mroczek, D. (2008). Personality trait change in adulthood. *Current Directions in Psychological Science, 17*, 31–35.

Roberts, B. W., Walton, K. E., & Viechtbauer, W. (2006). Patterns of mean-level change in personality traits across the life course: A meta-analysis of longitudinal studies. *Psychological Bulletin, 132*, 1–25.

Roberts, R. D., Schulze, R., O'Brien, K., MacCann, C., Reid, J., & Maul, A. (2006). Exploring the validity of the Mayer-Salovey-Caruso emotional intelligence test (MSCEIT) with established emotions measures. *Emotion, 6*, 663–669.

Roberts, R. E., Roberts, C. R., & Chan, W. (2006). Ethnic differences in symptoms of insomnia among adolescents. *Sleep, 29*, 359–365.

Roberts, S. M. (1995). Applicability of the goodness-of-fit hypothesis to coping with daily hassles. *Psychological Reports, 77*(3, Pt. 1), 943–954.

Robins, L. N., & Regier, D. A. (Eds.). (1991). *Psychiatric disorders in America: The Epidemiologic Catchment Area Study.* New York: Free Press.

Robins, R. W., Fraley, R. C., Roberts, B. W., & Trzesniewski, K. H. (2001). A longitudinal study of personality change in young adulthood. *Journal of Personality, 69*, 617–640.

Robinson, L. A., Berman, J. S., & Neimeyer, R. A. (1990). Psychotherapy for the treatment of depression: A comprehensive review of controlled outcome research. *Psychological Bulletin, 109*, 30–49.

Robinson, N. M., Abbott, R. D., Berninger, V. W., & Busse, J. (1996). The structure of abilities in math-precocious young children: Gender similarities and differences. *Journal of Educational Psychology, 88*, 341–352.

Robles, T. F., Glaser, R., Kiecolt-Glaser, J. K. (2005). Out of balance: A new look at chronic stress, depression, and immunity. *Current Directions in Psychological Science, 14*, 111–115.

Robles, T. F., & Kiecolt-Glaser, J. K. (2003). The physiology of marriage: Pathways to health. *Physiology and Behavior, 79*, 409–416.

Rockafellow, B. D., & Saules, K. K. (2006). Substance use by college students: The role of intrinsic versus extrinsic motivation for athletic involvement. *Psychology of Addictive Behavior, 20*, 279–287.

Rodenburg, R., Benjamin, A., de Roos, C., Meijer, A. M., & Stams, G. J. (2009). Efficacy of EMDR in children: A meta-analysis. *Clinical Psychology Review, 29*, 599–606.

Rogers, C. R. (1942). *Counseling and psychotherapy.* Boston: Houghton Mifflin.

Rogers, C. R. (1951). *Client-centered therapy: Its current practice, implications, and theory.* Boston: Houghton Mifflin

Rogers, C. R. (1961). *On becoming a person.* Boston: Houghton Mifflin.

Rogers, C. R. (1970). *Carl Rogers on encounter groups.* New York: Harper & Row.

Rogers, C. R. (1980). *A way of being.* Boston: Houghton Mifflin.

Rogers, C. R. (1986). Client-centered therapy. In I. L. Kutash & A. Wolf (Eds.), *Psychotherapists' casebook* (pp. 197–208). San Francisco: Jossey-Bass.

Rogers, M. A., Yamasue, H., Abe, O., Yamada, H., Ohtani, T., Iwanami, A., et al. (2009). Smaller amygdala volume and reduced anterior cingulated gray matter density associated with history of post-traumatic stress disorder. *Psychiatry Research, 174,* 210–216.

Rogers, N. L., Szuba, M. P., Staab, J. P., Evans, D. L., & Dinges, D. F. (2001). Neuroimmunologic aspects of sleep and sleep loss. *Seminars in Clinical Neuropsychiatry, 6,* 295–307.

Rogers, T. B. (1995). *The psychological testing enterprise: An introduction.* Pacific Grove, CA: Brooks/Cole.

Rogoff, B., & Chavajah, P. (1995). What's become of research on the cultural basis of cognitive development? *American Psychologist, 50,* 859–873.

Rohan, M. J., & Zanna, M. P. (1996). Value transmission in families. In C. Seligman & J. M. Olson (Eds.), *The psychology of values: The Ontario symposium* (Vol. 8, pp. 253–276). Mahwah, NJ: Erlbaum.

Rohrbach, L. A., Grana, R., Vernberg, E., Sussman, S., & Sun, P. (2009). Impact of Hurricane Rita on adolescent substance abuse. *Psychiatry, 72,* 222–237.

Roisman, G. I., Clausell, E., Holland, A., Fortuna, K., & Elieff, C. (2008). Adult romantic relationships as contexts of human development: A multimethod comparison of same-sex couples with opposite-sex dating, engaged, and married dyads. *Developmental Psychology, 44,* 91–101.

Roisman, G. I., & Fraley, R. C. (2006). The limits of genetic influence: A behavior–genetic analysis of infant–caregiver relationship quality and temperament. *Child Development, 77,* 1656–1667.

Rolls, E. T. (2000). The representation of umami tastes in the taste cortex. *Journal of Nutrition, 130,* 960–965.

Rooney, N. J., Bradshaw, J. W. S., & Robinson, I. H. (2001). Do dogs respond to play signals given by humans? *Animal Behavior, 61,* 715–722.

Rosch, E. (1973). Natural categories. *Cognitive Psychology, 4,* 328–350.

Rosch, E., Mervis, C. B., Gray, W. D., Johnson, D. M., & Boyes-Braem, P. (2004). Basic objects in natural categories. In D. A. Balota & E. J. Marsh (Eds.), *Cognitive psychology: Key readings* (pp. 448–471). New York: Psychology Press.

Rose, A. J., Carlson, W., & Waller, E. M. (2007). Prospective associations of co-rumination with friendship and emotional adjustment: Considering the socioemotional trade-offs of co-rumination. *Developmental Psychology, 43,* 1019–1031.

Rose, A. J., & Smith, R. L. (2009). Sex differences in peer relationships. In K. H. Rubin, W. M. Bukowski, & B. Laursen (Eds.), *Handbook of peer interactions, relationships, and groups* (pp. 379–393). New York: Guilford Press.

Rose, J. E., Behm, F. M., Salley, A. N., Bates, J. E., Coleman, R. E., Hawk, T. C., et al. (2007). Regional brain activity correlates of nicotine dependence. *Neuropsychopharmacology, 32,* 2441–2452.

Rose, R. J. (1995). Genes and human behavior. *Annual Review of Psychology, 46,* 625–654.

Rose, S. A. (1980). Enhancing visual recognition memory in preterm infants. *Developmental Psychology, 16,* 85–92.

Rosen, J. B. (2004). The neurobiology of conditioned and unconditioned fear: A neurobehavioral system analysis of the amygdale. *Behavior and Cognitive Neuroscience Reviews, 3,* 23–41.

Rosen, J. B., & Donley, M. P. (2006). Animal studies of amygdala function in fear and uncertainty: Relevance to human research. *Biological Psychology, 73,* 49–60.

Rosenblith, J. F. (1992). *In the beginning.* Newbury Park, CA: Sage.

Rosenhan, D. L. (1969). Some origins of the concerns for others. In P. Mussen & M. Covington (Eds.), *Trends and issues in developmental psychology* (pp. 134–153). New York: Holt, Rinehart & Winston.

Rosenhan, D. L. (1973). On being sane in insane places. *Science, 179,* 250–258.

Ross, M. W. (1980). Retrospective distortion in homosexual research. *Archives of Sexual Behavior, 9,* 523–531.

Roth, S., & Cohen, J. L. (1986). Approach, avoidance, and coping with stress. *American Psychologist, 41,* 813–819.

Roth, T. (2005). Prevalence, associated risks, and treatment patterns of insomnia. *Journal of Clinical Psychiatry, 66,* 10–13.

Roth, T., Krystal, A. D., & Lieberman, J. A., III. (2007). Long-term issues in the treatment of sleep disorders. *CNS Spectrum, 12,* 1–13.

Roth, T., Schwartz, J. R., Hirshkowitz, M., Erman, M. K., Dayno, J. M., & Arora, S. (2007). Evaluation of the safety of modafinil for treatment of excessive sleepiness. *Journal of Clinical Sleep Medicine, 3,* 595–602.

Rothbart, M. K., Ahadi, S. A., & Evans, D. E. (2000). Temperament and personality: Origins and outcomes. *Journal of Personality and Social Psychology, 78,* 122–135.

Rothbaum, B. O., Hodges, L. F., Kooper, R., Opdyke, D., & Williford, J. (1995). Effectiveness of computer-generated (virtual reality) graded exposure in the treatment of acrophobia. *American Journal of Psychiatry, 152,* 626–628.

Rothbaum, B. O., Hodges, L., Watson, B. A., Kessler, G. D., & Opdyke, D. (1996). Virtual reality exposure therapy in the treatment of fear of flying: A case report. *Behavior Research and Therapy, 34,* 477–481.

Rothbaum, B. O., Rizzo, A. S., & Difede, J. (2010). Virtual reality exposure therapy for combat-related posttraumatic stress disorder. *Annals of the New York Academy of Sciences, 1208,* 126–132.

Rouch, I., Wild, P., Ansiau, D., & Marquie, J. C. (2005). Shiftwork experience, age, and cognitive performance. *Ergonomics, 48,* 1282–1293.

Rowe, T. (2006). Fertility and a woman's age. *Journal of Reproductive Medicine, 51,* 157–163.

Rowlett, J. K., Cook, J. M., Duke, A. N., & Platt, D. M. (2005). Selective antagonism of GABAA receptor subtypes: An in vivo approach to exploring the therapeutic and side effects of benzodiazepine-type drugs. *CNS Spectrums, 10,* 40–48.

Ruark, J. (2009, August 3). An intellectual movement for the masses: 10 years after its founding, positive psychology struggles with its own success. *Chronicle of Higher Education.*

Rubin, K. H., Lynch, D., Coplan, R., Rose-Krasnor, L., & Booth, C. L. (1994). "Birds of a feather . . .": Behavioral concordances and preferential personal attraction in children. *Child Development, 65,* 1778–1785.

Rubin, S. S. (1993). The death of a child is forever: The life course impact of child loss. In M. Stroebe, W. Stroebe, & R. O. Hansson (Eds.), *Handbook of bereavement. Theory, research, and intervention* (pp. 285–299). Cambridge, UK: Cambridge University Press.

Ruderman, A. J. (1985). Dysphoric mood and overeating: A test of restraint theory's disinhibition hypothesis. *Journal of Abnormal Psychology, 94,* 78–85.

Rudgley, R. (1998). *The encyclopedia of psychoactive substances.* New York: Little, Brown.

Ruffin, C. L. (1993). Stress and health: Little hassles vs. major life events. *Australian Psychologist, 28*(3), 201–208.

Ruffman, T., Slade, L., & Redman, J. (2005). Young infants' expectations about hidden objects. *Cognition, 97,* B35–B43.

Rumelhart, D. E. (1980). Schemata: The basic building blocks of cognition. In R. Spiro, B. Bruce, & W. Brewer (Eds.), *Theoretical issues in reading comprehension* (pp. 33–58). Hillsdale, NJ: Erlbaum.

Ruscio, A. M., Brown, T. A., Chiu, W. T., Sareen, J., Stein, M. B., & Kessler, R. C. (2008). Social fears and social phobia in the USA: Results from the National Comorbidity Survey Replication. *Psychological Medicine, 38,* 15–28.

Rush, M. C., Schoel, W. A., & Barnard, S. M. (1995). Psychological resiliency in the public sector: "Hardiness" and pressure for change. *Journal of Vocational Behavior, 46*(1), 17–39.

Rushton, J. P., & Jensen, A. R. (2005). Thirty years of research on race differences in cognitive ability. *Psychology, Public Policy, and Law, 11,* 235–294.

Rushton, W. A. H. (1975). Visual pigments and color blindness. *Scientific American, 232,* 64–74.

Russell, C. J., & Keel, P. K. (2002). Homosexuality as a specific risk factor for eating disorders in men. *International Journal of Eating Disorders, 31,* 300–306.

Rutherford, W. (1886). A new theory of hearing. *Journal of Anatomy and Physiology, 21,* 166–168.

Saadat, H., Drummond-Lewis, J., Maranets, I., Kaplan, D., Saadat, A., Wang, S. M., et al. (2006). Hypnosis reduces preoperative anxiety in adult patients. *Anesthesia and Analgesia, 102,* 1394–1396.

Sachs, G. S., & Rush, A. J. (2003). Response, remission, and recovery in bipolar disorders: What are the realistic treatment goals? *Journal of Clinical Psychiatry, 64*(Suppl. 6), 18–22.

Sackett, P. R., & DeVore, C. J. (2001). Counterproductive behaviors at work. In N. Anderson, D. S. Ones, H. K. Sinangil, & C. Viswesvaran (Eds.), *Handbook of industrial, work and organizational psychology* (Vol. 1, pp. 145–165). Thousand Oaks, CA: Sage.

Sadker, D. (2000). Gender equity: Still knocking at the classroom door. *Equity and Excellence in Education, 33,* 80–83.

Sadler, W. A. (2000). *The third age: Six principles for growth and renewal after forty.* New York: Perseus.

Sah, P., Faber, E. S. L., Lopez De Armentia, M., & Power, J. (2003). The aymgdaloid complex: Anatomy and physiology. *Physiological Reviews, 83,* 803–834.

Sajatovic, M., Valenstein, M., Blow, F., Ganoczy, D., & Ignacio, R. (2007). Treatment adherence with lithium and anticonvulsant medications among patients with bipolar disorder. *Psychiatric Services, 58,* 855–863.

Sakari, M. M. (1975). Small group cohesiveness and detrimental conformity. *Sociometry, 38,* 340–357.

Salend, S. J. (2001). *Creating inclusive classrooms: Effective and reflective practices* (4th ed.). Upper Saddle River, NJ: Prentice Hall.

Salgado, J. F., Viswesvaran, C., & Ones, D. (2003). Predictors used for personnel selection: An overview of constructs, methods and techniques. In N. Anderson, D. S. Ones, H. K. Sinangil, & C. Viswesvaran (Eds.), *Handbook of industrial, work and organizational psychology* (Vol. 1, pp. 166–199). Thousand Oaks, CA: Sage.

Salkovskis, P. M., Westbrook, D., Davis, J., Jeavons, A., & Gledhill, A. (1997). Effects of neutralizing on intrusive thoughts: An experiment investigating the etiology of obsessive-compulsive disorder. *Behaviour Research and Therapy, 35,* 211–219.

Salthouse, T. A. (2004). What and when of cognitive aging. *Current Directions in Psychological Science, 13,* 140–144.

Salvatore, J.E., Chun-Kuo, S.I., Steele, R.D., Simpson, J.A., & Collins, W.A. (2011). Recovering from conflict in romantic relationships: A developmental perspective. *Psychological Science, 22,* 376–383.

Samarel, N. (1995). The dying process. In H. Wass & R. A. Neimeyer (Eds.), *Dying: Facing the facts* (3rd ed., pp. 89–116). Washington DC: Taylor & Francis.

Sanaktekin, O. H., & Sunar, D. (2008). Persuasion and relational versus personal self-esteem: Does the message need to be one- or two-sided? *Social Behavior and Personality, 36,* 1315–1332.

Sanchez-Hucles, J. V., & Davis, D. D. (2010). Women and women of color in leadership. *American Psychologist, 65,* 171–181.

Sanders, J. D., Happe, H. K., Bylund, D. B., & Murrin, L. C. (2005). Development of the norepinephrine transporter in the rat CNS. *Neuroscience, 130,* 107–117.

Sanderson, C. A., & Cantor, N. (1995). Social dating goals in late adolescence: Implications for safer sexual activity. *Journal of Personality and Social Psychology, 68,* 1121–1134.

Sanes, J. N., Dimitrov, B., & Hallett, M. (1990). Motor learning in patients with cerebellar dysfunction. *Brain, 113,* 103–120.

Sangrigoli, S., & de Schonen, S. (2004). Recognition of own-race and other-race faces by three-month-old infants. *Journal of Child Psychology and Psychiatry, 45,* 1219–1227.

Sansone, R. A., & Sansone, L. A. (2011). Personality pathology and its influence on eating disorders. *Clinical Neuroscience, 8,* 14–18.

Santelli, J. S., Lindberg, L. D., Abma, J., McNeeley, C. S., & Resnick, M. (2000). Adolescent sexual behavior: Estimates and trends from four nationally representative surveys. *Family Planning Perspectives, 32,* 156–165, 194.

Sanyal, S., & vanTol, H. M. (1997). Review the role of dopamine D4 receptors in schizophrenia and antipsychotic action. *Journal of Psychiatric Research, 31,* 219–232.

Sapolsky, R. M. (2000). The possibility of neurotoxicity in the hippocampus in major depression: A primer on neuron death. *Biological Psychiatry, 48,* 755–765.

Sapolsky, R. M. (2002). Chickens, eggs and hippocampal atrophy. *Nature Neuroscience, 5,* 1111–1113.